Sports Illustrated™

THE BASKETBALL VAULT

Great Writing from the Pages of *Sports Illustrated*

Edited and annotated
by Chris Ballard

TRIUMPH
B O O K S

Library of Congress Cataloging-in-Publication Data available upon requ

This book is available in quantity at special discounts for your group
organization. For further information, contact:
  Triumph Books LLC
  814 North Franklin Street
  Chicago, Illinois 60610
  (312) 337-0747
  www.triumphbooks.com

Printed in U.S.A.
ISBN: 978-1-62937-956-2
Design by Patricia Frey

THE BASKETBALL VAULT
CONTENTS

ICONS

Introduction

On August 9, 1954, a magazine called *Sports Illustrated* debuted on newsstands across America. Had you been around to read the early issues, you may have been a bit perplexed. Alongside stories on baseball and football, the magazine went deep on polo, safaris and yachting. One early cover featured a picture of fall foliage with the title "A Walk Into Autumn."

Basketball coverage? Not so much.

Then again, the game held little sway over the country at the time. It had only been five years since the Basketball Association of America merged with the National Basketball League to form the National Basketball Association. At the time, players took set shots and competed below the rim. Most if not all needed second jobs; few made more than $10,000 a year.

Then, in 1957, Bill Russell entered the league, followed two years later by Wilt Chamberlain. The game changed (for the better), became more diverse and, ultimately, more popular. By the early 1960s, *Sports Illustrated* had also started to find its footing and the magazine's writers gained unparalleled access to the NBA's top players. When these stars wanted to make a statement, they came to SI. Russell spoke out on race. So did Lew Alcindor. Chamberlain opened fire on the commissioner, coaches and owners in a story titled "My Life in a Bush League."

It's hard today to imagine the sway a magazine held at the time. But, in an era before cable TV or the internet, SI was one of the few truly national outlets. So writers like Frank Deford developed friendships with athletes and traveled with teams. Later, in the 1980s and 1990s, Jack McCallum chronicled the reign of Magic, Larry and Michael from the inside.

With seven decades of material, it's impossible to fit SI's best pro basketball stories in a single volume. Some writers, such as Deford, McCallum, Gary Smith and Lee Jenkins, merit their own anthologies.

Instead, we've aimed to include a range of pieces that span eras and recall icons of the game. So within are stories featuring Wilt, Russell and

Kareem; Bird, Magic and Michael; Kobe, Shaq and LeBron; Steph, Giannis and Durant; Leslie, Taurasi and Hammon.

You'll find deep-dive profiles on stars, coaches and one commissioner; deconstructions of single games or historic shots; and tales of crime and courage off the court. The goal: that each story is either timeless, as illuminating and entertaining to read now as when published, or that it provides a telling snapshot of a particular era, such as the 1963 piece by Gil Rogan on Bill Russell or Chris Mannix's dispatch from the surreal COVID-plagued 2020 playoffs held in the bubble.

You'll find features reflecting the evolution and rise of the women's pro game, including Shelley Smith on a young Lisa Leslie; Johnette Howard on Sheila Tighe's quest to get one more look; and Deford's origin story on Diana Taurasi. (Sadly, there were far fewer stories by and about women to choose from for this anthology. For decades, both *Sports Illustrated* and the industry at large lagged in covering women's sports and employing female writers [the same goes for writers of color]. While this is changing, we've still got a ways to go.)

You'll also find stories that were themselves news, like when LeBron announced his return to the Cavaliers and Jason Collins became the first active NBA player to come out.

Sometimes, as with Jackie MacMullan's piece on Charles Barkley, the stories include a personal connection between writer and subject. Other times, as with S.L. Price's takedown of Knicks owner James Dolan, no punches are pulled.

Throughout, we've endeavored to showcase a range of writers, each with their own writing style, from the effortless prose of Phil Taylor to the intricate structuring of a Gary Smith feature to Selena Roberts's turns of phrase. Also represented are some of the magazine's current crop of talented writers, including Mannix, Chris Herring and Rohan Nadkarni.

While the sections are broken out by theme, this book is meant to be dipped into rather than read in a linear fashion. Start with Popovich and then head to Van Gundy, or go deep on the disappearance of Bison Dele and then return to a profile of Larry Legend. Seven decades of stories await.

INDELIBLE MOMENTS

JULY 2, 2012

The Greatest Game Nobody Ever Saw

The toughest competition faced by the best team in basketball
history was, in fact, its own; at a closed scrimmage in Monaco
between sides led by Michael Jordan and Magic Johnson,
the details of which remained secret for nearly 20 years

BY JACK McCALLUM

*What if some of the best players in league history played a game in an empty
arena, with only pride and bragging rights on the line? From Jack McCallum,
who also wrote* Dream Team, *the definitive book on the 1992 U.S. Olympic
squad, which changed the global game forever.*

You have a tape?" Michael Jordan asks. "Of that game?"

"I do," I say.

"Man, everybody asks me about that game," he says. "It was the most fun
I ever had on a basketball court."

It befits the enduring legend of the Dream Team, arguably the most
dominant squad ever assembled in any sport, that we're referring not to
a real game but to an intrasquad scrimmage in Monaco three days before
the start of the 1992 Olympics. The Dreamers played 14 games that summer
two decades gone, and their smallest victory margin was 32 points, over a
fine Croatia team in the Olympic final. The common matrices of statistical
comparison, you see, are simply not relevant in the case of the Dream Team,

whose members could be evaluated only when they played each other. The video of that scrimmage, therefore, is the holy grail of basketball.

A perfect storm hit Barcelona in the summer of the Dream Team. Its members were almost exclusively NBA veterans at or near the apex of their individual fame. The world, having been offered only bite-sized nuggets of NBA games, was waiting for them, since Barcelona was the first Olympics in which professional basketball players were allowed to compete. The Dreamers were a star-spangled export from a country that still held primacy around the world.

This debut couldn't have been scripted any better, and when the Dream Team finally released all that star power in a collective effort, the show was better than everyone had thought it would be ... and everyone had thought it would be pretty damn good. The Dreamers were Johnny Cash at Folsom Prison, the Allman Brothers at the Fillmore East, Santana at Woodstock.

Most of the 12 names (Michael Jordan, Magic Johnson, Larry Bird, Charles Barkley, Scottie Pippen, Karl Malone, Patrick Ewing, David Robinson, John Stockton, Chris Mullin, Clyde Drexler and Christian Laettner) remain familiar to fans two decades later, their cultural relevance still high. It's not just that Danger Mouse and Cee Lo Green christened their hip-hop duo Gnarls Barkley, or that other artists have sung about Johnson (Red Hot Chili Peppers, Kanye West), Pippen (Jay-Z), Malone (the Transplants) and Jordan (impossible to count). Consider this: The name of Stockton, a buttoned-down point guard, is on a 2011 track by Brooklyn rapper Nemo Achida, and the popular video game *NBA 2K12* features Jordan, Magic and Bird on the box cover—not LeBron, Dirk and Derrick.

Yet the written record of that team during the summer of '92 is not particularly large. The Dreamers, like the dinosaurs, walked the earth in a pre-social-media age. Beyond newspaper stories, there are no detailed daily logs of their basketball activities (*Bird shot around today, but his back is sore*) and no enduring exclamations of chance meetings around Barcelona (*OMG, jst met ChazBark at bar & he KISSED me on cheek; hez not rlly fat LOL*). Much of the story is yet to be told, and the scrimmage in Monte Carlo may be the most tantalizing episode of all.

Negotiating for the team to train in the world's most exclusive gambling enclave started, believe it or not, with commissioner David Stern, who at the time was understood to be fervently antigambling and terrified of betting lines. But he also recognized that a training camp in, say, Fort Wayne, Ind., was not an inducement for players such as Jordan and Magic to buy in. So he began talking to a friend, New York Giants co-owner Robert Tisch, who also owned the showpiece Loews Hotel in Monaco. From there, NBA deputy commissioner Russ Granik and Loews chairman Robert Hausman reached a deal with the principality.

Players, coaches and schlub journalists like me said bravo to the decision. The Dream Team did get in some work during its six days in Monaco, but on balance it was more like a minivacation. The team's daily schedule called for two hours of basketball followed by 22 hours of golf, gambling and gaping at the sights. Nude beaches and models were a three-point shot away, sometimes closer. "I'm not putting in a curfew because I'd have to adhere to it," said coach Chuck Daly, "and Jimmy'z [a noted Monte Carlo nightclub] doesn't open until midnight."

The Dream Team flew into Nice at midnight on July 18 and made a crash landing at the Loews, or Jet Set Central, about 20 miles away. During a security meeting before the team arrived, Henri Lorenzi, the legendary hotel manager, had complained about the number and the aggressiveness of the NBA's security people. "Do you realize who is gambling in my casino right now?" Lorenzi said to the NBA's international liaison, Kim Bohuny. Lorenzi ticked off the names of politicians, movie stars and even tennis immortal Björn Borg. "No one will care that much about this team," he said.

"Well, we'll see," replied Bohuny.

When the team bus pulled up, there was such a rush of fans to see the players that some fans crashed through the glass doors at the entrance. "I get your point," said Lorenzi.

The Loews casino was located in the middle of the hotel, thereby serving as kind of theater-in-the-round when the Dream Teamers were there, the regulars being Jordan, Magic, Barkley, Pippen and Ewing, the same group that had started playing a card game called tonk back at the team's first training camp, in La Jolla, Calif., and would play right through the last night in Barcelona. On one occasion Barkley, feeling like the luckiest blackjack player in the world, hit on a 19; it would be a better ending to the story to say he drew a deuce, but he busted. From time to time Jordan even reserved his own blackjack table and played all five hands.

Each afternoon, after their workout and lunch, a gaggle of players trod through the foot-thick casino carpets in golf shoes, sticks on their backs, bound for the Monte Carlo Golf Club, a 25-minute ride away. The course wasn't a jewel, but it was hilly and commanded wonderful views of the Riviera. One day, after practice, *Newsday* writer Jan Hubbard arranged a foursome with Barkley, Drexler and me. Barkley was at that time unencumbered by the neuropathic-psychosomatic disorder that has come to plague his golf game, which at this writing remains a wretched smorgasbord of tics and stops and twists and turns. He hit the ball far and had a decent short game, though he was subject to lapses in concentration. Drexler, whom Barkley called Long and Wrong, was just learning the game. With a full, aggressive, coiled swing, he routinely hit 300-yard drives, usually 150 out and 150 to the left or right.

Our merry group played nine, then picked up Robinson at the turn. He was fairly new to the game and, in the fashion of a Naval officer who had built televisions with his father as an adolescent, was working on it with consummate dedication. Robinson was as enthusiastic as anyone about being a Dreamer; as the sole returning member of the 1988 U.S. Olympic team, which won only the bronze medal, he was on a redemptive journey. But Robinson was, to a large extent, a loner. "He wasn't driven like myself and most of the other players," Jordan says. And years after Barcelona, Robinson still seemed unable to fully comprehend the thirst-for-blood competitiveness of his teammates. He told me a Jordan story from the first time they met, at a 1988 exhibition game. "I go back to meet Michael because, like everybody else, I'm big fan, and you know the first thing he says to me? 'I'm going to dunk on you, big fella. I dunked on all the other big fellas, and you're next.'

"And he said it almost every time we played. I'd go back at him: 'Don't even think about it. I will take you out of the air.' And Michael would always promise to get me."

And did he? "Eventually," Robinson said. "It was a two-on-one with him and Scottie. Michael took the shot and I went up to block it, but I didn't get there, and he dunked it and the crowd went crazy. 'Told you I was going to get you one day,' he said. Man, what a competitor. He never forgot anything, never let you get away with *anything*."

By Dream Team time, Robinson had, as he puts it, "been born again in Christ." He didn't drink or swear and was finding it uncomfortable to be around those who did. But a golf course—certainly one with Charles Barkley on it—is a very tough place for a true believer. Our fivesome played on, insults and four-letter words flying. At one point Robinson complained to Hubbard about Drexler's cussing and also wanted Barkley to tone it down. Charles seemed to comply, but then—I believe around the 14th hole—he let loose with another barrage, all of it in good humor but salty. So Robinson shook his head, smiled, picked up his bag and left.

In my mind's eye, I still see Robinson walking off the course on that day. Most athletic teams and most athletic relationships are built on sophomoric humor, insults and d-- jokes, all wrapped in testosterone. To stand with your team yet somehow to have the guts to stand alone from time to time ... now, that takes a particular kind of man.

If the gentleman from Italy—whose name nobody remembers—had it all to do over again, I'm sure he would toss the ball to his fellow referee, assistant coach P.J. Carlesimo, and proceed rapidly to the nearest exit of Stade Louis II, the all-purpose arena in the Fontvieille ward of Monaco. For soon he will become the unluckiest person in town, and that includes all those who are surrendering vast quantities of French francs at the tables.

He tosses the ball up between Ewing and Robinson, and Robinson taps it—on the way up, illegally—toward his own basket. Robinson's teammate on the Blue Team, Duke's Laettner, the only collegiate Dreamer, races the White Team's Pippen for the ball. Take note, for this is the first and last time in history that this sentence will be written: *Laettner beats Pippen to the ball.* Laettner sweeps it behind his back to his Blue teammate Barkley, who catches it, takes a couple of dribbles and knifes between the White Team's Jordan and Bird. Jordan grabs Barkley's wrist, the whistle blows, and Barkley makes the layup.

"Shoot the fouls, shoot the fouls," Chuck Daly yells, sounding like that character in *Goodfellas*, Jimmy Two Times. It's morning and almost no one is in the stands, but Daly is trying to install gamelike conditions because even the best of the best need a kick in the ass from time to time. As Jordan calls for a towel—it is extremely humid in the arena, and almost everyone is sweating off a little alcohol—Barkley makes the free throw.

Magic Johnson's Blue Team 3, Michael Jordan's White Team 0.

And so the Greatest Game Nobody Ever Saw gets under way.

About 12 hours earlier the U.S. had finished an exhibition game against France. It was awful. The players were still getting used to local conditions—meaning the steep fairways at the Monte Carlo Golf Club and the nocturnal bass beat at Jimmy'z—and even the seemingly inexhaustible Jordan was tired after walking 18 holes and arriving back at the Loews not long before the 8:30 p.m. tip-off. The Dream Team was sloppy and allowed France leads of 8–2 and 16–13 before it woke up and went on to win 111–71.

It didn't matter to the fans, though, who had gobbled up the 3,500 available tickets in a 15-minute box-office frenzy. The opposing team's guys, at least half a dozen of whom had brought cameras to the bench, were deemed heroic by dint of being slain. Happiest of all was the French coach, Francis Jordane. "He was very excited because he figured that his last name would give him special entrée to Michael," recalls Terry Lyons, the NBA's head of international public relations. "We took a photo, and sure enough, there is Jordane right next to Jordan, with his arm around him."

By breakfast this morning Daly had decided that his team had better beat itself up a little bit. The Dream Team had scrimmaged several times before this fateful day, a couple of the games ending in a diplomatic tie as Daly refused to allow overtime. He normally tried to divvy up the teams by conference, but on this day Drexler was nursing a minor injury and Stockton was still recovering from a fractured right fibula he had suffered in the Olympic qualifying tournament. Lord only knows how this morning would've gone had Drexler been available. Jordan had already taken it upon himself to torture the Glide in scrimmages, conjuring up the just-completed NBA Finals—in which Jordan's Bulls had beaten Drexler's Trail Blazers in six games—and taunting Drexler, "Stop me this time!"

So with two fewer Western players than Eastern players, and only two true guards (Magic and Jordan), Daly went with Magic, Barkley, Robinson, Chris Mullin and Laettner on the Blue Team against Jordan, Malone, Ewing, Pippen and Bird on the White.

The gym was all but locked down. The media were allowed in for only the last part of practice. A single cameraman, Pete Skorich, who was Chuck Daly's guy with the Pistons, videotaped the day. It was a closed universe, a secret little world: 10 of the best basketball players in the world going at each other. Daly had a message for them: "All you got now. All you got."

The absence of Drexler means that Magic and Jordan are matched up. "Those two going against each other," Dream Team assistant coach Mike Krzyzewski told me in 2011, "was the pimple being popped."

Jordan dribbles upcourt, and Magic yells, "Let's go, Blue. Pick it up now." This is what Magic has missed since he retired because of his HIV diagnosis in November 1991: the juice he got from leading a team, being the conductor, the voice box, the man from whom all energy flows. A half hour earlier, during leisurely full-court layup drills, Magic had suddenly stopped and flung the ball into the empty seats. "We're here to *practice!*" he yelled. That was his signal that the players were half-assing it, and the day turned on that moment. Magic had promised Daly back in the U.S., "I will see to it that there will be no bad practices."

Bird gets the ball on the right side, guarded by Laettner. With an almost theatrical flourish Bird swings his torso as if to pass to Jordan in the corner. Bird made better use of body fakes than anyone who ever lived, his remedy for a relative lack of quickness. Laettner bites, and Bird is free to drive left into the lane, where he passes to Malone on the left baseline. Malone misses a jumper, Ewing misses an easy tip, and Laettner grabs the rebound.

Magic dribbles upcourt and goes into his Toscanini act, waving both Laettner and Mullin away from the right side and motioning for Barkley to isolate on the block. Bird has him on a switch. "Go to work, CB!" Magic instructs. "Go to work!" Barkley up-fakes Bird but air balls a jumper. Laettner is there for the rebound and lays it in.

Johnson's Blue Team 5, Jordan's White Team 0.

Playing tit for tat at the other end, Malone posts up Barkley on the left side. But the Mailman misses an easy jumper, and Laettner—player of the game so far—gets the rebound. At the other end Laettner drives baseline on Ewing, who shoulders him out-of-bounds. "Don't force it if we don't have it," says Magic, directing the comment at Laettner.

After the inbounds pass, Magic dribbles into the lane and spins between Jordan and Pippen, a forced drive if there ever was one. (It is incumbent upon Magic's followers to do as he says, not as he does.) The gentleman from Italy blows his whistle, and no one is sure what the call is, including the gentleman from Italy. Bird, a veteran pickup-game strategist, turns to go upcourt, figuring that will sell the call as a travel, but Magic is already demanding a foul. He wins.

"That's a foul?" Jordan asks in his deep baritone.

(Years later I will watch Magic in a pickup game at UCLA, this one without referees, and he will win the foul battle virtually every time, standing around incredulously until he is awarded the ball, and on defense pointedly playing through his own fouls and acting like a petulant child when an infraction is called on him.)

A minute later Barkley bats away Pippen's shovel pass to Ewing and storms pell-mell to the other end. Bird is ahead of him but overruns the play, and Barkley puts in a layup.

Johnson's Blue Team 7, Jordan's White Team 0.

Jordan is now getting serious and calls out, "One, one!" Pippen gets the ball on the right wing, fakes Mullin off his feet and cans a jumper to break the drought for White.

Johnson's Blue Team 7, Jordan's White Team 2.

Mullin, always sneaky, taps the ball away from a driving Jordan, and Barkley again steamrollers downcourt, this time going between Malone and Ewing for another full-court layup, taking his two steps from just inside the foul line with that sixth sense all great players have about exactly when to pick up the dribble. "Foul! Foul!" Barkley hollers, but he doesn't get the call.

Johnson's Blue Team 9, Jordan's White Team 2.

Malone misses another open jumper; Magic rebounds, heads downcourt and yells, "I see you, baby" to an open Mullin. Mullin misses but Barkley rebounds and finds a cutting Laettner, whose shot is swatted away by Ewing. Laettner spreads his arms, looking for the call, soon to be joined by his more influential teammate.

"That's good!" Magic yells, demanding a goaltending violation.

"He didn't call it," says Jordan.

"It's good," Magic says again.

"He didn't call it," says Jordan.

Magic wins again. Goaltending.

Johnson's Blue Team 11, Jordan's White Team 2.

Bird goes right by Laettner and takes an awkward lefthanded shot in the lane that misses. His back is hurting. Laettner has a layup opportunity at the other end off a quick feed by Magic, but Ewing blocks it, a small moment that presages Laettner's NBA career. He isn't springy enough to dunk or physical enough to draw a foul.

"Dunk that s––, Chris," Jordan says. "Dunk that s––." (Years later Jordan will tell me, coldly and matter-of-factly, "Anybody who had Laettner on the team lost. He was the weak link, and everybody went at him.")

Bird misses an open jumper, and Magic goes over Pippen's back to knock the ball out-of-bounds; nevertheless Magic flashes a look of disbelief when the ball is awarded to White. Ewing swishes a jumper.

Johnson's Blue Team 11, Jordan's White Team 4.

Magic drives, a foul is called on Ewing, and Malone, no fan of this Magic-dominated show, is starting to get irritated. "*Sheet!*" he yells at the gentleman from Italy. "Everything ain't a foul!"

His mood is no better seconds later when he gets caught in a Barkley screen, and Mullin is able to backdoor Pippen, get a perfect feed from Magic and score a layup. "Whoo!" Magic yells as he heads back upcourt.

Johnson's Blue Team 13, Jordan's White Team 4.

(Years later Pippen will go on a nice little riff about Mullin's ability to read the game. "Mullie just killed me on backdoors," Pippen says, watching the tape with me. "He wasn't that fast, but he knew just when to make his cut.")

Jordan is now looking to score. He forces a switch off a Ewing screen, takes Robinson outside and launches a three-pointer that bounces off the backboard and into the basket. A lucky shot. Magic calls for the ball immediately—tit for tat—and Jordan retreats, fearing a drive. But Magic stops, launches a jump shot from just outside the three-point line and yells, "Right back at you!" even before it reaches the basket. It goes in.

Johnson's Blue Team 16, Jordan's White Team 7.

There is little doubt that if Jordan played Magic one-on-one, he would drill him, because Magic simply has no way to defend MJ. Magic is bigger but not stronger; he can't jump as high; he's nowhere near as quick; and Jordan's predaceous instincts are unmatched in one-on-one challenges. But this morning it's Magic's one-on-one game against Jordan's. Going one-on-one against Jordan, however, not only is a flawed strategy but also goes against Magic's basketball nature. Johnson is a conciliator. I'll bring everybody together is his mantra, just as it was back at Everett High in Lansing, Mich., where the principal used to call upon Magic to settle racial disputes among his fellow students. "You understand the respect I have for Michael," Krzyzewski will say years later, "but one thing about him—he cannot be kind."

Jordan, with the surety of an IRS accountant, is starting to get into the game. He initiates a play from the point, goes through the lane and out to the left corner, gets a pass from Ewing and hits a jumper as Magic arrives too late to stop him. At the other end Magic waits until Barkley sets up on the left low block, and then Magic passes him the ball. Barkley turns around and hits a jumper.

"Take him, Charles, all day," says Magic.

Jordan dribbles slowly downcourt and motions Malone to the right block. Jordan makes the entry pass, and Malone turns and quick shoots over Barkley. Good. Tit for tat.

Johnson's Blue Team 17, Jordan's White Team 11.

Bird air balls a wide-open jumper. He looks 100 years old. White gets the ball back, and Jordan signals that the left side should be cleared for Malone to go against Barkley. The entry pass comes in, and Malone clears space by slapping away Barkley's hand. He turns toward the baseline and, legs splayed, releases a jumper. Good.

"Right back at you," Jordan yells.

Johnson's Blue Team 18, Jordan's White Team 13.

After a couple of futile exchanges, Magic races downcourt and throws a pass ahead to Robinson. "Keep going, David," he hollers, and Robinson obligingly drives to the basket, drawing a foul on Ewing. "All day long," Magic hollers. "All day long." Then he gets personal. He yells, "The Jordanaires are down."

Jordan is not amused. About halfway through the Greatest Game Nobody Ever Saw, Magic may have sealed his own doom. "Hold the clock!" Jordan hollers, clearly irritated, making sure there is enough time to strike back. Robinson makes one of two.

Johnson's Blue Team 19, Jordan's White Team 13.

A minute later Barkley spins away from Malone on the right block, and Malone is called for a foul. "Called this same f--- s-- last night," Malone says to the gentleman from Italy, referring to the game against France. "This is *bulls--*!" To add to Malone's frustration, Daly hollers that the White team is over the foul limit.

"One-and-one," says Daly.

"*Yeah!*" Magic yells. "I love it. I *love* it! We ain't in Chicago Stadium anymore." He punctuates the insult with loud clapping.

Throughout his career Jordan has heard complaints that the referees favor him. At a Michael-Magic-Larry photo session, Magic quipped, "You can't get too close to Michael. It's a foul." Jordan is tired of hearing about it, particularly from Magic.

Barkley makes one of two.

Johnson's Blue Team 20, Jordan's White Team 13.

Now amped up, Jordan goes through four defenders for a flying layup, then Pippen steals Mullin's inbounds pass. Jordan misses a jumper, but Pippen rebounds, draws a foul on Mullin and gets an enthusiastic palm slap from Jordan. As Barkley towels himself off from head to toe, Pippen makes both. Perhaps they are in Chicago Stadium.

Johnson's Blue Team 20, Jordan's White Team 17.

Bird grabs the rebound off a missed Robinson shot, and Jordan cans a jumper to bring White within one. Magic, still determined to make this a one-on-one contest, spins into the lane and misses badly. Barkley is starting to get irritated at Magic's one-on-one play and will later complain to Jordan and Pippen about it. Jordan races downcourt with Pippen to the left and Ewing to the right. You know where this is headed. Pippen catches the ball and throws down a ferocious lefthanded dunk.

Jordan's White Team 21, Johnson's Blue Team 20.

Mullin drives and draws a reach-in foul on Pippen. "Wasn't that all ball?" says Jordan. Mullin makes one free throw, misses the next.

Jordan drives the lane, and Magic, now visibly tired, gets picked off. Robinson, the help defender, is whistled for a foul. After Jordan misses the first, Magic knocks the ball high in the air—a technical in the NBA, but who cares?—and keeps jawing. "Let's concentrate," hollers Daly, trying to keep everyone's mind on the business at hand.

Jordan makes the second.

Jordan's White Team 22, Johnson's Blue Team 21.

Malone comes down hard on his right ankle after making a layup off an assist from Jordan. His bad mood has grown worse. Malone walks it off—a normal man would've gone for ice—as Pippen and Bird come over to slap palms and Jordan yells, "Way to go, Karl."

Jordan's White Team 24, Johnson's Blue Team 21.

In March 1992, a few months before the Dream Team got together, I asked coaches and general managers around the league this question: If you were starting a team and could take either Malone or Barkley, which one would you select? Malone-Barkley had the ingredients of a Magic-or-Larry debate. Mr. Olympia vs. the Round Mound of Rebound. Mr. Reliable vs. Mr. We Hope He Isn't in a Bar Sending a Drunk Through a Window.

Malone won the poll 15–7. His supporters invariably mentioned his loyal-soldier quality and contrasted it with Barkley's penchant for controversy; Barkley's backers felt there was no substitute for talent and that Charles achieved more with less, having no Stockton in Philadelphia to deliver him the ball. Even considering the full flush of their careers, it's a difficult call. Malone, the second-leading scorer in NBA history, behind Kareem Abdul-Jabbar, averaged 25 points per game, compared with Barkley's 22.1. Barkley outrebounded Malone by 11.7 to 10.1. Both have been accused of folding under pressure, but the big picture reveals that each was an outstanding postseason player with numbers almost identical to his regular-season metrics. Bill Simmons, in *The Book of Basketball*, has Malone and Barkley together in his pantheon of best players, at 18th and 19th respectively.

But there is always the root question in sports: Who was *better*? You have that moment when you can give only one person the ball, and whom would you choose? I'm sure that if players spoke honestly, Jordan would always get the ball. And I'm equally certain that the Barkley-or-Malone nod would go to Barkley. Charles had that ineffable something that Malone didn't have. He wasn't more important to a franchise, he wasn't as dependable, and he wasn't as good over the long haul. He was just ... *better*.

Of all the Dreamers, though, Laettner came closest to paying Barkley the ultimate compliment. When I casually commented that everyone believed Jordan was the best, Laettner pursed his lips and considered. "I guess," he said, "but by a very, very small margin over Charles."

Now, at the morning game in Monaco, Jordan and Pippen walk up the court together. "He's tired," Jordan says of Barkley. As if to disprove him, Barkley plows into the lane, and Malone is called for a block. Taking a cue from Magic, the Mailman bats the ball high into the air. Seeing a profusely perspiring Barkley at the line, Jordan moves in for the kill. "A man is tired, he usually misses free throws," says Jordan. This is a recurring theme for His Airness. "One-and-one now," says Jordan, wiggling two fingers at Barkley.

Barkley makes the first—"Yeah, Charles, you gonna get your two anyway," sings Magic—but Ewing bats the second off the rim before it has a chance (maybe) to go in.

Bird misses another open jumper but decides to make something of this personal nightmare. As Magic yo-yo dribbles on the left side, Bird suddenly comes off Laettner and steals the ball. He bumps Magic slightly, but even the gentleman from Italy is not going to call that one. As Magic tumbles to the ground, Bird takes off, Barkley in pursuit, *pursuit* used lightly in this case. In fact, *takes off* is used lightly too. Bird fakes a behind-the-back pass to a trailing Jordan, and Barkley takes a man-sized bite at it, his jock now somewhere inside the free throw line. Bird makes the layup. "Way to go, Larry!" Jordan yells. "Way to take him to the hole. I know you got some life in you."

(Years later I watch some of the game with Mullin. When Bird makes this turn-back-the-clock play, Mullin calls to his wife, Liz, "Honey, come here and watch this. Watch what Larry does here." And we run it back a couple of times, Mullin and his wife smiling, delighted by the sight of the Bird they love. A couple of months after that, I remind Jordan of the play. He grows animated. "That's Larry, man, that's Larry," he says. "Making a great play like that. That's Larry Bird.")

Jordan's White Team 26, Johnson's Blue Team 22.

Laettner makes two free throws, and at the other end Jordan feeds Malone for a jumper. Barkley misses a jumper, but Robinson, an aerial acrobat, a giant with a past as a gymnast, leaps high over Ewing and taps the ball in off the board.

Jordan's White Team 28, Johnson's Blue Team 26.

Jordan launches a jumper from the top of the key, outside the three-point line, as Mullin flies out to guard him. "Too late!" Jordan yells.

Jordan's White Team 31, Johnson's Blue Team 26.

Now mostly what you hear is Jordan exhorting his team, sensing the kill. Magic backs into the lane, Malone guarding him on a switch. The gentleman from Italy blows his whistle ... and the Mailman blows his top. "Oh, come on, man," he yells. "Stop calling this f——— *bullsheet*." Jordan comes over and steps between Malone and the ref. "Forget it, Karl," says Jordan. "Don't scare him. We might need him."

Magic shoots the first, which rolls around as Jordan, hands on shorts, yells to Ewing, "Knock it out!" Too late. Magic swishes the second.

Jordan's White Team 31, Johnson's Blue Team 28.

Pippen pops out from behind a Ewing screen and swishes a jumper. At the other end, Mullin loses the grip on a Magic pass, and Bird recovers. Jordan begins a break, motions Ewing to join him on the left side and watches in delight as Patrick takes a few pitty-pat steps and makes a jumper.

Jordan's White Team 35, Johnson's Blue Team 28.

Ewing is whistled for a foul on Robinson, who makes both. At the other end Jordan feeds Malone, who draws a foul on Barkley.

"One-and-one?" the Blue team asks.

"Two shots," says Jordan, who has taken over the whistle from Magic. Malone misses both. Robinson grabs the second miss and gives it to Barkley, who steams downcourt and passes to Laettner, who goes up and fails to connect but is fouled by Jordan. *Dunk that s——, Chris.*

"Every time!" yells Magic from the backcourt, desperately trying to regain the verbal momentum. "Every time!"

Laettner, who has been and will remain silent throughout the game, makes both free throws.

Jordan's White Team 35, Johnson's Blue Team 32.

Magic is called for a reach-in, and now he goes after the gentleman from Italy, trailing him across the lane. Magic lines up next to Ewing and pushes his arm away as Ewing leans in to box out on Jordan's free throws. Jordan makes both. Magic is steaming.

At the other end the gentleman from Italy calls an inexplicable moving screen on Robinson, which delights Jordan. "My man," he yells, clapping his hands. "My man, my man, my man." *We might need him.*

"Chicago Stadium," Magic yells. Malone backs Barkley down, and the whistle blows, and now it's Barkley attacking the gentleman from Italy. "Come on, man!" he yells. "That was clean!" For a moment it appears as if Barkley might strike him. Malone makes one of two.

Jordan's White Team 38, Johnson's Blue Team 32.

Laettner makes a weird twisting layup. On the sideline Daly is beginning to pace, hoping this thing will come to an end before a fistfight breaks out or one of his players assaults the gentleman from Italy. As Robinson lines up to shoot a free throw, Jordan and Magic begin jawing again. "All they did was move Bulls Stadium right here," Magic says. "That's all they did. That's *all* they did."

"Hey, it is the '90s," Jordan says, reaching for a towel.

Robinson makes both.

Jordan's White Team 38, Johnson's Blue Team 36.

Jordan dribbles out front, running down the shot clock, pissing off Magic all the while. Finally he drives left, goes up for a jumper and draws a foul on Laettner. Before Jordan shoots, Magic moves in for a few words. They are not altogether pleasant. Jordan makes the first. Magic keeps jawing. Jordan takes the ball from the gentleman from Italy, slaps him on the rump and says, "Good man." He makes the second.

Daly watches in relief as the clock hits 00:0. He waves his hands in a shooting motion at both baskets, the sign for players to do their postpractice routine, ending the Greatest Game Nobody Ever Saw.

Jordan's White Team 40, Johnson's Blue Team 36.

Except that it isn't over. Not really.

"Way to work, White," Jordan yells, rubbing it in. He paces up and down, wiping himself with a towel, emperor of all he sees, as Magic, Barkley and Laettner disconsolately shoot free throws.

"It was all about Michael Jordan," says Magic. "That's all it was."

It's no joke. Magic is angry.

Jordan continues to pace the sideline. He grabs a cup of Gatorade and sings, "Sometimes I dream...." Jordan has recently signed a multimillion-dollar deal to endorse Gatorade, and the ads feature a song inspired by *I Wan'na Be like You*, the Monkey Song in the animated film *The Jungle Book*. The Gatorade version's lyrics are:

Sometimes I dream/That he is me/You've got to see that's how I dream to be/I dream I move, I dream I groove/Like Mike/If I could be like Mike.

As Magic looks on in this sticky-hot gym, sweat pouring off his body, towel around his neck, there is Jordan, captain of the winning team, singing a song written just for him, drinking a drink that's raking in millions, rubbing it in as only Jordan can do. And on the bus back to the hotel? Jordan keeps singing, *Be like Mike.... Be like Mike....*

The game would have reverberations in Barcelona as Michael and Magic relentlessly continued to try to get the verbal edge on each other. And in the years that followed, this intrasquad game became a part of basketball lore, "kind of like an urban legend," as Laettner describes it.

And not everybody loved it. "You have to look at who relishes that kind of thing," says Malone. "As they say, it's their *geeeg*." By *their* he means Jordan's and Magic's. (Last year I asked Malone if he wanted to watch few minutes of the video. "No," he said. "Doesn't interest me.")

But Krzyzewski, no fan of trash talk, looks back on the game fondly, remembering almost every detail. "Every once in while I'll be doing something and a line from that game will just flash into my head," he says. "*They just moved Chicago Stadium to Monte Carlo.* It just makes me smile.

"A lot of players talk trash because the TV cameras are on. But the doors on that day were *closed*. This was just you against me. *This is what I got—whatta you got?* It taught me a lot about accepting personal challenges. You know, if somebody could've taped the sound track of the game, not necessarily recorded the basketball but just the sounds, it would be priceless."

Well, I got the original VHS tape, converted it to DVD and even got a specialist to make a CD of the sound track. It picked up almost everything. The Greatest Game Nobody Ever Saw was not about the hoops. It was about the passion those guys put into playing, the importance they placed on winning and on personal pride.

Years later Jordan brought up the game before I had a chance to ask him about it. "In many ways," he said, "it was the best game I was ever in. Because the gym was locked and it was just about basketball. You saw a lot about players' DNA, how much some guys want to win. Magic was mad about it for two days."

Magic, for his part, estimates that his anger lasted only a few hours. "Let me tell you something—it would've been worse for everybody if he lost," says Johnson. "Because I could let something go after a while. But Michael? He'd never let it go. He never let *anything* go."

— POSTSCRIPT —

Jack McCallum: Stop me if you've heard this, and there's a chance you have. I've talked about this story more than any other I've written in my 50 years as a journalist. Briefly: There was reportedly no video of the famous intrasquad scrimmage that the Dream Team played in Monte Carlo prior to the 1992 Olympic Games in Barcelona. But in the course of my reporting for the book Dream Team, I found that Pete Skorich, coach Chuck Daly's personal videographer who worked for the Detroit Pistons, had indeed taped the entire session.

Pete gave me a copy of the CD, I paid to have it touched up and sound-edited, paid someone to make an actual box score of the game and made it a chapter in *Dream Team*, which SI excerpted. Not a month goes by when somebody doesn't ask me if they can get a copy of it, but the NBA took control of it when they found out they had it. I wouldn't have dreamed of selling it anyway, but I always thought that Skorich should've gotten something out of it. "I was just doing my job," Pete always said.

DECEMBER 23, 2013

Anatomy of a Miracle

Ray Allen's Game 6 three-pointer didn't just swipe the
NBA title for Miami. It capped a beautifully frenetic half-
minute that, for better and worse, no one can stop reliving

BY LEE JENKINS

*For the better part of a generation, the Spurs defined success in the NBA. This
story is not about their many victories but instead about their most famous
loss. Lee Jenkins, one of SI's most talented and astute reporters, deconstructs
an all-time comeback.*

The best shots remain airborne forever, in driveways and alleys, at parks
and YMCAs, amateur imitations of Magic Johnson's junior skyhook over the
Celtics, Reggie Miller's turnaround against the Knicks, Michael Jordan's step-
back versus the Jazz. They live in dusty old gyms like the one at Santa Monica
High, where on a warm November morning, a 64-year-old former professor
and Air Force intelligence officer strides across the key to the right corner.
He glances down at the strip of hardwood separating the three-point line
from the sideline and marvels at how narrow it is. Someone shooting from
that corner would have only three feet to leap and land—not much room for
a man who is, say, 6'5" and wears size-15 sneakers. It's like asking a giant to do
gymnastics on a wire. "This son of a gun sprints all the way back here, turns
his body, gets his balance, takes his time and sets up perfectly," the professor
says. "He can't rush it. He has to follow through. And he does it all because

18

he's done it a million times before. He's waited his whole life for this shot."
Then Gregg Popovich pantomimes the stroke that broke his heart.

Popovich has demonstrated in hundreds of sideline interviews that he
is loath to discuss many subjects—his success, his emotional state, anything
having to do with momentum, whether he is "happy" about a development
or "surprised" by it, and how a team "got hot" or "went cold." Ask the Spurs'
coach to re-create the most excruciating moment of his career, however,
and he grows as animated as Metta World Peace on Jimmy Kimmel. His
players, wrapping up a morning shootaround before a game against the
Lakers, eye him curiously. Is he ... ? Is that ... ? Yes, he's doing the Ray Allen.
"It goes through my mind every day," Popovich says. "It's gone through my
mind every day since the game, and I'll be happy when it only goes through
my mind once a week."

Jill Popovich noticed her father sulking around his San Antonio home
in the weeks after the Heat beat the Spurs for the NBA championship, and
she exacted every sideline reporters' revenge. "I'm tired of this," Jill said.
"You've been to the Finals five times and won four. Greggy can't lose one?
Well, aren't you special!"

"You're right, honey," Popovich replied. He flew to San Francisco with his
assistant coaches for their annual summer retreat and dissected the video
of Game 6. Miami had won the series in seven games, but it was the sixth
that ate at Popovich: The Spurs, 28.2 seconds away from clinching their
fifth title in 14 seasons, blew a five-point lead and lost 103–100 in overtime.
The video session took seven hours. Popovich then presented the footage
to players on the first day of training camp. The Spurs weren't hiding the
wound. They were exposing it so it could heal. "I didn't want anybody going
into the season thinking, Oh, gosh, we got screwed, the basketball gods took
one away from us," Popovich says. "That's bulls--. There's a healthier way to
move on. It wasn't just one shot. It was 29 seconds."

:28

Losing the Finals, players will tell you, is a little like being in a car
accident. "Everything slows down," says Miami center Chris Bosh, "and you
see things you don't usually see, hear things you don't usually hear. It's kind
of terrifying." Trailing 94–89, the Heat huddled around coach Erik Spoelstra
during a timeout. "I thought it was over," Bosh says. "I was having flashbacks."

AmericanAirlines Arena looked the same to him as it did late in Game 6
of the 2011 Finals against the Mavericks. Security guards surrounding the
floor, bent at the waist, holding yellow ropes in anticipation of another
team's celebration. Staffers waiting in the tunnel, carrying duffel bags
stuffed with another team's championship hats and T-shirts. Fans rising
from their seats, stomping into the aisles toward the parking lots. Only one

image was different. Bosh's wife, Adrienne, so forlorn that night two years earlier, stood and applauded from her courtside seat across from the Heat bench. How sweet, Bosh thought, she doesn't know we're going to lose. "I figured if she was still clapping, I could still do my job," he says. "It was improbable, but I guess it wasn't impossible."

He looked at Spoelstra, scribbling a play. "Just focus on the clipboard," the coach said.

:27

Spoelstra sent out a lineup with five three-point shooters, leaving Bosh on the bench. Popovich countered by removing center Tim Duncan. As forward Mike Miller prepared to inbound near the Heat bench, Allen ran across the key, screening Manu Ginóbili and Danny Green to free LeBron James at the top of the circle. James caught the inbounds pass, but Green recovered and contested James's three-point attempt with an outstretched right hand. The shot, as hard and straight as a four-seam fastball, smacked off the bottom right corner of the backboard square. My God, Popovich thought to himself. We're up five and he just shot an air ball. The game might be over.

:26

Danielle Calixto, manager of a children's boutique in downtown Miami, sat among season-ticket holders in row 26, section 124. She had purchased two tickets on Stubhub for $287 apiece and brought her boss's eight-year-old daughter, Diandra. "The season-ticket holders were all getting up, shaking hands, telling each other, 'I'll see you next season,'" Calixto says. "I told them, 'You're going to regret this,' and they said, 'Yeah, you're funny.' Diandra started crying because everybody was leaving, and she didn't understand why we weren't leaving too. We were surrounded by empty seats. She wanted to call her mom. I told her, 'You just have to sit here right now and believe with me.'"

:25

If James had shot a standard brick, San Antonio forward Kawhi Leonard would have grabbed the rebound in his colossal 9.8-inch mitts and sealed the game at the free throw line. But the shot was so wild Leonard couldn't corral it, and the ball rocketed off his hand and straight in the air. The closest Heat player was guard Dwyane Wade, stuck behind Leonard, giving up three inches and nine years. Wade jumped off his right leg, the one with the bone bruises in the knee that require daily treatment and occasional prayer. "Kawhi has those claws—his hands are claws—and you're just doing anything you can to get a fingertip on the ball," Wade says. "I got just enough."

:24

Green was the Finals' breakout star, but here he made a costly mistake. Instead of shadowing James on the left wing, he assumed San Antonio would come away with the loose ball and drifted downcourt. "Most important rebound of the game and we have a player who's backing up," Popovich says. "All he had to do was pick up LeBron."

:23

Royce Young, a reporter for CBSSports.com, was packing up his laptop. Young was sitting at a press table in section 102 and wanted to beat the crowd to the Spurs' locker room. He already had his story. He was going to write about Tracy McGrady, San Antonio's 12th man, finally winning a championship in his 16th season. "I don't blame the Miami fans for leaving," Young says. "I think 29 other teams' fans would have left too. The game was over." Wade's rebound tip bounced off Allen to Miller, who shoveled it back to James.

:22

Andre Wade was five in 2003, when Miami drafted Dwyane Wade. "Daddy," Andre told his father, Ricky, a Jamaican expat who owns 14 McDonald's franchises in Palm Beach County. "That's D-Wade and I'm A-Wade. We have to get season tickets." Andre and Ricky have spent the past decade in row 19. "With 20-something seconds left, I blew a gasket," Ricky says. "I told my son, 'I'm busted and disgusted. We're leaving.'" Andre protested, to no avail.

"I was angry at the fans who left," Allen says. "This is it. This is Game 6. We don't win and it's summer." He saw the ropes, encircling the floor, as a metaphor for his rage. "When you get to the end of your rope," Allen says, "tie a knot."

:21

With Green scrambling back, James elevated on the left wing and buried an open three. "Suddenly the energy in the building totally changed," says Heat general manager Andy Elisburg. Young pulled his laptop back out of the bag. "Let me sit down just a second," he thought.

:20

Popovich used his final timeout. Spoelstra told his players which Spurs to foul and what play he would likely call after the ensuing free throws. James nibbled his right thumbnail. Allen swigged a bottle of water. "There was a play we'd worked on all season, but we didn't use more than once or twice," Spoelstra says. The mere mention of it induces an eye roll from Bosh. "We practiced it a million times," he says. "We never ran it."

:19

Duncan extricated his feet from the ropes along the sideline and inbounded to Leonard, who was promptly fouled. Allen waved his arms up and down, begging the crowd for noise, for life. Leonard missed the first free throw. Behind the San Antonio bench a woman in a white tank top and sunglasses waved a red foam finger over the players, like bunny ears. McGrady bowed his head. Leonard made the second: 95–92.

:18

All season the Spurs had taken Duncan out when leading by three late in games because they switch defenders on every pick-and-roll to blanket the three-point line. At 37, he is the slowest of the starters—and therefore the likeliest to be late on a switch. Duncan, who had 30 points and 16 rebounds, was replaced by Boris Diaw. Bosh, however, was back in for the Heat.

:17

Spoelstra called the play, the one the Heat never run. Point guard Mario Chalmers, who made the buzzer beater that forced overtime for Kansas in the 2008 national championship game, dribbled down the left side.

:16

Allen, like most snipers, didn't grow up shooting corner threes. He only discovered their value once he reached the NBA. The corners yield the highest percentage three-pointers, not only because they're closest to the basket, but also because teams swing the ball around the perimeter, forcing the defense to rotate. The last swing pass, and the last rotation, is to the corner. "I always go to the corner first," Allen says. He jogged down the right side. But he was nothing more than a decoy to space the floor for James.

:15

Chalmers continued all the way to the left elbow. "Some people thought we should foul," Popovich says, though Chalmers shot 79.5% from the line last season. "O.K., so you're three points up and you foul, now it's a one-point game and a free throw shooting contest. And we're one of the worst free throw shooting teams in the league. All we need is a rebound and it's over. I wouldn't give that up for a free throw contest."

:14

A panel of 11 voters, spread around the arena, chose the Finals MVP. NBA staffers radioed the picks to Tim Frank, the league's senior vice president of communications. Frank feverishly tallied the votes on press row so he could relay the result to commissioner David Stern for the trophy presentation.

:13

Bosh screened point guard Tony Parker on the left wing to clear James at the three-point line, and since San Antonio was switching everything, Diaw picked up James. But San Antonio committed another uncharacteristic error. Instead of switching back onto Bosh, Parker joined Diaw and lunged at James. "It was my job to screen Tony," Bosh says. "When he went under me, I was like, Oh, s--. I thought about screening him again, but I didn't want to pick up the foul." Bosh didn't yet recognize the opportunity Parker had handed him.

:12

"In 2011, the first year this group was together, we had so many failures in late-game situations," Spoelstra says. "We spent an inordinate amount of time fixing them. In 2013, during the 27-game winning streak, we had games where we were down in the fourth quarter and had to storm back. We realized we've been here before."

:11

James fired, Diaw in his face, Parker in his shorts. Bosh had nowhere to go but the rim. "He was all by himself at the top of the key," Popovich says. "He walked right into the lane."

:10

Bosh is no bruiser, but the Heat used him at center in the Finals to keep more shooters on the court. "He was making sacrifices that whole series," says former Miami center Alonzo Mourning, now a member of the team's front office. "He didn't score much, but people don't realize how much he focused on clogging that middle and getting those rebounds."

:09

James missed—albeit with a lighter touch this time—and the ball caromed off the left side of the rim. Ginóbili, guarding Allen in the right corner, abandoned him to track the rebound. He got one hand on the ball. Bosh got two. Ideally, the Spurs would have fouled immediately, but Bosh held the ball only for a second, and in that second he noticed something. Ginóbili, the man assigned to the best three-point shooter in NBA history, was falling down.

:08

As a young player in Milwaukee, Allen invented a drill in which he lies in the key, springs to his feet and backpedals to the corner. A coach throws him a pass. He has to catch and shoot without stepping on the three-point line or the sideline. In Allen's first training session with the Heat, just after Labor Day 2012, he performed the drill. "It was the first time I ever saw anybody do that," Spoelstra says. "He told me he does it for offensive rebounding purposes. He said, 'You never know when you'll be in a situation where you have to find the three-point line without looking down.'"

:07

Allen had followed Ginóbili into the key, even though Bosh was in a far better rebounding position. "Get where you need to be!" he told himself. He took five furious steps backward. "CB!" he shouted. "CB!"

"I used to have nightmares about Ray," Elisburg says. "The ball works around the three-point line, and there's Ray, and he's wide open in the corner, and you see it coming in slow motion. Now he plays for us, and it was in slow motion again. You see Chris looking at Ray and Ray running back.

It's make or miss, win or lose, live or die. But isn't that the beauty of sports?" Bosh backhanded the ball to Allen. "I wish I'd waited a little bit longer," Bosh says, but John Stockton couldn't have made a better pass. Allen caught it at his rib cage with his right hand, and as he gathered, he took two final steps back over the three-point line. He didn't look down. The next day Frank asked Allen if he knew his size-15s were over the line. "I hoped," he said.

:06

Mike Breen and his friends at Fordham used to follow the basketball team wherever it played. They sat in the stands, and when a Ram hit an outside shot, Breen yelled "Bang!" He incorporated the catchphrase into his broadcasts first as play-by-plan man for the school radio station and later as lead NBA announcer for ESPN. Breen arrives at arenas around three hours before tip-off. In Miami, and before that in Boston, and before that in Seattle, and before that in Milwaukee, one person was sure to greet him. "Ray was always on the court," Breen says. "He was always shooting."

Allen's game-day routine never changes. He naps after shootaround. He eats chicken and white rice for lunch. He arrives three hours before the tip. Game 6 was no different, but for the first 47 minutes and 54 seconds, he made just one basket, a layup. He was concerned enough about his rhythm, or lack thereof, that he retreated to the practice court at halftime for extra shooting.

:05

With Ginóbili down, a cavalry of four Spurs charged at Allen, led by Parker. But he wasn't rushing. According to an ESPN Sport Science segment, Allen's average shot release takes .73 of a second. This time he waited a leisurely .83. "If you didn't know the context—if you took a picture of my positioning, my body, and erased the backdrop—you'd just say, 'Oh, that's Ray shooting a three-pointer,'" Allen says. "It looked exactly the same."

Norris Cole knew first. "I was on the bench, in the opposite corner, so I had the best view of it," says Miami's backup point guard. "That's why I jumped so high." He tracked the flight of the ball, traveling at a 40-degree angle, and leaped three feet in the air. "Rebound Bosh!" Breen said. "Back out to Allen! His three-pointer! Bang!"

A viewing party at the AT&T Center in San Antonio fell silent. "Oh s—!" Heat forward Shane Battier yelled on the bench. "We're in it! We're here! We're here!" Even a security guard, holding the yellow rope behind Allen, pumped a fist. "There was a collective violence in the building," Elisburg says. "It was like an explosion."

At the scorers' table Frank stopped tallying MVP votes. In row 26 little Diandra bawled again, and Calixto tried to comfort her. "Someday you will understand all this," she said. "You will be glad you were here." And in section 102, Young thought about his wife, Keri, whom he called after Game 5 in San Antonio. He wanted to fly home to Oklahoma City and leave Game 6 to another reporter. "What if something amazing happens that you'll remember for the rest of your life?" Keri said. "You don't want to miss that."

Ricky and Andre Wade were walking through the parking lot when they heard the eruption. "I think the Heat came back," Andre said. "No," Ricky replied. "That's just the Spurs winning the bloody championship." They flipped on 790 AM, the Heat's flagship station, in their car. "The announcer was screaming, 'Ray Allen did it! Ray Allen did it!'" Ricky recalls. "My son was so pissed at me. He said, 'I told you. We got Ray Allen for a reason. Ray Allen is clutch.'"

Bosh heard Popovich's voice cut through the din: "Run! Run!" Popovich wanted the Spurs to inbound the ball, while the Heat were celebrating, and drive straight to the rim. "We've won games just like that before," Popovich says. But referee Joey Crawford stopped play to confirm that Allen was behind the three-point line. "He was clearly behind the line—that's why I was so livid," Popovich says. "But I talked to the league about it later, and I understand it intellectually. They wanted to make sure they got it right."

:04

As Crawford reviewed the replay, Spoelstra put James on Parker, to take advantage of his size as well as his adrenaline. James gathered the Heat, urging them to harness their emotions. "We need to commit together to finish this game," he said. "That shot is for nothing if we don't focus here."

:03

In 20 years, Spoelstra believes, people will forget that there were another five seconds left, plus overtime, plus Game 7. Fans outside the arena who learned of Allen's shot on their smartphones tried to force their way back in. But the doors, marked NO RE-ENTRY ALLOWED, were locked. "I asked one of the ushers what it was like, and she said people were banging on the doors, jerking the handles, trying to get them open," Young says. "She was nervous that if they did open one, she'd get trampled." The marooned fans watched through the windows on a television in the Heat souvenir store.

:02

Parker took the inbounds pass and drove down the left side, but he couldn't turn the corner on James, who wore him like a second sleeve. Bosh raced over to contest, and Parker unleashed a one-legged fade-away as he fell across the baseline. It didn't reach the rim.

:01

Royce Young was not going to write about McGrady. Little Diandra would have to hang in there for five minutes of overtime. The real fans poured down from the 300-level into the expensive seats. "We needed a historic 30 seconds," Battier says. "And we got it."

:00

"Get those mother---- ropes out of here," Allen hollered as the buzzer sounded, and off went the security guards, off went the duffel bags, off went the Spurs' championship shirts and hats—eventually to impoverished regions of Africa as donations from the NBA.

After the Heat had won to force Game 7, Spoelstra retreated to his office and watched the last half-minute of regulation. "It crumbled me in my chair," he says. Breen went back to the Mandarin Oriental hotel and barely slept. Bosh went out to dinner and barely ate. "What's wrong with you?" friends asked. "What happened tonight," he replied, "never happens."

"But it happened!" they said.

"I know," Bosh explained. "We could play out that scenario a million times and maybe we win twice." He told his wife what a difference her applause made. "Really?" Adrienne said. "I was just trying to keep from crying."

Ricky and Andre Wade, elated but embarrassed, decided not to tell anyone that they bailed early. But TV cameras had captured them leaving the arena, Ricky in green pants and a white shirt, Andre in a white shirt and Heat hat. "We started getting calls from friends and family in England, Jamaica, South America, asking, 'What the hell were you doing?'" Ricky says. "I told my son, 'We are scandalized. The world knows we walked out.'" Ricky was offered $7,000 for his two tickets to Game 7, which the Heat won 95–88. He turned down the cash. "This has impacted us so significantly," Ricky says. "It teaches you, Never turn your back on something important to you. Stick it out until the end."

The day after Game 6, Popovich gathered the Spurs. "I know you don't believe this now," he told them, "but if that's the worst thing that ever happens to you, you'll lead easy lives. You've got jobs, you've got wives, you've got children. S-- will happen to you. It's called life. Mark this down as a tough one, but if it's the toughest, then you're lucky. So get over it and let's go play."

He delivered a variation of the same speech three months later on the first day of training camp. The Spurs, to no one's surprise, began this season 17-4. Six months have passed, and Allen sits in the cramped visiting locker room at Minnesota's Target Center, considering the consequences of his 3,209th NBA three-pointer. "If we don't win that game," he says, "I'm probably not here right now. This locker room is very different." Bosh would be the scapegoat. Spoelstra would be under fire. James would be back in the public crosshairs.

Instead, James won his second straight Finals MVP, and Spoelstra signed a contract extension. They're all kings. "I've been overwhelmed by people who saw that shot," Allen says. "Famous people, regular people, everywhere I go it's all anyone wants to talk about. But it's never really about my making the shot. It's always about where they were." He savors their stories. One friend, in Brooklyn, left a house party because the guests were too loud. He returned to his apartment just in time to see his buddy let fly. His shriek woke the building.

On a trip to Toronto this season Allen ran into Frank, and he was reminded of the notorious yellow ropes. "I know you guys were just doing what you had to do," Allen said. In a way, he's grateful for those ropes. They added a little more thread to a 29-second tapestry that will live in montages and driveways forever. The extra twine helped produce the unbreakable knot.

— POSTSCRIPT —

Lee Jenkins: Every epic comeback includes an equally staggering collapse, so when I started writing a retrospective of Ray Allen's three-pointer in Game 6 of the 2013 Finals, I realized I'd need the Spurs' point of view and I assumed they wouldn't be excited to share it. At that point, I only knew Gregg Popovich from the little he shared during press conferences and sideline interviews, flashing reporters either blank looks or death stares. I could only imagine how he'd respond when I sent a request to discuss the most excruciating moment of his career. Popovich agreed to meet after a shootaround at Santa Monica High. A lot of the great ones don't like talking about their victories. "How happy are you? How good does this feel? How do you win every time?" Those are the questions that earn the death stares. But ask Gregg Popovich about the time Ray Allen broke his heart with both hands and stomped on it in the right corner at American Airlines Arena, and he lights up. "It was 29 seconds," he said, deconstructing them frame by frame, as if studying the moments leading up to a train wreck. Several Spurs eyed Popovich during the interview, standing in the right corner of the court, mimicking the position of Allen's feet and the extension of his release. He was smiling as he pretended to let fly. He'd made peace with his worst moment, and if he had, then they could also. No surprise, six months later, they won the championship.

FEBRUARY 19, 1990

She Was Truckin'

Schoolgirl Lisa Leslie scored 101 points in the first half, and then the opposition went home

BY SHELLEY SMITH

Before she became a collegiate star, fashion icon and WNBA legend, Lisa Leslie was a high school prodigy trying to make her mark. And, back in 1990, before a successful women's pro league or widespread coverage of the women's NCAA tournament, sometimes the best way to do that was through outrageous feats: dunking a ball, taking on men's players, scoring an ungodly amount. Leslie did all of the above. Shelley Smith, who went on to a long career at ESPN, deftly captures a moment in time, both for Leslie and for women's hoops.

Lisa Leslie figured she would score between 25 and 30 points a quarter, or just enough to break Cheryl Miller's eight-year-old national single-game record of 105 points in a high school game. Just enough, she hoped, to solidify her position as the hottest high school player in the country. But a funny thing happened on the way to the record book.

"I heard a buzzer and looked up at the scoreboard," says Lisa, a 6'5" senior center at Morningside High in Inglewood, Calif. "It showed us up 49–6. I asked. 'Is this the half?'"

It was the end of the first *quarter*, and Lisa had scored all her team's points in a Feb. 7 game against an injured, overmatched squad from South Torrance High. By halftime Morningside, the defending state champion, had a 102–24 lead, and Lisa had added 52 points in the second quarter for a stunning total of 101, four shy of Miller's record. But she wouldn't get it. Lisa's opponents had seen enough. Two members of the visiting South Torrance team had already fouled out, and another was injured, leaving only four healthy players to contend with Lisa and her teammates. So, after taking a vote among the wounded during intermission, South Torrance coach Gilbert Ramirez decided to forfeit the game.

Upon hearing the news, Lisa asked Ramirez if his team would let her score three more baskets to surpass the record. The South Torrance players said no. The referees allowed Lisa to shoot four technicals, levied for delay of game, at the start of what would have been the third quarter. She made them all to gain what she thought was a place alongside Miller, who played for Riverside (Calif.) Poly High and starred at USC, in the record book. The points, however, were later nullified by Southern Section officials, who ruled that the game was over when Ramirez quit at the half.

The next day South Torrance's players, humiliated, limped back to school, where they met privately with principal John Schmitt, who said the team was "very upset." Schmitt then called an all-school assembly in which he voiced support for Ramirez, whom Southern Section officials suspended for one game for having forfeited. (He was subsequently reinstated and did not miss a game.) "This is not what we promote in high school athletics," Schmitt says.

Tell that to California state senator Diane Watson, who presented Lisa with a certificate of recognition two days after the massacre. "I heard how you burned up the court," Watson told her. "I heard how the other team was so in fear it had to leave. You are a winner."

South Torrance players knew before the game that they had been chosen as sacrificial lambs for Lisa, who was averaging 27.3 points, 15.1 rebounds, three assists and seven blocked shots for the season and in January was named the female recipient of the Dial Award, given annually to the nation's outstanding high school scholar-athlete. For the past three years Morningside coach Frank Scott has given one senior the chance to break the school's single-game scoring record in the team's final home game. South Torrance wasn't the Lady Monarchs' final home opponent this season, but a bench-clearing fight had broken out the last time Morningside played its last home foe, Centennial High, and Scott was worried the game could turn ugly again if Lisa attempted to break the record against the Apaches. Thus, South Torrance was led to slaughter.

"Lisa could have broken the record her sophomore year," says Scott. "And if I'd let her, she could have averaged 50 points a game instead of 27." Even so, perhaps Morningside's thoughtless tradition should be reexamined.

To her credit, Lisa did not dunk, something she does early and often in most every other game, on the smaller South Torrance players. And she didn't turn hostile when South Torrance quintuple-teamed her, swatting and scratching in futility at her shots, most of which were short-range jumpers. Lisa didn't escape unscathed, either. She suffered a cut lip and more than a few bruises, some of them coming from salvos fired at her the next day by the local media and by angry callers to radio talk shows, all of which decried her lack of sportsmanship in flogging an obviously helpless opponent. Of the criticism, Lisa shrugged and said, "I can handle it. I won't be here forever."

Having reached 6'2" by the time she was in the ninth grade, Lisa has perfected the Teflon approach to fielding insults. Life has not been easy for her. She met her father just once after he left the family when Lisa was four years old. He died five years ago. To support her three daughters—Dionne, 22, Lisa, 17, and Tiffany, 10—Christine Leslie bought an 18-wheel rig in 1982 and began taking to the road for months at a time, leaving a live-in housekeeper to care for the three girls. Christine doesn't like leaving her children, but the money she earns is too good to pass up. And every penny goes home.

"There were some sad times," says Lisa. "Mom had to travel so far and so long. But we understood she had to do it. It made me mature really fast. I had so much to do."

When school let out for summer vacations, Christine packed Lisa and her younger sister into the rig and drove across the country. Most of the time they all slept on a bunk in the back of the truck. "It was 36 inches wide," Christine says. "All of us would jam in there. We had to hold on to each other. That helps us now. We all hold on to each other in a lot of ways."

Lisa started playing basketball in the seventh grade, and by last season she was recognized as the best high school player in the nation. Last summer she starred on the U.S. Olympic junior national team that toured Spain. She has a 3.5 grade point average and has been class president three of her four years at Morningside. Recruited by hundreds of colleges, she says she has narrowed her choices to Long Beach State, Southern Cal and Notre Dame. In fact, women's basketball at the collegiate level has been praying for someone like Lisa to come along since Miller, a four-time All-America, finished at USC in 1986. So, no matter where she goes, everyone will benefit—except, of course, her opponent of the moment.

Lisa's performance against South Torrance did earn her a place in the record book in one category—most free throws made in a game. She converted 27 of 35 shots from the line. Lisa also converted 37 of her 56 field goal attempts in her 16-minute flurry. Looking back, she doesn't regret trying to break the record, only that she didn't make it. Of the South Torrance players, she says she's sorry if they feel bad.

"It wasn't personal," says Lisa. "They knew I was going for the record. I thought knowing that would take some of the hurt away."

NOVEMBER 13, 1995

55

Last spring, the newly unretired Michael Jordan lit up
Manhattan, the Knicks and the NBA itself with what may
have been the most thrilling performance of his career

BY ALEXANDER WOLFF

*In 1995, Alexander Wolff set out to recount one of Michael Jordan's most
legendary performances: the night he dropped 55 points against the Knicks
at Madison Square Garden in just his fifth game after returning from his
short-lived retirement.*

*Wolff faced a formidable obstacle, however. A year earlier, SI had run a cover
on Jordan's baseball career with the headline "Bag It, Michael." Since then, MJ
had refused to speak to SI. So, even though Wolff had known Jordan for years,
dating back to his North Carolina years, he didn't even try to interview him.*

*Instead, as Wolff later recalled, "What that forced me to do was go other
places to recreate the circumstances. I got the tape, watched it, slowed it
down, rewound it and then tried to talk to as many people as possible."*

*The result is a hybrid story. "It's this great interplay between game action
and the other context, the human interest, that surrounds it," Wolff said. "So
much stuff dribbles out after a big game that you're never going to find on
deadline in the blush of those 90 minutes or so that you have. This story was
somewhat like a historical piece and a deadline piece."*

*There is no place like it, no place with an atom of its glory, pride, and
exultancy. It lays its hand upon a man's bowels; he grows drunk with ecstasy;*

31

he grows young and full of glory, he feels that he can never die. —Thomas Wolfe, on New York City

On March 27 of this year, on a Monday afternoon flush with the balm of spring, Michael Jordan arrived in Manhattan and checked into the Plaza Hotel. That evening he and four companions, including NBC commentator Ahmad Rashad, met for dinner downtown at Robert De Niro's Tribeca Grill. These were old friends, determined to liberate Jordan from the prison of his hotel room—to "keep it regular," as Rashad says. The game that Jordan and his Chicago Bulls were to play the next night against the New York Knicks at Madison Square Garden was only indirectly alluded to, but throughout the evening Rashad sensed something about Jordan—sensed that Jordan knew that if he had something to say, New York was the place to say it.

When Jordan returned to the hotel after midnight, CBS's Pat O'Brien was waiting for a previously scheduled interview. Jordan had stood him up for more than three hours, but O'Brien had spent that time well, drawing up the most prescient of questions. "When will fans see an explosion," he asked, "the kind of game in which you score 55 points?"

"It's just a matter of time," said Jordan.

Jordan wasn't accustomed to being measured against his past. Until he stepped away from the game for 17 months, beginning in October 1993, the public had always spun its wonderment forward, asking the question, "What's he gonna do next?" But with his return, the public imagination now ran backward, and to Jordan the rephrasing of the usual question must have come with daunting psychological g-forces: Can he possibly do those things again?

And, oh, those things he had done. There had been that moment during his final season at North Carolina, in the dying seconds of a victory at Maryland, when Jordan made off with a lazy Terrapin pass and threw down a breakaway dunk stunning in its suddenness, its playfulness, its remorselessness. As Jordan sat in the locker room, his eyes intent on the latticework of his shoelaces, a reporter asked him if he had intended the dunk to "send a message."

"No messages," he replied, scarcely looking up, like an efficient secretary.

Back then Jordan had no need to gild his game with ulterior meaning. But things were different now, 11 years, three NBA titles, two Olympic gold medals, his father's murder and a bush-league baseball misadventure later. Based on the first few games of Jordan's comeback from his sabbatical in the Chicago White Sox organization, a columnist in Florida had already declared him "finished." One New York tabloid had dubbed him FAIR JORDAN. And Doug Collins, an NBA analyst for Turner Sports who had been

Jordan's coach with the Bulls and soon would become coach of the Detroit Pistons, had committed apostasy. He had called Jordan "human."

So it was that, carrying a new uniform number, 45, and these fresh burdens, Jordan found himself in New York with a message to deliver. *While you were out....*

In a hype-saturated age, before a hype-inured crowd, in a building whose owners have enough chutzpah to call the place "the world's most famous arena," Jordan did more than live up to his extravagant billing that night. In his fifth game and 11th day back in the league, he somehow surpassed it. He did, indeed, go for 55 points against the Knicks—more than anyone had scored in the new Garden since it opened in 1968 and the highest total to that point in the NBA season. Dunking but once, he scored blithely, over and around six different members of a team notorious for its defense, until it came time to win the game. Then he did so with a pass.

With baseball still on strike, hockey scarcely off its lockout and football's most gifted and charismatic ballcarrier, its onetime MJ equivalent, being shuttled in handcuffs between a jail and a courtroom, the world of sports sorely craved what Jordan provided. But even he must have wondered if he was still capable of going off in such fashion—until three days earlier, in Atlanta. That's where he had fully reacquainted himself with the rhythms that in basketball come vertically, up from your feet, not horizontally, through your arms and hips, as a baseball player's do. Against the Hawks he had sunk 14 of 26 shots and scored 32 points, including the game-winning two on a hanging jumper at the horn. The performance sling-shot him on to New York, to find out, as the song says, if he could make it there.

On Tuesday the 28th, at the Bulls' game-day shootaround, the Garden is rank with the smell of elephants, the Ringling Bros. and Barnum & Bailey Circus having arrived five days earlier. But Jordan and a teammate, Ron Harper, are engaged in a game involving a different species: a version of H-O-R-S-E, half-court shots only.

"How much?" Harper asks, playing to Jordan's wagering jones.

"Fifty," says Jordan.

"I got you."

Three times they match each other, miss for miss, before Jordan bottoms one out. Then Harper launches his try into the air, and, amazingly, it too swishes through the hoop.

But here is what makes Jordan Jordan: His next shot, another 43-footer, is perfect. Harper is literally at a loss.

"Hah!" says Jordan, adding a sort of amen to an omen.

Every year the Super Bowl spends two weeks building itself up so 100 million Americans might be ritually let down. But there has been no fortnight of foreplay to Jordan's visit to the Garden, because two weeks ago he still was not officially under contract to play basketball.

As strobe lights and flashbulbs fire during warmups, the Garden is already full and charged with promise. Old hands, the ones who can recall the title fights of the Ali era and the Sinatra comeback concert held here, have a point of reference. But younger employees are thrown for a loop. "It was June all of a sudden, right in the middle of March," Chris Brienza, 30, the Knicks' director of public relations at the time, will say later. Brienza has issued credentials to some 325 members of the media (175 more than for a normal regular-season game) from a dozen countries. But only about half can be accommodated with seats, so an apology is distributed to every member of the press. "As you may have guessed," the handout begins, "tonight's Knicks-Bulls game is, shall we say, somewhat popular...."

Outside the Garden, the Bulls' team bus has taken 15 minutes to negotiate the half block from Seventh Avenue to the Garden's service entrance. Some people among the swells surrounding the arena bang on the sides of the motorcoach when they realize who's inside. Scalpers lucky enough to hold $95 lower box seats are getting as much as $1,000 a ticket. At Gerry Cosby & Co., the sporting-goods store in the Garden concourse, clerks are selling number 45 jerseys right out of the boxes. "All Bulls stuff is going again after being dead for a year and a half," says Cosby's Jim Root.

Jordan is normally available to the press until the locker room closes 45 minutes before tip-off. He particularly likes to engage the New York writers, to consider their smarter-than-average questions. But tonight he hides out in the training room, playing solitaire on his portable computer.

Every playoff renewal of the rivalry between the Bulls and the Knicks during the early 1990s has featured an incident with Jordan at its center. In '91, in Chicago's 103–94 Game 3 victory over New York, Jordan dunked over 7-foot Knick center Patrick Ewing as the Bulls swept the series. On the eve of Game 7 a year later, Michael asked for advice from his father, James, whose body would be found in a South Carolina creek 15 months later; Papa's counsel—"Take over"—worked just fine, with Michael going for 42 and the Bulls winning by 29.

In 1993 Jordan took his infamous gambling trip to Atlantic City between the series' first two games, both Chicago losses, yet he rose to block one of 6'10" forward Charles Smith's four unavailing shots under the basket as Game 5 wound down, and the Bulls eliminated the Knicks once more. Why, in Game 4 Jordan scored 54 points. (Imagine ... 54 points!)

The Bulls' route to each of their three crowns went through New York. Yet in 1994, with Jordan having been taken to task by a certain weekly sports magazine for "embarrassing" baseball, the Knicks finally beat Chicago and advanced to the NBA Finals. Thus, to New York fans, Jordan ought to seem like a Sisyphean rock. Yet there's affection in the voice of Mike Walczewski, the Garden's P.A. announcer, as he introduces Jordan, and unambivalent cheers from the crowd—a crowd that jeers the other Bull starters.

Jordan will later say that he had never felt less confident before a game. But the way he walks to the center circle for the tip-off, pausing halfway there to paw at the floor with his shoes like some ready-to-strike animal, hints at what is to come.

How does a pro basketball player score 55 points? Even if you're Michael Jordan, it helps if you've essentially been ordered to do so by your coach. The request unburdens the conscience, leaving you free to let fly. For the better part of two seasons, Chicago coach Phil Jackson has run up against the skinflint New York defense too many times without Jordan not to take full advantage of his presence now. "They'd smothered us," Jackson will say. "We needed scoring. So I said, 'Go for it.'"

The first option of the Bulls' basic triangle set comes off the fast break. The team's most potent offensive threat nestles into the low post, hoping to get the ball there and make a move before the defense can entirely establish itself. During Jordan's absence, forward Scottie Pippen usually played this role, called post-up sprinter, but in Chicago's pregame meeting Jackson told Jordan to take up in the hub of the Chicago offense. "Everything else is pretty much a moot point if he can make his shots," Jackson will say afterward. "And we knew within a few minutes that he was making his shots."

His first, a short pull-up jumper in transition, comes on a pass from forward Toni Kukoc, the Croatian emigre who arrived after the Bulls' third title and had so looked forward to playing with Jordan that he broke down in tears the day Jordan announced his retirement. Jordan's second shot comes after he has set up as the post-up sprinter, and the Knicks are called for an illegal defense. He takes the subsequent inbounds pass and shows John Starks, who's attempting to guard him, a little mambo with the ball and a left-to-right rock before leaping up to shoot and score.

During the first quarter he'll do this again and again, having his way with the 6'5" Starks. Sometimes Jordan doesn't so much as show his face to Starks before spinning into a fallaway. The first time he feels Starks rest a forearm on his back Jordan spins past him and along the baseline for a layup. The next time he spins in the same direction, only to fall back and unspool another perfect jumper. Starks, with no recourse now, is whistled for a hold. As if to highlight the defensive quandary they're in, the Knicks are cited for their second illegal defense violation five minutes into the game.

Midway through the quarter, on consecutive baskets, Jordan knocks down two shots that are mirror images of one another: He takes two dribbles to his right, soars and feathers in a jumper (10 points now), then takes two dribbles to his left, leaps and sinks another (13 and counting). It's as if he's a basketball camper doing station drills, and the Knicks scarcely exist.

Here, finally, New York decides to dispatch some help to Starks. When Jordan next catches the ball on the low block, he finds Ewing rushing at him. Jordan spins to avoid the double team but, sealed off by the baseline, he's forced to leap up and throw a pass that's picked off.

In spite of this momentary success, the Knicks call off the double team. The move baffles Jackson, but New York coach Pat Riley has his reasons: In spite of Jordan's performance so far, the Knicks hold the lead and will for most of the game, at one point by as many as 14. And there's no team in basketball more adept than the Bulls at swinging the ball out of a double team and into the hands of an open shooter. "Their shooters and their spacing are so good," Riley will say, "that if you start running all over the place, they're going to get everything."

As the quarter winds down, Jordan seems joyous with each touch of the ball. One time he seems to bring his right knee up, in a sort of mummer's strut, as he rises into his shot (15 points now). "It's rare that players can live quite up to New York," Jackson, himself a former Knick, says later. "I've seen a lot of them fall flat on their faces because of the pressure to perform there. But he had the whole evening in the palm of his hand. Sometimes the game just seems to gravitate into his grasp."

At one point the Knicks throw a new jersey at him, 6'8" forward Anthony Bonner. Jordan has schooled the smaller Starks on the blocks; Gulliver here he takes outside, draining his longest jumper of the evening thus far, with a little leftward float thrown in to make it interesting (17 points). Then he bottoms out a three-pointer, only the second of 11 attempted treys to this point in his comeback (20 points). The Knicks lead at the quarter 34–31, but Jordan has sunk nine of 11 shots.

"I'm going to miss him," Starks had said upon hearing of Jordan's retirement. "He brought out the best in me."

"I think he forgot how to play me," Jordan will say after the game.

So many celebrities are in the Garden that if the Oscars hadn't taken place in Los Angeles the night before, the whole country might be listing alarmingly to starboard. The usual potted plants, Knick regulars Woody Allen and Spike Lee, are rustling their leaves courtside. Tom Brokaw, Peter Falk, Bill Murray, Diane Sawyer and Damon Wayans all have taken the trouble to rearrange their busy schedules. There's Christopher Reeve, pre-accident, and Mario Cuomo, post-Pataki. And tonight the stars seem to come in pairs. Phil and Marlo. Connie and Maury. Lawrence Taylor and fellow pro wrestler Diesel. Even pairs that should be together: Itzhak Perlman, recording artist, and Earl (the Pearl) Monroe, now a recording executive.

As Jordan goes for the speed limit, announcer Al Trautwig, working the sidelines for MSG Network, approaches a large man sitting courtside. "Excuse me," he asks. "Are you Al Cowlings?"

In spite of having its own financial market and international flights to 65 cities, Chicago has a woeful dearth of celebrities. Joe Mantegna and Oprah can only take a town so far. Chicago is so star-poor that, months later on Monday Night Football, a Bear fan diving 30 feet from the stands in pursuit of an extra point will end up with the same agent as Jim McMahon.

Thus the city must get all it can out of its single world-class celeb. Two nights after Jordan's New York epic, SportsChannel Chicago will air 24 hours of highlights and documentary footage of, and interviews with, the man himself. And a Windy City radio station will poll its listeners on the pressing matter of whether Jordan should be named King of the Universe.

It's a wonder that only 41% say yes.

In the second quarter Jordan seems to slip the bounds of the Garden and reinvent his surroundings—to pull asphalt under his feet and the spirit of New York's playgrounds into his bloodstream. Fifteen of the Bulls' 19 points this quarter will be his: his 28th and 29th of the game on his staple, the simple fallaway over Starks; his 30th and 31st after jabbing with each shoulder, then spinning into another fallaway that beats a dying shot clock. In a glimpse of foreshadowing, up for a jumper near the end of the half, he passes up the shot, pitching instead to a 7-foot teammate, end-of-the-bencher Bill Wennington, who pitches it right back.

Jordan's tongue comes out often as he makes these moves, of course. But at one point he flashes a trace of a smile. His mirth is evidently contagious; later in the game Starks will head downcourt unable to suppress a laugh at the ridiculousness of what he has become a victim of. "In a game like this," the former supermarket checkout clerk says later, "you just have to hope he starts missing."

Jordan hardly has missed as he leaves the court at the half. The Bulls trail 56–50, but Jordan has sunk 14 of 19 shots. As he files through the tunnel an adolescent girl reaches over the railing above, risking getting singed as Jordan's hand meets hers.

A Garden basketball crowd is famous for its ability to make the syllables of the word defense sound like invective. Yet Jordan and his 35 points have reduced 19,763 people to disorganized murmuring. Going back nearly four decades New Yorkers have been quick to root for the home team, but they've also been appreciative of the great opponent. The Knicks sucked rotten eggs during the early 1960s, but the undercard of an NBA doubleheader back then might have featured the Boston Celtics or the Philadelphia Warriors, and fans would fill the old Garden for a 6 p.m. tip-off to behold the conjurings of a Cousy or the majesty of a Chamberlain.

Yet through the 1990s Jordan haunted the Garden in part because some of that connoisseurship seemed to spill from the loges and infect the Knicks themselves. From power forward Charles Oakley, the team's enforcer and an ex-Bull who adores his former teammate, to Starks and that laugh he'll let slip, the entire Knick family seems to have a streak of the fan in it.

Not that anyone in the stands is going to take the Knicks to task for falling under Jordan's spell, least of all tonight, anyway; they too are his hostages, suffering from a sort of Stockholm syndrome. "More than anything else, the fans wanted to see him have a great game," Jackson will say. "It was like they'd gone to a Broadway show."

Intermission over, Jordan scores points 40, 41 and 42 on a three-point shot. Forty-seven, 48 and 49 come on another trey. No one in the NBA should be able to jump-shoot his way to a total like this, least of all against a team of bogarters like the Knicks, least of all Jordan, whose J is a jumble of knocked knees and limbs akimbo even when it's clicking, and it hasn't been clicking since he returned. Yet here he is, on his way to scoring 55 the way Larry Bird might have scored 55.

The Bulls' Steve Kerr may be the best three-point shooter in the league. Yet friends will tell him later that he looks starstruck as he sits on the bench, watching as Jordan sends shot after shot whispering through the net. The reaction of players like Kerr worries Jackson. The Bulls were so dependent on Jordan prior to Jackson's taking over the team in 1989 that then assistant coach John Bach referred to the team's "archangel offense." To transform Chicago into the group that won three straight titles, Jackson took on twin missions: to jawbone Jordan into involving his teammates more through the triangle offense, and to persuade the "Jordanaires" that the team's goals weren't being served if they stood around gawking during number 23's levitations. Jackson's membership on the 1973 Knick title team, a squad founded on balanced scoring and a commitment to finding the open man, established his bona fides as he made that sale.

At first Jackson and Jordan coexisted in delicate balance—the coach with his higher truth of championship basketball, which Jordan so desperately sought; the superstar with his worldly gift, the ability to manufacture baskets when Jackson's beloved triangle broke down. By the time the Bulls won their first crown, Jordan had become so committed to team play that he accepted the ritual "I'm going to Disney World" endorsement opportunity only when the other Bull starters were included. Yet now Jackson wondered if he would have to make both pitches all over again. No one on the team had played with Jordan before his return other than Pippen, center Will Perdue, swingman Pete Myers and guard B.J. Armstrong, who as a rookie had actually checked out a library book on Einstein and Mozart, hoping they would give him insight into genius and make him a more sympathetic teammate to the great one. And would Jordan come to understand that the team, which had been playing well when he rejoined it, didn't need a savior?

As if to provide Jackson with Exhibit A in that case, Chicago seizes its largest lead, 99–90, precisely when Jordan is taking his longest rest of the evening, for more than five minutes at the start of the fourth quarter. The Bulls knew they could score by letting Jordan go one-on-one. Now they have proved they can prosper without him at all.

Still, Jackson might wonder: Can the team click with Jordan a constituent part?

As the game enters its final minutes Jordan and Ewing are taking turns. Another Jordan jumper over Starks—points 52 and 53—gives the Bulls a 107–102 lead. After Starks counters with two free throws, Ewing adds one of his own; then, finally coming over again to help Starks on a double team, he blocks a Jordan shot, making possible a slam from Starks that ties matters at 107. Jordan dishes off for his first assist of the game, to Pippen for a bank shot, and Chicago leads 109–107. Ewing's two free throws reknot things at 109 with 39 seconds left on the clock.

It's felicitous that Jordan and Ewing, Ewing and Jordan, are engaging each other down the stretch. In a few months they will be leading an uprising against the players' union. At the Plaza earlier this afternoon Jordan met with Charles Grantham, at the time the executive director of the players' association, to bone up on issues pertaining to a new collective bargaining agreement. By tonight's lights, could there be any better pair to make the case for how very productive NBA labor can be?

At Turner Broadcasting in Atlanta the suits know that the Nielsen ratings took their usual dip at halftime. But they spike up with the start of the third quarter, the result of tens of thousands of *Hey, are you watching this?* phone calls. Through the final two quarters the numbers creep upward in 15-minute increments, from a 5.2 to a 6.0 to a 6.8 to a 7.4 to an 8.0, ultimately averaging a 5.0 rating—a record for a nationally telecast game on cable.

Steve Smith of the Hawks yapped at Jordan three nights earlier, proving anew that, all things considered, mouthing at Michael isn't a prudent thing to do. "Who's going to get the shot?" Smith asked Jordan as the Bulls prepared to put the ball in play for the last time.

"Pippen," Jordan said, before taking the inbounds pass with 5.9 seconds to play, moving up the floor and beating his interlocutor with the game-winner.

Tonight, as adrenaline gets the better of Starks, he can't help himself. "Hey, how ya doin'?" the Knick guard asks Jordan late in the game, renewing acquaintances, after a fashion. "What's been goin' on?"

The same free-flowing juices that set off Starks's mouth cause him to bite for any fake Jordan offers, including this one. Starks is on his way down, helpless, as Jordan rises up for his final attempt, and final basket, of the night. The score now stands at 111–109, Chicago.

Jordan has squeezed off 37 shots. Twenty-one have found their mark, three from beyond the arc. Throw in his 10 foul shots and Jordan, as Spike Lee will put it, has dropped "a double nickel" on the Knicks.

During the 1994–95 season, Chicago's second-most celebrated basketball player may have been a West Sider named William Gates. He's the costar of *Hoop Dreams*, the acclaimed documentary film that traces Gates's life from age 14, when he was only a whisper in the Cabrini-Green housing projects, through high school, to the day his world-weary mother and washed-up older brother tearfully send him off to Marquette on a full scholarship. In a moment that gets just right the suddenness with which parenthood can steal up on adolescents living in places like Cabrini-Green, the film cuts to a shot at the Gateses' kitchen table. Encircling it are an infant girl, Alicia; her teenage mother, Catherine; and William, who, it becomes quickly clear, is Alicia's father. They are discussing the day Alicia was born and Catherine's request that William be in the delivery room—a request that went unfulfilled. "I can't miss a game just because an incident occurs, you know, unless it was like a death or something like that," William says.

"Something like that!" says Catherine. "This is a once-in-a-lifetime thing! Like the girl is born every day...."

"Especially around that time of the year, too, state tournament," says William.

Last night, Oscar night, Gates was in the Garden, playing in the Golden Eagles' 87–79 NIT semifinal defeat of Penn State. Gates didn't intend to let the Bulls pass through town tonight without looking in on his homeboys, and, a movie star now, he lined up courtside seats with Lee. But at 6 a.m. Catherine, now Gates's wife, called to tell him she was again going into labor, more than five weeks early.

It's an instructive epilogue to the film that Gates headed back to Chicago to witness the birth of his second child, William Jr. "Catherine's getting me back," Gates thought to himself as he headed for the airport. "Michael saved that performance for me, and I missed it," he will say upon hearing what had occurred in his absence.

Gates never did make it back for the NIT final, which Marquette lost 65–64 in overtime to Virginia Tech. Yet his decision bespoke a maturity that developed only after *Hoop Dreams* finished filming. He seems to have learned that you can hoop-dream all you want, but ultimately reality will settle back in–and in reality there's much more to life than a basketball game.

The foul that puts Starks on the line, where his free throws will tie the game at 111, is Perdue's sixth. Jackson sends Wennington in at center, and the Bulls call a timeout.

In the huddle the Bull staff points out that the Knicks have permanently changed their defensive thinking. After letting Starks (and such others as Greg Anthony, Hubert Davis and Derek Harper) be used and abused for most of the game, New York has sent Ewing over the last three times Jordan probed the Knick defense. Jackson and his aides remind Jordan that there will be a vacuum in the middle into which a teammate might slip.

Jordan dribbles to precisely the same spot from which he sank his last shot, the right elbow of the foul lane. Starks tracks him all the way. Sure enough, Ewing rushes over. "I'd be lying if I said I was coming out to pass the ball," Jordan will say later. "I was coming out to score. But then Patrick came over to help...."

It's an article of basketball faith that a player who's double-teamed finds the open man. But Jordan has been so individually mesmerizing to this point that his pass to Wennington, who looks like a leper alone under the basket, seems like a revelation.

From Jackson's vantage point it looks as if Jordan has pulled an Amazing Kreskin, bending his pass around the onrushing Ewing. Starks has been so fooled by Jordan's sudden pass that, after biting on another fake, he stumbles, spraining his left ankle. From the Garden floor Starks's view must have been obscured; following the game he believes Perdue has scored the dunk that wins the game 113–111.

Before the Bulls strung together their three titles, critics returned again and again to three quibbles with Jordan: That for all his individual greatness, he wasn't a winner; that his heedless defensive wanderings left the rest of the Bulls vulnerable; and that when he was double- and triple-teamed, he couldn't reliably find his teammates. Not that he needs to, but within a few seconds Jordan provides a tidy set of refutations, one for each canard: The Bulls win. When Starks fumbles away New York's last chance in the final three seconds, it is under pressure from Jordan. And the winning shot comes on Jordan's pass.

To Jackson, a son of Pentecostal ministers and a relentless proselytizer for team play, that last act is the night's transcendent moment. "Justice," Jackson says of that pass. "Poetic justice. It brought reality and order back to the evening."

No longer able to dictate to their lavishly paid charges, NBA coaches are all social workers now. The best ones have found ways to reach their players almost subcutaneously. Jackson's style of management is particularly indirect. As he explains in his new book, *Sacred Hoops: Spiritual Lessons of a Hardwood Warrior*, Jackson prods and pokes, trying less to drum into each Bull a set of cold facts than to nudge him to a heightened state of awareness. As a result players often come to Jackson after they've realized what he wants them to grasp.

Several days after the Knick game Jordan approached Jackson. "I've decided to quit," he said. "What else can I do?" Jordan was kidding. But he soon became serious. Jackson had encouraged him to fire away that Tuesday night. But Jordan told Jackson that he understood how his outburst in the Garden had to be an aberration if this fragile and reconstituted team were to challenge for the title. "You've got to tell the players they can't expect me to do what I did in New York every night," Jordan said. "In our next game I want them to play as a team."

As glad as Jackson was to hear Jordan say that, things wouldn't be so easy. The whoopee over his return cleaved Jordan from his teammates. As he searched for privacy, Jordan cocooned himself inside his retinue of friends and followers—a natural and perhaps necessary reaction, but one that alienated him from the group. The confidence and trust the team had developed before Jordan's return began to dissipate. Nowhere was this more evident than in two games in the Eastern Conference semifinals against the Orlando Magic. Rust and unfamiliarity with his teammates led Jordan to bollix up critical plays late in Games 1 and 6.

To reemphasize to Jordan and Jordanaires alike their interconnectedness during those ill-fated playoffs, Jackson had read the team a favorite passage of his from Rudyard Kipling. It's a text Jackson is sure to return to this season, as the Bulls make another run for a title, this time while integrating into the team the iconoclastic personality of Dennis Rodman.

Now this is the Law of the Jungle—
as old and as true as the sky;
And the Wolf that shall keep it may prosper,
but the Wolf that shall break it must die.
As the creeper that girdles the tree trunk,
the Law runneth forward and back—
For the strength of the Pack is the Wolf, and the strength of the Wolf is the
Pack.

Basketball's great wolf had his howl on that Tuesday night in the Garden. But having delivered a message, he was ready to return to the game's ultimate truth, a lesson his coach regards as holy writ: That if you're not in it together, you're not in it to win it. And if you're not in it to win it, double nickels ain't nothing but chump change.

JULY 11, 2014

LeBron: I'm Coming Back to Cleveland

LeBron James explains to SI's Lee Jenkins why he's returning to the Cleveland Cavaliers after spending four seasons with the Miami Heat

BY LeBRON JAMES (As Told to Lee Jenkins)

A landmark story for a star and a city (and a magazine). The moment it hit the web, the balance of power in the league tilted.

Before anyone ever cared where I would play basketball, I was a kid from Northeast Ohio. It's where I walked. It's where I ran. It's where I cried. It's where I bled. It holds a special place in my heart. People there have seen me grow up. I sometimes feel like I'm their son. Their passion can be overwhelming. But it drives me. I want to give them hope when I can. I want to inspire them when I can. My relationship with Northeast Ohio is bigger than basketball. I didn't realize that four years ago. I do now.

Remember when I was sitting up there at the Boys & Girls Club in 2010? I was thinking, This is really tough. I could feel it. I was leaving something I had spent a long time creating. If I had to do it all over again, I'd obviously do things differently, but I'd still have left. Miami, for me, has been almost like college for other kids. These past four years helped raise me into who I am. I became a better player and a better man. I learned from a franchise that had been where I wanted to go. I will always think of Miami as my second home. Without the experiences I had there, I wouldn't be able to do what I'm doing today.

I went to Miami because of D-Wade and CB. We made sacrifices to keep UD. I loved becoming a big bro to Rio. I believed we could do something magical if we came together. And that's exactly what we did! The hardest thing to leave is what I built with those guys. I've talked to some of them and will talk to others. Nothing will ever change what we accomplished. We are brothers for life. I also want to thank Micky Arison and Pat Riley for giving me an amazing four years.

I'm doing this essay because I want an opportunity to explain myself uninterrupted. I don't want anyone thinking: *He and Erik Spoelstra didn't get along.... He and Riles didn't get along.... The Heat couldn't put the right team together*. That's absolutely not true.

I'm not having a press conference or a party. After this, it's time to get to work.

When I left Cleveland, I was on a mission. I was seeking championships, and we won two. But Miami already knew that feeling. Our city hasn't had that feeling in a long, long, long time. My goal is still to win as many titles as possible, no question. But what's most important for me is bringing one trophy back to Northeast Ohio.

I always believed that I'd return to Cleveland and finish my career there. I just didn't know when. After the season, free agency wasn't even a thought. But I have two boys and my wife, Savannah, is pregnant with a girl. I started thinking about what it would be like to raise my family in my hometown. I looked at other teams, but I wasn't going to leave Miami for anywhere except Cleveland. The more time passed, the more it felt right. This is what makes me happy.

To make the move I needed the support of my wife and my mom, who can be very tough. The letter from Dan Gilbert, the booing of the Cleveland fans, the jerseys being burned—seeing all that was hard for them. My emotions were more mixed. It was easy to say, "O.K., I don't want to deal with these people ever again." But then you think about the other side. What if I were a kid who looked up to an athlete, and that athlete made me want to do better in my own life, and then he left? How would I react? I've met with Dan, face-to-face, man-to-man. We've talked it out. Everybody makes mistakes. I've made mistakes as well. Who am I to hold a grudge?

I'm not promising a championship. I know how hard that is to deliver. We're not ready right now. No way. Of course, I want to win next year, but I'm realistic. It will be a long process, much longer than it was in 2010. My patience will get tested. I know that. I'm going into a situation with a young team and a new coach. I will be the old head. But I get a thrill out of bringing a group together and helping them reach a place they didn't know they could go. I see myself as a mentor now and I'm excited to lead some of these talented young guys. I think I can help Kyrie Irving become one of the best point guards in our league. I think I can help elevate Tristan Thompson and Dion Waiters. And I can't wait to reunite with Anderson Varejao, one of my favorite teammates.

But this is not about the roster or the organization. I feel my calling here goes above basketball. I have a responsibility to lead, in more ways than one, and I take that very seriously. My presence can make a difference in Miami, but I think it can mean more where I'm from. I want kids in Northeast Ohio, like the hundreds of Akron third-graders I sponsor through my foundation, to realize that there's no better place to grow up. Maybe some of them will come home after college and start a family or open a business. That would make me smile. Our community, which has struggled so much, needs all the talent it can get.

In Northeast Ohio, nothing is given. Everything is earned. You work for what you have.

I'm ready to accept the challenge. I'm coming home.

— POSTSCRIPT —

Lee Jenkins: On July 4, 2014, I was at a neighborhood Fourth of July party when a representative of LeBron James called and asked me to be ready to interview him the following week, probably in Las Vegas. I'd pitched the interview a couple months earlier. James was a free agent and I thought a first-person story could be an effective way of revealing his decision and describing the reasons he made it. I didn't necessarily think he'd agree and remained uncertain even on July 8, as I flew to Vegas and checked into the Wynn hotel, where James was staying. Speculation about where James would play, and how he would announce his choice, was rampant. Everyone had a theory. Everyone had a source. After waiting 24 hours, I was invited to James's suite. His existence often reminded me of the Jim Carrey movie, *The Truman Show*, but never more than that day. As the talking heads on his television debated his decision, he laid out the reasons he was returning to Northeast Ohio. It was probably the easiest story I've ever written. I transcribed the tape, arranged the sentences, and booked a flight to Cleveland, so I'd be the first national reporter there after the news broke. When I was greeted on the ground by TV cameras, I realized this was much different than my standard NBA profile. Four years later, the Cavaliers beat the Warriors in the Finals, and I cornered James in the visitor's locker room at Oracle Arena. "This is what I had in mind," he said.

MAY 6, 2013

I'm a 34-Year-Old NBA Center. I'm Black. And I'm Gay.

I didn't set out to be the first openly gay athlete
playing in a major American team sport. But since
I am, I'm happy to start the conversation

BY JASON COLLINS

*In 2013, near the end of his career as a solid reserve center, Jason Collins
made international news with this announcement.*

I wish I wasn't the kid in the classroom raising his hand and saying, "I'm different." If I had my way, someone else would have already done this. Nobody has, which is why I'm raising my hand.

My journey of self-discovery and self-acknowledgement began in my hometown of Los Angeles and has taken me through two state high school championships, the NCAA Final Four and the Elite Eight, and nine playoffs in 12 NBA seasons.

I've played for six pro teams and have appeared in two NBA Finals. Ever heard of a parlor game called Three Degrees of Jason Collins? If you're in the league, and I haven't been your teammate, I surely have been one of your teammates' teammates. Or one of your teammates' teammates' teammates.

Now I'm a free agent, literally and figuratively. I've reached that enviable state in life in which I can do pretty much what I want. And what I want is to continue to play basketball. I still love the game, and I still have something to offer. My coaches and teammates recognize that. At the same time, I want to be genuine and authentic and truthful.

Why am I coming out now? Well, I started thinking about this in 2011 during the NBA player lockout. I'm a creature of routine. When the regular season ends I immediately dedicate myself to getting game ready for the opener of the next campaign in the fall. But the lockout wreaked havoc on my habits and forced me to confront who I really am and what I really want. With the season delayed, I trained and worked out. But I lacked the distraction that basketball had always provided.

The first relative I came out to was my aunt Teri, a superior court judge in San Francisco. Her reaction surprised me. "I've known you were gay for years," she said. From that moment on I was comfortable in my own skin. In her presence I ignored my censor button for the first time. She gave me support. The relief I felt was a sweet release. Imagine you're in the oven, baking. Some of us know and accept our sexuality right away and some need more time to cook. I should know—I baked for 33 years.

When I was younger I dated women. I even got engaged. I thought I had to live a certain way. I thought I needed to marry a woman and raise kids with her. I kept telling myself the sky was red, but I always knew it was blue.

I realized I needed to go public when Joe Kennedy, my old roommate at Stanford and now a Massachusetts congressman, told me he had just marched in Boston's 2012 Gay Pride Parade. I'm seldom jealous of others, but hearing what Joe had done filled me with envy. I was proud of him for participating but angry that as a closeted gay man I couldn't even cheer my straight friend on as a spectator. If I'd been questioned, I would have concocted half truths. What a shame to have to lie at a celebration of pride. I want to do the right thing and not hide anymore. I want to march for tolerance, acceptance and understanding. I want to take a stand and say, "Me, too."

The recent Boston Marathon bombing reinforced the notion that I shouldn't wait for the circumstances of my coming out to be perfect. Things can change in an instant, so why not live truthfully? When I told Joe a few weeks ago that I was gay, he was grateful that I trusted him. He asked me to join him in 2013. We'll be marching on June 8.

No one wants to live in fear. I've always been scared of saying the wrong thing. I don't sleep well. I never have. But each time I tell another person, I feel stronger and sleep a little more soundly. It takes an enormous amount of energy to guard such a big secret. I've endured years of misery and gone to enormous lengths to live a lie. I was certain that my world would fall apart if anyone knew. And yet when I acknowledged my sexuality I felt whole for the first time. I still had the same sense of humor, I still had the same mannerisms and my friends still had my back.

Believe it or not, my family has had bigger shocks. Strange as it seems today, my parents expected only one child in 1978. Me. When I came out (for the first time) the doctors congratulated my mother on her healthy, seven-pound, one-ounce baby boy. "Wait!" said a nurse. "Here comes another one!" The other one, who arrived eight minutes later and three ounces heavier, was Jarron. He's followed me ever since, to Stanford and to the NBA, and as the ever-so-slightly older brother I've looked out for him.

I had a happy childhood in the suburbs of L.A. My parents instilled in us an appreciation of history, art and, most important, Motown. Jarron and I weren't allowed to listen to rap until we were 12. After our birthday I dashed to Target and bought DJ Quik's album *Quik Is the Name.* I memorized every line. It was around this time that I began noticing subtle differences between Jarron and me. Our twinness was no longer synchronized. I couldn't identify with his attraction to girls.

I feel blessed that I recognized my own attractions. Though I resisted my impulses through high school, I knew that when I was ready I had someone to turn to: my uncle Mark in New York. I knew we could talk without judgment, and we did last summer. Uncle Mark is gay. He and his partner have been in a stable relationship forever. For a confused young boy, I can think of no better role model of love and compassion.

I didn't come out to my brother until last summer. His reaction to my breakfast revelation was radically different from Aunt Teri's. He was downright astounded. He never suspected. So much for twin telepathy. But by dinner that night, he was full of brotherly love. For the first time in our lives, he wanted to step in and protect *me.*

My maternal grandmother was apprehensive about my plans to come out. She grew up in rural Louisiana and witnessed the horrors of segregation. During the civil rights movement she saw great bravery play out amid the ugliest aspects of humanity. She worries that I am opening myself up to prejudice and hatred. I explained to her that in a way, my coming out is preemptive. I shouldn't have to live under the threat of being outed. The announcement should be mine to make, not TMZ's.

The hardest part of this is the realization that my entire family will be affected. But my relatives have told me repeatedly that as long as I'm happy, they're there for me. I watch as my brother and friends from college start their own families. Changing diapers is a lot of work, but children bring so much joy. I'm crazy about my nieces and nephew, and I can't wait to start a family of my own.

I'm from a close-knit family. My parents instilled Christian values in me. They taught Sunday school, and I enjoyed lending a hand. I take the teachings of Jesus seriously, particularly the ones that touch on tolerance and understanding. On family trips, my parents made a point to expose us to new things, religious and cultural. In Utah, we visited the Mormon Salt Lake Temple. In Atlanta, the house of Martin Luther King Jr. That early exposure to otherness made me the guy who accepts everyone unconditionally.

I'm learning to embrace the puzzle that is me. After I was traded by the Celtics to Washington in February, I took a detour to the Dr. King memorial. I was inspired and humbled. I celebrate being an African-American and the hardships of the past that still resonate today. But I don't let my race define me any more than I want my sexual orientation to. I don't want to be labeled, and I can't let someone else's label define me.

On the court I graciously accept one label sometimes bestowed on me: "the pro's pro." I got that handle because of my fearlessness and my commitment to my teammates. I take charges and I foul—that's been my forte. In fact, during the 2004–05 season my 322 personals led the NBA. I enter the court knowing I have six hard fouls to give. I set picks with my 7-foot, 255-pound body to get guys like Jason Kidd, John Wall and Paul Pierce open. I sacrifice myself for other players. I look out for teammates as I would my kid brother.

I'm not afraid to take on any opponent. I love playing against the best. Though Shaquille O'Neal is a Hall of Famer, I never shirked from the challenge of trying to frustrate the heck out of him. (Note to Shaq: My flopping has nothing to do with being gay.) My mouthpiece is in, and my wrists are taped. Go ahead, take a swing—I'll get up. I hate to say it, and I'm not proud of it, but I once fouled a player so hard that he had to leave the arena on a stretcher.

I go against the gay stereotype, which is why I think a lot of players will be shocked: *That* guy is *gay*? But I've always been an aggressive player, even in high school. Am I so physical to prove that being gay doesn't make you soft? Who knows? That's something for a psychologist to unravel. My motivations, like my contributions, don't show up in box scores, and frankly I don't care about stats. Winning is what counts. I want to be evaluated as a team player.

Loyalty to my team is the real reason I didn't come out sooner. When I signed a free-agent contract with Boston last July, I decided to commit myself to the Celtics and not let my personal life become a distraction.

When I was traded to the Wizards, the political significance of coming out sunk in. I was ready to open up to the press, but I had to wait until the season was over.

A college classmate tried to persuade me to come out then and there. But I couldn't yet. My one small gesture of solidarity was to wear jersey number 98 with the Celtics and then the Wizards. The number has great significance to the gay community. One of the most notorious antigay hate crimes occurred in 1998. Matthew Shepard, a University of Wyoming student, was kidnapped, tortured and lashed to a prairie fence. He died five days after he was finally found. That same year the Trevor Project was founded. This amazing organization provides crisis intervention and suicide prevention to kids struggling with their sexual identity. Trust me, I know that struggle. I've struggled with some insane logic. When I put on my jersey I was making a statement to myself, my family and my friends.

The strain of hiding my sexuality became almost unbearable in March, when the U.S. Supreme Court heard arguments for and against same-sex marriage. Less than three miles from my apartment, nine jurists argued about *my* happiness and *my* future. Here was my chance to be heard, and I couldn't say a thing. I didn't want to answer questions and draw attention to myself. Not while I was still playing.

I'm glad I'm coming out in 2013 rather than 2003. The climate has shifted; public opinion has shifted. And yet we still have so much farther to go. Everyone is terrified of the unknown, but most of us don't want to return to a time when minorities were openly discriminated against. I'm impressed with the straight pro athletes who have spoken up so far—Chris Kluwe, Brendon Ayanbadejo. The more people who speak out, the better, gay or straight. It starts with President Obama's mentioning the 1969 Stonewall riots, which launched the gay rights movement, during his second inaugural address. And it extends to the grade-school teacher who encourages her students to accept the things that make us different.

By its nature, my double life has kept me from getting close to any of my teammates. Early in my career I worked hard at acting straight, but as I got more comfortable in my straight mask it required less effort. In recent days, though, little has separated "mask on, mask off." Personally, I don't like to dwell in someone else's private life, and I hope players and coaches show me the same respect. When I'm with my team I'm all about working hard and winning games. A good teammate supports you no matter what.

I've been asked how other players will respond to my announcement. The simple answer is, I have no idea. I'm a pragmatist. I hope for the best, but plan for the worst. The biggest concern seems to be that gay players will behave unprofessionally in the locker room. Believe me, I've taken plenty of showers in 12 seasons. My behavior wasn't an issue before, and it won't be one now. My conduct won't change. I still abide by the adage, "What happens in the locker room stays in the locker room." I'm still a model of discretion.

As I write this, I haven't come out to anyone in the NBA. I'm not privy to what other players say about me. Maybe Mike Miller, my old teammate in Memphis, will recall the time I dropped by his house in Florida and say, "I enjoyed being his teammate, and I sold him a dog." I hope players swap stories like that. Maybe they'll talk about my character and what kind of person I am.

As far as the reaction of fans, I don't mind if they heckle me. I've been booed before. There have been times when I've wanted to boo myself. But a lot of ill feelings can be cured by winning.

I'm a veteran, and I've earned the right to be heard. I'll lead by example and show that gay players are no different from straight ones. I'm not the loudest person in the room, but I'll speak up when something isn't right. And try to make everyone laugh.

I've never sought the spotlight. Though I'm coming out to the world, I intend to guard my privacy. I'm making this blanket statement in part to keep rumors and misunderstandings at bay. I hope fans will respect me for raising my hand. And I hope teammates will remember that I've never been an in-your-face kind of guy. All you need to know is that I'm single. I see no need to delve into specifics.

Look at what happened in the military when the Don't Ask, Don't Tell policy was repealed. Critics of the repeal were sure that out military members would devastate morale and destroy civilization. But a new study conducted by scholars from every branch of the armed forces except the Coast Guard concluded that "cohesion did not decline after the new policy of open service was put into place. In fact, greater openness and honesty resulting from repeal seem to have promoted increased understanding, respect and acceptance."

The same goes for sports. Doc Rivers, my coach on the Celtics, says, "If you want to go quickly, go by yourself—if you want to go farther, go in a group." I want people to pull together and push ahead.

Openness may not completely disarm prejudice, but it's a good place to start. It all comes down to education. I'll sit down with any player who's uneasy about my coming out. Being gay is not a choice. This is the tough road and at times the lonely road. Former players like Tim Hardaway, who said "I hate gay people" (and then became a supporter of gay rights), fuel homophobia. Tim is an adult. He's entitled to his opinion. God bless America.

Still, if I'm up against an intolerant player, I'll set a pretty hard pick on him. And then move on.

The most you can do is stand up for what you believe in. I'm much happier since coming out to my friends and family. Being genuine and honest makes me happy.

I'm glad I can stop hiding and refocus on my 13th NBA season. I've been running through the Santa Monica Mountains in a 30-pound vest with Shadow, the German shepherd I got from Mike Miller. In the pros, the older you get, the better shape you must be in. Next season a few more eyeballs are likely to be on me. That only motivates me to work harder.

Some people insist they've never met a gay person. But Three Degrees of Jason Collins dictates that no NBA player can claim that anymore. Pro basketball is a family. And pretty much every family I know has a brother, sister or cousin who's gay. In the brotherhood of the NBA, I just happen to be the one who's out.

$-$ POSTSCRIPT $-$

Here is **Jon Wertheim**, writing in 2013 about the story's genesis:

At some point the idea of having no openly gay athletes in a league might sound as unimaginable as a ball field segregated by race. But today Collins becomes the first active male athlete in a major U.S. team sport to come out of the closet. Yes, that's a lot of qualifiers. Yes, it may be an artificial construct. But it is a milestone. Tens of thousands of men have played in the NFL, NBA, NHL and Major League Baseball. Until today none had expressed his homosexuality before retirement.

Collins didn't do this to make a political statement, much less to satisfy a sponsor. To his great relief, he didn't do it under duress; that is, he wasn't outed or "caught" by the smartphone paparazzi, "a fear that has trailed, trust me," he said more than once, "this is not a choice."

Collins had simply grown tired. Tired of being alone; tired of coming home to an empty house; tired of relying on Shadow, his German shepherd, for company; tired of watching friends and family members find spouses and become parents; tired of telling lies and half-truths—"cover stories like a CIA spy," he says with his distinctive cackle—to conceal that he's gay. He was also tired of...being tired. For most of his life, he's had trouble sleeping, which he attributes to struggles with his sexuality.

He's known "forever" that he's gay. But until last year it was personal, don't-go-there territory. "I kept telling myself the sky was red, but I always knew it was blue," he writes in this week's cover story for

Sports Illustrated. Last summer, at 33, he finally came out to a small group of family members and friends, though none of them is in the NBA. Bolstered by their unconditional support, he decided he was ready, at 34, to go public. "Now," he says, "it's time to live my life genuinely."

P.S. to the postscript: At the time that Collins's story ran, it felt like perhaps the beginning of a sea change in the league. And yet, while active players have come out in a myriad of other sports, as of the writing of this book, in the summer of 2022, Collins remains the only active NBA player to come out.

GIANTS AMONG MEN

MAY 10, 1999

The Ring Leader

The greatest team player of all time, Bill Russell was the hub of a Celtics dynasty that ruled its sport as no other team ever has

BY FRANK DEFORD

Thirty years after Bill Russell, as player-coach, led Boston to its 11th title in his 13 seasons in uniform, Frank Deford wrote this definitive profile, which won a National Magazine Award.

It was 30 years ago, and the car containing the old retired basketball player and the young sportswriter stopped at a traffic light on the way to the airport in Los Angeles. (Of course, in the nature of things, old players aren't that much older than young writers.) The old player said, "I'm sorry, I'd like to be your friend."

The young writer said, "But I thought we *were* friends."

"No, I'd like to be your friend, and we can be friendly, but friendship takes a lot of effort if it's going to work, and we're going off in different directions in our lives, so, no, we really can't be friends."

And that was as close as I ever got to being on Bill Russell's team.

In the years after that exchange I often reflected on what Russell had said to me, and I marveled that he would have thought so deeply about what constituted friendship. It was, obviously, the same sort of philosophical contemplation about the concept of Team that had made him the most divine teammate there ever was.

Look, you can stand at a bar and scream all you want about who was the greatest athlete and which was the greatest sports dynasty, and you can shout out your precious statistics, and maybe you're right, and maybe the red-faced guy down the bar—the one with the foam on his beer and the fancy computer rankings—is right, but nobody really knows. The only thing we know for sure about superiority in sports in the United States of America in the 20th century is that Bill Russell and the Boston Celtics teams he led stand alone as the ultimate winners. Fourteen times in Russell's career it came down to one game, win you must, or lose and go home. Fourteen times the team with Bill Russell on it won.

But the fires always smoldered in William Felton Russell, and he simply wouldn't suffer fools—most famously the ones who intruded upon his sovereign privacy to petition him for an autograph. He was that rare star athlete who was also a social presence, a voice to go with the body. Unafraid, he spoke out against all things, great and small, that bothered him. He wouldn't even show up at the Hall of Fame when he was inducted, because he had concluded it was a racist institution. Now, despite the importunings of his friends, he is the only living selection among ESPN's 50 top athletes of the century who hasn't agreed to talk to the network. That is partly because one night he heard an ESPN announcer praise the '64 Celtics as "Bob Cousy's last team." Cousy was retired by then.

Russell says, "They go on television, they're supposed to know."

Cousy says, "What the Celtics did with Russ will never be duplicated in a team sport. Never."

Of course, genuine achievement is everywhere devalued these days. On the 200th anniversary of his death, George Washington has been so forgotten that they're toting his false teeth around the republic, trying to restore interest in the Father of Our Country with a celebrity-style gimmick. So should we be surprised that one spectacular show-off dunk on yesterday's highlight reel counts for more than some ancient decade's worth of championships back-before-Larry&Magic-really-invented-the-sport-of-basketball?

Tommy Heinsohn, who played with Russell for nine years and won 10 NBA titles himself, as player and coach, sums it up best: "Look, all I know is, the guy won two NCAA championships, 50-some college games in a row, the ['56] Olympics, then he came to Boston and won 11 championships in 13 years, and they named a f——— tunnel after Ted Williams." By that standard, only a cathedral on a hill deserves to have Bill Russell's name attached to it.

But then, too often when I try to explain the passion of Russell himself and his devotion to his team and to victory, I'm inarticulate. It's like trying to describe a color to a blind person. All I can say, in tongue-tied exasperation, is, You had to be there. And I'm sorry for you if you weren't.

Russell was right, too. The two of us did go our separate ways after he dropped me at the airport. He left the playing life exactly 30 years ago this week, on May 5, 1969, with his last championship, and my first child was born on May 7. So there were new things we both had to do, and in the years that followed we were together only a couple of times, briefly.

Then a few weeks ago we met at his house in Seattle, and for the first time in 30 years I climbed into his car. The license plate on the Lexus reads KELTIC 6, and on the driver's hands were two NBA championship rings: his first, from '57, and his last, from 12 years later. We took off together for the San Francisco Bay Area, there to visit Bill's father, Charlie, who is 86 and lives in a nursing home. It was 13 hours on the road. We stopped along the way at McDonald's and for gas and for coffee and for a box of Good 'n' Plenty and to pee and to buy lottery tickets once we got over the California line, because there was a big jackpot that week in the Golden State. In Oakland we found a Holiday Inn and ate a fish dinner at Jack London Square, where a bunch of elderly black ladies sat at the next table. "I was thinking they were old," Bill said, nodding his gray head toward them. "Then I remembered, I'm probably their age." I laughed. "Hey, what are you laughing at?" he roared. So, like that, wherever we happened to be going in the car, our destination was really back in time.

Back to the Russell Era. Back to the Celtics and the University of San Francisco Dons, to the Jones Boys and Cooz. Yes, and back to Wilt. To Satch and Heinie and the sixth men. Red, of course. Elgin and Jerry. But more than just the baskets, more than just the '60s. Russell's family experience describes the arc of a century. Why, when Charlie Russell was growing up in Louisiana, he actually knew men and women who had been slaves. He told me about "making marks in the ground" to help his illiterate father calculate. I was baffled by that expression. "It's from the old country," Bill explained. That is, from Africa, centuries before, passed along orally. And as we were talking, and the old man—wearing a jaunty red sweat suit and a green hat—reminisced about more recent times, he suddenly smiled and said something I couldn't quite make out. I leaned closer. "What's that, Mr. Russell? How *what*?"

"No, *Hal*," he said. "All on account of Hal DeJulio." Charlie remembered so well, after all this time. You see, if young William hadn't, by chance, been there on the one day that DeJulio showed up at Oakland High in the winter of '51, none of this would have happened. None of it at all. But life often hangs by such serendipitous threads, and sometimes, like this time, we are able to take them and weave them into a scarf for history's neck.

The long trip to Oakland was not unusual for Russell. He enjoys driving great distances. After all, he is most comfortable with himself and next most comfortable with close friends, cackling that thunderous laugh of his that Cousy fears he'll hear resonating in the afterlife. *Playful* is the surprising word that former Georgetown coach John Thompson thinks of first for Russell, and old number 6 himself always refers to his Celtics as "the guys" in a way that sounds curiously adolescent. Hey, guys, we can put the game on right here!

Cynosure on the court though he was, Russell never enjoyed being the celebrity alone. "I still think he's a shy, mother's son," says Karen Kenyatta Russell, his daughter, "and even now he's uncomfortable being in the spotlight by himself." Maybe that's one reason the team mattered so to him; it hugged him back. "I got along with all the guys," Russell says, "and nobody had to kiss anybody's ass. We were just a bunch of men—and, oh, what marvelous gifts my teammates gave to me."

"He was just so nice to be with on the team," says Frank Ramsey, who played with Russell from 1956 to '64, Russell's first eight years in the NBA. "It was only when others came around that he set up that wall."

Russell loves nothing better than to talk. "Oh, the philosophizing," recalls Satch Sanders, who played with Russell from '60 to '69. "If he started off and said, 'You see,' we just rolled our eyes, because we knew he was going off on something." Yet in more recent times Russell went for years without permitting himself to be interviewed. "If I'm going to answer the questions, I want them to be my questions, the right questions," he says—a most unlikely prerogative, given the way journalism works. O.K., so no interviews. Privacy edged into reclusiveness.

On the other hand, as upside-down as this may sound, Russell believes he can share more by not giving autographs, because instead of an impersonal scribbled signature, a civil two-way conversation may ensue. Gently: "I'm sorry, I don't give autographs."

"You won't?"

"No, *won't* is personal. I don't. But thank you for asking." And then, if he senses a polite reaction, he might say, "Would you like to shake hands with me?" And maybe chat.

Utterly dogmatic, Russell wouldn't bend even to give his Celtics teammates autographs. One time this precipitated an ugly quarrel with Sanders, who wanted a simple keepsake: the signature of every Celtic he'd played with. "You, Satch, of all people, know how I feel," Russell snapped.

"Dammit, I'm your teammate, Russ."

Nevertheless, when the shouting was over, Russell still wouldn't sign. Thompson, who was Russell's backup on the Celtics for two years, is sure that Russell never took pleasure from these sorts of incidents. "No, it bothered him," Thompson says. "But doing it his way, on his own terms, was more important to him. And that's Bill. Even if it hurt him, he was going to remain consistent."

Russell speaks, often, in aphorisms that reflect his attitudes. "It is better to understand than to be understood," he told his daughter. "A groove can become a rut," he advised his teammates. And perhaps the one that goes most to his own heart: "You should live a life with as few negatives as possible—without acquiescing."

So, alone, unbothered, one of the happiest times Russell ever had was driving around the West on a motorcycle in the '70s. When he takes a long automobile trip by himself these days, he listens to National Public Radio, CDs and tapes he has recorded to suit his own eclectic taste. On one tape, for example, are Stevie Wonder and Burl Ives. On another: Willie Nelson and Aretha Franklin. But also, always, Russell sets aside two hours to drive in complete silence, meditating. He has never forgotten what Huey Newton, the Black Panther, once told him: that the five years he spent in solitary confinement were, in fact, liberating.

Russell returned twice to the NBA after he retired as the Celtics' player-coach following the 1968–69 season. As coach and general manager of the Seattle SuperSonics from 1973 to '77, he built the team that would win the championship two years after he left. A brief tenure with the Sacramento Kings during the '87–88 season was, however, disastrous and unhappy. On the night he was fired, Russell cleaned out his office; returned to his Sacramento house, which was contiguous to a golf course; and stayed there, peacefully by himself, for weeks, venturing out only for provisions and golf. He didn't read the newspapers or watch television news. "To this day, I don't know what they said about me," he says. He put his house on the market immediately, and only when it sold, three weeks later, did he return to Seattle, where for 26 years he has lived in the same house on Mercer Island, one tucked away into a sylvan hillside, peeking down at Lake Washington.

Divorced in 1973, Russell lived as a single parent with Karen for several years, until she left for Georgetown in 1980 and then Harvard Law. Alone after that, Russell says, there were times when he would hole up and practice his household "migratory habits." That is, he would stock the kitchen, turn on the burglar alarm, turn off the phone and, for the next week, migrate about the house, going from one couch to another, reading voraciously and watching TV, ideally *Jeopardy!* or *Star Trek*—just bivouacked there, the tallest of all the Trekkies, sleeping on various sofas. He was quite content. The finest team player ever is by nature a loner who, by his own lights, achieved such group success because of his abject selfishness. You will never begin to understand Bill Russell until you appreciate that he is, at once, consistent and contradictory.

Russell began to emerge from his most pronounced period of solitude about three years ago. Shortly after arriving in Seattle in 1973, he had gone into a jewelry store, where he hit it off with the saleswoman. Her name is Marilyn Nault. "Let me tell you," she sighs, "working in a jewelry store is the worst place to meet a man, because if one comes in, it's to buy something for another woman." But over the years—skipping through Russell's next, brief marriage, to a former Miss USA—Marilyn and Bill remained friends. Also, she impressed him as a very competitive dominoes player. When Bill's secretary died in 1995, Marilyn volunteered to give him a hand, and all of a sudden, after more than two decades, they realized they were in love. So it was that one day, when Marilyn came over to help Bill with his accounts, she just stayed on with him in the house on the hill under the tall firs.

There is a big grandfather clock in the house that chimes every hour. Like Bill, Marilyn doesn't hear it anymore. She has also learned how to sleep with the TV on, because Bill, a terrible night owl, usually falls asleep with the clicker clasped tightly in his hand. Usually the Golf Channel is on. Imagine waking up to the Golf Channel. Marilyn has also learned to appreciate long car trips. Twice she and Bill have driven across the continent and back. Their lives are quite blissful; he has never seemed to be so at peace. "They're the ultimate '50s couple," Karen reports. "They have nothing but kind things to say about each other, and it's part of their arrangement that at least once a day, he has to make her laugh."

Yet for all the insular contentment Russell has always sought in his life, his play was marked by the most extraordinary intensity. If he threw up before a big game, the Celtics were sure everything would be all right. If he didn't, then Boston's coach, Red Auerbach, would tell Russell to go back to the toilet—order him to throw up. Rookies who saw Russell for the first time in training camp invariably thought he had lost it over the summer, because he would pace himself, even play possum in some exhibitions, to deceive pretenders to his throne. Then, in the first game of the real season, the rookies would be bug-eyed as the genuine article suddenly appeared, aflame with competition. It was as if the full moon had brought out a werewolf.

Cousy says, "The level of intensity among the big guys is different. You put a bunch of huge guys, seminaked, out there before thousands of people, and you expect them to become killers. But it just isn't in their nature. Kareem [Abdul-Jabbar] probably had the best skills of all big men, and he played till he was 42. If he'd had Russ's instincts, it's hard to imagine how much better he'd have been. But he'd have burned out long before 42."

Sanders: "There's no reason why some centers today couldn't block shots like Russ did. Only no one has the intestinal fortitude. A center blocks one shot now, the other team grabs the ball and scores, and the center stands there pouting, with that I-can't-do-everything look. Russell would block three, four shots in a row—I mean from different players—and then just glower at us."

Russell: "Once I blocked seven shots in a row. When we finally got the ball, I called timeout and said, 'This s— has got to stop.'" Some years Russell would be so exhausted after the playoffs that, as he describes it, "I'd literally be tired to my bones. I mean, for four, five weeks, my bones would hurt."

Russell believes that Wilt Chamberlain suffered the worst case of big-man syndrome; he was too nice, scared that he might hurt somebody. The year after Russell retired, in the famous seventh game of the NBA Finals at Madison Square Garden, Willis Reed, the New York Knicks center, limped onto the court against the Los Angeles Lakers, inspiring his team and freezing Chamberlain into a benign perplexity. Russell scowls just thinking about it. "If I'm the one playing Willis when he comes out limping," he snarls, "it only would have emphasized my goal to beat them that much worse." Russell would have called Six—his play—again and again, going mercilessly at the cripple, exploiting Reed without remorse. The Celtics would have won. Which was the point. Always.

"To be the best in the world," Russell says, all but licking his lips. "Not last week. Not next year. But right now. You are the best. And it's even more satisfying as a team, because that's more difficult. If I play well, that's one thing. But to make others play better...." He grins, savoring the memory. "You understand what I mean?" Bill often says that, invariably when there is no doubt. It has to do with emphasis more than clarity. In fact, I can sort of visualize him saying that after he blocked a shot. *You understand what I mean?*

Yes.

It is difficult to comprehend whence came Russell's extraordinary will on the court. Karen recalls only once in her life that her father so much as raised his voice to anyone. "I just never saw the warrior in him," she says. "As a matter of fact, as I got to understand men better, I appreciated all the more how much of a feminine side my father has." Ironically it was Russell's mother, Katie, who appears to have given him his fire, while his father, Charlie, instilled the more reflective component.

What do you remember your father telling you, Bill?

"Accept responsibility for your actions.... Honor thy father and mother.... If they give you $10 for a day's work, you give them $12 worth in return."

Even more clearly, Russell recalls the gritty creed his mother gave him when he was a little boy growing up in segregation and the Depression in West Monroe, La. Katie said, "William, you are going to meet people who just don't like you. On sight. And there's nothing you can do about it, so don't worry. Just be yourself. You're no better than anyone else, but no one's better than you."

One time, when he was nine, William—for that is what he was called till basketball made him just plain Bill—came home to the family's little shotgun shack after being slapped by a boy in a gang. Katie dragged him out to find the gang. She made her son fight every boy, one by one. "The fact is, I had to fight back," Bill says. "It wasn't important whether I won or lost."

When he and I visited his father, Charlie said this about Katie: "She was handsome and sweet, and she loved me, and she showed it by giving me children." Bill was very touched by that, subdued. Then Charlie smiled and added, "She played some basketball too—the bloomer girls."

Bill shot to his feet, screaming, "Daddy, I never knew that!" Then there was such vintage Russellian cackling that the old fellow in the next bed woke up, a little discombobulated by all the fuss.

If Katie Russell had any athletic instincts, though, they paled before her passion for education. It was an article of faith with her, a high school dropout, that her two sons—Charlie Jr., the elder by two years, and William—would go to college. Bill has a vivid memory of his mother taking him to get a library card. That was not mundane; that was a signal event. And this is what he remembers of West Monroe, altogether: "I remember that my mother and father loved me, and we had a good time, but the white people were mean. But I was safe. I was always safe. In all my life, every day, not for one second have I ever thought I could have had better parents."

Then, in 1946, when William was 12, his mother died of kidney failure, with very little warning. Katie Russell was only 32. The last thing she told her husband was, "Make sure to send the boys to college." The last thing she told William was, "Don't be difficult for your father, because he's doing the best he can."

The Russells had moved to Oakland not long before, after Charlie was denied a raise at the mill in West Monroe because he was black. Now the father and his two sons boarded the train with Katie's casket to return to Louisiana to bury her. It was after the funeral that young William heard Katie's sisters arguing about which one of them would take the two motherless boys to raise. That was the custom in these matters. Charlie interrupted. "No," he said, "I won't let you. I'm taking the two boys back with me." Though there was still much protesting from the aunts, that was that.

"I told my two boys they'd lost their best friend," Charlie says, "but we could make it if we tried." The goal remained to get them through college. Charlie Jr. was developing into a pretty good athlete, but his father couldn't spend much time thinking about games. After all, he'd had to quit school to work; unlike Katie, he'd never even been able to play basketball. It certainly never occurred to him that now, for the first time, there were people like Hal DeJulio around, scouting black teenagers, eager to give the best ones a free college education just for playing some ball.

The radar detector on the Lexus beeped. Russell slowed down. A bit. We had driven through Washington and most of Oregon, too. A billboard advertised the Seven Feathers Casino. Ah, fin de siècle America: casinos, cable, cosmetic surgery and scores from around the leagues. Russell, who just turned 65, is fairly pragmatic about the new ways of the world. He never put on any airs— witness that amazing laugh of his, which is the loud leitmotif of his life. "I try not to stifle anything," he says. "It isn't just my laugh. If I have to sneeze, I just let it go. You understand what I mean?"

He is also helped by the fact that even as a young man, he looked venerable. Other players would dart onto the court, all snappy and coltish. Number 6 would stalk out hunched over, stroking that dagger of a goatee, and stand there dark and grim. We always talk about teams "executing." All right, then: Russell appeared very much an executioner.

Jerry West, who was denied about a half-dozen championships strictly because of Russell, remembers. "When the national anthem was played, I always found my eyes going to Bill. He did that just right, stand there for the anthem. He was a statue, but there was a grace to him. Even just standing still: grace."

Whereas Russell is disappointed by much that he sees on the court today, he does not lambaste the players. He is just as prone to blame the coaches for taking so much of the spontaneity out of basketball. "The coaches dumb players down now," he says, clearly irritated. "They're stifling innovation. They're not letting them play outside the system." Pretty soon, it seems, the Celtics' fast break, which was the most gloriously coordinated rapid action in sport, will be nothing more than athletic nostalgia, like the dropkick.

And the players? Well, it's not just them. "All the kids in this generation— they really don't have a clue," Russell says. "They don't know, but they really don't care. A lot of my peers are annoyed that the players accepted a salary cap. I'm not. I know there's not supposed to be a limit on what you can make in America, but then, the NBA may also be the only place where there's a high roof for a minimum. When I speak to the players, I just say they have a responsibility to be caretakers. When you leave, there should be no less for those who follow you than there was when you arrived."

We started up Mount Ashland, whose other side goes down into California. Russell said, "Of course, a lot of my peers are also annoyed with all this money these kids are making. Me? I love it when I see a guy get a hundred million, because that says something good about what I did. You understand what I mean?"

This is, however, not to say that some of the guys making a hundred million—or getting by on only 50 or 60—have a clue about what Bill Russell did. It took years of hectoring by some of his friends to persuade Russell to step out of the safe shadows, to display himself again. His legacy was fading. John Thompson fairly bellows, "Nobody cares when some turkey like me won't give interviews. But Bill Russell! I say, Bill: You owe it to the people you love not to take this to your grave. I want my grandchildren to hear you talk about all you were."

So, while sometimes it mortifies Russell that he is, like everybody else, marketing himself—"I can't believe I'm doing all the things I swore I'd never do," he moans—there is the reasonable argument that truth nowadays must be packaged; otherwise, only the hype will survive as history. So Russell is planning a speaking tour and an HBO documentary about his life, and Karen is working on a book about motivation with her father, and a huge charitable evening to honor Russell is scheduled at the FleetCenter in Boston on May 26, when his number 6 jersey will be ceremonially re-retired. Russell is even selling about 500 autographs a year, and when we went to ship some signed basketballs to a sports collectibles store, I felt rather as if I had gone over to Handgun Control and mailed out some Saturday Night Specials.

So, O.K., it's the millennium, it's a different world. But we're not that far removed from the old one. Look at Bill Russell in 1999. His grandfather Jake was of the family's first generation born free on this continent. When this fading century began, Jake Russell was trying to scratch out a living with a mule. The Klan went after him because even though he couldn't read or write a lick, he led a campaign to raise money among the poor blacks around West Monroe to build a schoolhouse and pay a teacher to educate their children at a time when the state wouldn't have any truck with that.

At the other end of Jake's life, in 1969, he went over to Shreveport, La., to see the Celtics play an exhibition. By then his grandson had become the first African-American coach in a major professional sport. Jake sat with his son, Charlie, watching Bill closely during timeouts. He wasn't quite sure what he was seeing; Celtics huddles could be terribly democratic back then. It was before teams had a lot of assistants with clipboards. Skeptically Jake asked his son, "He's the boss?" Charlie nodded.

Jake took that in. "Of the white men too?"

"The white men too."

Jake just shook his head. After the game he went into the decrepit locker room, which had only one shower for the whole team. The Celtics were washing up in pairs, and when Jake arrived, Sam Jones and John Havlicek were in the shower, passing the one bar of soap back and forth—first the naked black man, then the naked white man stepping under the water spray. Jake watched, agape. Finally he said, "I never thought I'd see anything like that."

Of course, it was hardly a straight line upward to brotherhood. Nor was Bill Russell afraid to point that out to America; he could be unforgiving and sometimes angry, which meant he was called arrogant by those who didn't care for his kind. Russell invested in a rubber plantation in Liberia, and at a time when African-Americans were known as Negroes, and the word black was an insult, Russell started calling himself black. In the civil rights movement he became a bold, significant figure far beyond the parquet.

Thompson says, "It took a long time for me to be able to accept him as a person, as another guy, because I admired and respected him so. Russell made me feel safe. It was not that he was going to save me if anybody threatened me. Somehow I knew it was going to be all right so long as I was with him. I was going to be safe."

Often, edgy whites misunderstood him, though. Once a magazine quoted him as saying, "I hate all white people." Russell walked into the cramped old Celtics locker room, where equality reigned: Every player had one stool and two nails. Frank Ramsey glanced up from the magazine. "Hey, Russell, I'm white," he said. "You hate me?"

The two teammates looked into each other's eyes. "I was misquoted, Frank," was all Russell said. That was the end of it; he and Ramsey remained as close as ever. A few years earlier, too, there had been a big brouhaha in Kentucky, Ramsey's home state. Russell and other black Celtics had pulled out of an exhibition game there because the hotels were segregated. There was a lot of talk that Russell should not have embarrassed Ramsey that way. None of the talk came from Ramsey, though. Then, in 1966, when Russell succeeded Auerbach and became the first black coach (while continuing to play), he accepted the job only after trying to persuade Ramsey to return to basketball, from which he had retired in 1964, and coach the Celtics. Russell thought that would be better for the team than for him to make history.

The Celtics really did get along the way teams are supposed to in sports mythology. Russell threw Christmas parties for his teammates and their families. In 1962 he took the astonished rookie Havlicek around town to get a good price on a stereo. "All of us were strangers in a place far from home,"

Russell says. "But we made it into a unique situation. Cousy started it. He was absolutely sincere about being a good teammate."

Still, it was different away from the warm cocoon of the Celtics. One night in 1971 the team assembled in the Boston suburb of Reading, where Russell lived, to be with him as the town proudly honored their captain. It was the first time Heinsohn ever saw Russell cry, he was so happy. A few months later some people broke into Russell's house, rampaged, smashed his trophies, defecated in his bed and spread the excrement over his walls. They didn't want any black man in their town. But in the locker room Russell never talked about the terrible things that happened to him so close to the Celtics' city. "He was too proud to let people know," Heinsohn says.

Cousy still feels guilty. "I wish I'd done more to support Russ," he says. "We were so close, as teammates, but we all should have been more aware of his anger." Cousy draws a deep sigh. "But you know jocks—all into the macho thing. Always afraid to let the conversation be anything more than superficial. We mature so much later than anybody else."

So they just had to settle for winning.

Russell drove the Lexus into Oakland. When he was a little boy, after rural Dixie, his big new California hometown seemed such a wondrously exciting place. But Oakland wasn't Valhalla. "I couldn't even go downtown," he says. "The cops would chase the black kids away. And you still have those soldiers in blue in the streets. In terms of economics, things are certainly better in America today. But the criminal justice system hasn't improved."

Still, even if the police ran young William out of stylish Oakland, he grew up in contentment. Even after Katie's death, the Russells enjoyed the sort of family embrace that is denied so many black boys today. Charlie Jr. would graduate from college and become a social worker and a playwright. William, for his part, was a bookworm. For someone who ended up 6'10", he grew very late and wasn't much noticed on the basketball court. But then, he also wasn't much good. Frank Robinson, the great baseball player, was on the McClymonds High basketball team with Russell, and he says, "He couldn't even put the ball in the basket when he dunked." Russell was scheduled to graduate in January 1951, whereupon it was his intention to get a job in the shipyards and save up to go to college part time.

This is surely what would have happened, too, except that Hal DeJulio, who had played at the University of San Francisco and occasionally steered young players toward the school, went to an Oakland High–McClymonds game one day to help the Oakland coach. USF was a struggling urban Catholic college that didn't even have a gymnasium; the team had to settle for leftovers and overlooks. As a consequence, DeJulio noticed McClymonds' center, the unknown string bean with the incredibly long arms, who had a rare good game that day. A week later DeJulio showed up unannounced at the Russells' house and offered William a scholarship to San Francisco. Only then did he tell Dons coach Phil Woolpert about his find. Woolpert was skeptical but agreed to take William on.

It was that close to there never being a Bill Russell. "It gives me chills," Karen says.

Even as Russell won his first NCAA title, in 1955, his coach—like most everybody else—couldn't yet fathom that Russell was this genius who had, in effect, created a whole new game of basketball. For instance, Woolpert concurred with the conventional wisdom that to play defense you must not leave your feet, "and here I was airborne most of the time," Russell recalls. Although the Dons' victories piled up, Woolpert kept telling Russell he was "fundamentally unsound." He would say, "You can't do that." Russell would respond, "But I just did."

Nevertheless Russell liked Woolpert—"a fine and decent man," he calls the coach—who was being excoriated for starting three black players: Russell, K.C. Jones and Hal Perry. Woolpert was flooded with hate mail, and rival coaches snidely called him Saperstein, after Abe, the coach of the Harlem Globetrotters. Although the NCAA championship won by the 1965–66 Texas Western team, with five black starters, has over time been painted as a watershed event, the fact is that Russell was as much pioneer as avatar. The African-American domination of basketball traces to two teams, his teams: USF in college, Boston in the pros. Texas Western was but the end product of what Russell inspired—and what he had suffered through—a decade earlier.

K.C. Jones remembers an occasion in Oklahoma City, where USF was practicing, when local citizens threw coins at the players as if they were clowns in the circus. Inside, Jones raged. But Russell, smiling sardonically, picked up the change and handed it to Woolpert. "Here, Coach, hold this for me," was all he said.

"Then," Jones says, "he took it out on the opposition."

"I decided in college to win," Russell says matter-of-factly. "Then it's a historical fact, and nobody can take it away from me. You understand what I mean?"

Indisputably, his race diminished Russell in the eyes of many biased observers, but, withal, it was the rare fair-minded expert who could comprehend the brilliance of this original force. Indeed, even as Russell won every year in the NBA, the fact that Chamberlain averaged skyrocket numbers was more beguiling to the unsophisticated. Meanwhile, in Boston, the stylish—and Caucasian—Cousy continued to hold the greater affection. Auerbach recalls one time when Cousy was injured but the Celtics swept a five-game road trip, with "Russ blocking a million shots." When the team returned home, it was greeted by a headline that made no reference to the victory streak, asking only, WILL COUSY PLAY TONIGHT? "This coulda killed my team," Auerbach says. He felt obliged to order the exhausted players to go directly from the airport to the Garden, there to air the matter as a team.

Russell was a great admirer of Cousy, though, and the two led together. If they called a team meeting, they'd start off by soliciting opinions on how they—Cousy and Russell—were lacking. After that, who could bitch about anybody else? Jones cannot recall a single instance, either in college or in the NBA, when Russell "jumped on anyone's butt. But Bill definitely had his Machiavellian side. Anybody who didn't fit in, he'd just dismiss him."

Russell's simple key to a successful team was to encourage each player to do what he did best. "Remember," he says, "each of us has a finite amount of energy, and things you do well don't require as much. Things you don't do well take more concentration. And if you're fatigued by that, then the things you do best are going to be affected." The selfishness of successful team play—"I was very selfish," he declares—sounds paradoxical, but a team profits if each player revels in his strength. Still, Russell points out, there is a fine line between idealistic shared greed and typical self-gratification. "You must let your energy flow to the team," he says.

And sometimes, of course, you simply must sacrifice. For instance, one of the hardest things Russell had to learn to accept was that if he filled one lane on a fast break and Heinsohn was on the other flank, Cousy would give Heinsohn the ball—and the basket. Every time. "He simply had so much confidence in Heinie," Russell says. "So I had to discipline myself to run that break all-out, even if I knew I wasn't going to get the ball."

Above all, though, the key to Russell's success was that his greatest individual talent was the one that most benefited the team. It was not only that he blocked shots; Auerbach estimates that 80% of the time Russell could also direct the blocked ball into Celtics hands, usually fast-break bound. Moreover—and here is why statistical analyses of Russell's play are meaningless—the mere threat of a Russell block made opponents think twice about shooting, while the other Celtics could gamble aggressively on defense, knowing that number 6 would save them. "Other teams, all you hear is 'Switch!' 'Pick!' 'Help!'" Thompson says. "On the Celtics you'd only hear one word: 'Russ!'"

Although Russell made his *team* nearly invincible, the singular image that survives is of that one extraordinary athlete. That's the trouble with old sportswriters: They remember the beauty they saw far better than people today can visualize it from reading statistics. "It wasn't just that Bill was the whole package—and he was," West says, "but there was such presence he brought to the game."

By himself, in fact, Russell was hugely responsible for changing the way the public thought about big men in basketball. Before Russell, the giants were often dismissed as gawky goons or, like Chamberlain, bully-boy Goliaths. But Russell was as comfortable in his shape as he was in his skin, and it showed. "I am tall," he says. "O.K.? And if that's the only reason I can play, that's all right too. Don't deny your biggest asset. I'm a tall black guy. O.K.? No apologies, no bragging." In a game that was much more choreographed than the one today, no one could fail to see the elegance of Russell—this great winged bird swooping about, long angles that magically curved, rising high before your eyes. In fact, Russell saw himself as an artist, his play as a work of art. "If you can take something to levels that very few other people can reach," he says without vanity, "then what you're doing becomes art."

Unashamed, he sought to play the perfect game. "Certain standards I set for that," he says. "First, of course, we had to win. I had to get at least 25 rebounds, eight assists and eight blocks. I had to make 60% of my shots, and I had to run all my plays perfectly, setting picks and filling the lanes. Also, I had to say all the right things to my teammates—and to my opponents." Ironically, the closest he ever came to achieving that ideal was one night when he lived up to all his standards except the most obvious one: He did not make a single basket in 11 attempts.

Never mind. There were many discrete exquisite moments that made up for never quite attaining that comprehensive dream. "Sometimes," Russell told me in the car, breaking into a smile at the recollection, "sometimes if I could do something exactly the way I wanted, it was such an exhilarating feeling that I wanted to scream."

That memory was so joyous, in fact, that he missed the turn to the airport. Yes, 30 years later, he was driving me to an airport again. We had seen his father that morning, so our mission was accomplished. And now Karen was coming up to visit Charlie, so three generations of Russells would be together, Bill in the middle.

Karen returned, not long ago, from her first visit to West Monroe. "We're like so many other Americans, all scattered to the winds," she says, "and it was, for me, like finding my lost tribe. It also put my father's incredible journey into a context I'd never been able to put it before." She visited Katie's grave, and it made Karen think: "She had the vision for my father, as he had the vision for me."

Charlie was touched when Karen hugged him and told him this. Bill looked at them—the father who had a sixth-grade education and the daughter who'd graduated from Harvard Law. There they were, a whole century's worth of one American family. When Bill was young, in his game, players like him were known as pivotmen. Now, in his family, he is something of that again, the axis on which the Russells, ahead and behind him, turn. But then, it was the same way with basketball. Bill Russell was the pivot on which the whole sport turned. You understand what I mean?

— POSTSCRIPT —

Deford passed away in 2017. Here he is, in 2014, talking about this story with SI's Ted Keith:

Russell had approached me.... because friends of his were saying, "Bill, you're being forgotten." He was very reclusive. Now he's ubiquitous, he's everywhere, but in the period leading up to 1999, Russell had sort of disappeared. And as a consequence, he approached me with some friends of his. I met him down on 42nd street in New York City at a hotel next to Grand Central Station. And everybody said, "How do we get Bill publicity?" The main thing I did first was a documentary on HBO. They were thrilled with the idea. "Russell wants to do a documentary? Yeah!"

Then the idea came up at SI at about the same time of doing all these pieces about the turn of the century. SI came to me and said we want you to do a story on Russell as the greatest team player, which I certainly agreed with. I was the logical choice to do it because a) I had covered him when he was a player and b) I had done a story with him—he wrote it, I did the ghostwriting part—when he retired in 1969.

All those things led together and he was delighted to do the story.

He suggested the drive. He said, "I'm going down to see my father, why don't you come along." So I flew out to Seattle and spent the night at his house. The next morning we got in the car to drive off to Oakland. The deal was we'd switch off driving but Bill drove the whole damn way. He wouldn't give up the wheel.

When we got to Oakland we couldn't get a hotel room. It's a long drive so we showed up too late and we finally got into the Holiday Inn or something like that. That was a very unique story because it wasn't the usual kind of [reporting process]. It created a wonderful framework for a story.

A Different Drummer

After years of moody introspection, Kareem Abdul-
Jabbar is coming out of his shell. But whether at
home, as here, or on a basketball court or in a roller
disco, he still steps to the music he hears

BY JOHN PAPANEK

*In choosing a Kareem story to include, we considered running an early first-
person piece from 1969 when he took direct aim at the sports culture of the
day (titled "A Year of Turmoil and Decision" and written when he was still
Lew Alcindor, you can find it online). But this 1980 feature by John Papanek
captures a wider view of this complicated, talented man, freezing him in a
moment—toward the end of his playing career and before he evolved into a
scholar and writer—when Kareem was still figuring out who he was and where
he fit in the game.*

It happened on a perfectly beautiful Southern California afternoon following nine straight days of devastating mid-February rains. Nearly 16,000 Los
Angelenos went indoors—and on a Sunday, no less—to watch a basketball
game. Moreover, it was a game between the Lakers and the Houston Rockets,
which lets you know straight off that it wasn't a particularly big one, except
that playoff time was near and it had been many years since the Lakers
were fun to watch.

The P.A. announcer for The Forum, Larry McKay, was informing the
crowd that the great Laker center, Kareem Abdul-Jabbar, had called in sick

with migraines. No one booed. In other years the fans would have hooted the roof off the Fabulous Forum and a dozen beach-bound Mercedes would have piled up at a parking-lot exit. Some sportswriters, with wicked glee, would have seized the opportunity to blast a favorite target for showing once more that he cared for nothing and no one except himself. And at least one would have begun typing: "The Lakers' 16-game home winning streak came to a s-Kareeming halt yesterday because Kareem Abdul-Jabbar rolled over in bed and said, 'Not today. I have a headache.'"

But no one wrote anything of the sort. On this Sunday afternoon the working-stiff Lakers, without their leader, slopped through two and a half periods, somehow staying barely ahead of Houston. Then a second remarkable thing happened. The crowd suddenly went berserk. Standing ovation. Players on the floor froze in mid-fast break. Abdul-Jabbar had arrived. He had tried to sneak to the bench inconspicuously, an attempt foredoomed by his 7'2" height. (Officially he is 7'2"; his lady friend Cheryl Pistono says he is closer to 7'5".)

Abdul-Jabbar entered the game immediately and swatted five Rocket shots out of the air. He rebounded ferociously, passed with élan and hit six of the seven shots he took, two of them "sky hooks" over Moses Malone, who a year earlier had seemed ready to end Abdul-Jabbar's 10-year reign as the most dominant player in the sport. Of course the Lakers won. The score was 110–102.

"I knew it was too good to be true," moaned Houston Coach Del Harris. "Bringing in Kareem is like wheeling out nuclear weapons."

"Is Kareem better than Malone?" the Rockets' Rick Barry was asked. "What kind of ridiculous question is that?" Barry said. "Kareem is probably the best athlete in the world."

The fans at The Forum wouldn't have disagreed. Their Lakers were about to overtake Seattle, and they were considered the No. 1 contender to unseat the defending champions because, at 32, Abdul-Jabbar was playing like a kid again, having his finest season in five as a Laker. He was playing with vitality and emotion, leading fast breaks, dunking with authority, slapping palms and occasionally—you could be sure because he had finally gotten rid of those infernal goggles after four years—smiling. And he had not missed a single game.

In the Lakers' dressing room Abdul-Jabbar sat in front of his locker. Usually he is in the shower before the press arrives, dresses before he is totally dry and dashes out, saying as little as possible, as though he has a bus to catch. This day he sat there, and the media people approached him as they always do—verrry carefully.

Someone asked him how he felt, and he began to answer. In an instant he was mobbed.

"I haven't had a migraine bad enough to make me miss a game in two years," he was saying. "They're a mystery of medical science. No one knows what causes them. The pain was so bad this morning, I was crying. I couldn't move. I had to lie in a dark room in total silence. You know what it felt like? It felt like the Alien was inside my head, trying to get out my eyes."

The image was clear enough even to those who had not seen the movie *Alien*. He was asked why, with all the pain, had he bothered with such an unimportant game? Abdul-Jabbar seemed to expect the question. If anything about him has been constant throughout his career, it has been his pride. "These guys are my teammates," he said. "But they are also my friends. They needed me."

Those familiar with Abdul-Jabbar knew there had been migraines before, usually in times of extreme tension. There had been bad ones in 1973, while he was playing for Milwaukee. They developed after seven people—a friend and six relatives of Abdul-Jabbar's Muslim mentor, Khalifa Hamaass Abdul Khaalis, members of a group called the Hanafi—were murdered, allegedly by rival Black Muslims, in a Washington, D.C. house that Kareem had purchased for them. Abdul-Jabbar was thought to be a target as well, and he was accompanied by a bodyguard for several weeks. The immobilizing headaches came on again in 1977, after Khaalis and his Hanafi group sought revenge by invading three Washington buildings, including the national headquarters of B'nai B'rith. They held 132 hostages for 38 hours, leaving seven wounded and one dead. Khaalis went to jail, and the Jewish Defense League threatened to kidnap Abdul-Jabbar. This latest series of headaches—and more would follow—seemed to coincide with Abdul-Jabbar's pending divorce suit.

There are those who have always believed that a man who can dunk a basketball without leaving his feet should be the NBA's Most Valuable Player by default. Because size seems to be the primary requisite for getting the award—centers have won it 19 times in the 24 years it has been given, including Abdul-Jabbar in 1971, '72, '74, '76 and '77—the distinction isn't esteemed as highly as MVP honors in other sports. Maybe that is why smaller players—Cousy, Robertson, West, Baylor, Frazier, Erving, Havlicek, et al.—are accorded greater devotion than the giants who have played the game—Russell, Chamberlain, Abdul-Jabbar, Walton. They are *expected* to dominate.

Bill Russell, of course, was the perennial champion, the quintessentially unselfish team player/philosopher with the twinkly eyes and the thunderous laugh. Dominant though he was, you had to love Russell. Wilt Chamberlain, of imposing size and strength, once scored 100 points in a single game and averaged 50.4 in one season. But he was a colossus who evoked little affection. Bill Walton, one of the best all-round centers in history, has been beset by injuries; giants aren't supposed to be fragile.

And then there is Abdul-Jabbar, the first, the only player to incorporate every desirable element of the modern game into his own. He has the speed and grace of Baylor, the skill and finesse of West, the size and very nearly the strength of Chamberlain. He is a superb shot-blocker and a better passer than some think; he has seldom had teammates worth passing to. And he has been amazingly consistent, averaging nearly 30 points and 14 rebounds a game during his career. He has constantly been harassed by defenses, often by two opponents. Perhaps he has made what he does look too easy. He is not often "spectacular." But it is astounding how often he gets a "quiet" 32 points.

"He's always been my idol," says San Diego's Walton. "To me, he's the greatest."

"He does things to you that make you ask, 'Damn, now how could a man his size have done something like that?'" says Milwaukee's Bob Lanier.

A good bet to top off this, his 11th season, with his second championship ring, Abdul-Jabbar is also likely to accomplish what only one other professional athlete in any sport has done before him—win his sixth Most Valuable Player award. (Gordie Howe had six in hockey.) In pro basketball Russell won five and Chamberlain four.

Abdul-Jabbar's athletic competence is not limited to basketball. He is a powerful runner, swimmer, bicycle racer and tennis player. He worked out last summer catching passes at the Minnesota Vikings' training camp with his friend Ahmad Rashad, and he practiced a form of kung fu for several years with the late Bruce Lee. Moreover, he is a terror on wheels at Flipper's Roller Boogie Palace in Hollywood, which he often goes to after Laker games. On a recent night he skated past two girls and heard one squeal to the other, "It's Wilt Chamberlain!"

Which brings up the perennial question: who ranks first among the great centers—Chamberlain, Russell or Abdul-Jabbar? Modesty prevents Kareem from saying what he truly believes—that it is he. "Kareem is a *player*," says West, his former coach, although he had become angry with Abdul-Jabbar at times when Kareem seemed to be playing less than inspired ball. "A great, great, great basketball *player*. My goodness, he does more things than anyone who has ever played this game. Wilt was a force. He could totally dominate a game. Take it. Make it his. People have thought that Kareem should be able to do that too. No. That would not make him a *player* of this game. Russell was a *player*. The greatest. But he was playing a different game than they're playing now. You can't compare the two of them."

What Russell had, of course—what great players must have in order to win—were other *players* around him. Abdul-Jabbar has not always had that luxury, and it rankles him that this has never seemed to matter to the press or the fans. "It's the misunderstanding most people have about basketball," he says, "that one man can make a team. One man can be a crucial ingredient on a team, but one man cannot make a team. In the past I have played on only three good teams—in '71 when we won the championship, '74 when we lost to Boston in the finals and '77 here in Los Angeles. It was only when Milwaukee picked up Oscar Robertson and Bob Boozer that we became a good team. When I came to Los Angeles in 1975, the Lakers had to give up three excellent young players to get me. Those guys—Brian Winters, Dave Meyers and Junior Bridgeman—made Milwaukee a good team. I probably had my best year, and the Lakers finished next to last. In '77 we had the best team in the league, but we lost Kermit Washington and Lucius Allen just before the playoffs, and Portland beat us four straight.

"We were playing, more or less, with four guards and me. Don Ford was out-rebounded by Maurice Lucas something like 45–12. Yet everything written said that Walton had outplayed me. Walton played a great series. I played a great series. The Trail Blazers played a great series. The Lakers played a poor one. The press tried to make it seem like I was embarrassed. Walton made one dunk shot on me, and that was supposed to have signaled the end of Abdul-Jabbar being the best."

The press has apparently changed its mind—Abdul-Jabbar is the best again—because so many things have happened to make the Lakers fun once more. "I view that with total cynicism," Abdul-Jabbar says of the press turnaround.

First there was the arrival of the superb rookie point guard, effervescent Magic Johnson. He was going to be everybody's little brother, spark new life into the dour Kareem. Then came a new coach, Jack McKinney, to replace the problematical perfectionist, West. After McKinney suffered a serious injury in a freak bicycling accident 13 games into the season, *another* new coach, a bright Shakespearean scholar from LaSalle College in Philadelphia, Paul Westhead, took over. Presiding over all was a new owner, millionaire playboy-mathematician Dr. Jerry Buss, who had pumped new life into the town by actually promoting the Lakers, and into the team by rewriting contracts, throwing lavish postgame parties stocked with *Playboy* Playmates and Bo Derek imitations, and flooding the locker room with the likes of James Caan, Sean Connery and O.J. Simpson.

Said Connery to Kareem after witnessing his first pro basketball game, "Metaphysically as well as literally, you stand head and shoulders above the rest of the gentlemen."

Every one of the Laker changes has worked like Magic, who has, says Abdul-Jabbar, "incredible talents that he brings to the game. He creates things for us the way nobody ever has for this team." Just as important have been Jim Chones, Mark Landsberger and Spencer Haywood, three strong and talented rebounders who came along this season to remove much of the inside burden from Abdul-Jabbar and enable Forward Jamaal Wilkes to play like an All-Star.

"Early in the season," says Westhead, "everything was Magic this and Magic that. People sort of forgot about Kareem. In a way that was good, because, before long, everybody realized that Magic or no Magic, this team is nothing without Kareem. I mean nothing."

So many good things happening all at once sounds like some kind of Tinseltown fairy tale. But it so happens that at this moment Abdul-Jabbar is undergoing a rebirth, fighting his way out of the shell he has kept himself in for the past 15 years. It isn't easy. There has been racial hatred and distrust; violence perpetrated against his close friends and violence perpetrated by himself; a bad marriage; and now a messy divorce.

Abdul-Jabbar lives in a 10-room Bel Air house just down the road from Caan and O.J. and near the jazz musician and composer Quincy Jones. It is decorated with several of Abdul-Jabbar's valuable Oriental rugs and pieces of Islamic art he purchased in Africa and the Middle East.

The other day Abdul-Jabbar rather coldly told a visitor he had invited over to wait in the living room until he had finished dinner.

"Kareem!" came a loud, scolding female voice from the kitchen. "Tell him to come in here and sit with you!"

Whispers followed.

"Well, if you're going to be that way, I'll just have my dinner in the living room," she yelled, and came to the door, apologizing.

Cheryl Pistono is funny, friendly, delightfully smart-alecky, wise beyond her 23 years. Like Kareem, she has an uncommon odyssey behind her; somehow it fits that they should have ended up in the same place. She left a working-class family in LaSalle, Ill. at 16 to live with relatives on the Coast, went to Beverly Hills High School and got "into the high life. Hanging out at Hugh Hefner's, weekends in Las Vegas, stuff like that," she says. Like Kareem, she had been a disgruntled Catholic. Only she settled on Buddhism. "Some combination," she says, laughing. "Like oil and water, right?"

Last winter, when she brought Abdul-Jabbar home to meet her family, it was a big occasion. "Everyone was very excited, even though they didn't really know who he was," she says. "The funny thing is that my father is a really big basketball fan who had always loved Kareem, but when Kareem was in his house, he refused to come home. Couldn't handle the racial thing.

Now my grandmother, who's in her 80s and lives out here, really gets on him. She cuts the articles about Kareem out of the papers and sends them to him, just to needle him."

Abdul-Jabbar readily acknowledges that Cheryl has had a greater impact on his adult life than any of his teachers, coaches, owners, friends or teammates. She convinced him to seek a divorce from his wife Habiba, whom he married in 1971 but has not lived with since 1973. The divorce is now being settled in court. Cheryl attacks inconsistencies in his religious beliefs—he removes paintings and photographs of human figures from the walls, according to Islamic law, and hides them under her bed when devout Muslim friends visit, for instance—and she rails at him for choosing religious laws over conventional ones. She was horrified that he fathered two children with Habiba after their separation—they have three—and told him so.

"I met a person who had never received anything from anyone but praise," she said. "I mean, he was a god, right? No one ever told him, 'Hey, that's——. Why do you do that? That hurt that person.' People have always been afraid to tell him that they don't like him. I never praise him. Never. I'm the only person who ever told him he was full of——."

As if on cue, Abdul-Jabbar bursts from the kitchen, relaxed, beaming. "Cheryl, that was a *wonderful* dinner you prepared. Really praiseworthy."

"Kareem, you can be such a jerk...."

He laughed loud and hard until Cheryl left the room. Then he grew quiet and serious. He fingered a copy of *Heavy Metal*, his favorite science-fiction magazine. He was asked about the *Alien* metaphor. Could it be a metaphor for his life? "I suppose it could," he said. "Like there's an alien inside me trying to get out? Maybe. Maybe the alien is the real me that I have kept locked away for so long, like all my life. I've missed a lot of things, I know. I'm trying very hard to change all that."

In his mind he went back to when he was a boy growing up in the Dyckman Street housing project, a racially mixed community in the Inwood section of Manhattan. Too many bad things had happened over the past 15 years, he says, for him to remember those days with fondness. He was, after all, a different person then—Lew Alcindor, Catholic—and now he finds himself a 33-year-old Muslim. "I feel sometimes that I went right from being a kid to where I am now," he says. Cheryl maintains he is still a kid.

He has no intention of renouncing Islam and becoming Alcindor again. He is a fervent believer, if less zealous than he once was. He just wants to recross the bridges between his past and his present that got burned, and try to recapture what he calls "a sense of reality."

When he was six years old he attached himself to the first and only real hero of his life, Jackie Robinson. "Not because he was the first black baseball player in the majors," Abdul-Jabbar says, "but 'cause he was a hero. See, I understand now what was going on then in terms of what it meant socially. But at the time I didn't understand that. My parents didn't explain it to me. I didn't even *know* that he was the first black. I didn't even realize that everyone else was white. All I knew was that Jack was out there and it was like Jack against the world and Jack was going to win. Jack took no prisoners. Guys like Sal Maglie would throw at Jack, and Jack would bunt down the first-base line and try to spike the guy as he fielded the ball. Jack was serious. And that competitive intensity that he had—that I understood. But I didn't understand why it was the way it was. I loved Jack."

Because he was what he was, Alcindor soon began to learn all that he could have wanted to know about the two subjects that would dominate most of his life—basketball and racial prejudice. As a boy he could never understand why his white friends seemed to feel that there was something wrong with being black. One afternoon, when he was 12, his best friend, a white boy, and two others followed him home from school, shouting "Nigger! Black Boy! Blackie!" at him. That was when Abdul-Jabbar began constructing the wall.

At the same time, of course, he was becoming the greatest schoolboy basketball player of all time. In the eighth grade, when he was 6'8", he had his first brush with high-pressure recruiting. Manhattan's Power Memorial Academy and Coach Jack Donohue won out, and Lew Alcindor began attracting a lot more attention than most urban black children received in the middle '60s. In his last three years at Power his teams won 78 of 79 games and three city Catholic championships. But along the way there were more of those moments that reinforced Alcindor's feeling that it was himself against the world, just like Jackie Robinson.

In his junior year Power was playing St. Helena's, an easy opponent, the night before its big game with powerful DeMatha of Hyattsville, Md. As Alcindor recalled in SI (Oct. 27, 1969): "We played rotten and I played rottener than anybody, and at halftime we were only up by six points when we should have had the game settled by then. We went down to the coach's room, and Mr. Donohue started picking us apart one by one and telling us how awful we played, and then he pointed at me and he said, 'And you! You go out there and you don't hustle. You don't move. You don't do any of the things you're supposed to do. You're acting just like a nigger!'"

After Power won that game, and the DeMatha game, Donohue tried to laugh off the incident, saying, "See? My strategy worked!" But it worked instead to help shove Lew Alcindor into what he calls his "white-hating period."

"I was 17 years old, being cheered on the basketball court but being called a 'nigger' by those same people on the street," he says. That summer riots erupted in Harlem. "I stepped off the subway right into the middle of it. It was chaos, wild, insane, and I just stood there trembling. Cops were swinging nightsticks at everybody, bullets were flying, windows were being smashed, people were stealing and looting. All I could think of was that I wanted to stay alive, so I took off running and I didn't stop till I was at 137th and Broadway, several blocks away. And then I sat huffing and puffing and pondering about what I'd seen, and I knew what it was: rage, black rage. The poor people of Harlem felt that it was better to get hit with a nightstick than to keep on taking the white man's insults forever. Right then and there I knew who I was and who I had to be. I was going to be black rage personified, black power in the flesh."

He went to UCLA, influenced in part by a letter from a famous alumnus named Jackie Robinson. Three NCAA championships followed, and UCLA lost just two games in all that time, one being the celebrated Astrodome matchup against Houston and Elvin Hayes. That game took place just eight days after Alcindor suffered his first serious eye injury, a scratched eyeball.

Fame at UCLA did not make life any happier for Alcindor, who had already come to think of basketball as nothing more than business, though it was important for him to be the best. He nearly left UCLA for Michigan after his sophomore year, and after his junior year he incurred a great deal of resentment when he aligned himself with Harry Edwards and called upon all black athletes to boycott the 1968 Olympics. The boycott failed to materialize, although Alcindor himself stayed away, working with black children in New York instead. By his senior year he had retreated into his Islamic studies, had few friends and spent most of his time alone.

"Ever since childhood I had this ability to draw into myself and be perfectly contented," he said in 1969. "I *had* to. I had always been such a minority of one. Very tall. Black. Catholic. I withdrew into myself to find myself. I made no further attempts to integrate. I was consumed and obsessed by my interest in the black man, in black power, black pride, black courage. That, for me, would suffice."

After his Rookie-of-the-Year season in 1970 with Milwaukee, Alcindor made his conversion to Islam public and changed his name to Kareem (generous) Abdul (servant of Allah) Jabbar (powerful). "I never had any real trouble passing my change off on the public," he says now. "Because of my talent on the basketball court, people tended to avoid engaging me in any conflict if they could help it. The people in Milwaukee were good about it, they realized I wasn't some sort of idiot. The coach, Larry Costello, had some trouble. He kept stumbling—'Lew...Kareem...Lew...Kareem.' He was very self-conscious about not saying the wrong thing."

In 1971 the Bucks won the NBA championship, and Abdul-Jabbar picked up his first MVP award. They won at least 60 games in each of the next two seasons, and lost to Boston in the championship finals in 1974. But life was still dragging on Abdul-Jabbar. His friends had been murdered in 1973, his marriage had broken up, he was shuttered in Milwaukee, a town he was not enthusiastic about in the first place. "I would stay home, read, get into my music," he says. His frustrations built so, that after suffering his second serious eye injury in a 1974 exhibition game, he slammed a basket standard in disgust and fractured his hand.

When his contract expired in 1975 he did all he could to get back to New York, to play for the Knicks, which had been his lifelong dream. When that fell through he chose Los Angeles. He still kept mostly to himself, although there were more people he could be comfortable with—Muslim friends and jazz musicians like Wayne Shorter, Herbie Hancock and Chick Corea. Generally speaking, his teammates at the time did not fit that category. "My feeling about basketball then was that I was paid to play my best and that is what I did," he says, "not to pat guys on the behind and be their friend."

The worst year of his life was 1977. In March his friend Khaalis led the Hanafi Muslim siege on the B'nai B'rith building in Washington and ended up in prison. Abdul-Jabbar became the target of kidnap and death threats. Later in the spring the Lakers, with the best record in the NBA, lost four straight playoff games to Walton and the Portland Trail Blazers. The papers suggested that Abdul-Jabbar was washed up. That fall, on opening night of the 1977–78 season in Milwaukee, of all places, Abdul-Jabbar reacted to an elbow to the solar plexus from rookie Kent Benson by throwing a brutal punch that gave Benson a concussion and broke Abdul-Jabbar's hand. Again, his own violent reaction upset Abdul-Jabbar, but not nearly so much as the reaction from the public and the league office. He was fined $5,000, while Benson was not even reprimanded.

"Everyone's attitude was that it was totally my fault," says Abdul-Jabbar. "So again it was me against the world. I can understand how the punch happened. He was a rookie, he made a mistake. When he did that I thought of all the times I was provoked, abused, bullied, scorned, and I was not going to take one more thing. My reaction was extreme, no two ways about it, but the league's reaction was wrong. It was neither my fault nor Benson's, totally. It was the system's."

Just two months earlier Abdul-Jabbar had first met Cheryl. "I had no interest in him," she recalls, "because I never liked the people who were into the sports mentality, and despite everything else, he obviously was. He expected me to fall all over him. Women always had, but one day he brought me a rose from his garden. He was serious as hell! I thought, oh, I've got to get this person to laugh. All I could think of was to not hurt him."

Abdul-Jabbar insists that basketball was really what his life had been about all along. He loves it and expects to play, he says, "as long as I keep my mental and physical health." But in December of 1977 he was nearly ready to quit. Just a month after his hand had healed sufficiently for him to return to action, he witnessed yet another violent act when teammate Kermit Washington crushed the face of Houston's Rudy Tomjanovich with a punch. "He was miserable," says Cheryl. "I sent him air-express letters saying, 'Kareem, your career is not a jail sentence.' He felt so sorry for himself it was disgusting."

Cheryl "got serious" with him and told him what he had to do. How he had to be more than just a basketball player, he had to be a leader. How he had to stop pushing people away and start listening to what they had to say. How he had to forget about keeping his emotions inside of himself, because they would continue to come out as fits of rage. And they did. Hearing these things from her one evening, he became so enraged he broke two doors in his house off their hinges.

Gradually he has come around, has gotten less "serious." But when a person has been locked in so long, making changes is not easy. Cheryl introduced him to roller skating. It is a staggering sight to see a man his size doing disco moves on wheels with consummate grace. But he does, and he is happy, and he actually blends into the bizarre crowd at Flipper's. Even so, sometimes he closes up. One night a young fan approached Kareem to tell him how great he was. Kareem gave a blank look and the tiniest nod, but would not speak. The fellow skated off in a huff and confronted Cheryl. "Hey," he said, "how can someone be so great on the court and such a —— off it?"

Cheryl felt terrible. "Did he nod to you?" she asked. "If he did, it came from his heart, believe me." Then she chastised Kareem.

"It bothers me that people interpret me the way that they do," Abdul-Jabbar says. "I don't mean to be intimidating. I'm about respect. I want people to respect me, that's all. It's something I get from my father. He's a cop—a big, strong man, very quiet. That intimidates people. He was my example, I'm just like Big Al, that's what I always thought.

"Now I realize what happened to me. O.K., I was big. That never bothered me. I always liked being big. But because I was a basketball star, all my life people had gone to a great amount of trouble to insulate me from things. It was necessary, it seemed then. My high school coach had to insulate me from the flesh peddlers, and there were hundreds of them in New York. At UCLA they had to insulate me from the press. In Milwaukee I signed a very large contract and they were careful not to overburden me. Beautiful. It was all so easy to accept. I liked it that way. And even the people I learned about Islam from felt that it wasn't necessary for me to learn it the way it was generally taught, because that wasn't good enough for me, so they made my environment as pure as possible. My parents were part of it, too. When I was under their guardianship they always told me to go along with the program. I bought it all because there were immediate rewards—winning basketball games. Later I won basketball games and made a lot of money. Looking back on it now, I don't think any of it did me a whole lot of good.

"I didn't realize that I was missing so much. So a lot of the things I'm going through now, the things Cheryl has spoken about, have to do with reviewing my life and picking up on things I did wrong. Now I'm dealing with my life, by myself, for the first time in my life."

Westhead, the rookie interim coach, marvels at the man he had known, by reputation, as "the aloof Kareem." "I expected there to be this so-called 'chill factor,' but there is none of that at all," he says. "Maybe it is his soft personality. The guys seem to thrive on it. It's like he's their big brother. He's got so many stories. O.K., maybe a half hour before games, everybody gets quiet and waits for Kareem to tell one of his stories. He tells these special tales about growing up in New York, characters he's met. It's story time, then everybody goes out and plays basketball."

It is true. One day Kareem is telling about how Wilt took him out to dinner when he was a senior in high school: "He had the Bentley and the racehorses and every beautiful woman in Manhattan, and he takes me to his pad and there is the finest woman I have ever seen in my life. I'm 17 and my eyes are big as apples and my jaw is hanging open...." Another day he tells about "the toughest dude who ever lived in Harlem, Sugar Stamp," so named because he used to connive to get sugar-ration stamps during World War II. "One time Sugar hit the number and two guys ambushed him, shot him three times in the stomach. Man, Sugar chased 'em both, beat one to pieces and about caught the other when he finally checked out...."

Once he told about the most amazing player he had seen, a visitor to Harlem from Philadelphia for a playground all-star game. "This dude brought his own *cheering section* from Philly, man, and I had never even heard of him. Before the game they start screaming, 'Jesus! Black Jesus! Black Jesus!' I thought, who *was* this dude? He was about 6'3", and the first play of the game he got a rebound on the defensive end of the court and started *spinning*! Man, he spun four times! Now, he's 90 feet from the hoop and this dude is spinning. Well, on the fourth spin he throws the ball in a hook motion. It bounced at midcourt and then it just rose, and there was a guy at the other end and running full speed and he caught it in stride and laid it in. *A full-court bounce pass!* After I saw that I could understand all the Black Jesus stuff. I didn't find out the dude's real name until way later. It was Earl Monroe...."

An evening at the Bel Air house with Cheryl and Kareem has grown late. Kareem has talked about a movie he has just made, a spoof on the *Airport* films, called *Airplane*, in which, wearing his famous goggles, he plays a co-pilot; a record album he is contemplating making, on which he will play conga drums along with Tito Puente's percussionist, Joe Madera; a shopping trip in Karachi, Pakistan, during which he purchased Oriental rugs and was followed around by 300 people who, because of his great height, regarded him as a rare curiosity; his father—"I escaped a lot of whippins in my time thanks to Big Al"—and the crowd at Flipper's, where, the night before, ex-football star Jimmy Brown had accidentally crashed into a girl and broken her leg.

Abruptly the conversation dries up. "Kareem!" Cheryl implores. "Tell about Magic."

"'Knee Deep,'" he says. "That's the name of a song Magic keeps playing on his box. He's kind of worn me out with that." He laughs.

"But he had all the stewardesses dancing on the plane after you beat Boston for the second time, Kareem, and he had you dancing too."

"No," he protests. "I wasn't dancing on the plane."

"Pat Riley got off the plane and told me you were in the aisle."

"Nah. Pat Riley wasn't in on it."

"He said you were standing in the aisle and...."

"I couldn't even stand up in the aisle if...."

"I don't believe you!"

"Well, maybe I did do some moves...in my seat."

He tried to be serious, but he and Cheryl laughed and laughed.

"Kareem, remember opening night in San Diego when you made that hook shot at the buzzer to win the game, and Magic leaped up on you and hugged you and everyone jumped up and down in the middle of the floor?"

"Yeah," said Abdul-Jabbar, laughing. "It was like we just won the seventh game of the championships."

"Maybe you did."

APRIL 21, 1997

Shaq's World

Since Shaquille O'Neal left Orlando and moved to
Los Angeles to play for the Lakers, he and his posse
have been livin' large—and unbelievably loud

BY RICK REILLY

*SI wrote often about Shaq, telling his origin story while he was at LSU
(by Curry Kirkpatrick), profiling him during his Orlando tenure (John Ed
Bradley), covering his complicated partnership with Kobe (Jack McCallum
and Phil Taylor) and, finally, catching up with him during his swan song with
the Cavs (I wrote that one). This feature captures the big man just after he
signed with L.A., at the height of his powers—and celebrity. It's a good match
of writer and subject.*

BEVERLY AND ROBERTSON, WEST HOLLYWOOD

We are stopped, yet the can of Mountain Dew in the cup holder is doing the
watusi. The windows are closed, yet my hair is doing a scene from *Twister*.
The truck roof is bouncing up and down like popcorn in a pan.

Poltergeist? No, just Shaquille O'Neal turning up the 3,700-watt stereo
system in his blue Ford Expedition until the sound is akin to what you would
hear if you lived in a small compartment inside the engine of a DC-10. It is
very loud in here. Oh my god, is it loud.

In the backseat, the man called Dirt seems to be laughing. Outside,
people in chichi restaurants are looking up in horror from their sun-dried
radicchio. Shaq is grinning his crazy lopsided cross-eyed grin.

"DO YOU ALWAYS PLAY IT THIS LOUD?" I inquire.

"WHAAAT?" he replies.

"DOES IT HAVE TO BE THIS LOUD?"

"NO, BRO, I HAVEN'T LOST ANY POUNDS."

Sigh. This is going to be a *very* tough interview.

THE FORUM, INGLEWOOD

The sound is excruciating. The spectators' faces at a pregame shootaround are contorted. These people are in pain. This is because Shaq is practicing free throws.

Since Shaq left his personal Mousetrap in Orlando on July 18 and signed professional sports' most ridiculous long-term deal yet—$120 million over seven years—with the Los Angeles Lakers, he has put the Fabulous back in the Forum. By the end of January the Lakers were in first place in the Pacific Division and had the best record in the Western Conference this late in the season for the first time since 1991, and Shaq was the only man in the NBA in the top five in four major categories (scoring, rebounds, shooting percentage and blocks). Then, on Feb. 12, Shaq hyperextended his left knee, fracturing a bone and partially tearing a ligament in the process. The Lakers lost 12 of their next 28 games and fell to the fourth playoff spot in the Western Conference. Last Friday night Shaq came back in a home game against the Phoenix Suns, and L.A. expects nothing less than a Frank Capra ending to break out.

Some good things have happened because of the injury. Shaq has realized how much he wants to be a great Lakers player. "I want my jersey up there someday," he says, pointing to the Forum wall where the retired numbers hang. He has labored obsessively to rehab the knee, lifting, bicycling, running and, recently, for two hours every day, working on his game with Magic Johnson. Shaq has also realized how much he respects his new teammates. "I wouldn't mind coming off the bench," he said before his comeback.

The bad thing is that with all that time on his hands, Shaq has logged even more hours at the free throw line, and Shaq on the free throw line is not a pretty thing. Of the 130 players in the league who have made at least 125 foul shots, Shaq ranks dead last. His free throw percentage has dropped every year he's been a pro, down to his current .469, which is even lower than Wilt Chamberlain's sorry lifetime mark of .511. Shaq has turned the foul line into the *Yipe!* stripe, and he has become everyone's favorite fourth-quarter welt post.

"Everybody in the league knows to foul Shaq," says Magic. "Kareem [Abdul-Jabbar] was a clutch free throw shooter. He wanted it at the end." If you have a narrow lead, you do not want Shaq on the line at the end. You do not win NBA titles when your go-to guy in the fourth quarter can't make a free throw to save his car stereo.

"He doesn't have a good touch with the ball," says Abdul-Jabbar, the Lakers' last monster center before Shaq. "Any shot that he takes from more than two feet that he can't jam seems to lack touch. He's not selfish, he plays hard, he plays for the team, but there's just not much progress with the soft touch."

Not that he isn't trying. Before he was injured, Shaq arrived an hour before practice to shoot free throws and stayed long *after* practice to shoot some more. Nightly during his rehab he went to a Manhattan Beach gym and worked on his foul shot. Yet it seems hopeless. Watching him practice free throws is like watching a man try to throw a grapefruit into a milk bottle. "I don't know what's wrong," says Magic. "His shot, he just, he just has got *no* rhythm."

UCLA, WESTWOOD
The knee does not keep Shaq out of the driver's seat. He pulls the Mobile Earache into the second floor of the parking garage at UCLA, where he works out with Magic. Two car alarms go off.

USC, NEAR DOWNTOWN L.A.
Oh, the places Shaq can go in L.A.—and if there is anything Shaq loves to do, it's to go places. Today he approaches a retired English teacher and asks him the same question he always asks him. "What's my word for the day, Pop?"

Pop is Sam Armato, USC professor emeritus and father of Shaq's agent, Leonard. "Ancillary," the professor says. He explains that the word means subordinate, secondary, a side dish.

A few nights later Shaq tells reporters, "I do have other interests, but they're ancillary."

Ancillary? You could employ a small country helping Shaq pursue his ancillary interests. This is what he has going in Los Angeles as we speak (*ready? Inhale!*): This summer he will appear in his third movie (*Steel*, produced by Quincy Jones); he has his own record label and line of clothing (TWIsM: The World Is Mine); he is promoting his third rap CD (*You Can't Stop the Reign*); he is developing his own TV series (*Hoops*, a basketball-themed show); he has been nominated for a Grammy as a contributor to a music compilation produced by Jones (*Q's Jook Joint*); he has his own Web site (www.shaq.com); he has marketing relationships with more than

10 companies (which he sometimes plugs ad nauseam—when he signed with L.A., he said the way for the Lakers to win was, "Play hard, drink Pepsi and wear Reeboks"); he is a partner in the entertainment company A.S.E. (Armato is Shaq Entertainment—get it?); he and the Universal Studios theme park are developing a Shaq "entertainment venue," in which you will be able to pursue your favorite Shaqtivities, such as recording rap music, playing video games and jamming basketballs—but not, at least so far, sitting in a car and having your ears turned to Gerber's. (*Exhale.*)

"In the last year?" says Bucky, Shaq's driver-personal assistant-gofer. "I've had one day off. I mean, the guy never stops."

LA CIENEGA AND MELROSE, WEST HOLLYWOOD

"Dirt, why do you think Shaq loves it in L.A. so much?" I ask.

"More roads," says Dirt.

Shaq has always loved U.S. road travel. Coming home from his first day at preschool in Jersey City, he refused to get off the bus. His mother asked what was up. "Wanna keep riding," he said.

After losses at the Forum, Shaq will keep riding, sometimes for four hours. After wins, though, the route is always the same. It includes his favorite streets—Wilshire, Sunset, Melrose, Third, Beverly—a stop at Jerry's Famous Deli for a sausage-and-cheese omelette and pancakes, and then home. When you are Shaq, there are only two places you can hide: your house and your car. And even though Shaq lives in a 5,000-square-foot penthouse with a 360-degree view of L.A., he likes the car better. In the car he also has the privilege of using the bass to realign his spleen.

He says, "Mllnghrose, bro, thzzwhr I rnngmb cnk itup."

It is so very loud in here. "I'M SORRY?" I shout.

"MLLNGHROSE, THZZWHR I RLLY CRNK INGUP!"

"MELROSE IS WHERE YOU REALLY CRANK IT UP?"

Oh god. We are turning onto Melrose. He reaches for the little joystick that controls the colossal power of the world's cruelest sound system. "That's O.K.," I say nervously. "You already—"

But it is too late. The system is cranked, and there is nothing that can be done by any human, save Shaq, to uncrank it. Arm hairs stand. The volume numbers climb...20...people on the street look up in shock...35...the heads of old men in barbershops snap up in horror...42...I am trapped inside Dick Vitale's larynx.

Shaq rolls his window down and grins wildly at the stunned people on the street. Two blocks later, he turns the dial down to 3. "I *love* to see the reactions, bro," he says. "Old people just *hate* it."

THE FORUM

Cripes, it's loud in here. This is because Shaq has just spun a 360-degree vortex move ending with a Herman Munster jam in the slack-jawed face of Mike Brown of the Phoenix Suns. This is last Friday night, Shaq's first night back after missing 28 games in rehab. He is only supposed to play a little, but he gets carried away, ding-ding-dinging up a game-high 24 points along with 11 rebounds, two assists and three blocked shots. The Lakers win 114–98, flushing the Suns' winning streak at 11, and all is right with the great Los Angeles basin and one very big knee. Shaq is baq. On Sunday he nails a baseline jumper at the buzzer to beat the Utah Jazz 100–98.

"It's like the '80s are here again," says an usher. Since Shaq came to L.A., stars are leather-to-leather once more at the Forum (so far this season: Jack Nicholson, Jim Carrey, Arsenio Hall—he's back!—Cindy Crawford, Garry Shandling, Denzel Washington, Brandy, Sharon Stone, Dennis Miller, Pete Sampras, Kevin Costner, Evander Holyfield, the usual assortment of Baldwins, Robert Shapiro and everybody else you can think of from the O.J. trial).

All-Star swingman Eddie Jones has been terrific. Rookie center Travis Knight has been nice. But Shaq is the main reason L.A. is hot. No Laker has scored like this since Abdul-Jabbar in 1980–81. No Laker has rebounded like this since Abdul-Jabbar in 1978–79. No Laker has blocked shots at this rate since Abdul-Jabbar in 1979–80. Shaq is the leader of the team: He climbed all over La-Z-Boy forward Elden Campbell early in the year, he's chaperoning rookie guard Kobe Bryant through his teenage years ("Can you believe how loud that stereo is?" says Bryant), and he's keeping point guard Nick Van Exel somewhere in the vicinity of this planet. "We had heard he wouldn't do much voicing of his opinion here," Lakers coach Del Harris says of Shaq. "But he has."

Folks in Orlando might think he is doing a little too much voicing of his opinion. "The general manager here actually *played* in the league," Shaq says of the Lakers' Jerry West (who is actually executive vice president of basketball operations), as opposed to Magic senior executive vice president Pat Williams. (Replies Williams: "I know I don't have Jerry West's jumper. But I have a hoop in the backyard now, and I'm working on it.")

More L.A.-versus-Orlando Shaqrimony: "These fans *know* the game," Shaq says, presumably dissing crowds at the O-rena. He relishes being with a franchise in which he is part of great basketball history, not the *entire* history.

He seems to like the coach in L.A. better, too. At Magic's Sports Star Award dinner on Jan. 21, Shaq got up and said, "I'd like to thank Del Harris for calling my plays." Emphasis on the plural. In Orlando, Shaq's basic play was to set up on the right block and let the power forward cut through. Now he gets the ball on the right block, left block, free throw line, left wing, right wing, places with room to demonstrate his handsome ball-handling skills. Remember, this is a guy who as a kid always wore Magic's jersey, not Kareem's.

The only problem is that all those bright lights in the Forum have revealed flaws in Shaq's game. After five years in the league, he still seems to have only four shots: the two-handed earth-shaking dunk, the one-handed Inglewood-shaking dunk, the sky-throw and the fadeaway air ball.

"I love Shaq," Magic says, "but he needs another shot. Kareem had more moves. Shaq needs the drop-step move Kareem had."

"Ever thought of having Kareem in to show you a few tricks?" I ask Shaq.

"Ahh, bro," he says. "I've got all that. I just ain't showing it yet. And remember: I'm the only one who sent Michael Jordan home."

May 18, 1995, Eastern Conference semifinals, Orlando over the Chicago Bulls, four games to two.

LAX

Typical rich jock. Takes another babe to the airport. Gives her a big kiss goodbye. Tells her he'll think of her all the time. Promises to call her four times a day.

Wait a second. This rich jock *does* think of the babe all the time. *Does* call her four times a day. Wears her name in gold and jewels around his neck. Records his voice on a tape for her to play over and over when she misses him. Enters malls all across America and comes out with armfuls of presents to ship to her. Doesn't want to *marry* her, of course—but can't wait to change her diapers again.

The new babe in Shaq's life is Taahirah O'Neal, a nine-month-old beauty by way of his longtime girlfriend, Arnetta Yardbourgh. Taahirah and Arnetta live in Houston but are constantly being sent for by the boss.

"Daddy's right here," Shaq recorded on a tape for Taahirah. "Daddy's right here. Daddy, Daddy, Daddy." He also put her ABCs on the tape, and a few of his rap songs, and parts of the dictionary (Shaq's mother used to read the dictionary to him when he was a boy), and some soul music. The man is seriously in love. He even took Lamaze classes for Taahirah's birth and was there all the way, except for the moments when, according to his 6'3" mother, Lucille, "I thought he was going to faint."

That's another thing that drove Shaq from Orlando—the way people in the town dealt with Arnetta's pregnancy. "They said, 'So, where'd he meet her, in a hotel?'" Shaq says. "'How much money does she want?' They just assumed it was some dirty thing. Now people want to know why she isn't living with me. She's going to school [masters program, communications, Houston]. What am I gonna do, say, 'No, you need to move here right now'?"

"You thinking of marrying her?" I ask.

"Bro, for all you know, I might already be married."

We checked. As far as we can tell, he isn't.

JERRY'S FAMOUS DELI, WEST HOLLYWOOD

Shaq hates to wait for traffic, success or food. The first time he walked into Jerry's with his posse of payrolled relatives, security guys and wall leaners—the Men of Unclear Purpose—he asked the waiter, "What's the biggest tip you ever got?"

"Mmmm...fifty bucks," the waiter said.

"If we eat fast, I'll quadruple that."

You cannot imagine how fast you can get a few sausage-and-cheese omelettes at Jerry's Famous Deli if you put your mind to it.

Yes, Shaq is happy in L.A. The city seems to have given him room to swing his 45-inch arms. A military kid, he moved around a lot—Newark, Jersey City, West Germany, San Antonio—but L.A. is really his home. He has come here every summer for the past eight years, since he was 16, just to hang, to work out with Magic or to make movies. One year he came out and sold trailer-park lots. One year he did nothing but ride around in a friend's Volvo. Now he is here with a wad of 100's in his pocket and a big lopsided grin on his face.

"I think he's happier here, in an environment where he can flourish," says Leonard Armato. "He's not under an unfair magnifying glass. If he misses a free throw, O.K., he missed a free throw, and the press can rip him for that, but not for *more* than that. He's not being unjustly criticized down to the smallest thing."

In Orlando small things seemed to pile up on the big man. He hated the poll the *Orlando Sentinel* took in his last season, asking, "Is Shaq worth $115 million?" and he hated the predictable answer: 91.3% said, Hell no. He hated the power struggle with his coach, Brian Hill. He hated being such a big fish in a medium-sized tank. In L.A. he is one of hundreds of very big fish in the biggest and brightest fish tank in the world.

"I never dreamed I'd be playing for the Lakers," Shaq says in a rare quiet moment. "When I was a kid, I hardly had any self-esteem. Did you know I skipped first grade? And it was like there were some things I wasn't good at. I used to be coloring and thinking I was doing pretty good, and then I'd look at the kid next to me, and his drawing would be so much nicer, you know? Neater. All inside the lines. When I was 13, I was 6'7" and couldn't dunk. And the kids would say, 'Man, you so soft! You can't even dunk!'

"I've always listened to the iffers. They'd be like, 'Yeah, you doin' good in high school, but if you get to the McDonald's All-America game you ain't gonna do s—-!' And then it was, 'Yeah, you an All-American at LSU, but if you get to the pros, you won't be nothin'!' And now it's, 'Yeah, you got all these movies and ads and rap CDs and stuff, but you ain't never won a championship.' Well, I'm glad I got my iffers, because they keep me hungry."

PACIFIC THEATRE, EL SEGUNDO

Now wait a minute. How did Shaq and the Men of Unclear Purpose find a movie theater with *nobody* in the seats?

"I bought every ticket, bro," says Shaq, smiling lopsidedly. "I said, 'How many seats in your theater?' And the lady said, 'Two hundred.' And I said, 'I'll take 'em all!' Seven bucks a ticket!"

That's another reason Shaq loves L.A.: It's Movietown, and Shaq was raised on movies. *Rocky IV* is what made him start lifting weights. The *Superman* movies gave him an alter ego. He keeps an original Freddy Krueger prop glove and one of the masks from Jim Carrey's *The Mask* at his penthouse, where he sits in front of his DirecTV screen and orders up movies by the dozen—he has seen his own Kazaam more than a dozen times—at $2.99 each. "I must *own* this company by now, bro," he says gleefully, for he is never so happy as when he is spending money at ungodly rates.

If he keeps making movies as dreadful as *Kazaam*, he will soon have a little less to spend. His next movie, *Steel*, is supposed to be better. Based on the comic-book series of the same name, it's the story of a former military metallurgist who dons a suit of armor and fights crime. The movie was Shaq's idea, naturally. He handed the comic book to Quincy Jones and said, "This is me." Replied Q: "Let's star you in it!" At that very moment, 5,000 classically trained actors working as waiters blanched.

In this movie, which was filmed last summer and should be released in August, Shaq did most of his own stunt work, possibly because every other agile 7'1", 300-pounder was already employed in the NBA. Shaq ran under a burning helicopter. He jumped off a moving train. He jumped from the top of one 20-story building to another.

"Shaq," I say, "you've got another job making $17 million a year. Are you out of your cranium?" Dirt muffles a laugh.

"Bro, me and Dirt used to do that stuff all the time back home [in Newark]," Shaq says. "Roof to roof? We'd do that s—- *daily*."

LITTLE SANTA MONICA BLVD., CENTURY CITY

As we extend the record for Longest Interview with Fewest Words Exchanged, there is not much to do besides wonder how life will be when we're as deaf as Pete Townshend—and, of course, take stock of the subject at hand. For a genetic freak, Shaq is perfectly proportioned. Standing in a field 100 yards away, he looks like anybody else. It's only when you get close that your flabber gets gasted. From his belt to the floor you could fit Ross Perot. His neck is 19 inches around. His size-22 sneakers are so big that whenever he signs a pair and they are taken back up to the Lakers public relations office, people gather around and take turns stepping into them—shoes and all— giggling all the while.

Unlike many of the tall, Shaq doesn't slouch, and often, when he gets dressed up, he wears fedoras that make him even taller. He wears either sweats or gorgeous high-collared suits—nothing in between. He paints his toenails. He is a wonderful dancer, as I see sometimes when we park and he gets out and starts dancing to his four-wheel concert. His voice is nice, even Shaqapella.

His hands are huge and soft, and at Lakers practices he likes nothing more than leading a fast break. "He's got a crossover dribble," gasps Bryant. "A seven-footer with a crossover dribble!"

He has an easy way about him and likes to pull legs. If you introduce yourself as Steve, he might say, "Nice t'meetcha, Doug."

"Steve," you'll say. "It's, uh, Steve."

"Sorry?" he'll ask, bending down to hear.

"It's, uh, not Doug, it's Steve."

"Oh, sorry," he'll say, looking away again, "George."

MELROSE AVENUE, HOLLYWOOD

You half expect Shaq to pull into the Paramount Pictures lot, get a half-caf, half-decaf skinny latte, maybe do lunch with some execs. But he does not pull in. Shaq does not want to be a corporate entity moonlighting three hours a day as an NBA center. He is serious about business—he likes his friends to call him Enrico Gates, after Roger Enrico, CEO of Pepsi, and Bill Gates of Microsoft—but he is twice as serious about hoops. He makes movies only during the summer and insists on having an NBA basket outside his trailer. (While filming *Steel* he practiced free throws, and he and Bucky played two set painters two-on-two for hours every day.) Shaq does no ads, appearances or rap recording on game days. "He's committed to basketball," says Harris. "He works as hard as anybody. And I don't think making movies ruins your basketball career. It hasn't seemed to hurt Michael Jordan."

Says Shaq: "People expected me to freak out here. Well, I didn't."

In fact, one night when we were at his penthouse, the Men of Unclear Purpose informed him that he was invited not only to the premiere of the

Rodney Dangerfield movie *Meet Wally Sparks* but also to a Damon Wayans party.

"Nuh-uh," said Shaq. He also didn't go to the Grammys. "Couldn't," he says. "Why not?" I ask.

"Because, bro. That's just what they wanted me to do."

MANCHESTER AND LA BREA, INGLEWOOD

A cherry Impala lowrider pulls up next to an unsuspicious-looking blue Ford Expedition. The driver of the lowrider is playing his stereo very loudly.

Behind dark tinted windows, Shaq grins lopsidedly. He turns the volume on his own system to 12, which is slightly louder than the lowrider's offering. The lowrider counters with a small avalanche of noise. This knob-a-knob goes a couple of more rounds. Now the traffic light is about to go green. With a small tweak of his giant thumb, Shaq visits upon his poor challenger's tympana an apocalypse of noise—35 by the stereo's count, and we know too well the hell this can bring. The Impala's driver jerks upright and looks over in horror. Shaq rolls down his window halfway, grins at the man and peels off.

I can lip-read what he says to me, because he does it with such relish: *Love to tease 'em, bro.*

WILSHIRE CORRIDOR, BEVERLY HILLS

What with the baby, Shaq has decided that he needs a crib with more rooms, so we are out hunting. The first place we go to must be the world's largest town house. The owner—Sheldon Ausman, the man who is trying to build a football stadium in downtown L.A.—has a 100-gallon saltwater fish tank in the living room filled with very big fish. Shaq was no A student at LSU, but he recognizes symbolism when it slaps him in the face. Big fish in a big tank. Shaq in L.A. Shaq points. Shaq grins from here to Canoga Park.

Later, in the lobby of a swank high-rise, the elderly owner sniffs, "I believe an acquaintance of yours is one of our residents."

"Really?" says Shaq. "Who?"

"A Mr. Doggy Dogg?"

Dirt melts in laughter, and Shaq will feed him lines the rest of the afternoon.

"Yes," says Shaq snootily. "A package for Mr. Doggy Dogg?"

LOYOLA MARYMOUNT, WESTCHESTER

Alone again, Shaq is at the Lakers' practice site before his comeback, clanking free throws as though he were still in his *Steel* armor. Then he sinks a succession of shots and gets cocky. "When I come back, I ain't missin'," he says. "And you can quote me! I ain't missin'!" But then he starts missin'. Magic has been working with him, getting him to bend his knees and take his time.

Shaq shoots too low is what the problem is. The ball leaves his hand at about 8' feet and never gets past 10. He misses free throws right and left and short and long, but they are always too low. He clanks them, shanks them and even tries to bank them, but they are too low. They have no arc. They have no backspin. Giant orange knuckleballs. I cannot take it anymore.

"Shaq," I say. "Look how little you break your wrist. You're shot-putting 'em. Why don't you bring your wrist back parallel to the floor so you get some backspin?"

"Because I can't," he says.

"You can't?"

"No, bro. I broke my wrist when I was a kid in Germany. Fell out of a tree. The thing fused or something. Look at this." He can bring his wrist back only a few inches, as if he were wearing a cast.

"You can't!"

"No, bro. My s—- is all messed up. It comes off all to the right."

Says Abdul-Jabbar, "That would explain a few things."

THE PENTHOUSE, WILSHIRE CORRIDOR

If you were as rich as Shaq, you would probably live like he lives. He has hired half his family and some friends, too. As we said, it is unclear exactly what these people do, but Shaq would do anything for his relatives and pals, including pay and, in many cases, house and feed them. There is Kenny, Shaq's cousin, whose main job seems to be to remind Shaq of things. Today, for instance, Kenny reminds Shaq that he has a radio show to do at 5 o'clock. But you would not say Kenny is Shaq's personal scheduler, because that is Uncle Mike's title. This means that Uncle Mike gets the day's personal schedule from Armato and in turn gives it to Shaq. Why Armato cannot give it to Shaq himself is unclear.

Uncle Mike also seems to have something to do with security, but that seems to be the official job of Uncle Jerome, who is not Shaq's uncle at all but was Mike's partner on the Newark police force. It is also unclear why a 25-year-old giant who has practiced martial arts needs a full-time security man 13 years older than he is, but this is none of our business, and besides, Jerome looks like he could turn a reporter into a large blood clot.

Bucky is Shaq's driver, but then so is Dirt, although I did not see either of them drive Shaq anywhere. Still, Bucky is always driving somebody, and, as a native Angeleno, he must stand by at all times for emergency routing calls from Shaq. "I'm by the big doughnut," Shaq might phone to say. "Is there a shortcut home from here?"

Joe, Shaq's chum from high school, has a very clear job. He handles the mail.

There is also Thomas, Shaq's personal chef. Shaq hired Thomas away from a Hyatt Regency near Orlando at twice his salary because of the exquisite way he made Shaq's club sandwich one day. It is unclear how much job fulfillment there is in Thomas's position. For instance, as part of Shaq's unbreakable game-day ritual, Thomas makes two beautiful Dagwood sandwiches for Shaq, who takes one bite out of one sandwich and leaves the rest. Thomas also seems to warm the baby's milk a lot. This is life in Shaq's World: One day you are working in a giant hotel's restaurant operation, and the next day you are making a small fortune dabbing milk on your wrists.

Since the injury, there is even less for Thomas to do, because Shaq has cut back his colossal intake of food and eats mostly salads and fruits. (One day after a workout, Shaq pulls up his sweaty size XXXXXL shirt and shoves his bagel-sized belly button against my thorax. "Pinch an inch," he challenges. I try. I cannot. Still, this is much closer to an interview subject than I care to be.)

Mostly, though, the Men of Unclear Purpose stand around the pool table in Shaq's penthouse and shoot a lively game of craps. Then many of them go home to Shaq's Manhattan Beach house, which they have to themselves because Shaq doesn't like it anymore. ("Too many people knockin' on the door," he grumbles.)

It is wonderful work if you can get it.

CULVER CITY

With the hearing I still have left, I make some calls about this stereo business. Even Haas Auto Stereo, the company that installed the system in Shaq's Ford Expedition, doesn't know how powerful it is. "Our meters don't go that high," says Jeff Haas. The folks at Haas do know, however, that when Shaq's car is parked in their warehouse and one of its windows is cracked and the system is cranked up, the breeze moves the pages on a wall calendar 15 feet away.

Scott Genaw of ListenUp! Audio and Video in Denver says that 3,700 watts in a Ford Expedition would probably produce about 130 to 140 decibels. "That's like taking all the noise in the Seattle Kingdome and sticking it in a car," he says. OSHA guidelines say consistent exposure to 115 decibels for longer than 15 minutes will begin causing permanent hearing damage.

I am ready to bring all this up to Shaq. Unfortunately Dr. Dre has the floor.

"YOU'RE GONNA GO DEAF!" I holler.

"NO, BRO, WE KEEP GOING STRAIGHT HERE!"

Double sigh.

THE FORUM

Leaping from roof to roof on cue, churning out rap CDs, carrying entire ad campaigns, starring in feature-length movies and designing his own line of clothing are simple. Performing one of the easiest feats in all of sports is another matter. Shaq clanks on.

His failure as a free throw shooter kills people in the Lakers organization, because they all like the kid so much. Shaq has made the Lakers fun again. (Note to Lakers reserve center Sean Rooks: Guess who filled the pocket of your red sport coat with lotion?) Though he's big-time, Shaq does not do much big-timing. "Anything I ask him to do," says Lakers public relations man John Black, "he does." Shaq's huge "Shaqsgiving" turkey and "Shaq-a Claus" toy giveaways in Watts this past holiday season were big successes, and he wants to double his donation next year. "He's one of the nicest kids I've ever been around," says Jerry West.

Soon, though, the Hollywood honeymoon will be over, and nobody will remember that it took Chamberlain four years to bring a championship to L.A. and Abdul-Jabbar five. The fans will want an NBA title *now*.

But nobody will root harder for Shaq than Rudy Garciduenas, the Lakers' equipment man the past 11 years. When Shaq arrived, he couldn't believe Rudy was using his girlfriend's beat-up Hyundai to get all the team's equipment from the Forum out to Loyola Marymount.

"Man, you need a new ride," Shaq kept teasing Rudy. Yeah, yeah, big joke. Rudy had heard it for years. But one day Shaq went up to Rudy and said, "No, *seriously*, you need a new ride"–and bought him a new Ford Ranger.

The day it arrived Rudy had a misty look in his eyes. He walked toward the big man with open arms, and....

"No, no, no," said Shaq. "No hugs, bro."

Which only goes to show that even if a man can't make free throws, he can still be a soft touch.

MY HOUSE, DENVER

There is this ringing in my ears. No, hold on. That's the phone. It's my editor in New York.

"You're late on the Shaq piece," he says.

"WHAAAAT?" I inquire.

"ARE YOU EVER SENDING IN THE SHAQ PIECE?"

"I CAN'T COME BACK EAST RIGHT NOW, I'M TRYING TO FINISH THE SHAQ PIECE!" *Click.*

This could get very convenient.

JANUARY 3, 2017

Freak Unleashed

The Bucks have handed the reins to the ridiculously athletic
6'11" Giannis Antetokounmpo, making him the tallest—
and most intriguing—point guard in NBA history

BY LEE JENKINS

*Before he began racking up MVPs and dominating the league, Giannis was
something of a basketball outlier. (O.K., so he still is.) In this early story, Lee
Jenkins captures the wonderful possibility of Giannis, the player, and the
curiosity and work ethic of Giannis, the young man.*

On the worst nights, when the fadeaways are short and the pocket passes
are late, Giannis Antetokounmpo skips the showers. He storms out of the
Bradley Center in full uniform, from home locker room to player parking
lot, and hops into the black Explorer the local Ford dealer lent him. He turns
right on North 4th Street in downtown Milwaukee, steers toward the Hoan
Bridge and continues six miles south to the Catholic seminary in St. Francis,
where the priests pray and the Bucks train and The Freak dispenses his
rage. Alone, Antetokounmpo reenacts the game he just played, every shot
he clanked and every read he missed. Sometimes, he leaves by 1 a.m. Other
times, he stays until three, sweating through his white jersey for a second
time. "I get so mad, and if I go right home, I'm afraid I'll never get that anger
out," Antetokounmpo says. "This is how I get the anger away."

He used to administer his form of self-flagellation on the court, because
that's what he saw Chris Paul do after a Clippers loss in L.A. But he noticed

some fans lingering in the lower bowl with their cellphone cameras and he didn't want anybody to think he was putting on a show. So he retreats, in space and time. Here he is not the $100 million man with the catchy nickname and the barrel chest who studies Magic Johnson's fast breaks and Russell Westbrook's mean mugs, who wrestles LeBron and mimes Dirk, who hears MVP chants and references *40-balls*. Here he is not even the spring-loaded first-round pick who arrived wide-eyed in the United States three and a half years ago, tweeting breathlessly about his first smoothie, refusing to use the auto-pump feature on his gas nozzle because he was so excited to pump it himself, chirping after a burger at In-N-Out in Westwood Village: "This is America right here! The real America! Isn't it beautiful?"

No, here he is the lanky hustler from Athens, peddling watches, sunglasses, toys and video games, on the streets near the Acropolis while his parents feared that police would demand their papers and deport them back to Africa. Much of his backstory has been told, how Charles and Veronica Antetokounmpo emigrated from Nigeria to Greece in 1991 for a better life, had four boys there, and bounced from one eviction notice to another. But the further Giannis gets from his childhood, the more it resonates, in different ways. "I can't push it to the side," Antetokounmpo explains. "I can't say, 'I've made it, I'm done with all that.' I will always carry it with me. It's where I learned to work like this." He could sell all day, serenade tourists with Christmas carols at night, and return home without enough cash for dinner. Still, he laments, "The results were never guaranteed." Therein he finds the biggest difference between his life then and now. "If I work here," he says, "I get the results. That's the greatest feeling ever for me." It keeps him coming back to the gym—straight from the arena after losses, straight from the airport after road trips, straight from the bed after back-to-backs.

Antetokounmpo stands 6'11", with legs so long opposing coaches constantly complain that he is traveling, until they review the tape. "He's not," says Wizards coach Scott Brooks. "It's just that we've never seen somebody with a stride like this." Among the NBA's legion of stretchy giants, Kevin Durant is the scorer, Anthony Davis the slasher. Antetokounmpo is the creator, traversing half the court with four Sasquatch steps, surveying traffic like a big rig over smart cars. Durant and Davis try to play point guard. Antetokounmpo actually does it, dropping dimes over and around defenders' heads, leading the Bucks in every major category; 23.8 points, 8.9 rebounds, 5.9 assists, 2.0 blocks and 2.0 steals. This season he will be the team's first All-Star since Michael Redd in 2004, and before you learn to spell his surname, he will be much more.

Growing up, his customers occasionally mentioned his cartoonishly long limbs, but he shrugged. He didn't need a 7'3" wingspan. He needed a sucker to buy those knockoff shades. He viewed himself less as The Greek Freak than a Greek grinder. "I didn't really look at my body and think about what it meant," Antetokounmpo says. "I didn't figure it out." He glances down at his 12-inch hands, bigger than Kawhi Leonard's, bigger than Wilt Chamberlain's. He finally knows those names. "A lot of players will tell you, 'When I was a kid, I watched Kobe Bryant, Michael Jordan, LeBron, Magic, and I wanted to be just like them,'" Antetokounmpo says. "For me it wasn't like that at all." He laughs, because at last he grasps the magnitude of his gifts and the ways they can be unleashed. He understands that a 22-year-old with his build and his drive should never go home hungry again.

Antetokounmpo lives in a modest three-story townhouse near Saint Francis de Sales Seminary, in the same complex as his parents. Like any hoop phenom, he subsists on Wingstop and NBA TV. But when he needs to steady himself amid his unimpeded ascent, he heads west to Omega restaurant, where 24 hours a day he can order gyros and lamb chops with sides of nostalgia and perspective. "I think about where I was four years ago, on the streets, and where I am today, able to take care of my kids and my grandkids and their grandkids," Antetokounmpo marvels. "I'm not saying that in a cocky way or a disrespectful way. But it is a crazy story, isn't it?"

On March 28, 2013, Bucks general manager John Hammond sat in a dining room at the Bradley Center before a game against the Lakers and explained why his team could not acquire a superstar. Hammond was in his fifth season, with a record of 181–206, never good enough to contend and never bad enough to tank. The stars he had brought to Milwaukee, if you can call them that, were Brandon Jennings, Monta Ellis, John Salmons and Carlos Delfino. Hammond outlined the two most obvious ways to land a prospective headliner: Finish on the fringe of the lottery and turn a lucky Ping-Pong ball into the first overall draft pick, which has about a 1.8% chance of occurring. Or pitch a premier free agent on a small market with a frigid climate and a mediocre roster, which comes with even steeper odds.

At the end of an otherwise dispiriting conversation, Hammond mentioned casually that he was leaving town the next day. "Where are you going?" I asked.

"Greece," he said.

Memories of the trip have become blurred in the recounting: Antetokounmpo's coach, idling outside the gym on a scooter, smoking a cigarette; Antetokounmpo's teammates, nearly twice his age, coming straight to pregame warmups from their day jobs; Antetokounmpo's parents, sitting high in the stands, as their beanstalk son deftly ran the point for Filathlitikos in the Greek second division. Hammond flashed back to a line that coach Larry Brown once told him. "For some people the game goes 110 miles per hour. For others, it goes 70." Afterward Antetokounmpo's Greek agents drove Hammond through Athens. "I don't know what's going to happen to this guy," the GM said from the backseat. "But his life is about to change in a major way."

The 18-year-old Antetokounmpo was no secret among scouts, but many organizations were scared to draft him, given that he couldn't even score an invitation to the Nike Hoop Summit. But Hammond, desperate for that elusive star, was ready to take a risk. The Bucks picked Antetokounmpo 15th overall in 2013, recognizing that there is yet another way to secure a difference-maker: Steal him.

The day after the draft Antetokounmpo walked out of the elevator at The Pfister Hotel in downtown Milwaukee, where former Wisconsin senator and Bucks owner Herb Kohl was coincidentally sitting in the lobby coffee shop. Antetokounmpo was self-conscious about his broken English, but Kohl's top lieutenant, JoAnne Anton, happened to be fluent in Greek. "I remember how his eyes lit up when he heard her voice," Hammond recalls. "It was a small thing, but you couldn't help but think, 'Maybe this is meant to be.'"

So began an endearing affair between Antetokounmpo and Milwaukee. He moved into a two-and-a-half-bedroom apartment in St. Francis that he shared with his parents and younger brothers, Kostas and Alex. Bucks guard O.J. Mayo sent him a U-Haul filled with furniture. Caron Butler and Zaza Pachulia helped him pick out clothes for road trips. Hammond and assistant general manager David Morway taught him to drive, parallel parking on the seminary grounds, and assistant video coordinator Ross Geiger lent him his maroon Subaru Outback Legacy. Geiger was Antetokounmpo's best friend in Milwaukee, the one who oversaw his graduation from EDM to hip-hop, and instructed him on which lyrics he could sing in public and which he could not. But when they ate dinner, even at McDonald's, Antetokounmpo insisted on splitting the bill. Either he didn't comprehend how much more he earned than a video guy, or he couldn't bear to part with the cash.

Milwaukee went 15–67 in Antetokounmpo's rookie season, which dampened his enthusiasm not a bit. He memorized lines from *Coming to America* and *Next Friday*. He learned to throw a football with Morway's sons, Michael and Robbie. He begged teammates to play the shooting game two-for-a-dollar that he picked up from power forward John Henson. When a Greek TV station came to visit, he told Geiger they would need a customized handshake, "so we look like we know what we're doing." The Bucks were brutal, and The Greek Freak averaged only 6.8 points, a reserve small forward who spent most of his time marooned in the corner, probing for open spaces and put-back dunks. But he provided highlights and hope. "I love Milwaukee!" Antetokounmpo told teammates over lunch at the facility one day. "I'm going to be in Milwaukee 20 years! I'll be here so long they'll be sick of me!" He feared that somebody would wake him from his dream and send him home. "That they'd take it all away from me," he says.

To Bucks vets, Antetokounmpo supplied comic relief during a dismal winter, but Geiger sensed he was capable of more. One night they were watching a game on television when Antetokounmpo shouted, "Whoa! Did you see that?" Geiger hit rewind. Antetokounmpo was always amazed he could rewind live TV. "There it is!" Antetokounmpo yelped. "Look at the action on the help side and how that opens up the whole play!" Another night Geiger invited him to dinner at a friend's house and Antetokounmpo barely uttered a word. On the way home, he told Geiger, "You're really close with Erik, but you're not that close with Matt."

"He was right," Geiger says. "He knows how to read people and situations. That's because of how he grew up. He couldn't waste his time selling you something for five minutes if you weren't going to buy. He had to read body language and move on."

When Antetokounmpo reminisces about his rookie year, he sounds as if he is talking about another era and another person. "I was like a kid in the park, seeing all the cities, seeing LeBron and KD, having so much fun. But that kid—the kid with the smoothies—I'm not really that kid anymore."

Pro sports age everybody. There was the night in his first season when Antetokounmpo's agent at Octagon, Alex Saratsis, told him that a Bucks assistant coach believed he wasn't working hard enough. "You can tell me I'm not playing well," Antetokounmpo replied, tears in his eyes. "You can tell me I'm not doing the right things. But you cannot tell me this. I won't accept it." And there was the night in his second season when the Bucks' new head coach, Jason Kidd, banned him from shooting three-pointers. "I want to shoot threes," Antetokounmpo argued. "How can I not shoot threes?" Geiger left for the Suns. Morway went to the Jazz. Nate Wolters, Antetokounmpo's best friend on the team, was waived. "I didn't know all that would happen," Antetokounmpo says. "You build these relationships, know these people, and then all of a sudden you get a text in the summer: 'I'm not coming back.' What? You get mad. You learn this is a business."

The first time Kidd benched him, Antetokounmpo was irate. "I was like, 'Let's see what this guy did in his career, anyway,'" Antetokounmpo recounts, and called up Kidd's bio on his phone. "I saw Rookie of the Year, NBA championship, USA Olympic gold medal, second in assists, fifth in made threes, blah, blah, blah. I was like, 'Jesus freaking Christ, how can I compete with that? I better zip it.'"

At 6'4", Kidd is one of the best point guards who ever lived. "But I wanted so badly to be 6'7" or 6'8"," Kidd says. "Guys like Magic are looking through a window that's so high. They can make passes I could only dream about." He detected enough playmaking ability from Antetokounmpo to try him at point guard in the 2014 summer league and again in the '15 preseason, but he wasn't satisfied with the results. Last Feb. 20 in Atlanta, with the Bucks 11 games under .500 and Michael Carter-Williams coming off the bench, Kidd put the ball in Antetokounmpo's massive mitts. "We didn't talk about it," Kidd says. "We didn't make a big deal out of it. There was no pressure. We just wanted to try something different."

The Bucks won that night in double overtime as Antetokounmpo had 19 points and three assists, and afterward Kidd embarked on an audacious experiment: building the biggest point guard anybody can remember. Kidd oversees the project, but assistant coach Sean Sweeney runs it, accompanying Antetokounmpo to his midnight workouts, deconstructing his pick-and-rolls, furnishing him with clips of Magic but also less predictable influences such as Kiki Vandeweghe's post moves and Shawn Kemp's transition dunks. Antetokounmpo hung a photo of himself, facing up against the Raptors, in Sweeney's office. Sweeney has repeatedly taken the picture down, but somehow, it always returns. "Don't forget about me!" Antetokounmpo sings.

This summer they worked out twice a day for two-and-a-half weeks at Long Beach State's Walter Pyramid, picking strangers out of the bleachers to fill fast breaks. "It was an inordinate amount of time going through situations," Sweeney says. "We'd start with the running game. 'First look is to the big running to the rim. Next look is up the side to the wing. Next look is across the side. Now can you get it and go full speed? Now you can get it and go and pitch it back to a trailer who can shoot?'"

"You know what I liked about using all those strangers?" Kidd adds. "He had to speak. You don't know these people, but you have to tell them what to do. They're looking at you for direction and you have to give it to them. That's what a point guard does. He has to know his teammates better than they know themselves."

The Bucks acquired Matthew Dellavedova in July and made him their de facto floor general, but Giannis is the one making the decisions and feeling the consequences. "If this guy gets the ball five times, I know he's happy, and if that guy gets it once, I know he's not," Antetokounmpo groans. "So I'm like, 'Oh, man, I've got to get that guy the ball.' It's hard to satisfy everybody."

Actually, it's impossible, which is another of the lessons Kidd is imparting. There are things stars do, like pick up the bill at McDonald's, and things they don't, like placate everyone in their presence. "To make the next step, I've learned you need a little cockiness inside you," Antetokounmpo says. "I can be a little cocky." As a rookie, he jawed with Carmelo Anthony. In his second season, he body checked Mike Dunleavy. But the Bucks have been seeing his snarl more often of late, after pep talks from Kobe Bryant last season and Kevin Garnett last month, as well as daily skull sessions with veteran Bucks guard Jason Terry. "I'll tell him something at a timeout like, 'Watch the curl, and if the curl isn't there, the slip will be wide open,'" says Terry. "And he'll always tell me, 'I got you, bro.'" He searches for the slightest edge, because a highlight a night is not enough anymore. He needs 25/12/8 with a win. "I've definitely become more serious," Antetokounmpo says. "I have a franchise on my shoulders."

On 28-and-a-half acres around the Bradley Center, the Bucks are constructing a new practice facility that will open later this year and a new arena that will open next year. Next to the site is a billboard, featuring Antetokounmpo's muscled back, over the slogan THE FUTURE LOOKS STRONG. Hammond, it turns out, proved himself wrong, and possibly twice. He found a star, and he might have snagged another, drafting forward Jabari Parker second in 2014. The Bucks currently sit seventh in the East, but outside of Cleveland, their long-term outlook is as bright as anybody's.

Hammond and Antetokounmpo talk often, though no longer about the perils of right turns on red. "He's trying to figure this whole thing out, what he's going to be," Hammond says. "We're seeing this more focused side of him, but it's a fine line. You still want to enjoy the game, the fun part of it." His trust is difficult to earn. Private trainers with renowned NBA clients offer to work with Antetokounmpo every summer. He turns them all down, sticking with Bucks staffers.

"Because my parents were illegal, they couldn't trust anybody," Antetokounmpo says. "They were always nervous. A neighbor could be like, 'These people are making too much noise, their children are making too much noise,' and the cops could knock at our door and ask for our papers and that's it. It's that simple. So you're always a little closed. I'm outgoing when I feel comfortable, but it took me 21 years just to invite a girl to meet my friends. I'm closed too."

Around familiar faces, like his live-in girlfriend, his innocence is impossible to extinguish. When Saratsis mentions the All-Star Game, Antetokounmpo hushes him, so as not to jinx it. When Geiger visits, Antetokounmpo hands him the Wingstop menu, with the addendum, "I'm buying!" And when Kostas left home for the University of Dayton this fall, big brother drove six hours to move him into his dorm, stopping only at Wal-Mart. "Here is Giannis at midnight, with 80% of the freshman class, walking up and down the hallway carrying bedsheets," recalls Dayton coach Archie Miller.

Giannis functions as the family patriarch, with his father adjusting to the United States and his older brother, Thanasis, playing in Spain. When Giannis inked his four-year, $100 million extension in September—after postponing the signing by four hours to accommodate a morning workout—he called Bucks co-owner Wes Edens at his hotel in Ireland. "I just wanted to say thank you for the money," Antetokounmpo started. "It means so much to me and my family. I'm going to work very hard for it." Then he offered to buy friends and family steak at the Capital Grille in Milwaukee for lunch. When the meat arrived, with appetizers and side dishes, Giannis looked alarmed. "I don't know who's paying for all this," he cracked, "because I only said I'd get the steak."

Three months later he walks into the practice gym the morning after a home-and-home with the Cavaliers, 76 minutes in close proximity to LeBron James. "You feel different after you play him," Antetokounmpo reports. "Your legs, your body, you're sore everywhere. Sometimes you have to lie to yourself, lie to your mother: 'Yeah, I'm good, I'm good.'" The team has the day off. "But where else do I have to be?" he asks. He plays two-on-two. He shoots along the arc with Sweeney. Rookie Thon Maker mops the floor. Antetokounmpo's three-point percentage, 29.3 this season, right around his career mark, is still the source of much consternation. Judging by his practice sessions, it will spike soon, and then there won't be any way left to defend him. "When I'm coaching," muses the 39-year-old Terry, "he'll be pretty much unguardable."

The next night, against Washington, Antetokounmpo starts the game with a reverse layup, a midrange pull-up, a pair of sweeping hooks and finger rolls. The Wizards can't keep him out of the lane or off the free throw line. He dunks off a Eurostep, a lob, a back-cut and a put-back. He dunks over Kelly Oubre, Otto Porter and Markieff Morris, flexing as they wince. When Morris fouls him hard on a breakaway, Antetokounmpo sprints over to ask him about it. He has 24 points in the first half, Milwaukee has 73, and the Cream City Clash in Section 222 chant: "Can't Stop Gian-nis!" He looks as long as Durant, as strong as Davis, as ferocious as Westbrook. He's got Dirk's fadeaway, with the right knee raised, and a nifty two-handed scoop all his own.

He finds Parker for a dunk and a layup, Henson for a layup, Dellavedova for a short J. Leading the break, he whips a pass to Terry in the corner for three. *I got you, bro.* In the post he backs down a trio of Wizards and kicks out to Malcolm Brogdon for another three. With 6:26 left he stands on the free throw line, and the locals break out a rare MVP chant. He has a career-high 39 points. He craves the 40-ball. He tries to settle himself, but the second free throw rims out, and Kidd calls him to the bench. The Bucks lead by 27, which will be their final margin. He winks at Alex, his youngest brother, behind the courtside seats.

In the locker room afterward, players scatter for Christmas, two days away. "Stay out of the gym!" swingman Tony Snell cautions, and Antetokounmpo surreptitiously shakes his head. "I don't know," he mutters. A few minutes later the black Explorer turns right on North 4th Street, toward the snow-covered bridge, taking the league's most unlikely driver to a place only he can see.

AUGUST 18, 1986

Doing Just Fine, My Man

At 50, Wilt Chamberlain has finally mellowed some;
however, he remains, as always, larger than life

BY FRANK DEFORD

Cast as a villain early in his career, Wilt Chamberlain never relished the role as some might. Instead, he learned to live with it.

Because of his size and skill, Wilt could never hide. So he chose either to be alone or, when not, to embrace and further his own mythology, for better and for worse.

Of the many words written about Wilt, few capture the man in all his complexity like this piece by Frank Deford, which ran 13 years before Chamberlain's death, at 63.

Come ahead, and with one bend in the road, imagine yourself in Seoul, late in September of 1988 as the U.S. Olympic basketball team takes the court for its opening game against Spain. The starting five for the Spaniards is introduced: Creus and Villacampa at the guards, Sibilio and San Epifanio at the forwards and Martin at center. And then the Americans: Lebo and Rivers at the guards, Ellison and Manning at the forwards and Chamberlain at center. The cheers are so great for the one player, the last man, that the referee, Fiorito of Italy, delays the jump for three minutes, until finally the roar of the crowd dies down. "O.K., my man," the big fellow says, taking his crouch.

It does not seem possible (except, of course, that time flies when there are no free throws to shoot), but next Thursday, Aug. 21, at the end of Leo, on the cusp of Virgo, the most incredible physical specimen ever to walk the earth will turn 50 years old. Even now, save perhaps for a tiny white fringe in his beard, he doesn't look a day older than the legend. He favors black, revealing garb—usually tank tops and tight-fitting pants—and unfettered feet. Even on the pavement of Manhattan he goes barefoot, donning shower clogs only on the most demanding, formal occasions. The deep, resounding voice (with the curious, contradictory little boy's occasional stutter) has not risen so much as half an octave, and he is even trimmer than when he played, 25 or 30 pounds down; but, more important, as far as he knows, he has not shrunk a whit from the seven feet one and one-sixteenth inches, which he says he is but which no one ever believes. How's the weather up there?

He was, always, the Giant. But he was also the Monster. "Nobody loves Goliath," Alex Hannum, one of Wilt's coaches, once said. Yet the benign irony of Chamberlain's middle-aging is that while he has lost the villain's stigma, he yet retains the giant's stature. Wilt is still the very personification of height, for good or for caricature. Even now, 13 years after his career ended, 24 years after he scored 100 points in an NBA game against the Knicks before 18,000 screaming fans at Madison Square Garden, grandfathers don't say to tall boys: "My, you're going to be a regular Ralph Sampson." Or "...a regular Manute Bol." They say, "My, you're going to be another Wilt the Stilt." If you have something to sell involving a point you're trying to make about size or stature—like a car or an airplane seat or a brokerage house—you still call Wilt Chamberlain and have him represent your product because then people get the point right away even if they never saw a basketball game or weren't even born when Wilt Chamberlain was playing.

For all the times that Bill Russell trumped Chamberlain—and while he was at it, almost broke Wilt's heart—for all his championship rings, still, Russell would walk into a coffee shop somewhere and little old ladies would come over and ask "Mister Chamberlain" for his autograph. Years later, at the height of his career, Kareem Abdul-Jabbar would suffer the same fate. But nobody ever mistook Wilt for anybody else until, he reports proudly, the last couple of years when, every now and then, people call him "Magic." Magic Johnson is 23 years his junior.

But the tragedy to Chamberlain was that although he was probably the greatest athletic construction ever formed of flesh and blood, a natural who was big and strong and fast and agile, accomplished in virtually every challenge he accepted—for all that, he was never allowed to win. If, by chance, he did win, it was dismissed because he was the Monster. If he lost, it was his fault. He was a road attraction, the guy to root against. And Wilt, baffled that his bigness and bestness were the very cause of that disaffection, fought back in the worst way, with more bigness and bestness. If the most points would not win him love, then he would grab the most rebounds, tally the most assists; or he would make the most money, eat the most food, go to the most places, drive the fastest cars, sleep with the most women.

As, through the ages, men who could pull off only one or two of these feats found out, it doesn't necessarily assure satisfaction, accumulation doesn't. Al Attles, an old friend and teammate, now vice-president of the Golden State Warriors, says, "I don't think Wilt would ever admit this, but he would try to do things just to get acceptance from other people. But people would never be happy with what he did, and beneath that veneer, I knew how much it was hurting him. He was so misunderstood. So few people took the time to try and appreciate Wilt. Most everybody just assumed that a great player couldn't possibly also be a great person."

Chamberlain was on holiday on the Adriatic in the summer of '74 when it occurred to him that he would finally hang it up. It wasn't anything dramatic that made him quit. Good Lord, he could sure still play. (Twelve years later, just this past April, the New Jersey Nets reportedly offered him nearly half a million dollars to play out the last couple weeks of the NBA season—and he was 49 by then.) He didn't have any special new career plans back in '74 either. No, there was just one thing: "The more I thought about it, the more I realized that there was always so much more pain to my losing than there ever was to gain by my winning."

And so he walked away. Not long after, he published his autobiography, and in it he unequivocally declared that his happiest year had been the one with the Harlem Globetrotters, the one when nobody asked him to break any records, but just to go out there, put his rubber bands on his wrists like always, have fun and help other people enjoy themselves.

Is that year with the Globies still your happiest? Wilt drew his bare feet across the tiles. Los Angeles stretched out below him, his great house soaring above. "Oh, no, my man," he said with a big smile. "There's been 10 great years since then. There's been 10 *straight* happier years."

No one comprehends better than Wilt himself that he had to lose all those many times to satisfy other people, so that then, after basketball, he could live happily ever after.

Wilt is aiming his white Ferrari down the freeway at a considerable speed. "I've never had any bad habits for spending money except on cars," he says. He has a classic Bentley—baby blue—back in the garage, and is involved, in England, in a project to build a $400,000 custom sports car that will be ready soon, known as the Chamberlain Searcher I. Peter Bohanna, an automotive designer who worked on special effects for James Bond films, is personally developing the Chamberlain. There will be a prototype mold so that 20 copies can be run off, should you want to order one.

The white Ferrari is something like 8' centimeters from road to roof, but Wilt fits in comfortably, a revelation that infuriates littler people. These people hate to think that big people can ever be comfortable, especially in a) cars and b) beds. Little people are always asking Wilt how he sleeps, and they are mightily upset to learn that he sleeps like a baby. Little people forget that everybody starts off their existence sleeping all tucked up, and it's not really all that hard for tall people to revert to that when a bed is too short.

But then, little people no longer aggravate Wilt. After 50 years of this, he just laughs—down—at them. "I know that, subconsciously, little people feel anybody tall has enough going for him, and so there's envy and they try to belittle your height," Wilt explains. "People will never come up to a stranger and say, 'Gee, you're small,' or 'How much do you weigh, fatso,' but nobody ever minds asking anybody tall how tall they are. It doesn't make any difference what you tell them, either, because if you're tall, no matter what you answer, little people will say, 'Oh no, you're taller than that.' You think I don't know how tall I am, and they do? But it doesn't matter. I could say, 'Oh, I'm ten-foot-three' and the guy would say, 'Oh, no, you're taller than that.'"

Little people, Wilt says, get it all wrong even when they're trying to be polite. For example, whenever he gets on an airplane, the top of the door is about at his belt level, but the stewardess will always say, "Don't forget to duck." Wilt shakes his head. "What am I going to do?" he asks. "Bump into the door with my stomach?" In a world where doors and doorknobs, mirrors, shower heads and everything else is built for little people, big people learn to duck instinctively all the time. Wilt laughs at the fact that when little friends spend time with him, after a while they all start to duck, subconsciously, just from being around him. Actually, it is little people who bump their heads most, because they're not used to the occasional low-hanging thing. Little people are the ones stewardesses ought to really worry about.

"I wouldn't say it's always been the easiest thing being seven feet and black, but never once in my life did I ever feel like I was a misfit," Chamberlain explains. "Athletics probably had a lot to do with that." Still, it is not just that he is extremely tall. Wilt's is a phenomenal, overwhelming presence. Tom LaGarde, who tops out at a mere 6 ft. 10 in., was a member of the 1976

U.S. Olympic team. He remembers being on court before a game in Montreal when Wilt strolled into the arena. Several people on the floor were as tall as Wilt, or nearly so. It didn't matter. Everything just stopped. Everyone just stared. Bob Lanier, 6 ft. 10 in., 270, one of the hugest men anywhere, filled out a questionnaire recently that asked him to cite the most memorable moment in his entire athletic career. Lanier wrote: "When Wilt Chamberlain lifted me up and moved me like a coffee cup so he could get a favorable position."

No matter how well one knows Wilt and, presumably, gets used to him, no one is ever able to consciously accept his majesty. Wilt's oldest friend, since third grade, is Vince Miller, a schoolteacher in Philadelphia, a man of better than average height himself. Yet, no matter how many times they play each other in tennis, Miller never fails to lob too short when Chamberlain comes to the net, and as the overhead comes screaming back, there is Miller shouting, "I just never remember how tall you really are."

And how strong was he exactly? How fast? How high could he jump? How long? Who knows? By now, the myths of what Chamberlain did at his leisure (or might have done, if he hadn't been concentrating on basketball) compete in memory all too much with whatever did happen. Wilt is not averse to embellishing his own legend here and there, either. At the moment, Lynda Huey, an old friend, a travel agent by trade, a track nut by passion, is trying to get Wilt to enter the World Veterans Championships in track and field (50-year-old division) next year in Melbourne. "Wilt will rewrite all the record books," Huey says blithely.

And what event would you enter, Wilt? The discus, the 200, the high jump? "Almost anything," he shrugs. These days, for typical daily amusement he competes (against others or himself) in the following activities: basketball, racquetball, volleyball, tennis, polo (yes, the kind with horses), rowing single sculls, swimming, running races, lifting weights, hurling objects, performing the martial arts, aerobics and walking long distances. He still holds his own in scrimmages with current NBA players. The Nets' offer, while obviously of considerable publicity value to a team somewhere out in the suburbs that nobody knows exists, was perfectly legitimate. Wilt finally turned it down only because he was afraid he would disappoint people, afraid that even though he was sure he would acquit himself proudly, playing in the NBA in his 50th year, nothing he could do would be enough to satisfy expectations. He would lose again.

But maybe, Wilt, maybe you could shoot free throws better now? Wilt shakes his head in tolerant chagrin, suffering another fool as best he could. No matter what, he is never going to escape from free throws. He could always score and rebound and run and jump and arm wrestle and throw shot puts and god knows what all, but he couldn't shoot free throws. It just goes to show you: Everybody really is human. Nobody Can Do It All. In fact, one theory was that deep in his soul, Chamberlain wanted to miss free throws so that people would see, at last, that he had human limitations, too. Certainly it was psychological—"totally, a head trip," he says—because early in his basketball life he did quite well shooting free throws. That night at Madison Square Garden, when 50,000 fans jammed in to see him score his 100, he went 28 for 32 at the line.

Countless suggestions were proffered. He shot underhanded, one-handed, two-handed, from the side of the circle, from well behind the line. Hannum suggested to Wilt that he shoot his famous fadeaway as a foul shot. Hannum checked the rule book and said he found that you had to be behind the line only *when* you shot, so he proposed that Wilt start near the basket and fade back to the line. Wilt thought the idea had merit, too, but he was just too scared to try the scheme and bring even more attention to his one great failing. And so he never did learn to shoot free throws as well as a man as he did as a boy. It was a very peculiar Achilles' heel.

When Wilt was negotiating to fight Muhammad Ali in 1971, his own father, who was 5 ft. 8' in. and a boxing fan, said, "You'd be better off if you gave back those gloves right now and went down to the gym and worked on foul shots."

For whatever reason, Chamberlain has always been a loner. His favorite sport to this day remains track and field, an individual game—not basketball, with its team clutter. His fondest early recollections in sports are of his going over to a field at the Philadelphia Rapid Transport Company and throwing the shot. It was something he enjoyed the most because he could do it all by himself. Perhaps he became a loner simply because he was so much bigger and stronger than everyone else. It is also true that he sucked his thumb until he was in junior high. But, he says, "you've got to like yourself more to be a loner," and anyway, Wilt never has lacked for friends.

His closest friends—most of whom have always called him Dipper or Dippy—go back 20 years or more; his advisers, as well, have been tight with him for decades. Chamberlain also numbers among his buddies women who were once lovers—whom he always describes, most properly, as "young ladies"—but for all his affairs there has been little real romance, and never once has he come close to getting married.

His reputation precedes him. During a time when Groucho Marx was a neighbor, Groucho would suddenly appear at Wilt's house, cigar in tow, walking in his crouch, the whole bit, come in, smirk, say only, "Where're the girls? Where're the girls?" and then slink away. And, like free throws, the subject of Chamberlain's bachelorhood forever clings to him. "I just don't think I'm the sort of person who could be with one soul," he explains. "I'm too individualistic...and too gregarious with the young ladies. And I'll tell you this, too, my man: I have no need to raise any little Wilties. Not any—especially in a world where overpopulation is our biggest problem."

In many respects, Wilt, even at 50, looms as the perpetual adolescent—playing games by day, chasing women by night, no family responsibilities, plenty of money. One could even say he is narcissistic. But it is not quite as simple as that. All along, as his old teammate and friend Tom Meschery says, "what Wilt was on the outside identified him as a person. It's that way with many athletes, but it's all the more so with Wilt because there was more on the outside of him than anybody else."

The well-adjusted athlete can, in effect, grow beyond his body when the time for games is over. The weak ones have trouble. "Many athletes hang on because they're afraid of the real world," Wilt says. "They miss the limelight, the young ladies on the road. So maybe I was lucky. The fans were so fickle with me. I *had* to learn that self-acclaim is more important than what anybody else says." In all his years in the NBA, he never once gave a young lady a ticket to one of his games.

Still, unlike other athletes who could retire from sports, Chamberlain could not retire from his body. It's not unlike the famous story told of Winston Churchill, when the lady next to him at dinner said, "Why, Mr. Churchill, you're drunk." And he replied, "Yes, madam, but when I awake tomorrow I will no longer be drunk, but you will still be ugly." A lot of athletes will wake up some tomorrow, and they won't be athletes anymore; they'll be insurance salesmen or restaurant owners or TV color men. But it didn't matter when Chamberlain gave up basketball—that was nearly coincidental—for he would forever be one of the most imposing creatures in the world, never able to retire from his body.

Not that he minds. "I have to exercise three, four hours a day," he says. "If I miss just one day, my body tells me. I don't sleep as well. I get irritable. But then, maybe it's not so bad for me to depend on something. Most people depend on some*one*. Besides, I work hard at keeping my body in shape, because that's been my money-maker, you understand. Most of the commercials that I still get wouldn't have been mine if I had gotten fat. You see, my man, it's still important that I look like I could do it."

And, just as he turned down the Nets' six-figure offer for a few weeks' work, so does Wilt pick and choose his jobs around the globe. He remains very much a worldwide phenomenon, and, indeed, almost wherever Wilt goes he is sure to meet someone who tells him how he was personally there in the Garden, along with 475,000 others, SRO, the night Chamberlain went for his 100. When Wilt does agree to work, he is most often involved with the movies—as a budding producer or as an actor of sorts in the latest of the *Conan* films—or in commercials, for the variegated likes of Drexel Burnham, Foot Locker and Le Tigre. He can be most discriminating, for few other athletes ever invested so wisely. Chamberlain made money in traditional areas, such as stocks and real estate, but also at his famous Harlem nightclub, Smalls Paradise, and in something as risky as broodmares. His house and the Bel Air hilltop it stands on may be worth eight figures. He remains in demand. "I'm still something of a yardstick," he says. "They say, 'When you're hot, you're hot.' But I've always been hot."

In his spare time, he works with young amateur athletes, often as a patron. He has sponsored volleyball teams, the Big Dippers (men) and the Little Dippers (women), and track clubs, Wilt's Wonder Women and Wilt's A.C. (WHERE THERE'S A WILT, THERE'S A WAY, reads the slogan on the team bus.) Currently, mid-Olympiad, he is concentrating his support on a few individual comers, and dreaming dreams of 1988 in Seoul for himself, too.

It's amazing what it will do for a man when, suddenly, his size is only an object of awe, and not an instrument of might. The worst thing in sports is to be expected to win, and then to lose. The second worst thing is to be expected to win, and then to win.

Nothing, of course, in all Wilt's life so affected him, so undid him, as his rivalry with Russell. "Wilt always played his best against Russell," says Meschery, now a teacher living in Truckee, Calif., "but then it wasn't just that Russell's team always beat Wilt's team. It was that somewhere along the way, Russell became the intellectual, the sensitive man, the more human, the more humane. And Wilt wasn't supposed to be any of those things. Well, that was a bad rap. Wilt was every bit as good a person as Bill, and you could tell how much he was hurt by the way he was perceived."

The argument about who was more valuable, Chamberlain or Russell, will never be resolved. The variables of team, the subtleties of contribution, temperament, achievement and synthesis, are all too complex—even contradictory—ever to satisfy truly dispassionate observers. But whatever, Russell clearly enjoyed much the better press and public image. Also, it seems, he got the best of Wilt personally. When Russell quit, Chamberlain was shocked at the criticism Russell suddenly unleashed about him.

"Friends had told me that Bill had been conning me," Chamberlain says now. "I didn't want to believe them. You want to believe that somebody likes you for yourself. But now, I'm afraid that they were more right than I was."

For all the criticism he suffered, though, Wilt remains remarkably charitable about the past. "All that stuff is beyond me," he says. "Besides, I think it's even better for a person to change his attitudes. That's a bigger thing to do than to be born with all the right ideas." Only Russell's old coach and mentor, Red Auerbach, still draws Chamberlain's ire. He refers to Auerbach not by name, but as "that man I don't like"—but even then, he goes on to credit Auerbach for his professional successes.

"Looking back, maybe I was luckier than Russell," Wilt says. "Working with so many coaches was probably more character-building for me, as opposed to Russell, who had only one coach, that man I don't like.

"I know this, my man: It took a lot for me to go out there year after year, being blamed for the loss. I'd be in a crowd somewhere in the middle of the summer, and someone would holler, 'Hey, Wilt the Stilt, where's Bill Russell?' But after the Celtics would beat us, I'd always make it a point to go into their locker room—and maybe those losses were good for my life. Everybody would like to have a few more rings, but I wouldn't trade the experiences I had. If you win like that, like the Celtics did, year after year, if you win everything when you're a young man, then you expect to win everything for the rest of your life."

Curiously, while everything about the physical Chamberlain is in the extreme, he is a man of moderate instincts. He even chose to support Richard Nixon instead of liberal Democrats. His upbringing in Philadelphia was stable and middle class. He was raised in a large family by two southern parents who "never stressed anybody's race or religion." His neighborhood in west Philly was mixed, his closest neighbor a white numbers banker. Overbrook High was largely Jewish at the time, and then he went to the University of Kansas, which put him in touch with middle America, and the Globies, which introduced him to the world. Wilt possesses a perspective that is more global than that of most Americans, let alone most Americans who grew up in the parochial world of locker rooms.

"Look, my man, I'm proud to be black, but I'm even more proud of being an American, and I'm proudest of all of being a member of the human race," Wilt says. "I know some of my brothers in the 'to [the ghetto] won't appreciate me saying this, but, all things considered, I think America's dealt with the racial situation as well as we could have. You have to look at it in comparison with similar problems in the rest of the world—in Ireland or India, wherever. I've never allowed bigotry to make me bitter, you understand, and I've seen an incredible change for good in my lifetime.

"I feel so strongly about here, about California being the Mecca, the melting pot of today, the hope. It all works so well here, all types of people. But I also know I can be naive, because I want it to work so much. And I always know the Birchers and the KKK are never far away. But we're getting there, you understand.

"And then we get hung up on the wrong things. I don't find it shocking that if 90 percent of the people are white, then more of the kids identify with Larry Bird than some black player. So what? Physiologically, it's apparent that blacks are better built to handle the game of basketball. We're quicker. We can jump. Whatever the reason: genes, environmental conditioning—who knows? It's like the little black kid who says, 'Mommy, why do I have curly hair?' And she says, 'Well, son, you have kinky hair to keep the tropical sun from baking your brain.' And the kid says, 'But, Mommy, I live in Cleveland and it's 22 degrees out.' 'I'm not the Maker. I don't know why.'

"But these kids today, they've got no concept of history. They're always coming up to me and saying, hey, Wilt, aren't the Celtics racist? And I say, look, that man I don't like is still running that team, but he was the first coach to play a black, and the first to start five blacks, and the first man to hire a black coach. Now all of a sudden he's a racist?

"Or these kids, they're trying to tell me the players today are better. Let me tell you, my man, that I played in the golden age of basketball. They say, look at the shooting percentages today. Are you telling me any of these guys today can shoot better than Jerry West or Bill Sharman? Well, they can't. One game I saw on my dish this year, and I counted, and the two teams shot 57 layups. In one game. I guarantee you, nobody *ever* shot 57 layups in a *week* of games I played in. It's a good game now, you understand, but it's a different game. They're flashier. They have more flair, but they're not necessarily any better. And hell, Elgin was doing all that stuff 30 years ago."

Wilt leaned back in his chair then, stretching out to his full 7 ft.1 1/16 in.(although he is, of course, much taller than that) and he spoke about his own game. While with the Lakers in 1969, he tore a tendon in his right knee, and while he was recuperating, running on the beach, he discovered volleyball. Periodically since then there has been talk that Chamberlain wanted to play on a U.S. Olympic volleyball team, and while he still entertains such thoughts, now he is also thinking seriously about trying out in '88, when he would be a growing boy of 52, for the discus or the U.S. basketball team.

His past professionalism might well not be an obstacle. Pro soccer and ice hockey players participated in the 1984 Games, and the International Olympic Committee is now considering a revision of the rule governing eligibility, which could open the door for any athlete to compete.

Wilt would dearly love the opportunity. "Of course, maybe I'd get thrown out of the Hall of Fame if I messed up," he says. Or maybe they would build a new wing for him if he sank a couple of clutch free throws against the Soviets. He chuckled at that thought, and scratched at the patio with his bare feet. The young lady he was with looked at him with even more fascination. One minute, he was talking about playing games in the deep past before she was even born, and in the next, he was talking about playing games in the years ahead, with people even younger than she.

One of the reasons Chamberlain likes to travel the world is that it allows him to be even more content when he gets back to his castle on the hill. It is totally his domain. Time does not operate here as it does outside the gates, for Wilt remains the most nocturnal of men; often, he will not call it a day before the sun comes up. Apart from the hours he sets aside for his exercise, there is no pattern to his existence. He does not even live a diurnal life as we know it. He will, for example, go on a complete fast, eat nothing at all for three days, and then suddenly, at 4:30 in the morning, devour five greasy pork chops. He has driven across the country—the whole United States—on the spur of the moment. He is as independent as anyone in the world.

His house is as unique as he is, like a great cloak that surrounds him. Wilt conceived the house and helped design it—and it was completed in 1971, during the time he was leading the Lakers to their record 33 straight wins. At its highest point, the mansion reaches 58 feet. The ceilings are cathedral, and much of the glass is stained. "Everywhere I've been in the world, the prettiest things are the churches," Wilt says. There is not a right angle in the place. The front door is a 2,200-pound pivot. There is a huge round table, a Jacuzzi and sauna, a weight room, a pool room, a room that is entirely a bed, and so forth. And a moat surrounds much of the house. On the next rise over, but down from Wilt's mansion, lives Farrah Fawcett. The rest of the City of Angels is below that.

All the doors are high so that he never has to duck, but there are only two other concessions to Chamberlain's height: one large chair downstairs, and a master bathroom with the toilet and shower head set high. From his bed, Wilt can push a button and fill a sunken bath at the other end of the room. He can push another button and roll the roof back, "so I can get my tan in bed." Except for the young ladies who pass through, and friends who stay over, he is alone, save for two jet-black cats, whose names are Zip and Zap. "At last," Al Attles says, "he is so secure, so at peace with himself."

An eclectic collection of mostly modern art decorates the halls, but in all the house there are only two trophies. One is a huge eight-foot carving that the late Eddie Gottlieb, the Mogul, Wilt's friend and first NBA owner in Philadelphia, presented to him once for something or other that Wilt can't recall anymore; the other, on his bureau, is his citation of membership in the Hall of Fame. "I gave all the other stuff away," he says. "It makes other people happier." Attles, who was Philadelphia's second-leading scorer with

17 points the night Wilt tossed in his 100 before 1,872,000 paid at Madison Square Garden, has the ball from that game.

Downstairs, in the kitchen, lies a copy of *The New York Times* of Aug. 21, 1936, the day Chamberlain was born. An old friend had just sent it to him as an early birthday present. The Spanish civil war was the lead story; Alf Landon's campaign was in high gear in Omaha; Trotsky was on the run from Stalin's Russia. And Jesse Owens was on his way back to America, to triumph and segregation, after starring in the Olympic Games of Berlin.

Fifty years, someone mused.

"Well, it takes awhile, you understand," Wilt replied. "The first time I was in Russia, they'd give me the best caviar, and I'd dump it and ask, 'Hey, where're the hot dogs?' Basketball inhibited me. It took me awhile to find out it's not all bouncy, bouncy, bouncy." By now, he just thanks the people who tell him how proud they were to have been there in Madison Square Garden the night he got his 100.

Curiously, Wilt Chamberlain himself was in Hershey, Pa., that evening, because that's where the Knicks and Warriors played before 4,124 fans when he got his 100.

He laughs and strides across the sunken living room. There he is: black on black, the beard, the tank top, the skin-tight pants, the bare feet, this great human edifice that hardly seems touched by the years. But something seems to be missing. What is it? What's wrong with this picture?

Suddenly—yes. The rubber bands. Or rather: There aren't any rubber bands. Chamberlain always wore rubber bands around his wrists. It was his signature as a player, something he had started as a kid, to make sure he always had extras to hold up his socks on his long, skinny legs. And then when his legs got fuller and stronger, he kept wearing the rubber bands, just for effect. And even when he finished playing basketball, he still wore rubber bands. Where are the rubber bands, Wilt?

"I kept wearing them because it reminded me of who I was, where I came from," he says. "Then suddenly, about two years ago, I felt that I just didn't need that reminder anymore. So I took off the rubber bands." He hasn't worn any since that day.

Wilt is strictly on his own now. The Giant is 50 years old, but the Monster didn't live that long.

ICONS

DECEMBER 20, 1999

Michael and Me

Reflecting on his stellar career, Charles Barkley credits the friend
who was there for him every step—and misstep—of the way

BY JACKIE MacMULLAN

His first shot as a professional was a dunk, and that was a tremendous relief
to Charles Barkley, a 21-year-old rookie forward for the Philadelphia 76ers, a
plump kid from Auburn who had never averaged more than 16 points a game
in his life. When he was drafted with the fifth pick in 1984, some thought he
was too small to rebound in the pros, but Barkley, who measured 6'4¾" in
his stocking feet, wasn't worried about that. He was terrified, however, that
he might not be able to score. "My attitude going in was, I wanted to average
10 rebounds a game for 10 years and make a million dollars in one season,"
he said last Friday.

His friend Michael Jordan, picked two spots ahead of him by the Chicago
Bulls, assured him there was a place for him in the NBA. They first drew
close to each other during the 1984 Olympic trials. Barkley, mingling among
players from highly regarded programs such as Georgetown and North
Carolina, was intimidated by the talent. Jordan, after watching Barkley
attack the glass with abandon and pound the ball up the floor like a point
guard on steroids, wondered why. "I figured if they were on television, they
had to be better than me," Barkley said. "But about halfway through, I called
up [Auburn coach] Sonny Smith and told him, 'Coach, I'm just as good as
these guys. All except one.'"

Already Jordan was special. He and Barkley played cards, drank beers,
shot hoops, shared dreams. Barkley was cut; Jordan went on to win a gold
medal. It was a pattern that would repeat itself through the long careers of

these two elite athletes: Charles coming up just short, Michael hauling off the big prize.

On Dec. 8, in a game between his Houston Rockets and the Sixers, Barkley's glittering 16-year career was ended by a torn left quadriceps tendon, abruptly terminating what was supposed to be a yearlong farewell tour. In a lengthy interview with SI in Boston last week, Barkley expressed only one regret—that he didn't start lifting weights sooner. "Michael was always on me about it," Barkley said. "It was one of the few times I didn't listen to him."

His reflections on his basketball life are inextricably entwined with recollections of His Airness. Who knows how Barkley's career would have differed had he not played opposite the greatest player of all time? Barkley doesn't care. "Michael Jordan was the single biggest influence in my career," Barkley said. "He has been my closest friend since the day I started. He has been there for me in ways you could never understand, as a basketball player, a personal friend, a financial adviser."

When Barkley wore a garish sweater to a game early in his career, Jordan called him and told him to wear a suit, to be professional. "Are you trying to look like a basketball player or do you want to appeal to corporate America?" Jordan scolded. One day, when Michael read how much Nike was paying Sir Charles, he set Barkley straight again. "Insist on stock options," Jordan told him. "You don't need the cash right now. You've got plenty." Barkley took the advice, and, he says, it was worth millions in extra income.

What cemented their friendship, though, was their willingness to stand by each other during hard times. When Jordan was dogged by the details of his extensive gambling in 1992 and '93, Barkley was his most vocal supporter, both publicly and privately. When Barkley landed in jail for a few hours after heaving a bar patron through a glass window in Orlando in 1997, Jordan was the first to make contact, offering help and begging Barkley to hire a bodyguard. (He did.) When Michael received the call in 1993 telling him that his father, James, was dead, Charles was standing beside him while the two were on a West Coast golf outing.

The public never knew the depth of their friendship. They were an odd pair: Barkley living by the seat of his pants and telling the truth as he saw it, even though he knew the repercussions would be ugly; Jordan measuring his words, mindful of political correctness, always seeking to avoid controversy. Barkley abhorred the idea of being a role model; Jordan carefully crafted his life to become one. Though Barkley knows he often pinned the bull's-eye on his own back, it bothers him that the shots he took as a result may affect his place in NBA history. "I've done some stupid things," Barkley concedes. "But how does that diminish my game?"

The numbers don't lie. The kid who fretted about scoring averaged 22.2 points along with 11.7 boards in 1,072 games. He won the rebounding title in 1986–87, outfoxing men eight inches taller and 40 pounds heavier. He was an 11-time All-Star and, in 1992–93, the league's MVP. Three years ago he was named one of the game's 50 best players of all time. He, Kareem Abdul-Jabbar and Wilt Chamberlain are the only players in NBA history to have 20,000 points, 10,000 rebounds and 4,000 assists. In Barkley's ongoing game of one-upmanship with Jordan, that last distinction gives Charles one of his few chances to say *Take that, Michael.*

In the eyes of the public, Jordan was impeccably stylish, like a shiny new Jaguar; Barkley was a powerful pickup truck with all sorts of nicks and dings on the door. In 1991, when Barkley was a Sixer, a heckler at New Jersey's Meadowlands Arena made a racial comment, and Barkley exploded. He spit at the man but hit a little girl instead. "It was a watershed moment for me," Barkley said. "I sat in my hotel room that night thinking, Everyone in the f––– world is going to hate me tomorrow."

The phone rang. It was Jordan, offering...what? Condolences? A strategy for damage control? His friend and rival kept it simple: "I'm here if you need me," Jordan said.

But Barkley had to sort through this one alone. He was up all night, wondering how he had become so consumed with winning, so obsessed with chasing down the elusive championship he was constantly reminded he didn't have, that he had abandoned his sense of decency. "Let's say I did spit on the person I was aiming for," Barkley said. "That was wrong, too. I sat in that room, and I told myself, You better figure out what's important, because this sure as hell can't be it."

The incident, he said, changed him profoundly. The public did not see his contrition or his pain, but he made a decision. Winning wasn't everything—it couldn't be. He forced a trade from Philadelphia to the Phoenix Suns before the 1992–93 season, and basketball was fun again. He averaged 25.6 points, 12.2 rebounds and 5.1 assists and won his one MVP trophy. He and Jordan talked about meeting in the Finals. When it happened, the media caught wind of their friendship and began chronicling their golf, dinner and nightclub meetings.

Magic Johnson, an NBC commentator for the Finals, condemned the fraternizing between Barkley and Jordan. Barkley was stung by this, and a bit amused as well; just a few years earlier Magic was the one kissing his Detroit Pistons pal Isiah Thomas before each game of the 1988 and '89 Finals. But after the Suns stunned the Bulls in Game 5 to send the series back to Phoenix with Chicago up three games to two, Charles told Michael he would pass on the golf, dinner and cards when they got to Arizona. "We were down one game," Barkley said. "I thought I'd try something different."

He was home in Phoenix less than 10 minutes when the phone rang. "Charles," Jordan said firmly, "we'll be friends long after we've stopped playing basketball. Have your clubs ready."

They played golf. The Bulls won Game 6 and sealed their third straight championship. Barkley was left empty-handed for the ninth straight season. As he sat slumped at his locker, head in his hands, a familiar voice called out to him. It was James Jordan. "I want you to win a championship so badly," the elder Jordan told Barkley. "I know my son is in the other locker room, but I was rooting for you, too. You deserve to have your own ring."

Barkley hugged James, who was wearing his Bulls cap. "Well, then," Charles told him, "how about I see you here the same time next year?"

One year later James Jordan was dead, murdered near Lumberton, N.C., by two teenage thugs looking to rob someone. His distraught son had quit basketball and was playing minor league baseball in Birmingham. And Barkley was home watching the Rockets, the team that had eliminated his Suns in the second round, win their first championship. He would never taste the Finals again. Jordan unretired and collected three more titles, just like that. Friends wondered why this didn't eat away at Barkley's relationship with Jordan. "Because," Barkley told them, "our friendship means more than that."

Whenever they played each other, Charles and Michael had dinner together the night before. During one of those meals, in the middle of the 1997–98 season, Jordan told Barkley he was retiring again, this time for good. By then Barkley had gone to Houston, still in search of a championship. After he surrendered $1.2 million in salary so that the Rockets could acquire Scottie Pippen before last season, Barkley was hopeful. Instead, Pippen struggled in Houston's post-up offense, demanded a trade in the off-season, publicly vilified Barkley as fat and overrated, then attached a damning kicker: He said Michael had told him Barkley would never be a winner.

Jordan was on vacation but tracked down Barkley within minutes of hearing Pippen's quotes. "I don't know if Michael was madder that Scottie said all that stuff or that he dragged his name into it," Barkley said. "I told him I was O.K. with it. I knew about Scottie. The whole league knew he was a guy you couldn't count on. You can fool the media and the fans, but you can't fool the players. Scottie was exposed long before this."

In October, Barkley announced he would retire at the end of this season. He was 36 years old, and while he would make $9 million and could still put up numbers, Houston was rebuilding after Pippen's departure, and there would be no ring. Barkley was struggling with the idea that his career would soon be over and frustrated by the team's erratic play. Jordan and Tiger Woods flew out to spend a couple of days with him two weeks ago. Charles was cheered by their visit. "I'm going to make sure I go out in a big way," he told them.

His last shot was a post-up move, the alternative to a dunk when your legs don't have the spring they used to. Barkley tried an up-fake on 7-foot Sixers rookie Todd MacCulloch, who swatted the shot away rudely, with no sense of history. Philly ran down the floor in transition, with Barkley chugging in pursuit. As forward Tyrone Hill moved toward the basket, Barkley leaped at him, trying to block his shot. Barkley made contact, landed awkwardly, grabbed his left knee. He immediately signaled for trainer Keith Jones, his leg hideously distorted.

Barkley watched the rest of the game in a knee brace, signed a hundred or so autographs, cracked some jokes. ("Just what this country needs—another unemployed black man.") He went out with his teammates and reminisced about the game he loved. "What you hold on to is the feeling you had when you realized you had something special going on and, unless Michael was on the floor, you were going to be the best, and nobody could stop you," Barkley said. "At the end of the night you'd have 25 points and 12 rebounds, and all they'd talked about before the game was how to slow you down."

As he limped back to his hotel room in Philadelphia, the city where it all started, he remembered that feeling of invincibility. Then he sat down on the bed and cried.

His message light was flashing, as he knew it would be. There were dozens of messages, but the first one was from Michael, telling him how sorry he was. "I'm here if you need me," Jordan's voice mail said.

Though it was late, Barkley considered calling his friend. Then he realized it was pointless. Charles Barkley will never play professional basketball again. Even Michael Jordan can't help him with that one.

— POSTSCRIPT —

Jackie MacMullan: The ever-accommodating Charles Barkley promised me an exclusive interview during his NBA farewell tour. "Right after we play Philly," he assured me in December of 1999. "We play Boston after that, and we'll talk."

I was in Philly to witness what happened next: Sir Charles ruptured his quadriceps tendon in front of the fans who first welcomed him to the league 15 years earlier as the fifth overall pick. It was a devastating end to a truly memorable career. There was no need to come to Boston; Barkley was headed for surgery.

But Charles came anyway. "Out of respect to Celtics fans," he told me. "I always loved playing there." He sat with me at the Ritz-Carlton, his leg propped with pillows, and shared how Michael Jordan shaped his career, both on and off the court. We reminisced about his past triumphs—and transgressions—and then he convinced me to break my long-standing rule of never socializing with subjects I cover. We clinked glasses and sipped champagne to toast his amazing career.

In subsequent years, Jordan would stop speaking to Barkley over his candid comments that His Airness had surrounded himself with "yes" men in his front office. Perhaps Michael will reread this piece—and then reconsider his stance.

Mister Clutch, Master Builder

Jerry West won only one NBA title as a player, but as general manager he has wrought a Laker dynasty

BY RICHARD HOFFER

In this story, Hoffer captured the essence of West: the tormented genius, the passion, the self-laceration, the unquenchable fire. No man has made his mark on more decades of the NBA, from perennial All-Star to coach, from GM of the Lakers to, later, sounding board for the Warriors and Clippers. For writers, he has long been a dream subject: welcoming, intelligent, complicated and brutally honest.

Friends remain puzzled by the man's anguish, a public torment that is at once spectacular and unnerving. Over the years it has abated somewhat, and the man's wife reports that so far, as the NBA playoffs near, her husband's stomach has not required its seasonal medical attention. This is a good sign, you don't know how good. Once, when he was still coaching the Los Angeles Lakers, he didn't speak to her for three weeks. It was their first year of marriage, and she was too scared to talk to anyone but her mother about it. Later he told her it was nothing personal. It was playoff time.

Another good sign: It used to be that after a Laker loss, his mood might require her to seek another ride home. But when a division rival pasted the Lakers recently and Magic Johnson went down and out with an ankle injury (that is to say, the world came to an abrupt and fiery end), the family repaired to a movie that he actually remembers seeing. "He even spoke to us," says his wife.

So, good signs all around. Yet—good signs aside—he maintains a strange misery that neither friends nor success can lift, a cultivated gloom that, like his clutch play for 14 Laker seasons, is practically a work of art.

Who wouldn't want to be Jerry West, to achieve all that he has? Who would dare dream the life Jerry West has led? Not even Jerry West—Zeke from Cabin Creek, dribbling a ball on the West Virginia dirt on winter nights 40 years ago, a country boy's solitaire—could have created this life from his imagination.

"I was my own best friend," he says of those days. "I was everything, actually. Player, coach, announcer, even the timekeeper. It was amazing to me how many times in those imaginary games there'd be one second left, my team one point down and me with the ball, and I'd miss and—the really amazing part—there would still be time for another shot, or 10." Not that many years later, the timekeeper no longer his best friend, he would make a 60-foot shot at the buzzer to send a 1970 NBA championship game into overtime. Not even his dreams, as fevered as they may have been in the Appalachian twilight, anticipated the glory of real life.

Real life: West became one of the greatest guards to play the game, a perennial All-Star, a rich man, later a winning coach and, after a brief retirement to country-club life and a one handicap, the architect and curator of the 1980s' dominant professional sports franchise. Life's lottery winner. As general manager of the Lakers since 1982, West is the man who risked the 26th pick in the '89 NBA draft on Vlade Divac, strictly a Yugoslavian novelty act (popular opinion), and came up with Kareem Abdul-Jabbar's successor for the next decade or so (new popular opinion). After everyone else passed, West took a chance on A.C. Green out of Oregon State and developed a Laker mainstay. He stole Mychal Thompson and Orlando Woolridge to keep Magic surrounded by winners. And now the Lakers are going after NBA title No. 6 in 11 years. Does West have a golden touch? "Well," says Pete Newell, his longtime friend and onetime boss, "he's the only guy I know who went into oil for a tax loss and struck a gusher."

So watch West at a Laker game, enjoying all this success: He covers his eyes, pounds the armrests of his seat near a Forum tunnel—"It feels like an electric chair," he says—jumps up and...leaves.

"I've never followed him," says Mitch Kupchak, West's assistant general manager. Kupchak doesn't dare. "But I think he leaves the building. I think he's out in the parking lot by himself, walking around."

So this is the unnerving part: Sometimes your dreams come true. West considers this as if for the first time and laughs. "Pretty scary, huh?"

The Lakers, taken part by part, are an unlikely dynasty. The owner, Jerry Buss, surrounds himself with celebrities and conducts a life of such apparent hedonism that it would keep the Church Lady in business for many a season. Buss strides about his various holdings in blue jeans held up by a huge cowboy belt, and he has been known to entertain party guests— that is, a tableful of young women—by setting his chest hair on fire. This goofiness is only heightened by strange stabs at dignity. "Dr. Buss returning your call," a secretary will announce. Yet the chemistry Ph.D. from USC has proved to be a genius in real estate and has shrewdly applied the important principles of that business to the operation of an NBA franchise: Identify the market (show-biz rich) for an appropriate property (more and better show biz) and calculate, to the penny, the market's ability to pay (did we mention show-biz rich?). Courtside seats at the Forum cost $350, and they're sold out every year.

The coach, Pat Riley, is an equally unusual component. His hairdo is as well known by now as Don King's. The sheer stylishness of the man gives him a kind of Hollywood sheen. In fact, film director Robert Towne tried to talk his friend Riley into starring in *Tequila Sunrise*, the idea being that the move from Laker coach to movie star was strictly lateral. Riley declined, so Towne appropriated his character for Kurt Russell to play, slicked-back hair and all. Yet Riley, for all his glamour, had the grit to push his team to back-to-back NBA titles, and almost back-to-back-to-back. Behind locker room doors he is believed to play Joan Crawford more often than Cary Grant.

The team itself is a happy combination of separate and interlocking talents—workaday players like Green alongside improvisational artists like Magic. You can say the Lakers are all Magic, but Buss points out, "Lots of teams have superstars and still don't win." The team isn't just Magic, and it was never just Magic and Abdul-Jabbar. It's a blend that draws as much on the spirited character of Magic as on his no-peek passing, and it has produced not only fast-breaking entertainment but championships, too. With five NBA titles and three other trips to the finals, the Lakers moved well beyond the Boston Celtics in the 1980s. Now the Lakers compare themselves not with the best of the NBA but with the best of the sports world (Edmonton Oilers, four NHL titles in the '80s; San Francisco 49ers, three Super Bowl victories).

But, truly, the man behind this run of NBA titles has been Jerry West, all the while discounting success and envisioning failure, championship ring by championship ring. As the team's special consultant from 1979 to '82, he scouted college players for then general manager Bill Sharman. As G.M.

since then, he has picked and signed the talent and kept everyone happy. But with the Lakers, as with any winning team, there are special problems.

West was talking about these problems recently as he set forth from Inglewood to scout the Final Four and the year-end college camps and all-star games. It was basically a fool's errand, frustrating to a man who can really appreciate talent. "What we do," he says, "is identify the 20 best players. And then we cross them off. Just cross them off. Not the most fun thing."

The NBA tries to enforce parity through its draft, giving the high picks to the losers, reserving a pool of leftovers for the winners. The curse of winning every year is to be consistently denied a chance at the top talent, which presumably will turn a winner back into a loser over time. Is seven years time enough? In his tenure as general manager, West has had no draft pick higher than 23, and twice he did not pick until the third round. Do you wonder why he is superstitious, driving the same route to the Forum for 22 years now—off the San Diego Freeway at Manchester, then down a series of side streets he can't name? ("This can be a problem," he admits in all seriousness, "given the traffic of Los Angeles.") This kind of success is fragile enough to collapse of its own weight; better not to disturb it with the slightest deviation from ritual.

West is more likely to attribute the Laker record to his Forum route than to any decisions he has made. His is a near-pathological humility, a refusal to set himself apart from anyone else by his deeds. In his house in Bel Air there is his 1960 Olympic gold medal (which reminds him of the last time basketball was really fun), a painting of him done by former teammate Gene Wiley, and the ball with which he scored his 25,000th point. That ball has scored a few more in his driveway; some of his five sons—three from his first marriage and two from his second—have used it in pickup games. Otherwise, there are no reminders of West's career, no emblems of ego.

"We've been fortunate" is how he begins any discussion of the Lakers' continued success. He lays it all to Magic and the recently retired Abdul-Jabbar. "Two of the greatest players to ever play the game, on one team," he says, "and that rarely happens. Our job is so much easier when those people have been around. The complementary people, which we have been able to get, have helped us. But someday we're going to need more than complementary people, no question. I shudder to think when Earvin's gone. I just shudder." He thinks about it and finds an opportunity to be miserable. "We'll probably have to be real bad before we get good again."

This is pure West. Not only is he incapable of accepting credit, but he is an uncomfortable winner—doesn't even think of himself as a winner. He ends an interview by saying he hopes the story does not end up rubbing any noses in the Lakers' success, because if you want to know the truth, he's just a loser waiting to happen, just like the rest of the guys in the league, just like always.

Tell it to the rest of the guys. The NBA is a clubby organization, a sort of roving fraternity party. The general managers and the scouts set out for some college game and invariably run into each other and settle into a courtside klatch. Even so, West seems especially beloved and respected by the competition, and by the establishment. NBA commissioner David Stern is impressed by West's grasp of such administrative tangles as the salary cap. "Jerry has disproved the notion that you have to be a lawyer to master that," he says, "and the lawyer in me hates to admit that. He's just an excellent executive. He'd be a success in any business."

Even more impressed are his colleagues. Billy McKinney, director of player personnel for the Minnesota Timberwolves, calls West the "most underrated sports executive in America. People don't understand the mechanics of keeping a team great."

Like McKinney, the rest of the NBA is most appreciative of West's fine eye for talent. Of course, West has been sharpening that eye a long time. When Tommy Hawkins was West's teammate and roommate, the two would show up at an arena well before the other Lakers and, if there was a high school game that preceded theirs, sit through it, comparing notes on what they saw. "He'd say, 'Watch how this kid gets out of a jam,' or 'Check his attitude,'" Hawkins recalls. "These were high school kids."

When Jack Kent Cooke owned the Lakers, he regularly called West in to evaluate talent before a trade or draft. (Today, West calls Magic in for the same reason.) "It was very unusual to do that, to ask a player for advice," says Cooke, whose relations with West were not always so comfortable. "But the passage of time invariably showed him to be right."

For a player it was largely an irrelevant talent, a parlor trick. But West could not help himself. He saw everything and he remembered it. Kupchak thinks back to 1972, when the Lakers were playing the Knicks in the NBA finals. Kupchak was being recruited by Duke out of a Long Island, N.Y., high school and was being led through the Laker dressing room at Madison Square Garden. Duke coach Bucky Waters introduced him to a number of players, including West. Nine years later, having just been signed by the Lakers, Kupchak was boarding the team bus when he bumped into West, then a Laker consultant. Kupchak, jittery in West's presence, made some small talk. "You know, we met way back in...."

"At the Garden—1972," West said. "Bucky Waters brought you by."

That reminds Kupchak of one more story: He and West were driving down a freeway once, and Kupchak noticed some commonplace commotion off to the side. "Did you see that?" he asked. And West said, wearily, "I see everything."

For a general manager, though, this ability is no burden. Rather, it's a marvel. Consider Green, the 6'9" forward who as of mid-April had missed only three games in his five-year NBA career. Green has been the Laker defensive leader while steadily increasing his scoring, season by season. After 22 players had been selected in the 1985 draft, he was still there. "You went to see A.C. Green," says Pat Williams, then the G.M. at Philadelphia, "and you did not see a special player. He was just another forward."

West agrees that there was nothing obvious about Green. "He came out of Oregon State and a system that didn't score many points. He was a player who did not particularly show well in the all-star games, either. Played O.K., not great." But West and Riley both were in the market for a big, dirty-work kind of guy, and to the amazement of some of the Laker players, they plucked him. Abdul-Jabbar remembers somebody telling him that the team had drafted a kid out of Ralph Miller's slow-down offense up north. Kareem covered his eyes. "A kid who passes 17 times before he shoots? How's he going to help the Lakers?" Says West, characteristically, "He could have been a bust."

Not likely. What other general manager takes his 23rd pick onto the floor to share a few moves with him? Or offers advice on where to set up housekeeping, or asks if he has a financial adviser? "He took responsibility for me," says Green, "but not to save face for a draft selection. That's just him." Half a dozen players picked ahead of Green have either left the NBA or been relegated to the bench.

The rest of the Laker roster was put together in similar fashion. When it became apparent that Abdul-Jabbar could play only almost forever, West dealt off two players, two draft picks and some cash for Thompson, an underwhelming center at Portland and then, briefly, San Antonio. The upshot of that is expressed by Magic: "If we don't get Mychal, we don't win."

It's not easy to see what West sees. Of course, there are other general managers who are also good at identifying talent. But West looks for more than just talent. It's evident by the Lakers' luck in this era, when everybody knows that a missed practice can mean something besides the car didn't start, that he checks out character as well. Laker scout Gene Tormohlen says that's why a lot of obvious picks slide right on by the team. "We usually announce it differently," he says.

Not that the Lakers are living in another world. Woolridge has made a nice comeback from drug rehabilitation, but only after West addressed the issue head-on with him. "He doesn't beat around the bush," says Woolridge.

But what mainly guides West—better articulated by Abdul-Jabbar—is this: "He takes people he would have liked to play with."

In 1983, West made the Lakers' single most unpopular trade when he gave Norm Nixon to the San Diego Clippers for the rights to Byron Scott. "I hated it," says Magic. Everybody did—even, truth be told, West. He left the Forum with tears in his eyes. "Terrible, absolutely terrible," he says. "Absolutely no fun." But Nixon was 28 years old, Scott 22. Scott has become a high-scoring guard alongside Magic. Nixon is now retired.

There is hardly anybody on the roster besides Magic who is not some kind of steal, one of Jerry's Kids. After last season, Buss sat down with West in the Polo Lounge for one of their regular chats, and both agreed that they needed a backup guard. "So we pick up Larry Drew," Buss says. "Now, why don't other teams pick up guys like Larry Drew? They tried. Both Drew and Orlando Woolridge had offers that exceeded ours. I think they were swayed [to sign with the Lakers] by the prestige of Jerry West."

But these players are examples of petty thievery compared to Divac. He is the Great Train Robbery, the Thomas Crown Affair and the Brink's Job rolled into one. Divac is 7'1", 22 years old, and can run, block shots and score. In addition, the bearded one has become a crowd favorite at the Forum, no small consideration. "Do you understand what Divac is?" asks Kupchak. "He's the equivalent of a top-five pick, the kind of player you've got to lose 50 games to get. What he does is make us set for 10 years."

In fact, Divac was a top-26 pick, the kind of player the Lakers needed to lose just 25 games to get, and Kupchak, like everyone else on the Lakers staff, had doubts about him all the way.

Oh, the NBA knew Divac was a talent, no question. And the Lakers expected him to be one of the first 10 or 15 picked. But as draft day approached, the rest of the league began to cool on Divac. "He scared a number of scouts with a lackluster performance in the European championships, when he was playing down to the competition," says Divac's agent, Marc Fleisher. "But besides that, and the language problem, and the issue of whether he would come at all, there were these rumors. He smoked, he drank, he jumped off the balcony of a girls' dorm."

Meanwhile, West was organizing his own scouting report, though he figured to have no chance at Divac. He called Fleisher for some videotape, since the Lakers, unlike the Celtics and many other NBA teams, did not scout Divac in Europe. He called former Laker Bob McAdoo in Italy for reassurance, which he received.

So when Divac slid to No. 26, the Lakers were presented with an unexpected dilemma. Divac or another seven-footer, Missouri's Gary Leonard. Kupchak and scouts Tormohlen and Ronnie Lester all voted for Leonard.

Tormohlen says, "I told Jerry I was scared. Mitch and Ronnie were afraid of the deal. The bottom line is, if every team knew how good Divac was, why was he still there?"

And to solve the dilemma, the Lakers had exactly five minutes. West called Buss in Hawaii to report his choice. "Early on with the Lakers, I made a strong suggestion about a draft choice in the first round," says Buss. "It was the last time I stepped out of line. So when he told me about this seven-foot Yugoslavian and said, 'What do you think?' I said, 'Go ahead. In our position we should gamble.'"

That was what West wanted to hear. Today the rest of the league sniffs that Divac is not much of a risk when you're picking 26th. Says Celtics patriarch Red Auerbach, "In the first 15, you can't take a chance. They had nothing to lose." The Celtics, who ordinarily pick down low with the Lakers, had the 13th pick last year and were so giddy about the comparative availability of talent that they practically expected to develop another Larry Bird. They didn't—their choice, 6'10" forward Michael Smith of BYU, has contributed little—and meanwhile the Lakers get to develop a solid replacement for Abdul-Jabbar.

Once he made the pick, West quickly solved all problems, paying off Divac's former team and settling on a three-year contract worth close to $2 million, which is not exactly No. 26 money. How good was the deal? "Well," says Kupchak, "the tribute to the deal is that you don't read about Kareem anymore, as in, 'If only the Lakers still had Kareem....'" Leonard, by the way, is with the Minnesota Timberwolves, used sparingly.

It is suggested to West that he must feel pretty proud of having landed Divac. He waves his hands. "Oh, my," he says, "we've done some terrible things here. We drafted Earl Jones [a 23rd pick in 1984] and he didn't do a darn thing, a terrible mistake and all my fault. We traded for Billy Thompson, who was put on the expansion list. We passed on Dennis Rodman. That wasn't the best move we could have made. Now, Vlade's done a real nice job for us, and he's a breath of fresh air, but the measure of any player is after three years, knock on wood...."

Never mind.

Jerry West is naturally distrustful of success, and he is always surprised, but never pleased enough, when it comes his way. He was a two-time All-America at West Virginia, the only college player you could mention in the same breath with Oscar Robertson, but he was astonished when the Lakers, just then picking up to move from Minneapolis to Los Angeles, drafted him in the first round in 1960. "I didn't think I was good enough to play in the NBA," he says. "No, really." Then, after a bad game during the Olympic trials that year, he almost gave up on the Olympics, too. Pete Newell, the U.S. coach, had to explain to him that if West wasn't on the team, neither was he. "But that was Jerry," says Newell.

His career with the Lakers is storybook stuff. But if it was unexpected to West, it was also unsatisfying. This is how it went for the game's greatest guard: He would start every night with his stomach in knots and end every season with a loss. Now 51, he still can't help but hark back to that annual loss. "The albatross around my neck," he says. Of course, West exaggerates— the Lakers finally won an NBA title in 1972—but it did not go unremarked that he was one of sport's beautiful losers. Six times before '72 he helped the Lakers to the NBA championship round, only to lose to Boston. In 1969 he was so heroic in defeat that he was voted MVP. All this, you should know, came after his college team was beaten in the 1959 NCAA finals by the University of California.

He was driven. Hawkins recalls that West never had back-to-back bad nights. West hardly ever had single bad nights, but if he did, he would return to their room and do a stream-of-consciousness replay. "A thorough recapitulation," says Hawkins. "I never thought it silly—maybe a little excessive."

How seriously did West take it all? Hawkins remembers that once during introductions at the Forum, West looked up at the crowd and said he felt just like a Roman gladiator. "He had very grandiose notions about what this thing was, more than an arena, more than a game."

To have this approach and still lose took quite a toll. The NBA championship in '72 was pitiful recompense, though not entirely unappreciated. After the Lakers beat the Knicks, West wandered off by himself and sat in the trainer's room, "I thought how differently we'd be perceived from then on. Instead of a bunch of losers and chokers, suddenly we were champions. It was amazing." But the toll mounted, resuming the strange momentum of defeat that had plagued his career: two more frustrating finishes to seasons, losing to the Knicks in the '73 finals and to the Bucks in the first round of the '74 playoffs. The broken noses and the final stomach pull that led him to retire in '74, way early. He was 36 and still one of the best in the game. "But I didn't want anyone to hit me again, I didn't want another needle stuck in me, and I was tired of losing. I woke up one day and said, I don't like this, and I don't like myself."

His first marriage was unraveling, his life's work was prematurely completed, and he had only one championship to show for it. The NBA wasn't about to forget him: Among the ways he has been immortalized is by the league logo, which depicts West dribbling left handed. But he barely kept track of his old team. The dream career was over, and the payoff was he was essentially lost.

Gary Colson, then basketball coach at Pepperdine, used to run around with West during this period, a time of vigorous bachelor life, by most accounts. "You hear about movie stars who have done it all and just go fruitcake?" says Colson. "Here you go. I had this fear, you know, a Marilyn Monroe type of thing. What else was there? What would he do now that the cheering had stopped? He was searching for something. It was a depression that all great actors and athletes go through."

West, unoccupied and unanchored for the first time in his life, threw himself into golf. Every day, all day. Eddie Merrins, the pro at Bel-Air Country Club, stood back and watched West attack his game. "I think he felt, in his own mind, that he'd just switch from one game to another, play professional golf," says Merrins. "He was a very good club golfer, and he did shoot that 28 on our back nine [in a friendly round in 1974], which nobody else has ever done. Yet he was reluctant to enter competitions. He wasn't perfect, and it was as if he didn't want to embarrass himself with a poor round."

Since a poor round always lurked around the corner, golf ultimately wasn't his game. West rarely plays today, though when he does, he must be somewhat comical to watch. He plays speed golf. "Once," says former teammate Rod Hundley, "we were creeping up on this foursome and they said, 'Why don't you play with the two following you, the ones way back?' I said, 'We were playing with them.'"

But the golf was necessary therapy during a strange time, when West seemed frantic to shed his past life, layer by layer. Colson used to help West move from one bachelor pad to another, and West was always giving him stuff, artifacts of an unsatisfying life: jewelry, clothes—"I'm wearing his shorts right now," Colson says, laughing—and belts. "I'd take these belts home, and on the back of one of them is Hickok. You remember the Hickok Award [the S. Rae Hickok Award for professional athlete of the month, won by West in April '69 and January '72]? He gave me two or three All-Star rings."

One day in 1974, Colson invited West to a Pepperdine basketball affair. West was seated next to a Pepperdine cheerleader, Karen Bua, and for reasons she still can't tell you, he blurted out his life story to her. She was slack-jawed. "I had never met the man, and he just basically told me everything," she says. "He was just starting a divorce and was not a happy person. Very famous, had done everything and was just empty. I felt, what a sad human being." Having spilled these astonishing confidences, there was nothing for West to do but marry Karen, which he did four years later.

Civilian life was a struggle. One awful consequence: He now was famous for no reason. He couldn't stand it. He was on a scouting visit to Rutgers in the late '70s when some players noticed him and came up for autographs. "He began perspiring profusely," says Jack McCloskey, then his assistant coach. It was a physical reaction. Karen has watched him sign autographs silently and stone-faced, and has wanted to tell him, smile, talk to these people. But she finally recognized that it was not arrogance but embarrassment.

If unemployment was a problem, what to say of West's coaching stint for Cooke from 1976–77 through 1978–79? It was the most disastrous 145–101, three-time-playoff job ever turned in. Oh, the first year was a dream. West took a team that hadn't been in the playoffs in two years to the best record in the NBA. "In some respects, of all the things I've been involved in, that was the most fun year I've ever had in basketball," he says. But Cooke liked to tinker. "Mr. Cooke was good to me, other than him wanting to be my assistant coach," West says. Championships continued to mock him. And the job quickly turned him into the kind of man who might not speak to his wife for three weeks and then say, "Nothing personal."

Cooke was equally exasperated by his protégé. "I expected nothing like perfection from Jerry, and he didn't fail me," he says. "He was only moderately successful as a coach, because he could never understand why average players couldn't do the things he did so easily."

Another morning dawned with West's waking up and discovering, "I did not like myself. I was absolutely miserable." He quit, and though Buss later got down on his knees—"literally," says Buss—to beg him to return, West never again considered coaching. (In 1981, after firing Paul Westhead, Buss named West and Riley Laker co-coaches. But West said he was only helping Riley and returned to his consultant's role after two weeks.)

West had no reason to think himself qualified for anything but dribbling a ball, or showing others how. So his competence as general manager, a job arranged by his predecessor, Sharman, and Buss, surprises him. "This is a side of me I never knew existed," he says. Lucky again. Because this may be the happiest time in West's life. "His proper niche," says Cooke. His competitive drives and his abilities have, for once, found a healthy outlet in his job. And Karen says he comes home, by whatever strange route, and plays with the kids, and is relatively relaxed, nearly normal.

Not completely, of course. For one thing, he is as quirky as ever. He won't travel with the team. (The last time he did, during the 1983 playoffs, the Lakers were swept by Philadelphia.) And even when the Lakers are home, he maintains his rituals. Game nights, he goes into his office and right back out. No reason. He is, despite recent improvement, surely tormented, always distrustful of his charmed life. It's what happens when your dreams come true, and you realize you shot too low.

The core torment is this: There should have been more, and West knew it all along. "Those winter nights as a kid," he says, "playing until your fingers cracked and bled. Dreaming. Winning the game with a last-second shot, being somebody you could look up to. All those things came true for me, everything happened except one thing, and that's winning a championship. And I thought I had the ability to do something like that. I thought I was gifted with greater skills. I thought I was responsible. I've often wondered what my life would have been like if we'd won."

He means, won all the time. If you remember West at the end of a close game, you remember a man demanding the ball. They called him Mr. Clutch for the way he took charge. It wasn't because he wanted the two points—nobody has ever heard him discuss his scoring—but because he wanted and expected the win. West was enslaved by his own greatness, doomed by his own dreams, haunted by responsibilities nobody else in the game has ever shouldered. He suffers them still, pacing outside in the Forum parking lot, the din of the game now distant, ticking off defeat after defeat, each one his fault. You imagine he promises the California night air, it won't happen again.

FEBRUARY 18, 2002

Ahead of His Class

Ohio high school junior LeBron James is so good that he's
already being mentioned as the heir to Air Jordan

BY GRANT WAHL

*A cover story, and photograph, that became iconic. In 2002, SI dispatched a
young college hoops scribe named Grant Wahl to write about a young phenom
named LeBron James. Twenty years later, James is now in the twilight of his
own career, passing on a mantle as Jordan once did to him.*

Resplendent in a sleek navy blue suit, his burnished dome gleaming in
the light, Michael Jordan steps into the tunnel of Cleveland's Gund Arena,
flashes a million-watt smile and gives LeBron James, the top high school
player in the country, a warm, we're-old-pals handshake. "Where's Mama?"
Jordan asks.

"She's in New Orleans," LeBron says, grinning at the memory of how well
his mother, Gloria, had gotten on with Jordan when they met in Chicago
last summer.

It's 10 p.m. on the last night of January, and the moment feels charged,
even a little historic. Remember that photograph of a teenaged Bill Clinton
meeting JFK? Same vibe. Here, together, are His Airness and King James,
the 38-year-old master and the 17-year-old prodigy, the best of all time
and the high school *junior* whom some people—from drooling NBA general
managers to warring shoe company execs to awestruck fans—believe could
be the Air Apparent.

Jordan has just hit another buzzer-beater to sink the Cavaliers, but another game is afoot. A spectacularly gifted 6'7", 225-pound guard who averages 29.6 points, 8.3 rebounds and 5.9 assists for St. Vincent–St. Mary High in Akron, LeBron is thought to possess all the elements necessary to do for some apparel company what Jordan did for Nike. Not only does he have the requisite high-flying game and an Iversonian street cred that Jordan himself lacked, but he can also turn on the charm when necessary. It's why LeBron is a year from signing what's expected to be the most lucrative shoe deal in history for an NBA rookie, estimated at $20 million over five years, and why Jordan, who represents his own division of Nike athletic wear, would want LeBron in the Swoosh family.

Tonight, however, LeBron is wearing a black coat and stocking cap bearing the logo of Adidas, his high school team's sponsor, which Jordan can't help but notice yet chooses to ignore. They schmooze for a few minutes, bantering about LeBron's upcoming game, until Jordan leaves, offering this piece of advice: "One dribble, stop and pull up. That's what I want to see."

LeBron nods and smiles. "That's my guy," he says. All things considered, it's hard to decide what's more impressive—that LeBron could be hailed as the best high school player even though he's only a junior, or that many NBA scouts believe he would be the first pick in *this year's* draft (if league rules didn't forbid his entering it), or that he can get an audience with Jordan as easily as a haircut appointment.

Then again, the world behind the velvet rope is nothing new to LeBron. Last summer he was the only schoolboy invited to play in Jordan's top-secret workouts in Chicago. LeBron speaks regularly with Boston Celtics star Antoine Walker, who is his best friend among NBA players. Those floor tickets to the Cavaliers game? LeBron's surrogate father, Eddie Jackson, simply made a call to Cleveland coach John Lucas. Already LeBron has hung out with Michael Finley, Tracy McGrady and Jerry Stackhouse, to say nothing of his favorite rapper, Jay-Z. "He's a cool guy too," LeBron says. "We went to his hotel first, and then I had backstage passes."

Did we say LeBron just turned 17?

"At this age LeBron is better than anybody I've seen in 37 years in this business, including Kevin [Garnett] and Kobe [Bryant] and Tracy," says Sonny Vaccaro, the Adidas rep who signed the first shoe deals with Jordan (for Nike), Bryant and McGrady.

Says Germantown (Pa.) Academy coach Jim Fenerty, who watched LeBron pile up 38 points and 17 rebounds in a 70–64 defeat of his Patriots in December, "We played Kobe when Kobe was a senior, and LeBron is the best player we've ever played against. LeBron is physically stronger than Kobe was as a senior, and we've never had anybody shoot better against us."

"There are only four or five players in the NBA that I wouldn't trade to get LeBron right now," says former Phoenix Suns coach Danny Ainge.

If that sounds like enough hot air to pump up all the tires in Akron, check out LeBron's résumé. Last season, while leading St. Vincent-St. Mary to its second straight Division III state title, he became the first sophomore to win Ohio's Mr. Basketball award. His stock skyrocketed last July at the Adidas ABCD Camp, where he won MVP honors, and it threatened to soar off the charts after he totaled 36 points, nine rebounds and four assists to almost single-handedly keep the Irish close in a 72-66 loss to national powerhouse Oak Hill Academy in Trenton, N.J., on Sunday. Must have been the shoes: LeBron was wearing special American flag-themed Adidases given to him last Friday by Bryant, who was in nearby Philadelphia for the NBA All-Star Game.

"A lot of players know how to play the game," LeBron says, "but they really don't know how to *play the game*, if you know what I mean. They can put the ball in the hoop, but I see things before they even happen. You know how a guy can make his team so much better? That's one thing I learned from watching Jordan."

Indeed, while NBA scouts are universal in their praise of LeBron's all-around package—his shooting range, his fluid handle, his disarming explosiveness—their most common comparison is with another breathtaking passer, Magic Johnson. "The most surprising thing is that a guy who could dominate offensively is so unselfish," says one scout. "Most of these young guys don't know how to play, but he looks to make the pass first, and he's great at it."

"If I were a general manager, there are only four or five NBA players that I wouldn't trade to get him right now," says former Phoenix Suns coach Danny Ainge, who was in Trenton to see LeBron play for the second time. "I love Jason Williams at Duke, and I've heard of the Chinese guy [7'6" Yao Ming], but if LeBron came out this year, I wouldn't even have to think about it. I'd take him No. 1."

It's a moot point, though. After causing a stir last summer by saying that he might become the first high school junior to declare for the draft—and challenge the NBA rule which prevents players in this country from being selected until their high school class graduates—LeBron vows he'll stick around to get his diploma from St. Vincent-St. Mary in the spring of 2003. "The rule's not fair, but that's life," says LeBron, who has a 2.8 GPA. "I'll stay another year because my friends are here. The only thing I think is bad, they let that 17-year-old golfer [Ty Tryon] on the PGA Tour. You've got tennis players competing professionally when they're 14. Why not basketball players?"

With LeBron staying at St. Vincent–St. Mary another year, the buzz around him should rise to an unprecedented level for a high school athlete. "This is like a mid-major college environment right now," says Frank Jessie, the school's athletic director. This year the Fighting Irish moved their home games to the University of Akron's 5,100-seat James A. Rhodes Arena. Some 1,750 season tickets were sold (at $100 to $120 a pop), and St. Vincent–St. Mary is drawing 4,075 fans, almost double the attendance of the university's men's team.

LeBron may be the reason for the hysteria, but he isn't your typical high school hoops phenom. For the last two years, in fact, he has risked career-threatening injury as an all-state wide receiver on the St. Vincent–St. Mary football team. At first Gloria refused to let LeBron play last fall, but after the 22-year-old singer Aaliyah died in a plane crash last August, he persuaded her to let him play. "You're not promised tomorrow," LeBron says. "I had to be out on the field with my team." Though LeBron did break the index finger of his left (nonshooting) hand, he helped lead the Irish to the state semifinals.

Gloria knows she can protect LeBron for just so long. She gave birth to him at 16, and after her mother died two years later, she and LeBron drifted from apartment to apartment around Akron. (On one occasion their building was condemned and bulldozed by the city.) "I saw drugs, guns, killings; it was crazy," LeBron says. "But my mom kept food in my mouth and clothes on my back."

The Jameses' nomadic existence and unsettled home life took a toll, however. In the fourth grade, LeBron says, he missed more than 100 days of school. Nor did it help that Jackson, who has been in a relationship with Gloria since LeBron was two, spent three years in jail after pleading guilty to a 1991 charge of aggravated cocaine trafficking.

Late in the fourth grade LeBron moved in with the family of Frankie Walker, his youth basketball coach. "It changed my life," LeBron says. "The next year I had perfect attendance and a B average." By the sixth grade LeBron was splitting time between the Walkers' home and Gloria's, and soon Jackson reentered the picture, providing financial support, Gloria says, from his work as a concert promoter and a full-time drug counselor at an Akron outreach program. LeBron, who has never met his biological father, refers to Jackson as Dad.

LeBron has been Akron's rising star ever since he led his eighth grade team to the finals of a national AAU tournament. Though he says he's considering Duke, North Carolina, Florida, Ohio State and Louisville, no one believes he'll go to college. Meanwhile Gloria, 34, and Eddie, 35, are busy crisscrossing the country, "listening to folks, letting them give their sales pitch, weighing the options," as Gloria puts it. They attended the Super Bowl in New Orleans after having met with "some representatives there in regards to some marketing" for LeBron, which is all Gloria will say.

Adidas already has a relationship with LeBron through its sponsorship, now in its second year, of the St. Vincent–St. Mary team (LeBron even got to help design the Irish's uniforms) and of an Oakland AAU team that he has played on the last two years. Gloria and Eddie have visited the suburban Los Angeles home of Vaccaro, and LeBron has attended Vaccaro's ABCD Camp in Teaneck, N.J. Nike has gone to a full-court press as well, hosting Gloria and Eddie in Oregon for a meeting with company chairman Phil Knight. "Why go through the middleman when you can go straight to the top?" Gloria says. "Nike's *very* interested."

Jordan could play a role too. "This is going to be like a Shakespearean drama," Vaccaro predicts. "Basically, only two people are involved: me or Michael? Adidas or Nike? Whoever it is, LeBron's going to translate far and wide. I believe that."

"A lot of NBA players who wear Nike have never gotten to meet Phil Knight, but it's also an honor to meet the Adidas people like Sonny Vaccaro," Jackson says with perfect politesse. Either way, Jackson knows LeBron's in the driver's seat, yet he also knows firsthand that the distance from jail to the office of a multinational's chairman is shorter than you'd think. Not long before his meeting with Knight, Jackson pleaded no contest to a disorderly conduct charge and received a suspended 30-day sentence for his role in an altercation last July at an Akron bar.

For now LeBron exists in a weird netherworld between high school student and multimillionaire, between dependent child and made man. He's both, of course. At Gund Arena during the Cavaliers game, middle-aged fathers and mothers asked him to pose for pictures; LeBron dutifully complied. Later, an 11-year-old boy in a Jordan jersey collared him for an autograph, one of dozens he signed during the evening. Even Cleveland Browns coach Butch Davis chatted up LeBron after the game. "Hey, LeBron! How you doing?" Davis said, slapping him on the back. "Want to be a wide receiver for us? Just for the red zone, how about that?"

It's heady stuff, but in so many other ways LeBron remains a kid. During a Cavaliers timeout, he frantically waved his arms as the rally crew shot plastic miniballs into the crowd. (He eventually snagged one, which he was still clutching when he met Jordan after the game.) On the ride back to Akron in a reporter's car, LeBron simultaneously blasted Jay-Z over the stereo, gabbed on his cell phone and checked his two-way pager for messages from pals like Sebastian Telfair, the Brooklyn whiz kid who's regarded as the nation's best sophomore.

He's *almost* there, but not yet. Only one more year—with no injuries, no complications—and he'll make it. Then he can worry about the next step. Above the television in the Jameses' modest west Akron apartment, LeBron keeps an ersatz SI cover featuring his photograph and the cover line Is He the Next Michael Jordan? It's preposterously too early to answer, of course, yet judging from young LeBron's unprecedented rise, it's a question that is at least worth asking.

— POSTSCRIPT —

Grant Wahl: Whenever you write a story about a tantalizing prospect, you hope that when you read the article 20 years later at least some of it will hold up. By no means is that guaranteed. I wrote a magazine piece on the soccer phenom Freddy Adu in 2003, and Adu never became the star his promise suggested. So for a high school junior named LeBron James not only to meet but exceed the overwhelming expectations that came with my SI cover story in 2002 is something that I still find astonishing.

The sports media landscape in 2002 was such that an SI story could still more or less introduce an athlete to the country. And I remember every detail of my reporting visit: Meeting LeBron and his buddies at their high school practice; spending time with them in LeBron's small West Akron apartment; driving them to see Michael Jordan in a Wizards-Cavaliers game; and lurking in the background while Jordan met LeBron after the game in what turned out to be the lead scene of my story.

When SI managing editor Bill Colson decided to put LeBron on the cover— during the middle of the Salt Lake City Winter Olympics—I was both pumped and hopeful that the kid would live up to the hype. The idea for the cover line (THE CHOSEN ONE) came from SI college basketball editor Greg Kelly, and I guess LeBron liked it, because he eventually got CHOSEN 1 tattooed across his back.

I don't have many SI stories that are commemorated on their anniversary every year, but that LeBron cover—shot by Michael LeBrecht II—is one of them. Not long ago, I reread my story and smiled. It held up.

NOVEMBER 24, 2003

Geno Auriemma + Diana Taurasi = Love, Italian Style

A pair of paisans at UConn share a passion for hoops that
makes a perfect match of cocky coach and fearless player

BY FRANK DEFORD

*An origin story for perhaps the best women's player ever and also a profile
of the most successful coach in the women's game. Like all Deford stories, this
one heads far afield.*

On one of those rare occasions when he was alone, unbothered, in his office,
the coach sat listening to Pavarotti. Interrupted then, he reluctantly turned
off the music. "Love songs," he said wistfully to the interloper. "All the best
love songs come from Naples."

This is one of those, of a sort.

East of Naples, in the mountains, in the province of Avellino, sit two small
villages. One of them is so small, in fact, that it is almost impossible to find,
hidden as it is in the Calore valley, surrounded by vineyards, watched over
by its patron saint, San Marciano. It is called Taurasi.

Forty years ago a five-year-old named Mario Taurasi left the hamlet of
his name. His parents took him to Argentina, where he grew up, and then,

in 1980, he took his wife to California. Their daughter, Diana Lurena, was born shortly thereafter, and a few years later, in the fourth grade, she took up basketball. It was immediately apparent that the kid had a facility for the game.

About 30 miles from Taurasi, due east of Vesuvius, up in the Picentini range, is the town of Montella. At the highest point in the village is the Holy Saviour, sister church to one of the same name in Norristown, Pa., a working-class suburb of Philadelphia. One day in November 1961 Marsiella Auriemma and her three children left Montella for Norristown, where Marsiella's husband, Donato, was already settled, laboring in a candy factory for 15 to 20 bucks a week. Their oldest child, Luigi, who was called Geno, was seven. The ride from his village to the port in Naples was the first time he had ever been in a car. He had never had so much as a coin in his pocket. He could not speak a word of English.

In Norristown, at the parochial school, St. Francis, the nun who taught second grade explained to Geno, through an interpreter, the way things worked there. At the end of the school year, she said, the boys who passed went on to third grade. Those who didn't stayed back in second. There would be no remedial help, no English-as-a-second-language class. Pick it up on your own.

In June little Geno went up to third grade. It was obvious right off that, in any language, the kid had a way with words.

Four Octobers ago, Diana Taurasi was a senior at Don Lugo High in Chino, Calif. She had become the best girls' basketball player in the country, and she was boarding a flight from Los Angeles to Hartford to visit the campus of the University of Connecticut, where Geno Auriemma was the coach of the second most eminent women's basketball program in the country. Tennessee was still first, but Auriemma had the Lady Vols in his sights. He had grown up slick and ambitious, driven as much to chase down the big time as to outrun the nebulous fears that dogged him. "I don't know—all the obvious ones," he says. "I'm the oldest, immigrant family, couldn't speak English. I'm Italian, Catholic—hey, that's enough guilt. What more do you need? I felt inferior. I grew up scared of everybody."

No one would ever imagine this, of course. To the women coaches who despise him and to their teams' furious fans who see him on the court, Geno—just Geno—is an arrogant little dandy. Worse, he's one good-looking guy. The azure eyes, the perfect head of swept-back curly hair: Finally, we know what became of Frankie Avalon after *Beach Blanket Bingo*. Worse: the cock-of-the-walk gait. "Geno's natural walk is a strut," says Rebecca Lobo, the star of his first championship team, in 1995. Sometimes he even snaps his fingers when he struts, daddy-o style. But then, it's enough that Geno just stands there at the side of the court, hands on his hips, as if he is simply not going to put up with these stupid broads anymore. Then there's the stylish tie that's always undone—perfectly undone, as if he has a valet just to perfectly undo his stylish ties. Come on, this cocksure, suave little s.o.b. is running scared?

"The worst fear of all is fear of failure," Geno says. "The year Jen Rizzotti was a sophomore, she was a chem-bio major, and she had to get a four-oh. *Had to.* I asked her one day what drove her. 'I hate to lose,' she said. 'Well, then,' I told her, 'you're my point guard, so we'll get to the final eight, maybe the Final Four, but we'll never win till you replace that *I hate to lose* with *I wanna win.*' And eventually Jen did, and then we won." He pauses. "But me, I'm still motivated by fear of failure."

Because you've got no coach who can change that in you?

"Yeah. That's right."

That day in October four years ago, Geno waited at Bradley International Airport for Diana's plane to come. She'd had the luxury of living in a universe far different from the one he had lived in. Four decades had passed since little Geno had walked off the boat. If there was any anti-Italian prejudice in the California Diana had grown up in, she wouldn't have allowed herself to notice. Geno was hardly surprised. His own three kids—two girls and a boy—don't have a clue about the insecurity he suffered, the sneering prejudice. *Dago. Greaseball.* All around us now, after all, are Italian clothes, Italian food, Italian wine. Charming Italian men, gorgeous Italian women. The world has come to love all things Italian. Ciao. *Va bene.* One of Geno's favorite players, Meg Pattyson (class of '92), came to him. "You'll never guess," she said. "I'm in love with a guinea." He hugged her. "It's about time you got smart," he said. *Forza Italia!*

Anyway, coaches had never seen anyone like Diana Taurasi. She never doubted herself, never expressed any trepidation. The first time Geno saw her she was at an all-star camp, only a sophomore but clearly the best player there. He never coveted a player so much in his life. All this and a *paisan*, too. But would a Southern California girl go cross-country, Backeast, to a campus at a crossroads named Storrs in the middle of some farmland in northeastern Connecticut?

Not only that, but there was also Diana's mother to contend with. The last thing Lili Taurasi wanted was for her baby to move 3,000 miles away. Geno was well aware what a formidable obstacle Lili posed. "You know," he says, "that stereotype about the tough Italian father who slams his fist down and everything runs his way is wrong. Italians have real strong mother figures."

Except that Geno on the recruiting beat is a formidable presence. Not for nothing does Auriemma mean *golden gem*. Jamelle Elliott, one of his assistants, remembers when she was a high school prospect in 1992 and saw him coming to recruit her, strutting through her tough neighborhood in Washington, D.C. "Geno was the only white guy—the only one—I'd ever seen come down my street, and he just walked in as if he'd been there 10 times before."

Diana says, "I know this will irritate a lot of coaches, so I never said it then, but I wanted to play for a man. Anyway, Geno was different from all the other coaches. He'd tell me things that were real. And 99 percent of it was true."

Auriemma helps clarify this. "You know what I do better than most anyone?" he asks. "I deal with women. And the way I do it is to tell them exactly what I think. I don't think they're used to that from men."

When he was recruiting Diana, one of the most sought-after high school players in the history of women's basketball, he told her that basically she was full of it. "No matter what she said to me, I didn't believe it," Geno says. "I said to her, 'Look, I've already lived your life. I didn't have the talent, but I lived it, growing up. Your parents have no idea, do they?' See, I conned my parents. Report card? They never saw mine, because they didn't know a kid brought report cards home. My mother never set a foot in school. I said, 'Diana, it's not my parents' fault they didn't know. They just didn't have a frame of reference for what it's like to grow up in America. The same with your parents. So I know who you are, and I know that's exactly why you're going to come to Connecticut because I know *you* know you've missed the kind of structure and discipline you can get there.'"

Diana didn't let on, but she thought, *I want to play with the best. I want to be a lot better, and who can help me? Coach Auriemma is the only one who has the nerve to challenge me.*

Another time Geno told her, "You know, Diana, you have a good chance to be the best player there ever was." She replied only, "I just wanna win." Geno liked that, so he let it go.

Still, there was Mrs. Taurasi. She got off the plane in Hartford with Diana, already mad that her daughter was visiting this crazy place, Backeast. And she wasn't going to cut it any slack. "At one point," says Chris Dailey, Geno's associate head coach, "Lili said she didn't like Connecticut because it didn't have enough traffic. I said, 'Lili, you gotta be the first person in history to complain because a place doesn't have enough traffic.'"

Lili told Geno, "I don't like Connecticut. It's too dark."

Geno said, "Lili, for God's sake, it's 10:30 at night. When it's 10:30 in California, it's dark there, too."

Well, Lili did soften a little because Marsiella Auriemma, now a widow, was there, and the two ladies could talk in a mixture of Italian and English. And Kathy Auriemma's eggplant parmigiana was a big hit. And when Geno pulled out a bottle of wine he'd found with the Taurasi label, straight from the vineyards in the Calore valley, that trumped any move any Anglo coach had made. But in the end Geno just told her, "Look, Lili, if Diana goes to UCLA, you'll be happy at first, but if she isn't happy, then you won't be. If she goes here, maybe you won't be happy at first, but when you find out how happy she is, you'll be happy for a long time." And then, in that way he deals with women, he put it head-on: "You know, Lili, we're recruiting Diana. We're not recruiting you."

Probably Lili already knew the jig was up. "She had to have known," Diana says.

After all, going across the country didn't intimidate the kid. When she was 11 her father, discouraged and homesick, packed up the family and returned to Argentina. The Taurasis lived there for a year, but it didn't work out, and they came back. Because Diana won't admit that anything fazes her, she says moving around didn't bother her. Argentina, Storrs—she could handle it.

When she enrolled at UConn, Geno told her again that she could be the best player ever. This time he asked her directly, "You want that?" Diana took a moment, then said, "Yeah, I do."

Geno says, "Once she said that, it was like a license for me to do anything I wanted to with D."

He just calls her D. Among themselves, though, the other UConn coaches call her Little Geno.

Diana Taurasi is not just hard to read. She actually looks very much like that other famous inscrutable Italian lady, Mona Lisa. Diana is friendly, outgoing and full of laughs, but underneath she doesn't let on, doesn't give in. In fact she still maintains that she had no trouble adjusting to Backeast. Her coaches thought otherwise. "She fought conforming to what the Connecticut ideal is," Dailey says. "She wanted it—after all, that's why she came here—but she was struggling with it."

Geno says, "I called her Eddie Haskell. Everything was, No problem. Everything was a lark. D will say, 'I don't care what anyone thinks of me.' That's her style. That's what she says, and that's her stren'th"—he says *strength* Philly-style, without the g—"but sometimes your greatest stren'th is your greatest weakness, and I knew there were times when D was dying inside."

Her freshman year the Huskies had the whole 2000 championship starting lineup back, but late in the season two All-Americas, Shea Ralph and Svetlana Abrosimova, went out with injuries. "D just decides that she's going to take on both of their roles," Geno says. "Now remember, she's a freshman. She hadn't even started at the beginning of the season. But she does it." Geno ran isolation plays, clearing out for Diana. She was the Most Outstanding Player of the NCAA East Regional.

Then, against Notre Dame, in the semis of the Final Four, disaster struck. The other Huskies were hot, but Diana was ice-cold. The freshman kept getting open, though, kept taking good shots...and kept missing. Notre Dame came back from 15 down in the second half to win going away. Diana made only one basket; she missed 14 shots, and when she fouled out, for once even Ms. Mona Lisa couldn't hold back the tears. Geno tried to console her. "Hey, man, relax," he said, grabbing her as she fled down the bench. "We wouldn't be here if it wasn't for you."

Amazingly, the terrible performance didn't haunt Diana. She'll even joke about it to bolster a teammate who has a bad game. "Hey, that's nothing," she'll say. "I shot 1 for 15 in the Final Four."

Bonnie Henrickson, the coach at Virginia Tech, says, "In many respects the most important game Diana ever played was that one against Notre Dame. That would have crippled a lot of players. With Diana, it elevated her."

"See," Geno explains, "in her mind it never happened. D lives in the moment more than anybody I've ever seen. The past is gone, and there is no future. It is only right now."

Anyway, after that came the wonder year. Taurasi's sophomore season UConn went 39–0; it really wasn't fair. Her four fellow starters, all seniors, would be among the first six players taken in the WNBA draft. The Huskies were on another planet. The *latest* lead anybody held on them all season was with 26 minutes to go. John Wooden said UConn was playing prettier basketball than any of the men's teams were playing. In the backcourt with Sue Bird, the college player of the year, Diana averaged 14.5 points. It could have been twice that. In a lopsided game she wouldn't shoot; she said she got a bigger bang from an assist than a basket.

What everybody says, one way or another, is that she *sees*. D sees things on the court that God hasn't arranged for other people to pick out.

In its own way, though, last season may have been more amazing than the golden gem the year before. The team was made up of Diana, some holdover subs, two redshirts and some callow frosh. The coaches were figuring six, eight, maybe even 10 losses. The first day of practice was a debacle. Afterward, though, Diana blithely bubbled, "This is going to be the ugliest undefeated team in history."

Diana had to do two things that were in utter conflict: carry the team yet build up the confidence of the other players so she wouldn't have to carry them. Jamelle Elliott says, "Geno kept preparing Diana for the double and triple team. 'You can't get frustrated, D. You gotta keep moving. You gotta make everybody else better.'" The Huskies started out winning. Then they kept winning. They beat Tennessee in Hartford, and a month later they took on No. 1 Duke in Durham. It was the first time Cameron Indoor Stadium had ever sold out for a *girls'* game. The Crazies came to cheer Alana Beard and the Blue Devils, confident of beating up Geno's kids and Diana. Coming into the game, Geno fed the Dookies red meat, ragging on their private-school elitism. "There are just as many Duke graduates working as waitresses as UConn graduates," he declared. "Of course, I'm sure Duke graduates work at better restaurants." The crowd hooted at him, pretty much ignoring the visiting players.

Diana loved it, Br'er Rabbit in the briar patch. "Duke was such a kick, man," she exults. "All the stuff those guys were screaming...." It perfectly illustrated what Auriemma tells his top recruits: "You're an artist, right? You need a stage. And if you think you're a great performer, you need the biggest stage. You wanna be on the stage in St. Louis—" He pauses, considering the possibility that someday there will be a player in St. Louis he covets. "I got nothing against St. Louis, you understand, but you wanna be on the stage in St. Louis or on Broadway?"

Certainly UConn is the Great White Way of women's basketball. "Everybody brings their A game against us," Diana says, licking her chops. All the home games are SRO. And many on the road, like Duke, bang out too. And in Durham, as the crowd screamed at Geno, Diana led the Huskies to a huge upset, 77–65. Her teammates were getting better, but they had to because Diana was injured and in pain. She had a bad back, a bum ankle and a foot problem called plantar fasciitis, which, in English, means *your heels feel like they're on fire.* Her coaches figured she was operating at only two thirds of her potential, but behind those searching almond eyes she wouldn't reveal anything. Sometimes Geno would force her to sit out practice on threat of being kept out of a game.

Geno has had so many All-Americas, but sometimes he would simply watch Diana in awe. "I love going to practice every day," he says. "I love watching the kids get better. I tell you what's worth everything: when one of your players says, 'I could never have been this good without you.'" But Diana was beyond that. It wasn't so much that he was coaching her as that she was channeling him. "I'll say, 'D, I've got this vision in my head' about, say, coming over the top, and right away she'll just say, 'Uh-huh.' She just sees it before I can say it. Not only that, but she takes it from where I saw it and goes to another level." Geno shakes his head. "Next year I'm gonna say the same thing to some normal kid, and she's not gonna say 'Uh-huh,' and then I'll know, I finally gotta forget about D."

For all she could do, though, Diana's injuries never really healed last year, and the Huskies finally fell apart—once, in the last few minutes of the Big East championship game. After 70 straight victories they lost to Villanova, but Geno convinced them that it was a blessing in disguise. Sure enough, Diana then led them to another national title. The year before, the Huskies had been a juggernaut. This squad was different. It was not a one-woman team, you understand, but rather one woman's team. At the buzzer of the NCAA championship game, Diana flew into Dailey's arms. "I get it, CD!" she screamed. "I finally get it!"

It was all stren'th now; there was no weakness left, Backeast.

Playing on teams was what confirmed young Geno as an American. Being a part of something, sharing the camaraderie. Team is sacred to him. He was actually best at baseball, but basketball "seduced" him, he says. Baseball was too much of an individual game for him; football had too many players. "But basketball," he says, almost in reverie. "Basketball. If just one fifth of the guys don't do their job, your possibility of winning goes down drastically."

He fit in on the team. "You see, that made me bigger than I was—and not just because I was only five-seven. I was satisfied passing the ball to guys who were open, helping out on defense. The team was what I lived for. I wasn't going to get the Diana Taurasi [glory]. I needed the team."

Geno knows it sounds crazy, but there is still a part of him that regrets that the military draft ended just in time to spare him from Vietnam. He would have loved being with the guys in basic training and in battle. "Look, I didn't want to get shot or anything, but...." But, you see, combat must be the ultimate game, platoon the ultimate team.

The UConn women don't wear their names on their uniforms. The coach has a long, semicomical explanation that he gives fans when they ask about it. But then he sighs and draws his finger across his chest and says, "The short answer is, It's all about what's across here." UCONN. One year, by mistake, the uniform company shipped the jerseys out with the players' names on them. The team voted to send them back. Geno says, "I tell 'em when I recruit 'em, look, after a big game you're gonna have to go into that media room, and you might be looking at 20 TV cameras, and if you win, here's what you say: 'I couldn't have done it without my teammates.' And if we lose, you say, 'I blew it.'"

Walt Frazier was Geno's favorite player. This figures. Frazier had this dichotomy to him. Off the court he was all show, the Beau Brummel, cool, hip, today. Clyde. But on the court he was Walt, the consummate playmaker, solid, controlled, classic. As a coach, for much the same reasons, Geno is very much an heir to Al McGuire. McGuire had the glib patter, the showman's persona. But on the court he was the opposite: conservative and controlling. Geno is much more adaptive in his strategy than McGuire was, but he has the same split personality. He's the snappy barker out front, but once he gets you into the tent, he's quite traditional, jammed up with values and do-right. On a team trip to Europe a few years ago the Huskies hardly ate any of the strange food prepared for them at a stop in Belgium. Geno marched them all into the kitchen and made them apologize to the cooks.

"I remember a few days after we won [the NCAAs], and I was sitting in his office when this fan came in," says Lobo. "She was gushing, asking us to sign all kinds of things, and when she left I made a snide remark. Geno snapped, 'Don't act like that, Rebecca. Don't ever be one of those players who don't appreciate.'"

He discovered his aptitude for coaching the way other people find out they can play the piano the first time they sit down at one. He had figured maybe he would be a history teacher. It was easier than what his old man did, working in a factory, and besides, Geno noticed that teachers drove nice cars and got the summer off. Then one day when he was 21, working his way through West Chester State, he got a part-time job coaching ninth-grade girls. It was an epiphany. "The first time I did this," he says, "I knew. It's still the only thing I've found that I'm any good at."

Coaching basketball?

"Yeah." He pauses. "No, I don't know if that's it. What I can do is, I can see what they can't see." It's a gift. His wife is almost scared by how intuitive he can be. "I always wanted to be one of those guys who could make you do something," Geno explains, which, in a nutshell, is what good coaching is.

He coached both girls and boys, but newly married to Kathy, he also tended bar, stocked shelves, taught gym and worked construction to pay the bills. When Phil Martelli, who is now the coach at St. Joseph's, turned down a chance to be the women's assistant at Virginia because he wanted to stick with men, he suggested Geno for the job. Geno demurred, afraid to venture into the world outside of Philly; the Big Five was his immigrant's glass ceiling. Martelli urged him to at least take a look. Instantly, in the baronial luster of Charlottesville, Geno was bug-eyed—"Me, a little boy from Norristown, at Mr. Jefferson's university," he says.

Debbie Ryan, who is still the coach at UVA, hired him for $13,000 a year. It might've helped that Ryan's a Natale on her mother's side. "Yeah," she says, laughing, "but it was evident right away how aggressive and bright Geno was. And he was well grounded because he'd carried the load for his family from a very young age. He has a wonderful working-class mentality, and he never forgets where he came from." Ryan laughs again. "And if you forget, Geno'll remind you."

Suddenly Geno, the hang-out team guy, had entered this parallel universe where skirts ruled. He had never been a ladies' man, either. Probably that's good. His high school coach had told him that a boy could be a student, a player and a lover—but only two out of the three. Geno had stuck with what he knew best. Now he was not only an assistant in a women's program, but Kathy had given him one daughter and was expecting another soon. Every day his life was like those red-light neon signs that blink, GIRLS! GIRLS! GIRLS!

Only a few male coaches who are wired right can make the adjustment and play second fiddle to the fairer sex. It is also true, though, that whereas male coaches never hire female assistants for men's teams, some women coaches have a special, practical reason for bringing a male on board to coach women. "I always want a man on my staff," Ryan says, "because a lot of players can use a male role model since they don't have one at home." The UConn staff is like a nuclear family, with Geno the daddy; Chris Dailey, his right-hand woman from the start, as the mommy; and two younger assistants, Tonya Cardoza and Jamelle Elliott, as the big sisters. "I told you how my mother was strong and self-sufficient," Auriemma says. "My thinking was that every woman must be like my mother, so ever since, I've tried to surround myself with strong, self-sufficient women."

Curiously, nobody attributes Geno's success to any variation on the theme of *being good with women*. Rather, the women he has worked with and coached conclude that he gets through to women because he gets through to people. *I wanted to be one of those guys who could make you do something.* It was just happenstance that he ended up coaching women, and although sometimes he thought the women's side was a dead end, when the head-coaching job opened up at UConn he applied. The Huskies were perennial losers. The women's basketball office was one small room with black rotary phones. The team had to share a locker room with men's soccer. During basketball practice the track team ran around the outside of the court, while, close by, weightlifters hoisted in time to their music. Geno thought he could use the job as a stepping-stone to a really classy program.

Pat Meiser-McKnett, who's now the athletic director at Hartford, was chair of the UConn search committee that year, 1985. Geno was only 31, and he'd never been a head coach anywhere, and he was a man, but he blew them away. "Geno was absolutely captivating," Meiser-McKnett says, "but there was also such subtlety, friendliness and warmth." In other words

Auriemma showed his soft, feminine side. The players told Meiser-McKnett that they didn't give a hoot what chromosomes their new coach had. They'd just like maybe to win for a change. UConn signed Geno for $28,229 at a Dunkin' Donuts.

He got in under the wire. Nowadays a man would have no shot at a high-profile women's college basketball job. The sport is too visible for such an athletically incorrect move. Geno is the last dinosaur.

Of course, the antimale process is probably being speeded up because of Geno himself. "I'm quite sure that women don't like me as the face of women's basketball," he says, cat-with-canary, knowing very well that the declaration will ensure that women will like him even less. "A kid like D, a program like ours—it transcends the sport. It's bigger than the game. We've gotten too good for our own good." It's instructive that even though the Huskies won another championship last year as a long shot, the (mostly female) coaches' association voted Gail Goestenkors of Duke, who coached the beaten favorite, coach of the year.

In 1989, back at the beginning, Geno had led the Huskies to a Big East championship and into the NCAAs in only four years, but he didn't get a single other coaching inquiry. Why was that? He cocks an eye, checking to see who just fell off the turnip truck.

Because you're a man? "Yeah." But then, as a gentleman of intuition who does not fear telling the truth, Geno amplified that. "Also, I guess I rub some people the wrong way."

The classic example of the difference between how males and females respond to coaching is, If a coach tells a women's team that some players aren't doing the job, every player will duck her head and think the coach is singling her out. If a coach tells a men's team the same thing, every guy will think, At least he doesn't mean me. "If my players think I like 'em, then I can say and do whatever I want," Geno says. "You've got to be careful how you phrase it, how you approach it. The difference with women is, they can't see that when you criticize something they did, you're not down on them personally."

Nevertheless, he can be a fierce taskmaster. He has always been especially hard on his best players, Diana most prominently included. The only All-America he eased up on was Nykesha Sales, whom the other coaches facetiously called Precious for getting off so lightly. But even Sales once spent a whole week so mad at Geno that she wouldn't talk to him. Lobo can remember the whole team getting so angry at Geno that Jen Rizzotti would call everybody together and say, "'Screw him. Let's just do this for ourselves.' Which, of course, was exactly what Geno wanted."

Lobo's mother had cancer her junior year. "Geno never let up on her, though," Rizzotti says. "Never. He'd call her 'the dumbest smart player I ever saw.' He was brutal."

"But the thing is, Geno couldn't do enough for me off the court," Lobo says. "He was always there when I needed him."

It is this dichotomy that befuddles so many of Geno's female competitors in the game. Why do his players—always "my guys"—put up with this smug, curly-haired little Philly smoothie who can be so sarcastic and rude and man-mouthed? What's the matter with these girls? Meg Pattyson, who played for him and then served as one of his assistants, tries to explain: "He's the kind of man I could tell, 'I got my period, I got cramps, I'm all bloated.' Or, 'My boyfriend's acting like a jerk.' You could talk to Geno about anything. How many men can you do that with?"

In '91 Pattyson was a stalwart on the first UConn team to get to the Final Four. The team was slow, but it had some shooters, so Geno just had them jack up threes. That was pretty revolutionary stuff in women's basketball at the time. With only a few seconds left, against Clemson, Pattyson botched a pass, and the Lady Tigers scored. Geno screamed for a timeout. It was the first time a Huskies game had ever been televised, and with the camera right in his face he yelled, "Meg, what the f---are you doing?" You didn't have to be much of a lip-reader to get it.

Pattyson went back out and made a spectacular shot to ice the Huskies' trip to the Final Four. Afterward, at the victory party, her father approached Geno. "Did you say to my daughter on TV what I thought you did?" he asked sternly.

With an angelic smile, Geno said, "I certainly did. I said, 'Meghan, dear, didn't your father teach you to come meet the ball?'" That got a big laugh out of Mr. Pattyson.

And that's the kind of crap Geno gets away with that drives so many of the women in women's basketball crazy. *Arrogant* is the word that's bandied about the most. And, just for spite: *little*. Geno topped out at 5'10". He's not only a man coaching women's basketball, but in a big man's game, he's a short-legged runt.

In 1998, near the end of Sales's senior season, she ruptured her Achilles tendon. She had scored 2,176 points, one short of the UConn career record. The next game was against Villanova, which is coached by Harry Perretta, another dinosaur. Geno and Harry cooked up a scheme: Let Sales score a basket at the start of the game, then a Villanova player would get a matching freebie, and Sales would go out of the game with the record.

When Geno told the team what was going to happen, Dailey says, "it was the first time since Nykesha's injury that the kids felt good." But when Geno and Harry pulled it off, there was a firestorm. The purists in the media went berserk. Where was the respect for the Sanctity of the Game? The genteel Guardians of Pure Sport who inhabit sports radio were especially put out. Thomas Boswell was in high dudgeon. *The New York Times* was aghast. *ABC World News Tonight* got on the hot story.

"You know, when it happened there were maybe 4,000 people in the stands at Villanova, and they all thought it was terrific," Geno says. "They gave Nykesha a standing ovation. It wasn't until the next day, when they read the newspapers and listened to the radio, that they found out that they were really all a------s."

"But you see," says Elliott, "he just thought it was right and didn't care what anybody else thought."

So much of Geno is still a reflection of his high school coach, Buddy Gardler. "I listened to him," Geno says. "My son comes home from practice and says, 'Hey, you know what my coach told me?' You think my son ever listens to *me*, even if I say the same thing? But kids listen to high school coaches." Geno sighs. "What I've tried to do, ever since I started this, since I was 21 years old, was to practice two hours a day as well as I can and learn something new about my players, so then I can go home and sleep well."

But, of course, he doesn't look the part of Old Pop Coach, taking the boys out for hot chocolate and cookies. What people see is *slick*. Or they hear that he's a sarcastic martinet in practice. Or they hear his wise-ass digs. For his "guys," though, that's just the guy in him. Cardoza says, "Arrogant? Cocky? He's not that kind of a person. Every player on the team likes him, and every player he ever had likes him." Come on—every? "Every. Because they all figure out that he has their best interests at heart."

"We all just liked him so much," Rizzotti says. She's a head coach herself now, at Hartford, where, she says, she bases "only everything" she does on the way Geno ran his show. "People outside don't know what a good sense of humor he has. You know, some coaches, you make fun of them behind their backs. We'd make fun of Geno to his face."

Also, most of them figure out that Geno really likes women. If you're in men's sports, who are you with all the time? You're with men, that's who. So there's just not much preparation for being with women—a whole lot of women. It can be a revelation. "Girls are much more concerned about the social scene," Geno says. "A boy interested in making the NBA, what does he care about anything in school but basketball? But girls need to know what pajamas everybody's wearing. Of course, girls tend to be more conscientious. *Tend to be*. But here's the main thing: Growing up, girls don't have as many jerks hanging around them as boys do."

You mean that's because boys hang around with other boys?

"Exactly. When you think about it, women are terrible judges of character, probably because they want someone to be better than he is. How many couples do you know, the woman is terrific and he's a jerk, and everybody wonders, How did he get her?"

Lots.

"Right. And then, how many couples do you know the other way round, where he's terrific and she's a jerk? How many?"

Not many.

"O.K., so what's the only possible reason for that?"

There are more good women than good men?

"Exactly."

Feminists come in funny packages. "You're married, right?" he says. "How many times have you gone and done something stupid and your wife says, 'But why didn't you think of it this way?' My coaches are the same. They give me the right approach I never thought of, and I go back to my players and they just melt in my hands."

On the court Geno assembles his Huskies. They stand there, surrounding him, 13 players, three coaches—16 women, most of them taller than he is, listening as he addresses them. Auriemma gives his orders and watches. Seldom is he pleased. On those rare occasions when he is, the dumbfounded associates refer to him as Mister Rogers. He passes quickly through that neighborhood. Sometimes he is caustic. Sometimes he sprinkles in barnyard words. His most scathing epithet, though, is "girlie-girlie."

Diana Taurasi says, "He'll pound away at you. There were times I hated to come to practice because it was so mentally demanding. He'd put you in situations where you couldn't win. But it's like he says: 'You're going to prove me right. Or prove me wrong.' And I'm always determined to prove him wrong. You see, you hate him in a way you need to."

Diana is forever intent, utterly engaged. Form three lines: layups, pull-up, cut off the high post. Rote stuff. Pass, then back to the end of the other line. Next time shoot, then back to.... But after Diana has taken part, when she goes into the next line, she shuffles backward. She doesn't want to miss her teammates even working a silly drill. Ms. Mona Lisa is always watching.

"Girls are dumb as rocks," Geno declares. "At basketball I mean. They don't play enough. I ask my players, 'How many days do you think a guitarist plays guitar? Every day. Well, basketball is your art. Do you talk the game every day, touch a ball every day?' D does. D's different. She plays all the time. So she's picked it up. I mean, how do you teach someone to stick her ass out when she goes up on a shot so she can draw a foul? D knows that. But most of 'em just don't play enough."

Implicit in all of this is the wistful belief that if Geno were coaching men, they'd all be as dedicated as Diana. And, of course, if he were coaching men, more people would take him seriously. He'd be *a coach* then, instead of what he is now: *a coach on the women's side.* Geno's trouble is that as much as the Huskies mean to him, he's always an outsider, the odd man out in a woman's game, an odd duck for not coaching men.

"I could do it with men for a while," he says. "For a while. It really isn't that different—what you're trying to do. But see, you try to teach a man something, he's much more inclined to view it as, *Hey, what difference does it make? What difference does it make if I come off a screen and catch the ball exactly like you tell me to?*

"I wonder too. I wonder if I were a men's coach, if I'd end up a p----like most of 'em. How many drill sergeants, working with 18-, 19-, 20-year-old guys, don't end up p----s, at work, anyway? How can you help it? Have I been spared that? I think so. I don't have to be a p----. I can coach and still be sensitive. See, over here, the players listen to you, they actually *want* to please, they do what you want them to do. Men's coaches have never had a situation like this. No, this is the perfect place for me."

But certainly there is a part of him that aches some, that would like to be Coach Geno Auriemma, not Geno Auriemma, women's coach. He goes to clinics and listens to the masters, men who haven't achieved anything near what he has but who've done it on the men's side. "I'm in awe of old coaches," he admits, tenderly. "I met Tex Winter. I just stared at him. Hubie Brown. Cotton Fitzsimmons. Johnny Bach. I could listen to them for hours. I love that. I'm playing golf with Jim Boeheim and I'm thinking, Gee, this is *Jim Boeheim* I'm playing golf with."

And part of it, he knows, is that very few of his male colleagues look back at him with that sort of admiration. If he hasn't been asked about this a lot, he certainly has thought about it a lot. Even for a guy with such a silk tongue, his answer is too perfectly framed by half. "Look," he says, "my wife thinks I do a good job. My players believe in me unquestionably. And my coaches. And I believe my administrators think I'm the best coach in the country. Then everybody else will tell you I just win 'cause I have good players. Ninety percent of the women coaches resent me because I'm a man. The other 10 percent appreciate what I do and are my good friends. Ninety percent of the men's coaches are jealous that I get all the attention I do for coaching women. The other 10 percent know me and give me a fair amount of credit."

Anyway, he'll be 50 on his next birthday, and he knows the cards have been dealt faceup. He must keep on winning with the women. "It's like that expression: A taste of honey is worse than none at all," he says. "I want more. I'm a perfectionist. Besides, I make an ungodly amount of money, so I'm supposed to win."

He looks around Gampel Pavilion, 10,000 seats. Every game, they all get filled up—as do the 16,000 for the Huskies' games at the Hartford Civic Center. He calculates the box office gross. The Huskies also have a five-year, $4 million in-state TV contract. Believe that? Women's college hoops: seven figures, in a small state. Geno, who is paid a base salary of $700,000, plus incentives, adds in the merchandise sales and the million or more he knows comes in for special contributions. "All of a sudden we're an eight-, nine-million-dollar-a-year business," he says. "We lose three or four games, it's like *what's wrong this year?* We lose four or five, I guess my family's gonna need police protection. And all this on the back of some 19-year-old kid who's fighting with her boyfriend, and she's got her period, and she has to make a foul shot. And then all of a sudden I start thinking, If I don't recruit this one good kid, is all this jeopardized? I mean, how much longer can it keep going up and up?" He lifts his hand, like a plane rising skyward, but in counterpoint he shakes his head mournfully. "It's gotta blow up sometime."

But you just won another title.

"Misery," he shoots back.

You mean, then, you've reached a point where you can't be happy?

"Yeah, you really can't be. Not for yourself. I'm just happy for the kids. I can't share what they have. But what I can do is try and teach them how to share it among themselves the same way I did when I was on a team."

He wins national championships with women, but it's still not quite as dear as it was to come off the bench as a boy for Buddy Gardler at Bishop Kenrick. Geno always throws a big party at the Final Four so his buddies can come, and for once it's not just Geno and his women. It isn't easy loving the team and being the head of the team but never being able to really be part of the team. "You know what I miss?" Geno asks.

He's at the head table, at a UConn alumni dinner in Danbury, where he had just wowed the crowd, cracking wise. All these fans of women's basketball. Wide-eyed girls with cameras. Adoring older women. And: men. Guys 40-50 years old who never even knew UConn had a women's team when they went there and are now cheering Geno, asking him about his plans for rotating substitutes and who's gonna bring the ball up, Diana or Maria? You're not going to get this anywhere else in America. And the season is still seven weeks off. This is what Geno has built. Only it's a house that he can't really live in.

Meg Pattyson, his old player and assistant, has come with him to the dinner. "So, all right, Geno, what is it you miss?" she asks.

"I miss being able to be with the guys. You know, hanging out, drinking beer, playing cards."

"Telling dirty jokes," Meg says.

"Yeah, all right. But you got it wrong. I'm talking about *hanging out*. You know how many times I been to a strip joint?" He made a circle with his thumb and forefinger. "Never. I don't need that, Meg. I'm just talking about hanging out with the guys."

It isn't easy being a dinosaur. "But I got one more year of D," Geno says, chuckling almost devilishly. "It's a timeout. I'm just talking to D. I look over at the other coach, and she's talking to the whole team. And I know—duh— we're better because I'm talking to D. Every day I'm gonna go to practice and just enjoy her from the first minute to the last. Then I'm leaving."

But he won't. It's too much fun getting up every morning and strutting into the bathroom and looking into the mirror with those baby blues and seeing the face of women's basketball, shaving.

APRIL 27, 1998

Show Time!

Is Kobe Bryant the second coming of Magic or
Michael? The playoffs are the place to find out if he's
truly a prodigy or merely a creature of hype

BY IAN THOMSEN

*No NBA compilation can be complete without a Kobe story. We could have
chosen a story from his title years; a snapshot after his sexual assault case
in Colorado; an examination of his competitive drive; an homage after his
final 60-point farewell; or many others, all worthy. But in this illuminating
Ian Thomsen feature we get the origin story of Bryant, hearing the classic
early tales—of West and Michael Cooper and Magic Johnson—and glimpsing
what's to come.*

Last December, before the Los Angeles Lakers' annual pilgrimage to Chicago,
the team's director of public relations, John Black, quietly warned 19-year-
old Kobe Bryant that the press was about to open public hearings into the
matter of whether he was, indeed, the next Michael Jordan. Bryant could
have gone into a slump right then.

"It doesn't bother me," he responded. "I expect to be that good."

Now he was really asking for trouble. For Jordan is the American Zeus, an
utterly commercial god who scores, plays defense, wins championships and
appears in the advertisements during timeouts. A few weeks after Bryant
had been interviewed for the position in Chicago (he scored 33 points,
many of them while being guarded by Jordan, who had 36), he was being

promoted on one side of a full-page newspaper ad for the Feb. 8 All-Star Game. On the opposite side of the page was the requisite picture of Jordan, his tongue dangling like a royal flag.

"I said, 'Cool,'" Bryant says. "It was like they were making it out to be some big one-on-one showdown."

Others were more concerned. "Wasn't Harold Miner supposed to have been the next Michael Jordan?" asked New Jersey Nets assistant coach Don Casey. Miner vanished from the league as if he had been caught staring at the Lost Ark of the Covenant. Grant Hill, exhibiting the wisdom of a Duke graduate, seemed to turn away from comparisons with Jordan at the last moment, but the unexplainable forces of the universe punished him nonetheless by making him play for Jordan's former coach, Doug Collins, the screaming Hydra.

It is because Bryant is so completely unaffected by fame that the league and its network partner, NBC, felt they could safely extol his virtues. In so doing, they almost turned him into the anti-Jordan. Western Conference coach George Karl benched him in the fourth quarter of the All-Star Game, and several of the older players—but then they were all older, weren't they?—were apparently fed up with everything Bryant stood for. Karl Malone recalled trying to set a pick for him. "The guy told me he's got it," the 34-year-old Malone said. "Like I told Coach Karl, when younger guys tell me to get out of the way, that's a game I don't need to be in. I was ticked."

"I still don't remember that play," Bryant says. "I probably did it—I'm sure I did it—but there's nothing wrong with it. I was just being aggressive. When somebody told me what he said, I thought it was funny."

It was not meant to be funny. It was meant to lump Bryant in with the prematurely rewarded nine-figure millionaires of his generation. Malone's complaint is that the league's young stars have walked into a vault of public goodwill and unmarked bills that was unlocked for them by the older players, and they are shortsightedly spending the principal when, really, they should be content just to live off the interest. Their preposterous salaries have given them a sense of power long before many of them have even contended for championships. When Malone, the league's reigning MVP, saw that he had been replaced on the All-Star Game marquee by a 19-year-old who doesn't even start for his club—well, you can't blame Malone for assuming the worst.

Bryant's second NBA season has been one long, inconclusive argument. His play since All-Star weekend has seemed to confirm suspicions that he is a creature of hype. In the 24 games between Feb. 10 and March 25 he shot an anemic 37% from the floor and averaged just 12.1 points, or 5.8 less than he had during the first half of the season. Not the numbers of the next Michael

Jordan. Worse, Bryant admits that some of his teammates have confronted him about being selfish on the court. Lakers coach Del Harris has vowed to teach Bryant a lesson about the "team game." Bryant "didn't learn it in high school, and he didn't go to college, so he has to learn it here," says the 60-year-old Harris. "The only way he can learn it is by reduced playing time until he accepts it." During one 10-game stretch after the All-Star break, Harris cut Bryant's playing time by almost seven minutes a game; by the end of the season the chastened Bryant was back near his prebreak average of 26.7 minutes.

But the playoffs are here. The haggling is finished. Over the last month the Lakers have been reinstalling Bryant into their offense with the understanding that they can't go far in the postseason without him. Harris worries, too, that they can't go far with him. The young man is being asked to fulfill his potential immediately. The Lakers need his creativity in the half-court offense, and yet they haven't married themselves to him for better or for worse, in good times and in bad. Will he be the Bryant of the first half of this season, full of energy and confidence, or the Bryant of the second half, who has been fatigued and criticized? The Lakers are going to find out the hard way, by running their engine at the highest temperatures without the proper testing.

Someday, Magic Johnson firmly believes, Bryant is going to look back on this season and realize that he is the only one who remembers his struggles. "People forget," Johnson says, as if speaking about himself.

The believers—Johnson, Jordan, Lakers center Shaquille O'Neal—exhibit the same faith in Bryant that they have in themselves. In him they see a self-made man, a prodigy who taught himself the game by correspondence course. Perhaps no player has ever made more use of his imagination. Compared with the older stars, Bryant seems to have been raised far away in a basketball convent. In truth he was.

Where is the incentive to improve if the money and the praise—the full-page advertisements—are lavished on players before they accomplish anything? Johnson looks at many young stars as if they've inherited their wealth; when they actually take over, he worries, the business he helped to build will fall apart. He was especially distressed by the uninspired performances by basketball players at the 1996 Olympics, in which no money changed hands. "A lot of these guys are not worthy and not deserving," he says. "They don't go out and do it for their country. They want the money, but they don't want the responsibility that comes with the money. Kobe is different. He wants all of it."

In Johnson's day TV was just becoming infatuated with the NBA, principally because of him and Larry Bird, and the new exposure made the games seem larger and made the players richer and more famous. That drove the league's profits ever higher, so that a player today can enjoy the life of a champion without winning a title. If Bryant is unique, it might be because he didn't see the game as a way to improve his life. He was connected to the circuit by his father, a former NBA player, and the things Johnson did coursed through the little boy's mind like the blood that pumped through the rest of him. At the same time, Kobe was isolated and sheltered from the excesses of the superstar life. His version of the American Dream differed fundamentally from that of his current NBA peers. They believed in the jackpot. Bryant grew up believing in the mythology.

"My wife and I used to prescreen movies before we'd let the kids see them," says Joe Bryant, Kobe's father. "We used to push the kids under the seat when the actors would start kissing." Joe and his wife, Pam, were still editing Kobe's entertainment a couple of years before he signed his three-year, $3.5 million contract with the Lakers in 1996. He didn't see *The Godfather*, his favorite movie, until last year. "It reminds me of my family," Kobe says. "Not because of the violence, but because of the way they all pulled for each other no matter what."

The Lakers were skeptical when the 17-year-old Bryant came looking for a job a few weeks before the '96 NBA draft. The league's successful high school prodigies—Moses Malone (who began his career in the ABA), Darryl Dawkins, Kevin Garnett—had been big men who were pushed ahead by financial and in some cases academic imperatives. Bryant was different. He was 6'5", which meant that, after playing basketball in the U.S. for less than five years, he was asking teams to wager a first-round pick on his chances of thriving at shooting guard or small forward, arguably the most competitive positions in professional sports. Second, with an SAT score of 1,080, Bryant could have entered most U.S. universities on his academic talents alone, and third, his family didn't need the money; his father had recently completed a 16-year playing career in the NBA and Europe.

When Lakers general manager Jerry West asked Bryant to jump, he might have thought he was watching a coiled spring release: Bryant touched the top of the backboard square. West then put him through a kind of obstacle course, pitting him against Michael Cooper, the former Lakers defensive whiz who used to guard Bird. Cooper bullied and shoved Bryant, trying to use his strength and experience, but the youth moved like a fish under water. West then introduced Bryant to Dontae' Jones, the star of Mississippi State's 1996 Final Four team who was also working out for the Lakers and would be drafted in the first round by the New York Knicks. Both young men were starving for opportunity. A ball was tossed between them, and everyone stood back. Bryant devoured the moment smoothly, like a lion with excellent table manners.

West turned to an aide and said with a buried giggle, "I've seen enough. Let's go." West, who calls Bryant the best prospect he has ever put through a workout, was so impressed that he arranged to send the Lakers' starting center, Vlade Divac, to the Charlotte Hornets for Bryant, whom the Hornets chose with the 13th pick. Freed of Divac's salary, the Lakers then signed O'Neal to a seven-year, $120 million contract, restoring the team to title contention for the first time since Johnson's better days.

The Lakers still aren't sure how Bryant made up so much ground so fast. "Kobe is at least as mature as any player we have now," West says, "and you cannot discount his family's contribution to that."

But how did a teenager learn the fundamentals so thoroughly while spending the better part of eight years in relative basketball isolation in Europe? The smartest general manager in the game has no ready explanation. He finds himself saying, "You watch Stevie Wonder and you marvel at how he and Ray Charles have overcome handicaps, yet they are wonderfully talented and gifted."

When Joe Bryant left La Salle in 1975 after his junior year to turn professional, it was because his family needed the money. "The rule back then was that you had to prove that you were in financial hardship," he says. He was a 6'9" forward with a guard's mentality, and he was chosen in the first round by the Golden State Warriors. He held out for more money. The Philadelphia 76ers traded for him, offering a reported $900,000 over five years, and that, he says, was that. "I was on the East Coast, so they put me under the basket," he says. "That used to be big, that East Coast–West Coast argument: If Magic had been in New York, would he have had the same kind of freedom he had in L.A.?"

Kobe was born a year after the 1977 NBA Finals, the premature peak of his father's eight-year NBA career. (Joe was a defensive specialist on the Sixers' second unit, behind Julius Erving and George McGinnis, as Philadelphia was dissected in six games by Bill Walton's Portland Trail Blazers.) Kobe, Joe says, "was named after a Kobe steak house in King of Prussia, Pennsylvania. But I don't know if I should say that, because they might want the rights to his name."

In 1984, after Joe had finished his NBA career with the Houston Rockets, he and Pam and their three children set off on a family adventure with all kinds of unforeseen benefits. They moved to Rieti, Italy, where Joe began his European playing career. For eight years, during which he played for four teams, he moved his family from one town to the next like an actor in the theater, settling wherever he could find a production that had a role for him. In the meantime his son was developing a romance with basketball that he might never have experienced in America.

Six-year-old Kobe was enrolled in first grade in a school in Rieti where his two sisters—Shaya, then seven, and Sharia, eight—were entering the second and third grades, respectively. Because they were just learning to speak Italian, they had to work harder than other students. Perhaps had Kobe been a star soccer player, he would have been treated as someone sacred, but his talent for basketball carried no great weight. "In Italy they told me, 'You're a great player over here, but when you get over to America, it won't be like that,'" he recalls.

Basketball became his private hobby, and he had little choice but to be humble about it. "After school I would be the only guy on the basketball court, working on my moves, and then kids would start showing up with their soccer ball," he says. "I could hold them off if there were two or three of them, but when they got to be 11 or 12, I had to give up the court. It was either go home or be the goalkeeper."

By U.S. standards Kobe and his sisters enjoyed an unusually well-rounded life: The streets were safe at all hours, and children mixed easily with their parents in the bright cafe bars. "In America, families break apart because the son has to take a job in South Dakota," Joe Bryant says. "In Italy you'd see whole families living in one big villa. That's what our kids saw. We would go have a meal and end up sitting at the table, eating and talking, for three or four hours."

The Italians were impassioned believers in their basketball clubs, carrying team flags and scarves and wearing their team colors. Fans would throw coins at visiting players, hop in place together, chant in a single voice or sing in a bellow throughout each game. Whether Joe was playing for Reggio di Calabria near Sicily or Pistoia to the north—the sorts of small towns where Italian basketball thrives—he was a cult figure, a 30-points-per-game scorer, the direct opposite of his role in the NBA. "They used to sing songs for my father," Kobe says, and in Italian he sings one: "*You know the player who's better than Magic or Jabbar? It's Joseph, Joseph Bryant!*"

"If we upset one of the big teams in Italy, I didn't have to pay for a meal for the rest of the week," Joe recalls, laughing. "One year we upset somebody, and the town was like a festival. So much passion."

During the week Joe would practice with his club twice a day, a time-wasting European custom, but for the first time in his working life he took his meals at home. His club would play every Sunday and occasionally in midweek. On Saturday afternoons he would take the family for walks into the mountains. On Monday, his usual day off, Americans who were playing for other Italian clubs would bring their families and meet in the nearest big city—Florence, Rome, Venice—at McDonald's. Sharia and Shaya remember making friends with the daughters of ex-Sixer Harvey Catchings, Tauja and Tamika, who are now basketball stars at Illinois and Tennessee, respectively. "I have pictures of them walking through Venice with Kobe," Joe Bryant says.

On weekdays after school Joe would take Kobe to practice with him, something he couldn't have done in the NBA. While the team worked out, Kobe would shoot baskets in a corner, like a shadow thrown by his father. Italian basketball cognoscenti still remember Kobe shooting around during halftime and being shooed off the court as his father's games were resuming. "The crowd would be cheering me," Kobe says. "I loved it."

"Sure, we were in Italy, but he was around basketball all the time, playing against older guys," Joe says. "He was always wanting to play my teammates, and, you know, the older guys, they would pretend that they were falling down."

"I used to set them up," Kobe says. "I'd say, 'Come on, you're playing a little kid.' Then it would come to game point, and they'd start getting serious, and I knew I had them. My father would be on the sideline talking trash: 'You're gonna let a little 10-year-old bust you up?'"

"I've never seen somebody who can see a move that another guy does and learn it as quickly as he can," Robert Horry, a Lakers forward, says of Kobe. "Usually it takes so long to get a move down, to learn the footwork. Sometimes it takes all summer. But he'll work on it, and two days later you'll see it in his game."

The videotapes used to arrive in Italy every couple of days, like letters from home. Kobe's grandparents would tape the biggest NBA games, as well as TV shows and movies, and Joe would receive tapes of other games from a couple of NBA scouting services to which he subscribed. In all he and Kobe watched the Lakers about 40 times a year. Joe loved seeing the work of an NBA guard his own size. "He comes into the league with all that fancy stuff, and they call it Magic," Joe told reporters near the end of his NBA career. "I've been doing it for years, and they call it 'schoolyard.'"

In a closet in the house the Bryants still own near Philadelphia is the little Lakers jacket that Kobe wore as a baby. Later he graduated to a Lakers letter jacket with leather sleeves. In his room in Italy was a life-sized poster of Magic Johnson. The Lakers were based more than 6,000 miles away, but that only deepened Kobe's appreciation of the way they played. Because the games he saw were on videotape, he didn't see them just once. He memorized them. "He would watch those games like they were a movie, and he knew what the actors were going to say next," says Shaya Bryant, now 20.

The play-by-play analyst for these games was Kobe's father. As they watched tape together, Joe would predict where the ball was headed and why, which made him seem like a wizard to his little boy. Kobe would sit in front of the TV and study what a player did with his shoulders, his feet, his head, as if that were the whole point of watching, to decide how the man was balancing his weight without betraying his intentions. "Genius at first is little more than a great capacity for receiving discipline," wrote the English novelist George Eliot more than a century ago. It may seem as if Kobe was analyzing basketball technique. But as far as he knew, he was just getting to know his heroes.

After watching the tapes over and over, Kobe would go outside, alone, and try to beat the world's best players at their own game, more dependent on his imagination than any kid growing up in America. As a result he gives credit for his fallaway jump shot to Hakeem Olajuwon. "My baseline jumper, I got it from Oscar Robertson," he says. "Oscar liked to use his size against smaller players. That's what I try to do." From Earl (the Pearl) Monroe he realized how to "shake one way, then go back the other way." In Europe Kobe taught himself the fundamentals of basketball. Not until he returned to Philadelphia as an eighth-grader did he develop a crossover dribble and other street moves. "I learned all my dribbling moves from God Shammgod [at summer camps]," Bryant admits happily.

All he had needed, in retrospect, was the firsthand experience of his father, access to videotapes and a basketball court free of soccer players where he could do his homework. He could not have developed in this way 20 years ago. There would have been no videos in the mail. For the fundamentals he would have had to go to college. If today he plays with a sense of joy, a sincerity, then he learned it from watching Magic Johnson and from hearing the passion of the Italian crowds who sang for his father. "I was like a computer," Bryant says. "I retrieved information to benefit my game." He could have been raised just as successfully in Australia, Iceland, South Africa—just so long as he remained within reach of his father's occasional loose elbow, which kept him from daydreaming too deeply.

"I didn't beat him one-on-one until I was 16," Kobe says. "He was real physical with me. When I was 14 or 15 he started cheating. He'd elbow me in the mouth, rip my lip open. Then my mother would walk out on the court, and the elbows would stop."

In November 1991, Joe and Pam were awakened by one of those dreadful 2 a.m. phone calls. Pam's parents wanted them to hear the shocking news from somebody they trusted. Magic Johnson had just retired from basketball after learning he was HIV positive. Pam and Joe talked it over, and in the morning, without mentioning Johnson's prognosis, they told their 13-year-old son that his idol had been forced into retirement.

They were living in Mulhouse, France, at the time. The boy was crying, and it took all the father's strength not to cry along with him as they took their 45-minute trip across the Swiss border to the international school the children attended.

"I was sad because Kobe was sad," Sharia says. "I never imagined feeling that way about somebody I'd never met. It hurt him as if it was a family member. For a week he was missing meals. It was really, really hard for him."

The Mulhouse club, for which Joe was playing, was shaky financially, and it was also time for the Bryant children to prepare themselves for college in the U.S., so the family moved back home a few weeks later. Kobe turned out to be a much better player than his Italian friends had thought. He launched himself into the American system without hesitation, joining the famed Sonny Hill summer league in Philadelphia. There a counselor scolded him for listing "NBA" as his future career on his application. "The guy said NBA players are one in a million," Bryant recalls. "I said, 'Man, look, I'm going to be that one in a million.' You see Magic, Michael—they made it. What's different about them? The whole thing kind of pissed me off."

No doubt Bryant was lured away from Duke, Michigan and North Carolina—his three college choices—by the prospect of a millionaire's contract, but the powers of his imagination should not be ignored. Jordan and Johnson were back in the NBA, and in Bryant's mind's eye, they were waving him onto the court. "I wanted to get in the league and play against those guys," he says.

"See, the kids in America, they don't do the work that Kobe did," Johnson says. "That's a problem with the young people now. They don't have the fundamentals." Johnson, now 38 and a Lakers vice president, says he learned about Bryant's special feeling for him "because of his family telling me some things after he joined the Lakers. I also knew because he was always calling here at the office, telling me, 'Let's work out,' or, 'Where are you working out?'"

A lot is made of Bryant's similarity to Jordan. He jumps like Jordan. ("Like Julius, too," his father adds.) He slashes and creates his own shots, much like Jordan (and Julius), and when he needs the extra moment to aim his jump shot, he can hang there, bent forward slightly, as if his shoulder blades have become little wings.

Every now and then, though less often recently, the Lakers turn the Bryant-Jordan comparison around. "Sometimes you say Michael could do things Kobe does," Lakers guard Jon Barry says, "and sometimes it's unanimous that he couldn't."

Sometimes Bryant even sounds like Jordan, answering an interviewer's question the way Jordan would. "That's a by-product of him studying those tapes," says Joe Carbone, Bryant's personal trainer.

Yes, Bryant has a personal trainer, just like Mike. "I just have so much energy," Bryant says. On a game day, early in the morning, he is usually in the gym with Carbone, lifting weights and stretching before meeting his teammates for the shootaround. Some nights he will call Carbone and arrange to meet him at a gym even though the Lakers practiced that afternoon. This summer, regardless of how far the Lakers go in the playoffs, Bryant plans to work out at least five hours a day, half of the time in the weight room, the other half on the basketball floor. "That's when I'm going to pick up my game another five notches," he says.

"It's going to be hard for him to do, because he's not going to get in a lot of quality games over the summer," warns Harris. "What he has to work on is his team game."

Wasn't this the same thing Jordan heard the first seven years of his career? Until June 1991, when he escorted Magic's Lakers out of the NBA Finals, the mantra Jordan heard was that he would never be considered as great a player as Johnson or Bird until he won a championship and proved he could elevate the play of his teammates.

Jordan was stubborn about it. He was the league's top scorer for four consecutive seasons without taking Chicago to the Finals. During the Bulls' five subsequent NBA title runs, he has continued to lead from the front. Bryant's circumstances in Los Angeles are different. By no means is the team built around him, the sixth man; in fact, he says some of his teammates have complained to him that he should be less aggressive on offense.

"If you watch Jordan, you'll see he's not looking for the spectacular play anymore," Harris says. "His highlight films are of him kissing the trophy."

Jordan, meanwhile, has been giving his protege the opposite advice, as he did after the All-Star Game. "We were talking, waiting to go into the room for interviews," Bryant says. "Michael said, 'It's important for you to stay aggressive. You just have to continue to be aggressive.'"

O'Neal has been offering Bryant similar advice. "When you look at the NBA champions, most of them had a one-two punch," says O'Neal, imagining himself and Bryant as that combination.

This debate—should Bryant be more aggressive or more of a team player?—is going to define his career. He is the Lakers' best one-on-one player, and his ability to create his own shot, as well as dish off to his teammates, will be crucial to the team's success in the playoffs. Bryant is under the most intense scrutiny, knowing that he will receive a large part of the blame if the Lakers lose. He will have to trust his instincts if he is to become the great player who leads his teammates to a title.

"I've been fighting the people around me this year, as far as them questioning my shot selection and how I should adjust to them," he says. He has adjusted somewhat. In a recent road game against the Toronto Raptors he could be seen looking first for the open man, receiving the ball in different positions and passing when he could—things often asked of less gifted players. But he also will have to be stubborn. If he continues to develop his vision, as Johnson believes he will, the Lakers will have to adapt to his strengths, on his terms.

Johnson predicts that Bryant will learn to read the game, to let it flow through him as if he were part of the circuit. "It's going to take him two more years," Johnson says. He has been of this opinion since the conference semifinals last May, when he watched the Lakers' postseason end in Game 5 against the Utah Jazz with four Bryant air balls—one on the final shot of regulation, three more in the disastrous overtime. It was as if Johnson were looking at himself on the TV screen. Twice in his first five years he was blamed for playoff elimination: in the first round against Houston and in the Finals against the Celtics. Each time Johnson recovered to win a championship the following year.

Last May, on the first morning of the Lakers' off-season, a few hours after the team's plane had returned from Utah, Johnson was in the gym at UCLA when who walked in but the 18-year-old himself. "That was just like me," Johnson says. "I loved seeing that from him. That's how I reacted, too. This is where he needs to be."

So it's settled, then. If the rest of us are forever trying to balance our feminine and masculine sides, the great basketball players are trying to bring their Michael side into balance with their Magic side. The Magic side is the one Bryant must develop.

It's certainly there inside him, circulating through him like something passed down by his father. It's the kind of personality trait that can develop only in certain environments. It wouldn't have grown on the East Coast in Joe Bryant's day, it probably wouldn't blossom in Chicago now, and it certainly wasn't going to bloom on the courts of Italy or Lower Merion High, which Bryant led to the Class AAAA Pennsylvania state championship two years ago.

"It could only have happened in L.A. for Magic," Joe Bryant says. "When Kobe was heading out to L.A., I was telling people, 'Look, what Kobe is living is a dream, and hopefully he is going to a place that still believes in dreams.' That's what L.A. is. You go around there, and everyone's searching for that big movie deal or trying to become a star. Then you look at Magic."

"I'm a positive person," Johnson says when you ask him about his health. He has been so aggressive and optimistic in his treatment that doctors can no longer find traces of HIV in his blood (which is not to say that the virus has disappeared). "Kobe's a positive person, too," he continues. "It's like God blessed that trade so that Kobe could come out here and be around a guy who can help him by sitting and watching him every night. I'm going to take care of him, but I'm also going to criticize him when he has to be criticized. Like the other night, when he went out and shot five or six or seven times and wasn't even warmed up. Those are the kinds of things he's going to have to learn if he's going to be what he wants to be, and that's the best ever."

So does a happy ending settle with the evening sun in Los Angeles? In his room overlooking the Pacific, Kobe lies on his bed and watches a videotape of the Lakers, as he has always done. But now, instead of studying Magic, he watches himself. He imagined his future so deeply that he made it come true. Now he studies how he is doing, asks whether he should have rotated defensively or passed to the open man, and sometimes he looks into the corner of the picture, at the big man sitting courtside in the rich suit, at the amazing sight of Magic Johnson watching him play.

Bryant knows that after this game ended, he returned backstage to the very locker that Magic used to occupy like a king on his throne. The Lakers say locker assignments are made by chance, but perhaps an astrologer would argue differently.

When Kobe comes out of his bedroom, it's as if nothing has changed. His parents are still living with him, by his choice; he is still only 19, after all. In fact, apart from the view of the ocean and the expensive fixtures, this might be any one of the places they rented in Italy. He didn't even have to leave home to make his dream come true.

"And if he keeps on growing?" Magic says, because Kobe is now 6'6", an inch taller than he was a year ago. "If he grows to be as tall as Joe?" That will mean he's as tall as Magic. "Then it's just over," Magic says. "Oh, my goodness."

NOVEMBER 9, 1981

Gifts That God Didn't Give

Larry Bird was blessed with his height, but lots of work made
him the NBA's most complete player since Oscar Robertson

BY JOHN PAPANEK

*An insightful portrait of Larry Bird—Celtics savior, long-range assassin and
a man who aimed to be unknowable. As Bird says in the story, "I just don't
explain myself to people. I want to keep 'em guessing. The way they take me
is the way they take me."*

Outside the gym it's a chilly and gray Brookline, Mass. evening. Inside it's
steamy and hot and marginally violent. It is the first of October, the last
day of a rite known as orientation camp, and eight players, including one
promising rookie and one has-been, are scrimmaging for their lives against
the home team from Hellenic College. The following morning the veterans
would check into camp, and soon afterward, most of the members of the
orientation class would be checking out. The veterans, after all, are the real
owners of the green jerseys—the World Champion Boston Celtics.

It is seven o'clock, and the real Celtics are at once celebrating the official
end of summer and dreading the transition from champions to defending
champions. No NBA team has successfully defended a title since the 1969
Celtics, so this last night of liberty is to be cherished. But not by Larry Bird,
who can't wait until morning.

His premature appearance in the Hellenic College gym, calculated, as
always, to be as unobtrusive as possible, is, as always, anything but. The

176

pair of worn sweatpants, the navy-blue sweat shirt and the blue baseball cap bearing the inscription West Baden Police that is pulled down over his straw-blond hair (but not his blue eyes) fail to mask Bird's truly, 6'9", ultra-white identity. There is a palpable skip in the beat of the practice when everyone realizes he is in the gym. All the would-be Celtics nod to him in careful reverence, and what they are thinking shows even more clearly now that *he* is here. Bird knows what they're thinking, but he wants them all to relax. He recognizes his responsibility to them, even though most will never get to play on his team.

"You guys gettin' your asses beat again?" he calls out in his southern-Hoosier twang as he sits down next to some rookies. The tension eases, and the players go even harder as Bird calls out encouragement across the gym from where Coach Bill Fitch has been hollering commands all evening. Bird salts his Herb Shriner Hoosierisms with a dash of Redd Foxx vulgarity and the players love it. Bird is a champion. He has proved it. But more than that, he is what the Creator had in mind when he invented the teammate. For this moment—and for this moment only—all the rookies and free agents and Larry Bird are one. Celtics. Eight minds cry out at once: "Please grant me the chance to play with Larry Bird!"

When the court clears and everyone leaves the gym, Bird ventures onto the floor, alone with a basketball and a goal to shoot at—a creature in his natural habitat if ever there was one.

He begins his routine by setting the ball down by his feet—lovingly, if that is possible—and then jumping rope vigorously for five minutes to warm up. When he finishes, he bends down to the ball, but instead of picking it up he gives it a hard slap and it springs to life, leaping up to Bird's hand like an eager pet. He never holds it, just begins striding briskly down court while the bouncing ball weaves itself intricately in and out of his legs. He quickens his pace from a walk to a jog, from a jog to a run—stopping, starting, darting, spinning. The basketball is his dancing partner, never causing Bird to reach for it or to break stride in any way. When Bird begins to feel loose, he flings the ball against a wall and back it comes, in rhythm. Off a door, off a chair... the ball seems to be at the end of a rubber band attached to his right hand.

Now he finds himself making layups, 10 with his right hand, 10 with his left. No misses. Then hooks from eight feet: 10 and 10, no misses. He backs away along the right baseline for 15-foot jump shots. He misses three in a row, and for the first time the ball goes its own way and Bird has to chase it. When he catches up with it, he flings it, a little bit angrily now, off a wall or a section of bleachers. Once, when he has to go way into a corner of the gym for the ball, he spots a small trampoline lying on its side. *Thwang*—he hurls the ball into the netting and it shoots back to him. A new game. He passes into the trampoline 25 or 30 times, harder each time, until the ball is a blur flying back and forth, powered by nothing but flicks of his wrists.

He catches the last pass from the trampoline, spins and shoots from 35 feet—and the ball hits nothing but net. Three points. Not only is the shot true, but the ball hits the floor with perfect spin and, bouncing twice, comes right into his hands at 15-foot range on the left baseline. With his body perfectly squared to the basket, the fingers of his right hand spread behind the ball, the left hand guiding the launch, he makes another jump shot. He moves three steps to his right and the ball is there—as expected—and he swishes another. He continues to move "around the world" all the way back to the right baseline, making 10 15-footers without a miss and without reaching for the ball. It is always there to meet him at the next spot. Then he goes back the other way and never misses. From 20 feet he makes 16 of 20, and then he begins all over again, running up and down, dribbling the ball between and around his legs, heaving it off a wall every now and then, putting it down for the jump rope, then calling it back into action.

After two hours of this, Bird shrugs off a suggestion that his performance has been slightly short of incredible. "Nah, I was really rusty," he says. "I've missed it. Being out there all alone...I've always liked it best that way. At midnight, like that, when it's really quiet, or early in the morning when there's nobody else around."

If Bill Russell symbolized the Boston Celtic ideal of humility, teamwork and excellence through 11 championship seasons, the torch was passed to John Havlicek, then Dave Cowens and now to 24-year-old Larry Joe Bird. Bird, in fact, carries humility to an extreme. He spurns publicity (and untold thousands of dollars) and doesn't enjoy sharing with strangers his innermost—or, for that matter, outermost—feelings. To some, he is every bit what he calls himself—"Just a hick from French Lick." He went through most of his senior season at Indiana State without talking to print reporters because, he explained, he wanted his teammates to get publicity, too. "When Larry makes up his mind to do something, nothing can change it," a Celtic official says. That intense resolve goes a long way toward explaining Larry Bird. "How do you differentiate the great athletes from the good ones?" asks Cowens, sitting in his athletic director's chair at Regis College in Weston, Mass. "It's a savvy, or something. Larry's got it. Something mental that other players with more physical talent don't have. If I were starting a basketball team, I'd look for a great center, but if I couldn't find a great one, I'd take Larry Bird."

The image of the dummy, the hick, is one more thing that Bird uses to his advantage, like his jump shot or, more to the point, his head-fake. "Like I tell people," he says, "I'm not the smartest guy in life, but on a basketball court I consider myself an A plus. Not that I'm dumb. I can keep up with 90 percent of the people in this world. I just don't explain myself to people. I want to keep 'em guessing. The way they take me is the way they take me."

This is the way to take Bird: He is the most *complete* basketball player to come along since Oscar Robertson. Bird may not be the best player—at least he doesn't think he is—but no one playing the game today can do as many different things on a court as well as Larry Bird. The year before he joined the Celtics, 1978–79, the team won 29 games, lost 53 and finished last in the NBA's Atlantic Division with the second-worst record in the league. In that season, Bird, averaging 28.6 points and 14.9 rebounds, led Indiana State from obscurity to 33 straight victories and the NCAA finals. In 1979–80, his NBA Rookie of the Year season, Bird averaged 21.3 points, 10.4 rebounds and 4.5 assists; led the Celtics to the NBA's best record (61–29); and carried them to the Eastern Conference playoff finals, which they lost to Philadelphia. Last year Bird averaged 21.2 points(he scored four fewer points than in 1979–80 over the 82-game season); upped his rebounding average to 10.9 and his assists to 5.5; led the Celtics to a 62–20 record, tying them with the 76ers for best in the NBA; and then averaged 21.9 points, 14 rebounds and six assists in the playoffs as Boston won its 14th NBA championship. Bird finished second to Philadelphia's Julius Erving in the balloting for the league's most valuable player.

When you thumb through basketball history to find the one player who could score, rebound, pass, play defense, lead a team and—this is Bird's greatest gift—see the court better than all others, your finger stops first at Robertson, the great guard for the Cincinnati Royals and later the Milwaukee Bucks. But then it continues, past Havlicek, past Rick Barry, past Erving, past Jerry West, past Earvin (Magic) Johnson even, and comes to rest at Larry Bird.

At 6'9", Bird, who plays forward, is four inches taller than Robertson, but height would seem to be Bird's only natural advantage over Robertson or anyone else for that matter. Bird looks like a soft, fleshy adolescent. He is slow as NBA players go, and in the words of an NBA scout—not the only one who thought Bird would be a mediocre pro—he suffers from "white man's disease." That is, he can't jump. How, then, can Bird be so great? "I would say my vision, my court awareness and my height are God-given," Bird says. "Everything else I've worked my ass off for."

Work—at least work on a basketball court—is what Bird loves. It has been that way ever since he was old enough to dribble a basketball up and down the hilly streets to the playgrounds of French Lick. Ind. Because his two older brothers, Mark and Mike, generally dominated the ball and the neighborhood games, Larry had to wait his turn. And when he got the ball—late at night or early in the morning, when no one else wanted to play—he would usually take it to the park by the old high school and work by himself for hours on end, just as he does now. Nothing else mattered to him but mastery of the ball and the game to which it belonged. When Bird gets into a game with four other players, his greatest gift—his court awareness—makes that unit work. He performs as though he not only sees everything as it develops, but also as though he sees everything before it develops.

"Larry is the best passing big man I've ever seen," says Celtics President Red Auerbach, who coached nine NBA championship Celtic teams and has been around the NBA since 1946. "Barry was damn good, but he wasn't in a class with Bird. This guy is unique. He's like a Bob Cousy up front, and Cousy, without question, was the greatest passer who ever played the game. Larry will probably go down in history as one of the great forwards of all time, if not the greatest."

Says Havlicek, "What Larry does doesn't surprise me because our minds think alike. When I watch a game I know what *should* be done, but 99 percent of the time it isn't. When Larry's in there, 99 percent of the time it *is*." Says Bird, "When my teammates get open I hope to God I can get 'em the ball. If you don't get 'em the ball, you'll tell 'em you seen 'em but it was too late. I don't know how many times last year I'd cut right down the middle and [Cedric] Maxwell would pass the ball a second before I was open. And he'd come right to me and say, 'My fault, I missed you.' It just carries over. And I know I might have started that. When you get that going, it means that everybody's always looking for the open man, and that's all they care about. The other teams better watch out."

What most impresses the people who know Bird—from his few new friends in Boston, to those in Terre Haute, where Indiana State is located, to the French Lickers who have known him since he was an itty-bitty thing with a basketball under his arm—is that nothing has changed him. Not the celebrity. Not the money—$650,000 per year. Nothing. The quintessential team player in the quintessential team game still wears blue jeans and baseball caps, and he still derives a third of his pleasure from being alone with a basketball and a goal to shoot at. Another third comes from being part of a team. "I've never known another player who is so loyal," says Celtic Kevin McHale. "If you're Larry's teammate, you're one of the most important people in the world to him." The rest of his pleasure comes from winning, mowing his lawn, drinking beer, hunting squirrels, fishing, playing golf, and being with friends and family. Those who know Bird have a saying: "That's Larry." And they always say it smiling.

"If I say Larry Bird is the best player," Celtic Guard Tiny Archibald comments, "people say, 'He's on your team, that's why you're saying that.' I still say he's the best all-around player. He does more things for us than any other player does for his team." Other Celtics echo Archibald's sentiments. Chris Ford: "Larry is a living textbook of basketball." Fitch: "I call him 'Kodak' because his mind is constantly taking pictures of the whole court."

Bird used to crawl into the nearest corner when people said such things about him. He would look down at his feet and, without thinking, mumble whatever words came first—anything to get these stupid questions over with and let's play ball. But during last year's playoffs Bird was the Celtics' most eloquent spokesman—after Fitch.

Bird doesn't receive star treatment on the Celtics—"That's the way I like it, too,"—and always heaps praise upon his teammates: "If it weren't for Tiny, for Max, for Robert Parish...you know, I could be out there but we wouldn't have won anything." They, in turn, heap praise upon Bird. Archibald says, "Guys appreciate his talent and what he sacrifices. We know he's the main focus on the team, but everybody on the team likes him because he's just Larry."

There is, however, another side of Larry Bird. When he gets loose, has a few beers and gets himself into comfortable company, he'll sit back, look up rather than down, his blue eyes sparkling and his face shining like a little boy's, and suddenly his Hoosier voice will become musical and full of confidence in his own marvelous talent.

"There are a lot of good players in the league," he'll say. "And on any given night any player can get hot and do anything he wants to. Some guys are very consistent and some guys are just great, but there are probably about 20 guys up there all the time. Now, I figure three out of four nights I'm going to play better than anybody else in the game. If you want to know who the best player in the league is, I'll put my money night after night on Kareem Abdul-Jabbar. He's the best. After him I'd probably take Julius Erving. And then, when it comes to a player who can do everything consistently, you'd have to say Elvin Hayes. There are just so many good players."

Bird is reminded of a stretch in the middle of last season when the Celtics won 25 of 26 games. "O.K.," he says. "I was playing great basketball for about a month. I reached my potential. For one stretch there, I was averaging about 28 points, 14 or 15 rebounds and seven assists. I felt like I had control of every game I played." But then came a nasty injury—one of Darryl Dawkins' massive knees caught one of Bird's comparatively delicate pink thighs just before the All-Star Game, and Bird's thigh turned ugly purple for two weeks.

"I've been hurt before, but I never had pain through my leg and back like that," Bird says. "It felt like my hip came out through my ear. And Darryl didn't even know he hit me! A while later I see him and he says, 'I'm sorry, Larry. I thought I felt something against my leg that night. I read in the paper the next morning that I hit you.' I never did get it back until the playoffs."

Bird didn't miss a game, though. Never has, college or pro. And when he "got it back," it was just in time to beat Dawkins and archrival Philadelphia in the regular season's final game. That win gave Boston a bye in the first round of the playoffs and Bird a week to let his bruised thigh heal.

Boston's first playoff opponent was red-hot Chicago—which had won 15 of 17, including a two-game sweep of the Knicks in a mini-series—and the Celtics dispatched the Bulls in four straight. "I made the best shot of my life in that series," Bird says. "Fourth game, tied up, their place, time out just before the fourth quarter and they got about 20,000 fans just going nuts. Coach Fitch says, 'Let's do something to quiet this crowd down.' We threw the ball in, messed around with it for a while, I made a three-pointer, then stole the ball, went back, laid it in.... We went up five within 40 seconds. I mean, that crowd just went 'Whoooo!' Stopped. From then on it was over."

After that it was Philadelphia again, and Boston's miracle comeback: Down three games to one, the Celtics rallied from six points behind with 1:51 to play to win Game 5; rallied from 17 points behind to win Game 6 at the Spectrum; then rallied from seven points behind in the closing minutes to outscore the 76ers 9-1 and win Game 7—and the series—91-90. In the final moments of that Game 7 Bird made two key steals, a couple of free throws, a crucial rebound, swatted a layup into Erving's face, then canned the winning basket on a 12-foot bank shot. "I wanted the ball in my hands for that last shot," Bird said after the game. "Not in anybody else's hands in the world."

The championship series against Houston was supposed to be a formality, but the Rockets extended the Celtics to six games. In Game 1, Bird executed a play that Auerbach called "the greatest I've ever seen." He grabbed the rebound after his own missed 18-footer from the right wing, shifted the ball from his right hand to his left in midair and banked it in as he went sprawling across the baseline. In Game 6 the Rockets came from 17 points down in the fourth period to pull within three with 1:51 left. Bird caught a pass from Archibald and, just as calmly as if he were all alone in a gym at midnight on the first of October, hurled in a three-pointer that put away the championship. "I didn't even know it was a three-pointer," Bird says now. "I caught the ball in shooting position; nobody was around, I just released it. Heck, when I'm open like that for a shot I usually feel like I can't miss it. And when I have a shot like that to get us a game [in this case, a championship], I got to take it because I know I have an excellent chance of making it."

Can Bird feel when a shot is going to go' in? And when it's not? "I used to in college, not anymore," he says. "For one thing, I don't like the basketball they use in the NBA [the seams on the pro ball are wider than those on the college ball]. In college I never had to worry about anybody blocking my shot. I could take my time. The defense is so much better in the pros. I always have somebody like Bobby Jones to worry about. You can never fake them out. You just have to make your move and shoot it quick. In college I followed my shot a lot. In the pros you can't afford to. If you follow your shot, you get burned at the other end. And there's one other thing...."

Bird laughs a little bit and holds up his right index finger. "This," he says. The finger is shaped much like a boomerang, permanently bent toward his thumb at a 45-degree angle. Two operations have failed to straighten it; he can bend it only halfway to his palm. "I didn't have this in college," he says. He broke it playing softball the summer before his rookie year, trying to catch a wicked line drive off the bat of his brother Mike. "Mike hit a shot that knuckled like nothing I ever seen and that sucker hit my finger and I dropped it. So I picked it up and threw to second base, only the ball tailed up and away and clear over the second baseman, and Mike went all the way to third base laughing like anything. I had to laugh, too, because I didn't know why the ball did that until I looked down at my hand and saw my finger broken at about a 90-degree angle."

How great a baseball player would Mickey Mantle have been if he hadn't torn up his knee early in his career? One wonders what kind of shooter Bird would be now if he had a straight finger.

"That's what Red was telling me when I was trying to sign," Bird says.

Larry Bird was born in French Lick on Pearl Harbor Day, 1956, and he'd just as soon let the personal stuff go at that. The folks in the beautiful old hillside resort town honored their favorite son by renaming Monon Street as Larry Bird Boulevard, and they acknowledge the fact that Georgia Bird had to work all her life to raise her daughter Linda, 26, and five sons, Mike, 29; Mark, 28; Larry; Jeff,17; and Eddie, 14. (Larry's father and mother were divorced in Larry's junior year in high school; his father committed suicide about a year later.) But they don't say much else. Close friends have been conditioned to say nothing more. Larry is a town treasure, and even though the townspeople would love to use his fame for their own fortune, as their elders once used the famous mineral springs to attract the cream of American society, they refrain. "I could tell some stories about some real nice things Larry has done but I wouldn't unless Larry said it was O.K.," says one close family friend. Another, a restaurateur, has thought of how his business would improve if he renamed his place "The Bird's Nest," but he knows Larry wouldn't go for it. "I'll say this much," the man says, "you won't find a finer person than Larry. He hasn't changed one little bit. He comes back here in the summer every year and doesn't want anyone to know he's around except his closest friends."

Mrs. Bird isn't working at the moment, and has been troubled with blood clots in her legs. She has worked in just about every restaurant in town and several of the factories. Her most recent job was as a dietary supervisor at a local nursing home. If you think the mother of a basketball millionaire shouldn't have to work, you don't think the way the Birds do.

"Larry thinks I should work," she says. "He believes everyone should work. That's how he got to be such a good player. My kids were made fun of for the way they dressed. Neighbor boys had basketballs or bikes. My kids had to share a basketball. A friend of Larry's would say, 'If you can outrun me down to the post office, you can ride my bike for 10 minutes.' Larry used to run his tail-end off."

Now that Larry has made it, Mrs. Bird says she has never had it so good. The only thing she'd like is a new home. "Just once I'd like to have one without scratches in the wall or a warped door," she says. But that's easier said than done. There was a house she would like to have had—which a friend had passed up for $55,000. Mrs. Bird called a broker to inquire about it, and said her son Larry would be home soon to look it over. Suddenly the price jumped to $80,000. When Larry heard about it, he told his mother, "If that's the way it's gonna be, Mom, forget it. We ain't gonna pay more just because I'm a ballplayer."

"That's Larry," Mrs. Bird says with equal measures of parental pride and puzzlement.

For Bird, the pain of public exposure has been great from the beginning, when all he wanted to do was play ball. He didn't know what to make of the college recruiters who came to town. No sooner had he checked into Indiana University in 1974 than he checked right out. Same thing at Northwood Institute in West Baden, Ind., a few months later. In his first 18 years Bird never was farther than 40 miles away from French Lick for more than a weekend.

When Bird finally found himself a home at Indiana State in 1975, it was only through the persistence of Bill Hodges, the assistant basketball coach who would become ISU's head coach in Bird's senior season. "If it wasn't for Coach Hodges, who knows what I'd be doing today?" says Bird.

"He'd probably be a bum," says a French Lick friend, "pumping gas or working in the Kimball piano factory like the other boys."

Bird never considered that basketball was something he could excel at and make his living from. "I didn't care either," he says. "I was one of those guys that never looked ahead. When I was younger I played for the fun of it, like any other kid. I just don't know what kept me going and going and going. I remember we used to practice in the gym in high school; then, on the way home, we'd stop and play on the playgrounds until eight o'clock. I played when I was cold and my body was aching and I was so tired...and I don't know why, I just kept playing and playing. I didn't know I was going to college until I was there. I never thought about pro basketball until I got there. Now that I am there, I want to make the most out of it that I can. I guess I always wanted to make the most out of it. I just never knew it."

Bird takes for granted that one doesn't think he's just talking about money. "The way I live, I'd be happy making ten or twelve thousand a year," he says. But his agent, Bob Woolf, thinks in other terms. In his office on the 45th floor of Boston's Prudential Tower, Woolf has one entire rolling file cabinet filled with Larry Bird business. Woolf, a prominent sports attorney and meticulous keeper of scraps of paper and lists, pulls out the hotel bill from Larry's first visit to Boston. "Look at this," he says. "Three nights. Nothing but room and tax. Not a room service charge. Not a phone call."

The chance for Woolf to represent this most prized client came after a bizarre series of meetings set up by a committee of Terre Haute businessmen who "adopted" Bird, and still advise him on his finances. They reduced a list of three final candidates to Woolf after an eight-hour session. When Woolf met Bird over a dinner with the businessmen, he did his best to impress. Woolf wanted everyone to know what he thought Bird was worth, and he shared his insider's knowledge of salaries of basketball, football and baseball players. Woolf mentioned Tommy John of the Yankees, who happens to be a native of Terre Haute. The men on the committee blurted, "Yeah! How much does Tommy make?"

Woolf was about to divulge the numbers when Bird piped up for the first time: "Hey, please, Mr. Woolf. Tommy John's a friend of mine. I don't want to know how much he makes."

Woolf keeps a list that chronicles hundreds of calls from people who want something from Bird, beyond the usual bank and shopping center openings: Mary Hickey, age 23, wanted to have lunch with Larry; the *Boston Herald American* wanted him for an article on Boston's most eligible bachelors; Bob Hope's people called; Ted Kennedy's people called; *Sesame Street* called; the Opera Company of Boston called. No, no, no, Bird said. Then there was the man who stole the hubcaps from Bird's Ford Bronco, found out whose hubcaps they were—and returned them. Bird sent him tickets to a game. He did a tacky TV commercial for Chardon jeans—Why not? Free pants!—and a commercial for McDonald's McChicken sandwich.

Woolf, meanwhile, waits for June 1984, when Bird's five-year, $3.25 million contract expires. "The Celtics dare not call one day before then, offering an extension," Woolf says, "because I'm dying to see what kind of money he'll draw on the open market. He could become the highest-paid athlete in the world! Certainly in the NBA."

Woolf has served as a surrogate father to Bird. When Bird bought a home in the Boston area, he purchased one right next door to Woolf's in Brookline, just two minutes from the Celtics' practice site at Hellenic College. Last summer Bird bought a place on Cape Cod—right across the street from Woolf s. But now that Bird feels a bit more comfortable in the limelight, he no longer hides behind Woolf. Still, his reverence for home, family and charity hasn't changed. He mostly stays out of Boston, preferring the sanctuary of his house, which he shares with a 3-year-old Doberman named Klinger and a longtime girl friend named Dinah Mattingly. He tends to his lawn and apple trees obsessively. His friends are chosen with caution; sometimes. Bird admits, too much caution.

"I'm not really shy, but it depends on what situation I'm in," he says. "I used to be real bad. I'm not the kind of person to go up and shake hands with somebody, because I'm in a situation where everybody wants to be my friend. I guess I miss out sometimes. I'm just accustomed to a small environment. When I was young, I was never around more than five or ten people at once."

Almost without exception, those people whom Bird has allowed to get close to him treasure his loyalty. He's great with children; for them, he will indulge himself in situations in which he wouldn't give an adult the time of day. His two summer camps—one in French Lick, the other in the Boston area—are strictly labors of love.

Bird's favorite camp was the one he ran at his old high school. Springs Valley, immediately after last season's playoffs. "I had 260 kids and did I have a blast with them," he says. "The kids are like...like you own 'em. I had to baby-sit 'em, put 'em to bed, talk to their parents on the phone. It was the first time most of them were ever away from home." The younger the children were, the more fun Bird had with them. One day he was a sight—going one-on-five against 7-and 8-year-olds whose flailing arms could barely reach Bird's belt-line. Still, somehow the little ones managed to win. "This ain't fair," Bird yelled. "I need help." So he grabbed another tyke, tucked him under his left arm and dribbled around while six small boys squealed in ecstatic laughter.

"Larry, you really ought to bring the media in here. Let them see how you play with these kids," said a friend who was looking on.

"Never," said Bird. And that was that.

He supplied entire teams of French Lick youngsters with clothing and equipment. And he also has—though he would rather not have it known—a compelling affinity for the physically handicapped. "He's got an incredible memory," Woolf says. "If I told him something a year ago and change one word today, he'll catch me. He'll play a golf course once and memorize the location of every tree. I can go to a game and swear that Larry never saw me, and days later he'll tell me in which section I was sitting, who I was talking to, what I was wearing."

Woolf recalls that when a *Today* show crew came to tape a segment on Bird shortly after last May's playoffs, they wanted to show Larry watching a replay of the championship game against Houston. They threw the videotape on at a random point in the game and Woolf asked Bird if he could tell what part of the game was showing.

"Fourth quarter, 5:40 left," said Bird.

"How can you possibly be that precise?" Woolf asked. There had been no commentary and no score flashed.

"The song," Bird said.

"The song!" Woolf said.

"That fight song. That's the last time they played it. They played it three times during the game. This is the last time because the crowd is going nuts. Houston came from 17 down and there's about 5:40 left."

"You mean you were aware of the song?" Woolf asked incredulously.

"I was there, wasn't I?" Bird asked.

"I was there, too, but I don't remember any song," Woolf said. "And I wasn't playing."

Bird chuckled and went on watching the tape. He proceeded to call each play in perfect detail, about five seconds before it appeared on the tape.

"Larry's not subject to the normal persuasions," Woolf says. "He doesn't react to things the way normal people do."

But he did last spring. Four days after the Celtics won their championship, the financially beleaguered city of Boston turned out en masse to honor its team. Bird told a cheering crowd on City Hall Plaza, "I spent ten minutes in the Mayor's office with all these people going around getting autographs, and now I know why Boston is going bankrupt."

There was some nervous laughter, but Bird wasn't finished. Someone in the crowd held up a sign that made a scatological reference to Moses Malone, the Houston center. Bird spotted it and announced to the throng, "I think, after all the hollering and screaming, I look out in the crowd and see one thing that typifies our season. Moses does eat——!"

Bird later apologized to those he offended, including Malone, but it never occurred to him that the remark would be offensive. "That's me," he says with an impish grin. "I've said a lot of things I wished I never had, but hey, that's me. I'll do a lot more before I get older. There's nothing I can do about it once I've done it. What people think of me could hurt a little if they think bad. I'm sure there are people in this world who hate me, but there are a lot who love me. I'm just me. I try to be honest.

"Like I told this friend of mine in Terre Haute before I came into the pros: 'One of these days I'll be the best basketball player in the NBA.' I was with the guy last June after it was announced that Julius Erving won the MVP. First thing this guy says to me is, 'Well, hell! You lied to me again! You been in the league two years already and you haven't even come close.' I said, 'Well, maybe this year.'"

That's Larry.

NOVEMBER 18, 1963

'We Are Grown Men Playing a Child's Game'

The bearded man laughing at his daughter is Bill Russell, the most remarkable basketball player of our time. Sport, however, is one of his lesser interests. Here are his trenchant, often angry observations on today's Negro-white crisis and his role in it

BY GILBERT ROGIN

It's been 60 years since this story came out. Rogin was only 33 at the time and had just had his first piece of short fiction published in The New Yorker. *Here, he gives Russell the space to be himself, accepting him without judgment. (The story would hold up well enough that* Hang Up and Listen, *the excellent* Slate *podcast, devoted part of a 2020 episode to discussing it.)*

In hindsight, the piece serves as a reflection of the America that existed in the early 1960s. It also provides a glimpse into the mind of one of the most outspoken, and thoughtful, men to ever play.

Bill Russell, the dark, gainly and responsible man who is center and co-captain of the Boston Celtics, the perennial champions of the National Basketball Association, is, without question, one of the most remarkable athletes of our time, yet he regards his life up to now as a waste. "I don't consider anything I have done," he has said, "as contributing to society. I consider playing professional basketball as marking time, the most shallow thing in the world." Russell is not biting the hand that feeds him and his family; he is too canny and practical a man. He is not sullying basketball in any meaningful sense, either. It is, rather, that he is close to 30 years old and has made certain judgments that seem to him so correct and obvious that he is not afraid to enunciate them: basketball, or any other sport, is, at bottom, frivolous, and the imposition of being a Negro at this moment in history is an obligation that cannot be met on the floor of the Boston Garden. Where and how he can fulfill it Russell does not yet know.

In six full seasons with the Celtics, Russell has been selected four times by the players in the league as the NBA's most valuable player, including the last three years in succession; on the other two occasions he was runner-up. Before Russell joined the Celtics late in 1956, they had led the league in scoring for the five foregoing years but, nonetheless, each year the Celtics had been eliminated in the divisional playoffs. In Russell's tenure Boston has won six of seven championships. The only year it lost out—1958—Russell was injured during the final playoff series and did not play in two of the last three games. His contributions to his team's welfare are, however, often unsung. Not long ago, for instance, it was—who else?—Russell who found a teammate's contact lens on the court. "Do I have to do everything for this club?" he said, with an indulgent smile.

What makes Russell's achievements most noteworthy is that he is primarily a defensive player in what, prior to his time and success, was threatening to become an almost wholly offensive game. "Basketball," says Red Auerbach, the Boston coach, "is like war, in that offensive weapons are developed first, and it always takes a while for the defense to catch up. Russell has had the biggest impact on the game of anyone in the last 10 years because he has instituted a new defensive weapon—that of the blocked shot. He has popularized the weapon to combat the aggressive, running-type game. He is by far the greatest center ever to play the game." By Russell's own admission, he can block shots only 5% of the time, and even less frequently against such gifted shooters as Elgin Baylor and Oscar Robertson. What makes him such a formidable and dominant figure is, as he says, that "they don't know which 5% it will be."

Says Bill Russell: "Basketball is a game that involves a great deal of psychology. The psychology in defense is not blocking a shot or stealing a pass or getting the ball away. The psychology is to make the offensive team deviate from their normal habits. This is a game of habits, and the player with the most consistent habits is the best. What I try to do on defense is to make the offensive man do not what *he* wants but what *I* want. If I'm back on defense and three guys are coming at me, I've got to do something to worry all three. First I must make them slow up or stop. Then I must force them to make a bad pass and take a bad shot and, finally, I must try to block the shot. Say the guy in the middle has the ball and I want the guy on the left to take the shot. I give the guy with the ball enough motion to make him stop. Then I step toward the man on the right, inviting a pass to the man on the left; but, at the same time, I'm ready to move, if not on my way, to the guy on the left. I'm giving away all my secrets."

"What Russell really does," says teammate Tommy Heinsohn, "is demoralize. The other players are afraid to take their normal shots. Instead, they're looking to see what Russell will do." As Bill Bridges of the St. Louis Hawks said recently, "Russell told me I better bring pepper and salt to the next game. He told me I was going to eat basketballs." Indeed, the ball has come to be known by the pros as a Wilson burger, after its manufacturer.

"In my modest opinion," says Russell, who is not a particularly good shooter, "shooting is of relatively little importance in a player's overall game. Almost all of us in the NBA are All-Americas. We became All-Americas by averaging 20 points or more a game, so by the layman's standards all of us can shoot. It's the other phases of the game that make the difference. If you're going to score 15 and let your man score 20 you're a deficit. If your value to the team is strictly as a shooter, you are of very little value. Offense is the first thing you learn as a kid in any sport: catch a pass, dribble, bat, shoot. You learn the offensive aspects of a game long before you learn there even are defensive aspects. These are the skills you come by naturally. Defense is hard work because it's unnatural.

"Defense is a science," Russell says, "not a helter-skelter thing you just luck into. Every move has six or seven years of work behind it. In basketball your body gets to do things it couldn't do in normal circumstances. You take abnormal steps, you have to run backward almost as fast as you can run forward. On defense you must never cross your legs while running, and that's the most natural thing to do when changing direction. Instead, you try to glide like a crab. You have to fight the natural tendencies and do things naturally that aren't natural.

"In rebounding, position is the key. No two objects can occupy the same place at the same time. Seventy-five percent of the rebounds are taken below the height of the rim, so timing is important, because almost everyone in the league can reach the top of the rim. A really important part of rebounding is being able to jump up more than once. You have to keep trying for that ball. Sometimes you jump four or five times before you can get your hands on it. I used to practice jumping over and over again. When I was 6 feet 2, I could jump to the top of the rim 35 times, over and over.

"You have to have strong hands. Most of the time three guys will have their hands on the ball at the same time, and you have to be able to grab it away. I guess I just naturally have strong hands, but if I didn't I would exercise until they were strong. But getting the ball is only half the job. Then you have to do something with it."

The foundation of Russell's brilliant play, however, is not blocking shots, rebounding or his other purely physical skills. It is, rather, his admirable mind and purpose, his intelligence—he knows what to do with the ball—and his pride. "People don't realize," says Auerbach, "that this is a brain out there. People think of him as just a big guy with fantastic coordination, but he approaches being a genius once the game starts. I admire his mind off the court, too," Auerbach adds not entirely facetiously, "because he's smart enough to understand me."

"To sum it all up," says Heinsohn, "he's got a hell of a lot of pride. When he's playing his game it makes us almost unbeatable, and the secret to the thing is that he gets himself up so often. He's so nervous before a game he upchucks."

"He wants to be the best in everything he does," says Co-Captain Frank Ramsey. "He hates to lose. As long as the team's winning he's completely happy. As long as he's playing real great ball we're winning. Then he's the life of the party. You hear that laugh 10 miles around. He's only moody with himself."

Although Bill Russell has much to laugh about and does in his high, rackety way ("There are only two things that could make me quit coaching," says Auerbach. "My wife and Russell's laugh"), he is, at intervals, an angry, dissatisfied and aloof man of uncommon principle, and is no less remarkable as a person than he is as an athlete.

Russell's scraggly beard is a telling indication of the man. Not only is Russell nearly 6 feet 10 and black—circumstances, obviously, over which he has no control—but he has deliberately set himself further apart by being one of the few professional athletes to wear a beard. Ask him why he grew it and he will reply in time, if he feels like it: "I've thought about it, and I've thought about it. Why did I wear the beard, why do I? It's part of this thing—I've always fought so hard to be different and I am different without even trying, and maybe it's just my own little revolution. It just isn't done in polite circles, in a sense. But I do think it's part of my personality. When I first joined the Celtics I shaved the beard off. I did it on my own. It was none of their business, and if I had valued their opinion I would have asked them. I made a concession to conformity at that time. Then I grew it back. After we won the first championship I let Heinsohn shave it off, and then I grew it back again. It was a very childish thing, in the sense of defiance. I wear it now to let people know I am an individual. I do think for myself, and I'm very opinionated. Contrary to popular belief, I'm a living, thinking, breathing human being."

"They say I owe the public this and I owe the public that. What I owe the public is the best performance I can give, period. If someone asks me for an autograph I think it's a waste, but I sign them occasionally. Sometimes I just feel like being nice, or it gets rid of them. I personally don't care what people think of me. I don't think I think any different than anyone else, but I may act different. One thing I'm not is a liar. It's not a matter of morals—more a matter of ego. I think too much of myself to misrepresent myself. I'll do anything I can for anyone as long as it doesn't hurt me. But I have sympathy for very few people. Basketball—that's all people want to talk to me about. It's a waste, because they have nothing to say. I resent people who talk to you and have nothing to say. So I don't say anything. 'How's the weather up there?' 'How are things on Main Street?' That's where I live. What the heck kind of question is that? "You must be a basketball player, because you're so tall. Just walk up and put it in, eh?' No, I'm not a basketball player. I just kept growing. 'What size bed do you sleep in?' I hate for people to get personal. A big bed. 'How much do you eat?' It's ridiculous. If you mind your own business, life ain't bad. If you do the best you can that's the best you can do.

"We're a bunch of grown men playing a child's game. It's a child's game we've made into a man's game by complicating it. Silly, isn't it? We entertain people for x number of hours during the winter. They may talk about it for a few minutes, maybe an hour; then it's forgotten. Is this a contribution? No. Analyze it—it's a silly game. I'm also a silly man because I enjoy it. I enjoy baseball, too. Perhaps I'm a little dull."

It is not easy for a white man to understand or totally accept the vision of a black man; skin is the hardest boundary. The point is this: Bill Russell, or any other black man like him, does not want the white man's sympathy or, indeed, his friendship. What he wants is recognition and acceptance of himself as an individual, a black individual, who can meet the world on equal terms and fare unequally, according to his merit.

"A few things have happened," Russell says. "I've got three kids now, a certain amount of responsibility to them. I also have a certain amount of responsibility to a lot of other kids. I give most Negroes a certain amount of pride. Here's one of our guys doing all right, they say, the world can't be all bad. That contribution is very shallow. Of course, I'm practical. Where else but in basketball could I command this salary? [It is estimated in excess of $40,000.] Man does what he has to, but the contribution I'd like to make as a person—to my kids and little black kids all over the world—is to make life better, so their ambitions aren't stifled when they face the world, to give them the opportunity to do what they're most skilled at. I could have a burning ambition to give my kids a million dollars. If I gave them that alone, I'd be giving them nothing."

"The most any kid can ask for," says Russell, "is to succeed or fail on his merits. Success and failure are relative. Everyone doesn't have presidential abilities and everyone can't be an All-America. It doesn't necessarily mean you're a failure. My father's a foundry worker. This doesn't necessarily mean he's a failure—because another person's father is a lawyer. Society needs both. Some people are going to be laborers, but why say a man has to be a laborer because he's black? One right we never had in this country—we never had the right to be a failure or an individual. Why if one black man fails should all black men fail? That's what the struggle is about; whether it's through love, as with Martin Luther King, or through pride, as with the N.A.A.C.P., or through hate, as with Malcolm X and Elijah Muhammad.

"What does the American Negro want? the editorials ask. I find this very stupid. We're all products of our society, and the acceptable standards are the same. We want the same things. When they write about Birmingham, the papers refer to 'outsiders' and 'racial agitators.' To the black people of the U.S. there is no such thing as an outsider. There's been too much play on words in this country. Negroes have to earn their rights, they say. My oldest son, Buddha [William Felton Russell Jr.], was born on November 2, 1957. Suppose 50 kids were born around Boston that day. Why does my son have to earn any more than any of those 50 kids? I was born on February 12, 1934. Why do I have to earn more than anyone else?

"There used to be a lot of emphasis on the first Negro to do this, the first Negro to do that. It's unimportant who's the first or who's the last. The important thing is—how many? The rest is tokenism. When Thurgood Marshall was made a judge it made me feel real good, because he never attempted to disassociate himself, like some educated Negroes. Some Negroes live in a twilight zone, closing themselves off into a small, white society. The Negro world doesn't concern them. I feel sorry for them—to an extent. Education is the acquiring of the ability to think for oneself; anyone can get through college on memory courses. If a Negro judge says, 'I don't think of myself as a Negro, just as a competent judge,' he's not facing life the way it is in our society. It's harder to face it the other way, but you can sleep at night—every night."

Although everyone in his family is a life member of the N.A.A.C.P., Russell has not played a major role in any single Negro organization; he does not look upon himself as a leader, and is uncomfortable in crowds. He views the

Negro movement as being various in means but single in aim, and feels that its factionalism is not divisive but a search for the most effective way.

"I would have loved to go to Birmingham," Russell says, "but I'm not passive. Sometimes I think I have tendencies to violence. I've been mad enough to fight three times in my life, and each time I wanted to kill the man. You know the athletes I admire? Ted Williams, Jackie Robinson and Sonny Liston. It's easy to be easygoing and friendly to everyone. I think a man has to be what he is. If he feels good, he is good; if he doesn't, he isn't. I'm an admirer of Floyd Patterson, too. These are honest people in the sense of representing themselves. Some Negro athletes don't show me much. I'm disappointed in them. They are politicians in the sense of saying the right things all the time.

"If I went down there to Birmingham and let someone spit on me and didn't do anything about it, it wouldn't be me. If you never really express dissatisfaction concretely, people tend to ignore it. If you believe in something you've got to say it. This passive kick—if it doesn't work, how can they keep preaching it? It is predicated on the premise that people are basically moral. If they are right, this is wonderful. If they are wrong, the religious phase of the movement will be destroyed. If Martin Luther King is wrong he has failed as a leader. Maybe I'm becoming a fatalist or whatever you call it. Morality is a very large word. Morality and love have a lot in common. Who can really define it? What is moral and what is immoral? It is relative.

"I've been reading about the Black Muslims. A lot of things they say express the way I feel perfectly, or, rather, a great deal of the things they say I cannot disagree with. Can the races get along? Yes. Will they get along? That's the question. The Muslims say the white man's a devil. I don't agree with that, because I don't think there is such a thing as a devil. They say the white man is evil. I wonder about that in the sense that I wonder whether all men are evil. I dislike most white people because they are people. As opposed to dislike, I like most black people because I am black. I consider this a deficiency in myself—maybe. If I looked at it objectively, detached myself, it *would* be a deficiency."

In 1959 Russell first went to Black Africa on a tour for the State Department. The continent had such an impact upon him that he bought part ownership of a rubber farm in Liberia and named his baby daughter Karen Kenyatta after Jomo Kenyatta, the prime minister-designate of Kenya and onetime Mau Mau leader, whom Russell greatly admires. Russell is thinking quite seriously of settling in Liberia. "I found a place I was welcome because I was black instead of in spite of being black," he says.

"The basic problem in Negro America is the destruction of race pride. One could say we have been victims of psychological warfare, in a sense, in that this is a white country and all the emphasis is on being white. Whiter than white. According to the law, immigrants from northern European countries are more desirable than any others. When a white man says his folks come from Ireland, he says it with a certain amount of pride. He probably can trace his family tree for generations, for whatever it's worth. This is not true of the American Negro. Until the emergence of the independent African countries all we knew about Africa was from the Tarzan and Jungle Jim movies. How stupid they made the natives! One white man—Tarzan—was the best and smartest at everything. Even King Kong, after accepting the sacrifice of blacks for years, when he was offered a white girl he didn't kill her. He fell in love with her! Pride in being black was practically destroyed by seeing stupid things like this; there was almost a sense of self-degradation. Also, until very recently, the so-called Negro elite was fair-skinned.

"The problem I see in Africa is that it has to build a middle class. All your great political and social changes have been brought about by the middle class—merchants, artisans, technicians. Africa's needs are not necessarily administrators but people who can do—plumbers, tool-and-die-makers, draftsmen. Black Africa is stepping from carrying things on the head to carrying them in airplanes. They've skipped the wheelbarrow, the horse and buggy and, practically, railroads. They have problems so immense, where do you start? You educate as many as you can. But everyone who gets an education wants to be an administrator. People have to realize there are stations in life, forms of success. Everyone wants to have the ultimate success. Everyone can't have it. Someone must roll their sleeves up and go to work. I find it a very perplexing problem, whether I should go to Africa or stay here. I've thought about it a great deal. If my contribution would be more concrete here, no doubt I should stay here.

"When I look at the struggle of the American Negro I can't help but be very, very proud. With what we've had to work with we've done a pretty good job of surviving. But we still have so far to go.... It would be a hell of a country.... It's a great country as it is. Now we have to define great; an ambiguous word. Great industrial empire, standard of living.... I think it would be so much greater if everyone had an equal opportunity in every field. There is no way to speculate how much brainpower this country has lost. And we don't have to like each other to live together peacefully and equally. Have you ever read how in the time of drought all the animals use the same water hole? The lions stay with the lions, the tigers with the tigers, the elephants live with elephants, but they all use the same water hole."

Of course, because of his wealth and position, Russell's experiences do not parallel those of most black men most of the time. He lives on a white block in a white town, has white baby-sitters and drives a 1964 Lincoln Continental convertible. The fact that owning a big car is considered a Negro stereotype does not concern Russell. "I've passed the stage," he says, "where I have to prove anything. I happen to like watermelon, too. There may come a time when I have to ride a bicycle. It won't bother me. It just won't be as fast or convenient." In Boston, Russell's celebrity is so great he can no longer enjoy himself at the ballpark or at nightclubs; he gets too much attention. Once in a while, however, the ineradicable fact of being black, which he has never forgotten intellectually, falls upon him and wounds him like a blow.

"In the summer of 1962," Russell said the other day, "I took my two sons to Louisiana, where I was born and lived for nine years, to see my grandfather. I make a reasonable living, I'm a reasonably intelligent person; I bathe regularly, so I'm pretty much a normal human being. But from the time I left Washington, D.C., we couldn't eat. I had only driven the road once before, so I was following the map, staying on the main road. We couldn't stop and eat. Or sleep. I wasn't really hungry. I was just trying to get food for my kids. I wasn't interested in socializing, or rubbing elbows. Some Negro entertainers try to show the whites that they are nice people. All of us are nice people, but this movement is not a popularity contest. I don't care if the waitress likes me when I go into a restaurant. All I want is something to eat. I drove a pretty nice car, had a few hundred bucks on me—legal tender—but I couldn't stop to eat or sleep. I bet any Russian you name, from Khrushchev on down, would have had a nice trip to Louisiana. What can you tell a kid 5 and a kid 3? No one can justify this to me. Customs and traditions and all that junk!

"One of the greatest crimes is apathy. I'm kind of hardheaded. You're either against me or for me. Being neutral you support the status quo. You see this going on—you say that's sad, it really shouldn't be. Say it to a few people, and it makes you feel better. This is apathy. All I ask is that you practice good citizenship. Vote and try to accept people for what they are as persons. If you do that you give everyone an equal chance. If you come to me and say you're not prejudiced, you're lying. I think all whites feel guilty, but I'm not sure they know what they feel guilty about."

Bill Russell's life is founded on the facts that he is black, was poor and grew taller than most men. He was born in Monroe, La. and moved to Oakland, Calif. when he was 9. When he was 12 his mother died; he was raised by his father. "When my mother died," Russell says, "my father was a young man and he could very easily have shipped me and my brother off with relatives, but we stayed together. It wasn't all good and it wasn't all bad; some of the bad things that happened I have come to understand. When you're poor it's a different world.

"My brother used to run track. Did the 100 in 10.2, 10.4—that's not bad—and my father came out one day and raced him with work shoes on. My brother says he won, and my father says he won, and I say it was a dead heat. It's not important. The important thing was that my father got in the race. I remember this field in Louisiana where the grass grew very tall. Sometimes we'd all play hide and seek—the four of us—in that field. When it was time to go in, my father would pick me up with one arm, pick up my brother with the other arm, my mother got on his back, and he ran us all the way home. Everybody had a great time...."

Russell was hardly an outstanding basketball player as a youngster. In fact, in McClymonds High in Oakland, he was not even third-string junior varsity. There were 15 uniforms but 16 players. Russell and another substitute shared the 15th uniform, dressing for alternate games. In the second semester of his junior year Russell was cut from the jayvee. He would have quit basketball in despair except for the foresight of the varsity coach, who had been his homeroom teacher in junior high school; he had Russell join the varsity where he became, at last, a full-fledged third stringer. The coach's name is George Powles; he is a white teacher in a school that is almost totally Negro. "I have never met a finer person," Russell says. "I owe so much to him it's impossible to express." In his senior year Russell finally became a starter and was the sixth or seventh highest scorer. "It was an act of kindness on Powles's part," he says. "He used to tell the guys I'd be a pretty good basketball player. I couldn't see it. He gave me money so I could join the boys' club and play every day. It was frustrating. Most of the kids wouldn't let me play. I had to play with the little kids, and who wants to play with them when you're 6 feet 2!" McClymonds won the league championship, but Russell did not even make third team all-league, and there were but six teams in the league. It was due only to the divination of Hal De Julio, who played on the University of San Francisco team that won the National Invitation Tournament in 1949, that Russell got an athletic scholarship at USF; his solitary offer. At USF Russell blossomed overnight; he was twice an All-America and led his team to 55 straight victories and two NCAA championships. In 1956, at Melbourne, Russell was a standout on the undefeated U.S. Olympic team.

Russell also excelled at track and field. At USF he ran the 440 in 49.5 and high-jumped 6 feet 9¼ but, curiously, the only reason he went out for the sport was to get a varsity letter as a freshman; in basketball he had to settle for a freshman numeral. "I didn't think I was very good," he says, "but I found I could see all the great athletes from a good seat. It was sheer enjoyment, even more as a spectator than as a participant. It was like being at a carnival. It was like being invisible and being some place you always wanted to be."

Although he speaks highly of the Boston Celtic management, Russell feels that the NBA has quite some way to go before it is accepted as a first-class league. He complains, for example, that the NBA has no pension fund and that the league bungled and lost its TV deal by putting on too many shows between mediocre teams. "The papers made a big deal about the rivalry between Wilt Chamberlain and myself," he says, "and we were on TV together three times in two years." He regards officiating as one of the NBA's weakest points. "I acknowledge it's a difficult game to referee," he says, "but there should be more than three good referees in the whole league, which is all there are. The only way to get the best referees is to make it worth their while. The referee is just as important as the players. With a good referee the better team will win. In basketball, the referee can influence the game, set the tempo. If the price is right—$10,000 to $15,000—and you put them under contract, you'll get a lot of good ones."

Although Russell is just now entering his prime as a player, he often ponders quitting basketball. "When I think about it," he says, "there are a lot of things to consider, but it never has anything to do with quitting on top. First of all, I'm very much afraid of airplanes. Secondly, the game takes a lot out of me. I call it a nine-hour game, two hours getting mentally prepared, two hours for the game itself and five hours before I get to sleep. Sometimes, even then, I can't get to sleep. I feel that if I don't have a good game we will probably lose, and it will be my fault. During the playoffs it's a 16-hour game. People say Floyd Patterson should quit. I don't think so. Because he's not champion he's not a failure. I think it's false values if a guy feels he has to quit on top. There are few enough pleasures in life not to do the thing you want to do.

"One of the saddest things that has happened to me," Russell said the other day, "is that in basketball so many good things have happened to me it's hard to get a real thrill any more. You know what I get excited about now?—when my kids say funny things or I get two new speakers for my stereo, although I had a perfectly good system before that."

In Russell's home in Reading, a Boston suburb, he has installed a $2,100 stereo system—he has 1,500 LP albums and who knows how many 45s—and some $5,000 worth of electric trains are in the basement. Recently, his wife Rose began displaying some of Russell's basketball trophies around the house. "If it was up to me, I'd put them away again," Russell says. "As far as I'm concerned, there should be no pictures of the man of the house in his home. And no trophies. Outside achievements don't belong in a family setting. But Rose has her own ideas, too. She's the finest person I ever met. I've told her many times that if I was married to anyone else I wouldn't be married. It's difficult to live with a person of my character. I'm moody and demanding, in some ways inconsiderate. In other ways I'm a pretty nice guy, I think."

When Bill Russell permits you to get to know him, you discover quickly that he is more than just "a pretty nice guy." You discover a first-rate and rewarding person. And when you are talking to him, or listening to him, or beating him in gin rummy—he's no ace at that game—you do not think of him as a basketball player, or a giant, or a Negro, finally, but as someone it is worth your while to be with.

SEPTEMBER 26, 2005

Wonder Women

BY STEVE RUSHIN

For many years, Rushin, one of the most gifted writers to appear in the magazine, penned a column titled "Air & Space." Here, he contrasts the men's and women's pro games, 10 years after the founding of the WNBA. (Rushin has a unique vantage point; he's married to Rebecca Lobo.)

In most sports, child support is a court-ordered payment. In the WNBA, child support is the front-loading baby carrier worn by new mom Tina Thompson, an All-Star forward for the Houston Comets. (It's Gucci.)

NBA players possess luxury cars. WNBA players *repossess* luxury cars. "I can't tell you all my tricks," says Sacramento Monarchs All-Star center Yolanda Griffith, who once worked as a repo woman in West Palm Beach, Fla., to support her daughter, Candace. "Let's just say some people would smash the window or jimmy the door, then hot-wire it."

NBA stars cash checks. WNBA stars *speak* Czech. "*Dobrý* means 'good' and *clona* means 'screen'," says Connecticut Sun All-Star forward Taj McWilliams-Franklin, who lives in Italy, will spend the winter in South Korea and speaks only Italian and Spanish to her daughters, Michele and Maia, to sharpen their language skills.

Last week Griffith's 25 points and nine rebounds led Sacramento to a Game 1 win over Connecticut in the WNBA finals. Then McWilliams-Franklin's 24 points and 16 rebounds led Connecticut to an overtime win in Game 2. (On Sunday the Monarchs took a 2–1 lead in the best-of-five series.) The

WNBA postseason may not be the Mother of All Sporting Events, but it does seem, at times, to be a Sporting Event of All Mothers.

But then who could *possibly* care about women who are Willis Reed on the court (Sun guard Lindsay Whalen played Game 1 with a broken bone in her left knee) and Donna Reed off it (McWilliams-Franklin owns three sewing machines and made the dress she wore to Game 1)?

"I'm a good Southern girl," says the 6'2" McWilliams-Franklin, who turns 35 next month. "My dad, from West Virginia, thought a girl should cook, clean, wash, sew, make dinner and go to work or she'd never get a good husband."

She does all that *and* is one of the best rebounders in basketball. Even Dennis Rodman didn't make his own dresses.

Clearly (as sportswriters love to point out) this will never be the NBA. Players seldom refer to themselves in the third person and are even shy about the first person. After she hit a three-pointer to send Game 2 into overtime, Sun forward Brooke Wyckoff said her principal emotion was relief that "I wasn't the dork who missed the last shot."

NBA players are given $98 a day in meal money on the road. By comparison WNBA players get peanuts (or pretzels). Last Friday night at New York's Kennedy airport, 7'2" Sun center Margo Dydek collapsed like a folding ruler into her coach seat on Jet Blue to fly across the continent to Sacramento. Her teammates always ask the person on the bulkhead aisle to switch seats with Large Marge. "Usually," says Sun guard Katie Douglas, "it's a 5'2" guy who refuses to move."

Only gentlemen seem to give up their seats to chicks who set picks, and at least one of them has taken his old-fashioned values overseas: Army Sgt. Reggie Franklin, who is stationed in Vicenza, Italy. In October, Sergeant Franklin will report to Germany for a month of specialized training, then to Iraq for a year, beginning in January. Taj's father was almost right: She didn't get a good husband, she got a great one.

McWilliams-Franklin, meanwhile, will play a short winter season in South Korea so that she can be home in Italy for daughter Michele's high school prom and graduation. On Sept. 7, when Taj was in Indianapolis for a playoff game, Michele turned 17. She called her mother in tears and said, "I understand why you can't be here. But I still wish you were home."

"The worst thing [about playing] was missing my daughter's eighth-grade graduation," says Griffith, 35, the MVP of the WNBA in 1999 and a two-time Olympic gold medalist. "We had our home opener for the Monarchs that day, so I had no choice. Candace got to the arena with about seven minutes left in the game." It was then that the entire Monarchs team congratulated

Candace (who's now 16) with a taped message played on the Arco Arena scoreboard.

McWilliams-Franklin and Griffith were both teenagers when they became single mothers. McWilliams-Franklin left Georgia State to have Michele, then enrolled at St. Edward's in Austin, where she worked in a TCBY store. Griffith left the University of Iowa after her first semester to have Candace, then enrolled at Palm Beach Community College, where she learned how to legally hot-wire cars for cash. At St. Edward's, McWilliams-Franklin sat through classes with half her chair in the lecture hall and half in the hallway so she could keep one eye on her toddler daughter playing in the corridor. "I needed to have my degree," she says now. "It was my duty. And basketball was the way to get it."

That, in the end, may be the fundamental difference between the NBA and the WNBA. When McWilliams-Franklin says she's just trying to feed her family, it's literally true.

DECEMBER 1, 2016

Sportsperson of the Year: LeBron James

In 2016, Northeast Ohio's favorite son used his incomparable
skills to deliver a title to a suddenly revitalized city,
while using his voice to have an even wider impact

BY LEE JENKINS

*After leading the Cavs back from what seemed an insurmountable deficit in
the NBA Finals, LeBron was an easy pick for SI's Sportsperson of the Year.
Here, Lee Jenkins explores James's childhood and the forces that shaped him.*

After midnight, when the kids are down and the streets are still, LeBron
James asks his wife if she wants to go on a cruise. That's the term he uses,
and because Savannah has been with him since high school she knows he is
not referring to a yacht in the Caribbean. They head to the garage, grateful
somebody can watch the children, and select one of the more inconspicuous
cars from their fleet—usually the pickup or an SUV. And as Northeast Ohio
sleeps, they turn out of their gated mansion 20 miles south of Cleveland and
continue another 20 miles down Interstate 77, through the darkness and
into the past.

The cruise does not follow a defined route. It can start in West Akron or
North Hill, Merriman Valley or Lane-Wooster, but it always traces the same
stops on a boy's urban odyssey. There's no need to fire up the GPS. "I don't
know every address," James says. "But I can find the places I'm looking for."

Hickory Street, where Big Mama's house used to sit high atop the hill, before the city tore it down. "My first home," James says. His mother, Gloria, who gave birth to him at 16, raised him there with her mother, Freda, across from the low-slung lawn maintenance center. All that's left on the property is an asphalt driveway in the woods and railroad tracks running through hickory trees in what used to be the backyard.

Overlook Drive, up the block, where he and Gloria lived with the Reaves family after Big Mama died and they struggled to pay the electric. "The Reaves cut out the bottom of a crate and nailed it to the telephone pole," James remembers. "I hooped all day on that crate." Now the neighborhood kids have a real portable basket and a trampoline on the corner of Overlook and Hickory.

Silver Street, where he moved in with Uncle Curt and ran alongside Mount Peace Cemetery, a block away on Aqueduct. "I dreamed of being Batman, of making the NBA, of buying a house for my mom, of being the Fresh Prince of Bel-Air—the Fresh Prince of Akron," James laughs. "It was as big as I could dream."

The Elizabeth Park projects, two hulking concrete buildings in the basin under the Y-Bridge, down the street from the single-story Baptist Church with the brick façade. "That's when things got really tough," James winces. "It was a mess. It was survival. There was violence. I saw so much I wouldn't want my kids to see." The blighted structures have since been leveled, turned into the Cascade Valley Apartments, a collection of two-story condos with multi-colored wood paneling.

Woodward Avenue and the three-story white house with green trim flanked by twin maple trees out front. James walked the two blocks to Harris Elementary School, also since razed and turned into parkland. "It was nice being that close to school, but you start to wonder, 'How many more times are we going to do this? How many more times are we going to move?' But I wasn't going to ask my mom those questions. She was making the best choices for us that she could."

Frederick Boulevard, Crestview Avenue, Moon Street. There are others he forgets. The order blurs. Did he sleep on a couch or in a bed? Did the place belong to an uncle or an uncle's friend, a cousin or a friend he just called a cousin? "I know Moon Street was fourth grade," James recalls, "when I missed the 82 days of school because I couldn't get across town." He'd often stay inside and eat from the same box of cereal for breakfast, lunch and dinner. "A bag of potato chips was like a steak."

Hillwood Drive, the green-and-white traditional with peeling paint and a tiny teddy bear hanging from the roof of the front porch, where youth football coach Frank Walker opened his doors. "Here is a married couple with a son and two daughters," James says. "Here is structure. Here is stability. It was the first time I'd felt that since Hickory."

Spring Hill Apartments, a six-story white shoebox on Rentar Lane, with units tucked behind sliding glass doors and vertical blinds. Gloria and LeBron were on the top floor above the playground. She made him leave his sneakers on the deck because they smelled so bad after school and practice. "That was it," James sighs. "Finally, just me and my mom, united. Friends came over, wanting to spend the night, and I was like: 'You guys have moms *and* dads but you want to stay with *us*?' I thought that was so cool. I got there in sixth grade and didn't leave until 12th. So for all the painful memories, there are bright ones. That's a bright one."

The cruise, which he takes about every six months, ends back at the mansion gates before sunrise. "Blessings on top of blessings," James says. "It makes you appreciate them all." Among professional athletes, and particularly NBA players, James's childhood journey is not unique. But he clings to it as a subject of reflection and a source of inspiration.

"When you grow up the way I grew up, I don't think you ever really get past it," he continues. "I think it's part of you forever. Life is like a book and I think you have to go back and read your book sometimes, to learn from it. Maybe I'm at Chapter 8 right now, but you can't sit down and start reading a book at Chapter 8. You have to go back to Chapter 1."

With 2 minutes and 27 seconds left in the first half of Game 7 and the Cavaliers trailing the Warriors by three points, Tyronn Lue called timeout. "Bron, you've got to be better than this," the Cavs coach implored.

"What do you mean?" James asked, incredulous. He had just scored 41 points with 16 rebounds in Game 5 and added another 41 with 11 assists in Game 6, evening a series that was essentially over. He'd sent his teammates impassioned late-night group texts, showed them the commencement address Steve Jobs delivered at Stanford and convinced them during a post-practice bus ride across the Bay Bridge that the championship was their destiny. *It's already written*, he shouted from the back.

"What more do you want me to do?" he pressed Lue.

"Stop being so passive!" the coach barked. "Stop turning the ball over! And guard Draymond!" James's numbers looked fine—12 points, seven rebounds, five assists—but he had unleashed a few sloppy passes and Draymond Green, his primary assignment, was 5 for 5 from three-point range. "Bron was mad, pissed off at me, and then we went into the locker room at halftime and I told him the same thing in front of all the guys," Lue recalls. "He was mad again, pissed off again."

After Lue finished, he saw James approach assistant coach Damon Jones in the locker room and overheard their exchange. "It's messed up that T Lue is questioning me right now," James said. The Cavaliers trailed by seven. The season was slipping.

"Everything I read all year is that you want to be coached, want to be held accountable, and trust T Lue," Jones replied. "Why not trust him now?"

James was still rankled. He moved on to James Jones, his long-time teammate, who has ridden shotgun to the past six Finals. "I can't believe this," LeBron said.

"Well," Jones responded, "is he telling the truth?"

Lue, ducking in and out of a back office, kept an eye on LeBron. "He stormed out of the locker room," Lue says. The coach laughs as he tells the story. "I didn't really think he was playing that bad," Lue admits. "But I used to work for Doc Rivers in Boston, and he told me, 'I never want to go into a Game 7 when the best player is on the other team.' We had the best player. We needed him to be his best. I know he might have been tired, but f-- that. We had to ride him. And he had to take us home."

With 1:08 left in the game and the Cavaliers in another timeout, James sat motionless on the bench at Oracle Arena. He had cooled Green in the second half. He had swatted Andre Iguodala on the crucial breakaway. He had put up six straight points, and the score was tied. "I will never forget that timeout because he was so calm—and we were so calm because he was so calm," remembers Cleveland power forward Kevin Love. "I could see Adam Silver in the stands over here. I could see Phil Knight over there. Everything was kind of moving in slow motion."

Cavaliers general manager David Griffin flashed back to a game at Quicken Loans Arena in November 2014, shortly after James returned to Cleveland. "We were dropping confetti for every regular-season win at home," Griffin recounts, "and three wins in, Bron was like: 'Can you do something about the confetti? We haven't accomplished anything yet.'" Griffin asked the game operations staff to quash the confetti, which they did, but after the Cavs vanquished the Hawks in the Eastern Conference Finals, James noticed unwelcome debris tumbling from the rafters. In an otherwise jubilant post-game locker room, he spotted the GM. "Griff," James grumbled, "how 'bout that confetti tonight?"

"Dude," Griffin shot back, "we won the East."

"That's *a* trophy," James deadpanned.

The Warriors took the hardware he wanted, and for a year, the NBA belonged to Steph Curry and Klay Thompson, two splashy sons of the suburbs reared by dads who played in the league. "LeBron tells everyone he's gotten to the point where you give it your best effort, and if you don't win, it is what it is," Griffin says. "I think that's bulls--. I think he was consumed by that trophy in a way that was probably not healthy, and when he didn't get it, I don't think he was the same person for a while. I think it bothered him deeply and he came back a radically better version of himself."

Golden State went 73–9 last season, a record no team had ever reached, and seized a 3–1 lead in the Finals, an advantage no team had ever overcome. "But the thing is, when you have LeBron James, you're never afraid," Griffin continues. "You're never David against Goliath because you have Goliath. So fear does not really exist. Every circumstance we put ourselves in, we expect to get out of, because we have him. He makes you believe you can do anything because he is present, and we all get to succeed because we're in his sphere. I imagine that's how it was with the Yankees and Babe Ruth, but I've never seen anything like it."

Griffin points out a photograph of James, hanging in a hallway of the Cavaliers practice facility, taken moments after Kyrie Irving hit the three and Love made the stop and Tristan Thompson did the double-take as the horn sounded. James's arms are wrapped around Love's neck, his head tilted skyward, eyes squeezed shut. He is standing on the tiptoes of his black-and-gold Soldier 10s. Love could feel an actual weight lifting from his teammate's 250-pound frame. "Look at LeBron's face," Griffin says. "Look at that joy. I don't know what he can do that's bigger than this. I really don't. It's like if the best player on this year's Cubs were from Chicago, or the best player on the 2004 Red Sox were from Boston. He broke the curse *at home*."

James knows the picture. He passes it almost every day. "I didn't cry when José Mesa blew the save for the Indians," he says. "I didn't cry when Earnest Byner fumbled at the 1 for the Browns. I didn't cry when MJ hit the shot over Craig Ehlo. I would have been pulling for Jordan because that's who I wanted to be. But I'm part of this community and I know what those moments meant. So the first thing I thought about were the fans who waited 52 years. Then I thought about my family. And then I thought about my upbringing, the people who supported me when I didn't have a dime to my name, and my life was a struggle. There were so many emotions—too many to hold onto." He rattles off names of the uncles and cousins, coaches and teammates, friends and strangers, who once offered a sofa and a cereal box, or more. He mentions the fourth-grade teacher who gave him a stack of worksheets for extra credit so he could see fifth. He scoffs at the suggestion that he was protected because he was gifted.

"There are a lot of gifted nine-year-olds," he counters. "They did it because they cared."

He never owed his hometown a debt. He repaid it anyway, with back-breaking interest.

LeBron James is SI's 2016 Sportsman of the Year because of those three games in June. Considering the opponent, the deficit and the stakes—for himself and his region, eternally entwined—it is hard to find a more prodigious championship performance in sports history, much less basketball history. Afterward, as the Cavaliers flew from the Bay Area to Las Vegas for their victory party, James approached Lue on the plane and thanked him for the final push. "I needed it," he said.

By traditional measures, 2015–16 was not his best season, not even close. His rebounds were up but his assists were down and his scoring was static. In a pop-a-shot league, he laid bricks outside the paint, barely scraping 30% from three-point range. "But that's not how you measure the greatness of somebody like this," says Wayne Winston. "You have to look deeper, at what he does for his team."

A statistics professor, Winston designed the famed Lineup Calculator for the Mavericks in 2000 to gauge the effect players have on each other. Plug James into the calculator for '15–16 and he nearly breaks it. "A great player is worth nine to 10 points for his team per 48 minutes," Winston says. "In other words, if he played an entire game with four average players against five average players, his team would win by nine to 10 points. Last season, LeBron was worth 19.4 points per 48 minutes, the best year of his career."

When James was on the court, the Cavaliers were better than the NBA average, no matter who was with him. And when he was off the floor, they were worse than the average, no matter who was replacing him. "We're *The Sandlot*," Love says. "And he's Benny the Jet." When Love was on the court with James, for example, the Cavs were 12.2 points better than average. When Love was without him, they were 4.1 worse. When Irving was with him, they were 9.7 points better than average; without him, 1.3 worse. The results were similar with role players. Channing Frye, for instance, was plus-22.6 with James and minus-5.1 without him. Not much changed in the playoffs, either. Tristan Thompson was plus-14.7 with James and minus-22.9 without him. Cleveland's most effective post-season lineup was actually James and four subs. "When LeBron runs the team with four journeymen," Winston says, "the team is amazing."

Players don't need the calculator to grasp the phenomenon. In January '15, J.R. Smith and Iman Shumpert flew to Cleveland, having been traded from the Knicks to the Cavaliers. Shumpert was devastated. "It was the first time Shump had been traded and I told him, 'I know the feeling, I know where you're coming from, but this could be a great thing,'" Smith recalls. "'The pressure isn't on us anymore. We can just be free and play. That's what LeBron lets you do. He lets you go out there, with heart and energy, and just play.'"

To acquire Shumpert, the Cavaliers had to absorb Smith, best known for his clubbing, tweeting and lead-foot driving. "I've got him," James told Griffin when trade talks began. On Smith's first full day in Cleveland, James was rehabbing an injured back and found him in the weight room. "People say you only care about offense, offense, offense," James told Smith. "I think you can become one of the top five defenders in our league." Smith, an unconscionable gunner, didn't know if James was joking. "I sat there for a minute and started thinking, You know what, he might be right," Smith says. "I'm not going to be able to shoot step-backs at will anymore here. I have to use my athletic ability, my speed and strength, in a different way." They became workout partners that day.

Smith feared his reputation would never change, no matter what he did, a concern he shared with James. "We talked about that," Smith says. "I try not to talk about it around anybody else. I'm an insecure guy when it comes to my game and he's the same way in a sense. That's why he's always working on jump shots, free throws, areas he doesn't feel good about." Smith grew close enough to James that he felt comfortable texting him late at night after the Cavaliers dropped Game 4 of the Finals, falling behind 3–1. "I told him, 'No disrespect to anybody else, but we can't win without you being aggressive,'" Smith recounts. "'I don't care about turnovers. I don't care about missed shots. We need you to be you.'"

James needed Smith to space the floor. In the 2015 Finals, Smith shot a meager 29.4% from three, and in the rematch he wasn't much better. At halftime of Game 7, he was at 31.7% for the series and 0 for 4 on the night. While Lue worried about James, James fretted about Smith. "I was really down on myself," Smith says. "It felt like the year before was happening all over again. Bron came up to me at half and was like: 'Don't worry about that. Let it come. You're going to hit some big shots and we're going to get right back in this thing.'" Smith scored eight points in the first two-and-a-half minutes of the third quarter, drilling two threes, and the mighty Warriors buckled.

The caricature of J.R. Smith—the parties, the GIFs, the speeding tickets—appeared buried. And roughly eight hours later it was resurrected, as he sprayed $23,000 worth of champagne into the crowd at XS Nightclub in Vegas, evidence that a man can only change so much. But Smith had already morphed from renegade to darling, in the time it took to peel off his championship T-shirt. The Cavaliers trusted Smith enough to award him a four-year, $57 million contract extension in October, or maybe it's more accurate to say they trusted James enough. During free agency, the Cavs essentially bid against themselves for Smith, as other organizations questioned his value without James. Smith, after 11 scattered seasons and four stops, had finally discovered the place where he could prosper.

"I'm never going to leave Cleveland," Smith says. "Even if they trade me someday, I'm going to live here forever."

On the Sunday before the presidential election, James and Smith sit on white plastic folding chairs in a backstage hallway at the 94-year-old Public Auditorium in downtown Cleveland, waiting for Hillary Clinton. James is no political firebrand, and when Clinton's campaign first asked him about appearing at a rally over the summer, he was apprehensive. He endorsed her, in an op-ed for *Business Insider*, but giving a speech was another matter. He decided that if the race was close at the end, and he could make a difference, he'd muster a few words. "I get nervous," James admits. "People give me notes, bullet points, but I don't know what I'm going to say. I just talk from the heart."

Clinton did not know James personally but she watched Game 7 on a small TV next to a recovery room at Columbia Medical Center in New York after her daughter, Chelsea, gave birth. "As big as you are, as busy as you are, it humbles me that you'd take the time to do this," Clinton tells James, when they meet backstage. "Of course," James responds. He introduces Clinton to Smith, who vows to keep his shirt on. "Oh, you look good either way," Clinton cracks, and James howls. He then introduces Smith's eight-year-old daughter, Demi, whom James calls his niece. He explains that Demi was just in Washington D.C. visiting monuments. He snaps a photo as the girl describes what she saw.

The time has come. James walks across the tiled floor into the auditorium, up five metal steps, to a blue carpeted stage. Applause engulfs him. "I want people to understand how I grew up in the inner city," James tells the crowd. "I was one of those kids and was around a community that was like, 'Our vote doesn't matter.' But it really does. It really, really does." He speaks for less than two minutes, but the campaign is thrilled. Not only did the most famous man in Ohio appear with the candidate, he had also posed backstage with the staff, as they stood on chairs around him. Only one person was missing from the shot. "Should we get HRC in here?" an aide wondered. "No, that's okay," another chirped, and Clinton shrugged good-naturedly. She hung off to the side, out of the picture for the first time in about six months. "I think this may have happened once before," an aide mentioned, "with Brad Pitt."

Two days later, James and his wife stayed up until 4 a.m., watching the state and the country choose Donald Trump. "When I was growing up, I didn't have my father, so you looked up to people in positions of power,"

James says. "It could be athletes or actors or leaders, like presidents. I think parents could use some of those people as role models. But when we elect a president who speaks in a disrespectful way a lot, I don't know that we can use him in our household." The next morning, James and Savannah ate breakfast, before the Cavaliers flew to D.C. for their championship ceremony with President Barack Obama. "I think we're going to have to do more," he told his wife. "I think we're going to have to step it up more."

This was the year of athlete activism, and James honored the greatest of all, donating $2.5 million to support a Muhammad Ali exhibit at the Smithsonian National Museum of African American History and Culture in D.C. James reveres Ali, as a revolutionary as much as a fighter, and feels a responsibility to speak out when stirred. He voices an opinion on virtually every subject reporters ask him about, from police brutality to NFL ratings. But his form of engagement differs from Colin Kaepernick's, and for that matter, Ali's. "I understand protests, but I think protests can feel almost riotous sometimes, and I don't want that," James says. "I want it to be more about what I can do to help my community, what we can do so kids feel like they're important to the growth of America, and not like: 'These people don't care about us.' I'm not here to stomp on Trump. We're here to do our part, which starts in the place we grew up, street by street, brick by brick, person by person."

James's philanthropic efforts are well chronicled. His foundation sponsors every at-risk third grader in the Akron public school system, following them through high school. With his first class currently in eighth grade, the foundation partnered last year with Akron University to guarantee four-year college scholarships for any of the students who graduate high school with a 3.0 grade point average. "It was huge," says Michele Campbell, executive director of the LeBron James Family Foundation, who currently counts 1,100 students in the program. "But we try to stay ahead of our kids and we started thinking about what their life would look like in college. We learned that the dropout rate for African-American students, between freshman and sophomore year, is really alarming." Campbell called James into the office in Akron after the All-Star Game and shared the statistics she'd found, that 18.6% of first-time African-American students at U.S. public universities graduate within four years of starting, according to the *Digest of Education Statistics*. "We can't get them all the way there," she said, "and see them drop out."

In October, the foundation announced plans to create a 7,000 square-foot institute at InfoCision Stadium on the Akron campus, which will become a 24/7 haven for the students. "Even though the university is in their backyard, I think there's sometimes a feeling that it's for someone else and not for them," Campbell says. "We needed a place where they can feel safe and carry that home-away-from-home feeling." Campbell and James have five years to figure out what exactly they will do with the space—they've assembled a board of experts to make recommendations—but they could use it for tutoring, counseling or social events. They like that the site is in the football stadium, partly because the exterior wall is glass, looking out over Akron.

James weighs in on a lot of sensitive issues but his cause—underprivileged children and families in Northeast Ohio—is clear. It informs even some of the choices he makes for his production company, SpringHill Entertainment, when he and business manager Maverick Carter are picking projects to back: *Cleveland Hustles*, an unscripted series in which aspiring entrepreneurs pitch a panel of investors their ideas for small businesses in Cleveland; *There Goes the Neighborhood*, a comedy in which a white family moves into a gentrifying African-American section of Cleveland; *The Wall*, a game show in which $12 million will be on the line every night. "What always appeals to us are real stories that are authentic and inspire people," Carter says. "That's the common thread."

"I sometimes look at LeBron and see that six-year-old boy in him, who grew up in a place that was cold and gray and poor, and everybody told him that you can't do anything here and you have to leave," Griffin says. "And now he is living out every single childhood dream he ever had, literally everything he ever could have thought of. I remember being that little kid. We all remember being that little kid. And I know he's inspired me to dream bigger than I ever did before. I think he's inspired a lot of people to do that. He's Ohio's favorite son—again—and he's using that to the full extent of its bandwidth. He's making this as big as any other place."

Cleveland has hemorrhaged population since 1950, from 900,000 to 400,000, and the first decade of the new millennium saw a 17% drop. But in the past five years, the drain has slowed significantly, to 1.46%. "Something is happening," says Richey Piiparinen, senior research associate of The Center for Population Dynamics at Cleveland State. "The river burned in '69. The mayor lit his hair on fire in '72. Everybody left. We were defined by Rust Belt shame. We were the first region that died. And then recently, we've seen trends pointing to this return migration, this boomerang effect. LeBron is the face of it because his boomerang was so iconic."

The shift was caused primarily by the growth of Cleveland's health-care industry, not the presence of a basketball player. But Piiparinen studies a discipline called psychogeography, how the emotions evoked by a place determine whether people choose to live there. "It's part of what makes a city hot," Piiparinen explains, "and there's no doubt LeBron ties into it." When James announced in '14 that he was coming back to Cleveland after four years in Miami, 7.4% of the city's population was age 25 to 29, a figure that had barely fluctuated since '09. A year later, the number had spiked to 8.3%, while the national average held steady at 6.9. Owners of downtown apartment buildings were among the biggest beneficiaries. According to Joe Marinucci, president and CEO of the Downtown Cleveland Alliance, housing in the area has hovered above 94% occupancy for the past 16 quarters.

"There's a group here called Look Up To Cleveland that puts high-school students through one-day sessions about things going on around Northeast Ohio, good and bad," says Jacob Duritsky, the vice president of Strategy and Research at Team NEO, a nonprofit economic development organization. "I give the presentation on the economy, and at the end, I always ask these 17- and 18-year-olds how many of them intend to come back to Cleveland after they go away to college. I started asking six years ago, and out of 50, 10 or 15 would raise their hands. Last year, 43 or 44 raised their hands. I don't know anyone who says they are moving back just because LeBron James did, but he's an important piece of a change in momentum."

One of Duritsky's colleagues, Mike Stanton, grew up in West Park and Fairview Park. In '09, he graduated from Ohio State and served in the Army for five years. After that, he worked for a plastics manufacturer in Pittsburgh and Atlanta, before Team NEO called last spring. He interviewed in Cleveland on a Wednesday, during the Eastern Conference semifinals, and flew back to Atlanta that night. "I got in my car, on the top deck of the parking garage at Hartsfield Airport, and turned on the radio because the Cavs were playing the Hawks," says Stanton, 30. "The Cavs were up by 25. They'd make like 20 three-pointers. The announcers were talking about how obscene it was. You're looking for some reassurance and that kind of provided it. 'The decision is made. I'm coming home.'"

Cassi Pittman grew up in East Cleveland and didn't apply to one college in Ohio. She went to the University of Pennsylvania and earned her Ph.D. in sociology and social policy from Harvard. Then she followed the crowd to New York, where her father went to college, at Columbia. He used to tell her, "The only people who don't stay in the city after graduation are the ones from California and Cleveland." She moved back in July '14 as an assistant professor of sociology at Case Western. "LeBron was not the catalyst," says Pittman, 33. "But I did tell everyone we made our decision mutually."

Likewise, 32-year-old Jessica O'Rielly wrote a *Coming Home* essay when she resigned from a New York media company last June, moving with her husband to Shaker Heights. And 31-year-old Valerie Malloy insisted on a chalk toss when she wed her longtime boyfriend, Elliott, after a move from

Omaha in September '14. "One of the groomsmen brought the chalk," says Malloy, married at Ariel International Center in Cleveland. "But it was the dustless chalk so it didn't work."

On June 19, Father's Day, Valerie and Elliott visited both sets of parents and grandparents before heading downtown to watch Game 7 at a bar. But Winking Lizard was packed and the air conditioning at Huron Point Tavern was out. They finally secured a table at Becky's with eight friends. "I was crying, and not just because there was champagne and beer in my eyes," Malloy says. "It was probably the greatest day of my life."

Two days before the ring ceremony, James walked from the weight room to the court at the Cavaliers practice facility. "Is this what you thought it would be?" Griffin asked.

"No," James replied, "it's so much more."

When the Cavs drafted him in 2003, placing 40 years of a city's dashed hopes on his shoulders, it was a burden. "Just learn as much as you can, soak up as much as you can and get better," James told himself then. Fronting a franchise, at 18, was challenging enough. Healing a region's damaged sports psyche was too much. At times, he seemed to rebel against the role that was handed to him, famously doffing a Yankees hat before a playoff game against the Indians at Jacobs Field in '07.

Juxtapose that image with the scene at the World Series this fall, James wearing Indians hats and jerseys to his suite at Progressive Field, leaving Beats by Dre headphones in the home clubhouse with notes that read: *It's your turn.* "LeBron James pretty much is Cleveland," says Indians closer Cody Allen, "and when he is on your JumboTron, going nuts with his guys, that stuff gets ingrained in your mind. Things in this city changed when the Cavs won. People took that excitement and optimism and shifted it right over to us. I don't necessarily think we needed that, but it breathed something into us. Everywhere you went, you'd see Cavs gear and Indians gear. They went together. In front of mom-and-pop stores, you'd see Cavs banners with Indians banners. It was like small-town high-school football pride."

When the Tribe was on the road, James watched at TownHall in Ohio City. "Long way from the kid in the Yankees hat," he laughs. "I still love seeing the Yankees play baseball. That was part of my childhood. But it's different now. I think it takes a while to understand your purpose and who you are. When you find that out—and it happened for me in Miami, when I was by myself and had to be more independent—you realize, 'This is what I'm supposed to do.' I'm here to represent for Ohio but mostly for the youth that look up to me. When you find your calling, everything else is easier." Last summer, after Dwyane Wade hit the free-agent market, James did not try to steer his friend. But when it became clear that Wade would join his hometown Bulls, James told him: "Those are the people who watched you grow from a kid into a man."

On a crisp, cloudless Sunday morning in the first week of November, the subject of James's sports apparel is once again at issue. The Browns are hosting the Cowboys and James has reserved a suite at FirstEnergy Stadium. One of his friends calls, before brunch at Urban Farmer, to make sure he is not wearing any blue-and-silver stars. James grew up a Dallas fan, ever since he played youth football for the South Rangers, whose uniforms looked like the Cowboys'. James assures his friend he has already decided to go neutral.

In a gray Nike hoodie and a black ALWAYS BELIEVE hat, James watches from the front row of his suite, next to Tristan Thompson and Khloe Kardashian. Bernie Kosar swings by to say hi. With 23 seconds left in the first half, Cleveland receiver Terrelle Pryor Sr. grabs a 12-yard touchdown pass in the corner of the end zone. Instead of savoring a rare highlight, Browns' fans sitting below James turn to check his reaction. He smiles and claps three times.

"Lakers-Suns tonight at 9:30," James announces, before retreating inside the suite for a halftime game of cards. He does this a lot, blurting out random matchups and tip times that would only pique the interest of a devoted League Pass geek. Bucks-Wolves! Hornets-Pelicans! "He knows every team so well, he could run the pregame walk-through by himself," says Jordan McRae, the Cavaliers second-year guard. "Every young guy should get a chance to play with him, even just for a little bit."

"There's always something on his mind," Griffin adds, "something he's planning, something he wants to achieve, and we're all a part of it, but there's no way to know exactly what it is." If the first month of this season is any indication, it has to do with playmaking. James is averaging the fewest field goal attempts of his career, 17.2, and the most assists, 9.7, whipping four-seamers to Cleveland's bevy of oversized shooters. When reporters recently asked him about records he most admires, the first one he mentioned was Scott Skiles's 30 assists in a game. He wants to help Irving win an MVP, and in the process, he may wind up snatching another for himself. The more immediate concern is Smith, mired in a wretched shooting slump, and demonstrating some familiar flakiness. In one defensive possession at Milwaukee, he comically left his man to hug Bucks reserve Jason Terry.

Two days before Thanksgiving, James sits on a bench next to the Cavaliers practice court, leaning against a black pad that supports his back. "Where are your shoes and socks!" he hollers. "Go put on your shoes and socks!" His youngest son, nine-year-old Bryce, is playing barefoot with Irving. Bryce is in fourth grade now, the same grade James was in when he lived on Moon

Street and missed the 82 days of school. Someday, he may take Bryce on a cruise, but for now he just wants to sit back in this basketball palace and watch his boy rebound for his point guard.

"This is amazing, isn't it?" James asks. "This is my life."

— POSTSCRIPT —

Lee Jenkins: At SI, the debate about who will win Sportsperson of the Year starts in the fall, usually around the World Series. You don't know who it will be or whether you will be assigned the story. In 2016, things were different. I knew LeBron James would win it, and I knew I'd probably write the story, from the moment the Cavaliers came back from 3–1 down to beat the Warriors in the Finals. When I showed up in Cleveland that November to interview James—just four years after interviewing him for his first Sportsperson of the Year award—his fame had reached a new peak. He was campaigning with Hillary Clinton in her presidential bid. He was partnering with the Smithsonian National Museum of African-American History and Culture on a Muhammad Ali exhibit. He was openly chasing Michael Jordan's six championships. I asked him how he was grounding himself, in this new stratosphere, and he described drives he took in the middle of the night with his wife through the deserted streets of Akron, visiting the many houses and apartments where he lived as a child. He started rattling off the addresses, like he was recounting plays, along with memories of each one, some warm and some painful. I furiously jotted them down, and the next day, started down the same roads James did. Every year, it seemed, there was a different address, a new challenge. He overcame them, without ever forgetting them.

APRIL 23, 2001

How Allen Iverson and Larry Brown Learned to Live Together

Two fiercely competitive small men in a big man's game,
two sons of hardworking single moms—Allen Iverson and
Larry Brown are so much alike that only their mothers
could tell them apart...and bring them together

BY GARY SMITH

*Few players in league history had as profound an impact in as short a time
as Allen Iverson. He turned scoring into art, chafed at authority, influenced
fashion and culture and, in 2001, put together a season for the ages, becoming
the smallest player to be named MVP. (Iverson was generously listed at six
feet and 165 pounds.)*

*Iverson led the Sixers to the NBA Finals, losing to the Lakers. Here, Gary
Smith drills down on the relationship between Iverson and his peripatetic
coach, Larry Brown, seeking to understand what drove both men.*

Two women waited in a tunnel, outside a door. Light danced off the diamonds
dangling from the black one, and a red rose jiggled in her hand. She was 39.
She couldn't stand still. The white one stood by the wall, unornamented,
holding her 92 years and her silence.

The door began to open and close. The younger one sang out greetings to the tall men coming out. Both women's eyes stayed fixed on the door.

At last the two shortest men of all exited the locker room. One wore the tailored suit, short gray hair and wire-rimmed spectacles of a tenured professor. The other's hair was stitched in cornrows, his skin covered with baggy clothes and tattoos. It was unusual that they walked out together. They had always been so far apart.

"That's my boy!" cried the younger woman. "My baby won the game!"

"That's *my* boy," the older woman said quietly. "He *coached* the game."

The women turned to face each other for the first time. "What's your name?" said the younger one.

"I'm Ann," said the older one. "I'm Larry Brown's mother."

"Oh my God! My name's Ann too!" hollered the younger woman. "I'm Allen Iverson's mother!"

"Oh, I know who Allen is," the elder said. "You've got a good little boy."

Ann Iverson thrust her rose into the other Ann's hand. Larry's mom gave Allen's mom her phone number at the nursing home and urged her to call. The two sons watched all this, then headed away, each with his own mother, into the night.

Larry and Allen always did that—walked off, with their histories, in different directions. Theirs was the most studied relationship in the NBA, watched as closely as a weather vane to see if the storm clouds on the league's horizon were about to blow in and burst. If the 60-year-old Jewish grandfather and the 25-year-old rapper, arguably the best coach and the best player in the game, could emerge from their cultural bunkers and work together, then perhaps the growing divide between players and coaches, between philosophies and generations, could be bridged as well.

Larry and Allen had so much in common, if they just stopped fixating on their differences. Both were raised by single moms. Both were the smallest guys on every court they played on, all heart and hunger—Larry diving across floors so often he now hobbled on replacement hips, Allen skidding and bouncing toward the same fate. Each so sensitive that one word or look from the other could inflict deep pain. Both, even with their 35-year difference in age, going home every day to the noise, toys and sticky hugs of small children: Allen to his three-year-old boy and six-year-old girl, Larry to his three-year-old daughter and six-year-old son. Both living in multimillion-dollar Main Line estates on the outskirts of Philly, only a few miles apart. Both feeling terribly misunderstood.

Anyone who witnessed a 76ers game, who saw the veins pop on Larry's forehead as he sat coiled on the bench, who watched Allen dip and dart relentlessly when he didn't have the ball and hurl his 165-pound body into the mayhem when he did, knew immediately that they were the two men who cared the most. Their passion entwined them: Each needed the other, completely, to have a prayer of doing what they both *had* to do. Win. Everything.

They began to grope their way toward each other this season after a summer when all seemed lost, when Larry nearly took the North Carolina job and Allen was all but gone in a trade. Their turn from the brink altered team dynamics so dramatically that it hurtled the Sixers to the league's second-best record this season. Still, it remained the most volatile of relationships, so painful at times for Larry that his wife, Shelly, told him a few months ago that maybe he should quit, so charged with potential that he and Allen could end up side by side on a float rolling down Broad Street this June.

It's none of my business, of course. But with so much at stake—in a sport that hinges, more than any other, on relationships—why let those two mothers and sons walk away, as they did that night in Miami two years ago? Why not sit them all down and have the Anns tell each other's son their tale? *Defy* those two boys to remain misunderstood....

Ann Iverson would order up a glass of blush wine before telling her story, stick a straw in it and ring that straw with lipstick, flaming red. She'd wear what she wears to Sixers games: mink hat and mink coat over a custom-made IVERSON'S MOM number 3 jersey flapping down to her knees over a shirt festooned with the same words and images that are tattooed on her son's skin, along with a pair of Reebok sneakers and a couple hundred thousand dollars' worth of jewelry. She'd be ready to talk all night, because she'd slept all day. Her nickname is Juicy.

Allen Iverson was conceived without intercourse. That was 1 a.m. on Sept. 22, 1974 at my grandmother's house in Hartford. I'd made up my mind that on my 15th birthday I'd have my first sexual encounter, with Allen Broughton. He was a point guard, and the leader of a gang called the Family Connection—he was only a year older than me, but he had 40- and 50-year-old men under him! We'd been goin' together since I was 12, but I'd told him I wasn't gonna have sex with him till I was 15. I thought that was a decent time to wait.

We had it all planned. At midnight of my birthday, when everyone was asleep, he tapped on the back door. I was in my pj's and robe. We went down to the basement and used an old mattress that was down there. He started grindin' against me—he never put it in—and before you know it.... Then I heard the bathroom door upstairs—Grandma was awake! I got him out of the house quick. Eight weeks later I took a physical for basketball, and they told

me I was eight weeks pregnant. I said to the doctor, "You're tellin' a story!"
They took the test again, and the doctor called my grandma in and said,
"Your granddaughter's gonna have a baby, but she hasn't been penetrated."
I'm tellin' ya, I look at Allen and I say, God had a plan for him and me.

Ann Brown would order cranberry juice but leave most of it in the glass.
She doesn't have much thirst or appetite any more. Her name, officially, is
Mrs. Alpern—that was the name of her deceased second husband—but she'd
answer to Mrs. Brown for those likelier to know her by the surname of her
two coaching sons and her deceased first husband. She'd wear slacks and a
sweater, and a scarf to give her some color now that her red hair has gone
to wispy curls of white. Her only jewelry would be a wristwatch and a 1988
Kansas national championship brooch on a necklace tucked beneath her
blouse. She'd say that brooch meant everything to her, but no one needed
to see it.

I met Milton in Brooklyn when I was 26. He was a furniture salesman.
Milton had loads of personality. We looked like brother and sister. He was a
worker, and so was I. Herbert was born first. He was colicky, such a crybaby
I'd have to take him out in the hallway—I'd go out of my mind. I had an
appendix attack when he was three weeks old. A second child? I didn't want to
have another one after what I'd gone through, but Milton insisted. He thought
something was wrong with me when it took so long to have another one.

Four-and-a-half years later, Larry was born. He was an angel, so quiet
and gentle. I never had to correct him. Herb was wonderful as well, but he
would flare up, more like his father. Larry was like me. I don't think he ever
got in trouble, thank God! Does it sound like I'm saying this in conceit? He's
so polite, just a very good soul. It's so nice to be nice, don't you think? Now
I'm bragging to you, and I don't mean to brag. I'm sorry.

The Sixers did leg lifts at the beginning of practice. Larry lay down and did
them with the team. Allen lay still and stared at the ceiling. Then the Sixers
and Larry rolled over and did push-ups. Allen rolled over and grunted, but
his body didn't leave the floor.

How many NBA coaches stopped practice a half-dozen times to teach
their players the right way to execute a pick-and-roll? Exactly where the
feet should go, when the teammate should rub past, how the pick-setter's
hips should turn to the basket. Larry did. He lived to teach the game. He
lived for practices.

Allen listened for a moment. Then his feet did a little hop, his arms a
little dance move. Suddenly he hurled a basketball the length of the court.
It slammed off the backboard, its echo bouncing off the walls.

We come from slaves down in Georgia. My father's name was Willie Lee Iverson—6'5" and good-lookin', and Papa was a rollin' stone, yeah, yeah. He had 17 children by four women, and I was the oldest one, and they say I'm like him. I didn't wear no dress. I climbed trees and kicked ass. My mother was a waitress. She died when I was 12, when they tied her tubes wrong and her bowels got infected, and that was the most devastatin' thing of my life. I was sittin' in a chair that night with a sheet pulled over my head so I could talk on the phone in privacy, when I hear my sister Jessie say, "Ann, somethin' wrong with Mama." Pulled that sheet off and Mama was doubled over.

The ambulance came and I was squeezin' down the steps beside her and I told her I wanted to go with her. She said, "No, you watch Jessie and Stevie and Greggy for me." And I said, "I'll do that." I didn't realize it then but I sure did later—she didn't mean watch my sister and brothers just that night. She meant for good.

They had to pay us for the mistake they made on my mother. We got 3,818 dollars and 18 cents. Don't forget that 18 cents.

I cried in bed 'most every night after she died. I remember one night she came to me in a dream and told me to stop cryin', that things would get better. I felt good, seein' her...but there were still roaches runnin' cross the floor when I woke up.

My grandmother decided us four kids needed to stay with her instead of my father. Ethel Mitchell was the sweetest human being. Her husband said he was done raisin' kids, so she gave up her house and her marriage for us, two months after Mama died, and raised us up. Family stayin' together, that's what that woman was all about.

Five months pregnant with Allen Iverson, and I'm still playin' basketball. I'd go into a game and try to take it right then and there, run ahead of all my teammates. "Slow down! Pass the ball!" Coach Evans used to holler at me. Coach would paddle me when I needed it, but she never disciplined me in the street, never in front of people. Never disrespected me. She kept it in the family.

Then I got in a fight with a girl who wanted Allen Broughton. Still pregnant. My 38th fight and I'd lost only once—to twin boys. But that was it for my grandma. She packed that house up in one week and moved us to Hampton, Virginia, where she came from.

That's where Allen was born. When the nurse brought him to me, I looked at his little body and saw those long arms and said, Lord, he's gonna be a basketball player! His uncles, Bubba and Chuck, wanted me to nickname him after them, so I nicknamed him after both. All his family and friends call him Bubba Chuck.

My cousins moved in with us, six of 'em and their mom. That made 13 of us in a two-bedroom house—six teenagers, the rest under 10. Bubba Chuck was more like a little brother to me than a son. Here I was a 15-year-old worryin' each mornin' about a baby and gettin' my sister and two brothers off to school. I'd wake up at night and feel Allen's chest, make sure his heart was beatin', and think, dag, this is my baby. He's relyin' on me. If I don't do right, he won't do right.

He had a picture in his mind. In its foreground sat Michael Jordan and Scottie Pippen, appearing year after year at all those playoff press conferences against a backdrop bearing the NBA logo, wearing $2,000 suits with pressed shirts and silk ties. Pure class, thought Larry, who himself has been known to order 10 suits, 15 ties and 20 shirts on a stroll through a custom clothing store.

He knew one picture like that could begin to relax all the white people made tense by Allen's tattoos and cornrows and 'do rag. That's what Larry wanted to do for Allen when the Sixers finally made the playoffs. So in April 1999, Larry required coats and ties for the first-round trip to Orlando. Allen removed his untied boots, his floor-sweeping jeans, his untucked T-shirt and double-sized leather jacket. He wore a grey pin-striped Versace suit into the locker room. "See how good you look?" said Larry. Allen took the suit off and left it in a ball on the locker room floor.

My father was the baker for the czar of Russia. My mother's family was in the junk business. I was one of eight. We came to Brooklyn from Minsk in 1910, but I can't tell you anything about it. I was three when we left Russia and I don't remember it, and my parents never talked about it—they were too busy in the bakery. Everyone was too busy. I grew up on my own. I started at about 12, washing dishes, then working the counter. My father kept selling bakeries and buying new ones. He made money that way, I guess. We moved like gypsies.

My father had a heart attack when he was 50. After that, he sat in a chair near the front door and kissed the women as they came in, and gave out samples of rugelach. That's a pastry with cream cheese, nuts and raisins, rolled into twists. Everyone loved him—he was like the mayor. My mother took over running the business, but she died of walking pneumonia when she was 57. So my brothers, who were supposed to get an education, ended up staying in the bakery too. We were always there for each other. Never thought I'd end up in a bakery all those years. But who ever thought Milton....

What happened was this: Milton got a new job, a promotion, traveling all over Pennsylvania as a sales representative for his furniture company. Used to worry me sick, him driving hundreds of miles back to Brooklyn every

Friday night to be with me and the boys for the weekend. How those boys loved him. He'd take them to games, play ball with them. I'd sit on the stoop and tie a rope around Larry's waist while he'd play around with a ball.

I couldn't stand Milton having to drive that far, so we moved to Pittsburgh when Larry was six. Milton insisted on buying our first house. We were just about to move into it when Milton came home on a Friday from work. He said he didn't feel well....

Allen woke up feeling like hell. The shootaround was scheduled for 11 a.m. late last season in Miami. Sure, he'd been out till 1:30 at the All-Star I in South Beach, but that wasn't a late night for him. His body ached from slamming into men a foot taller and a hundred pounds heavier every game, and his ankles and feet hurt so much he had to wear slippers around the hotel. If only they would do away with practice. If only he could just hole up all day and recover, he'd be ready to go to war again by game time that night. He picked up the phone, but he didn't call Larry. He called the trainer and said he had a headache.

At the shootaround Larry looked at his watch. To ensure that he was never late, Larry set his clocks at home so far ahead that he often arrived at places 20 minutes early. He looked at the trainer. Wasn't aspirin invented for headaches? What was this, the 40th or 45th time this season Allen had been late or hadn't shown up? Not to mention all the times he had hidden in the bathroom and gorged on tacos while the rest of the team lifted weights.

That night Allen sat slumped in the locker room. He couldn't believe that he'd been suspended and that his coach had criticized him in front of the media. "I've been here four years," he said. "They know who I am as a competitor. So don't question my heart."

When Bubba Chuck was three, I told him, "You're the man of the house. You gotta do whatever you gotta do to become a man." I'd just moved out of Grandma's and moved in with Michael Freeman. He was a welder at the shipyard. I moved out two months later to be on my own, but he'd come over and visit after work most days, stay a few hours. He's the father of Allen's two sisters and he's a good man—the drugs he sold and went to prison for weren't for buyin' fancy cars and jewelry; they were uttingttin' food in our refrigerator. But Bubba Chuck was the man of the house.

We moved to the ghetto, and five kids jumped Allen. He ran to get his fishin' rod to fight with. I took him back and told him he had to fight one-on-one with fists. He beat two of 'em. Rest backed off. Bubba Chuck was—what?—seven? He played football in my grandmother's backyard with my brothers and the kids next door. They were all much older. They'd pick him up and throw him against the house, and he'd come in cryin'. I'd send him right back out. I wanted him to play basketball, but he said basketball was too soft. Michael Freeman took him to the court to let his ass get hammered. He was 10. Look how he gets beat down today and keIttin' back up.

I worked for Amway, and they taught me to set goals so I could realize my dreams. Can you believe that—bunch of white people tellin' me to set goals but that was the best thing I could've had. 'Cause all I had in the 'hood was people tellin' me how to sell drugs. I'll be honest, it was white people who lifted me up. Not black people.

Had to do lots of things to get us by. Can't tell you everything, gotta save some things for when I do my book. I drove a forklift. I was a secretary at Langley Air Force Base. Was a welder at the shipyard. Worked the counter at a convenience store, watched men walk right in and steal beer. Made the money I needed to bury Grandma playin' bingo. Men would lend me money till my SSI check came for my daughter—she was disabled with seizures. Bubba Chuck? He never worked a job—no! It was my job to take care of him. Only chore he ever had to do was take out the garbage. I cleaned his room my daggone self.

One day I came back to the projects from visitin' relatives in Hartford. All of a sudden, they're tellin' me I owed $32 and had to leave my house. I had $360 in my pocket but they wouldn't let me pay—they evicted us! My daughter and I went into a shelter for homeless mothers, but Bubba Chuck wouldn't go; he couldn't bear it. He moved in with his old football coach Gary Moore. He was 14 years old.

I didn't hide none of it from him. Whenever I took a bump, he was right there with me. He knows everything there is to know about me. But my kids didn't wake up every mornin' and see a different nigga in my bed or a different pair of shoes under it. I taught Bubba Chuck to go straight at a problem. Call me a top-dog bitch. If I gotta be one, that's the way I carry.

"It's about f--in' time," snarled Allen, when Larry sent him back into a game two years ago against the Cleveland Cavaliers, after he'd been out for two minutes and three seconds. He often cursed when Larry pulled him out of games, then sat on the far end of the bench with a towel over his head, the way his mother used to do with a sheet when she needed to be alone in a crowded house. In five decades of basketball, Larry had never seen or heard anything like it, so he knew it wouldn't go down well the following season when he yanked Allen and four other starters with 8:15 left in the third quarter and the Sixers trailing the Detroit Pistons by 23 points, and never put Allen back in. "I've never been done like that in my career," Allen seethed in the locker room. "If that's the way it is, something needs to happen. Something's got to give. I mean every word I'm saying. Every single word."

Larry was standing 10 feet away. He didn't say a word. He just walked away.

We never talked about it, the boys and I. Not when it happened. Not afterward. I can't believe I'm talking about it now.

Milton didn't want to make a fuss. Finally he told me to call the doctor—doctors made house calls in those days—but the doctor had a birthday party to go to, so he didn't come until the next day. When he finally did, he said Milton should go to the hospital, but the hospital said there were no beds. So we waited another day. I took him at about seven that evening. I didn't tell the boys. They were at a movie. Milton didn't even want me to come up and see him in his room. I left after he got checked in, went home and got a call. He was dead. Imagine the shock. An aneurysm. By then the boys were in bed. When they woke up, the mirrors were covered with cloth. That's a Jewish tradition. My brother Joe and sister Edith had driven in from New York during the night. Herb knew something was wrong. But I couldn't tell him. Finally Joe told him his father had died, and Herb started punching him and crying. How could I tell Larry? He was six. He asked where his father was. We said he was on the road.

We sent him to a relative's house. You couldn't have a child that age at a funeral. We didn't tell him for a month that his father had died. We kept telling him he was off on business. He's still hurt that he wasn't told and didn't go to the funeral.

You know when I saw how much he still missed his father? I went to visit him once after he was married, and he had a cigar in his mouth. I said, "Larry, you don't smoke!" He said, "I just keep them in my mouth, I don't light them." Then he said, "Dad used to have cigars—didn't he?"

Two days after the benching in Detroit, they sat across from each other in a room. Allen with his arms wrapped around himself, smoldering. Larry with his head tucked into his shoulders, loathing confrontation, furious that team president Pat Croce was forcing them to spill everything on the table. The table, that's what Larry crawled under at restaurants when his wife asked the waiter to take her blood-red steak back and do it medium, the way she'd asked.

Croce was scared. Larry had demanded that Allen be traded or he himself would quit. Allen had demanded that Larry be fired or that he be traded. Croce felt the whole franchise quaking under his feet. "Allen," said Croce, "I don't think Coach likes you."

Allen erupted at Larry. "You say this team's a family when it's convenient, but then you go talk about me in the newspapers," he said. "If it's really family, then you keep it in the family! You don't disrespect me like that.

There are times when you're coaching me and I'm looking at you, trying to learn, and I can tell you're thinking I don't give a f-- what you have to say. You think I'm not listening because of an expression on my face. Well, I hear you. I hear everything!"

"Are you finished?" Larry said.

"Do I ask you if *you're* finished when you talk to me?"

"Coach," said Croce, "I get the feeling that the way you act toward Allen feels to him like what the police and the judicial system did in Virginia after he came out of that bowling alley."

Larry's jaw dropped. The biggest hero in his life was Jackie Robinson. He'd never dreamed he could come across like *that*.

Go look at the sidewalk at 3710 Jordan Drive. It says, FREE IVERSON, SIMMONS, WAYNE AND STEVENS. I took a stick and wrote that in wet cement. That's the four black kids got put in jail.

Allen come home one day with a lump on his head and a headache. Fight had started at the bowlin' alley between whites and blacks over somethin' said. He told me his friends had pulled him out, he hadn't done nothin'. "They didn't want me gettin' in no trouble," he said. "They my niggas." He'd just quarterbacked the football team at Bethel High to the state championship and was doin' the same with the basketball team. Next thing I know they're arrestin' Allen and three other black boys.

All his life, every day when I left for work in summer, I'd tell Bubba Chuck, "You watch your sister and be good. God see everything you do." And that's what came right back at me now. Allen said, "Mama, how can that be? If God see everything I do, why'm I gettin' charged with this?" My grandmother told him, "Don't question God," and he never complained a word after that.

That trial was the first time he wore a suit and tie. I made him wear one to court. He hates 'em now. They remind him of then. You can't expect guys who grew up like he did to be in a suit and tie.

He didn't cry when they took him off in handcuffs to jail. I didn't either— wasn't gonna let my son see that. But my tears got in my eyes after they took him. I cried every night he was in prison. Day he walked back through the door, we clenched so hard, I felt like I was goin' up to heaven.

He'd changed in jail. He'd seen the world right in front of his eyes, and he knew what people could do to you. But I liked the change. When he came out, he took no s--.

Larry came out of the locker room ashen. It had been another one of those nights when his star had played as if he didn't understand that a team was a family.

He looked down the tunnel. There stood Allen, hugging and kissing his mother, sisters, aunts, uncles, cousins, childhood friends, old coaches and teachers—the reunion that awaited him after nearly every home game.

Larry turned to greet his own family. Allen's face lit up when he saw Larry's wife and two kids. He came over and gave Shelly a hug, L.J. a high five and Madison a squeeze.

Larry walked in silence to his car. He'd turned the pieces every which way. And still they never fit.

Milton left no estate. My sisters and brothers were always there for each other, but I hated being a burden. I was afraid I wouldn't be able to pay them back. At first we had to move in with my sister Cassie and her husband, Irving. Cassie lost four fingers in a bread-slicing machine. Oh, it was terrible. Irving was from Hungary and he was gorgeous, but he was so mean to the boys, so mean I had to move us out. We moved into the rooms above the new bakery my family opened. It was in Long Beach, on Long Island.

I'd open the shop at 6 a.m. and work till 10 p.m. or sometimes midnight, seven days a week. I got varicose veins from being on my feet all day—I was exhausted. What I wanted was to be a toe dancer, or play the piano or take art lessons. But I never complained. Who would I complain to? I think I was an asset to the business. Does it sound like I'm saying that in conceit?

Larry was like me, hating having to depend on my family for money and things. Do you know, he'd go buy cookies from the A&P a couple doors down rather than come into the bakery and eat the cakes for free? A lot of days, I'd leave before the boys were awake and come back home when they were asleep. I worried they were lonely. I knew they were unhappy. I thought of them all day. But I always knew where they were. I could look out the window and see them playing basketball across the street at Central School. Larry became a wonderful player. Do you know he scored 50 points in a high school game?

We moved to different apartments, looking for a better place. There were wealthy children all around the boys, and they were embarrassed because we didn't have much. Larry was so upset when he only had an accordion player at his bar mitzvah and his friends had all had bands. I felt terrible, but I never told the boys I was hurt or how hard things were. I just wouldn't. I felt so bad for them, not having a father. I felt they were cheated. I couldn't even face them. It was easier in a way to work those hours. I'd forget everything when I worked. Then they'd go to camp for two months each summer. That was a wonderful experience for them, don't you think?

Larry walked onto the campus at North Carolina to play basketball in 1959, and his story was no longer one that his mother could tell. The Tar Heels were the closest he'd ever come to what he'd dreamed a family could be. All a boy had to do was sacrifice his ego and do things the Carolina way, the Right Way, to belong.

You set picks. Helped teammates on defense. Practiced over and over the footwork on a drop-step or a box-out or an L-cut. Hit the boards. Hit the floor. Hit the open man. Acknowledged the assist. *Celebrated* the assist. It all smelled so much like the first-generation immigrants' code he'd inhaled throughout his childhood: People who came along before you figured out the right way to do things. If you failed to follow them, you disrespected them, you put yourself above them. It spilled over to life off the court. Opening doors for people, hustling across the street to help an old woman carry her bags, being on time, dressing sharp, shucking off praise, controlling your emotions were all part of the Right Way. Once you got everyone around you doing it that way, the victories piled up, the family grew tighter, and years after you had left, you remained part of a clan that at any hour could call or visit the father who never left: Dean Smith.

Larry led the ABA in assists his first three years as a pro, set the ABA assist record with 23 in a game. Then he became a coach, the keeper of a legacy, a branch of his sport's most legendary family tree. James Naismith, who *invented* the game, taught Phog Allen. Phog Allen taught Dean Smith. Dean Smith taught Larry. It was a source of deep pride, the only thing Larry ever came even close to saying in conceit: "My background," he'd say softly, ducking his head, "is probably better than anyone's."

No coach was ever quicker than Larry at converting a collection of guys into a family. At UCLA he'd teach the freshmen at dinner how to start with the silverware on the outside. In the pros he took new players to look for apartments or cars and shoved restaurant tables together so his team could gather for a feast.

No coach was ever quicker at spotting the smallest misstep, the slightest detour off the Right Way. He could stop a slam-bang scrimmage and tell every player exactly what he'd done on his last two trips up and down the court, as if a camera were clicking at each instant, seeing each of the pieces in the swirling whole. He'd stop game film and inspect the body language of players on the bench to see who was truly committed to the Right Way.

It was a purist's approach that seemed more suited to college than the pros, yet it worked, almost instantly, everywhere. He took the next-to-last-place Carolina Cougars to a 57–27 first-place finish in his first head coaching job, in 1972–73, then, two years later, the last-place Denver Rockets on an ABA-record 65–19 ride. His first UCLA team started four freshman in 1979–80 and reached the NCAA championship game. Three years later he had the laughable New Jersey Nets humming at 47–29 when he left to coach at Kansas. Five years after that, he and his assistants felt so much like family

that they all squeezed their left testicle in crunch time for luck, and the
Jayhawks squeezed out their first NCAA crown since 1952. In the nine years
that followed, his San Antonio Spurs, L.A. Clippers and Indiana Pacers all
went further than they'd ever gone before.

At each new place, he arrived flush with hope that here he'd begin
carving out the long-lasting father-son relationships with his players that
he treasured. Somehow, though, his sensitive heart would begin recording
reasons why this was not the perfect family, the perfect home. Then—three
times in 50 months in one dizzying stretch—he'd be gone. Some players
would be bitter, some relieved. Many would cry.

He and his brother, Herb, a college and professional coach for 40
years, drifted apart, and barely spoke for years. His mother, aunts and
uncles wondered why they rarely saw or heard from Larry...and his wives
did too. He had two children in his first marriage, remarried and adopted
his second wife's daughter, then married a third time and had two more
children. Through it all, he remained one of the shyest, sweetest gentlemen
you'd ever want to meet.

Then, in May 1997, with time running out in his coaching life, came his
ninth team in 26 years—the worst-record-in-the-NBA 76ers. And the player
whom he'd already told himself he couldn't coach. Allen Iverson.

*I wanted Larry to get rid of him. He was so much trouble; Larry tolerated
him a great deal. But look at him now. He's the most exciting player to watch.
He's very alert. I just want those big fellas to leave him alone. I can't stand
the way they knock him around.*

*The trouble is, Larry keeps all his problems inside. He doesn't sleep. I'm
the same way. I miss him terribly, but he has no time—but I forgive him. He
hasn't got a meanness in him. He's given me so much pleasure. You can tell
him that.*

"Wherever I go, everyone goes. Whenever I eat, everyone eats." This Allen
promised his family and friends on the eve of his selection, at No. 1, in the
1996 NBA draft. He called that Keepin' It Real.

His eyes moist, he told his aunts and uncles that his talent was God's
compensation to the Iversons for all their pain and loss, for Grandma
Ethel's death in a diabetic coma in 1994, for the wrongful death of Ann's
mother's in the early '70s, for the fathers who had vanished and the poverty
that had rushed in to fill their place. He was the payback. He'd carry them
all to the top, buy them houses and cars and cut them checks, shout down
their squabbles on his cell phone in the bowels of arenas 40 minutes before
games, go out and drop another 40, and sometimes, when it was all too
much, check into a hotel rather than stay at one of his crowded houses. "I

make all that money," he said, "and it ain't enough. I gotta make more to help all the people around me."

That's how the Iversons saw life: It was a circle, forever arcing back to old times and old pain. Keepin' It Real meant keeping the same friends and girlfriend he'd had since he was 16, before jail and before fame made everything suspect. It meant covering himself with 21 tattoos, virtually all about loyalty and strength, and wanting desperately to wear the same team's uniform his entire pro career. It meant staying inside the circle, never looking beyond it to find himself. At 4 a.m., on his way home from a club, he'd dial his mother—the third time he'd spoken to her that day—and say, I just called to tell you I love you and to thank you for having me. When his shooting touch went cold, she hurried to the bench and rubbed holy oil on his forehead, while Larry did a double take.

Keepin' It Real permitted Allen to sell without selling out. Permitted him to accept $50 million to hawk Reebok sneakers—as long as they had to drag him from his bed to get to the Reebok ad shoot two hours late and he didn't have to backslap or small-talk anyone. Permitted him to take white man's money after white justice had flung him in jail. Permitted him to blow off shootarounds, as long as he treated every game like a bayonet charge. To be late for a team bus, then stroll aboard and crack up everyone with his impersonations of players and coaches, his uncanny caricatures of them sketched on napkins, his rendition of Michael Jackson's *Thriller* video, staggering zombies and all. To be the Man of the House, as long as he could remain the little boy. To launch 27 shots a game because life was not about winning the Right Way, but any freakin' way you could.

Is it any wonder what those first three years together held for the son of Ann Iverson and the son of Ann Brown? Any surprise that the kid who lived life in a circle and the man who lived it in a line—away, straight away from the past and the pain—forever bewildered and enraged each other? "This team," says Sixers general manager Billy King, "felt the tension between Larry and Allen every day."

Of Allen's story Larry knew but a little, mostly about the bowling-alley incident and his two years at Georgetown. Of Larry's past, Allen knew virtually nothing beyond what a few players on other teams had told him: The cat knows the game, but he'll try to get in your head, try to mess with your game, look out.

No, the only wonder was that they remained together. After all, Larry possessed complete control over personnel decisions, more power than he'd ever had over a franchise: He could have traded Allen whenever he wished. But where would he again find such a warrior, such a bundle of quickness and energy and heart? So, instead, he traded or cut everyone else, *literally*—including such offensive talents as Jerry Stackhouse, Jim Jackson, Derrick Coleman, Tim Thomas and Larry Hughes. He began surrounding Allen with so many players who did it the Right Way that Allen could do it some other way and it might still turn out right, and the Sixers might yet become a lopsided but lovable family that delivered Larry the one thing he didn't have to go with the Olympic gold medals he'd won as a player and as an assistant coach, and his NCAA title: an NBA ring.

That is, until last summer, when Larry couldn't bear another day of selling out Dean and Phog and James. He had King cobble together a four-team, 22-player trade. Allen paced the floor at night, unable to sleep or eat, tormented by the knowledge that Larry could leave him by the roadside.

Allen called Croce, the tattooed team president who sat with him in the trainer's room before every home game, one of the few white men he'd trusted since the handcuff creases had faded from his wrists, perhaps the only executive in sports who could have held this relationship together even as long as this. For an hour and a half, he said the same words over and over: I'm gonna change. I'm gonna get married. I'm buyin' a big house. I'm ready to be a leader. I wanna be a captain. I'm gonna be on time. I can do it. Croce believed him, but it was only the decision by one of the other players involved in the deal—Sixers center Matt Geiger's refusal to waive his contractual right to a 15% bonus should he be traded—that kept Larry from turning Allen into a Piston.

Allen met with Larry just before camp and repeated his vows. "I want to have the kind of relationship with you," he said, "that Magic Johnson had with Pat Riley and Michael Jordan had with Phil Jackson." Those words touched Larry. That's all he'd ever wanted, too. The reaching out began.

It's still a work in progress. Remember that, no matter what you might've read or seen on TV. It began in chaos, a training camp convulsed by controversy over lyrics on Allen's as-yet-unreleased first rap CD. Coach Brown held his tongue. Co-captain Iverson kept his vows. The Sixers shot out to a 10–0 start, opening a gap their Eastern Conference rivals never closed. Teammates who'd quietly resented Allen's trigger finger when he wasn't showing up in the weight room or at practice were satisfied now that he was, and the victories kept piling up.

No doubt you know about Larry and Allen's shiniest moment, when Allen's fourth-quarter explosion carried the East All-Star team, which Larry was coaching, to a back-from-the-dead win over the West, and Allen's first breathless words at the podium after receiving the game's MVP award were, "Where's my coach? Where's my coach?" What you didn't see was what the Jewish grandfather carried in his pocket the second half of the season: a black crucifix given to him by Ann Iverson.

What you didn't hear was Allen stepping into the van awaiting him after practice one day and announcing, out of the blue, to his bodyguard-driver, "Man, I'm gonna win this man a ring. He's been in the league all this time and come so close and never got one. His first one gonna be *my* first one. Can't wait to see his face when I pour that champagne on his head."

What you might've noticed was Allen beginning to dish the ball more often to teammates when he was double-teamed. What you might've missed was Larry making a point of smiling and saying hello to Allen's tribe as he departed the locker room. Allen making eye contact and nodding when Larry gave him on-court instructions. Larry asking Allen into his office for input before February's Theo Ratliff-and-Toni Kukoc-for-Dikembe Mutombo trade. Larry giving Allen pats on the butt, and Allen giving Larry hugs.

Each man keeps forcing the other to discover the piece of himself he'd left somewhere behind. Allen began learning that a little trust and responsibility didn't make him someone's lackey. Larry began learning that he could let go a little without the world spinning out of control. Maybe it's just a coincidence, but traces of the circle began appearing in his life. He asked his brother, Herb, to be an assistant coach with the Sixers this year, and the two men who once barely spoke now talk away the half-hour in the car on their way to and from games.

"I'm learning how to talk to him when I have a problem," says Allen, "and he's learning to talk to me. We've both learned a lot about basketball and life. I know one thing. Coach's voice will never leave my head as long as I live."

"There are things that still drive you crazy," says Larry. "I've never had a challenge like this, but it's happening in little steps. It's 8,000 times better than it was. I don't judge anymore. I don't look at things so much as right or wrong. I realize now he's not trying to disrespect his teammates or provoke a reaction. It's just the way he is. I keep reminding myself of how he treats his mother and his family. He's got such a big heart. If I were a player, he'd be one of my best friends. It's a joy to see people focusing on the good things. He could do more for the game than anyone because of who he was and how he's changing. It could be the story of what our league is all about."

In living rooms and NBA arenas everywhere, people who once recoiled from Allen now watched him in a conflicted state of grudging wonder at his will and his work ethic. But beware, because the bridge between Allen and Larry still trembles. Allen stormed out of a practice in December when Larry waived Vernon Maxwell, a buddy of Allen's. At a team breakfast meeting in Chicago that same month, Allen let his coach have it. Larry's ceaseless dissatisfaction, he said, was grinding down the Sixers, making them feel as if they were losers instead of a first-place team.

Larry waited—surely someone would come to his defense. The room remained silent. All the old pain flared through his heart, all the old need to leave before he was left rushed up his throat. He coached that night's victory over the Chicago Bulls in monosyllables, thinking it might be the last 76ers game he coached. Then he flew back to Philly so distraught that he felt ill, unable to step onto the practice floor but nauseated by the knowledge that if he didn't—if, in mid-season, he left an unheralded team that then owned the NBA's best record—his legacy would be sealed as a hit-and-run driver instead of as a Hall of Fame coach. He missed two practices. His wife, an unending source of encouragement, looked at his sallow face and told him that perhaps he should quit.

Larry returned, but a few months later, as pain kept stabbing his chest wall, he submitted to tests that revealed a hiatal hernia and acid reflux. Somehow, Mr. Brown, said his doctor, you'd better take more care with your diet and stop swallowing so much stress.

Before every Sixers playoff game this year, Larry's 94-year-old mother will turn on the television and sit in the green chair beside the flowery bedspread in her nursing home in Charlotte. If the Sixers cannot forge an early lead, she'll slowly rise, turn off the TV, grip her walker and pace the living room, kitchen and bedroom, noticing the spots that needed dusting, until she feels it's safe to return to the TV and check again.

Four-hundred-and-fifty miles north, in a house just outside Philadelphia, Allen's mother will wake up late in the afternoon, get all her "tootin' and burpin' out" on her abdominal exercise machine, then do a half hour on her cardiovascular machine to keep her blood pressure from climbing to the near-fatal numbers it reached a few years ago. She'll bathe, dress and work the phones, make sure no one in her vast clan is in need, then apply the finishing cosmetic touches. She'll gather her folder full of pictures of her son to sign and give, along with hugs and admonitions to stay in school and Keep It Real, to the children who'll flock around her. Right before the game starts, she'll look over at the bench, at her son and that man.

Every young man needs an old man. Because getting older is like climbing a mountain. Each year, the older you get, the higher you are, the more distance you can see. You can warn the people below you what you see, so they don't run up against things. An old white man told me that once.

Larry asked me to help him this year, and I am, because Bubba Chuck had so many people around him against Larry Brown. That means nothin', 'cause

I'm for him. Larry's got so much determination and caring in him—I can see it in his big brown eyes. Sure as my name is Ann Iverson, Larry Brown's gonna win a championship here.

I met him in the X-ray room when he came back to check on Bubba Chuck's shoulder during a game. I told Larry he was meant to be here. Why question it? Why run? Sure, soon as Larry takes Allen out of a game, there's gonna be a stink in the air. That's just how Bubba Chuck is. I told Larry if you let Allen Iverson think you're a softy, you'll lose Allen Iverson. But if Allen Iverson sees you stick to your guns, he'll respect you. Told Larry Brown, God put you here for a reason—to guide my child. Told Larry Brown, please don't leave my son.

COLORFUL CHARACTERS

Rodman Unchained

The Spurs' no-holds-barred forward gives
new meaning to the running game

BY MICHAEL SILVER

"Rare Bird," read the cover of the May 29, 1995 issue. It's difficult to appreciate now just how impactful the accompanying image was: a prominent Black athlete on the cover of a national magazine, wearing only a rhinestone dog collar, short leather shorts, a shiny vest and, for good measure, holding a blue parrot.

The story, written by Michael Silver, was unlike any that had come before in the magazine, or likely since. Silver had flown to Los Angeles before Game 6 of the Spurs-Lakers conference semifinals, hoping to get Rodman to open up. That night, after a series-clinching win, Silver found himself at a club in Beverly Hills with Rodman and comedian Jon Lovitz. "Dennis was just starting to get weird, and I knew he was supposed to be a guy who could drink," recalls Silver. "I'm like, 'I'm 29, he's 34, I party pretty hard. I can hang with one 34-year-old for one night. It's not going to be a problem.'" Silver pauses. "Cut to me pouring shots out under the table—and they're all the shots like kamikazes. I'm like holy s---,he's a freak of nature!"

A three-day odyssey ensued: a late-night flight to Vegas; an evening at a gay bar; observing Rodman in a near-showdown with then-Spurs GM Gregg Popovich; and, finally, a sleepless Saturday night at Rodman's house in San Antonio, Silver typing out his story on a bulky laptop surrounded by exotic birds while Rodman entertained himself with strippers.

The result is both a portrait of a unique NBA character and a record of a vastly different era in sports, and sports writing.

———————————

The Sunday morning topics at Dennis Rodman's house have ranged from gay sex to Pearl Jam lyrics to his own drunken failures at Las Vegas craps tables, and now America's most provocative athlete has a more compelling matter to discuss. "Let's talk about shot selection," says Rodman, his low voice barely audible amid the clatter of 15 exotic birds and two German shepherds who actually hail from Deutschland.

It is the day before Rodman's employer, the San Antonio Spurs, will open the Western Conference finals at home against the Houston Rockets. Is Rodman so consumed by basketball that he wants to discuss it here amid a gathering so eclectic it makes MTV's *Real World* look like *The Waltons*?

"Hell, no," Rodman says, then clarifies. He wants to talk about the magazine photo shoot that is about to take place, one he thinks should include shots of him wearing makeup and women's clothing or, better yet, nothing at all. "I mean, why not be a little risque?" Rodman asks. "Push the envelope."

The beauty of this attitude is not just that it is designed to test the boundaries of mainstream society but that Rodman has absolutely no concern for how his antics will play in the basketball community. And though he has a desperate and obvious need to draw attention to himself, Rodman doesn't give a flying halter top about what his NBA peers or employers think of his behavior. He is moved far more by the opinions of the people in his midst: Gregg, a manager for a mail-order company specializing in gay men's apparel; Lara, a dancer, model and horse trainer; Bill, who works for Rodman's excavation company; and several other guests.

"I don't give a –– about basketball anymore," Rodman says. "It's like the Back to the Future ride in Orlando, like virtual reality. I'm already out of life in the NBA. I'm just living my life the way I want to. I'm not an athlete anymore. I'm an entertainer."

An hour later, when Rodman emerges wearing a shiny tank top, metallic hot pants and a rhinestone dog collar, his guests ooh, aah and gawk in amusement. "Dennis is in one of his transvestite moods," says Rodman's friend Amy Frederick, rolling her eyes. Were it not Rodman, a man who dreams of playing his last NBA game au naturel, this behavior might be a bit shocking.

This Sunday at home falls near the end of a 72-hour odyssey of Rodman-inspired insanity, a boundless weekend bender that has spanned three states and five figures' worth of frequent flier miles, and collected an entourage that at various times included Hollywood celebrities and fawning women, awestruck gamblers and acid-eating Deadheads, sultry strippers and a Bill Laimbeer–sized drag queen. Above all, this weekend has provided a rousing demonstration that Rodman is a rare human with both the positioning and the resolve to live by his own rules and attack life without regard to the demands or plans or standards imposed by others.

Flashbacks to impressions of Rodman that began to form three days earlier—on Thursday night, to be exact—now seem like dim and distant memories.

It's an hour before tipoff of the sixth game of the Spurs' Western Conference playoff series against the Los Angeles Lakers, which San Antonio leads three games to two. The San Antonio players are gathered in the cramped confines of the visitors' locker room at the Great Western Forum. At one end of the room five Spurs are watching a video of Game 5 and quietly talking strategy. One man sits near that group but not with them, oblivious to his environs. Clad in plaid flannel pants and a white T-shirt, senses shielded by Oakley sunglasses and large headphones, the rebel hunches over in his chair, rocks out to the music and lets his mind run free.

At that moment it's impossible to tell where Rodman has flown off to. It's too early in the Rodman joyride to realize that the man who will be the catalyst for San Antonio's series-clinching victory is preparing for battle by listening to Pearl Jam at about 7,000 decibels and traveling via fantasy to places most people will never admit to venturing: horrific torture chambers, chosen suicide spots, bedrooms with various partners. This is a Rodman who is darker and weirder than his image—the one who, depending on your outlook, is either a selfish problem child or an authentic genius who transcends his sport. Most of the Spurs would choose the former, less-flattering description, and that would be hunky-dory with Dennis the Menace, who values the opinion of his basketball peers about as much as Albert Einstein valued his report card.

Right now all that has been revealed is a 34-year-old, sculpted 6'8" black man with hair of a red-orange color that looks like it was lifted off a 1977 Camaro. Eyes closed, Rodman is visualizing himself on stage with Pearl Jam, drumming to the beat of "Indifference": "I'll swallow poison until I grow immune. I will scream my lungs out till it fills this room. How much difference does it make?"

In L.A., Rodman is the difference. Having survived a full-game benching for insubordination earlier in the series, he assumes the incongruous role of battle-tested leader. One by one before the game, teammates Sean Elliott, David Robinson and Avery Johnson approach the man who owns the only two NBA title rings on the Spurs' active roster and ask, "What's the best way to approach a game like this?" Rodman tells them to stop thinking and thrust themselves into the flow.

There are reasons Rodman is the best rebounding forward in NBA history, and the most important one is not that he works his butt off or gets outrageously physical or has no fear. It has more to do with the fact that, like hockey star Wayne Gretzky, he sees the game like no one else and is two moves ahead of the competition. He is less athlete than artist. He gets into his flow and becomes one with the ball, and before anyone else knows what's happening, it is his. "It's a whole different game for me," says Rodman, the winner of the last four NBA rebounding titles. "I know where the ball's going to go."

Once the game begins the L.A. fans ride Rodman hard. They chant, "Rodman sucks," but it becomes increasingly clear as he plays to the crowd— at one point he playfully knocks the hat off a courtside heckler—that he is made for this town. Athletically, he carries a mystical beauty. He runs up and down the court like a gazelle, and his defense is a study in body control. Even the weakest part of Rodman's game, his offense, is deceptively potent. "He can control the tempo of a game without scoring, and that's amazing," says teammate Doc Rivers, an 11-year guard. "He's a great offensive player. He's so smart, and he sees the floor like a guard. He'll set the key screen or make the great pass. His pass might not lead to the basket, but it's the pass that leads to the pass that leads to the basket."

San Antonio wins 100–88. Every time the Lakers make a charge, a burst of energy from Rodman helps repel them. For the first time as a Spur he assumes the unlikely role of floor leader, directing traffic with emphatic arm waves and barking out commands. Afterward he strides off the court, past the locker room and into an empty corridor. "This is what gets me so jacked, winning a series in L.A.," he says. "This town gets me off."

Rodman refuses to talk to the media, saying his teammates deserve the attention. Later he relents. Then in the parking lot he charges a Laker fan, chasing him down and grabbing him by the throat. Rodman's explanation? "He reached into my bag and stole my shades. I told him to keep the damn things." A 12-passenger stretch limo is there to rescue Rodman and transport him to Sanctuary, a trendy Beverly Hills hangout.

"You need a name," yells Jack (Une) Haley, Rodman's friend, teammate and guardian angel. A seven-footer who seldom plays but has ridden Rodman's coattails to a small celebrity of his own, Haley is the Spurs' middle man, the guy who alternately explains Rodman to the world and explains the rules of the world to Rodman. Though Rodman seldom listens—"He rebels just to rebel," Haley says—the two form an odd couple who come with their own lingo. In exaggerated California accents the two bust out words like schnay, a rough equivalent of the term "not" that Rodman's ex-girlfriend, Madonna, helped popularize. The key word in this private language is june (pronounced gee-OOOON), which serves both as Rodman's nickname and as a verb form that can be substituted for virtually any act. Haley goes by the shortened Une, and now he's brainstorming. "I've got it! You're Si," he says, addressing me.

Sigh?

"No, Si—S.I., for your magazine."

I don't dare say schnay.

Sanctuary is filled with celebs, deal makers and ladies of the evening, but Rodman is the center of attention. His table includes Haley, models galore and comedian Jon Lovitz. Movie producers and agents come over to shake his hand and pine for his time. "I will be in show business," he says, "but I'm not going to play some weak-ass basketball player. That would be stupid." An agent who says he helped put together *Pulp Fiction* thinks Rodman would be a classic Quentin Tarantino villain. Rodman is interested, though he says he's also talking with Warner Bros. and Disney about big projects.

Later, in the jumpin' back room, shots of Jägermeister and Goldschläger are passed around. Rodman says that he has never been into drugs, but he can drink like a fish, and keeping up requires commitment. Haley, who played at UCLA, is getting autograph requests up the wazoo while Lovitz watches. Only in L.A. could Jack Haley be bigger than Jon Lovitz. "Hey," Lovitz protests, "he's not that much bigger than me. Only about a foot."

A woman with a sexy Middle Eastern accent wants to know what the deal is with the flame-haired dude. "Who ees this man?" she asks. "What makes heem so special? Why does everybody want so badly to speak with heem?"

The answer is that Rodman, after three decades of confusion, anger and longing for acceptance, turned a corner a couple of years ago. He became a man who strives to live for the moment, with no watch, no pager and few worries about how he may be perceived—but with a quenchless thirst to be noticed. His explanation: "I woke up one day and said to myself, Hey, my life has been a big cycle. One month I'm bleeding to death, one month I'm in a psycho zone. Then, all of a sudden, the cycles were in balance."

Rodman eats when he's hungry, sleeps when he collapses and does whatever the hell he pleases. Few celebrities can pull this off, and athletes almost never do. He lives more like a rock star, an updated version of Jimi Hendrix or Jim Morrison, than an athlete. There is a fatalistic side to Rodman, but he's more of a '90s dissident than a '60s insurgent. He thinks anything political is crap and has adopted a younger generation's everything-is-screwed-up-beyond-repair resignation. He is a man drunk on his own ability to do whatever he wants, a rebel without a boss.

Why don't more people in his position behave so freely? "They hide behind their money, fame and success," he says. "Then all of a sudden they have no opinion, or they're afraid to voice it because they're afraid someone will take away what they've got. You can be famous and still voice your opinion, as long as you don't hurt anybody. You can do anything you want."

It is not surprising that some of Rodman's friends, including Madonna and Eddie Vedder, are icons. Rodman met Vedder, the Pearl Jam singer, and other band members two years ago; he has hung out backstage for three shows, a number he plans to triple next month. "I'm going to tour with them for two weeks," he says. "They'd better let me sit in on drums, or I'm out of there."

He busted loose from Madonna a year ago, ending a hot-and-heavy romance, but not before he learned a great deal from her about shock value and self- promotion. It is 3:30 Friday morning, and a heated Rodman is out front of Sanctuary talking Material Girl with a bouncer. "She wanted to get married," he says. "She wanted to have my baby. She said, 'Be in a hotel room in Las Vegas on this specific day so you can get me pregnant.' She had ways of making you feel like you're King Tut, but she also wanted to cuddle and be held." Through her publicist, Madonna declined comment.

The Spurs return to San Antonio on Friday afternoon, and aside from a trip to a local workout facility, Rodman's day is relatively tame. That night he is back at his house with his inner circle, barbecuing. Included are Rodman's surrogate brother, Bryne Rich, whose family essentially adopted Rodman when he was 19; Rich's girlfriend, Frederick; and Dwight Manley, a Southern California rare-coin dealer who, despite being five years younger than Rodman, serves as his caretaker. Rodman has about 800 messages on his answering machine; he speeds through most of them and writes down nothing.

At 9 p.m., the meat still thawing, Manley announces Continental has a 10:40 flight to Vegas. "Let's do it," Rodman says, and an hour and 39 minutes later, the five of us sprint through the San Antonio airport like O.J. Simpson, circa 1977, making the flight with seconds to spare. As the plane takes off, Rodman is blasting his favorite Pearl Jam song, "Release," through his portable CD player—"I'll ride the wave where it takes me"—and laughing. "What are we *doing*?" he asks, and everyone cracks up.

Everyone in the group is drinking Bloody Marys immediately after takeoff—everyone except Manley, who talks about Rodman and how he met him two years ago at a craps table at the Mirage in Vegas. "Dennis and

Bryne were supposed to be out there for a few days," Manley recalls, "and they stayed for five weeks." Rodman has been known to drop as much as $30,000 on a trip but has won as much as $72,000 at a single sitting. Money, to him, seems incidental. "He makes $2.5 million a year," Manley says, "and he doesn't save a penny."

Rodman's father, Phil, deserted the family when Dennis was three. Rodman grew up in Dallas, around his mother, Shirley, and older sisters, Debra and Kim, both of whom were college basketball All-Americas. At 22 he was working as a janitor at the Dallas–Fort Worth airport before he got his life together through basketball and became a key member of the Detroit Piston teams that won NBA titles in '89 and '90. "He never got to be a rebel as a kid," Rich says, "so he's really going for it now."

Says Manley: "It's the classic case of a boy who grew up without a strong male role model. He is learning manhood on his own, and he's learning it with no one to tell him no. He can get away with anything. No one stops him. When you're raised without boundaries, you have to find them for yourself."

Vegas is going nuts on this warm Friday night. The Grateful Dead is in town, and Rodman receives glassy-eyed, LSD-inspired stares as he walks into the Mirage Hotel. He heads for the craps table and starts blowing dough.

The American public's lack of composure around celebrities never ceases to amaze, but Rodman handles it pretty well. One guy wants to trade his beat-up Vermont baseball cap for Rodman's black lid that says simply APHRODISIAC. "Schnay," Rodman answers. A pair of buxom Australian expatriates who have settled in L.A. end up with the crew and follow Rodman into the men's room. Later a man spots Rodman and lifts up his girlfriend's miniskirt, revealing her bikini underwear. Rodman smiles and moves on. Everyone wants to talk basketball, and he just wants to roll bones until dawn.

Sleep comes after Saturday's sunrise and is ended rudely at nine o'clock by the voice of Haley, who has tracked Rodman down and telephoned his suite at the Mirage. "What the -- are you doing?" Haley rails at Manley. After some back and forth, Manley wakes up Rodman, now $5,000 lighter, and puts him on the phone.

The dilemma here is nothing new. Rodman has been in trouble all season with the Spurs. San Antonio general manager Gregg Popovich, a former Marine, and coach Bob Hill set rules for the team, and Rodman decides the rules are stupid and disregards them. Rodman refers to Hill as Boner and has nothing very positive to say about the hard-line Popovich.

This time Rodman wants to blow off a Saturday afternoon film session and a team dinner back in San Antonio. Haley, in the name of stability, urges

Rodman to be there. The problem is, the harder you push Rodman, the more likely he is to rebel for the sake of rebellion. It's a dangerous prospect because he has already pushed his superiors and teammates near their limits. In San Antonio's Game 3 defeat by the Lakers, Rodman lay down on the floor with a towel over his head and took off his shoes during a second-half timeout. Hill sat him for the remainder of that game and all of Game 4, which the Spurs won, and held him out of the starting lineup for Game 5 as all the while he and Rodman engaged in a hissing match via the media.

"That's just immaturity," says Rivers, who joined the Spurs in December. "If you want to go out and party and have crazy hair, that doesn't make you a bad guy. But when your actions impact the team, that's not good. There have been guys who have decided we'd be better off without him. I haven't done that yet, but I haven't been here that long."

Despite Haley's protests Rodman wants to follow through with a plan to jet to Phoenix for Game 7 of the Sun-Rocket series this afternoon, "just to freak everyone out." Haley calls Hill, who promptly phones Rodman. After 20 seconds Rodman slams down the phone and launches into a tirade: "Yeah, I really want to go to a goddam dinner with all the wives and old people— that'll be really fun." Haley is relieved by Rodman's decision to attend the dinner, saying later, "The organization has been fair with Dennis. If he'd have blown this off, the players would have said, 'To hell with him.'"

It's Saturday afternoon, time to get down and dirty, though it takes a while to figure this out. Rodman is at a specialty store in the Las Vegas airport, buying a sheet of Elvis stamps, and I'm carrying four pieces of luggage and getting ready to fly home to Oakland. We walk to the gate for Rodman's 12:15 p.m. flight to Houston, and I start to say goodbye. "Why the hell don't you get your ass on this plane so we can do some talking?" he asks, and before a plausible answer comes to mind, we're sitting in first class, listening to Eddie Vedder moan, "Why go home, why go home..."

Sleep deprivation has turned us into a punchy and expansive pair. Rodman is talking about life, philosophy, his divorce and getting naked in public, which naturally leads to Madonna. Rodman has great respect for his former squeeze, who has done a lot to promote homosexual lifestyles. Rodman often goes to gay bars in San Antonio and doesn't shy away from hugging and kissing male friends. He says that's as far as it has gone, "but I visualize being with another man. Everybody visualizes being gay—they think, Should I do it or not? The reason they can't is because they think it's unethical. They think it's a sin. Hell, you're not bad if you're gay, and it doesn't make you any less of a person."

Rodman's eyes are glistening, but he is not laughing. I ask him if he thinks about dying young. "Sometimes I say I'm going to play basketball and go-go-go until I drop dead," he says. "I'm not afraid of dying at all. It's just the next boundary."

Does he contemplate suicide?

"Sure. Sometimes I dream about just taking a gun and blowing my head off. If I ever know it's time to die, I'll head for a waterfall and camp out for a day, knowing I only have 24 hours to live, fly off the waterfall and just juuune."

The next question is whether Rodman's fantasies include murder. "Yeah, I'd kill somebody—in my mind," he says. "All of a sudden I lose control of what I'm doing. I'm in a torture chamber, and I've got to fight my way out. I definitely come out with a vengeance."

And who, in this fantasy, does Rodman most want to kill? "The person I used to be. He tried to be something he wasn't. He wanted everybody to like him because he was an athlete who had this and had that. He was dead wrong."

Rodman and I get to Houston with an hour layover before the connection to San Antonio and head to an airport bar to watch the last quarter of the Rocket-Sun game, with the winner to face the Spurs. "We should be there, SI," Rodman mumbles forcefully, and then we're drinking beer and eating gumbo and talking about which NBA players have the most guts. Hakeem Olajuwon, who is leading the Rockets to victory, is an obvious choice. "Best center in the game," Rodman says, placing Robinson, his teammate, second. He also picks Tim Hardaway and Clyde Drexler and the underappreciated Danny Ainge. The Suns expire as we race to catch the flight.

Back in San Antonio, Rodman returns from the team dinner. "Ever been to a gay bar?" he asks.

At 11 p.m., propped up by adrenaline and chocolate-covered coffee beans, I'm in the passenger seat of Rodman's custom Ford monster truck. "Everyone in the state knows my truck," Rodman says of the pink-and-white vehicle, "and they all know where I live."

Much later, after a night of drinking and dancing at that hopping gay bar, we pull up to his house and find the trees out front streamed with toilet paper. A carload of young revelers passes by, leaving a wake of unintelligible yells. We walk through the back door, past the four bottles of Goldschläger in the backup refrigerator, and understand each other without speaking. I will write all night and then be gone, out of Rodman's whirlwind, leaving him alone to pursue his calling as an unfettered spirit. Rodman's German shepherds are barking unconscionably, and his exotic birds are squawking with abandon. The Spurs' 10 a.m. practice will begin in a few hours.

Something profound needs to be said as we separate, but the silence persists. I'm walking to my computer when Rodman's low bellow runs me down. "Have fun *juuuning* that story," he says merrily. "And wake me up about 10:30."

He seems to be kidding, but who can know?

— POSTSCRIPT —

When Silver's story came out, it nearly overshadowed the conference finals. Talk radio went nuts. Newspaper columnists weighed in. "The beginning of the end," wrote a concerned Mitch Albom. "Rodman Robs Game of Values," read the *Seattle Times* headline. "Rodman: Clown or Monster?" asked the *Miami Herald*. Rodman eventually appeared on *Letterman*. The attention nudged him ever further toward his new stated goal: to exist as "an entertainer" rather than a basketball player.

The story had a galvanizing effect on the LGBTQ community. This was two decades before Jason Collins came out. Rock stars like David Bowie and Freddie Mercury had played with gender identity but little precedent existed in the world of major men's sports. And now fans were reading quotes like this, from Rodman: "Everybody visualizes being gay—they think, 'Should I do it or not?' The reason they can't is because they think it's unethical. They think it's a sin. Hell, you're not bad if you're gay, and it doesn't make you any less of a person."

Silver witnessed the effect. "[Dennis] lived most of his life scared to show his weirdness," says Silver, who remained close with Rodman, writing the second of his four memoirs. "Once he showed it, he was so overwhelmed by how many people came out of the woodwork to support him. All the freaks, and that's a broad definition, anyone who's freaky in any way, he was their hero for speaking out. And he got all this positive reinforcement he hadn't seen coming. He was surrounded by other artists, people that didn't fit in, whether transgender or people who lived on the fringes."

In retrospect, Rodman had a remarkable platform. He could have become an advocate or cultural ambassador. That wasn't his style though. "Dealing with Dennis is like dealing with your best friend when you're 10 years old," says Silver. "There's nobody better. You love that guy. It's beautiful. But sometimes when you need to have an emotionally developed interaction or a logistically important interaction, it's like, I'm dealing with my best friend when I'm 10."

JUNE 1, 1998

One Last Shot

Quitting her job and pounding herself into shape, scrappy
former college star Sheila Tighe tried to break into pro
basketball—after 14 years away from the game

BY JOHNETTE HOWARD

*A wonderful dispatch from the early days of women's pro ball, when those
who'd been born too late finally got a shot at the big time.*

If you happened to be poolside at La Quinta Resort in Palm Springs, Calif., a
couple of weeks ago, perhaps you noticed the 36-year-old woman wearing
the god-awful black toenail polish—black because, she joked, she'd just been
to war. Or perhaps you glimpsed the bruises exploding like tiny fireworks on
her arms, or the angry red scratches around them. Perhaps you gasped at
the half-dollar-sized blisters on the bottoms of her feet, or the parchment-
colored dead skin that was peeling off because of the countless miles she'd
recently run. As she lay there on her chaise longue for four days, reading a
mystery novel and not wanting to move, those marks were the only clues to
who she once was. Or to what she'd just been through.

"And I gotta tell you," Sheila Tighe says, lapsing into her best Staten
Islandese, "when I started this five months ago, I was saying the same prayer
every friggin' night: 'Please, God, just let me make it through.'"

You see, once upon a time Sheila Tighe was one of the best players in
college basketball, a fiery 5'9" guard who scored 21.3 points per game at
Manhattan College in New York City, a two-time All-America who earned

an invitation to the '84 U.S. Olympic Trials and was a Wade Trophy finalist in 1983 and '84. Before college, at St. Peter's High, Tighe was a teenage basketball phenom whose face daily adorned a front-page corner of the *Staten Island Advance* with only the word SHEILA underneath, no last name necessary.

Tighe (pronounced TIE) was the most recruited player in the New York City area since Nancy Lieberman four years before. She received mail from 125 schools. But she stunned everybody by choosing nearby Manhattan, a tiny Catholic school where her family could see her play. Back on Staten Island, her fans shrieked, "What was she thinking?" They asked the same question in 1984 when Tighe, partly because she was despondent over her boyfriend's sudden death from an aneurysm, quit basketball cold turkey, even as offers from the European pro leagues rolled in.

The question *What was she thinking?* came up again last December when, after a 14-year hiatus from topflight basketball, Tighe closed up her Los Angeles apartment, put her successful career as a production manager for TV commercials on hold, moved into a one-room, $550-a-month efficiency in Philadelphia and embarked on a five-month odyssey to win a job on a team in the WNBA or the ABL.

"I'm not going to say someone doesn't have any chance at all if she hasn't been competing [at a high level] either here or overseas," Lin Dunn, head coach of the ABL's Portland Power, said at one of Tighe's tryouts. "But let's just say a player's chances of walking in here from nowhere and getting drafted are slim and none."

Tighe knew that. Yet she was undaunted. When she started training, she had no guarantee she'd land the three tryouts that she did. "I don't know if I came back because I just never played enough, or because of the way I quit," she said before the tryouts began. "Sometimes I think I was just born too soon."

To really understand Tighe's thinking, however, you have to go back to the Rock, Staten Islanders' nickname for their borough. Because more than anything, Sheila Tighe is Iron Mike Tighe's kid.

Though Mike and Mary Tighe had 12 children—eight girls and four boys—sports bound Mike to Sheila, his ninth child, more than to any of the others. Sheila was just like him: square-jawed and extroverted, willful and demanding and proud, with the same brown eyes that hardened in the heat of a game, then softened at the slightest wisecrack later.

As a child, she heard all the stories about how her dad had been the best high school playmaker in New York City, how he'd starred for Georgetown, then lasted until the final cut with the 1946–47 New York Knicks. On nights that Sheila had games, her father would pace the living-room floor until she got home, then they'd rehash every detail, often butting heads. She remembers that a boyfriend of hers would drop by and, before long, he and her dad might be reenacting some basketball play.

"I'll never forget the night of my senior prom," she says. "My date and two friends came to pick me up, and soon we were moving furniture in the living room, and my dad was saying to my ma, 'C'm'ere, hon, set a pick.' I finally said, 'Dad? *No*. I am *not* going to pick-and-roll in my prom dress.'"

Mike Tighe's detailed memory of basketball games amazed Sheila. So in 1987, the year she moved to L.A., she noticed immediately when her father began to act absentmindedly. The doctor's diagnosis was Alzheimer's. It would be 10 wrenching years before the disease killed Mike, at age 75, last June 25. "That absolutely had an effect on me," Sheila says. "If you interview 100 doctors, 50 will tell you Alzheimer's is hereditary. So I decided if there's something I want to do, somewhere I want to go, I do it. Now. I'm not going to wait or have regrets." After a pause she adds, "At the start of this whole thing, I thought it was just about basketball. But it became so much more."

Last summer, when the WNBA's Los Angeles Sparks launched their first season, Tighe was just a standout in her Saturday-afternoon recreation league. A few of her pickup-game friends said, "You should be playing pro," and Tighe replied, "Yeah, right"—until she attended a Sparks game, and something stirred in her. Soon she was having heart-to-heart chats with her sister Lynn, a fine point guard for Villanova from 1984 to '88 and now director of basketball operations for the ABL's Philadelphia Rage. One day Sheila was on the phone with a rec league acquaintance named Ann Donohue, a 43-year-old TV writer and the producer of series such as *Picket Fences, Murder One* and *China Beach*. Donohue kept asking Tighe, Why not come back?

As Tighe recalls, "I said, 'Ann, you don't understand. I haven't played in 14 years. I'd have to quit my job to train full time.' And Ann just said, 'Yeah, so?' Then she said, 'How much would you need—$10,000 a month, $15,000 a month?' And I nearly choked."

Donohue, laughing hard, says, "What did I know about what it would cost? I've lived in Hollywood a long time. I was like, 'You don't have a gardener, a landscaper, a masseuse?'" Still, Donohue agreed to sponsor Tighe, paying her living and training expenses.

The final piece of the puzzle fell into place when Lynn Tighe's boss, Cathy Andruzzi, then the Rage's general manager, offered Sheila a place to train. (In 1980, when Andruzzi was the coach at East Carolina, she had recruited

Sheila and been turned down.) So last December Tighe moved back East and began rising each day at 5 a.m. for 2½ hours of weightlifting, aerobic work and basketball drills with Andruzzi. Tighe would then practice with the Rage for two hours, grab a quick lunch, put in an hour or two of shooting practice by herself, have an early dinner, then play two hours of pickup games, usually against men. "I'd fall asleep by 9:30 p.m.," she says. "The next morning I'd call Cathy at five and say, 'You up yet, Sunshine?' and do it all over again."

In five months of training, Tighe took just three days off. When asked by her mother on a mid-April trip home if she'd been to confession recently, Tighe rolled her eyes and cracked, "Ma, I wish I had *time* to sin."

Thanks to a call by Andruzzi, Tighe landed one of the 66 spots at the ABL's April 22–26 predraft combine at the University of San Francisco—no small feat considering that 350 players had been considered for a precious invitation. In the two-a-day workouts, the competition was fierce. Players flung themselves into every drill, every scrimmage, every suicide sprint with their teeth bared. The tension was thick.

One coach estimated that the ABL's nine teams eventually might keep only a dozen players from the combine. (In the end 26 were drafted.) The long odds were what drove 5'6", 131-pound point guard Laurie Byrd, 38, who played sparingly last season for the San Jose Lasers, to disdain stitches and slap a butterfly bandage on a nasty slice over her right eye so she wouldn't miss a minute; they were what sent former Stanford guard Christy Hedgepeth bounding up the steps outside the gym two at a time for a quick visit to the dentist after two of her front teeth were nearly knocked out during the first evening session. Hedgepeth was back playing the next morning.

When May 5—draft day—arrived, the New England Blizzard selected Byrd, but no organization chose Tighe or Hedgepeth. For Tighe, the combine confirmed that she was in great shape. What hit her hard were the things she couldn't simulate in training: defenders flying out to challenge her shot, the physical pounding, the games all run at full speed. She played solidly, but, she admitted after the session, "I didn't stand out."

Tighe is most effective in a set offense, but the tryout scrimmages were run-and-gun affairs. "I know *how* to play," she said at the combine, "but I can't match some girls' athleticism." She had to laugh when Aneta Kausaite, 27, a guard from Emporia (Kans.) State, looked at her as they stretched one day and said, "How old are you, anyway?"

Even before she heard from the ABL, though, Tighe was back in Los Angeles for a May 3 tryout with the Sparks. By 8:30 a.m., an hour before the daylong session began at Loyola Marymount in L.A., she was bouncing in place. During warmups she drained five, six, seven jumpers in a row. "I feel good," she said. When play started, it was clear she had benefited from her ABL experience. Her game was more assertive, more confident. The coaches noticed: Tighe made the midday cut from 40 players to 24. But at day's end her name was not on the final list taped to the gym door, and she inhaled sharply, heartbroken.

After a sleepless night, Tighe caught an 8 a.m. flight to her two-day tryout in Sacramento with the WNBA Monarchs. By the last scrimmage of the second day, she could barely hoist herself from a courtside seat. Yet once on the court she fought through picks and somehow kept her feet jitterbugging on defense. She even elicited some applause when she posted up, stole a glance over her shoulder and bounced a one-hop pass to a galloping teammate cutting behind her for an easy layup.

On another play, Curtycine Jones, a rim-scraping 6-foot guard-forward from Texas who would sign with Los Angeles, blew by Tighe for a basket. The next time downcourt, Jones tried to take Tighe again, but Tighe stole the ball. When Jones went after her a third time, an irked Tighe didn't wait for her to throw a move—she karate-chopped Jones hard across both forearms. Players on both sidelines tittered and laughed.

Tighe later scored, and a teammate shouted, "I see you, Sheila." A few minutes afterward, a coach's whistle blew to stop the action. Tighe, sweat-soaked and spent, walked off and said, "Well, it's almost over."

Then she blinked and said, "What am I saying? It *is* over."

Tighe's name won't be found in any WNBA media guide or ABL box score this season. But let the record show that her last basket—the one with which she said goodbye to her dream of playing pro ball—was a sweet jumper launched from just to the right of the key. She caught the ball and, in perfect rhythm, sent it on its way, her calloused feet touching back down just as the ball whispered through the hoop. No glass. No iron. Nothing but net.

On May 11, the day that Tighe packed her rickety black 1990 Saab and made the two-hour drive to Palm Springs, the WNBA's 10 teams were convening for training camp. Though Tighe doesn't smoke, she celebrated the end of her quest with a rebellious puff on a Marlboro. Referring to the 30 or 40 phone messages on her answering machine, she said, "How do I call everyone back and say, 'Hey, I didn't make it'?"

Wedged among the how'd-you-do calls was one inviting Tighe to play in a summer league at the Hollywood Y. Games started the following Monday. "The first thing I thought was, Aw, I don't know," Tighe says. "The last time I played there, I yelled at my teammates in a huddle, '*Whoever doesn't want to set a pick for me can just get off the court now!'* and four other voices all said, 'Sub!' I thought, Maybe I need a break. Maybe I should think it over."

Who was she friggin' kidding?

"Count me in," she said.

— POSTSCRIPT —

Johnette Howard: One of the things that's always stayed with me about Sheila Tighe's quest to make a pro basketball team at the age of 36—beyond the nonstop laughs we had during the five months that photographer Lynn Johnson and I followed her—were the glimpses Sheila provided into an athlete's heart. Her chase of a roster spot in the WNBA or ABL after a 14-year break from world-class basketball was quixotic on its face—but only if you believe it was only about basketball or getting a roster spot. It was not.

Sheila was a hotly recruited schoolgirl sensation at St. Peter's High on Staten Island by 1980, and she had dozens of hilarious stories about, say, the nuns there who would sit behind the team's bench and rub holy cards on the players' backs to invoke divine intervention in tight games. She had known unsurpassed joy because of the sport—two nominations for national college player of the year while at Manhattan College, an invite to the 1984 Olympic trials—but, in time, she also associated great loss with the game. She watched her father, her greatest basketball hero, lose a brutal 10-year battle with Alzheimer's. Late in her senior year of college, she was sitting on the steps at home one day, waiting for her longtime boyfriend to pick her up for a date, and he didn't show. Hours later, she learned he'd been struck dead that afternoon by an aneurysm. The shock derailed Sheila so much she turned down offers to play in Europe, the only pro circuit for women at the time.

Infinite possibilities disappear when heartbreaks like those happen. You never know what could've been. Returning to basketball allowed Sheila to reconcile the one "what if?" she could still control. Basketball was freighted with a lot of stuff for her back then. All of it had to do with love.

JANUARY 24, 2000

Tower of Power

Ground-bound Raptors forward Charles Oakley made
his name under the boards with his elbows and his
heart. What goes on in his head is a mystery

BY PHIL TAYLOR

*Few players epitomized a team more than Charles Oakley did during the
1990s. Before the NBA changed its defensive rules, the Knicks championed a
style of play that could seem closer to football than basketball. Oakley was
New York's designated heavy—he would later title his autobiography* The Last
Enforcer*—but he was more than that. In this profile, Phil Taylor deepens our
understanding of the pugnacious power forward, exploding some stereotypes
along the way.*

---

*We're like Jekyll and Hyde, like Jack and Jill. You know, they all went up the
hill.*

Charles Oakley says things like this often enough that they have come to
be known as Oakspeak. They are like brainteasers; you want to rearrange
the words to reveal the hidden meaning. But as simple and straightforward
as the elements of Oakspeak are, the combination is almost impossible to
decipher, and once you have accepted that, you have begun to solve Charles
Oakley.

He cannot jump, which tells you right away that he goes against the grain
of convention. Nearly everyone in today's NBA can soar; it's as if the league

had obtained a restraining order against gravity. But Oakley, the Toronto Raptors' 36-year-old power forward, has legs with only slightly more spring in them than your coffee table's, a fact that bothers him not in the least. He actually seems proud of being relatively earthbound in a league of leapers, so much so that you begin to wonder if he is truly incapable of clearing a deck of cards when he takes off, or if he simply wants to make it look that way.

There are, after all, those who insist that Oakley hasn't always played as if the soles of his shoes were slathered with glue. Dave Robbins, his coach at Virginia Union, remembers that Oakley had a perfectly decent vertical leap when he arrived at the Richmond campus, and some of Oakley's former teammates at John Hay High in Cleveland recall him as a spectacular dunker who would blow kisses to the crowd after his landings. Oakley only smiles when asked about these recollections, refusing to classify them as either fact or fiction.

Whether he can't jump or won't jump hardly seems like a mystery worth solving, because either by necessity or by choice Oakley has carved out an exemplary career on the ground. He has grabbed more than 10,000 rebounds in 15 NBA seasons—now that Charles Barkley has retired, Hakeem Olajuwon and Karl Malone are the only active players with more—and in the process established himself as the epitome of industriousness. Oakley is not so much a player as he is a selfless laborer, the kind who takes care of odd jobs such as flinging his 6'9", 245-pound body into the stands in pursuit of loose balls and setting picks that rattle opponents' molars. A typical Oakley moment occurred in early December when the Raptors were trailing the Washington Wizards 93–92 with one second left. Toronto guard Dee Brown drilled a wide-open three-pointer for the win, but almost unnoticed was the reason that Brown was free for the shot: Oakley had not merely screened Chris Whitney, Brown's defender, he had all but placed him in custody.

"He's tough as a pine knot," says Robbins. "I don't know if you've ever tried to hammer a nail into a piece of pine with a knot in it, but it will bend the nail. That's how tough Charles is. He'll bend the nail."

If a superstar scorer is an NBA team's primary need, a player like Oakley is its second. He ignores an open shot to find a better one; he's a master of the hidden art of helping on defense; he becomes a more reliable shooter in the clutch. That's why Chicago Bulls general manager Jerry Krause wept when he traded him to the New York Knicks for center Bill Cartwright in June 1988. It's why 13 months after the June '98 deal that sent Oakley to Toronto for forward Marcus Camby, Knicks coach Jeff Van Gundy was in

Oak's living room, trying unsuccessfully to persuade him to rejoin New York as a free agent. It's why the Raptors believe Oakley can help lead them not only to the first playoff appearance in their five-year history but also deep into the postseason. He has done nothing to shake their faith, providing a steadying influence for the team's 22-year-old rising star, forward Vince Carter. Though the Raptors were 20–17 at week's end, Oakley, with characteristic clarity, says there's room for improvement: "If you've got a bakery and you're selling out the baked goods every week, you've got to keep baking. We built a bakery, but now we've got a store with a bakery sign but no bread or anything."

It's not surprising that Oakley has found a way to succeed without jumping, given that he has never been much impressed by fancy but unnecessary tools. He refuses to use any machinery in the chain of eight car washes he owns in Cleveland and suburban New York City because he hasn't seen the piece of equipment that can clean or wax more thoroughly than the human hand. John Hay High didn't have a weight room when he was a student there, so Oakley had a teammate stand on his back when he did push-ups and sit on his shoulders as he did squats. He even finds planes excessive, traveling exclusively–and extensively–by car in the off-season. After a decade and a half in the NBA, Oakley knows what's important and what's not, and he has determined that the ability to hang in the air long enough to rebraid his graying cornrows is not. "A rebound is still a rebound, whether you get it a foot above the rim or a foot below the rim," he says. "There's nothing wrong with the old-fashioned way."

So is it that this Oak remains rooted out of his affection for time-honored methods? Is it his way of proving that there is still a place among these high-flying whippersnappers for a man who excels on the ground? His game seems to be an homage to players such as Wes Unseld and Paul Silas, tough, granitelike big men of the '60s and '70s who waged their battles on land, not in the air. He also knows that keeping an opponent off-balance, nudging him, elbowing him, leaning on him one moment and backing away the next, is vital down low. "You can't come at people the same way every time, because then they figure you out," he says.

Oakley has the same philosophy off the court. He is a utilitarian player who wastes little motion, yet he dresses in colors Crayola hasn't thought of and thinks nothing of discarding a $2,000 suit after wearing it once. He will throw basic, fundamentally correct passes all evening long, then for some reason uncork a behind-the-back flip or a length-of-the-court outlet that sails out-of-bounds untouched. He believes hard work is its own reward, but he's just as interested in other rewards–financial ones–as any of his younger teammates. He proved that by shunning the more championship-ready Knicks and Los Angeles Lakers last summer and re-signing with the Raptors, who could offer him more money ($18 million over three years).

Somewhere along the line, Oakley will explode every assumption you make about him. "Oak will fool you," says Orlando Magic coach Doc Rivers, Oakley's teammate with the Knicks in 1992–93 and '93–94. "It's like he thinks you're getting too close to figuring him out, so he throws you a little curve. It's like he's saying, You think you know me? Well what do you make of *this*?"

Robbins points out that, to survive the punishment under the boards, Oakley gained about 35 pounds during his years at Virginia Union and that the extra weight might have robbed him of some jumping ability. That makes sense. Yes, that must be it. After all, he couldn't have been fooling us all this time, could he?

Oakspeak: *If it ain't broke, don't break it.*

Oakley is grumpy, even more proof that he's not of this era. You don't see grumpy much anymore, certainly not among athletes. Today's player is arrogant or charming or savvy or angry or any number of other things, but rarely is he a good old-fashioned grouch. Oakley isn't scary grumpy; he's grumpy like your grandpa, just enough to make you brace yourself a bit before you approach him. It is one reason he has never been married, although he does have a three-year-old son, also named Charles, who lives with his mother in Tallahassee, Fla. Oakley supports his child financially and spends considerable time with him in the off-season, bringing young Charles to visit him and his extended family. It is a measure of how closely he guards the details of his private life that many people who consider themselves friends of Oakley don't know he is a father. "Personal life is nobody's business," he says testily. "I'm not one of those stars people want to know everything about, anyway."

It doesn't seem likely that Oakley will become a husband anytime soon. "I think he's got such traditional values that it would take a '50s-style woman who wanted to stay home and devote herself to the family to really make him happy," says Billy Diamond, Oakley's friend and business manager. But he certainly doesn't need someone to cook and clean for him. Oakley keeps an immaculate house and is comfortable enough in the kitchen that Toronto forward Kevin Willis nicknamed him Chef. "I've been on my own so long that I had to learn," Oakley says. "And I like being able to make my food the way I want it."

Almost anything can bring out the curmudgeon in Oakley. "You don't have to listen, but he has to talk," says Rivers. "He has to tell you how his sneakers are tight, his uniform is stiff, his locker is dirty, the chicken has too much salt, the bus is leaving too early, the plane is leaving too late. You just put up with him because he's Oak and somehow he's still lovable."

Oakley seldom complains about the things he ought to complain about. The flavor of a birthday cake or the color of the locker room rug can be nitpicked, but work or pain are to be endured in silence. He returned to Virginia Union for the school's annual celebrity golf tournament last summer, about six weeks after the season. "When he walked into the gym, he had a lump on his elbow as big as an orange," says Robbins. "Not a lemon, an orange. He said he must have banged it up during the season sometime. He didn't think anything of it. I made him go see our team doctor, who drained it and said he'd never drained more fluid at one time than he did out of that elbow. Oak's toughness ain't no act."

Oakley's feelings have been bruised almost as much as his body, but he plays through that pain as well. He has no romantic notions about hard work making him deserving of some special reward. If the reward is being traded from the Bulls just when they're on the cusp of a dynasty; if it's losing almost 40% of his $10 million balloon payment in 1998–99 because of the lockout; if it's being traded from the Knicks before last season and watching them reach the Finals, so be it. That's the way life is. The trade from New York, where he was a Madison Square Garden favorite, hurt him, and he had harsh words for Ernie Grunfeld, the Knicks' president and general manager at the time. But for the most part Oakley has kept up the tough façade. "It wasn't hard to accept," he says. "I'm an employee, and I got transferred. Happens every day. You just move your pencils and your tools to another building and get yourself a new desk."

Still, there are places where he is the boss, such as Oakley's Wash House, the combination car wash and Laundromat Oakley founded in east Cleveland. His sister Carolyn and mother, Corine, oversee the operation, and it seems as if an Oakley is at every station, making sure the stainless steel washers and driers gleam like freshly polished silverware on one side of the business and running a soapy sponge over a Mercedes on the other. A block down the street are Hair Solutions and Nails EtCetera, salons started with seed money from Oakley and run by his sisters. "Charles takes care of family," says his sister Saralene. "He got this started, but we do the work."

The Wash House helps the image—a practical, no-nonsense business for a practical, no-nonsense player—and Oakley does more than just lend the place his name. While in town he can often be found with a sponge or cloth in his hand, working on customers' cars. "You can go down there some days and see Oak in an expensive Italian suit, scrubbing like he was in overalls," says Herb Williams, Oakley's friend and former Knicks teammate.

Oakley has never fancied himself anything but a working man. He once described his role with the Knicks as that of "a butler in a mansion. I'm just happy to clean up and make sure everything is all right." That's one of the reasons he has been so loved in the cities in which he has played. He generously tips anyone in the service industry: locker room attendants, hotel maids, even waiters in restaurants where he has sent the food back two or three times (a not uncommon occurrence). "I like to let them know that I respect the job they're doing," he says. "I see them the same way I see myself."

In ways Oakley is not so much the last of his breed, as he is often called, but a breed unto himself. If you understand this about him, it's not so disorienting to learn that when he's not in uniform, he trades in his blue-collar persona for a silk-suit sensibility. Not that there's anything wrong with that—the league is full of clotheshorses—it's just that you don't expect Oakley to be one of them. He is just as comfortable discussing how to coordinate an outfit as how to set a pick. The closets in his spacious house in Toronto are the size of studio apartments, which is about right for a wardrobe that includes more than 200 suits, by his estimation, though the number is in a constant state of flux. "I usually won't wear a suit twice," he says. "If I do, it won't be in the same city. If I wear something in Toronto, the only way I'll put it on again is if I'm on the other side of the country or somewhere I can be sure that not many people have seen me in it."

Once he is done with a suit, Oakley usually finds it a good home. In the past, he sent dozens to players at Virginia Union, and last year he shipped a few to Bulls rookie Elton Brand because he judged him to be roughly the same size. Oakley has hundreds of neckties—he's a Zegna, Hugo Boss man—all tied in neat Windsor knots and hanging from racks. The floors of his closets are lined with shoes of every kind, with the notable exception of sneakers. Almost all those are at the Air Canada Centre, because he rarely puts on his work shoes anywhere other than on the job site. "I wear tennis shoes all year long when I'm playing ball," he says. "I don't want to wear them off the court."

Oakley has his own sense of style, which until recently tended to favor hues not found at Brooks Brothers. He has worn lime-green pinstripes with color-coordinated shoes and fedora, eggplant-colored jackets, bright orange three-piece suits. When Oakley was sidelined with a foot injury for 32 games in 1994–95, while with the Knicks, the Madison Square Garden crowd was treated to some of the most flamboyant pieces from the House of Oakley. Every night was Name That Color. "I didn't dress that way to stand out," Oakley says. "I did it because those colors looked good with my complexion and because that was the style at the time."

Yet he wants to be unique. The Knicks were playing in Miami one afternoon, and Oakley came down to the hotel lobby before the game wearing a suit the color of orange sherbet. Amazingly, he found teammate Chris Childs sporting the same ensemble. Oakley, mortified, went up to his room and returned dressed completely in black, which wouldn't have been unusual—if it hadn't been Easter Sunday.

When his work is done for the season, Oakley hits the road. Again, he sees no reason to take to the air, choosing instead to take long, often solitary drives that crisscross the country. "I drive probably 20,000 miles in the summertime," he says. "Some trips will be 4,000, 5,000 miles."

He will drive from Toronto to his hometown of Cleveland, then south to Alabama, where he has a sister, aunts, uncles and cousins, then anywhere. Chicago to see old friends. Florida to see his son. New Orleans just because. Most of the time, his only company is a collection of rap CDs. "Don't need anybody sitting next to me telling me to take this exit or that exit," he says. "Don't need anybody saying they need to stop to go to the bathroom."

This is Oakley the Grouch, showing that his disdain sometimes extends to human interaction. But then you learn that he throws lavish parties at Little Jezebel, the Manhattan restaurant in which he has a stake; that whenever he has a game in his hometown of Cleveland, he invites the entire team to come to his mother's house for a home-cooked meal; and that when he was a Knick and the All-Star Game was held in Cleveland, he sent a limousine to pick up the New York beat writers and take them out for a night on the town. *You think you know me? What do you make of this?*

Oakspeak: *You know what they say about spilled milk—clean it up, go into the kitchen and get some more.*

Julius Moss was 6'3" and barrel-chested, which was fortunate, because a man had to be strong to work a cotton farm in Alabama with not much more to help him than a couple of mules. It was the 1970s, and Moss obviously had more sophisticated machinery available to him, but he didn't see the need to change the farming methods he'd been using all his life. He had his grandson by his side, but there was only so much help little Charles Oakley could offer—he was still in grade school.

Charles had been sent to live with his maternal grandparents, Julius and his wife, Florence, after his father's death in 1971. Oakley's father, Charles Oakley II, had a history of bad health until a heart attack took his life at age 35. Although he was seven when his dad died, Oakley has little memory of him. "He wasn't really with the family," he says. "I really didn't know him. I saw him sometimes, but I didn't really know him."

Being in Alabama provided Oakley with the first extended male influence he'd ever had. The change from the asphalt of east Cleveland to the dirt roads of York, about 100 miles southwest of Birmingham, was an adjustment, but before long he was tagging along with his grandfather. Moss would rise at 5:30 a.m. to head out to the fields. He would let Charles sleep, but before he had broken a sweat, his grandson was usually out to provide whatever help he could. "Mainly I just watched him," Oakley says. "I watched how hard he worked. If it took 18 hours, he put in 18 hours. I wanted to be just like him. I guess he rubbed off on me to a certain extent."

Even after his time with his grandfather, Charles, the youngest of the six Oakley children, had some toughening up to do. "Charles was pretty much pampered, being the baby of the family," says Saralene. "He never had household chores or anything like that. That's why it makes me smile when people talk about how tough he is. I remember when he was nine or 10, the kids who played ball wouldn't let him get in games because he was too little. Believe it or not, he was short as a child until he shot up in junior high school."

By the time he reached high school, Oakley had grown to 6'3" and was already taking charges and setting picks; he just hadn't developed a nasty streak. His coach, Loren Olson, talked him into going out for the football team, and he made all-league at defensive end, but it was his one-on-one games against Olson, who is 6'10" and 280 pounds, that did the most to harden him. "I'd beat the crap out of him," Olson says. "I'd tell him all the time that he was mine. I'd tell him that this is my lane, and if you want to come in here, you're going to pay. Then he got bigger and stronger. And I decided it was time for me to bow out."

When he arrived at Virginia Union, the essential Oakley was almost fully formed—smart, self-sacrificing, tough but not dirty. It was clear that he drew no distinctions, that he would exact his pound of flesh from any opponent with the temerity to approach his hoop, whether in practice or a game, whether in crunch time or garbage time. Robbins was reminded that his power forward had been all business all the time when Oakley sent 5'3" Muggsy Bogues hurtling to the floor in an NBA game. "I asked him if he thought he might have hit Muggsy a little harder than necessary, considering his size," Robbins says. "Oak just looked at me and said, 'He came in my lane, didn't he?'"

Along the way Oakley developed subtlety to complement his brute force. "He's the first player I've seen go out-of-bounds and then come back in to rebound on the weak side," says Miami Heat center Alonzo Mourning. Most of Oakley's tactics are designed to keep opponents as ground-bound as he is. He clutches their shorts, digs his knee into their legs and is a master of the arm lockdown, in which he hooks their biceps in the crook of his arm. "He may get on some guys' nerves, but everybody respects him," says Dallas Mavericks forward Gary Trent. "He's just Oak."

On defense Oakley is an ounce of prevention. He has a kind of defensive ESP that allows him to beat potential scorers to "the launching pad," the term players and coaches use to describe the point at which the offensive player is clear to go up for his shot. "He protects the basket as well as anyone who ever played," says Van Gundy. "I'm not talking about shot blocking; I'm talking about keeping the shot from ever being taken. Others react on defense, but Charles anticipates. He knows when a teammate is about to get beaten, so that by the time it happens, he's there to help. If there were a stat on how many points a player saves his team, Charles would lead the league."

Oakspeak: *You can't throw a hook on the side of the road and expect to catch a fish in the grass.*

He is not underrated anymore, not really. In fact, rarely has a player been so appreciated for being unappreciated. It is common knowledge by now that Oakley helps his team in ways that are almost invisible to the untrained eye, that his true value is apparent only on game tapes, with the help of the pause and the rewind buttons. But he remains underestimated in other ways. Straight-ahead men like Oakley aren't supposed to have any mystery to them, no layers beyond the one most obvious to spectators. He leaves so much of himself on the floor that it seems unlikely that there is anything more to him that we cannot see.

Consider, however, the Raptors' pregame introductions at the Air Canada Centre. Oakley, always the last starter to be introduced, rises slowly from his seat with the annoyance of a man forced to get up from his couch to reach the remote. The Toronto reserves follow him as he makes his way onto the court with a gait that is half jog, half hobble. Everything in his demeanor suggests that he considers himself too old for this commotion, that he would rather soak his feet in a bucket of Epsom salts than take on another opponent. But it is only one more piece of misdirection. He gives himself away when the rest of the Raptors huddle around him and begin a brief but frenzied slam-dance, bouncing off one another like kernels of popcorn over a flame. Oakley is in the center of the scrum, shoulders hunched, bashing into the bodies that are coming at him from every angle. It's obvious that he is not an arthritic old man but an energy source, and that the other Raptors need a jolt.

What do you make of all this? You think you know him after all these years, but you wouldn't be surprised if, when he is all alone, Charles Oakley still dunks and blows kisses to the crowd.

− POSTSCRIPT −

Phil Taylor: Charles Oakley thought this story would never get written, and if it did, it would never be published. That was one of the first things he said to me when I told him I wanted to write a profile of him. He was convinced *Sports Illustrated* only featured big stars, the guys who "score all the points and do all the dances," is how I believe he put it. He said that players who did less glamorous work didn't get big feature stories. I told him he wasn't entirely wrong, that hardworking players like him didn't get enough attention, and that was part of the reason we wanted to give him his due. I blathered on about how he had been one of the most respected players in the league for a long time and how fans didn't know enough about him as a person. Even though I could tell from the look on his face that he wasn't buying any of it, he agreed to do the piece and was very cooperative. But over the course of the couple of weeks that I worked on it, Oak more than once reiterated that it was all a waste of time because the story would never see the light of day. I insisted it would, even though I knew that SI had a graveyard full of feature stories that never made it into the magazine for one reason or another. I was relieved when the piece appeared in print. I didn't say "I told you so" to Oakley, because he's not the kind of man to whom one says "I told you so." But it did get published, Oak. And look, now it's been published *twice.*

Jimmy Butler Does Not Want to Be Your Hero

He's the most interesting man in the NBA, but
when it comes to your interest and adoration?
Says Dwyane Wade: "Jimmy don't give a f—-."

BY ROHAN NADKARNI

Jimmy Butler was and is upset the Heat didn't go into the bubble and do what they said they were going to do: win a championship.

Which meant Butler took it upon himself in the offseason to persuade point guard Goran Dragić, an unrestricted free agent, to return to Miami so they could make at least one more run together at a title. Butler was frustrated that the two didn't get to display their collective talents during the Finals, when Dragić's foot injury limited him to just 34 minutes. And the teammates had grown particularly close over the course of the longest season in league history.

So Butler pestered Dragić, a 12-year veteran, on FaceTime. Dragić was vacationing in his native Slovenia as he mulled his options. Butler wasn't interested in hearing them. "He said, 'You better sign with the Heat. If not, I know where you live. I'm going to hunt you down. And I'm going to beat you up,'" Dragić recalls with a chuckle.

"I said, 'G, we got to run this back, or I'm going to punch you in your head,'" Butler recalls with no hint of a smile.

One minute after the start of the NBA's free-agency period on Nov. 20, Dragić announced he would be returning to the Heat on a two-year, $37.4 million deal.

After years of bouncing from team to team, leaving a wake of flustered teammates in his path, Jimmy Butler, the tough Texan from tiny Tomball, is now...*endearing*. The black hat is gone. As we talk over Zoom, I'm explaining to him how a story I wrote about how he won the bubble despite losing the Finals resonated with readers.

"No offense, but I haven't read any article that you've written," Butler, 31, told me last month. "I'm sure your work is absolutely f——— incredible, but I don't pay attention to the media. One day they're going to like you, the next day they heard this so they write a story about it. But don't nobody know what's really going on."

What really goes on with Butler has been a constant source of fascination since he entered the league out of Marquette as the last first-round pick in 2011. The Bulls unloaded him in June '17 after deciding he couldn't be the leader of a championship team. He lasted a little more than a season in Minnesota, where he clashed with younger teammates, then one year in Philadelphia, where he clashed with his coach. Through all that, he missed the playoffs only once. When he joined the Heat through a four-team trade in the summer of 2019, Butler was still the trash-talking, supremely confident MF-dropper he was in his previous stops. The difference: He entered an environment that welcomed his brand of passion.

"I still don't think Jimmy looks at himself as a good guy," says Dwyane Wade, the Heat legend who spent a year with Butler in Chicago. "You won't see a change in him. If you like him? Cool. If you don't? Cool. Jimmy don't give a f— either way."

The new marriage resulted in not only a surprising run by the fifth-seeded Heat to the Finals but also an iconic championship performance by Butler, albeit in a losing effort against the Lakers. The 6'7", 230-pound forward averaged 26.2 points, 8.3 rebounds, 9.8 assists and 2.2 steals on 55.2% shooting over six games, logging 43.0 minutes per night, much of that time in an enervating effort to slow down the only person on the planet capable of putting up similar numbers, LeBron James.

Butler doesn't describe himself as a hero; instead he considers himself someone with a sickness, an obsession about winning. The Finals loss still eats at him. ("Motherf———, we were right there.") And in Miami, from president Pat Riley down to the 15th man, he's part of a group that's as obsessed as he is.

In his first practice with the Heat, Butler was his usual abrasive self. No one was spared, not even Dragić. Everyone was taken aback by such competitiveness so early in training camp. But as opposed to his previous NBA teammates, Butler found his new ones were willing to push back.

Duncan Robinson, a swingman who had fewer than 200 minutes of NBA experience, was one of the first to go toe-to-toe with Butler. "I wouldn't be surprised if he didn't even know who I was then," Robinson says. Once, the anonymous shooter took a handoff on the wing; when Butler went under the screen, Robinson hit a wide-open three. He not-so-politely advised Butler not to leave him open like that again. And it was just that sort of response that assured Butler he was finally in just the right environment.

"He had been all over *SportsCenter* because of how it had gone down in Minnesota, and on top of that his reputation preceded him," Robinson says. "It was funny to realize it was now happening to us. What surprised me the most were his intentions. It wasn't coming from a malicious place. It was coming from a place of, Let me see what we got here."

It didn't take Butler long to size up the Heat. He went nearly the whole season with a knowing smirk on his face. After about 30 games he began ending nearly every conversation with his teammates with "and we're going to win a championship." Whether it was a meeting, a film session after practice or a locker room discussion after a loss, Butler committed himself to instilling that belief in everyone around him. The Heat didn't quite buy it at first, but his persistence paid off.

"He was so adamant about what was going to happen," Robinson says. "It gets to the point where you hear it enough, you assume that mentality as well. You're buying into the psyche he's constantly perpetuating."

The Orlando bubble was practically built for someone as focused as Butler. Unlike most players, he chose not to bring his infant daughter, Rylee, her mother or any friends with him, to remain mindful of the job at hand. While the isolation was understandably difficult for many, the five-time All-Star relished it.

"I had a good time, man," Butler says. "I learned a lot about myself. I had a lot of time to think, about basketball or life in general. And I picked up a lot of new hobbies."

One of those was figuring out new ways to amuse his teammates—and himself. After rookie Tyler Herro scored 37 points in Game 4 of the Eastern Conference finals, Butler showed up to next practice wearing the 20-year-old's high school jersey. After the Heat clinched a trip to the Finals, he rocked coach Erik Spoelstra's No. 30 University of Portland jersey. While the playoffs brought out Butler's intensity, it also let him tap into his lighter side. He was serious about the experience, but he wanted it to be fun for those around him. (Butler is also serious about his jersey collection; he won't reveal how he received the threads, lest others copy him. But he does say he has more jerseys "in the chamber.")

Another one of Butler's pastimes was as the proprietor of Big Face Coffee, a hotel-room café Butler started seemingly with the sole purpose of upcharging his wealthy clientele. He had landed in Orlando with enough equipment to satisfy his own coffee needs but saw a business opportunity once he realized there wasn't a reliable caffeine option on campus. The Big Face menu was surprisingly expansive—ranging from pour-overs to lattes to cappuccinos—for a pop-up operation. But each drink, no matter the size, cost $20.

Butler used to be the kind of coffee drinker who would load up a run-of-the-mill cup with eight sugars. Then his trainer, James Scott, told him consuming higher-quality coffee in moderation could help with his training regimen. It wasn't long before the endlessly curious Butler, on his travels to Europe, would spend hours in cafés, talking to patrons about how they take their coffee.

He became as obsessive about beans as basketball and now is an arguably more versatile barista than backcourt player. He owns a scale, a Chemex, an espresso maker—you name it. ("I wish I could take five years off and open a café.") His preferred cup is a black pour-over. His preferred origin of bean is Brazil. He roasts and grinds everything himself. And one of his biggest offseason projects was practicing his latte art, which still needs some work before it reaches the Big Face menu. ("You have to pour it from a certain height and certain angle. It's taken up a lot of time, and a lot of mistakes.") Scott says while it's easy for Butler to gouge NBA millionaires when he has no competition, his concoctions are worth the price because of the attention that goes into each cup.

"That's the part of Jimmy nobody knows," Spoelstra says. "That guy in the Dos Equis commercial? Jimmy's like a version of that guy. He's literally one of the most interesting people in the NBA fraternity. If you talk about anything, he's like, I've done that."

Spoelstra learned that lesson in the summer of 2019. He was on vacation with his wife, Nikki, in Europe and rerouted his trip so he could meet the Heat's prized new acquisition face-to-face in Italy. The conversation shifted to travel, and Spoelstra mentioned to Butler how he had been promising to take Nikki on a wine tour of France.

"Of course Jimmy goes into a whole story about how much time he's spent there, and how he's friends with one of the more famous wineries there," says Spoelstra. He sat sheepishly as Nikki got more envious with each detail. "My wife, I could just see the steam coming out of her ears."

Spoelstra speaks in awed tones when describing Butler. He calls him a ferocious competitor who would have thrived in the rough-and-tumble NBA of the 1990s but is also happy biking around Amsterdam. Dragić, who said multiple times during the season that he had to calm Butler down because he wanted to fight someone, is acutely aware of his teammate's soft side as well.

Dragić was in a dark place during the Finals. He had left the court after tearing the plantar fascia in his left foot in the first half of Game 1, and when he returned in Game 6 he was a shell of himself. After first learning of the severity of his injury Dragić locked himself in his hotel room.

"Jimmy always checked on me," Dragić says. "After a few days he said, G, that's enough. Let's get out of your room, let's hang out. He was telling me injuries are part of sports. It happens. He's always such a positive guy. I'm really grateful for him."

Dragić wasn't Butler's only responsibility. After averaging only 4.5 points through the first two games against L.A., Robinson was feeling he had let his team down. Around midnight the night before Game 3, Butler came pounding on Robinson's door. For 20 minutes, Butler told Robinson not to lose his confidence, that his shooting would win his team a game. Then for the next hour they talked about everything except basketball. Robinson cleared his mind and averaged 16.5 points for the rest of the series, including a 26-point outburst in a Game 5 victory. "For him to show how much he really cared and valued my role on the team," says Robinson, "it meant a lot."

Butler was everything for the Heat during their Finals run. Scorer. Stopper. Jokester. Friend. Motivator. Butler says the biggest lesson he learned in the bubble was how much everyone on the team looked to him to set the standard. That only pushed him harder, until he was hunched over a railing along the baseline near the end of Game 5, having spent every ounce of energy. "That's why we're in this game, to push ourselves collectively to places you can't imagine," Spoelstra says. "Jimmy's performance in the Finals was truly inspiring."

"It was unbelievable," says Dragić. "I don't want to take nothing from LeBron, but Jimmy was guarding the best guy on the other team, and he was doing everything on offense for us. He was the best guy on the floor."

"Look, I was legitimately exhausted," Butler says. "But if I'm not exhausted, I can't tell somebody else you're not going hard enough. And I think that's why my word holds a little bit of weight."

Butler's words also hold weight because he has made relationships in Miami that—from the outside—didn't seem possible in his other stops. He considers Spoelstra a friend. He and Dragić are the NBA's odd couple. And the younger players eagerly seek his mentorship. Spoelstra says he used to imagine what it would be like to coach Butler when he was an opponent. Butler also noticed from afar how hard Spo pushed players, or as he puts it, "I know when motherf——— are not bulls—-ing."

When he saw Butler eschew the postgame round of cards or celebratory dinner to watch more film in Chicago, Wade realized quickly how well Butler's values aligned with Miami's, and urged Riley to pursue him when Wade rejoined the Heat. "Jimmy told me he wanted to be remembered for his greatness," Wade says. "The moment finally presented itself for him in the Finals. And he was ready."

Conversations about Butler always seem to come back to how rigorously he prepares; his 4 a.m. workouts have almost become a cliché. But that's not to say that Butler isn't still putting in the time.

Even during this truncated offseason he pushed himself. His latest obsession is neurocognitive efficiency. Scott likes to run Butler through a drill in which he's wearing 3-D glasses and staring at a set of 12 balls on a screen. Four balls are highlighted at the start, and then all of them will start moving around and bumping into each other. After a period of time, Butler has to identify which four balls were originally highlighted. If he picks all the right ones, the balls start moving faster for the next round. Scott will then gradually make the drill more difficult, making Butler stand on one leg or punch him with boxing gloves as he tracks the balls.

Butler has noticed all the comings and goings around the league. Miami mostly stood pat in the offseason, while the Lakers, Clippers and Bucks all added pieces, and Kevin Durant is set to return to the Nets. "I feel the same way I always feel: I'm betting on the Heat," Butler says. "All the movement everybody's doing? Don't scare me none. We truly don't care. What makes me smile, is every time we take the floor, the best player is on the Miami Heat."

Butler's bravado is hardly misplaced. At a T-Wolves practice two years ago, Butler—who had just requested a trade—infamously lined up with the third-teamers in a scrimmage and put on a dominant performance to prove his worth to management. In Game 3 of the 2020 Finals, Butler— with his two best teammates, Dragić and center Bam Adebayo, out with injuries—lined up with a 20-year-old rookie, an undrafted shooting guard, a journeyman forward and a 7-footer who'd gone from end of the bench to starter, and put up a historic 40-point triple double, leading Miami past a team headlined by two future Hall of Famers.

"Just know, this year we finna win it, man," Butler says. "I got something up my sleeve. I'm going to be better than ever. Just wait on it."

Jimmy Butler has a way of getting what he wants.

— POSTSCRIPT —

Rohan Nadkarni: This was the first real profile I reported during the pandemic. That meant Zoom and phone calls instead of a trip to Miami. It also happened in the aftermath of the NBA bubble, which meant bothering people during an incredibly brief offseason. (A major shoutout to Erik Spoelstra for jumping on the phone only a couple of days before Thanksgiving.) So I wasn't sure exactly what to expect from Butler. Would he be exhausted? Would conducting our conversations over the internet make it difficult for us to make a personal connection?

Those questions were answered within about the first minute of our chat, which is roughly how long it took for Butler to drop his first MF bomb of the interview. It was smooth sailing from there, even as Jimmy told me he didn't particularly enjoy media attention. (As is mentioned in the piece, Butler made it a point to note he didn't care about anything I've written about him.) He regaled me with tales from his trip to the Finals, often adding for emphasis, "I'm telling you, motherf——."

The writing was the easiest part. Butler and those around him had supplied plenty of great material. All I had to do was weave together the set pieces into something remotely coherent. Since the story, Jimmy's coffee obsession has only grown—he now sells expensive "Big Face" merchandise in addition to beans, and he told me he drinks several cups a day—and he's added another legendary playoff run to his ledger. He's made the story hold up better than I ever could have imagined.

TEAMS

This Is the Life

In eight splendid days as an assistant coach for the Phoenix Suns, the author took a hit from Shawn Marion, lost a bet on Amaré Stoudemire and learned to love the game in a whole new way

BY JACK McCALLUM

The hardest thing was putting on the shirt. Many years ago, en route to cover a Celtics game at the old Boston Garden for SPORTS ILLUSTRATED, I realized I was wearing green, the home team's color. I jumped out of a cab, ran into a department store and bought a different shirt. That's the extent to which a journalist will go to keep his professional distance.

But there I was on Phoenix Suns Media Day, Oct. 3, at America West Arena, sporting a black polo shirt adorned with the team's logo. Six weeks earlier the Suns had agreed to let me serve as an assistant coach in training camp, and now I had to dress the part. Over the next five days I attended every coaches meeting, every two-a-day practice, every team meal and every bleary-eyed, pizza-chomping film session. I spent 12 hours a day with coach Mike D'Antoni and his five assistants, and during that period they asked to go off the record only a half-dozen times. I chased down shots for 2004–05 MVP Steve Nash, got slapped in the face during a drill by a disturbingly gleeful Shawn Marion, lost $20 betting against Amaré Stoudemire, heard myself introduced as an assistant coach in front of 7,000 fans, charted plays from the bench and developed an even deeper love of basketball—the result, no doubt, of walking into a gym every day with guys who live it 24/7.

In the end my lone disappointment was that much of the play-calling and terminology remained tantalizingly beyond my grasp. I came in knowing Basketball 101 and left as a first-year grad student, but the NBA is coached at a Ph.D. level. Suffice it to say that nothing you will see from the Suns this season sprang from the mind of McCallum.

OCTOBER 1: THE HOBO AND THE KANDI MAN

The first day of practice at the University of Arizona, in Tucson, is three days away, but D'Antoni and his assistants—Marc Iavaroni, Alvin Gentry, Phil Weber, brother Dan D'Antoni and Todd Quinter—have been meeting on and off most of the summer, and at least one assistant was always present when players worked out at America West Arena. The addition of free-agent guard Raja Bell ratcheted up the intensity of pickup games. "We now have three stormers," says Weber—that is, three players who will storm off the court if the team loses, Nash and Stoudemire being the others.

During the season NBA assistants spend as much as 18 hours a day together. They are by nature intensely competitive, but they have to find a way to get along, to consider one another's opinions and still be assertive enough to gain traction within the organization. The Phoenix assistants seem comfortable together, their lingua franca a combination of insults and hoops jargon.

Iavaroni will probably be a head coach someday; he was interviewed for the Portland Trail Blazers' job during the summer before they hired Nate McMillan. He's sober-minded and skilled with X's and O's but also quick-witted and friendly. Gentry has run three NBA teams, and though he may never get another head coaching job, his knowledge and professionalism practically guarantee him employment as an assistant.

Weber is a skilled clinician who, as the lone unmarried assistant, is known for his Peter Pan lifestyle and for impeccable standards in female companionship. Quinter, the team's chief scout, is gone much of the time during the season and thus is more of an "assistant assistant." He's the ultimate Suns insider, though; he has been with the club since 1986 (he started as video coordinator) and has served under nine head coaches. Quinter doesn't get too involved in the game plan, but when he says something—"That's the way the Spurs run it" or "The Sonics started doing that in February"—the staff listens.

I bond instantly with Dan D'Antoni. In a way we're both outsiders. After 30 years as a high school coach in South Carolina, Dan knows basketball inside and out but not the NBA; after covering the NBA for 20 years, I know the league reasonably well but not basketball inside and out. While Dan has integrated himself into the group, it's impossible to forget that he is Mike's big brother, four years his senior.

If you came to the team with no knowledge of the pecking order and sat around for a few minutes listening to the Phoenix coaches lob insults at each other—as they are on this day in the main basketball office—you would have no idea which one was the boss. But after an hour you'd say that 54-year-old Mike D'Antoni, despite his easygoing nature and open-mindedness, is unquestionably in charge.

They talk about the NBA's new dress code, which is aimed at cleaning up the league's image. By and large the Suns are a dapper bunch, though Nash, their leader, perpetually looks as if he were headed for a Green Day gig. The respect and affection the staff has for Nash is endlessly evident: They love his competitiveness, his leadership, his smarts, his sense of humor and his absolute lack of pretension—in short, his ability to look like a hobo and play like a hero. "The bad news," says Mike, "is that Steve will be in violation even when he's dressed up."

When the conversation turns to Stoudemire, whose five-year, $73 million contract extension will be announced on Media Day, the coaches sound more like fans. "Last season he dunked on [the Houston Rockets'] Yao Ming and didn't even look at him," says Weber. "Yao is 7'6". How is that possible?"

"Yao wasn't looking at him, either," says Iavaroni. "He had his eyes closed in fear."

"I'm not sure his best dunk wasn't against Adonal Foyle in the Golden State game," says Gentry.

"The one against [the Minnesota Timberwolves' Michael] Olowokandi was better," counters Weber. "Olowokandi's 7'1" and his wingspan must be 9'6"."

"That doesn't count," says Gentry. "Olowokandi's a pussy."

"That's Gentry," Iavaroni says, turning to me. "G-e-n...."

OCTOBER 2: GETTING THE DRILL DOWN

It's 1 p.m., and the coaches are on the America West floor. The court had been taken up for a concert, and there are no lines on the concrete surface and no goals. "Stand here," Iavaroni tells me. "We'll pretend Jack is the low block."

Over the next hour I am astounded by the preparation that goes into the drills for the first day of camp. Iavaroni breaks down the specifics of a defensive closeout so intensely—using mincing chop steps to advance toward an imaginary offensive player and yelling, "Hey!" at the top of his lungs—that we all break up laughing, Iavaroni included. It's evident, too, that Dan D'Antoni is more comfortable working through drills than he is theorizing in an office. He suggests to Gentry a wrinkle in the defensive positioning used when shadowing the dribbler as he zigzags up the court.

"Guys, I like what Danny just told me," says Gentry. They watch Dan run through it and agree: His way is better. It's a small thing, but you can tell Dan is pleased.

The coaches seem satisfied with a plan for keeping their interior defenders from straying too far from the paint—until Gentry says, "Of course, if that's [San Antonio Spurs marksman] Robert Horry out there, we have to do something different." It's always like that. Just when they agree on an approach, one of them says, "Well, if this is [the Sacramento Kings'] Peja Stojaković shooting...." or "If we're playing Dallas, and this is [Dirk] Nowitzki...." But they don't want the team to become distracted too soon by these details.

Even within schemes, though, they have to make allowances. When Iavaroni demonstrates the way he will teach how to fight through picks, Mike says that he wants Nash to do something different. "Steve has to keep his hands up to ward off [screeners] before they come at him," says D'Antoni. "I'd rather see him push off and go behind the screen than try to squeeze through."

"You're right," says Gentry. "They come after him then."

"That's how we lost him last year," says Mike, referring to Nash's left thigh injury, which he incurred while fighting through an Indiana Pacers' pick. "We lost him for three games. And—what do you know?—we lost those three games."

OCTOBER 3: TIME TO MEET THE PRESS

The players officially report to America West today, and suddenly there's an intensity in the air. Over the summer Phoenix dealt three-point bomber Quentin Richardson to the New York Knicks for veteran power forward Kurt Thomas; shot blocking reserve center Steven Hunter, a free agent, defected to the Philadelphia 76ers; and most important, the Suns chose not to match a front-loaded $70 million offer by the Atlanta Hawks to restricted-free-agent swingman Joe Johnson. Instead, Phoenix worked out a sign-and-trade with Atlanta for 6'8" backup Boris Diaw and two conditional first-round picks. Replacing Johnson's across-the-board production—17.1 points, 5.1 rebounds and 3.5 assists per game, as well as 47.8% three-point shooting—will become the coaches' biggest concern during the preseason. (Until, that is, Stoudemire starts limping.)

The coaches lounge in their office while the players are in the locker room getting their physicals. "Do we run more double drags because we have Kurt and Amaré?" wonders Mike D'Antoni. (A drag is one of the keys to the Suns' transition offense; typically, Nash will be dribbling ahead of the pack and someone, often Stoudemire, will veer toward him, set a pick on the move, and then either roll to the basket or flare to the side for a jumper. A double drag would involve another pick being set a split-second later.) "Or do we run Kurt like we ran Shawn [Marion] last season, to the wing or short corner?" (The short corner refers to a spot on the baseline halfway between the basket and the corner.)

"I like double drag with Kurt being the last guy," says Gentry.

"Maybe then Kurt is free and can watch Amaré and play off him," says Mike. "Either [Kurt] gets in the drag or he runs to the wing."

"I can see Kurt in some quicks, too," says Iavaroni. In Phoenix's set offense a quick occurs when, as Nash dribbles above the top of the key, a player races to the corner to set a screen, freeing up a teammate to receive a quick pass from Nash for a shot. Last year both Marion and Richardson scored on countless quicks.

Many conversations come around to the faith that they have in Nash and Stoudemire, a tandem that is effective on the run and in the half-court. But, being coaches, they even worry about those two players. "They were so good last year because they relied on each other," says Mike. "If they stop realizing that, we're lost."

Some of the players stop by Mike's office to say hello. It's like the first day of school. When Stoudemire sticks his head in, Mike says, quietly and firmly, to the coaches, "Fellas, give me a few minutes with Amaré." (Later, Mike tells me the talk was pro forma: Make sure we're on the same page, let's have the same goals as last year, etc.)

Media Day passes uncomfortably for me; wearing the team logo, I try to avoid most of my colleagues in the press. Mike Tulumello of the *East Valley Tribune* spots me and asks, tongue-in-cheek, "What do you hope to bring to the Suns?" Tongue similarly placed, I answer, "I think they should slow it down this year. Nash and Stoudemire are out of control, and I want to rein them in."

OCTOBER 4: A COLD SLAP IN THE FACE

My first official coaching duty at training camp in Tucson is pulling up the tape that the Arizona women's volleyball team has used to outline a court for their practices. "This is nothing," says Dan D'Antoni, pulling along with me. "As a high school coach I swept the gym and kept count of every time I did it. I still remember the number—20,152."

"You're a long way from that now," I say.

"Apparently not," says Dan, ripping up another piece of tape.

Minutes later the Suns hold their first meeting at the McKale Center. Mike's opening remarks should be piped into locker rooms throughout the NBA, which has grown tedious from too little fast-breaking and too much play-calling. "We're in the entertainment business," D'Antoni tells his players. "Our fans came out last year because we were exciting to watch. The NBA wants an up-tempo game because they can sell it better. And when you start cutting up the pie, it's a lot bigger when the fans respond."

He goes over the offensive goals, one of which I find particularly interesting. The Suns were seventh last season in fewest turnovers committed, but he would like them to be in the top three. Running at breakneck speed would seem to induce a high turnover rate, but Mike doesn't see it that way. "We only make two or three passes a possession because we're looking to score quick," he tells his team. "So we should be real good in that area."

Assistant video coordinator Noel Gillespie has several fast breaks cued up. Mike provides the commentary. "Now, watch [Zydrunas] Ilgauskas on this play," he says, referring to the Cleveland Cavaliers' center. "He gets a dunk on us and, hell, he's feeling good. Next thing you know Ilgauskas is…. Oh, s-! There goes Amaré pounding up the floor, right by his sorry ass, for a dunk on the other end." Everyone laughs. "Fellas, you have any idea how that frustrates a team? We have *got* to keep running."

Out on the court, in the first of the two daily practices, Dan's zigzag variation goes well. It's time for Iavaroni's closeout drill, which calls for the coaches to work the ball around the perimeter, catching and pivoting as players chop-step toward them. It's much more intense than that, though. The players wave their arms, yell and, on occasion, take physical liberties. "The main reason Mike was happy to get the head job," Weber tells me, "was that he didn't have to be in any more drills."

I watch a couple of reps, and then Quinter signals for me to replace him. Before I know it, Marion is running toward me like a madman, yelling, to the extent I remember, "Hey! What you got! Where you going!" To punctuate his enthusiasm, he whaps me across the mouth with an open hand. The next few times I get the ball, I pivot more aggressively, holding my elbows out.

During a break I ask Dan, who has also just finished his first NBA drill, what surprised him. "The speed, size and quickness of the players," he says. "You get the ball, they're on you. The court seems small."

Later I ask Marion if he hit me on purpose. "Nah, man," he says with a smile. "It's just part of the drill. Coaches get hit."

OCTOBER 5: NOTHING LIKE A MASSAGE

On the way to McKale, I ask if I can borrow one of the coaches' rental cars after practice. "I have to find a Radio Shack," I say. "My phone's not taking a charge."

"Well, that's familiar territory," says Mike. "Nobody on our team takes a charge."

Phoenix's players and coaches don't like to hear criticism about their porous defense, but among themselves they joke about it all the time. It's human nature: We can tell you how bad we are, but don't you tell us how bad we are.

At practice the eternally upbeat Weber says to forward James Jones, "The word for the day is *serendipitous*. You know what that means?"

"Not exactly," says Jones, "but I saw that movie *Serendipity*. That the same thing?"

"Just about," says Weber.

A former Indiana Pacer who was acquired over the summer in a sign-and-trade, Jones came from a system with many set plays. Like fellow newcomers Bell and Thomas, he is having difficulty learning how to read and react on the fly. "By this time last year [Pacers coach Rick] Carlisle would have put in maybe one tenth of his playbook," Jones tells me, "and that would be a hundred plays."

I ask if this is more fun. "Oh, definitely," he says. "Coach Carlisle is a great coach, but it's all about efficiency of possessions. He doesn't run that much, because he worries that it puts his defense out of position. He would rather have a 24-second violation than try something with the shot clock running down."

I relate that to Mike D'Antoni. "Most coaches believe defenses are more vulnerable late in the shot clock, that you can get them out of position with a lot of passing," he says. "We think defenses are most vulnerable before they get set."

I tell Quinter (who 25 years ago was an outstanding high school basketball player in Nazareth, Pa., where I covered him for a small daily newspaper) that I need some more reps today. We trade spots on Coaches Shell, a defensive drill in which the coaches make passes around the perimeter and sometimes cut through the pack without the ball. It doesn't sound like much except that, per Iavaroni's orders, the defense is charged with "tagging" the cutter, or more euphemistically, "massaging" him. I get massaged on all sides and put one hand up in front of my face for protection. I am once again overwhelmed by the size and strength of the players. "With a hand in front of my face, I wouldn't have been in real great position to catch a pass," I tell Quinter.

"Don't worry," he says. "Wasn't much chance of you getting one."

At lunch Mike goes over Three-on-Three Convert, an exhausting fast-break drill he wants to use in the evening session for his regulars. The coaches are told to keep the bottom three players in the pecking order—forward Lucas Tischer, swingman Dijon Thompson and guard Anthony Lever-Pedroza, all rookies—from getting too many reps.

"We'll put Jack in charge of them," says Dan.

"Take them off to the side and play around with the heavy ball," says Mike. "That'll screw 'em up good."

That night, though, the three participate as much as anyone else. "We didn't have the heart to keep them out," Iavaroni tells me. "That's what you were supposed to do."

We gorge at a pizza joint, and everyone just wants to go to bed. But it's back to Mike's room for one more meeting.

After the usual wisecracks the mood turns somber.

"Amaré was a little out of it today," says Weber.

Mike nods. "Yeah, he was hurting a little. The knee."

The left knee. He began complaining about it during summer workouts but, when pressed by the staff, insisted it was O.K. But the intensity of two-a-days has clearly made it worse. This won't be the last we hear about the knee.

OCTOBER 6: SINCE WHEN DOES STAT HIT THREES?

Each day the coaches go a little harder on the players. They are pleased with their pace and effort but not necessarily with their execution. The fast break, for example, looks good in five-on-none drills but ragged against opposition. Mike knows that running is risky with so many new players, but he's adamant that the Suns have to score to win and have to push the tempo to score. "We've got to find a way to get to 110," he says. (Phoenix averaged a league-leading 110.4 points last season.) "We don't score 110, we're Dallas." He means a good but not great offensive team doomed, in all likelihood, never to get out of the Western Conference.

Some of the new players feel like they're racing around without a destination in mind. "Coach, you have to help me out there," Bell says to Dan during a break. "I feel like I'm speeding. I need to find some focus." While Dan is pleased that Bell has put his trust in him, the coach at times feels overwhelmed himself. "We always ran in high school, but not with athletes like these," Dan says. "They get up and down so fast that it's much more difficult to break down what happened. Plus as a head coach I always watched the ball, and now I've got to train myself to watch off the ball. That's where an assistant can really help."

Even within my limited duties things sometimes move too fast for me, and the intensity is too great. On this day Iavaroni and I have backups Thompson, Tischer, and 6'11" Pat Burke with three balls in play at a side basket for a shooting drill, the results of which will factor into how many down-and-backs this group will have to run at the end of practice. Coaches have to rebound or chase balls that roll away, then toss one to a passer, who then feeds a shooter. It's a bit of a juggling act and, during one particularly manic sequence, I turn into a clown. I get rapped in the head by a few shots and throw a couple of balls to the wrong player. "Come on, man," Thompson says after I throw a pass at him as he's shooting.

I must be thinking like a coach, because the Mustard Man (remember, his first name is Dijon) is starting to get on my nerves. A second-round pick out of UCLA, Thompson doesn't always work hard and has an I-don't-need-any-help attitude. I'm not the only one who notices, which is bad news for him. "That's why he's going to be in Albuquerque," Gentry says later, referring to Phoenix's National Basketball Developmental League affiliate. "He should study Raja Bell. Raja's got $24 million in the bank, and look how hard he plays."

One of the positive signs has been the blending of Nash and Thomas. The former Knick isn't nearly the runner and jumper that Stoudemire is, but he knows where to go on the break, and Nash knows where to find him. I mention that to Dan.

"No question," says the older D'Antoni. "But I worry if we start going too much away from Amaré." Dan has already learned one verity about the NBA: Behind every silver lining is a cloud. One player's touch is cause for another's unhappiness. The ingredients that go into team chemistry are forever flammable.

Concern over the condition of Stoudemire's knee has grown. He practices only sporadically, and then seems a little mopey when he's on the sideline. "Come on, STAT, get in here," Marion yells when the team huddles after practice. Stoudemire ambles over and puts his hand in the circle. STAT, by the way, stands for Stand Tall and Talented, a nickname Stoudemire gave himself. The acronym appears as a tat on his right biceps.

The coaches, and Stoudemire himself, have been going on about his increased shooting range. I'm in a wagering mood, so I bet Gentry $20 that Stoudemire will make fewer than 5 of 10 from three-point distance. I tell Stoudemire the bet. "O.J. will take the other side of the action," I say. Stoudemire calls Gentry O.J. believing the coach looks like the celebrated white Bronco passenger. (The other coaches don't see the resemblance but are happy to use the nickname just to ride Gentry.)

Stoudemire makes two in a row, goes cold, makes two more. If he hits the last shot, I lose. As Stoudemire prepares to shoot, Gentry grabs the ball out of his hands. "All right, just pretend I'm Steve Nash," says the coach, dribbling to the foul line. Gentry licks his fingers and brushes imaginary hair behind his ears, replicating the Nash tics, then fires a pass to Stoudemire in the corner. Stoudemire drains the shot. He hit only 3 of 16 three-pointers last season, and he nails this one.

"Some guys are money players," says Gentry. "You put it on the line, they come through. Amaré's one of them." As Gentry takes his $20, I still feel pretty good. Perhaps I've made STAT stand a little taller or a little more talented. Or perhaps he'll spend the season bombing ill-advised treys.

After a team dinner at a nearby restaurant, the staff heads to Mike's suite at the Westin. The reviews of practice and the strategizing for the next day's sessions have become more specific; the coaches have to get certain things out of each player. At practice I've been studying them all, trying to see what they need to work on, and sometimes I think I have it figured out. But I'm amazed at the awareness of my new colleagues. At root coaching is the same at every level. It's a matter of reading the team, motivating the players who are short on drive, propping up the ones who lack confidence and challenging the ones who are too self-assured.

Mike: "Guys, we have to watch James Jones a little bit, keep his confidence up."

Weber: "He was shooting before and after practice."

Mike: "I know. Sometimes when you're working that hard, though, it's because your confidence is down."

Weber: "He shot 40 percent on threes last year. There's a certain level of confidence that comes with that."

Iavaroni: "Emphasize the right things with him. That's because he's not going to come to you. You've got to give it to him."

Gentry: "But I do think he believes he's a good player."

Iavaroni: "Absolutely. Let's just make sure he knows we know that."

Mike: "I'd just like to see him get a little more aggressive. A little more vocal. A little more, Hey, I belong here."

Mike gets a phone call from general manager Bryan Colangelo. He takes it in his bedroom and returns looking glum. "Amaré's going to get another opinion on his knee," says Mike. "We know he can't keep playing like this."

OCTOBER 7: SHOOTIN' THE BREEZE

The best thing about this coaching gig is walking into a gym every day. There is a giant rack of perfectly inflated balls and a half dozen baskets. Alone, you shoot around or maybe just dribble up and down the floor a few times, get loose. Gradually the players come out. You toss a ball to one of them and assume a rebounding position, for this is their game. The ritual takes on a comfortable, familiar rhythm. Pass, shot, rebound. If a shooter comes into the lane, you offer some token defense, then box him out, all of it at half speed.

As they fire and you rebound, there's conversation. Over the week I heard swingman Jimmy Jackson and Dan talk about a high school game that Jackson played against former NBA point guard Kenny Anderson's team more than 15 years ago at the Beach Ball Classic in Myrtle Beach, S.C. I heard Nash, as he sank baseline jumper after baseline jumper—17 in a row by my count—talk about how his brother and sister were better athletes than him but that they didn't have his drive to succeed. I heard Marion discuss the house he built for his mother in Las Vegas. I heard Lever-Pedroza, a point guard on Mexico's national team, talk about his dreams of playing for an NBA club in a city with a vibrant Hispanic community. His mother is Mexican, his father is Lafayette (Fat) Lever, an Arkansas-born former All-Star guard for the Denver Nuggets.

I'm rebounding for Thomas, who smiles and glances toward the sideline. "You see that man?" he asks, pointing at John Shumate, a former Notre Dame star who's now a Suns college scout. "He was the coach at SMU, where I really wanted to go. But he thought I should go to junior college for a year because I hadn't played much high school ball. [Instead Thomas went to TCU, where he led the nation in scoring and rebounding as a senior.] I tell you, every time we went up against [SMU], I just played my butt off." The memory pleases Thomas.

"Hey," he says to me. "You want to shoot some?" It's one of the things that will stick with me: *You want to shoot some?*

The teams for tomorrow night's open scrimmage at the McKale Center were set a couple of nights ago. Nash, Jackson, Jones, Thomas, Burke, Lever-Pedroza, Tischer and guard Leandro Barbosa make up the White team to be coached by Iavaroni, Dan D'Antoni and, well, McCallum. Stoudemire, Marion, Bell, Diaw, Thompson, center Brian Grant and guard Eddie House are on the Orange team to be coached by Gentry and Weber, who are at each other all the time but like to be together. Mike D'Antoni will sit at midcourt and evaluate screwups by players as well as coaches. Since then, however, Stoudemire has been pulled because of his aching knee. Mike is talking on his cell to assistant general manager David Griffin, who has to finalize the rosters for the scrimmage.

"Without Amaré, the Orange needs another guy," says Mike. "We'll give them Tischer."

Gentry shakes his head. "Lucas Tischer for Amaré Stoudemire," he says. "Now there's a trade that will go down in history."

On the bus from the hotel to McKale, the radio pumps out classic rock, but the coaches' mood is dark. The results of a second opinion on Stoudemire's knee are in: The injury is much worse than expected and could keep him out for up to nine months. (Four days later he would undergo microfracture surgery to repair a lesion, and his projected return was sometime in February.) Mike has already uttered what will become the Suns' mantra: "We just have to make the playoffs." He brightens briefly. "I coached them last year when we won 62," he says to Iavaroni and Weber. "It's on you now."

The coaches kick around how to compensate for Stoudemire's 26.0 points and 8.9 rebounds per game. "Shawn's just got to be a monster," says Mike, "and he has to understand we need him at the four spot." Though he made the Western All-Star team last season by playing mostly power forward, the 6'7", 215-pound Marion has continually expressed a desire to play small forward.

"We've got to get one more runner to join the pack," says Weber.

"No use looking to make a deal," says Mike. "There's no big men around like Amaré."

He claps Gentry on the back. "All right, Alvin, you coached the Clippers," Mike says. "What do we do now?"

At the arena Mike gathers the team around. His speech is breezy but direct. "I guess most of you guys know about Amaré," he says. "Looks like the best it can be is that he's out a month. Or he could be out six months. So we just have to band together and get it done another way. I don't have any doubts whatsoever. Just make sure you take care of yourself. Get in your extra shooting, talk to Aaron [trainer Aaron Nelson] right away if something comes up medically. Because you know what? We have to find a way to score 110 points. We have plenty here to do it, but we've got to find a different way from last year. So let's band together and go bust somebody's ass and get it done."

Practice is spirited but, again, ragged. The question hangs in the air: How will they get 110 a night without Amaré? The best answer to that—Marion— is the subject of the nightly meeting in Mike's suite. Though he makes spectacular plays and is a tenacious rebounder and defender, Marion is hard to read and to reach. The coaches are also concerned that he is doing too much bitching about others' mistakes.

"Shawn'll be all right," concludes Mike. "We don't need to worry about him."

OCTOBER 8: OF THE ORANGE AND THE WHITE

The morning practice passes quickly, and families and friends of the Phoenix coaches and players start arriving for tonight's scrimmage. Managing partner Robert Sarver, whose ownership group bought the Suns last year for $401 million, has proclaimed this Family Day and invited the public to spend the afternoon with the team. McKale has been transformed into a street fair with basketball clinics, raffles and photographers, along with appearances by the team's dancers and longtime mascot, The Gorilla. Mike D'Antoni tells the players, "You know you have to hang around a little while. Smile, say hello, sign some autographs and get out of there nicely."

It falls on the upbeat Weber to conduct the clinics for the kids. (The coaches call him Drill Phil.) As I leave the gym, I spot the D'Antoni brothers standing together, watching their children—Mike's 12-year-old son, Michael Jr., and Dan's eight-year-old daughter, Morgan—dribble upcourt together under the tutelage of Weber. I'm not even sure the dads appreciate what a fine scene this is.

Five hours later I walk back into the gym for the scrimmage. There are already a couple of thousand people in the stands. The pep band is warming up. Reporters are lounging on press row. I walk back to the locker room. The guard is unsure whether I'm legit, but the team shirt gains me access without question. Old school rap is playing loud. I wander back out and think, Man, this would be a great way to make a living.

The White team coaches—Iavaroni, Dan and I—huddle on the bench. We seem to be taking it more seriously than our counterparts in orange, probably because two of us are rookies and Iavaroni is, well, Iavaroni. He wants Dan to chart the offensive plays and me to chart the early offense (how many times we shoot within seven seconds) and deflections (steals, blocks or just getting a hand on the ball). "Uh-oh," says Quinter when he sees me, "Marc has you doing deflections? You know, he's going to go back over the tape and see if you screwed anything up." He's kidding. I think.

As the lineups are announced, I hear "...and coaches Marc Iavaroni, Dan D'Antoni and, from Sports Illustrated, Jack McCallum." I look over at a smiling Quinter. Tell you the truth, it felt good.

Iavaroni gathers the team around and shouts instructions: "O.K., we're blacking on the side. We'll gold when there's not an overload. And on offense we want to start with a drag." Incredibly, I know what this means. He wants to force everything baseline when the ball is on one side of the floor (black), wants everyone to front his man (gold) unless double-teaming help is warranted and wants the first offensive set to be a pick-and-roll (drag).

"The last time I was sitting on a bench," I say to Dan before tip-off, "I was coaching the Bethlehem Hurricanes in the Lehigh Valley Knee-Hi Basketball League."

He claps me on the knee. "In a way," he says, "this is no different."

On our first possession Thomas hits a jumper off a pick-and-roll, just like we drew it up. (All right, just like Iavaroni drew it up.) The game is a blur after that. Hands move fast and deflections are hard to calculate. I get so involved watching the symmetry of fast breaks that I almost forget to note a quick shot. My colleagues are immersed in the game; they have gone into a third gear of competitiveness.

"No way we should only be up two," Iavaroni says angrily in the second quarter. "We take [Nash] out and everything goes to s–." He sounds like it's June and the conference finals.

White is ahead by eight at halftime. Mike gathers both teams in the locker room and makes some general comments. "We're putting on a good show," he says. "We're running. We're playing some defense. We've had some lapses, but that's going to happen. At the end of the day what we're looking for is scoring more points than the other team. We were plus-seven last year, second best in the league to San Antonio. Good teams outscore their opponents by a big margin on average. That's what we want to do."

He is unremitting in his message: Run. Score. Keep running. Keep scoring. Put on a good show.

Marion hits four shots in a row for Orange to open the second half, and suddenly we're on our heels. Timeouts take on new importance when you're a coach, but Iavaroni can hardly make himself heard with the background cacophony. The Gorilla is normally a pleasant diversion; now I want him to sit the hell down so the crowd will shut up.

Over the week certain relationships have developed between player and coach, none closer than the one between Barbosa and Dan. The head coach will do most of the communicating with Nash, so Dan has taken it upon himself to work with Nash's backup. "Way to be, LB!" he says in a piercing drawl. "Good positioning, LB!" Barbosa listens, wide-eyed, to everything Dan says; the 22-year-old from Brazil is grateful for the attention and picks up a lot.

In the third quarter Barbosa takes a quick jumper and misses. "I don't like that one shot and out," says Iavaroni.

"Hell," says Dan, "that's the way we play."

Late in the third quarter Nash sits down for a breather. He looks at my pad. "I'm charting deflections," I say, "and I note that the 2005 MVP doesn't have any." A few minutes into the fourth Nash has three. "Did you get them?" he asks during a timeout.

With about 1:10 left, Sarver, the managing partner, hollers down the bench. "Mr. Iavaroni," he calls, "would you take a timeout, please." It's not a request exactly; more like a gentle order. "He's not going to pull a Nixon and send in a play, is he?" I say to Dan. Iavaroni obliges, and Steve Kerr, an Arizona legend who is now a Suns minority investor and adviser, walks to midcourt. He thanks the fans and the university for the hospitality it has shown the team during camp. A nice moment.

With 24 seconds left, the score is tied at 83 and we have the ball. "At the risk of demonstrating my genius," I say to Dan, "I think we should run something for Nash."

"You'll be a head coach someday," says Dan.

Nash, guarded by the tenacious Bell, dribbles down the clock and gets a screen from Thomas on the right side. Bell fights through and leaps at Nash as he takes an off-balance jumper. No good. "What! No foul?" I hear myself scream when I transcribe the tape later. I don't even remember yelling it, nor was it anything but a terrific defensive play by Bell. Typical coach. The scrimmage ends in a tie.

Afterward the Phoenix staff is reasonably happy. As we screen a tape of the scrimmage in Mike's suite, I am astounded by the almost total recall the coaches have of every play. As one sequence unfolds, Iavaroni says, "This is a basket-cut layup right here. Jimmy [Jackson] doesn't get over." That's exactly what happens.

Everyone agrees that Bell (24 points, four threes, flypaper defense) was the star of the evening, a gutty and confident team player who has fit in perfectly. "So, Mike, who do you like better," says Iavaroni, "Quentin Richardson or Raja Bell?" It's a rhetorical question. The coaches appreciated the three-pointers and the swagger that Richardson provided last year, but they are enamored with Bell's versatility. Alas, that's not the issue.

"What we have to do," says Mike, "is get Raja up to Joe Johnson numbers."

OCTOBER 9: BUT I KNOW THE INBOUNDS PLAYS AND...

It's 9 a.m. in the Westin lobby. Weber has his Diet Coke. The D'Antonis work their crosswords. Gentry reads the paper. Iavaroni peruses his defensive statistics. Camp breaks today, and the Suns will return to Phoenix. I'm saying my goodbyes. Everyone slaps me on the back as they leave. Dan gives me a quick hug.

I drive to a nearby Starbucks, wearing the last of my clean shirts with the Suns logo.

"Um, are you with the Suns?" a young lady asks me.

"Well, sort of, yes," I say. It's just too complicated to explain.

"Are you, like, a coach?" she says.

"Well, sort of, sure." I feel kind of proud until she gets to the essence of the conversation.

"Do you, like, know Steve Nash?"

Next time, I come back as a player.

— POSTSCRIPT —

Jack McCallum: For whatever variety of reasons, the Phoenix Suns said yes to my 2005 request to spend a week with them in training camp as a kind of quasi (more like half-assed) assistant coach. For whatever variety of reasons, coach Mike D'Antoni and his staff put precious few restrictions on what I was allowed to report. For whatever variety of reasons, the Steve-Nash–led team didn't sweat my presence. The result was the most behind-the-scenes story I ever wrote, which led to a behind-the-scenes book, *Seven Seconds Or Less*. Sometimes you just get lucky.

FEBRUARY 18, 2015

Warriors Come Out to Play

One dimensional and one-and-done last postseason, Golden
State has morphed into a multifaceted favorite this year.
The catalyst? Start with the bony, spiky-haired coach

BY CHRIS BALLARD

*The year was 2009 and the Warriors were mired in a decades-long slump.
Ownership was suspect and talent in short supply. The Warriors used the
seventh pick on Steph Curry, an undersized point guard from a mid-major
program. Wispy and baby-faced, he did not have the look of a franchise
savior.*

*I covered his first game for the Warriors and, living in the Bay Area, stuck
around the team over the ensuing six years, filing occasional columns and
features. The early going was rough. Losses, injuries, an unwelcoming Monta
Ellis. And then: new ownership, new coaches, new GMs and savvy draft picks.*

*By 2014, the table was set for the arrival of coach Steve Kerr and a system
that utilized Curry's unique talents. Like Steph, Steve Kerr had been a lights-
out shooter once considered too small, too unathletic and too slow to make
it at the NBA level. Like Steph, he was molded and shaped by a father he
admired.*

*This story, written the February before their first title, captures Kerr,
Curry and the team on the brink of a dynasty. Looking back now, in the wake
of the Warriors' fourth ring in eight seasons, it's remarkable how much of the
core and ethos of the team remains.*

The giant in the yellow T-shirt lumbers across the concrete, advancing on his target.

It's a Wednesday evening in late January, in the cavernous underbelly of Oracle Arena, minutes before the first-place Warriors are to host the Rockets. Golden State's primary owner, 59-year-old Joe Lacob, has just finished speaking to a bunch of venture capitalists in North Face vests. Straddling a stool in a private room, Lacob spoke of penciling profits and leveraging assets and the general awesomeness of Steph Curry. But now he's headed toward the tunnel to his courtside seat. Before he can get far, however, the giant intercepts him.

"Thank you Joe!" the man bellows.

Lacob peers up and recognizes the looming figure of Bill Walton, whose son Luke is a Warriors assistant coach and who, for reasons that never become totally clear, crashed the VC event and asked a handful of relatively complex financial questions.

"Thank you!" Walton shouts a second time, pumping Lacob's hand. "Thank you for everything you've done!"

Lacob smiles, nervous. "It feels weird when people say that," he says. "We haven't accomplished anything yet."

"But you have!" booms Walton, becoming serious. "You've changed *everything*. You've made people *believe* again."

Belief. When it comes to pro basketball in the Bay Area, it is a recession-proof currency, forever propped up by an enduring fan support that even team COO Rick Welts calls, "unexplainable." This is a franchise that has taken and taken from its fans while providing little in return.

No one expected change to come this quickly, though. Five years ago, when Lacob and Peter Guber bought the team for $450 million, the Warriors were 25–56 and coming off a stretch of 14 losing seasons in 16 years. The roster was riddled with D-Leaguers. The previous owner, the reclusive Chris Cohan, was loathed by fans. The coach—Don Nelson, in his final, melancholy, hangdog iteration—was already daydreaming about his beachfront home in Maui.

And now? Now, the Warriors are riding a 107-game sellout streak. At points this season they've had the top-ranked offense *and* defense. Their core is young and talented, their coaching staff deep, their owner committed and their executives earned the "Sports Team of the Year" award from *SportsBusiness Journal* for 2014.

Which leads to the question that all the North Facers want answered: How, in just five years, and without a draft pick higher than No. 6, did the Warriors go from a joke of a franchise to one of the best in all of sports?

The answer is about basketball and business, of course, but ultimately it's about people. It involves a prideful preacher and a mad scientist, a spindly point guard and a passionate power forward, an impatient multimillionaire and a UCLA walk-on. And, in perhaps the most crucial role in the months to come, a professor's son with a knack for diplomacy.

At 49, Steve Kerr still looks more like a YMCA All-Star than an NBA player, all bones and elbows and spiky blonde hair. During his years with the Bulls and Spurs, Kerr was the guy who, sizing him up, you figured you might be able to take on a good day. Skinny, short, bereft of hops. And yet, somehow, magically, he won five titles, earned the trust of Michael Jordan and retired as the game's all-time leading three-point shooter.

Now, as a coach, Kerr can give off a similar vibe: The Guy Who Just Got Lucky. He merely inherited a great team, Kerr tells you. It's all about the players, he stresses. *Don't talk to me, talk to my assistants—they're the ones doing the real work.* This story? Kerr doesn't want it to be about him. Really, he says, there are more important things to write about.

Sorry, Steve. Not going to happen. Because there's one major difference between last year's Warriors, which finished 51–31 before losing to the Clippers in the first round of the playoffs, and this year's team, which returned its top seven rotation players and entered the All-Star break with the best record in the NBA at 42–9. And that difference looks a lot like a spiky-haired YMCA All-Star.

Kerr always planned on coaching, but it wasn't until two years ago, while working as a broadcaster for TNT, that he says he began preparing in earnest. That summer he attended a sports leadership conference at the Aspen Institute in Colorado and ran into Jeff Van Gundy, whose work Kerr admired. Van Gundy told Kerr what he tells all aspiring coaches: Write down everything. Everything you've learned, everything you want to do. Everything you'd change. It'll organize your thoughts. Develop your philosophy.

So Kerr created a Word file on his laptop. Some days he added a few notes; other days he filled pages. During four years of college and 15 seasons in the NBA, Kerr played for Lute Olson, Lenny Wilkens, Phil Jackson and Gregg Popovich. His teammates included Mark Price, Tim Duncan, Scottie Pippen and Jordan. There was a lot to write, and no detail was too small. He jotted down offensive sets and defensive philosophies, but also included the little stuff—everything from a policy for families traveling on the road to whether players are required to do 20 minutes of cardio after a game if they don't play a certain number of minutes.

Kerr began collecting plays too, pausing games on the flat-screen at his San Diego home whenever he saw an action he liked—a backdoor lob off an inbounds or a particularly potent flare screen. Then he'd shoot an email to Kelly Peters, a friend and coach at nearby Torrey Pines High (and now a Warriors advance scout). Peters pulled the footage and compiled it using iMovie. Week by week, Kerr's file—named ATOs, for "After Timeouts"—grew.

By the spring of 2014, the video library had swelled to over 50 plays and the Word file had morphed into a detailed Power Point presentation. Kerr loved broadcasting, just as he'd enjoyed playing, but friends believed coaching was, in the words of Bruce Fraser, a Warriors assistant who's been close to Steve since the two played together at Arizona, "his calling." Now, with two of his three children off at college, it was time.

The plan was simple, and seemingly foolproof: Follow his mentor, Phil Jackson, to New York. But then the Warriors, coming off a second straight playoff appearance, did something unexpected: They fired their coach, Mark Jackson.

San Francisco Chronicle columnist Bruce Jenkins, the dean of Bay Area sportswriters, called the move a "risky gamble," labeling Lacob as "meddling" and "pathetic." "I don't buy this notion that, with a new coach, these same Warriors reach the NBA Finals next year," wrote Jenkins. "Dead wrong. Zero chance of that."

Privately, Lacob fumed. Publicly, he conducted a high-powered coaching search. In early May, he offered the job to Kerr who, after consulting with Popovich, as well as family and friends, took it, thereby breaking Phil Jackson's heart. But the Warriors offered a better roster, proximity to his family and a stronger organizational structure. Still, it was a weird situation to enter. Expectations were simultaneously high and low. *You'd better win at least 51 games. But we don't think you can do much better.*

To find success, Kerr knew he needed people to buy-in. He began with the most important man in the franchise.

Of the 15 players on the Golden State roster, it is strange to think that the 26-year-old Steph Curry is now the longest-tenured. Especially because he never should have been a Warrior.

The year was 2009 and Don Nelson couldn't believe it. The Minnesota Timberwolves had just taken two point guards in the first six picks and neither was named Curry. Nelson had long been enamored of Curry, seeing in the skinny Davidson star the playmaking and shooting skills of Steve Nash. Nelson and then-GM Larry Riley had Curry ranked second overall in the draft, behind only Blake Griffin. "And there wasn't really anyone else we liked," says Nelson. When the Timberwolves took Ricky Rubio and Jonny

Flynn, shouts of joy echoed in the Warriors draft room in Oakland. Curry was theirs.

It would be the last significant contribution Nelson made to the Warriors. He was fired soon after Lacob took over, but Curry remained. Beset by ankle injuries and mismanaged by interim coach Keith Smart, who often pulled the young guard after bad turnovers and in favor of veterans, Curry flourished under Mark Jackson, whom Lacob hired in June of 2011 to replace Smart.

As a point guard for 18 years in the league, Jackson had catered to stars, setting up players like Patrick Ewing and Reggie Miller. Now, as a coach, he did the same. He encouraged Curry to run endless pick-and-rolls and go one-on-one. The rest of the team? Much of the time their job was to set screens for Steph. Or feed Steph. Or guard the opposing point guard while Jackson hid Curry on a weaker offensive player. The strategy worked in at least one important respect: Curry got better. He was allowed to make mistakes. His confidence grew. He became an All-Star.

Meanwhile, the Warriors evolved as a team, due in part to Jackson's influence. He emphasized individual skill development, mandating that every player put in at least 15 minutes of extra work with an assistant coach. A pastor at a non-denominational church in Reseda, Ca., Jackson had an uncanny knack for fostering an us-against-them mentality. To this day, the Warriors still exit each huddle yelling "Just Us!", a unifying chant that began in the Jackson era. Upon his hiring, Jackson had immediately—and foolishly—promised that the team would make the playoffs in his first season. The Warriors didn't, and wouldn't for two more years, but Jackson's formidable public confidence and oratorical skill—which, says one team source, is what got him the job over then-Spurs-assistant Mike Budenholzer, because, "Of course Mark's going to win the interview"—buoyed the players' confidence.

Jackson was the right man at the right time. In many respects, though he was the wrong man for the long run.

Golden State GM Bob Myers looks younger than his 39 years. Tall and lanky, with a thatch of dark hair and big eyes, he has both the physical presence of a former athlete—he walked on at UCLA and still plays intense full court 1-on-1 games after Warriors practices against advance scout Chris DeMarco—and the social acumen of an agent, which he was for 14 years. Hired in 2011 to apprentice under Riley as an assistant GM, Myers impressed Lacob so much that he was elevated to general manager in only a year.

From the beginning, Myers and Lacob followed a plan. It revolved around a few key tenets. First, that the future of the league lay in position-less players. Size, length and versatility were more important than traditional designations. Second, despite recent trends, they believed that centers still mattered. Third, they believed that organizations flourished when stocked with high-character people. "I'd noticed that sometimes the most talented people don't help the bottom line in regards to winning," explains Myers. The executive motto became, in Myers' words, "Size, then character." They began with a significant advantage, possessing in Curry a tiny Tim Duncan. "Our best player is arguably our highest character player," says Myers. "It's like having a CEO that exhibits the highest character. Everybody else falls in line."

Meanwhile, Lacob set about changing the business side. In an effort to create both literal and figurative transparency, he ordered executive office walls to be replaced with glass. He informed basketball operations that, instead of being the team that sold draft picks, they'd now be buyers. And he took aim at the best in the business, luring Jerry West to become head consultant and then recruiting Welts, who dreamt up the concept of All-Star Weekend and the Dream Team during a 20-year stint with the NBA. This would prove to be Lacob's MO heading forward: Always go for the gold.

In March 2012, the Warriors traded Monta Ellis, the team's most popular player but a redundant piece next to Curry, to Milwaukee for center Andrew Bogut, an elite defensive big man. They drafted one big, long position-less wing after another—Klay Thompson (6'7"), Harrison Barnes (6'8"), Draymond Green (6'7")—and hit on a surprising number of them. They filled in holes with free agents like Jarrett Jack and Carl Landry, and acquired Andre Iguodala (6'6"), yet another long-limbed wing, while unloading the bloated salary of Andris Biedrins. In a business where 50% is a good success rate on personnel decisions, it was a remarkable hot streak.

By last spring, Lacob's five-year plan was ahead of schedule. Golden State had the talent and the mindset. There was just one more move to make.

During Kerr's three-hour interview last May, at an airport conference room in Oklahoma City, many things impressed Golden State's decision makers. First was the Power Point presentation, which by then ran 16 pages. It began with a section titled "Why I'm Ready To Be A Head Coach" and included segments on leadership, relationships, analytics and everything from dress code to dieticians to yoga instructors to sleep specialists. Kerr also included detailed thoughts on Warriors players, including potential rotation changes. But what sealed it, at least for Lacob, was Kerr's list of potential assistants. At the top, along with David Blatt (now the Cavaliers' coach), were Alvin Gentry and Ron Adams, two of the top strategists in the business. Here, Lacob knew, was a man who wouldn't feel threatened by those around him.

This, in the end, had been part of Jackson's undoing. Upon joining Golden State, he'd instituted a rule forbidding assistant coaches from talking to the press. Even so, assistant Mike Malone received credit for the team's improved defense, which angered Jackson (who declined to comment for this story). Within the team, he pitted players against each other to gain loyalty. "He'd say, 'You're my guy, and so-and-so is a clown,'" recalls one person with knowledge of the situation. "Then he'd go say the same thing to the other player, only reversed." When Jackson became frustrated with Malone's growing profile, he gave the defense to someone he could trust, Darren Erman. At the time, Erman, a former lawyer, was a recently-promoted assistant with no experience running an NBA defense. Fortunately for Jackson, Erman thrived in the role, molding a top-tier defense.

Then, last spring, things got downright strange. In March, without explanation, Jackson reassigned Brian Scalabrine, a well-liked assistant, to Golden State's D-League affiliate; in April, Erman was fired for violating team policy. (Jackson later cited "disrespect" in Scalabrine's firing; Erman was reported to have secretly recorded team meetings.) Players became wary of publicly crediting assistants, lest they incur Jackson's wrath. Meanwhile, the Warriors were heading into the postseason with a depleted, relatively inexperienced coaching staff and a number of troubling losses. To the Knicks, Hornets and Timberwolves at home. To the Spurs at home even though San Antonio sat its starters.

While Jackson excelled as a leader, he was not interested in the minutiae of coaching, according to sources. He so rarely watched film that the video team eventually stopped loading clips onto his laptop. He didn't draw up plays during huddles, or carry a clipboard. He often looked at his cellphone during practice, even when management was around. His relationship with the front office grew more strained.

There were other, cultural concerns. Jackson often emphasized his faith with the players. "It's fine to be religious," says one Warriors insider, "but it's a different thing to bring it to your work." When Jason Collins publicly announced his homosexuality in April 2013, Jackson told reporters, "I know Jason Collins; I know his family and am certainly praying for them." This seemed particularly tone-deaf considering that Golden State COO Rick Welts, the first high-ranking sports executive to come out, worked in the same building. Welts says he approached Jackson and had "a nice conversation, like grown-ups," adding, "He knew how I felt, I knew how he felt. I'm sure he thought it was an opportunity to educate me, and I thought it was an opportunity to educate him."

By the time the season ended, Lacob felt the situation had become too dysfunctional. Jackson no longer fit with his larger vision for an integrated, inclusive operation. As he later told a venture capital luncheon, by way of explanation: "You can't have 200 people in the organization not like you." (Afterward, Lacob felt bad about the comment. "I didn't know it was being taped," says Lacob of the event. "But that's no excuse.")

With Kerr's hiring, Lacob hoped to restore stability. One of the new coach's first moves involved a reclamation project.

Harrison Barnes was shocked when Kerr called him last May and said he wanted to meet him wherever he was. "That's big, actually making the commitment to fly out and see guys," says Barnes, who was in Miami at the time. "It would've been easy for him to fly and meet Steph and just call everybody else."

A talented 22-year-old forward, Barnes was coming off a miserable season. As the leader of the second unit, he was expected to score, and often out of isolation sets. It hadn't worked. "The best players in the league shoot only 20%, 30% or so on iso plays," Kerr said when they met, at the Four Seasons in Miami. "Any idea how well you shot?"

Barnes grimaced. "Probably way lower than that?" he ventured.

Kerr nodded. "I don't think you were used last year in a way that was best for you. But if you buy into what we're saying, you have a chance to be successful."

Over the weeks that followed, Kerr met with a number of other players, including flying to Australia to see Bogut. He gave them all the same message. *Here is what I'm hoping to do, here's why and here's how.* The players, some of whom had been conspicuously silent when Kerr got hired, appreciated the no-BS approach. "I think he was destined to be a coach," says Klay Thompson. "Just the way he's composed. He's got a real good way of dealing with people."

This may have something to do with Kerr's upbringing, which is well-chronicled. When Steve was 18 and a freshman at Arizona, his father, Malcolm, was working as the president of American University in Beirut. On January 18, 1984 as the elder Kerr headed to work, he was shot twice in the head and killed. Three years later, as a Wildcats senior, Kerr became a central character in John Feinstein's book, *A Season Inside*, which paints a portrait of a scarred yet uncommonly mature young man. In 1987, Arizona coach Lute Olson told the *New York Times* that Kerr was, "the smartest player that I've ever coached or ever seen." At an age when most young men were still forming their identity, Kerr already knew exactly who he was.

Now, as a coach, he wanted to be both firm and fair. And that meant making tough decisions. The first, and potentially riskiest, involved Barnes. After two weeks of training camp, Kerr knew that Barnes needed to start to fulfill his potential, so he could play off of Curry and Thompson. And that meant telling Andre Iguodala, a former All-Star who'd started the first 758 games of his career, that he was going to the bench.

Iguodala was skeptical at first. "But it's important not to dismiss things immediately so I thought on it," he says. Kerr had made some good points. The second unit, so ineffective the previous season, needed Igoudala's leadership and playmaking. And Iguodala appreciated Kerr's directness. "I agreed with his larger vision," he says. Plus, he adds, "I've been in this league 11 years and I want my professionalism to be something that stands out." In the end, he accepted the demotion gracefully. "Who else is going to complain now?" says Kerr.

Then, in November, Kerr got lucky. David Lee got hurt, straining his left hamstring. A two-time All-Star and a favorite of Lacob and many fans, Lee is a gifted playmaker and finisher. He is also a subpar defender who lacks the range to be a stretch four. Assistant coaches had pleaded with Jackson to move Lee to the bench the previous season in favor of Green, arguing that it would tighten the starting unit's defense and provide a desperately-needed offensive boost to the bench, but Jackson stood firm.

Kerr claims he intended to do the same. "If David Lee doesn't get hurt, he's still starting for sure," says Kerr.

But Lee *did* get hurt. And thus Kerr unleashed upon the league a unique, and uniquely voluble, defensive force.

It's a Warriors home game in late January and Draymond Green is hearing it.

"He's too little! TOO LITTLE!"

That's the Denver bench, shouting at Green, who just got ducked in twice—hoops jargon for scoring on deep inside position—by 6'8" Nuggets power forward Kenneth Faried, who is springy and muscular. And now Green, who is 6'6" without shoes, not much of a leaper and won't be on the cover of *Men's Health* anytime soon, is being told that he's too little. And, as Green says, "That does not sit well with me at all."

His whole life, Green's been told that he's too this or not enough that. An older sister used to sit on him and twist his legs to see if he could break free. One of his brothers, springy and athletic, challenged him to jumping contests in the house, knowing he'd win. The men down at Civitan Rec Center in Saginaw, Michigan mocked the chubby kid. Even after Green won high school state titles and led Michigan State to two Final Fours, the talent people projected him as a "tweener." Which is code for—you guessed it—too little.

What they overlooked was Green's versatility and mindset. He is, in the best sense, the perfect pick-up hoops teammate, willing to do whatever's necessary to help a team win. That's how he earned respect at Civitan and MSU and, later, in workouts with the Warriors. "His team just kept on winning all the drills," says Myers. Meanwhile, assistant GM Travis Schlenk remembers something else from that workout: "Draymond kept blocking jumpshots," says Schlenk. "He must have blocked three on the perimeter. You know how unusual that is?"

Now, Green is the unlikely anchor of the Warriors' top-ranked defense, one of the few humans who can guard both Dwight Howard and Chris Paul. As of the All-Star break, he leads the league in defensive rating and defensive win shares and is being mentioned as a potential Defensive Player of the Year. "The thing I love about him is he hates to be scored on," says Adams, the team's Yoda-like assistant coach, "and that's all you want in a defensive player."

Under Adams, the Warriors run a "shell" protection scheme predicated on length, anticipation and the ability to think and act decisively. They switch most every pick and roll, taking advantage of all their interchangeable parts, and Adams expects everyone to contribute. To him, there's no such thing as an innately poor defender. In Chicago, he helped Kyle Korver become part of a top defensive scheme and now he wanted to do the same with Curry. "I don't think you're a bad defensive player," he told Curry last summer, "but you don't play enough possessions well." (He also said, "Prove to me you're better than your dad.") Steph embraced the challenge. Though he now regularly covers opposing point guards, he's improved from an average to above-average defender, posting one of the top 10 defensive ratings in the league while leading the NBA in steals, which he accrues without gambling in passing lanes.

Still, Green is the heart of the defense, banging and bodying and talking trash (Tim Duncan is the only forward Green says he won't jaw with, partly out of respect and partly because, "You say something to Timmy, he just look at you with that Timmy face like, 'Wow, you're talking to me!'"). And yet, Green disappoints himself daily. "I feel like each possession is a battle and you never want to lose a battle," Green explains after a recent practice. "And if somebody scores on me, it really bothers me. It doesn't make me feel any better if it's Kevin Durant and he hits those shots on everybody. Well, I'm not everybody." Green leans forward, getting fired up. "People say, 'That's great offense, there's nothing else you can do.' No, I could have done something else, because he scored."

Which brings us back to the Nuggets game. On four other occasions already, Faried has tried to post Green and tossed up, in Green's estimation, "garbage shots." But that doesn't matter, because Green can't stop thinking about the two baskets Faried did make. "The one thing you know about Faried is that he's going to duck in, every time," explains Green. "Going into the scouting report, I should have known to sit on that duck in every time. Now, when he ducked me in the first time, I thought, man, I went to help and tried to come back a little bit and he ducked me in. The second time, I'm like, man, I had to step off a little bit and he ducked me in. So I went to the bench and there was a timeout. I said to the guys, 'If I'm going to help, y'all gotta help me.'"

As the half wore on, however, Green continued to replay the sequence in his head and came to a different conclusion. Maybe he had helped too far. Maybe Faried did just get good position. "And then I realized, damn, I think I just got ducked in," says Green. So at the next stoppage he went to Adams. "I said, 'I been replaying the play and...I could be wrong. I think I just got ducked in twice. So I'm going to go talk to the guys.'" Confirms Barnes: "He came right over and apologized."

By the way, the Warriors won that game by 43 points.

As important as Green's ascension has been, the Warriors defense was already stout before Kerr arrived. It's on the other side of the ball that the coach has had the larger impact.

Last season, the Warriors offense was often stagnant, and it frustrated Jerry West in particular. He couldn't understand how a team blessed with shooters like Curry and Thompson, and passers like Bogut and Lee, could be last in the NBA in passes per possession.

That was Jackson's preferred style of play, though, which resembled classic NBA basketball from the 80s and 90s—isolation and pick and roll. Kerr's approach has been a stark contrast.

Many first-time head coaches begin their career by mimicking a mentor. Think of Erik Spoelstra in Miami or Budenholzer in Atlanta. But Kerr has the advantage not only of multiple Hall of Fame mentors but also a respected offensive sidekick in Gentry, whom he hired last June. Together, they created what Gentry calls a "melting pot" system on offense. Watch Warriors games and you'll see the high-post action of Phil Jackson's triangle offense, the drag screens and sideline tilts favored by Mike D'Antoni's Suns (where Kerr served as GM from 2007–08 to '09–10), the low post splits from the old Jerry Sloan Utah handbook, and, most prominently, the motion offense and loop series of Popovich's late-generation Spurs.

The result is a system in which the only sin is standing still. "Ball movement and people movement," is how Gentry describes it. The bigs use dribble hand-offs, the shooters curve and cut in a continual churn and everyone, eventually, gets to touch the ball. To Kerr, who had the advantage of watching the Warriors up close as a broadcaster, this was the best way to utilize a roster stocked with bigs who are better-suited to passing than diving to the rim (in particular, Kerr calls Bogut "a witch with the ball.")

After debuting the offense in summer league, Kerr and Gentry installed it in training camp, while simultaneously focusing on conditioning. Initial results were mixed. There were moments of gorgeous passing and cutting, but there were also turnovers. Lots of turnovers. Seven games into the regular season, the Warriors were averaging 22 a game. For a coach like Kerr, who believes ball movement, limiting mistakes and defending are the keys to basketball, it was painful to watch. "I had so many ideas in my head," Kerr admits now. "I put in too much."

So he simplified the offense, from over 20 plays to a core of four or five sequences. It worked. The Warriors, one year after finishing last in the league in passes per game (245.8), are now 11th (313.6). They lead the NBA in both assists (1,389, tied with the Hawks) and hockey assists (8.1 per game), and they've cut their early-season turnover rate by a third (from 22.1 to 14.6). In previous years, Curry and Thompson often ended up launching difficult jumpers, and Thompson rarely ran off screens. This year, Thompson's improvement is due in large part to the evolution of his game, but he and Curry are also getting easier shots. "No one ever knew how good Klay really was last year," says one opposing coach. "Because Mark never ran any plays for him." Which, in retrospect, may help explain why the Warriors opted not to trade Thompson for Kevin Love. Perhaps they knew something the rest of us didn't after all.

There's another trickle-down effect to the offense, however: as reserve guard Justin Holiday says, "everybody gets a taste." Two role players in particular have benefited. The first is Barnes. As a cutter and kick-out threat, he's now shooting over 50% from the field and making 43.2% of his threes.

Barnes' improvement might have been predicted. The same can't be said for another Warrior.

Many coaches would have given up on Mo Speights. The Warriors originally targeted the 6'10" reserve forward in free agency for one reason: he could hit midrange jumpers. But last year Speights showed up 30 pounds overweight and not even his jumper could keep him on the court. Even when in shape, Speights profiles as the opposite of Kerr & Co.'s preferred player: an unwilling passer and passive defender. "I wouldn't have blamed Steve for ignoring him and counting the days until they could get rid of him," says one Eastern Conference GM. "To me, incorporating Mo is the most impressive thing Steve's done. How many coaches even try?"

This season, Speights is averaging 12.0 ppg on 50.3% shooting while displaying surprising flashes of defensive intensity and voluntary passing. All of which, teammates believe, ties back to coaching. "No one ever ran plays for Mo before," says Barnes. "Now there's a play, it's literally called 'Mo's Play,' to get him an elbow jumper."

Kerr, as is his nature, deflects credit. That's all Mo, he says. I just told him if he came to camp in good shape that he'd have a chance to really help the team. It was assistant coach Luke Walton, a former teammate of Speights' in Cleveland, who ran sprints with Mo every day after practice. And all this may be true, but it's overlooking the advantage of a coach like Kerr: like Phil Jackson and Riley before him, he understands life on the margins. "I know what all those guys are going through, and it sucks," says Kerr of the reserves. "I have great compassion for all the bench guys."

Kerr strives to mimic Phil Jackson, who, "never let anybody rot at the end of the bench." Says Kerr: "In ways the guys at the end of the bench define your chemistry. And if you ignore them, and they never play, they're going to get bitter. And all of a sudden it becomes insidious."

So Kerr rewards good practice play with playing time, and gets mad at himself when he misses an opportunity to play bench guys (he says his biggest regret of the season was not getting Brandon Rush into an early season game when Thompson didn't play). "Steve is an extremely positive guy, but he's no one's fool," says Adams. "He gives people opportunity. So the opportunity may come and it may go. There's no browbeating."

So far, the players appreciate Kerr's approach. Barnes credits his new coach for, "empowering the players," while Green likes that he and Kerr can have a dialogue. "Earlier this season I yelled at him during the game and he yelled back," says Green, who to be fair spends much of every game yelling at or with somebody. "Afterward I walked over to the sideline and said, 'My bad.' He said, 'Nah, you're fine. I love your passion, why would I try to stop that? That makes you the player who you are.'"

Lacob describes Kerr as, "exactly who he sold himself as," which, says Fraser, is one of Kerr's best attributes. "There's no bulls--tting about him," says Fraser. "He may be a bit nerdy, but you can't say he's not an honest, real guy. He does a good job of explaining and talking, not just commanding."

As for Curry, he says he likes that Kerr didn't, "try to come in and be the hero and reinvent the wheel when it came to what we were good at." "He's very mature for a first time head coach," says Curry. "To be able to have an awareness of the bigger goals, not just having the best record right now."

Green agrees: "He don't let us settle for mediocrity in anything."

One place that Kerr certainly does not abide mediocrity: the stair stepper. After most every practice, Kerr engages in a one-man assault upon the hulking black machine in the corner of the Warriors' practice facility, after which he does pushups and planks. Unless, as on a recent afternoon, he is challenged.

"Coach Kerr," says Curry. "You want some today?"

As Curry says this, he is in the midst of hitting either 39 or 40 free throws in a row—it's hard to keep track when the number gets that high. Hearing this, Fraser, who is Curry's shooting coach most days, walks over and waves his arms at Kerr from afar, pointing at Kerr and then at Curry, mimicking free throws.

Kerr dismounts and prepares for battle. Though he was an 86.4% free throw shooter, he knows the odds are against him. He and Curry typically play a game to 10, shooting two free throws at a time, where each make is worth one point but a swish is worth two. And, as you might imagine, Steph does a lot of swishing. At one point, says Kerr, the two had battled 11 times, during which time he had made roughly 84 out of 85 free throws—and won only once. "Steph swishes them all."

On the surface, the competition seems a fun diversion. But, like most things with Kerr, it's more than that. What is coaching if not a power balancing act? Here is Kerr, one of the best shooters in NBA history and a famously (if quietly) competitive man, willing to publicly lose, repeatedly, to his star player. That takes a certain innate confidence that carries over to other areas. At the end of timeouts, he often asks the team if they're seeing anything he isn't. Earlier this year, reserve Leandro Barbosa suggested a late-game play. Kerr not only listened; he used it.

The shooting contest also aligns with a core Kerr concept, which he talks about with Fraser often: maintaining the joy of the game. It's why he once held impromptu 2-on-2 football route-running competitions instead of traditional warm-ups before practice. It's why he took the team bowling, as he did two weeks ago in Minneapolis, overseeing a 2-on-2 competition in which all players were seeded based on perceived ability (in a complete shocker, Curry's team won).

Kerr is also a believer in process and preparation. He asks the video staff to load the previous five games of an upcoming opponent on his laptop leading up to a game. Last July he visited Pete Carroll and was impressed with how Carroll used music to energize the Seahawks in practice. Now the Warriors do the same thing. Following an example set by both Carroll and Bill Belichick, Kerr hired as his personal assistant Nick U'Ren, a 28-year-old who'd spent the previous five years as an assistant video coordinator with the Suns. Explains U'Ren: "The idea is that rather than have a 45-year-old woman behind a desk answering mail as your assistant, why not instead use that spot to add another young basketball mind to the staff." So now U'Ren does both; on any given day he might book Kerr's travel, splice video footage and spend 20 minutes breaking down game strategy with his boss. As far as he knows, he's the only person in the NBA with his job.

Other times, Kerr's moves are diplomatic. From day one, he has made a point of consistently praising Mark Jackson, which built good will with his players. Similarly, he downplays his impact on the team at every turn. "In the end both Pop and Phil taught me the players are the ones that do all the work," says Kerr. "You just want to guide the team in the right direction to play the way that they're best going to utilize their talent and skills." In pro sports, this mindset is unusual. "Usually winning breeds arrogance but he's a rare guy," says Van Gundy, who makes a point to also praise Mark Jackson's work as Warriors coach. "I think Kerr's fully aware that he's done an outstanding job. You don't play as long as he did without great pride and ego. But the way that Steve has handled himself, forget the coaching. What I have such great respect for is his humility with this success. Very, very few people I've known in coaching would have this humility with this success."

That Kerr is also comfortable with the media doesn't come as a surprise. As a former broadcaster (and one-time sports columnist for his high school paper), he understands the power of narrative. Take the famous story of how he and Michael Jordan got into a fight after practice, oft-cited as proof of Kerr's fire and toughness. "Let's be honest," says Kerr. "If we were losing right now, the narrative would be, 'This is a guy that got beat up by Michael Jordan.' We just tailor the facts to however the story is going."

If that's true, the facts aren't cooperating on this day. After a few warm-ups, Kerr bricks his first two free throws. Then Curry bricks one of his first two. "Oh no, I tried to go for the swish!" he yells.

Presently, both begin making their shots and, as usual, Curry goes on to win on yet another moonball swish, after which he runs off in celebration before returning to pantomime a golfer's handshake. But, for a moment, it was interesting to see the two of them there, disgusted with themselves and trying not to show it.

Two men bent on winning, united by a momentary failure.

FEBRUARY 11, 2022

The Harden-Era Nets Instantly Become One of NBA's Strangest Cautionary Tales

Why Brooklyn's Big Three experiment is over before it really got started

BY CHRIS HERRING

From Chris Herring, a requiem for the train wreck Brooklyn Nets, an experiment in taking the Super Team concept to its illogical extreme. Herring is an insightful observer of the league and here he places the Nets into both a modern and historical context.

When taking stock of the Brooklyn Nets and whatever the hell has taken place within the organization over the last 31 months, it feels fair to invoke the poem "Ozymandias," which became a part of broader pop culture after *Breaking Bad* gave a key episode that same name back in 2013.

The poem itself, an 1818 work by Percy Bysshe Shelley, describes a wrecked statue in a vast desert, and is meant to illustrate the downfall of an overly arrogant, once-powerful juggernaut. But forcing that poetic fit—much like the Nets forced their on-court one between Kevin Durant, Kyrie Irving and James Harden—overlooks the fact that Brooklyn never managed to win it all. (Hell, the club never even won the Eastern Conference.) That Big Three was as fleeting as it was dominant; an otherworldly talented group that absolutely shined when it played together—but also one that was unnecessary from the jump, as the Nets already had boatloads of talent and drama prior to bringing Harden to Brooklyn.

Through the first 13 games of last season, which predated Harden's time as a Net, the club already ranked sixth in offensive efficiency. And that was with Irving having missed six of those contests. Durant was an elite offense by himself, while Durant and Irving were a basketball version of Bonnie and Clyde. Harden was supposed to add a layer of inevitability; someone who could give Brooklyn a solid chance even if the Big Three suddenly became a Big Two due to a significant injury. (The Nets almost pulled this off last postseason, nearly beating eventual NBA champion Milwaukee after Irving got injured and Harden played through a bad hamstring tweak.)

Yet beyond the depth questions Harden's addition created—and ones that have been exacerbated by sharpshooter Joe Harris's lengthy absence—there was always the more fundamental issue of whether these players were solid enough to tether the entire franchise to them. Not in terms of talent, but in terms of their resolve. Not only to win at all costs, but to put their minds together to figure things out if and when they hit a rough patch, as just about all teams do.

In Boston, Irving had told Celtics fans he'd stick around, only to then leave months later. And that was after he demanded to be moved out of a contending situation alongside LeBron James in Cleveland, where he'd already won a title. Harden ended up with the Nets after shooting flares into the sky to have someone save him from Houston, where his effort dipped to an embarrassingly low level. (Some may levy that accusation in this instance, too, as he left with Brooklyn in the midst of a nine-game losing skid—one that now stands at 10 games, the longest in the league currently.)

It's here that the Nets organization deserves a solid degree of blame. Brooklyn couldn't force Irving, who's decided against being vaccinated for COVID-19, to get the shot. Yet while the club initially said it wouldn't allow Irving to be a part-time player by allowing him to play in just road games, the Nets later reversed course and said they'd play Irving on the road as the virus wreaked havoc on the NBA.

To what degree Harden was annoyed by this is unclear. But as we wrote months ago, when Irving expressed his stance on the vaccine, refusing to get it went beyond being merely a personal issue because—aside from public health—that made it a team issue as well. Players like Harden would have to shoulder more burden because of Irving's choice. Perhaps Durant, a close friend of Irving's who more or less decided to join the Nets as a package deal with him, could live with his friend's decision. But Harden didn't necessarily sign up for that. And perhaps those frustrations come to light even further when Durant is out with injury, like he is now, necessitating that Harden run the offense all by himself during home games.

The need to trade Harden, who could've left as a free agent this summer, is stunning nonetheless. It illustrates just how far removed the Nets are from where they were a couple years ago, when they'd established a playoff club with coach Kenny Atkinson and talented players like Jarrett Allen, D'Angelo Russell, Caris LeVert and Spencer Dinwiddie, who'd jelled while operating in a highly efficient system.

But those younger players moved on. And so did Atkinson, who mutually parted ways with the Nets just months into his first season with Irving and Durant on the roster. Then, upon the Nets hiring Steve Nash into that role, Irving said he thought of the coaching situation as collaborative. "I don't really see us having a head coach," he said. "KD could be a head coach. I could be a head coach." Irving also missed seven games in a row at one point last season due to personal reasons, a stretch in which Nash said he hadn't heard from his point guard about why he was sitting out.

To be fair, these gambles are ones plenty of NBA clubs would have made if they'd been in position to pull it off. And on truth serum, Nets general Sean Marks might even tell you that he'd still make the same choices if Irving's vaccination status had been different, which would have balanced Brooklyn's situation out in a number of ways. The data, while incredibly scant, was always clear: The Nets were close to unstoppable when all three stars played together.

Durant, Harden and Irving played just 365 minutes total over 16 games; 10 regular-season ones and six playoff matchups. The Nets logged 119 points per 100 possessions—an offensive efficiency rate that would shatter the NBA record—with those three on the court during regular-season contests. (Even with those three not playing much together, last year's Nets hold that record.)

But get this: they scored *far more* in the playoffs, notching an insane 137.2 points per 100 possessions. As a club, Brooklyn had an effective field-goal rate of 65.1% and a true-shooting percentage of 70.7%—Nikola Jokić–type numbers, except better, and on a team scale instead—in the 130 postseason minutes the trio spent on the floor, according to data from Stats Perform.

The stars had a chance to be worth all the headaches. With Durant on the way back from injury, Irving and Harden simply didn't prioritize the notion of winning over everything else.

That's not to suggest Brooklyn can't accomplish anything now that it's moved on from Harden. It may not be fair to assume anything about Ben

Simmons and his game (or his mindset) after having gone this long without playing. But he immediately becomes the Nets' most valuable, versatile defender, and gives them a pace-setting, playmaking presence—things they can use when Irving isn't playing, and qualities that should work just fine even when Brooklyn is whole again.

Things move quickly in the ever-changing NBA. We often come to revere the all-time winners, and we have ways of remembering the most tragic teams, and the most unthinkable misses that fall just short. The Harden-era Nets—fantastic, fleeting and ultimately flawed—will fall in the middle of the Venn diagram as one of the strangest experiments the league has ever seen. One that saw greatness tumble and shatter before it was ever fully assembled in the first place.

MAY 6, 1974

All Red, So Help
Them Henna

To make this team a girl has to dye her hair but she
also has to be a first-rate athlete. Then she can play
200 nights a year, humiliating out-of-shape men

BY WILLIAM JOHNSON AND NANCY WILLIAMSON

*Two years after Title IX, William Johnson and Nancy Williamson went on
the road with the barnstorming All-American Red Heads and their owner, a
misogynistic, small-minded man named Orwell Moore. The result: a portrait
of women's "pro" basketball in its early days, an era when the best player in
the world, Karen Logan of the Red Heads, competed in shabby high school
gyms and her team shared gate money with the local student council. Johnson
and Williamson let Moore hang himself in the story while providing sketches
of the young women and their tie to the game.*

This is the best women's basketball team in North America. That can be
said unequivocally, and you do not even know their names—the player-
coach, Jolene Ammons; the superstar, Karen Logan; the sparkplug, Donna
(Spanky) Losier; the captain, Cheryl Clark; the twins, Lynette and Lynnea
Sjoquist; the rookie, Paula Haverstick.

If they were men, they would be famous. They would be rich. They
would be on a first-name basis with Cosell, Schenkel, Whitaker and Gifford,
perhaps even Cavett and Carson. They would have played before hundreds

of thousands in the Garden, the Spectrum, the Forum, the Astrodome—tens of millions on television.

However....

On this dark night January rain is falling in the town of Barlow, Ky. Yet the lights are blazing at the high school gymnasium and cars gleam in the rain in the parking lot. Tonight the best women's basketball team on the continent is performing in Barlow and the proceeds from the gate will be split with the Ballard Memorial High School student council, which is planning to use the money to buy, among other things, a new water cooler. All the women on the team have blazing red hair, ranging in hue from near-tangerine to deep cinnamon. They are called the All American Red Heads. They are wearing red, white and blue uniforms, stars, stripes, etc. Tonight, as they do 200-plus nights each year, the All American Red Heads are going to play a man's team, the High School alumni. As always, the men are an assortment of sizes, shapes and basketball skills, a fair cross section of American manhood. Some are still willowy and lithe. Others have soft paunches and fat arms; they will soon be gasping like beached fish, their jowls slick and sweaty. They are dressed in motley clothes, a variety of sneakers. One is wearing black anklets. They are not basketball players anymore; they are barbers, bartenders, teachers, truck drivers, and they play the game from memory. They would be home watching *Maude* on television if they were not here playing basketball.

On this night, as before all of their games, the All American Red Heads spend a little time wandering through the crowd in their uniforms, selling programs for a dollar apiece. At the same time, the student council is selling homemade brownies and cookies and coffee. The money made this way is not split between Red Heads and the student council; each group keeps what it makes. The Red Heads program is red, white, blue and silvery. Large block letters shout 35TH ANNIVERSARY CELEBRATION! This is not quite accurate, for the All American Red Heads were founded in 1936, but it does not really matter. There is a drawing of a lovely smiling Red Head wearing a tiara, sneakers and knee guards, perched saucily on a globe of the world, spinning a basketball on one finger. There is a series of star-marked blurbs on the program that describe the Red Heads: THRILLING BASKETBALL... RATED FAMILY ENTERTAINMENT...CLEVER...BRILLIANT...POWERFUL ACTION... and so on.

The gymnasium is not full. There are about 1,400 people and the student council will not get as much money as it hoped for; neither will the All American Red Heads. Possibly the winter rain is the cause of the mediocre turnout. No, says the student council adviser in his soft Kentucky drawl, that is not the case. "We had the Red Heads here five years ago and they sure filled up this gym. We cleared $1,100, a record. I think the reason they aren't drawing so well is that five years ago we had a preliminary basketball game with women—housewives, mothers—from P.T.A.'s all over the county. They really drew 'em because people turn out to see their kinfolk perform, now don't they? The Red Heads themselves couldn't have got that big a crowd in Barlow."

The game begins after flowery introductions of the Red Heads: "...and here she is, the Magic Passer! Miss Basketball! The World's Greatest Ball Handler! A 20,000-point champion! Miss Everything...Player-Coach Jolene Ammons!" The Ballard High School alumni score quickly; the men are taller and can jump higher than any of the women. But the Red Heads are slick ball handlers and their passes snap with precision. Many are thrown behind the back, perfectly. The women are wearing bright red lipstick and blue eyeshadow, as if they were going to the theater. But here they are, perspiring like mad and playing basketball like demons. They drive swiftly down the court. They shoot with deadly accuracy. They shout at each other, shrilly, crying out play patterns. Sometimes they shriek jokes at the men. Their precision dazzles the crowd and, even though they are playing against butchers and insurance men and car salesmen, the All American Red Heads are plainly a splendid basketball machine. Sometimes they stop the action to clown, doing ball-spinning tricks, crawling between their opponents' legs, taking shots piggyback, offering such guffaw gags as "The Pinch"—a routine in which the Red Head comic, Spanky Losier, pretends that a man has pinched her behind and insists that a personal foul, "a very personal foul," be called. The crowd loves it. Small boys fairly roll on the floor at such funny stuff.

At the end, the All American Red Heads have won 79–69, and at this point in late January their season's record is 104 victories, 17 losses. The money is counted and the gate is split—$800 to the student council, $1,200 to the Red Heads—and the Red Heads, dressed in bright warmup suits, file out of the gymnasium into the rain.

Outside, a strange white limousine awaits them, a Toronado 28 feet long, emblazoned with huge red letters saying ALL AMERICAN RED HEADS across the four doors on each side. The women climb inside. Rain drums on the roof and the grand white vehicle rolls hissing over the wet parking lot and out onto Route 60. The seven heads of red hair can be seen, but barely, through the streaming windows. The All American Red Heads are sealed inside the car they call "Big Whitey," insulated from the outside world as if in some kind of rolling space capsule. Here is where they spend far more of their lives than they do on a basketball court. Tonight they will stay in Paducah, 25 miles away. In the morning darkness they will rise and drive 400 miles, nine hours, across much of Kentucky and most of Tennessee to still another town where they will play another high school alumni team that night.

A man from Arkansas named Orwell Moore owns the All American Red Heads. He is essentially a man of small-town hopes and minimal dreams. He likes to call the Red Heads' home office in Caraway, Ark. "The General Store" and, at times, Orwell Moore does look as if he should be wearing a bib apron behind a cracker barrel, ready to slice a slab of rat cheese off the wheel on the meat counter. Ordinarily, Orwell Moore stays home in Caraway to mind the office. This season he has two troupes of Red Heads on the road, the team touring the border states in January being by far the better. It is not a simple job, laying out an itinerary and calendar for the Red Heads: each unit travels some 60,000 miles a season and plays in more than 200 hamlets, villages and various wide spots along the road. Moore's wife, his brother Jack and a secretary are usually engrossed in booking phone calls, sending out endless mailings of Red Head publicity and posters, as well as trying somehow to link a game for the Lions Club in Waseca, Minn. on Dec. 12 with one for the Kiwanis in Joliet, Ill. on Dec. 14 and one in Sioux Falls, S. Dak. on Dec. 13. It is a Chinese puzzle at times, and Moore does not always solve it so neatly. When the Red Heads played in Barlow and then stayed in Paducah, they drove 400 miles to Morristown, Tenn., then turned around and drove 390 miles back to Murray, Ky., which is a mere 40 miles from—yes—Paducah.

So, though Moore ordinarily does not stray far from the store and the booking lists, he has decided to travel with his Red Heads No. 1 team for a few days. He has driven up from Caraway, and the Red Heads rendezvous with him on Interstate 55. Moore takes up the lead in his Pontiac Bonneville, rolling at the sedate pace of a funeral procession while Big Whitey purrs along behind, the seven redheads alight in the sunshine streaming through the windows, Jolene Ammons at the steering wheel as she almost always is.

Moore is expansive about his enterprise, full of a salesman's bombast. He is a big man with a paunch not quite as big as a basketball. His hat is perched jauntily on the back of his silvery yellow wavy hair and his features are strong and blunt and big; his green eyes are quite small and often gleam like small gems when he smiles, which he does often. Moore speaks in a hog farmer's drawl and punctuates what he says by adding "Raaaahght" or "Know what I mean?"

He is full of windy enthusiasm. "I tell the girls, 'Every day is Christmas when you're an All American Red Head.' I tell 'em, '*Happiness* is being an All American Red Head.' Raaaahght. Do you have any idea how much *good* the Red Heads have done for America? Bringin' good clean family fun to every state in the union, except Hawaii, and helpin' in any number of good causes, charities for blind people and poor Indian children and the like. Know what I mean?"

A hawk circles above flats of plowed soybean fields, and a green water tower of West Memphis, Ark. slides past. Moore drawls on. "Lions Clubs are our biggest sponsors, though Kiwanis and Rotary all like us, too. When we come to town it's like the circus. But furnishin' the folks a hee-haw is not our only objective. We also play a very classy game of basketball. Raaaahght. We have originated many of the tricks on the basketball court, such as the Piggy-Back Routine, the Referee Act and the La Conga Out of Bounds Play. I make it a point never to mention the Harlem Globetrotters, but when they claim to have originated many of the tricks that the All American Red Heads actually began, then I feel I must speak out. Know what I mean? The Globetrotters bring their own opponents along. We don't know who we're gonna play from night to night. You play over 200 games a year against men, more'n seven months on the road, well, a girl's got to love basketball with a passion to do that. And the All American Red Heads do love it with a passion."

A sign along Interstate 55 says WELCOME TO MISSOURI and the mini-caravan crosses that border, headed toward the mighty confluence of the Ohio and Mississippi rivers. Moore begins to explain his philosophy of business. His eyes gleam shrewdly, he smiles with relish as if he has discovered Rumpelstiltskin's secret, a way to weave gold thread out of straw. "We have an operation we can control. We keep it small. The meat of the traveling professionals is in the small towns. No overhead, no operating expenses." Moore speaks almost confidentially. "You get the gymnasium for nothing. No rent, no insurance, no light bills. No advertisin' costs, either. Say the Lions Club is sponsorin' the game. In these little towns the Lions Club is the elite. Raaaahght. The Lions Club can go to the local paper and say, 'Now I want these pictures of the All American Red Heads run on the sports page and I want a nice long story to go with 'em.' A Lion'll say that, and, yessir, it will be done. So the Red Heads have no advertisin' costs—the Lions take care of it. We have a suggested price for tickets—$2 adults, $1 kids. I always make sure they got adults at the doors. You get kids takin' tickets and they let all their friends in free."

He tilts his hat forward and says, "The biggest crowd the Red Heads ever played for was 11,500 in the Chicago Stadium. That was before I took over the team. We got $4,500 out of it, but I can't tell you how much it cost advertising, buying stories in the papers. You don't get publicity for nothin' in the big cities and you don't get the gym free either.

"If you wanted to book into the Memphis Mid-South Coliseum, it'd cost, say, $1,000 rent, $250 for insurance, *pay* for ticket attendants, *pay* for the union men who turn on the lights and turn off the lights, *pay* for the scoreboard keeper, *pay* for the referees. Know what I mean? Then there'd be $600 to $700 to buy ads in the Memphis papers and *twice* that much to buy ads on TV. Oh, no, once you start payin' people to run ads, you make a mistake. It costs $140,000 a year to run the All American Red Heads organization. People think if you don't have $1 million operating expenses, you're peanuts. I was offered $1 million for the Red Heads some time ago. I turned it down. It's a big farm for me, my general store, raaaahght."

Jolene Ammons honks Big Whitey's horn and Moore pulls over to a diner called the Sands Café. "Time for dinner," he says. The Red Heads primp and fuss, put on lipstick, brush their seven heads of red hair, check eye shadow, and enter the restaurant. The waitress tells them that the specialty today is homemade meat loaf with brown gravy and mashed potatoes, and since the Red Heads eat their big meal at noon, homemade meat loaf is it for most of them. Orwell Moore stands by their booths and beams down past his paunch. "Every day is Christmas with the All American Red Heads!" he booms. "These girls *love* their life because they all *love* basketball." The Red Heads nod and some smile. They all are eating with fierce speed. They are used to rapid and enormously efficient "pit stops."

On the *real* Christmas Day 1973, the All American Red Heads were in a motel in Joplin, Mo. They found a tiny Christmas tree and decorated it with shaving cream. They held a make-believe Miss America contest, which was won by Lynette Sjoquist, one of the twins, who was then awarded a pickle. They celebrated by drinking Coca-Cola and Dr Pepper.

By the end of January the Red Heads had traveled 35,000 miles since starting in October, been in 26 states, seen a normal person's lifetime quota of billboards, brown hills, used-car lots, junkyards, stray dogs, abandoned barns, gas stations and housing developments. They had visited a few (only a few) points of special tourist interest—the Will Rogers Memorial Museum in Claremore, Okla., Plymouth Rock, the Astrodome. And they had eaten uncountable pounds of McDonald's hamburgers; they often drive miles off the main highway looking for The Big Arch, as they call it. Most of the time they have only a vague idea of where they are.

The All American Red Heads began their odyssey on Oct. 4, in Mantachie, Miss. They have no idea, just now, where or when the journey will end. They don't know *where* because Orwell Moore, in his careful way, never allows the Red Heads to know their itinerary more than a month in advance. He says, "We have to give them their routes so their folks can write to 'em, but we never tell 'em beyond each month and they are generally sworn to secrecy about the schedule. If they told some reporter where they're playin', he might print the whole schedule in his paper and then some other attraction—donkey basketball, Gospel singers, some other basketball team—could see it and set up a date in the same town a week or two ahead of the Red Heads. That would kill us dead. There's only so much entertainment money around, know what I mean?"

The Red Heads don't know *when* their season will end because Moore doesn't know when the accumulation of gate receipts will be enough to show a profit. He says, "It's clearly understood that the girls are to play as long as I want them to play. We got to make ends meet at the store. Now the energy crisis cost five, six games canceled in Virginia in December. We got to make them up somewhere, so we'll be playin' into May this year. We've never got into June yet, but that's not sayin' it won't happen."

And so Big Whitey purrs along. At the wheel, firm and responsible, her normally dark hair now the color of burnt ginger, is Jolene Ammons, 32, born in Homerville, Ga., an All American Red Head for 11 years. Jolene is now player-coach, den mother, money collector, road accountant and chief chauffeur. On the court she is the playmaker. She is a lithe, handsome woman, though there is weariness in her face. There is nothing she does not do for her little coterie. She drives constantly and says she often sees ribbons of highway center lines streaming endlessly through her mind late at night. Over the years, both knees have been wrenched and twisted time and again, and many nights they throb with so much pain that she cannot sleep. Her coaching is sharp; a tough word here, a pointed question there gets rid of mistakes on the spot. Last year her Red Head team had a 188–13 record. Jolene's passes are hard and flat and she is deceptively fast; she has scored more than 21,000 points. She can spin basketballs on both hands at once, and does clowning exhibitions during halftime. Jolene Ammons would probably be a star on any woman's national team in the world, despite her age. The Basketball Hall of Fame in Springfield, Mass. has asked to display her jersey along with the uniforms of such male stars as Wilt Chamberlain and Jerry West. So far, Moore has not sent along Jolene's jersey; he has never been one to emphasize any individual stars on his teams, feeling he might inflame jealousies.

One of Ammons' nightly duties is to telephone reports to Caraway of money earned and individual points scored; if one woman is consistently rolling up too many baskets, Moore tells Jolene to make the offender cool off in order to keep peace. She is a gentle woman and her face often softens in laughter. She is pretty when she smiles. "I started playing basketball in the fourth grade," she says, "and the girl next door took dancing lessons. Every afternoon she'd walk off her front porch with her tutu and I'd walk off mine with my basketball. She got to be Miss Georgia and I got to be a Red

Head." Jolene admits, however, that she was her high school homecoming queen, replacing Miss Georgia the year after she graduated.

There is an Orwell Moore rule among the Red Heads that they must switch roommates each night and take different seats in Big Whitey each day to avoid cliques. So on this day Spanky Losier, 24, a former brunette of Gorham, N.H., whose hair is now dark red, is sitting in the seat behind Jolene. Spanky is fairly short (5'5"), almost tubby, a born comedienne and entertainer who burbles jokes while the Red Heads drive or helps pass the miles by singing in a sweet, clear voice accompanied by her guitar. She is given to spurts of laughter and frequent exuberant I-love-life eruptions about her role as a Red Head. "Hey, it's wonderful...I put my sneakers on and I'm raring to go. I love the game. Where else can you eat and breathe basketball 24 hours a day? I'm never bored. I'd never touch a drug, I'm too high on basketball...." At first it sounds phony, like Moore's evangelistic salesmanship. But it is true: Donna Losier is in a constant state of delight. She knows the words to 200 songs, can do imitations of everyone from Jonathan Winters to Richard Nixon, often snaps up out of a sound sleep giggling and tossing out lines like, "Hey, they say fish is brain food. Let's have a whale for lunch." She does the major comic routines at games, including the Big Pinch, and carries what she calls her "Crazy Kit," which contains, among other things, a top hat, a sequin covered whistle and a giant powderpuff, for her acts. As a serious basketball player, she is a polished ball handler and dribbler, a fine outside shot, an accurate and notably unselfish passer. This is Losier's seventh year as a Red Head, and every slab of homemade meat loaf still tastes like Christmas dinner to her.

In the next seat is the Red Head captain, Cheryl Clark, 24, formerly brown-haired, from Wetmore, Mich., six feet tall and exceedingly graceful. Her shoulder-length hair is chestnut now, and she wears tinted spectacles and looks almost scholarly. She is soft-spoken, the daughter of a schoolteacher, a writer of many letters during the long periods in the limousine. She says quietly, "I love basketball because I like the feel of running, the constant motion, the instantaneous decisions. Your mind stays active and that is stimulating." Cheryl glides so smoothly when she plays that her game seems almost gentle. She has perfected a driving shot from beyond the free-throw line that opponents never block, and which she seldom misses. This is her fifth season with the Red Heads; last year she performed with the other unit and it won 96 games in a row and finished the year with a 199-6 record.

The Sjoquist twins are sitting together today, large laughing girls with light strawberry hair. They seem almost coltish although each is 6'1" and weighs close to 190 pounds. Lynette and Lynnea, 20, are from a 400-acre farm near Cannon Falls, Minn. They alternate in the pivot for the Red

Heads, and sometimes alternate sentences when they talk. "We are from the farm, all right," says Lynette. "We'd eat our big meal—dinner—at noon and then Dad would have a nap," says Lynnea. "...and we'd go out with our three brothers and play basketball on a concrete court behind the barn," finishes Lynette. Both starred at a small Lutheran junior college and found it difficult adjusting to the Red Heads. "The hardest thing was getting used to the fact we're not the best anymore...." "Or even second best...." "But you have to go all out because people are paying to see us play...." "And you have to have a professional attitude." Both girls are strong under the basket. But this is their first season with the team and they tend to drop some of the veterans' swift, precise passes.

Another rookie is sleeping in the back of the limousine. She is Paula Haverstick, just 18, from the village of Sturgeon, Mo. She spends her days dozing, perhaps because she is by far the youngest on the team and shy to the point of pain. She almost never speaks, but when she puts on her Red Head uniform she suddenly comes alive. She usually substitutes for Jolene, and though Paula shoots well the team seems rudderless when Jolene is out of the game.

The finest athlete among the Red Heads is Karen Logan, 24, of Fortuna, Calif., a rangy woman with orange hair, who is perhaps not very far below the unmatchable Babe Didrikson in natural abilities. She probably would have made the 1968 Olympic team as a 400-meter runner except for a pulled tendon. In 1967 she won a California junior tennis championship, defeating Sharon Walsh who went on to be the U.S. junior champion in 1969. Logan drifted away from tennis because of a lack of confidence, but at Pepperdine University the men's basketball coach saw her play, encouraged her to perfect her game and urged her to get in touch with Orwell Moore. Karen has been riding the roads with the Red Heads since 1970, and is easily the best of them, averaging 23 points a game and playing always with a fierce intensity. Yet she is bitterly frustrated. For one thing, she would like to regain amateur status so she could try out for the 1976 U.S. Women's Olympic basketball team (this will be the first time the women's game has Olympic status). At the moment, that seems impossible. Beyond that, Karen is deeply troubled that there is really no way for the Red Heads to display their skill to the world, no way to prove that they are one of the best women's basketball teams on earth. "I'd give anything to play the Chinese team or the Russians," she says. "I'd love to have a chance at the AAU champions or any women's team anywhere. We could beat anyone in the world. I'm *sure* of it. But we'll never know. No one will ever know because we never play anyone but has-been men."

Seeing Karen play, even against once-upon-a-time high school stars, is like seeing a work of art. Her moves remind one of Pete Maravich. Her concentration during a game is almost fanatic; she plays with her shirttail flapping, her hair soaking wet, refusing to take a man's helping hand when she has been thumped to the floor, then, quick as a cobra, flicking the ball away from him at the next opportunity. Karen, too, was asked for a game uniform by the Basketball Hall of Fame. When she heard that only two other women (not counting Jolene Ammons) had ever been so honored, Karen instantly demanded to know where they live. She wanted to challenge them to games of one-on-one.

Such is the population of Big Whitey. What would one assume about a team of touring professional women basketball players? That they are tough, road-hardened pros? Actually, there is an aura of innocence inside Big Whitey. Traveling with the Red Heads, one does not hear so much as the word "damn" pass their lips. Nor does booze, or beer or any other artificial stimulant. Nor did any Red Head get kissed on this trip.

The first team of Red Heads appeared in 1936, a bunch of henna-haired girls who horsed around the Ozark Mountain countryside near Cassville, Mo., performing for the expressed purpose of drumming up business for a chain of beauty shops. The owner of the shops was Mrs. Doyle Olson, and her husband was the moderately famed C.M. (Ole) Olson who had for 22 years barnstormed the backwaters and barnyards of the land with a basketball team known as Olson's Terrible Swedes. They had stunned hicks the country over with such incredible tricks as the behind-the-back pass and the one-hand set shot. Olson had retired once from the itinerant basketball business before the original Red Heads appeared, but he found that there was enough interest in them to turn a good dollar. So he put them on the road, too. And except for a couple of years during World War II, a team of All American Red Heads has been on the highways of America. In 1948 Ole Olson hired Orwell Moore, then the coach and athletic director of Caraway (Ark.) High School, to be the Red Heads' coach. With Moore came his wife Lorene, or "Butch," a tiny wide-eyed birdlike woman who also just happened to be a talented basketball player. Little Butch Moore played for 12 years with the Red Heads and scored more than 35,000 points, and Orwell remained as coach until 1956 when Ole Olson sold him the franchise.

The early days of the Red Heads were bizarre at times. Moore recalls, "Even after 19 and 48, when I came aboard, we played in mighty shabby facilities, in church basements and on dance floors. We played once in an old factory in New Britain, Conn., where there was such a bend in the floor I couldn't see my team at the other end. We played on a skating rink once in New Castle, Pa. One place I remember the light was so dim they had to have small boys lying around the rafters holding little Aladdin's lanterns. Raaaahght. One night the lights went out due to an ice storm, and we played by car lights shining through the doors and windows so we wouldn't have to give the crowd their money back. We've played deaf and dumb boys, we've played the Boston Patriots, the Kansas City Chiefs. We've played on Indian reservations."

Moore pauses in his recollections, then lowers his voice. "The Red Heads were not always the lovely wholesome crowd of girls you see here today. Some of them carried on considerably in the old days. Lots of drinkin'. My first year I was out on the West Coast with the 'Young Unit' and in March things weren't goin' too well and, sure enough, Mr. Olson caught the other unit in a big beer party, know what I mean? He sent 'em all home. Olson wouldn't stand for that sort of thing.

"We're no part of Women's Lib and if any of the girls were to get involved in it—well, they better not let *me* know about it. I don't want the All American Red Heads tied to any causes. This is a wonderful livelihood for a girl, but I insist on high standards, *my* standards. Now, I don't tell them they can't smoke, but not many do. They are forbidden *ever* to smoke in the uniform of an All American Red Head. The children of America look up to and emulate the Red Heads. As for drinkin', well, I take a beer myself from time to time, but the Red Heads are not to drink. Now, you know, these men professional basketball players can walk in a bar and drink all they want. But let one redheaded woman basketball player sit down on a barstool and order up a beer and you upset the mores of a community, know what I mean?

"I think the successful people of this world have a high regard for the being of the Lord. Raaaahght. I am a Methodist and I believe we have got to have someplace to look for help and guidance. But I do not force that on the Red Heads. We have had girls of all persuasions—a Mormon, Indian girls, one Jewish and I believe there was even one Red Head who did not go along with the existence of the Lord, know what I mean?

"We prefer getting our girls young, fresh out of school. They are easier to coach, easier to fit the Red Head way when they are young. We got a scouting network all over the nation. Old Red Heads, high school coaches. The young girls themselves write to us and ask to play after they see the Red Heads. Paula did that. The twins, too. This is a wonderful life for a girl. Like a big happy family. These girls love basketball so much they don't care what they get paid. The salaries aren't very high. We only pay $40,000 a year to all the Red Heads. But it's not bad. The rookies can save as much money as a schoolteacher, $250 a month. They don't spend anything except on some clothes. Now Jolene, golly, she might save $1,000 a month. And they get five months off, most of 'em. Oh, it's a happy life bein' an All American Red Head. They got workman's compensation if they get hurt or sick.

"Yes, they got it pretty good with the Red Heads. But girls are girls. I sometimes call this the All American Matrimonial Bureau. They get married a lot. And being a Red Head gives a girl a brand of appeal she never had before. She goes home, know what I mean, after a year of bein' a pro basketball player and she's gonna have guys calling her she never knew about before. My girls marry the No. 1 eligible bachelor in their communities, bankers' sons, the rich ones with lots of dough, family dough. Due to their professional basketball career, they get the best jobs when they go home, the good job in the bank, for example. Even our stars stay only four, five years, as a rule. We have to get six new ones every year."

Moore pulled his Pontiac into a restaurant and gas station surrounded by massive trucks. Big Whitey followed him and the truckers stared and joked at the bizarre sight of seven doors snapping open and seven red-haired women emerging to stride across the lot into the restaurant. They sat down to a quick meal of hamburgers and coffee. "Every day is Christmas for the All American Red Heads," boomed Moore once again. After the meal he bade everyone farewell and left to return to the general store in Caraway. The Red Heads piled back into their car and began to cross Tennessee.

It was dark when the Red Heads arrived in Morristown, Tenn. and they were a little panicky, for they thought they were late for the game. At last they found a squad car and asked where the high school was. The cop pulled out in front of Big Whitey and gave the team an escort to the door of the school where they learned, to their immense relief, that they had rolled unknowingly through a time zone on the way and had plenty of time before the game. They had to wait to change into their uniforms because the men's team was using the locker room. It was not a room calculated to raise spirits or refresh the soul. The walls were dreary green and unwashed white. Exposed pipes cluttered the ceiling and the place was garishly lit by bare bulbs. There were some dented lockers, a wire cage full of equipment, two folding chairs, and two short benches bolted to the floor. Four ancient and rust-stained sinks lined one wall, each with a tiny mirror above it. The Red Heads crowded around to paint on their glossy game makeup. There were two stall showers, two toilets of the caliber of those found in a seedy bus depot. The floor was littered with tissues and paper cups. The Red Heads were subdued, even melancholy, as they dressed in the dismal setting, although Jolene remarked that this was a perfectly normal, average dressing room by the standards of the small-town schools they visited.

Karen Logan was dressed first and began to limber up. Soon the others joined her. Suddenly the dank place was filled with balls bouncing off the ceiling pipes, the walls, the floor, and suddenly the place seemed lighter, cleaner, prettier as the Red Heads, their bright hair shining, their red, white and blue uniforms aglow, began practicing their tricks. Now they were smiling, now one or two of them laughed. Suddenly the long drive and the dull hours in Big Whitey fell away like a dirty veil. They were playing basketball. They were happy and they took momentum from the shabby room and went into the gymnasium to play again the game they loved.

Even now as you read this, the All American Red Heads are somewhere out there. They are riding in Big Whitey, or splitting the gate receipts with student councils or faking out barbers in black anklets or sending little boys and girls into peals of laughter. They are somewhere in some small town fooling around like clowns and playing like demons. They are the best women's basketball team in North America, make no mistake.

BEYOND THE COURT

OCTOBER 23, 2013

Lost Soul

Bison Dele, once known as Brian Williams, left the NBA behind to explore the world. His quest carried him to a mysterious end near Tahiti. More than a decade later, his spirit sails on

BY CHRIS BALLARD

In March of 2013, I submitted a list of feature story ideas to the editors at SI. At the bottom, I pitched what I considered something of a dream story—the kind writers think about for years but never expect to get green-lit. It was about the disappearance of former Magic and Bulls center Brian Williams.

It stood as one of the great unsolved mysteries in the sports world. Supremely talented basketball player and son of one of the Platters (the Motown group) succeeds in the league and becomes the highest-paid player on the Pistons. A free spirit, he runs with the bulls in Pamplona and travels the world during the offseason, then changes his name to Bison Dele and abruptly retires at age 30 to try to find peace, or enlightenment, or whatever it was he felt was missing in his life.

Soon enough, I was headed to Arizona, and then Tahiti, and I began to hear strange stories, and conflicting accusations, and the truth became murky. More than once during the reporting, I was warned I should stop asking questions if I knew what was good for me.

It has been 11 years since the NBA player's catamaran went missing off the coast of Tahiti and the FBI descended upon this small island in the middle of the Pacific, flanked by journalists, asking questions about murder and love and fame. Eleven years since the TV reenactments and the breathless tabloid reports. Eleven years, and the mystery remains unsolved.

Many on the island have forgotten. Others prefer not to speak about what occurred. "It has been so long," they say, averting their eyes. "That has nothing to do with us." Tahiti relies on tourism, on its reputation as a paradise on earth; why talk about death?

Dig deeper, though, and you can find those who remember. Not just what happened, but what came before.

"The basketball player?" says Big Charlie. "Yes, I met him."

Big Charlie is tall and, like many Polynesian men with a taste for beer, thick of belly. Three brown teeth are visible when he smiles. Charlie works on the beach at the swanky Sofitel resort on Moorea, a small island neighboring Tahiti; he shows rich honeymooners how to chop a coconut. In his younger, slimmer days he manned the front desk at the Sofitel, and he remembers the handsome green-eyed giant who stayed in one of the over-water bungalows a decade ago. Such a kind man, says Charlie. Big heart. Was here three weeks, and Charlie never even knew he was famous. And his girlfriend—wow! You have never seen anyone so beautiful. Charlie remembers how the pair used to ride a little red scooter along the island's winding roads, the girl wedged between the player's legs as he steered them past hidden bays, oyster farms, lush forests and roadside stands selling papayas and pineapples. You could feel their love, Charlie says. He stops smiling. "It was sad, what happened."

Charlie says he is not the man to talk to, though. There is someone else. His name is Teva. He lives on the far west side of the island, out past the mile markers, and has no cell phone, but ask anyone in Ha'apiti and they will know him. Teva was with the basketball player and his girlfriend every day, for nearly a month, just before the end. He was their last friend. If you are looking for answers, Charlie says, maybe Teva has them.

Answers?

Those depend on which questions you ask.

It is June 13, 1997, and the United Center in Chicago is a cauldron of joy. The Bulls have just won the NBA championship—their fifth in seven years—in an epic series against the Utah Jazz that included two last-second game-winners and a remarkable flu-ridden performance in Game 5 by Michael Jordan. Now the team gathers on a portable stage erected on the parquet. Red-and-white confetti drifts down, and 24,000 Chicago fans roar. In the midst of it all is Jordan, hugging his Finals MVP trophy and grinning, a flake of red tinsel stuck to his right temple. To his left is coach Phil Jackson, bushy-haired and bearded, and next to him Scottie Pippen. Not far back is Dennis Rodman, scalp the color of a child's finger-painting, and Steve Kerr, holding his son on his shoulders. But the player closest to Jordan, the one standing just to his right, is Brian Williams, the Bulls' 6'10" forward-center.

The two men had become friends after the Bulls signed Williams as a free agent that April. Jordan pushed him to get in shape, to maximize his talent, to truly care about the game. Williams responded. He played a key role in the Bulls' championship run, logging nearly as many minutes as starting center Luc Longley. Kerr says the team wouldn't have won the series without Williams.

A childhood track standout who didn't try organized basketball until the 10th grade, the left-handed Williams played with uncommon grace on the court. He glided and swooped through the game. He was an excellent outlet passer and trailer on the break, if at times an apathetic player. He'd been a McDonald's All-American at Saint Monica Catholic High near Los Angeles and an honorable mention All-America at Arizona before being drafted by the Orlando Magic with the 10th pick in 1991. A season before joining the Bulls he averaged 15.8 points and 7.6 rebounds for the Clippers. Still, he'd never experienced anything like this moment in the United Center.

Which is what makes it so interesting in hindsight. Pull up the NBC footage and you can see the 28-year-old Williams on the stage behind Jordan, those pale green eyes staring over MJ's shoulder as the Bulls celebrate. This was Williams's first title, but you wouldn't know it. During what should have been the highlight of his professional career he looked distant, unsmiling, almost disembodied.

Friends recalled that look two years later when, after Williams changed his name to Bison Dele to honor his Cherokee and African heritage, he walked away from the remaining five years and $36.45 million of his contract with the Pistons. No one could believe it. Who walks away from $36 million?

Most assumed he would return. He never did. Instead, drawing on close to $16 million in career earnings, he traveled to the remote corners of the world, exploring the Australian Outback and sailing the South Pacific. His quest eventually took him to French Polynesia and to a woman named Serena, but it also attracted others to him.

That's the thing about escaping from someplace, or someone. No matter how far you go, you can't leave everything behind.

To understand why Dele ended up in Tahiti, you must first understand who he was. And few knew him better Patrick Byrne. They made an odd pair: Byrne the white, shaggy-haired son of a GEICO insurance magnate, and Dele, the towering son of a soul singer. They met in 1991 through a mutual friend,

Ahmad El Hosseini, the son of a former head of the Lebanese parliament. It was two months before Byrne learned his new friend, then still known as Brian Williams, was an NBA player.

Theirs was a friendship based on inhaling life. When Byrne was 21, he was diagnosed with testicular cancer. In remission after three years of treatment, he vowed to never waste a moment. He biked across the U.S. solo, trained in Brazilian jujitsu, earned a black belt in taekwondo and got a Ph.D. in philosophy from Stanford. In Williams he found a kindred soul. Williams had overcome a rough childhood to embrace all the world had to offer. In 1989 he journeyed to Beirut during Lebanon's civil war, ignoring a State Department ban. He ran with the bulls in Pamplona, attended art gallery openings and played the saxophone, violin and trumpet. He loved Wynton Marsalis and Miles Davis. He was enamored of William Blake's poetry and the films of Jim Jarmusch. He and Byrne spent long nights debating politics, race and philosophy. Williams was particularly fond of Friedrich Nietzsche. He read Beyond Good and Evil many times and was heavily influenced by Thus Spake Zarathustra, Nietzsche's philosophical novel about self-mastery and self-enhancement. Williams's favorite line: "We should consider every day lost on which we have not danced at least once."

Dancing was the least of it. Together, Byrne and Williams likely set an unofficial record for activities that violated an NBA contract. They biked together from Salt Lake City to Phoenix with no camping gear, going 50 miles at a time without access to water. They earned pilot's licenses and flew a single-engine plane from New Hampshire to Maine, Byrne in the captain's seat and Williams on his left, landing on remote lakes and sleeping under the wing. They wrestled and sprinted and skydived. They raced Go-Karts, crashing into each other at such speeds that Williams once sliced part of his Achilles tendon on the afternoon of a game.

Wherever they went, the pair attracted attention—or at least Williams did. One reason was his height and another was his fame, but there was something else about him, something magical. "He was the coolest cat," says Byrne. "Everyone wanted to hang out with him. You'd meet up and there was Eddie Vedder, or Billy Corgan. [Brian] was so naturally cool that they all wanted to be around him."

Williams had a particularly powerful effect on women. Lithe and graceful, he appraised the world from behind those green eyes, mysterious and self-confident. Women left him envelopes on his front doorstep. "Mr. Williams, you don't know me," one read. "I see you every day when you go to your car. I work in the hair salon [nearby]. I would do anything to spend one night with you, anything. I've told my husband. I don't care if he leaves me."

Byrne remembers watching Williams sort through the letters as most of us would the afternoon mail.

Williams had little tolerance for groupies, but he wasn't interested in long-term relationships either. He dated singers and starlets, including a Sports Illustrated swimsuit model and, for a while, Madonna. He enjoyed the novelty of dating the singer, but he found her self-absorbed. Eventually, when she called, he would hand the phone to Byrne, who would listen to her for 30 minutes, sometimes longer.

One woman was different. Serena Karlan had blazing blue eyes, dark hair and an almost feline face. Williams met her in 1997, when she was 25 years old and rooming with one of his high school friends. One night, returning with mutual friends from a concert in L.A., Serena asked, "Have you ever been in a crowded room and felt like you were the only one there?"

Williams was startled. "Yes, exactly," he said.

Later, he learned of her unusual background. How 30 people meditated and played music during her birth, in New York City on April 4, 1972. (Her head came out two minutes before the new day, her feet two minutes after, hence her middle name, Midnight). How her parents split when she was one, and she was raised by her mother in Berkeley, Calif. The granddaughter of Huston Smith, a renowned religious scholar, Serena grew into a thoughtful young woman. She came to believe in soulmates and true callings, and spent long nights with her best friend, Stacey Steele, eating coffee ice cream and talking about life. She also possessed deep reserves of empathy. Once, after her mother had broken up with a boyfriend, the six-year-old Serena comforted her by saying, "It's O.K., Mom. You just don't want anyone to leave." Her mother, grateful, and surprised by her daughter's insight, lay on Serena's bed until she fell asleep.

Though Serena and Brian had a connection, his peripatetic NBA career—five teams in eight years—made a relationship difficult. She moved on, working in retail but hating it. She turned down offers to model. One evening, at a nightclub in L.A., Prince invited her to his table and, later, out on the town in his limousine. They stayed in touch, and a few years later Prince hired her as a personal assistant. To Serena it was a strange arrangement: she, the rock star and his girlfriend hanging out together. She ended up feeling like a mother figure to the girlfriend. Eventually, wanting more from life, she left.

Every year or so she heard from Brian. Though she resisted his advances, her friends noted how she talked about him. Here was a man who was interested in more than her beauty, who saw the world as she did. That he was an NBA athlete wasn't important. If anything, Brian went out of his way not to talk about his job. Even so, he could seem emotionally unavailable.

In particular, Serena noticed there was one topic Brian rarely spoke about: his family.

At first it was just Eugene Williams and Patricia Phillips. She was a strikingly beautiful teenage bride; he was a soul singer. In 1966, they gave birth to a son, Kevin, and three years later to Brian. In 1970, Eugene was discovered at a nightclub by the R&B group The Platters. The Williamses ended up traveling the world with the band, but in Tokyo and other exotic places Eugene rarely ventured out from the hotel. He was no seeker. Early on it was clear the family's center wouldn't hold. Eugene and Patricia separated in '70 and later divorced.

Patricia remarried and settled the kids in Fresno, Calif., but that union unraveled as well. The boys' stepfather, Ron Barker, frequently berated them as Patricia looked on, Brian and Kevin later told friends. (Patricia says that Barker was "very strict" with the boys; Barker says he doesn't remember berating them.) When Brian was in the seventh grade, Patricia and Barker split up. She later told the *Rocky Mountain News*, "I have so banished that man from my conscious mind, I cannot tell you when I married him, how long I was married to him or when I divorced him."

Kevin grew to 6'8", but persistent asthma kept him from athletics. He could be socially awkward, and sensitive to a fault, but like his mother he was exceptionally bright. He read a full set of World Book encyclopedias in third grade. Brian was more sociable and naturally curious, with his father's artistic leanings. He too read voraciously, and played chess at the local Greek café against old men. He was fascinated by life's small moments of beauty. Once, he biked to the car wash and sat and watched, transfixed, as VWs and Fords were soaped all afternoon.

A gifted athlete who later kept up with future major league centerfielder Kenny Lofton during sprints at the University of Arizona, he settled on basketball, in part because of his height. Once he made the NBA, his family began contacting him, asking for money. As Brian blossomed, Kevin sputtered. He bounced from school to school. He attended De Anza College in Cupertino, Calif., but never graduated. He took steroids for his asthma, which was so severe that Patricia took him to the ER on several occasions. At times Brian paid Kevin's medical bills and watched over him. It was not easy. Kevin was moody and given to spurts of anger. He drank heavily. Every few months or so he'd contact Brian with another get-rich-quick scheme.

Brian tried to create distance from his family but found it difficult. He bought his mother a house and spent an estimated $80,000 to put her through college. He gave Kevin $50,000 on two occasions. At the end of his first season in the NBA, he and Byrne embarked on a bike ride from Salt

Lake City to Phoenix. Along the way, while at a Best Western in St. George, Utah, Williams told Byrne about his birth father: how Eugene was now a limo driver and lounge singer in Las Vegas, how he had become a coke addict. Spontaneously, Williams decided to spend $15,000 of a $25,000 NBA bonus check on a new Harley for his dad. When Brian proudly handed Eugene the keys to the motorcycle, Byrne says, "It was really touching. And his father just stood with his hand over his mouth, impassive." Finally Eugene said, "Son, next time just give me the cash."

Brian was crushed. He withdrew again and formed his own family, a web of friends and acquaints, none of them teammates. There was Byrne and Hosseini and Jen Gheur, an artist who became Brian's chef. Gheur remembers those days as the most exciting of her life. "B always opened doors to see what was behind them," she says. "He was a giant kid who ran wild like one of the Lost Boys in *Peter Pan*."

There was another friend, a buddy from college named Kevin Porter, whom Williams paid to be his assistant. Later Porter began referring to himself as Williams's "business manager" and "agent." But in FBI interviews, various people referred to Porter as Williams's "gofer."

Williams's friends felt he remained haunted by his childhood. While with the Magic he played only 21 games during the 1992–93 season as he battled clinical depression. He was erratic at practices, once passing out while guarding teammate Shaquille O'Neal in a five-on-five drill. One night he swallowed 15 sleeping pills. Another time he crashed his car into a pole. Williams later said the events were overblown, and he related both to his unhappiness in Orlando—he bemoaned the city as "sterile" and "made for tourists"—and the 2,000 calorie-a-day diet he was on. "I grew up a vegetarian, and I wanted to be superhealthy," he told SI in 1998. "Of course I wasn't consulting anyone on this. The lack of protein and iron in my diet finally ran me down."

NBA teammates remember Williams as a strange bird. He kept his distance, reading on plane rides while others played cards. In a league where money trumps all, he asked the Pistons to split his playoff share among ballboys, janitors and trainers. He once teared up while reading a biography of Miles Davis and told teammate Tom Tolbert that he wished he had the passion for basketball that Davis had for music. Another time, Williams's Detroit teammate Grant Hill asked him what book he was reading in the locker room. "*The Tarahumara*," said Williams, looking up from the academic text on the remote Mexican tribe. After practice in Denver once, the team found Williams in McNichols Center, where the ice had been laid down for an upcoming hockey game, joyfully gliding around on size-17 skates. "He was perceived as an athlete first but he had an artist's heart," says Tommy Sheppard, then the media-relations director for the Nuggets and now the Wizards' senior vice president of basketball operations. "I learned something from him which I've kept with me to this day: Don't let your job define who you are." Because Williams was so smart and charismatic, Sheppard says, people were often jealous of him. Back then, Sheppard had a description for Williams' approach to life: "He walked between the raindrops."

To those with an eye for it, there was also basketball greatness in Williams. Jordan saw it. Joe Dumars saw it. Kerr calls Williams, "maybe the most physically gifted player I ever saw." Most of all, though, Phil Jackson saw it. He said he had "a special relationship with Brian." After Williams left the NBA, in 1999, Byrne received an email with a message from Hampton Mears, the longtime Lakers scout and Jackson confidant. "If Brian is interested [in returning to the NBA] he should get in touch with Phil, or Jerry West.... They need and want him and start with high respect for Brian as a man and as a player."

Byrne forwarded the message to Williams, who never responded. He was off to explore the world. He lit out for Beirut, where he spent four months with Hosseini. He DJ'ed at nightclubs, invested in a bottled-water plant with his old friend, jet-skied in the Mediterranean. From there Williams made for Australia, disappearing for long stretches into the Outback. Byrne wasn't surprised. If anything, he wondered why it took his friend so long to leave the NBA. Says Byrne: "His great fear was to be another 40-year-old NBA player, paying the rent by doing car commercials."

"Maybe I know Teva," the shirtless man says. "Why do you want to see him?"

The man stands on his concrete steps, squinting. Elaborate tattoos cover much of his brown torso. Nearby, a pitbull lies in the dirt, collar secured to an iron post by a thick metal chain. A quarter-mile away, the shoreline of Moorea is visible, small waves frosting an endless expanse of blue. To the east the mountains rise, small shacks quickly giving way to thick jungle and, finally, serrated peaks smothered in clouds.

The man's name is Petero, and he runs a boarding house for surfers here, on the remote western coast of Moorea. He knows everybody in the area, or at least that's what the oyster farmer a few miles back, in Ha'apiti, said. That was after the man at the roadside stand in Vai'Anae had claimed to know Teva and provided directions to a nearby shack. All that turned up was a chubby teenager. The owner at the boat rental place said his name was Teva, but he'd never heard of a basketball player. Turns out there are *plusieurs* Tevas in Moorea. The better part of a day can be spent searching them out.

Big Charlie back at the Sofitel had anticipated this. That's why he'd mentioned that Teva's nickname was Ure. "Say that, and people will know him," Charlie had said. "But do not say this to women." Ure, Charlie, explained, means "the penis." It's a reference to Teva's skill with women. Charlie had smiled, revealing those three teeth, and said, "He likes it when you use this nickname."

Now, here at the surf lodge, there is finally someone who knows of Teva Ure. Petero is wary, though. He does not see many Americans here, and never journalists. What could a U.S. writer possibly want with Teva? He takes down a phone number and the writer's hotel name and room number. He will get a message to Teva, if indeed he knows him. If Teva agrees to talk, he will arrive tonight at the writer's hotel. If not, he won't.

It is an hour's drive back to the hotel, along the same twisting two-lane road that Brian and Serena once traversed on that red scooter. Tahiti is indeed stunningly beautiful, but it's different from Hawaii, with its polished tourist enclaves. There's a wildness to Tahiti, and especially the island of Moorea. People sell smoked chicken out of coolers on the roadside, wild dogs laze in the sun, children run around naked. The closest country is New Zealand, 2,500 miles away. The government is ramshackle, a combination of French administration and local graft.

It's a place where one can easily get lost. A place people go when they want to escape.

Kevin Williams always dreamt of going off the grid. According to friends, he never felt comfortable in his own skin. Worse, he lived in the shadow of his younger brother's success. Their resemblance made it even tougher. At 6'8" and 270 pounds, with a wide jaw and short hair, Kevin looked like a thicker, less handsome version of Brian. Growing up, the boys bickered endlessly. As an adult, Kevin felt underappreciated, overlooked. Paul White, his best friend since childhood, calls him "a complicated guy" with "a lot of emotion under the surface."

Like Brian, Kevin was given to bouts of depression. He tried to commit suicide on more than one occasion using medication. White traces Kevin's issues to his upbringing. "As a kid," he says, "you go through a divorce, you have a stepfather who's jealous of your intellect, your capabilities. And a mother who stands by and watches that happen." White continues: "Both of these boys were looking for something to fill the void inside of them because of their difficult upbringing. A void of feeling loved for who you are, for feeling safe."

Kevin drifted farther and farther from his family. By the time he showed up in New Zealand to surprise Brian in what Kevin termed an attempt to "heal the bond" in February 2002, it had been four years since either of his parents had heard from him. In the meantime, Brian had empowered Byrne to screen each of his brother's new business schemes—and those of Porter, who also sought money from Brian. In essence, this meant saying no on Brian's behalf.

By this point, Byrne had become quite successful on his own. In 1999, he founded an internet company that sold goods at closeout prices. He called it Overstock.com. As the company took off, Byrne began working 16-hour days. There wasn't time to meet Brian on a moment's notice or fly around the world with his old friend.

The two kept in touch via email, Byrne walking into the office every few months to see a new message from Zobilove@yahoo.com. (Brian's nickname among friends was Zobi.) Some emails were cryptic, others direct. There were thoughts, dreams, poems. In one, Williams wrote:

"Most people will never know the inherent goodness of their own ass because they never stop to find out if they have any. Most of the world just believes in luck, I say,

what you think you create,
what you create you express,
what you express you experience,
what you experience you are,
and what you are you think."

Another time, in July 2000, after Byrne beat back cancer again and rode his bike from San Francisco to Boston, his fourth cross-country trip, he received an email during the final push. It was from Williams, wherever he might be. It read: "Gooo Daddy Go".

Occasionally Byrne, Gheur and others heard updates on Williams from friends. He was in Monaco. He was chasing girls in Beirut. He was hanging out at a surf shop in Australia. He was camping out of a tricked-out old truck in Fremantle. Later the media would flesh out details. Like how Williams met a painter named Ollie McPherson at a pub in Australia and recruited him to be his traveling partner; they spent months camping in the bush before showing up in Adelaide so dirty that they were taken for aborigines. "He was trying to find peace," McPherson told an Australian newspaper. "Something was looming out there for him and he was heading towards it, like he was trying to cleanse his life or his spirit."

Hosseini worried about Brian. He knew Brian had taken to smoking marijuana regularly and dating young women. When Byrne spoke to Hosseini in 2000 and asked how their friend was doing, there was a long pause. Finally Hosseini said, "Zobi's methods have become unsound." Byrne wasn't sure. "It was Kurtz-like," he says. "Going village to village, the kids would get out of school and worship him and surf with him. [But] to me it sounds fantastic, to be out in a truck in the Outback."

In early 2000 Brian fulfilled a life-long dream and learned to sail. He bought a catamaran for $650,000 and named it *Hukuna Matata*, a misspelling of the Swahili phrase for "no worries." Built in 1997, the boat was 55.7 feet long, with a hull of fiberglass and reinforced plastic. Inside were several bedrooms, a kitchen and a living area that Williams outfitted with a wrap-around padded couch, bean bags and a TV. With a rotating cast of captains, mates and travel partners, Williams sailed the South Pacific from Australia to Paupa New Guinea to the small island of Vanuatu. Stories filtered out. How he'd dock in a small port, go ashore, and a whole village would come out and jam with him around the fire. How he'd project Bob Marley concert films onto the jib, and canoes would line up behind to watch.

The boat was part of Brian's pitch to Serena, when he contacted her again in 2001. Her journey had been full of false starts and frustrations, working in unfulfilling jobs in retail and PR, forever searching not for *a* job, but *the* job. Encouraged by one of her old elementary school teachers, she'd moved to New York City to work in real estate, showing listings. She was good at it but had no passion for the work. More than anything, she wanted to feel a purpose.

After the horror of Sept. 11, 2001, she heard from Williams. He was worried about her. He asked her to join him. Serena mulled the offer, then decided to go for two weeks. Two weeks turned into five. Upon returning, she told her mother she'd had an amazing time but didn't think it would turn serious. Brian had always been loath to commit. Besides, she wasn't sure about him yet. A couple weeks later she heard from him again. Come back out, he said. It's not practical, she replied. She had bills, financial obligations. Not long after, she received a small package from Williams. Inside was a check for $50,000 and a note that read, "This is what I think of your financial situation." This time he invited her not for a visit but to live with him. Serena talked to her mom and her friends. They encouraged her but knew she was going anyway. "She had deep connections with people," says her mother, Gael. "But Brian was the only one who got her that way."

In early 2002 Serena flew out to meet Williams in New Zealand. Whatever had kept them apart before was no longer an issue. Serena told friends she was ecstatic. She'd found something real.

A few months later, Kevin Williams made his unannounced arrival in New Zealand. He wanted to join them. Serena was dismayed. She called Steele, her best friend. It was, Steele says, "the first time I heard her speak negatively about another human being in the 17 years I knew her."

Here is what we know: Five months later, on the morning of July 6, the *Hukuna Matata* departed from a harbor in Pape'ete, the capital of Tahiti, bound for the island of Raiatea, 20 hours away, and from there to Hawaii. Four people were on board: Bison Dele, Serena Karlan, Kevin Williams (who'd changed his name to Miles Dabord, in honor of Miles Davis and a relative on his mother's side) and Bertrand Saldo, the boat's French captain.

Over the next two days, three satellite phone calls emanated from the boat.

After that, nothing.

At 6 p.m. the hotel phone rings. "There is a man here to see you," the woman at the front desk says. "He is down at the pool bar."

The sun has dropped below the horizon, but a pink glow remains. Near the beach, just past the sun-and-beer-glazed tourists and the bad acoustic guitar band covering Jason Mraz's "I'm Yours," sits a man with a ponytail tucked into a knit cap. He looks to be about 40 and as if he's made the most of those years. True to his nickname, he is already chatting up a 20-something blonde tourist, who sits next to him, giggling, a glass of Chardonnay in hand. The man gestures toward a quieter table. "When I heard someone was looking for Brian Williams, I knew I had to come," he says in French-accented English.

First, though, Teva wants to know why, after all these years, someone is looking for him, wanting to talk about the basketball player. Why now?

It's a fair question, and a hard one to answer simply. One could talk about the enduring mystery of what happened, or about the strange pull the story has had on so many people over the years—how it still affects lives in ways large and small. But how do you tell someone, in fractured French, that you want to know not about death, as everyone else does, but about an unfinished life? That you are more curious about what led Brian Williams on his quest than why it was never completed? That you want to know if, at the end, he found what he was looking for?

Teva listens, but he is skeptical. He hits his chest, hard, three times. "We were like brothers," he says. "Serena was like a sister. They are here, in my heart."

An attempt to turn on a tape recorder is waved off. The story is too private, Teva says, too revealing. He has never told it to anyone, at least no reporter. Finally he considers a trade.

"I will tell you the story," he says, peering over his beer. "For one hundred dollars."

For the first couple of months after the boat's disappearance, there was only confusion. Friends and relatives waited to hear something, anything. In late August, the U.S. Coast Guard sent a telex distress bulletin to all ships within a 1,000-mile radius of Tahiti. Scott Ohlgren, Serena's stepfather, put together a detailed 24-page "Summary Of Events" and tried to contact the FBI and the White House for help. Gael Rosewood, Serena's mother, held out hope.

Then, on Sept. 5, the first clue.

At 1:30 that afternoon, in Phoenix, a man claiming to be Bison Dele—a man who looked a lot like Bison Dele and possessed his passport and checkbook—attempted to purchase 460 one-ounce Gold Eagle coins from Certified Mint, Inc., a gold dealer on North Central Ave. The total cost, written in small, neat numbers on a First Union check: $152,096.

Two months after the disappearance of the *Hukuna Matata*, Kevin Williams was apprehended by the Phoenix police after he used his brother's passport and checkbook in an attempt to buy 460 gold coins.

The bank notified Kevin Porter, Dele's assistant, of the check, and Porter contacted Certified Mint and then the Phoenix Police Department, which in turn apprehended Miles Dabord, a.k.a. Kevin Williams. Porter flew in from Detroit. Five hours of questioning followed. Under interrogation, Dabord claimed he was buying the gold on behalf of his brother, who was O.K. the last time he saw him. Since Dele couldn't be reached to disprove this, the Phoenix P.D. allowed Dabord to leave. It was, the FBI would later say, a crucial mistake.

Phoenix is a world away from French Polynesia, but eventually the sequence of events leading up to Dabord's arrival in Phoenix would become clear. How a man matching the description of Miles Dabord was spotted on July 8 at the Pearl Resort, on Moorea, where he stayed for the better part of a week with his girlfriend, who had flown in to meet him from Los Angeles. The couple ate well and sat by the pool. Then, on July 16, a slightly damaged catamaran—registered as the *Aria Bella*, with the vinyl letters that had spelled *Hukuna Matata* removed from its stern—was piloted into Phaeton Bay on Tahiti's Southeastern shore by a man fitting Dabord's description. Dabord stored the boat and left on a flight to Los Angeles, after which he flew to Belize before arriving in Arizona.

Now, after being held overnight and released in Phoenix, Dabord ran. First to Palo Alto, to his girlfriend's place, and then to the border. He disappeared into Mexico. By now, the FBI was on his trail. So was Byrne.

Patricia Phillips, Brian and Kevin's mother, had heard from her older son. She said he called and said: "Mom, you know me. I could not survive prison." Byrne then spoke to her. He was in shock. Then he was angry. He caught the next flight to Phoenix. He met Porter, who put him in touch with Dabord.

I can help you, Byrne told Dabord. I've made a lot of money in my business. I can get you out of this situation. I don't care about the authorities—I just want to get B back. I can bring $150,000 in a suitcase. I'll meet you in Mexico.

Byrne thought that might work. Maybe he could bring in Dabord. Byrne made it past the border, stopped in a small town, asked around. There weren't many 6'8" black men in Mexico, after all. That's when he got a call from the Phoenix authorities. Reports had come back from Tahiti. The boat had been found. There was no sign of passengers. Authorities believed that Dele, Karlan and the captain were dead.

Standing on a dusty street thousands of miles from home, Byrne heard the words, and his eyes blurred. He'd spent his life being a fighter. He'd beaten cancer. He'd beaten his Wall Street detractors at Overstock. He hadn't let himself believe that Brian, who seemed so vital, who he referred to as his "superhero friend," could actually die.

Eventually Byrne dialed Phillips. He told her what he had heard. There was a long pause. Finally, Phillips said, "You know, Patrick, he never bought me anything."

Byrne was stunned. "Patricia, I thought he paid for you to go to UCLA," he said. "And he told me he bought you a $350,000 house."

"Patrick," she responded, "I've met other NBA moms who wear more than that on their wrist."

(Patricia denies saying that her son never bought her anything, and said that the comment about NBA moms was made in a different context, in a 2003 conversation about Dele's finances. She says it's a statement she will "always regret.")

Byrne never did catch up to Dabord. On Sept. 15, at 11:30 a.m., a patient described in hospital records as a "30 or 35-year-old gentleman who was found down in Mexico" was delivered to Scripps Memorial Hospital in Chula Vista, Calif. He had no reflexes. His pupils were nonresponsive. According to the hospital's emergency record, "The patient has areas on the right buttock and both wrists of...blistering, suggesting that he has been down and not moving for a significant period of time."

On September 26, 2002, at approximately 10 a.m., Kevin Williams a.k.a. Miles Dabord was taken off life support. He was pronounced dead at 8 p.m. the next day. The official diagnosis: "Suicide attempt with hypoglycemic brain damage with subsequent discontinuation of life support." Williams had overdosed on insulin and then lain down on a beach, waiting for someone to find him. The following day *America's Most Wanted* ran a segment on him.

At a joint funeral for the Williams brothers two weeks later, inside the white brick of the Trinity Baptist Church in central Los Angeles, Patricia Phillips said she loved both her sons. Then a cousin of the family, the Rev. Eugene Marzette, spoke. "The fact of the matter is," he said, looking out at the gathering of 200, "only God knows the truth."

Who is the author of a life's story? Who gets to decide who you were, after you're gone?

Patrick Byrne sits on a couch in a room at the Fairmount Hotel in Phoenix in June 2013. He is wearing black athletic shorts and a green long-sleeved shirt pulled up to his left elbow, so as not to interfere with the gauze-covered tube that protrudes from his forearm. He has not eaten for two days, and his thick blond hair is disheveled. The previous afternoon he was put to sleep for the 97th time—he keeps a count—as doctors at the nearby Mayo Clinic tried to fix an arrhythmia, another complication from the cancer that he has vanquished for spells but which never truly leaves. At 50, he remains vital. He speaks quickly, his eyes lighting up. He stands to act out stories, his 6'5" frame still thin and nimble, though after a few minutes he sinks back on the couch, winded.

Byrne cannot tell the stories fast enough now. He wants people to know who Brian was, how special he was.

In the years after the events of Tahiti, Byrne declined nearly all interviews. He hated how the TV shows gave credence to Dabord's account of what happened, the one he gave to his then-girlfriend, Erica Weise, before committing suicide. It remains the only first-person account. It goes like this: On July 7 Dele and Dabord got in a fight, and Dele accidentally punched Serena in the face. Her head thumped against a steel davit and she died instantly. Saldo, the captain, said they needed to report the death, but Dele became agitated and killed Saldo by hitting him on the head with a wrench. At that point Kevin says he had no choice: Out of self-defense, he shot his brother. Then, scared, he dumped the three bodies overboard and sailed back to Tahiti before fleeing, sure that no one would believe his story.

Byrne does not like to talk about the events on the boat—though he is certain Dabord's version is not true—and hates how others have tried to profit off his friend's death. He wonders why Dele's bank account suddenly dried up after he died. When talking about his friend, though, he becomes animated.

"I've been waiting 10 years for someone to ask about his life, not his death," Byrne says, and over two days the tales pour out. About singular moments, adventures shared, unbreakable connections. You can feel the love. Byrne feels his own mortality now, and he cannot tell the stories fast enough. He wants people to know who Brian was, how special he was.

At the same time, Byrne needs something to hold on to. That's why, along with Hosseini, he commissioned a piece of art made with Dele's final pairs of hightops. It hangs on the wall in his house an hour outside Salt Lake City: two basketball shoes nailed to a canvas above red ink, scrawled like blood. The quote is from one of Brian and Byrne's favorite writers, Hunter S. Thompson: "Too weird to live, too rare to die."

Patricia Phillips is harder to track down. Two years after Dele's death, she went to Tahiti to claim the boat, which she sold. Speaking from Chapel Hill, N.C., where she now lives, she alternates between anger and grief. She has not spoken publicly since 2002, and has her own version of the story. She says not to trust Porter, Paul White, Hosseini, Serena's parents, the FBI or Byrne. She believes Dabord was trying to assume his brother's identity but believes that there's no way he could have sailed the *Hukuna Matata* back by himself, that someone else must have been involved. "I had two sons," she says. "I'm still a mother to both of them. The only way I can maintain any modicum of sanity and understanding is to stick with the truth as I know it."

Patricia is the only remaining member of the nuclear family. In August 2008, Eugene Williams died in Las Vegas of pancreatic cancer at 64. His newswire obituary focused on his "five-octave voice" and his musical background—his own father had been a performing pianist. The only mention of his progeny came in the second-to-last sentence: "Williams was preceded in death by his sons, Kevin Williams and Brian Williams."

Dabord still has one defender. White, his childhood friend, says he became Dabord's attorney during the proceedings of 2002. White, whose office is in Los Angeles, says he is writing a book about what happened. That he's traveled to Tahiti. That people don't understand the whole situation. He talks about how Dabord always dreamed of going off the grid and how "he almost did it." He grants that Dabord had problems, that he clearly "never filled the void inside him," but he stands by his friend. "Just because you may seem like a loser," White says, "it doesn't mean you are a murderer."

Murderer? Theoretically, the French authorities in Tahiti, who conducted the primary investigation, could weigh in on that. Only when a reporter attempted to retrieve the public court records on the case and to interview the deputy prosecutor, Louis Bounan, it led to a strange scene. After arriving at the Palais de Justice in the capital city of Pape'ete, a two-story building accessible via a staircase manned by two armed guards with heavy smoking habits, the reporter handed over the required paperwork. The secretary said that Monsieur Bounan was gone "through August." It was early July. The reporter pointed out that he'd spoken to Bounan on the phone just an hour earlier. When pressed further, the secretary made a call and announced that, as it turned out, Bounan was at his desk. Bounan asked the reporter to leave the paperwork. A subsequent attempt to interview Bounan was moderately successful. Despite likely knowing English, he spoke only in French for 25 minutes. He said the case was a long time ago, that he barely remembered it. That it was sad but that it was an American. That the investigating judge on the case could no longer be reached. Then Bounan promised that all of the court records would be sent, via email, within "*deux semaines*" (two weeks) if not sooner. Three months later, they had yet to arrive, and Bounan had not responded to multiple follow-up emails.

As for Kevin Porter, Brian's friend and assistant, he has his own project. Earlier this June he called Byrne with a pitch, the first time Byrne had heard from him in years. Porter said he was shopping a screenplay about Dele and that he had momentum. Hollywood was hot for it. He just needed one thing: money. Maybe Byrne would like to put in some cash? Byrne saw red. He told Porter never to call him again.

Porter lives in suburban Atlanta these days, where he is a partner in an online cosmetics company and a manager at a nonprofit that teaches life skills to adults with mental and learning disabilities. He says he had many rough days at first, grieving for his friend, and still does occasionally. The timing of it all was tragic, he says. He believes Brian was ready to come back to the NBA before he died. (Byrne also believes this.) Porter confirms that he has written a screenplay, with a friend, and that it's about Brian's life on and off the court, as well as the tragedy.

Porter bristles when Brian's money is brought up. "Honestly, I didn't get one red cent from it, and that's O.K.," he says. "Obviously Patricia had not thought about me." He says he hasn't talked to her since Brian's death.

The postscript is less complicated on Serena's side. Here one finds mainly grief, and love. Stacey Steele, Serena's best friend, says she still misses Serena almost every day. Steele had her first child at 17, and Serena was like a second parent to him. "It was real hard on him at first, so I couldn't afford to mourn around him," Steele says. She takes comfort in what she can. "Her life was so clean and well-lived," Steele says. "She had zero things left unfinished."

Gael Rosewood, Serena's mother, still lives in Berkeley, where she works as a Rolf massage therapist. A diploma in osteopathy hangs on the wall of her office. Medical tomes line a bookshelf. At 66, Gael is thin, with gray hair and the same striking blue eyes as her daughter. She remains amazed at the effect Serena had on people. Two high school friends of Serena's still call Gael three or four times a year, just to talk.

Gael likes to think her daughter was happy in the end, with Brian. "I think they shared this sort of vast yearning for understanding the bigger picture of life and being connected to energy somehow," she says, sitting at a local cafe. "Brian had this enormous desire to break the chains of familial dysfunction and be free of that. I think that somehow this was something they were working on together."

The first few years after Serena's death were the worst for Gael. Then, one day she heard from a friend with a message: Serena had contacted her. It happened again with a different medium. And soon enough Gael felt like she was communicating with her daughter in small ways. A symbol here, a strange coincidence there. It gave her comfort. "I really went through a phase where I felt at the 10-year mark that I'm starting to heal," Gael says. "Then she stopped. I can't have conversations with her now. I don't know why. I think either she reincarnated or it's time for me to let go." Gael pauses, looking down into her empty tea cup. "I don't know."

For some, letting go is an emotional journey. For others, it is a factual one. Elizabeth Castaneda is the FBI agent who worked on the case. She's now retired from the San Francisco office, and she recently moved to Phoenix to be with her ailing grandmother. During her career, which began in 1983, she worked on all manner of cases: fugitives, bank robberies, drugs, pornography, violent crimes and abductions. More than most cases, though, Dele's stuck with her.

Along with 12 other agents, Castaneda went to Tahiti after the murders. Officially the case remains open, but there are no new leads. The only version of events the FBI got on record was Dabord's, but no one at the bureau bought it. "The explanation that Miles gave to Erica, his girlfriend, forensically it didn't pan out," Castaneda says. "According to him, Brian Williams struck the captain in the head with a wrench. That's going to cause blood spatter.... The top of the area where [they would have fought] had a ceiling. There was nothing there, and that's a massive bleed.... It just didn't make sense."

Indeed, the eventual scenario that was widely reported, and that the FBI put out to the public, involved Dabord, motivated by a desire to assume his brother's identity, shooting Dele, Karlan and Captain Saldo, then tying bodybuilding weights to their bodies and dropping them overboard. Castaneda thinks that explanation is close to the truth, but it still doesn't explain the lack of splatter, or bullet holes. She has a different idea about what happened between the brothers on that day, hundreds of miles from land, in the deep, shark-inhabited waters off the coast of Tahiti. Based on the forensics, she believes it is the only logical conclusion.

"I think Miles put them in the water at gunpoint in the middle of nowhere," she says, "and then he left them there."

Back on Moorea, Teva stares across the table. His beer is empty. The light is fading. The blonde is waiting, at the other table. Still, he has a story he wants to tell. Told his $100 price can't be met—that journalistic ethics prevent paying sources—he becomes frustrated and gets up to leave. Then he stops and leans back in. "O.K.," he says, "I will tell you the story. For only $50." In the end Teva shares his tale over a drink. He didn't come all this way not to talk about what happened.

"I never knew he was a star," Teva begins in good English. "After he died, I found out." When Williams showed up at the Sofitel resort, the two men struck up a conversation on the beach, a pair of free spirits connecting. Williams was friendly and carried a basketball with him, dribbling it when he could. He liked Teva's tattoo—a sun on his right shoulder—and called him Sunny. Serena was likewise outgoing. Says Teva, "She loved him totally." The three began hanging out. Drinks on the beach. Trips on the boat.

After a couple of weeks, Brian began asking questions about the island, enamored by it. Then one day he pulled his new friend aside. He pointed to a group of condos on a hillside, overlooking the ocean. He asked Teva who owned that land. Then he told Teva to look into it, that he wanted to buy three houses up there: one for himself and Serena, one for his mother and one for Teva. Teva's eyes widen as he retells the story. "I could not believe it."

Not long after, Dabord arrived. "But [he] wasn't nice," Teva says. "He was busy in the head, he was strange. But Brian loved his brother." Teva pauses, takes a sip. "The brother never talked.... I feel it, something was wrong. Brian was positive, and this guy was negative."

A couple of days later, Dele asked Teva to come with him on the boat. They were sailing for Hawaii. It would be an adventure. Teva asked his boss at the Sofitel, pleaded for the time off. His boss said no. Teva remains torn about this. Chances are, his life was saved. Then again, maybe he could have prevented Brian's death.

Teva has his own theory about what happened on the boat that day, and he's as sure of it as all the others are of their theories. There is no way to fact-check most of what he says. And yet in stories such as this one, maybe it comes down to what you want to believe. Stories are about perspective, after all. After a life of seeking, did Serena and Brian find what they were looking for? Were they finally at peace when they died? That depends on whom you believe.

Here is what Teva believes. He believes that Dabord intended to kill his brother in order to steal away Serena. Teva saw the way the man he knew as

Miles looked at Serena. Only something backfired. When Miles fired the gun that day on the boat, Serena leapt in front of Brian, taking the bullet. Teva is sure of it. It is heartbreaking. It is romantic.

Behind Teva, the bartender is now wiping down. It's been close to two hours, and the tourists are stumbling off to bed. Another day in paradise awaits. Teva has something else to say, though. None of this about the boat is what's important, he says. What's important is what Brian and Serena had in those weeks at the Sofitel. Brian never looked at other women, as all the other boyfriends and husbands did. And the look on Serena's face when she was with Brian was rapturous. "I am a hunter of women, you understand?" Teva says. "I know that look. I was happy for them."

Nearby, the acoustic duo begins to close up shop. The night is dark. Teva nods, now sure of himself. "It was," he says, "the beginning of a love story."

NOVEMBER 24, 2008

A Whoop-Dee-Damn-Do-Gooder

BY SELENA ROBERTS

After Rick Reilly left SI, a series of columnists took turns filling the "Point After" spot on the back page of the magazine. As one of them, I know how difficult the task was, trying to write a crisp 900 words with a point of view that would appeal to a national audience once it landed in their mailbox a few days later. Selena Roberts brought writing chops and a broader vision to the role. Here, she turns her sights on Derrick Coleman, the oft-maligned forward, to show a different side of him.

Plexiglass barriers had gone up along Linwood Street, encasing attendants at gas stations and clerks at liquor stores, sealing employees from harm but also human touch. Hard to slide a hug through a slot meant for credit cards, pens and pennies. After the racially charged riots of 1967, when the west side of Detroit burned, most of the remaining businesses installed bars, steel shutters and, of course, bullet-resistant glass, making every trip to the bodega feel like a prison visit.

Who could restore dignity to the neighborhood? Who could lift the spirits of residents, especially now, with the auto industry on empty? A renowned lazy ass. When I think of Derrick Coleman, I see a talented 6'10" NBA forward of the '90s with the smooth head and the body that always looked pulled from a hamper. He could defy coaches, dress codes and traffic laws, and still conjure 20 and 10. No utterance underscored Coleman's ethos of apathy

345

more than this response when he heard that a New Jersey Nets teammate had missed practice: "Whoop-dee-damn-do."

As it turns out, this was impatience speaking. A lot of athletes use the pros to escape their communities, but Coleman couldn't wait to use his basketball earnings—about $90 million over 15 seasons—to lay a breadcrumb path back to the neighborhood where he has long maintained a home. His is the one with the backyard basketball court, which friends tend to use as a parking lot.

Did he ever love his NBA job? "I didn't have a hard time [leaving]," Coleman says. "I don't miss playing the game." This sentiment won't square with anyone who celebrates Brett Favre's desire to speak in audibles till his last football breath. "Oh, we'd get mad at DC too," laughs John Johnson, a longtime neighborhood friend of Coleman's. "We'd see DC lying on his back with a towel over his head, not playing. We'd yell at the TV, 'DC, get in the game!'"

It's worth remembering what Favre said before reneging on retirement, when asked what he planned to do next: "Nothing," expressing a vacuum of purpose many players feel at the end. Coleman, 41, always knew the future would bring an adrenaline rush. On the drive back to Detroit from Syracuse in 1990, shortly before he would be drafted No. 1 by the Nets, Coleman told Johnson that when he retired he wanted to use his riches to right old wrongs. "As a kid I got tired of talking to people through glass," says Coleman. "Why can't I have a conversation with you without talking through glass?"

There is neither plexiglass nor steel bars in the four stores he owns in Coleman's Corner, a handsome strip mall of brick and stucco he opened last year, part of a $6 million (and counting) investment he has made into developing the first retail center on Linwood Street since the riots. So neighbors don't get haircuts in their basements anymore; they gather at the Barber Lounge, where they can talk politics and watch football on the tube every Sunday. So teens don't have to take two buses to a suburban mall for a job; they can walk a few blocks to punch a clock at Hungry Howie's, the pizza franchise Coleman owns and Johnson manages.

Johnson was the one who winced when Coleman refused to raise prices as gas shot to $4 a gallon and the cost of food skyrocketed. He was the one who saw a 2% drop in the ledger after Coleman decided to offer a dollar slice of pizza from 11 a.m. to 7 p.m. last summer. "Derrick remembered how, as kids, we'd take bottles in for a deposit," Johnson says. "He wanted kids to be able to buy a slice with them. I'd tell him, 'It's costing us.' And he'd say, 'That's O.K., school will be open soon. Then, we'll end it.'"

Some of those same children held an ear of corn for the first time when Coleman, a student of urban agriculture, brought a weekly farmers' market to a parking lot across from his mall. Who knew eating right didn't include a Fruit Roll-Up? "And you wonder why we, as black people, have a high rate of diabetes and high blood pressure," says Coleman, who hopes to ultimately own seven blocks in the area. He can talk green energy solutions, biofuels and the platform of his candidate for Detroit mayor, Dave Bing, the Hall of Fame guard and former Piston. Years ago, Bing built his manufacturing business in Detroit's inner city. "He has been my father figure," says Coleman, who stood next to Bing when he announced his candidacy last month. "I'm in his footsteps."

As even Bing acknowledges, there are safer places to invest than Detroit for millionaire athletes. "Yeah," says Coleman, "but if I don't try, how will I know?" A man of perseverance, this is the DC few knew beyond Linwood. All along, the NBA knucklehead wasn't misspending his talents, but saving for the day when his vision would shatter security glass.

JUNE 24, 1996

Crime and Punishment

After high school star Richie Parker was convicted of
sexual abuse, those who tried to salvage his basketball
career were scarred by their experience

BY GARY SMITH

*The winner of a record four National Magazine Awards, Gary Smith wrote
about people—the sports were almost incidental. His stories were the best
kind—they stayed with you, started conversations and, on occasion, made
you reconsider how you saw the world.*

*Technically, the following feature isn't about the NBA but it is about
basketball, at least partly. You won't be sorry you read it.*

One

Here is a man. Barely a man; he just ran out of adolescence. He stands
alone, 2,000 miles from home, beside a swimming pool, in a stucco-walled
apartment complex, in a city built on an American desert.

*Seton Hall chancellor Thomas R. Peterson buckled under to intense
pressure from media and alumni yesterday when he denied admission to
star basketball recruit and admitted sex felon Richie Parker.*

—NEW YORK POST, Jan. 24, 1995

It's too hot to run. But he must run. He strips to his trunks. He steps into
the pool. His body leans forward.

*The University of Utah ceased its recruiting of former Manhattan Center
basketball star Richie Parker in light of a barrage of media criticism and*

pressure from the university president regarding Parker's sexual abuse conviction.
—*NEW YORK NEWSDAY,* May 6, 1995

His hands ball up. His left elbow draws back, pushing against the water. Slowly his foot begins to rise from the floor of the pool.

George Washington University officials informed high school basketball star Richie Parker yesterday they "regrettably" would stop recruiting him and blamed "unbalanced publicity" for a wave of criticism that hit the school for pursuing the youth, who had pleaded guilty to a sexual assault.
—*THE WASHINGTON POST,* June 30, 1995

His foot gradually descends to the bottom of the pool. His other foot begins to push off. His shoulders tighten. The water pushes back.

Richie Parker will never wear a UTEP basketball uniform. UTEP has bowed out of its recruitment of the controversial basketball player, athletic director John Thompson announced Friday.
—*EL PASO HERALD-POST,* Feb. 24, 1996

His knee slowly lifts again. His arms silently pump.

USC on Wednesday terminated its recruitment of former New York City All-America point guard Richie Parker, a convicted sex offender. The decision came after...two days of sometimes heated exchanges among athletic department personnel.
—*ORANGE COUNTY REGISTER,* March 28, 1996

He climbs out finally and pants for air, in the desert that once was the bottom of an ocean.

Two

Here is a periodic table. It's the one you would see near the blackboard in any high school chemistry class, a listing of the 109 elements according to atomic number. Why is it being inflicted on you here, in a sports magazine? *Patience.* Remember, this is a story about higher education.

Near the lower lefthand corner of the chart is an element named cesium. Among its own—the metals surrounding it in the chart, such as sodium and potassium—cesium is a quiet, unassuming element. But because it has just one electron on its outer shell, one electron aching to leap to any atom that is lacking a full outer shell of electrons, cesium is a bomb in a suitcase when it leaves its neighborhood. On contact with oxygen, cesium will cause an explosion. Introduce it to chlorine, fluorine, iodine or bromine and look out! Almost everywhere it goes, trying to rid itself of the baggage of that one electron, another eruption occurs, and only those who understand what cannot be seen can make any sense of it at all.

Three

Here is an assistant principal. She works at Manhattan Center, the East Harlem high school Richie Parker once attended. Teenagers deposit their leather jackets in Ellen Scheinbach's closet in the morning for safekeeping, come to her at lunchtime for oatmeal cookies and advice. The phone's constantly ringing, teachers are always poking in their heads. "A lunatic asylum!" she calls her office, ambling about with her spectacles dangling from a neck chain. But now there's silence, and it's Richie's mother, Rosita, shuffling on her bad knees, clutching her envelope of articles clipped from the New York Post and the Daily News, extending them toward the assistant principal and asking her to explain.

Ellen Scheinbach is an authority figure, one of the few Rosita knows. Surely she can explain how all this could result from that one day in this building, in January 1994, when Rosita's 6'5" son, a junior then—a well-liked boy known for his silence, his gentle nature and his skill on a basketball court—was walking through these halls, having gone to the nurse's office with a sprained ankle and having found the nurse not there, was returning to class when he paused...and turned. And headed toward the bottom of a stairwell in the back of the school, where he and a schoolmate, Leslie Francis, soon compelled a 16-year-old freshman girl to perform oral sex on them. And how 15 minutes later, the girl came running up the stairwell, sobbing, and soon thereafter Richie and the other boy were being led away in handcuffs. And how from that moment on, virtually everywhere Richie would turn to rid himself of the baggage of those 15 minutes, another explosion would occur. How careers would be smashed, men fired, dreams destroyed. How some relationships would splinter and others almost spontaneously be fused. How secrets would burst from hidden places, and rage and fear would tremble in the air behind her lean, quiet son. The assistant principal can explain all this to Rosita, can't she?

Ellen throws up her arms. The incongruity of it all still confounds her. Richie Parker? Richie didn't drink. Richie didn't curse. Richie didn't get into arguments or fights; he had never even gotten detention. She knew lots of kids who would play peek-a-boo with a toddler in the bleachers for a few minutes, but Richie was the only one she knew who would do it for an hour. The only time she had ever seen him exert his will—to force any issue—was on a basketball court, and even there he did it so softly, so smoothly, that she would be startled to learn at the end of a game that he had scored 35 points. He would be rated one of America's top 50 high school seniors in 1995, a notch or two below Georgia Tech signee Stephon Marbury in New York's schoolboy hierarchy.

Two investigations—one conducted by a George Washington University lawyer and another by the lawyer of the stairwell victim, not to mention the searchlight sweep of Richie's life by the media—failed to turn up a single thread that would indicate that those 15 minutes in the stairwell were part of a larger pattern. Richie himself had insisted on his innocence at first, but eventually he pleaded guilty when the charges were lowered from first-degree sodomy to first-degree sexual abuse in January 1995. His sentence was five years of probation. So now Rosita's standing on the other side of Ellen's desk, holding a half-dozen full-back-page pictures of her son under screaming Sex Felon headlines, asking her what the world has come to that one rotten act by a 17-year-old could take on such monstrous proportions and why Seton Hall has just reneged on its promise of a scholarship for Richie as long as he didn't get a prison sentence...and it's only the beginning, because now the great American morality play is ready to hit the road, with actors and actresses all across the land raring to perform their roles, eager to savage or salvage the teenager from 110th Street in Manhattan—often knowing nothing more of him than his name. Ellen keeps shaking her head and blinking. Sports, having somehow become the medium through which Americans derive their strongest sense of community, has become the stage where all the great moral issues have to be played out, often rough and ugly, right alongside the games.

Ellen had tried to protect Richie from that. She had tried to smuggle him out when the media surrounded her school. She sat beside him at games when he could no longer play, to shield him from the media's popping cameras and questions. She went to Seton Hall and told administrators that she would trust Richie with her daughter, if she had one. But it was hopeless. In the same way that cesium needs to rid itself of that one dangling electron on its outer shell, Richie needed to take his sin to a university, to one of America's last "pure" places, and have it absolved so he could find his way to the promised land, the NBA. In the same way that fluorine longs for that extra electron to complete itself, the universities and their coaches were drawn to the basketball player who could enhance their profile, increase their alumni contributions and TV revenues. And the mutual attraction would keep causing explosions, hurling Richie and yet another university far apart, and Rosita would keep returning to Ellen, her eyes filling with tears. Hasn't her son, she would ask, done everything demanded of him?

Yes, Rosita, yes, he fulfilled the requirements of the criminal justice system and of the out-of-court settlement of the victim's civil lawsuit. He had met monthly with his probation officer, met regularly with a counselor, made both a private and a public apology to the victim, an acknowledgment that regardless of the details of the incident, he had done something profoundly wrong in that stairwell. He had promised to speak out against sexual abuse and to make financial restitution to the victim with a percentage of any money he might generate one day in the NBA. He had earned A's and B's at Manhattan Outreach Center, the school he was sent to in the wake of the court ruling, met NCAA qualifications on his fourth try with an SAT score of 830 and enrolled at Mesa (Ariz.) Community College, which refused to let him play ball but allowed him to be a student. And, yes, both the victim and her lawyer had requested that the country's media and universities let him move on. "He's rare among people who've committed a sexual offense," says Michael Feldman of Jacoby & Meyers, the victim's attorney. "He admitted that he did something wrong and committed to help the victim. How does it assist women to refuse him an opportunity now?"

"We believe Richie is truly sorry," the girl's father had told the *Daily News*. "We're religious people who believe in redemption. We don't believe in third chances. We do believe in second chances."

So how can Ellen explain to the 49-year-old woman with the envelope full of news clippings that the second chance, the fresh start, the comeback, the stuff of magazine covers and made-for-television movies, the mother's milk that immigrant America was nursed on and cannot—to its everlasting credit and eternal confusion—seem to wean itself from, has been denied to her son?

"What can I do?" Ellen cries. "I can't get the reporter from the *New York Post* fired. I can't speak to women's groups who are saying he shouldn't have the right to go to college and play basketball. What *is* a women's group, anyway? I know plenty of women, but what's a women's group? I can't call [Georgetown coach] John Thompson and tell him to give Richie a chance— you think he's going to listen to some little old Jewish lady? So I'm just left with this horrible frustration. It's like trying to comfort the survivor of a plane wreck when Rosita comes here. There's nothing I can do.

"He was 17 when this happened. For 15 minutes of rotten judgment, he's been crucified! These women's groups are talking about O.J. Simpson and Mike Tyson, and they're using Richie's name. When teachers here heard what he was accused of, they said, 'Are you kidding?' This is a kid who always tried to fade into the background, who wouldn't push back if you pushed him. Even when he wanted something, he'd just stand there and wait till you *asked* what he wanted. Look, I don't know what happened in that stairwell, but if he did it, he must've had a brain lesion. This kid is not a threat.

"If he were white, would this story have been written this way? But no, he fit the perfect stereotype. He has no money, and he's a black male teenager, so they could have a field day. What do people want—for him to fail, so he's out on a street corner? Are they saying you can never redeem yourself? If he wanted to be a doctor instead of a basketball player, would they say, 'You can't take biochemistry class'? Basketball is his talent, and while he's on probation he's entitled to play that the same way he'd be entitled to be a musician or an artist. Everyone thinks the NCAA is so macho. I've never seen so many wimpy men in my life."

Once, just once in the 2½ years of watching everything around Richie go to pieces, has Ellen feared that he might go to pieces too. She had never seen him cry, never heard him blame anyone else, never sensed a chip on his shoulder. But when it was clear that the board of education was about to suspend him from Manhattan Center in the middle of his senior season and that the media swirl was sucking down his teammates too, he came to her office with his mother and read his letter of resignation from the team. When he finished, he finally broke down and clutched his mother. "If not for you," he sobbed to her, "I don't think I could make it."

In the end, Ellen decides, perhaps there isn't much she can do to help Rosita, but there's something Rosita has done to help her. "I've learned a lot from her," says Ellen. "I've learned that no matter how frustrated and upset you get, you just keep turning to your kid and saying, 'I love you, and no matter what happens, there's one place for you that's safe.' When my son has a problem now I just try to hug him and say, 'Whatever decision you make I'll stand by you.' Because *it works*. I've seen it work. It saved Richie Parker."

Four

Here is a copy editor on the sports desk of a major city newspaper. She's smart, and she's funny, and if an office push-up contest or footrace suddenly breaks out, hopefully after deadline, she's the one you want to put your money on. Of course, because she's a woman, the sensitive stories go to Jill Agostino for editing. Anguish? That's a Jill piece. Morality issue? Absolutely Agostino. Not that it's ever actually stated in a sports department that men are bereft in those areas. It's just sort of understood.

So she gets the Richie Parker stories to polish for *Newsday*. And as she's scanning the words on her computer screen in early 1995, she begins to feel something tightening inside her. It's the old uneasiness, the one she dreads, the one she has no time for here, now, as the clock hands dig toward deadline; the one she might try to run into the ground tomorrow when she's doing her five miles, or scrub away in the quiet of her Long Island apartment, or stow away and convert to fuel someday, something to help flog herself through an extra hour of work when she has to prove her worth to some sexist idiot who dismisses her as a token woman in a man's world, a newspaper sports desk. But not now. Not here. No way.

She begins to sense it here and there between the lines—the implication that Parker is being treated unfairly—and her uneasiness starts to turn to quiet anger. She doesn't sleep much that night, doesn't feel like eating the next day. Another Parker story comes her way a few evenings later, then there's an afternoon drive to work listening to radio talk-show callers chew the issue to death, some of them actually sticking up for the kid, and her quiet anger curdles into a rage that no one knows, no one sees.

The writers like Jill. She's not one of those editors who must tinker with a story to justify their existence. One *Newsday* reporter writes an article that comes right out and says Parker is a good kid who made a mistake and deserves a second chance, and he calls Jill as she's editing it, cheerfully asking her how she likes his piece. There's silence on the phone. And then it erupts from her, something she has never even been able to tell her family.

"I've been raped," says Jill. "I don't agree with you."

"Oh, I didn't....Jill, I'm sorry," he says.

She feels like a jerk for making the reporter feel like a jerk, but it's too late now, the anger's out on the table, and it's not finished. *Mistake?* How can anyone call it that? Leaving your headlights on or forgetting your keys, *that's* a mistake—not humiliating a woman the way Jill had been nearly nine years earlier, at age 22, by a man on a boat on Queechy Lake in upstate New York. She goes into her boss's office, seething at a society where a man like Mike Tyson can walk out of jail a few years after raping a woman and be greeted by a thunderous roar and a paycheck worth millions of dollars, and TV commentators can blather on about all that *Tyson* has been through, as if the perpetrator was the victim and the real victim was yesterday's oatmeal. "I want to write a column," she tells her boss. "People need to know what it's like for the victim. I was raped."

His jaw drops. Well...uh...sure, Jill, but....

She barely sleeps that night. Her husband, Michael, says that if she's sure she wants to do this, he's behind her. She's sure. She sits on the couch the next day with a red pen, a blue pen and a notepad. The red ink is for her pain—the italicized sections interspersed in the column that recount that night on the lake where she swam as a little girl: *"I wanted to throw up every time I smelled the mixture of Grand Marnier and tobacco smoke on his breath as he held me down...."* The blue ink is for Richie Parker: "How often do you think Parker will think about this incident once he's on a college basketball court? For the victim, not a day will go by without that memory.... Parker's punishment should last until his victim is able to walk alone up the street, or through a parking lot, or down a dimly lit hallway and feel safe. Until the nightmares cease. Until a day goes by and she doesn't think about the horrible things these boys made her do. But it won't."

What are you doing? a voice inside her asks when she has finished writing. To her, this is not an act of courage, as some would take it. To her, this is Jill Agostino publicly admitting her most private pain just on the chance that it will make some men begin to comprehend how it feels to be violated, how it eats into a woman's life forever, how it can make her hold her breath when a stranger steps into an empty elevator with her, make her want to run when a man rolls down his car window and asks her for directions, make her stare into a mirror some days and hate her body because somehow it betrayed her.

She can't surrender to the urge to crumple up the notepad paper, because if she does, the man in the boat wins again, and she can't let him keep winning. He has won too many times, at night when she sits up rigid in bed from nightmares she can never quite recollect—only raw terror and the faint echo of all the world's laughter. He won every time she bought another size 8 blouse for a size 4 body, every time she froze when a colleague she didn't know well threw an arm around her shoulder, every time she couldn't sleep and had to caffeinate and will herself through the next day so that no one, except perhaps her husband, would ever dream that she was anything but the sharp, competitive woman that the world always sees.

Now comes the next agony. She can't let her family find out in a newspaper story. She must call her mother and father and brother and sister and tell them about the rape and why she buried it. She must listen to her mother cry and feel guilty for not protecting her daughter from something she couldn't possibly have protected her from. A few days later the story appears. Seven hundred and fifty thousand readers learn Jill's secret, and countless thousands more—including old boyfriends, old co-workers, old roommates—come across it in the newspapers across the country that run the story. Some of her colleagues are moved to tears by her column. Some confess to her their own buried stories of rape.

The eddies never seem to end. Radio talk shows call her to be a guest and ask her about her rape, and she has to keep reliving the worst moment of her life. The victim's lawyer calls to compliment her story and asks her if she would testify in his client's civil lawsuit against Parker. When that's settled out of court, he asks if she'd consider doing that in another lawsuit in which the jury needs to feel the long ripple of a rape, and she says yes, because how can she refuse to help someone who has endured what she has or allow so many people to keep insinuating that it's the violated woman who is to blame? SPORTS ILLUSTRATED calls a year later and asks to interview her, and she has to worry how that will affect the way her colleagues at her new workplace, *The New York Times*, will look at her, worry that *this* is who she is now to people, this is *all* she is. Each new episode will mean another week of barely eating, barely sleeping, a few more nightmares and 10 or 15 extra miles of running, but she can't back down. She has never met Richie Parker and no doubt never will, but Jill Agostino is paying for his crime, oh, yes, she's paying.

Five

Here is an assistant coach from the University of Utah. Once Donny Daniels, too, was a black teenager from a crowded city who lived to play basketball. And so even though he is the 40-year-old father of three, including two daughters, on this spring day in 1995, he is walking into his past when he walks into the Parkers' apartment. He finds Richie just as quiet and respectful as all his sources vowed. He sits in the living room with the 108 basketball trophies that take Rosita hours to dust. He looks into the kitchen where she cooks pots and pans full of baked chicken, ziti, collard greens, banana pudding and sweet-potato pies on Sundays and has half the neighborhood into her house, just like it used to be when she was growing up in North Carolina. He gazes around the home where Rosita and Richie's ever-so-quiet father, Richard, and Richie's two older sisters, Monica and Tanya, who have both attended college, eat and tease each other and laugh.

Donny talks to Rosita, who for years telephoned after Richie to make sure he had gone where he said he was going, who tried to seal her son from all the bad choices blowing around outside the window. No, Donny can't see her running a half-dozen times to the emergency room with high blood pressure at each twist her son's story takes; can't see her bent in half with chest pains six months after Richie's arrest, paramedics rushing through that front door and clamping an oxygen mask over her mouth, driving an IV needle into her arm, pushing a nitroglycerine pill under her tongue, trying to stave off the heart attack or stroke that's on the verge of occurring as her son watches, even more scared than he was on that long night when he lay awake smelling urine in a New York City jail. He can't see her lying in the hospital, realizing that if she doesn't stop letting the newspaper stories affect her so deeply, they're going to kill her. But listening to the mother and the son, he can feel it.

And it's all that feeling that Donny lets out when the *New York Post* reporter gets a tip and calls him a few days later to ask, "How can Utah consider rewarding a sex felon with a scholarship?" All that feeling from a man who senses that his and his university's integrity is being assaulted.

Of course, he has never walked into the *victim's* house and felt what a heart might feel there. "There are two victims here," he tells the reporter. "He doesn't evaporate into the atmosphere. He's not a piece of dirt. He has feelings and emotions.... They both made a mistake; they shouldn't have been there. But everyone's worried about the girl. What about him?... You don't see her name or picture, but Richie Parker is plastered all over.... She probably will get a doctorate and marry a successful guy and live in the Hamptons.... Will he ever be able to forget it?... Who's hurt more for life?"

Imagine the explosion this quote causes back in Salt Lake City, the ripping apart of molecules. Imagine how rapidly the college president and athletic director must run from that quote, how swiftly Richie's chance to attend Utah vaporizes, how many columns are written citing Richie as the prime example of America's coddling of athletes and Neanderthal treatment of women. Imagine how tightly doors shut to discuss what must be done with Donny.

He is luckier than others will be. He is placed on probation for a year and ordered to attend sensitivity training sessions with a director from the Women's Resource Center on campus. He gets a second chance.

A year later, when a writer from SI calls, Donny says he was wrong for saying what he did but wishes to say nothing more, and his boss, coach Rick Majerus, the most affable of men, seals his lips as well. Better to fence off the area and let the pieces lie where they fell, to be covered by the sediment of time.

Six

Here is a university president. Here is the picture of Teddy Roosevelt on his office wall. Which is which? Who's who? Mustache. Spectacles. Hair combed back. Eyes atwinkle. Robust body. Bent for bold action. Oh, so *that's* how you tell the two of them apart: Stephen Trachtenberg's the better politician.

He's the man who transformed the University of Hartford and George Washington, the one who gives big-idea speeches and writes ethics essays for books, magazines and newspapers. He knows something about everything. Even chemistry.

Yes, he's going to do it. He's going to give this Parker kid another chance, and he's going to satisfy the alumni and faculty and the women's groups and the media and the talk-show callers, and even the victim. He's going to introduce cesium to fluorine, and—*eureka!*—nothing's going to go *ka-boom!*

And why not? He's a master at problem-solving, a genius at persuasion. "He has a tremendous capacity to anticipate a whole variety of outcomes and the implications of those outcomes," says George Washington vice president Bob Chernak, "and then calculate how to move an issue toward the most favorable one. He's always three steps ahead of you. He's thinking of ideas in his sleep."

Stephen inherited a university with a profound identity crisis, not to mention a 1–27 basketball team, in 1988. In the wake of his brainstorms, applications have nearly doubled, contributions have soared, average SAT scores have rocketed, and the hoops team has become an NCAA tournament fixture. A new challenge? Bully! A fray? Fine! He would wade right into it and convince people he was right, the way he did during the student sit-ins at Boston University back in the 1960s as a bearded associate dean, persuading protesters not to risk a violent confrontation with police. He has built up a tall pile of chips at George Washington, and he's willing to ante up for Richie Parker.

Sure, he's eager to help his basketball team, but it's also something else. Sure, he's the son of one hell of a Brooklyn life insurance salesman, but he's also the son of a social activist, a mother who sent him to summer camps with Black kids and wanted him to become a doctor who would treat the poor, not to mention the grandson of a Ukrainian Jew who fled to America for a second chance. His record of helping kids out of deep holes is long. At Hartford he gave a scholarship to a young man with an eighth-grade education who had been convicted on drug-dealing and burglary charges. That man, John Richters—who played no sport—went on to graduate summa cum laude and get a Ph.D. in psychology and now works as a program chief at the National Institutes of Health in the study of chronically antisocial children.

A young deer—that's the image that forms in the university president's head when Richie enters his office in May 1995. Barely audible, Richie expresses contrition and an earnest desire to attend George Washington, and he's so hopeful that he buys a school hat and T-shirt. All the questions march through Stephen's head as Richie walks out of his office. Is it a college's job to mete out more punishment than the legal system does? Perhaps not, but isn't it a university president's job to make sure that a parent doesn't send an 18-year-old daughter to live in a dorm room next door to a sex offender? What if it were *his* daughter? If a sex felon shouldn't get a basketball scholarship, what about an academic scholarship? What about a thief, a mugger, an embezzler? A custodian or a waiter can return to his normal life after the legal system passes judgment, but a gifted basketball player cannot? Pro sports are fine for felons to play, but not college athletics? What kind of message does it send out when a sex offender gets a scholarship? When you remove the emotion from the question...but maybe you *shouldn't* remove the emotion from the question. All this confusion, does it signal a society lost in the wilderness...or one finally mature enough to look at questions it has always shut its eyes to? His mind gnaws at the bone, at every last bit of gristle. Beneath it all, he can sense what's going on, the vague feeling people are beginning to have that their love of sports—the sense of escape and belonging that they provide—is doubling back on them like some hidden undertow, pulling them all out to sea. It's not the ripest time for redemption.

But he takes a deep breath and begins constructing a master plan. He sends a university lawyer, a woman, to New York City to compile a massive dossier on Richie. If she finds any smudge, besides the stairwell incident, George Washington can retreat—but he keeps checking with her, and she doesn't. Shrewder still, he decides that *he* won't decide Richie's fate; he'll leave that to a blue-ribbon committee, one that he structures as if he were a supplicant at a Hindu shrine, bowing to a dozen different gods, to every possible political correctness: seven Blacks and eight whites, seven females and eight males, including a professor of law, an assistant chief of police, a minister, a campus chaplain, an academic coordinator, a faculty clinical psychologist, a director of multicultural student services, a superintendent of schools, two judges, two trustees and three students. "A Noah's Ark committee," he calls it. If the menagerie chooses to accept Richie, Stephen will have him redshirted for a year, ease him into campus life, save him from the jackals waiting at enemy arenas. And then, as the frosting on the cake, even before the committee makes its recommendation on Richie, he offers the victim, a valedictorian of her junior high class, a scholarship when she graduates from high school. A university lawyer warns him that one won't look pretty in a tabloid headline, but Stephen is determined. Win-win for everyone, right?

Do you recall Chernobyl? It all begins to rain down on Stephen Trachtenberg: the *New York Post* reporter, radioactive telephone calls, faxes and letters, scalding editorials, icy questions from the board of trustees, student petitions and condemnation from the faculty senate. Stephen, the father of George Washington University, is being called immoral, a fool, a calculating liar. Even his wife, Francine, in his corner all the way, warns him that he has underestimated what he's up against, that, politically speaking, he has made the wrong call. He's losing sleep. It's usurping his entire day and all of his night. The story moves to *The Washington Post*'s front page— *that's* trouble. If only he could buy enough time for his plan to incubate, for the score of Richie's last SAT test to arrive and the Noah's Ark committee to see the results of the nearly complete investigation, but no, Stephen looks to one flank, then the other and sees a remarkable alliance closing in on him. The feminists *and* conservatives, "the forces of the left and the forces of the right," he says, "coming together like the teeth of a vise." Eight years of working 12-hour days to build George Washington's image is being frittered away, and image is money. And he can't even try to persuade the public that he's right—the NCAA gag rule preventing school officials from discussing a recruit has stripped him of his greatest gift. Could he even lose his job over this, if the teeth keep closing? Could he?

One by one, those in his inner circle who admire the risk he has taken, or have simply indulged it, urge him to halt, even as his investigator's reports on Richie keep coming in, convincing him more than ever that it's right to go on. Finally it's just Stephen out there, hanging onto Richie by his fingernails as everything around them shakes. At last, he has to let go. Stephen looks at himself in the mirror. It's not Teddy he sees. It's not the man who could persuade almost anyone of anything. "I gave Richie Parker a moment of hope," he says, the light going out of his eyes, "and then I took it away."

Seven

Here is the victim. No, here the victim is not. She has never emerged from the shadows of that stairwell. She will not emerge now. Of her you shall only know this: For months after the incident she endured nightmares and telephoned threats from people who blamed her. She is an excellent student, but her grades dipped, and the taunts from schoolmates forced her to transfer from one high school, then another. She undergoes therapy. As she gets ready for her senior year, her family will not even reveal the borough where her current school is located.

She hopes to become a doctor. Her father is a social worker who deals with abused children, her mother a hospital nurse. Six years ago they and their daughter left Ghana and came to America, looking for another chance.

Eight

Here is a number. Such a nice, plump number. Say it: 500. Let them scoff at Dave Possinger, let them cringe at his intensity, let them ask him, like wise guys, to total up the traffic lights in the towns where he has coached, but this would be proof he could clutch all the way to the coffin: 500. One more win is all he needs. One more.

And no, this won't be 500 by dint of sheer endurance, a box turtle's milestone. Eighteen years is all it took Dave, an astonishing average of 28 victories a year. He is the best coach you never heard of, a 52-year-old man marooned in the bush country of NAIA and junior college basketball by bad luck and an old whiff of scandal. But it's summer, and the 1995–96 season is just a few months away, and on opening night his Sullivan County (N.Y.)

Community College team will no doubt pulverize Dutchess C.C. as it does every year, and he will join that invisible club: *500*.

He has envisioned the moment all summer, even as the man he has just chosen as his assistant coach, Charles Harris, has begun to grow intrigued by the never-ending newspaper accounts of a kid in New York City named Richie Parker. Richie is the last thing on Dave's mind. Dave has just coached his team to the national junior college Division III championship and is loaded to repeat in 1995–96, and he has no reason to think that Richie will end up with him in the bush country, at a low-level community college. Start making contacts and see what's out there, especially for the year after this, is all he has asked of Harris, a likable 40-year-old black man who Dave is sure will make a superb recruiter.

Everywhere Dave goes that summer, even on his vacation in the Philippines, he imagines the magical night that is coming: The limousine his girlfriend is renting to take him to the game. The official hoisting of the national-championship banner, his second in four years at the junior college in Loch Sheldrake, N.Y. Former players converging to congratulate him, a capacity crowd rising to recognize him. The plaque, the ringing speeches, the commemorative T-shirts, the late-night dinner for 100 in the Italian restaurant. "It dominated my thoughts every day," Dave recalls. "Even in places in the Philippines where there was no running water, no electricity, I'd see kids playing basketball and I'd think about 500. It would stand for all the years, all the kids, all the hard work." It would stand for his nine seasons at a New York NAIA school named St. Thomas Aquinas, where his 295–49 record helped make the program the country's winningest of the 1980s, on *any* level—yes, Dean Smith at North Carolina was second to Dave Possinger. It would stand for his four-year run of 133–5 at Sullivan County and ease the pain from the '89 scandal that forced him out after one year at Western Carolina, his one shot as an NCAA Division I coach, even though it was his assistant, not him, who was cited for minor recruiting violations. Perhaps 500 wouldn't mean quite so much if he had a wife and children, but no, it's just him and his basset hound Free Throw, and 500 stands for his life.

A few hours drive south, at a showcase game for unrecruited players, his soon-to-be-named assistant Harris is watching the one obvious jewel on the floor, Richie Parker. It's crazy, thinks Harris, who remembers inmates from the local prison taking classes from Sullivan County when he was enrolled there in the 1970s. "Everyone has something in their closet they're not proud of," Harris says, "and everyone deserves a second chance." A long shot, but what a coup if he could offer the kid the second chance that the four-year colleges wouldn't.

Harris gets clearance, he says later, from Sullivan County's athletic director, Mike McGuire, to have Richie apply to the school—not as a scholarship student but as any normal student would. Searching for a way to contact Richie, Harris calls the *New York Post* reporter. It's like the mouse asking the cat for directions to the cheese.

McGuire says now that if he heard the name Richie Parker, it didn't register. And that he definitely never gave Harris permission—even though Harris had been unofficially approved to go on contract in two months and had already invested countless hours and a few hundred dollars from his own pocket on phone calls and recruiting trips—to present himself to a *New York Post* reporter as a Sullivan County assistant coach and declare that Sullivan County was "committed to working" with Richie Parker.

You know what happens next. You know about the reporter's call to the president, asking if he knows that Sullivan County is recruiting a sex felon. You know about the next day's headlines, the ducking for cover. Richie, of course, will never play at Sullivan County. Harris's fate will hang in the balance for a few months while the school wrings its hands. In October, after he has spent weeks monitoring the players in study hall and working at practices without pay, hoping for the best, Harris is told he won't be hired.

Harris, with head-coaching dreams of his own, is crushed. Dave, who feels responsible for Harris, is devastated. There have been other slights from his superiors at Sullivan County, he feels, but to do this to a well-meaning man trying to give a kid a second chance—how can he go on working there and live with himself? But then, how can he walk out on his team two weeks before the season opener and deprive himself of the Holy Grail: *500*?

Simple, Dave's friends tell him. Win the opener, then quit. What a scene it would be, the man of the hour strolling to the microphone, saying, "Ladies and gentlemen, thank you. *I quit!*" But Dave's conscience won't let him do it. "If I start something," he tells his friends, "I have to finish it."

Five days before the opener, he quits. He can't sleep. A few days later he smirks and tells a reporter, "Your job is to tell me why I shouldn't jump off a building." His team goes on to win the national championship again, without him.

His record hangs there, rolling around the rim—499 wins and 116 losses—but athletic directors look right past him, searching for a younger man. Eight months later he still hasn't even received an interview. He takes a job as a regional director for National Scouting Report, a service designed to help high school kids get—what else?—college scholarships. "But there's still a claw in the back of my throat," he says, "a claw telling me, 'You are a basketball coach.'"

A week after he quits, Dave goes to his dresser drawer. He opens it and stares at what he purchased in the Philippines a few months earlier, and he makes a decision. Damn the math, they can't take it from him. It's there now, glittering in 18-carat gold from a chain around his neck: *500*.

Nine

Here is the girlfriend of the boy who has pleaded guilty to sexual abuse. She's tall and lean, a beautiful girl whose demeanor is so composed that everyone always assumes she's older than she really is, until that day when people are running to her in the hall, telling her to come quickly, something terrible has happened, and Richie's in the principal's office talking so helter-skelter that none of it makes sense, and the police are on their way, and she's nearly in hysterics.

He's the schoolmate Jaywana Bradley fell in love with in 10th grade, the one who taught her to play basketball so well that by her senior year she will be named by the *Daily News* as one of the best schoolgirl players in Manhattan. Who knew, perhaps they would go off together to trumpets, the king and queen of Manhattan hoops moving on, hand in hand, to set up court on a college campus...until this.

But what, exactly, *is* this? Jaywana keeps finding herself in bed, crying, wondering. People keep asking her, "You gonna leave Richie?" Some call her a fool if she sticks with him, and a few boys walk right up to her and say, "Why you going out with a rapist?"

She can't quite answer that. Maybe it's because her mother and father believe in Richie, her dad accompanying the Parkers to court hearings. Maybe it's just sitting there in the Parker apartment all those evenings, playing spades with the family and watching TV, feeling that relentless presence of Rosita—like a rock, a magnetic rock. Listening to Rosita talk about the past, telling how her father died when she was one, how her mother died of diabetic complications when she was 13, how her twin sister stepped in front of a car and was killed when they were five, leaving Rosita clutching the sleeve of the coat with which she had tried to yank back her twin. Maybe Jaywana, just like Richie, just keeps absorbing Rosita's relentless message: "Make your life what it's meant to be, and don't let anyone or anything stop you."

Maybe it's two young people pulling closer and closer together the more that forces try to drive them apart. Maybe she's a sucker for that playful, silly Richie, the side he only shows close family and friends. And maybe it comes from holding him, wiping away his tears the way she does when George Washington closes the door on him and she ends up getting the big-time basketball scholarship to Massachusetts that was supposed to be his.

He goes off to Mesa, to the junior college that decides not to let him play basketball, and she goes off to UMass, and they don't see each other for a long while. He has time to sort out what's essential, what he needs, now, sooner than he ever dreamed. When they come home for Christmas, he asks her to come over, calls her to his room and asks her to close her eyes. When she opens them, he's on his knee, asking her to marry him, and she says yes. And later, when she asks him when, he says, "As soon as we're done college."

More and more now, Jaywana finds herself daydreaming of a future. There is no city or people there, just her and Richie in a house surrounded by land and trees as far as the eye can see, a place where no one can touch them. Why the two of them against all odds? She can't explain. "I don't know what made me stick through it with him," she says. "All I know is that nothing anybody can ever say or do can pull me apart from him."

Ten

Here is death. Now, wait a minute—no one is going to be foolish enough to blame Richie Parker's 15 minutes in the stairwell or the administration of Mesa Community College or even the media for the death of a coach's father, but every event in life is chained to the next, and how do you ever separate the links?

This was supposed to be the year that Rob Standifer gave his father, Bob, a gift—perhaps the last one—in exchange for the gift his father had given him. All Rob's life his dad had awakened at 3 a.m. and reported to work three hours early at a construction company, logging 12- to 14-hour shifts. It didn't matter how badly his dad felt, with his bad back, his diabetes or his weak heart. Work made his father feel good, and his father had a knack of passing that feeling all around. The lesson Rob took into his bones was the old American one: Outwork everyone and you'll succeed in life.

And it seemed true. As a kid Rob was always the first one on the basketball court as a point of pride, shooting 1,000 shots a day, and sure enough, he found himself playing for the Mesa Community College team that nearly won the junior college title in 1987, finishing third in the national tournament in Hutchinson, Kans. He worked for nothing as a high school assistant and then for next to nothing for five years as an assistant at Mesa, and he was rewarded with the head-coaching job two years ago. He was only 27, but his dream, to coach a major-college team, was no longer quite so far away.

The pantry was bare his rookie year, but Mesa went 15–15. Then, doing it his dad's way—his typical off-season day ran from 7 a.m. to 10 at night— he ran the summer league, organized a computerized scouting system, cultivated his high school coaching contacts, recruited at hours when other coaches relaxed, pushed his players through an exhaustive weightlifting program and then nurtured them at night with so many phone calls that his friends called him Ma Bell. He was single and on fire. "I could be a maniac," says Rob, "and I was."

The pantry filled fast. Twice in the summer league in 1995 his players whipped a team with four former Arizona State starters on it, and Rob's target was clear. He was going to take his father and his team back to Hutchinson and this time win the whole damn thing.

Richie? He would sure make things easier. Rob had seen him play in the annual summer tournament at Arizona State, which Richie's New York City club team, Riverside Church, traveled to each year. Just like all the other coaches, Rob was struck by the distance between Richie and the world's image of Richie. Just like all the other coaches, he got that same feeling in the pit of his stomach when he saw a talented high school player—if you didn't get him dunking *for* you, he might soon be dunking *on* you. Besides, Rob knew Ernie Lorch, the Riverside director, and already had taken a few of Lorch's kids at Mesa. And so Rob, too, was drawn in. Mesa would be Richie's safety net, the faraway junior college where he could go to heal himself and play ball if all the Division I scholarship offers went up in smoke.

And because there was so much smoke, and Richie kept hoping and waiting for the next Division I chance, his decision to go to Mesa occurred at the last minute, just a few days before the start of school last August. And because Richie waited, Rob had to wait, and by the time he found out Richie was coming, there was no chance for cool heads to sit and debate this and perhaps construct a plan. Rob told the story of Richie Parker to three women—his mother, his girlfriend and his girlfriend's mother, and they all agreed with him. "What Richie did was flat wrong," Rob says, "but are you going to be part of the problem or part of the solution?" And he insists—*are you crazy?*—that of course he notified his superiors, two of them, about Richie and his baggage.

But the Mesa athletic director, Allen Benedict, says he was told nothing of Richie's past, that all he got was a 9 p.m. call from Rob telling him that a great player was coming from New York. The next morning, while Richie was at 30,000 feet heading west across the heart of America, the junior college president was on the phone with Benedict, saying, "Why did a reporter from the *New York Post* just call me...and who is Richie Parker?" And then the National Organization for Women was checking in, and cameras were peering inside the gym for a peek at Richie, and a TV truck was pulling up to Benedict's house. "Whether you do something wrong or not isn't the point sometimes," says Benedict. "It's the perception."

Rob was called in to a meeting less than two weeks before the first practice and forced to quit. Richie called Rob, nearly in tears at what he had wrought.

As for Richie, he could stay, but he couldn't play basketball. College athletics, Mesa president Larry Christiansen reasoned, are like a driver's license—a privilege, not a right. What the westward trip and the open spaces had done for so many others, they couldn't do for Richie Parker.

Richie had to decide, then and there, what was most important in his life. He chose to stay at Mesa, take courses and learn who he was without a basketball. He would work the shot clock at games, like one of those earnest guys in glasses that no one ever notices, and by the end of the year the administrators at Mesa would all say good things about him.

Rob had to tell his father the terrible news. He knew his dad was on the edge of the cliff—doctors had said that if not for the zest that Bob derived from his work, his heart would've likely given way three or four years before—so the son tried to shrug and keep his face a blank, so he wouldn't give his father that nudge. Bob was devastated, but as with all his other pain, he tried to keep it inside. He was bewildered, too. The ethic he had passed on to his only child—outwork everyone and you'll succeed—had failed, been displaced, it seemed, by a new one: Image is everything.

Rob didn't eat for three days after that, unless you count the antacid medication. He wouldn't even show his girlfriend, Danelle Scuzzaro, how badly this hurt.

On the fourth day after he was let go, he picked up a diamond ring at the jeweler's and took Danelle to dinner. Afterward, he dropped to his knee— cesium is the damnedest thing—and asked her to marry him. She said yes, and thank god.

Two weeks later, at 5:15 a.m., he got the call from his mother. His father's heart had stopped, at the age of 61. It might well have happened then anyway. "What happened to me didn't kill him," says Rob, "but it didn't help."

There was only one thing to be said for the timing. All the tears Rob had held back after losing his job could finally come out, and they did...again... and again...and again....

Eleven

Wait a moment. What about the reporter from the New York Post—isn't he here too? Sure, just a moment, he's still on the telephone. Gosh, look at him, just a kid, wouldn't even pass for 25. Just started at the Post, covering high school sports, when suddenly—whoa!—he has his teeth into the story of his life, and his incisors are wonderful.

Look at Barry Baum rolling out of bed in his Manhattan apartment and running, literally, to the newsstand at the corner of 79th and Broadway to check if the *Daily News* has scooped him on the Parker story. That has actually happened before, so Barry knows that sinking feeling. See him getting that 10 a.m. call from his editor, groggily picking up the phone—a medic on call in a tabloid war. "So what's goin' on with Parker today?" his editor demands. And Barry says, "I'll let you know," then shakes off the cobwebs and begins working the phones, looking for a tip. He loves this part, the detective work. And the most amazing thing keeps occurring. Because there's such an innocent charm about Barry, people *want* to help him.

Some high school scout or basketball junkie with his ear to the streets keeps slipping him the name of the next university showing interest in Richie, and then Barry plays his role, just as the university administrators and the coaches and the women's groups and the loved ones do. He becomes the Bunsen burner, the heat that agitates the cesium and fluorine molecules into rapid movement, more-violent collision. He leaps to call the university president and the campus women's center to ask that 64-megaton question—"How do you feel about your school recruiting a sex felon?"—and if they say they don't know who Richie Parker is, so they can't comment, he faxes them a pile of his Parker stories, and suddenly they have a comment. And all at once the coach and the athletic director are being called onto the president's carpet, or what's left of it, and then there's a follow-up exclusive story to write when they all abandon Richie, and there's no time to consider all the layers, all the moral nuances, because the editor's on the phone barking, "O.K., hurry, rewrite that for the second edition!"—just like in the movies. And then street vendors are snaking between the cars bottlenecked at the bridges and tunnels leading into the city the next morning, catching drivers' eyes with thick Sex Felon headlines, and every person who contributes his 50 cents confirms the *Post* editor's instincts and becomes another link in the chain.

"There were nights when I couldn't sleep, an adrenaline I had for a long time," says Barry. "I'd lie in bed, realizing I'd come to New York and made an impact on one of the biggest stories of the year."

Hadn't his editor at the *Post* told him, "We're going to put your name in lights," when he hired Barry in August 1994? Wasn't that music to his ears? Even as a little kid in Brooklyn Heights, he had dreamed of busting back-page stories for the New York tabloids. At 15 he talked his way into becoming the Knicks ball boy by rat-tat-tatting 10 letters to the team trainer, and then he parlayed that job into his own cable-TV show in Manhattan, *Courtside with Barry Baum,* by convincing the station of the wonderful access to big-name Knicks that a precocious 16-year-old ball boy had. He appeared on the televised dating show *Love Connection* three times, and when one of his dates sniffed about Barry's making the wrong turn on their evening out, he brought down the house by sniffing back, "Get a load of Miss Rand McNally, never made a wrong turn in her life!"

And then suddenly the kid who grew up calling *New York Post* and *Daily News* columnists with kudos and beg-to-differs is being lauded for his own back-page *Post* scoops on New York radio talk shows, being asked to appear on the all-sports station, WFAN, and invited to speak at a journalism symposium at Madison Square Garden with a poster board full of his Parker stories. Adrenaline, yes, but anguish, too, stuff you don't talk about when you're a guest on WFAN. Because the nasty phone calls to Barry's desk have begun, people hissing, "Leave Richie Parker alone!"

Then, when he's a guest on a radio talk show one day, a caller says, "Don't you see what you're doing? This is a black kid who comes from nowhere, and you're a white guy who probably comes from a lot of money." Barry blinks. "It hits me," he says. "That's true. I've always had everything, and I'd never even thought of the race factor." New York City high school coaches, his contacts, start saying, "C'mon, Barry, back off. What are you trying to prove?" Even his own father, Bruce, finally says, "Leave him alone already, Barry," and that stings.

"That even someone who knew me that well wouldn't realize that I'm just trying to do my job...." he says. "I mean, don't give me credit for keeping Richie Parker out of college, but don't blame me for it either. And the more people tell me to *stop* reporting a story, the more it means it *is* a story, right? But I keep wondering about Richie. All that time, I couldn't talk to him because his lawyer wouldn't let me, so I couldn't feel him. Finally they let me. You know, it changes things once you talk to him. Before that he was an object, and it was easy to write, 'Richie Parker, sex felon,' because I didn't know him. He was the predator and the girl was the victim, right? I talked to him at a Rucker League game last August, and he actually smiled at me. A smile is a big thing.

"Look, I've never had a problem with Richie playing college basketball. It's not the colleges' job to punish him further. He should be allowed to play—but not without students and their parents being notified, maybe by a letter from the university administration. You know, like Megan's Law, notifying people that a sex felon is in their neighborhood. It's funny. It's like *I've* become Megan's Law for these universities. I'm the one who tells them he's coming. It was amazing how quickly it played out with Oral Roberts. I reported that the school was interested, the story breaks across the country, the TV reporters arrive on campus—and the school announces it has already pulled out! It was like the fire trucks coming, and there's no fire, the local residents have already put it out. These universities have no backbone! Every university president I talk to, except for maybe Stephen Trachtenberg, it's like talking to the same guy. Every one of them says, 'I can't believe my coach did this and that isn't what we stand for' and blah-blah-blah. I'm convinced there's only one college president in the United States: He just keeps changing his name!"

One major-college coach, off the record, asks Barry what will happen if he takes the risk on Richie. What's Barry supposed to do, lie? He tells the truth, the coach says thank you and backs off, and—*poof!*—the chance is gone, the chemical reaction begun and finished before anyone ever even smelled it occurring. And it begins to dawn on Barry: "Somehow, I'm in this story. I'm not just the observer. People are making decisions based on my reporting. There I am, 25 years old and playing the part of deciding if this kid's going to get into college or not, and maybe, if he's good enough, even into the NBA. I have no agenda or angle at all, but he'd probably be playing now if I hadn't called Utah or GW or...."

"So where is the line? I've never been taught that line. I keep wondering, Am I doing the right thing? But I shouldn't have to make that choice. I started compiling a list in my mind of all the people whose lives I've affected, the people who have gotten fired, all the universities. And it tears me apart, because the last thing I want to do is hurt anyone. But I know if I stop reporting it and the *Daily News* gets the story, which you know they will, then my editor will call me and say, 'What's goin' on with Parker? What happened? Where are the words?' and what am I going to say? I can't win. So people blame me. It's like *I* was the one in the stairwell."

He stares off at the wall, catches his breath. "And it's not over yet," Barry says. "It's not over until I find out where Richie Parker's going."

Twelve

One day about a month ago Richie Parker stepped into an airplane in Arizona. The plane rose, and he looked through the window one last time at the desert and flew back across America, with no idea what would happen next. "I've learned I can survive without basketball," he said last month. "I've learned how the real world is and that I'm stronger than I knew I was. There's less fear now. I know myself more. I trust people less, but that doesn't make me sad. Just more aware of things. I can still live a good life." And he said a lot more, but it would be improper to let him do it here, for it might mislead the reader into thinking this was a story about Richie Parker.

This land is vast, and it contains so many kinds of people, and that is its grace. Two weeks ago Gale Stevens Haynes, the 45-year-old provost of the Brooklyn campus of Long Island University—and the Black mother of three teenage daughters—offered Richie Parker a basketball scholarship to her Division I school. She didn't pull the offer back when the *New York Post* reporter found out, and Richie accepted it. When asked why she did it, she said, "Unless there's an island that I don't know about, where we send people forever who have done something wrong, then we have to provide pathways for these people so they can rejoin society. If we don't, it can only explode. It can only explode in all of our faces."

— POSTSCRIPT —

In 2014, in an interview with SI's Ted Keith, Smith spoke about his process:

> A friend of mine named Cal Fussman, who is a writer with *Esquire*, was living on Long Island and he just started sending me envelopes every two or three days with two or three *New York Post* stories with big bold headlines about this kid named Richie Parker. They just kept coming for a month or so with a scrawled note in there that said, "You need to write about this, there's something with real depth to be written here."

> Finally, after that inundation I just said, he's right, and started the steps to follow the chain.

> That's really what that story was, following the links in the chain. Realizing the farther I went in that chain how much this story could suggest or reveal about America's relationship with sports and the torquing we have to do sometimes in that relationship and how compromised we can all get and the contortions we can all go into to justify our love of sports.

> So many things came into play there: morality, ethics and what really matters, where do we draw the line or do we just compartmentalize sports off to the side and say, I don't care very much if the performer is compromised.

> I was not coming in there to judge, I was going in there to understand. That gave the [people in the story] the safety to discuss what their fears were and how they could see the argument to just shut a kid off and cast him out of the gates.

> The more I went on with that story the more I realized the complexity goes on and on. The people we identify as the villains from a distance have a lot of good intentions and a lot of good reasons for those intentions. This is not an easy board game to move your pieces around on.

SEPTEMBER 7, 2020

'I'm Going Home.' Reflecting on Life Inside the NBA Bubble

Sports Illustrated senior writer Chris Mannix gives insight on what life was like living inside the NBA bubble

BY CHRIS MANNIX

In the fall of 2020, Chris Mannix penned a farewell column to the most surreal postseason in league history, one that played out in eerie silence against a backdrop of fear and uncertainty as COVID-19 shut down much of society. Mannix grew up on the game—before coming to SI he worked as a ballboy for the Boston Celtics—and his familiarity with the league and its characters and rhythms comes through in this column.

LAKE BUENA VISTA, Fla.—Goodbye, Bubble.

Goodbye, Orlando, Lake Buena Vista or wherever you officially were. After two months, 62 COVID-19 tests and a lifetime's worth of hand sanitizer, I'm going home. Farewell to my lizard friends on the stairwell, the mosquitos that swarm by the thousands and the monsoons that seem to spring from the sky. So long 7 a.m. alarms and midnight bus rides, the sprints to catch the end of one practice and the hustling to make the ride to the next. My watch has ended.

Goodbye, access, and I mean *great* access. I was initially concerned about how much value there would be in coming down here. We were warned that we would be separated from teams and not allowed to wander. Walk-and-talks, the lifeblood of any reporter, weren't allowed and one-on-ones weren't guaranteed. But I got time with everyone from Jayson Tatum to Devin Booker, Jacque Vaughn to Nick Nurse. Even Steven Adams answered a few goofy questions for *SI Kids*.

We didn't get LeBron James or Kawhi Leonard, but you *never* get James or Leonard. You did get to chat up Masai Ujiri in the hallway, pester Monty McCutchen when you had a question about a call and interrupt Tim Connelly on one of his power walks. More importantly, when Jacob Blake was shot and the NBA shut down, you didn't just get to hear players' reactions. You got to see them. You got to *feel* them. The despondence of Fred VanVleet. The frustration of George Hill. That mattered. It all mattered.

Goodbye, 314-square foot room, with your air conditioning that mysteriously shuts off in the middle of the night and your weird cactus art framed in every room. Honestly, two months in a hotel didn't bother me that much. Live in Manhattan for more than a decade, and anything with a private bathroom starts to feel like the Taj Mahal. Now if I only could figure out how to use a Keurig.

Goodbye, housekeeping, and rest assured I'm leaving you a large tip. Outside of my next-door neighbors—and apologies to you for having to suffer through a loud barrage of hot takes ranging from Damian Lillard's chances of shooting the Blazers into the second round to Canelo Alvarez's next opponent—I owe you folks the most. You probably had never seen so many picked clean buffalo wings in the trash bags, and I cringe at the number of half-finished cans of Bubly you poured out. I'm among the worst offenders but I know I'm not the only one, so to my fellow media members, make sure any paper you leave behind has Andrew Jackson's face on it.

Goodbye, snack size Krackels, Snickers and the junk food tables from hell the NBA set up in the media rooms. I arrived in Orlando anticipating a healthy trip. There was no Dominos delivery, so that eliminated about 4,700 carbs a week. Unlike Joe Vardon, the margarita master, or Marc Spears, a walking vineyard, I didn't plan to keep any alcohol in my room. I was coming out of this feeling good. Hundreds of mini Mr. Goodbars and dozens of Mickey's Ice Cream sandwiches later, and I'm leaving feeling bad.

Goodbye, Mack Weldon Ace Sweatpants, $78 and worth every nickel. Inside the waistband it reads For DAILY WEAR, and I took that literally. I often told people I had two pairs; I didn't. I said I dropped them in the laundry every few days, and that wasn't always true, either. These sweatpants belong framed somewhere in Advent HealthCare Arena, like Nate Robinson's jersey on the summer league wall.

Goodbye, NBA PR chief Tim Frank, with your Jon Cryer wardrobe, Kelly Williams and Country Club Christiano with your way too peppy morning emails. The NBA had some goofy rules—so I *can* camp out in a hotel hallway all day but I *can't* share a golf course with players for fear of, what, overhearing Kyle Lowry curse after shanking a putt?—and those proximity beepers...they were a little much.

Seriously though: Team and league PR staffs were terrific, always available, as helpful as they could be in a challenging environment.

Goodbye, ESPN's Tim Bontemps, you bleacher creature. I lost count how many times I would be walking through the arena and I'd get a call or text from Bontemps—doing yeoman's work for ESPN in Tier 2 throughout this—commenting on my wardrobe. Big Brother, weighing in from the upper deck. Follow Tim on Instagram, by the way, for compelling content like...scores.

Goodbye, Marc Stein, my hallway partner in the Coronado Springs. Stein and I had a similar strategy for the seeding games—don't go to them. With three practice floors in Coronado and teams shuffling in and out, a six-city trip through the NBA could be had in one afternoon.

Goodbye, Grant Williams. I have no idea who was hazing the Celtics rookie—word is it was Marcus Smart—but with Boston's meal room at the end of the Coronado lobby, I saw Williams make his way back and forth at least three times a day, bags of food in both hands. Someone was sending him on runs.

Goodbye, Malika Andrews, ESPN's permanent bubble resident. You want lessons on how to remain COVID-19 free? Talk to Andrews, who wears disposable gloves around campus—and Purells them when she gets in a car. Look after the *Orange County Register*'s Kyle Goon who is, I think, one abruptly canceled practice away from a complete meltdown.

Goodbye, Adrian Wojnarowski. I liked you better when you were at *The Vertical*.

Goodbye, masks—but not really. I admit, I find masks uncomfortable. Stifling, even. But they work. There are two constant safety measures inside the bubble: masks and daily testing. Testing looks to become more available, with $5 rapid tests reportedly on the way. Masks are available right now. The NBA reported zero positive COVID-19 tests among players in the last eight weeks. It wasn't because the league decamped in the only coronavirus free patch of land in Florida. It's because everyone was wearing masks. They're not an infringement on your freedom, folks. They are the way, for now, you can live a normal life.

Goodbye, coaches and players—no one could walk away from this experience without being enormously impressed. There were too many powerful moments to count. Rick Carlisle's daily references to important moments in Black history. Doc Rivers's, choking back tears, wondering why the country he loves "doesn't love us back." Donovan Mitchell's reminding the world of its social justice issues...just moments after a crushing Game 7 loss.

The microscope these players have been under is intense, the environment harsh. They are fighting for what they believe in, all while being told to shut up and dribble. They are telling you what *they* have experienced, all while right-wing crackpots argue the size of your bank account matters more than your skin color. Many, in their mid-20s, are picking up a mantle that should be carried by elected officials generations older. Don't tell me it hasn't had an impact. What has happened here will be remembered forever.

Goodbye, readers—at least for now. I've got a couple of stories in the can and I'll continue covering the postseason from afar. Michael Rosenberg will be Sports Illustrated's eyes and ears the rest of the way, so expect lots references to Brooks Koepka and glossy profiles on *anyone* who went to Michigan. I'm going underground for a few days. I'm going to download the new *Bill & Ted* movie. I'm going to stream *Cobra Kai*. I'll reemerge next week. Probably in the same pants.

— POSTSCRIPT —

Chris Mannix: In December of 2020, with the COVID-19 pandemic still raging and league officials sifting through options for the '20–21 season, commissioner Adam Silver, asked about the possibility of the NBA returning to the bubble, took it off the table. While safe, Silver said, the bubble "had a real impact on many of the participants in terms of their families, their mental wellness." Added Silver, "It's not easy being cooped up for months."

It's not. But, as the NBA quickly discovered, it's less disruptive. The NBA returned to home arenas just before Christmas. By mid-January, weekly COVID positives were registering in double digits. Some 21 games were postponed in January due to COVID-related issues. The Celtics lost almost a week of games from it. The Wizards lost nearly two. Even as the NBA plowed forward, key games were routinely compromised by rosters ravaged by new infections. In Utah, Jazz coach Quin Snyder coined a phrase: "Compete with COVID," giving the coronavirus the same weight as an opponent.

OCTOBER 3, 2005

Making It

Passionate players, delirious devotees and rising tv
ratings: as it approaches its 10th birthday, the WNBA
is showing signs that it can survive and thrive

BY KELLI ANDERSON

*Anderson covered much of the WNBA's first decade. Here, she provides a
snapshot of the league on its 10th anniversary, with profitability in sight.*

No one should doubt how important winning the 2005 WNBA title was to
Sacramento Monarchs third-year guard Kara Lawson. After commandeering
the game ball for the last 0.4 of a second of her team's title-clinching 62–59
Game 4 win over the Connecticut Sun on Sept. 20, Lawson, who had played
in two NCAA title games for Tennessee and lost both, pranced with it along
Arco Arena's press row in front of 15,000 screaming fans. Then, when she
returned home from celebrating late into the night with her teammates,
she slept with it. She declined to bring the ball to the parade that the city
of Sacramento had for the team the next day because, she says, "It would be
too easy to lose it."

The same can be said for a lot of things in the WNBA, be it a lead, a title
or the momentum that the league has started to build. After surviving
the WNBA's first best-of-five finals series, Sacramento became its third
new champion in three years, emphatically marking the end of the era of
minidynasties like Houston and L.A., which serially dominated the league
in its first six years. "Houston won it when the league was young," says

Sacramento's 35-year-old All-Star forward, Yolanda Griffith, who keeps adding elements to her game to ward off the influx of talented, athletic players after her job. "Now we're so competitive, you lose sleep thinking about what you need to do to win."

Better players and an anything-can-happen vibe are two reasons why more people seem to be catching on to what true believers have always known: WNBA games are great entertainment. The atmosphere is usually loud and buoyant, if not delirious—Arco's 15,000 faithful, many wearing purple or silver wigs, created a deafening din with their thundersticks for Game 4—and the play on the floor impassioned. Television viewers took note. According to the WNBA the finals had a 27% increase in viewership over last year even though the series featured none of the pro game's most marketed stars, such as Lisa Leslie, Sheryl Swoopes, Diana Taurasi, Lauren Jackson or Sue Bird. Viewership was up in the regular season, too, by 9%. (The league's average attendance dipped slightly, from 8,593 to 8,173.) The WNBA also continued its march toward profitability. New president Donna Orender, a former PGA executive who took over for Val Ackerman last April, expects to be in the black by 2007. "We're here to stay, and we're here to grow," says Orender, a former star in the old WBL, the women's hoops league that before the advent of the WNBA was the longest-lasting women's pro league in history. (It operated from 1978 to '81.) "We have a tremendous product."

Consider the Monarchs, who are all about team basketball, self-sacrifice, perseverance and hunger. After waiting nine seasons to make their first finals, Sacramento didn't waste their opportunity. Deploying a well-developed bench and a notoriously disruptive defense that is as exhausting to play as it is annoying to face—Connecticut coach Mike Thibault has likened it to a trip to the dentist—the Monarchs stifled the Sun's explosive offense, holding the Eastern Conference champs to 64 points and forcing them into nearly 15 turnovers a game.

Even in defeat, Connecticut, which made its second straight trip to the finals, scored a win for the league's evolving business model. The Sun, which is owned by the Mohegan Indian tribe and plays in the Mohegan Sun casino complex, is one of three WNBA teams not affiliated with an NBA team. (The others are the Washington Mystics and the Chicago Sky, who will start play in 2006 with former Hornets and Warriors coach Dave Cowens as coach.) "Everyone says [independent ownership] is the model of the future," says Orender. "I say the model is passionate, committed ownership, tied to passionate, committed fans, tied to passionate, committed sponsors."

Approximately 3,000 happy people showed up downtown at 5 p.m. on Sept. 21 to celebrate the Monarchs' victory, the city's first in a major professional sport. At a ceremony in which Monarchs owners, Gavin and Joe Maloof, were given a key to the city by Mayor Heather Fargo, the brothers gave coach John Whisenant, the 2005 Coach of the Year, the keys to a new Cadillac Escalade. They said they would have done the same for each of the players but couldn't because of the WNBA's limits on compensation. The players will get their bling in the form of a ring—"platinum," Griffith suggested into a TV camera for the Maloofs' benefit. But Lawson, for one, won't do anything as reckless as wear it. "I'll put it away for safekeeping," she says. In a young league, in a women's game, success is precious and must be handled with care.

JUNE 10, 1996

Hoop Dream? Dream On

The author had no shot at the NBA, but
the league indulged him—a little

BY JEFF PEARLMAN

During his seven years at Sports Illustrated, *Jeff Pearlman never wrote a boring story. He experimented with language and structure. He famously captured Braves pitcher John Rocker launching into a racist, sexist rant. And while Pearlman primarily covered baseball, he loved hoops. He played on the SI league team, deploying an exaggerated shot fake that predated D'Angelo Russell's. He profiled players, and later wrote a book on the 1980s Lakers,* Showtime, *that became an HBO series. In this, his first piece for SI, he wrote of doing something countless college kids had no doubt considered, late one night after a few beers, a classic "Why not?" premise played out in real life.*

The letter still exists, tucked away in a box with the keg taps and Greek memorabilia of my college days. It arrived on May 27, 1993. The night before I had gone out with my best friend to celebrate his 21st birthday. We were two college juniors confronting the reality of 9-to-5 futures. When I returned to my University of Delaware dorm in the morning, I found an envelope with the NBA insignia in the corner. "Maybe they want you, Pearl," my roommate joked. "The Sixers need help."

About two months earlier, at the urging of some fellow staffers at *The Review*, the college newspaper, I had informed the NBA of my intention to leave school early to pursue a pro basketball career. "I have nothing more

378

to gain from playing at the University of Delaware," I wrote to commissioner David Stern. "I believe I have what it takes to make it in your league."

I identified myself as a 6'2", 175-pound shooting guard. No lie, this. I said I had played at Delaware—and, indeed, I had, as a proud member of the Tools, two-time intramural runners-up. I also ran a year of track and cross-country.

Dear Mr. Pearlman:

As you know, the NBA requires any undergraduate basketball player who desires to become eligible for the NBA draft to forego, completely and irreversibly, his remaining collegiate basketball eligibility.

This will confirm that, by letter dated March 24, 1993, you notified the NBA of your decision to renounce your remaining collegiate basketball eligibility with the intention of inducing an NBA team to select you in the NBA draft scheduled to take place on June 30, 1993.

If the foregoing does not coincide with your understanding of the purpose and effect of your March 24, 1993 letter, please contact me in writing at the above address at least ten (10) days prior to the draft.

Sincerely, Joel M. Litvin General Counsel

Suddenly the blood rushed to my head. Not only was I going to duck out of school a year early, but I would also be making big bucks! Everyone knew Chris Webber would be the top selection, but after that, it was a toss-up. Shawn Bradley. Anfernee Hardaway. Jamal Mashburn. Jeff Pearlman. Two years earlier the Washington Bullets had used their first pick on LaBradford Smith. If they could spend $3.45 million for four years on a future CBA player, why not go cheap for an unknown like me?

A week later there was a message on my telephone answering machine from Rod Thorn, the NBA's senior vice president of basketball operations. "Call me," he said. "We need to talk." Thorn is a man with big concerns. Was he worried that I was too much for the league to handle? Like Dennis Rodman, I was an outlaw. I had a pierced ear; I shaved my head. Or perhaps Thorn wanted to warn me of the sharklike agents waiting for future stars to swim into their jaws.

"Hello, is Mr. Thorn in? This is Jeff Pearlman, from Delaware."

"Mr. Thorn isn't in," said the voice at NBA headquarters, "but our director of security would like to speak to you."

"Mr. Pearlman, this is Larry Richardson. We'd like to know if you're for real."

Ever notice how dreams have a way of imploding? There would be no Air Pearl Jams, no Wheaties box with my picture, no Letterman gigs. "Did you really play at Delaware?" Richardson asked.

Like all scam artists, I did what had to be done. "Yes," I said, thinking of track, the Tools, Frisbee outside my dorm.

"Nobody here has heard of you. Do you really think you're one of the best players in the world?"

"Not yet, but I can be. I think with proper development and a few other things"—a drastic reduction in basket height, the outbreak of a mysterious plague that renders all other NBA players clinically blind—"I can be something special."

"Have you thought about the CBA?"

"Yes." Many times—especially when I was 12 and got free cotton candy at an Albany Patroons game.

"How about Europe?"

"Who hasn't thought about that?"

Richardson, though skeptical, said that my name would be sent to all 27 NBA teams with the other early entries and that I should get an agent to help negotiate a possible contract. He wished me luck, adding, "You may need it."

The draft was June 30. I sat in front of the television for four hours. Late in the second round, the Indiana Pacers took a chance on a Delaware player. "This guy is a very smart pick," Hubie Brown commented on TNT. "I think Spencer Dunkley could be a surprise. A real sleeper."

For a moment—and this isn't just flowery prose to cap off a story—I closed my eyes and dreamed that Hubie had said something slightly different. "Jeff Pearlman could be a surprise," Brown was saying. "A real sleeper."

— POSTSCRIPT —

Jeff Pearlman: Although the Pacers wound up bypassing my services for those of Spencer Dunkley, the joke was on Indiana. While an overwhelmed, out-of-his-depth Dunkley reported to camp and was unceremoniously cut, I returned to school for my senior year and helped lead Edna's Edibles to the 1993–94 University of Delaware intramural championships game (where, ahem, we were crushed). Thus began a wayward 26-year basketball journey that likely ended last week when I showed up for an outdoor pickup game near my home and was greeted by the words, "I don't want the old dude on my team."

A Delaware player finally reached the NBA in 2020–21, when guard Nate Darling signed with the Charlotte Hornets. He has yet to thank me for paving the road...

APRIL 10, 2017

'You Can't Give In'

The death of Monty Williams's wife has taught the former
NBA coach two lessons: the beauty of forgiveness and the
need to move on, no matter how painful that might be

BY CHRIS BALLARD

*In two decades writing for SI I'm not sure I came across a human being as
universally respected as Monty Williams.*

The low point came last March. Or maybe it was April. Monty Williams isn't
sure. Time blurs.

For two weeks Micah and Elijah passed the stomach flu back and forth, as
five- and eight-year-olds do. They threw up on the carpet, in the bed, on the
bathroom floor. Everywhere but in the toilet and the trash can. Finally one
night, well after midnight, they combined for a particularly messy episode.
As his three teenage daughters slept in nearby rooms, Monty—who'd spent a
lifetime in basketball, first as a player and then as a coach, most recently as
an assistant for the Thunder—stumbled out of bed and herded the boys into
the shower, then into clean pajamas and back to sleep. Next he cleaned the
rug, scrubbed the tile floor and disinfected the toilet. He longed to go back
to bed but knew Ingrid never would have left the sheets to sit overnight in
the laundry room, clumped with all that sickness. Which meant he couldn't
either. He'd promised the kids nothing in their day-to-day lives would
change. If anyone's life was going to change, he'd said, it would be his.

So at 2:30 a.m., Monty trudged downstairs and out the back door into the cold Oklahoma night, where he hung the sheets over the fence. As he hosed them down he shivered and stared up at the sky, feeling lost. He was supposed to be sleeping next to his wife, or watching film, or on the road with his team.

Instead he was here, alone and overwhelmed. How in the world is this my life? he wondered.

The morning of Feb. 9, 2016, began like so many others. Monty awoke at 7:00, still groggy from the previous night's flight back from Phoenix, where the Thunder had beaten the Suns. Ingrid was already downstairs, conquering the morning. They'd been together 26 years, through five kids and eight cities, and he remained in awe of her. While many NBA wives contracted out the more mundane duties of parenting, Ingrid would not consider hiring a cook, a cleaner or a nanny. On game nights she bundled up the kids and brought them to the arena, but only after their homework was done. Then, at the end of the first quarter—sharp—they'd file out, because Dad may be an NBA coach, but nothing overrules bedtime.

On this morning Ingrid was out the door by 7:15, trailing five clean, neatly attired Williams children between the ages of five and 18, all of whom unfailingly addressed adults as Sir and Ma'am. She spent the rest of the day driving from this day care to that high school to this basketball practice to that doctor's appointment, in addition to making her regular stops at the church and the center for inner-city kids, where she volunteered.

So when Monty didn't hear from her that evening, as she returned from Faith's basketball game, it didn't strike him as strange. He was preoccupied anyway, at home preparing for the next Thunder opponent as Lael, his eldest, watched TV on the couch with Elijah.

Then, around 8:30, Lael's cellphone rang. It was Faith, calling her sister. Monty saw Lael's face fall.

This is what the police know: A little after 8 p.m., Ingrid was driving north on a four-lane road in downtown Oklahoma City in the family's SUV with Faith, then 15; Janna, 13; and Micah.

A sedan driven by a 52-year-old woman named Susannah Donaldson approached from the opposite direction. During the preceding hours, toxicology reports would show, Donaldson had taken a substantial amount of methamphetamine. Police also believe she may have been cradling a dog on her lap. By the time she approached the 1400 block of South Western Avenue, she was in the left lane, going more than twice the posted limit of 40. She swerved to avoid the car in front of her, sending her vehicle across the center line. Impact with Ingrid's SUV was head-on. Donaldson and the dog died at the scene. The Williams family was rushed to a hospital.

In the days that followed, local TV reporters stood by the road, grim-faced, noting the dark burn marks staining the asphalt, the spray of glass, debris lying on the side of the road. The newscasts showed photos of Ingrid and Monty together, her face frozen in that familiar smile, and her at a Thunder game. Interviews rolled with NBA coaches and players. They are difficult to watch, warned a reporter.

Monty clung to the fact that the children all survived, and without life-threatening injuries. For a while it seemed Ingrid might too, but the following afternoon she slipped away, at the age of 44.

Friends and family descended. Ingrid's parents drove through the night from their home in San Antonio. Clippers coach Doc Rivers, who'd played with and later coached Monty, canceled his vacation to fly in. Monty's pastors from Portland and New Orleans arrived. Gregg Popovich, his longtime mentor, reached out immediately. Charlie Ward, Billy Donovan, Sam Presti, Avery Johnson, Tim Duncan: They visited, called, texted. Anthony Davis and Ryan Anderson, players he was close to on the Pelicans, in town to play the Thunder, came to the house to sit with him. So many people sent flowers that Ayana Lawson, the Thunder's director of player services and appearances, finally contacted local florists and requested they send the gifts to one of Ingrid's charitable causes. Even so, Shaquille O'Neal managed to have a white orchid the size of a small tree delivered.

Monty couldn't process all of it. He knew people meant well, but he just wanted everyone to leave. Either that or to flee himself. Frustration and anger consumed him. The Lord could do anything. So why hadn't he moved that car? Why couldn't he have made Ingrid leave 10 minutes later, or a second earlier or a second later? Why did three of his kids have to suffer through that?

As a player, he used to hear Rivers tell him the same thing, over and over: "Get past mad." But that was basketball; this was different. Now a lot of people were mad. Rivers certainly was. He wanted to prosecute someone. Seek justice. The other woman was the one who stole a life. How could you not be mad?

Monty focused on just making it through the memorial service, on Feb. 18. Then maybe he'd take the kids and bolt to some state where no one knew him. Wyoming. South Dakota. Just hunker down and disappear.

First, though, he had to survive the week. He wished Ingrid were there. She'd know what to do. She always had.

They met in 1989, at a freshman mixer at Notre Dame. Monty was tall and skinny, with short hair and sleepy eyes. She was tiny, with dark hair, an electric smile and catlike brown eyes. Different, that's the word Monty comes back to. The girl drinking water instead of beer. The one not afraid to talk about her faith, right off the bat, but who never proselytized. To be on the outside who she was on the inside.

So what did Monty do? Like an idiot, he acted too cool, trying to play the role of the big-time hoops recruit. He even tried to set her up with a buddy instead. "Can you believe it?" he says now. "Dumb old Mont."

But he knows that's who he was then: dumb in so many ways. He'd grown up in Oxon Hill, Md., outside D.C., a neighborhood where, as Monty says, "you could either hustle and sell drugs or just not have." Often, the Williams family didn't have. His parents split when he was seven—Monty says he has "no real relationship" with his father. He was raised by his mom, Joyce, a strict, devout woman who worked as a data entry clerk. Sometimes she wondered about her only child; give the boy lunch money and, to her consternation, he'd often give it away to another kid who had none, then come home hungry. Still, he was well-liked and grew into a formidable small forward, fluid and athletic, averaging 30 points and 16 rebounds as a senior and leading Potomac High to the Class AAA state championship. He also graduated with a 4.0. "Never saw that boy take a bite of food without blessing it first," says his coach, Taft Hickman. "Even at McDonald's."

And yet Monty says he was putting on an act. Inside he was prideful, self-critical and prone to bouts of darkness. He spoke of faith but his was, he says, "nominal at best." When adults weren't around, he cussed up a storm. And when he prayed, what did he pray for? An NBA contract and fast cars.

For a young man who could go days without seeing a white face, who barely read a book a month, Notre Dame was a shock. Plato, genetics, philosophy, calculus? He just wanted to play ball. He failed his first test, then the next, then the one after that, after which he called his mom to say that maybe Notre Dame wasn't for him. Joyce wasn't having any of it. She hung up.

And if it weren't for Ingrid, he might not have lasted in South Bend. But a few weeks later he saw her on campus and did the smart thing: apologized. The next time they saw each other, at a party, they spent the whole night talking.

Next came joint study sessions. Though really, it was more like Ingrid teaching Monty how to study. Lay your books and notes in a semicircle, left to right. Prioritize. On breaks they took long walks around campus. She told him about her brother and her parents, blue-collar folks who worked in the automotive industry back in Michigan. She became his anchor in an unfamiliar world. Slowly, his test scores rose. It would be the first of many times she would save him.

His new teammates couldn't believe it. Who gets to college and immediately falls for a girl? What a rookie move. Monty didn't care. He knew this was someone worth holding on to. Ingrid wanted to take it slow. One afternoon he asked for a goodbye kiss after she walked him to practice and she pecked his cheek. A few days later she tippy-toed up to do it again and Monty pivoted.

The ensuing months were some of the best of Monty's life. Neither of them had much money, so date nights were at the dorm. Pizza from the basement snack bar, Corn Nuts and soda from the vending machines, then sit and talk. That summer he stayed on campus, while Ingrid went back home to Michigan. They wrote letters, hers arriving in envelopes covered in colorful drawings.

At the time he was just a smitten 18-year-old. It wasn't until later that Monty would realize that he hadn't just met the love of his life at Notre Dame, but he had discovered all the things he would become, through her. He'd joke about how his players got sick of him talking about Ingrid all the time, using her as an example, over and over. How when he met new players for the first time, he introduced her even if she wasn't there: "Hi, I'm Monty and you'll meet my wife, Ingrid." But who else was he going to talk about?

The day of the memorial happened also to be the NBA trade deadline. So Sam Presti, the Thunder general manager, told the rest of the league that he had his own deadline, at 1 p.m., an hour before the service. He ended up dealing two players that day, D.J. Augustin and Steve Novak. Both still showed up with their wives at Crossings Community Church, along with nearly a thousand others. Ingrid's life—their life—was there in the pews. Family and friends, of course, but also women from the ministry where she volunteered. Local police. A contingent from the Spurs, including Popovich, Duncan and David West, who flew in on the team plane even though they played later that night in L.A. Their opponents, the Clippers, were also represented, led by Rivers, his son Austin and Chris Paul. And on it went: Jeff Van Gundy and Brett Brown and P.J. Carlesimo and Kevin Durant, along with the whole Thunder organization. Members of the Pelicans—the team that fired Monty as coach less than a year earlier—folded themselves into a row. "Tallest funeral I've ever seen," says pastor Bil Gebhardt.

A little after 2:30, Monty walked to the dais, wearing a black suit and tie, his shaved head gleaming. At 6'8", and still fit at 44, he looked young enough to be a player. He placed a folded coach's card, containing some notes and scriptures, on the lectern. Then he took a deep breath and looked up.

Van Gundy wondered if it was a good idea for Monty to be speaking publicly. Monty had long been a pessimist, given to despair at times, and this could be too much. Others wondered if—even hoped that—he would condemn the other driver, as a coach calls out a player.

Monty had promised himself he wouldn't cry, the way he had the night before during the run-through with his family. "I'm thankful for all the people that showed up today," he began, his voice deep and more powerful than he expected. "It's a pretty tough time, not just for me but for all of you as well. I'm mindful of that."

He looked around the room but his only audience was his five children. He needed to show the way. "This is hard for my family, but this will work out," he continued. "And my wife would punch me if I were to sit up here and whine about what's going on. That doesn't take away the pain. But it will work out because God causes all things to work out. You just can't quit." He paused, looked around. "You can't give in."

You can't give in. How many times had she told him that? Like on that day in the doctor's office during his sophomore year, only a few weeks after Hickman had called to tell Monty that he was hearing he might be a first-round pick—not eventually, but next year. Now, Monty listened to a doctor tell him he had hypertrophic cardiomyopathy. A thickening of his left ventricle. Irregular heartbeat. Potentially fatal. All Monty heard was *No more basketball.* Not now, not next year, not ever.

Anger and depression consumed him. He pulled away from his teammates, his coaches, even Joyce. He got in fights. Punched through walls. He thought about transferring or dropping out, and at one point he even entertained the thought of taking his own life. For the next two years he became, as his mom says now, "not the nicest person" and "a different child."

Throughout, Ingrid was the one person who calmed him, "the one person I didn't want to hurt, no matter what." To leave school, or worse, would mean leaving her, and he couldn't bear that. If anything, they spent more time together: walking the campus, past the lake, stopping to pray at the Notre Dame Grotto. "The Lord will heal your heart," she told him, and something about the way she said it—so confident—made him believe her. So he poured himself into prayer, if for desperate, selfish reasons.

Ingrid's faith was different, though. Never convenient, never for show. Every week she disappeared for hours at a time in the afternoon. Finally, he asked where. So she brought him along and Monty watched, confused, as Ingrid spent two hours at a nursing home with a woman named Helen, one he was pretty sure was suffering from Alzheimer's. Ingrid brushed Helen's hair, talked with her, bathed her. As an athlete, Monty had been taught to perform charitable acts for the camera. But here was Ingrid, a young black woman, caring for an old white one, not for the cameras or a pat on the back. When he asked Ingrid why she did it, she looked at him funny. Wasn't this what Christ taught us to do? Monty was floored. "It was so real, and raw," he says.

For a while he accompanied her. Began to find his faith becoming more authentic. And then, in 1992, a Notre Dame trainer told him about an experimental test to determine if he could play with HCM. So he flew to the National Institutes of Health in Bethesda, Md. Five days of poking and prodding led to a final, frightening test. *We're going to stop your heart on purpose,* the doctors told him. *Trigger an arrhythmic episode. If it doesn't go well, it could kill you. You and your mom need to sign this waiver.*

What choice did Monty have? In his mind, there was no Plan B. For two years he'd gone against doctor's orders, working out furiously and playing in pickup games. In his mind it was basketball or nothing. Besides, he wasn't afraid of death. Or maybe, he'd later realize, he just didn't understand it yet.

Five doctors stood around the bed, just in case. Hours passed. Monty drifted in and out of consciousness. When he awoke, a doctor warned him not to sit up, or a vein could burst. Then he said there was something Monty should know. He was O.K. Not just O.K., but great. He could play ball again.

Monty sobbed. He had his life back. And can you blame him if his pride returned with it? He averaged 22.4 points and 8.2 boards for the Irish in 1993–94. After the Knicks picked him 24th, he spent his money on cars and lived like the big star he always thought he'd be.

But Ingrid? She never changed, not really. She told him the cars were a waste of money; "You can only drive one at a time," she'd say. They'd gotten married after his rookie season then moved city to city—five teams in nine years as a player. When he got the head job in New Orleans, she was eight months pregnant with Micah and yet she seamlessly integrated into another community. Players like Anthony Davis later described her as a "second mother." Along with Monty, she spoke to inmates, distributing copies of *Look Again 52*, the Bible study book they'd written together. They worked at a shelter for abused kids, donated shoes and equipment to the poor. In the off-season they went to South Africa with Basketball Without Borders.

Monty stresses that Ingrid was by no means perfect. She could be stubborn and headstrong. She could cut you down with one look. She was a loud talker, Monty always reminding her that "Hey honey, I'm sitting right next to you," to which she'd fume, because he was supposed to be listening to the message, not the delivery. And good luck changing her mind once she was set on an opinion. But all Monty knows is that when people have praised him for things in his life, it's usually Ingrid who was his ballast. Like in 2013, when Gia Allemand, the girlfriend of Ryan Anderson, committed suicide, and Ryan was the first one to find her, at her apartment. Hysterical, he called Gia's mom, then the police and then, as Ryan says, "the one person I knew in New Orleans that would be there for me no matter what." Monty arrived to find Ryan on the floor, a mixture of sweat and tears. The coach dropped to his knees, unsure what to do, and began hugging Ryan, rocking slightly.

When Monty finally got him into his truck, he thought about how he couldn't mess this up—how these are the tests that really matter. Back home, Ingrid had already taken control. She'd moved the kids upstairs and put them to bed, with instructions not to come downstairs for anything. After her own brother's unexpected suicide in 2003, she knew that the only thing to do was just be there for Ryan. So she and Monty sat with him in the family room, praying. When it got late and Monty tried to come to bed, she redirected him: No, you're sleeping downstairs, right next to Ryan. And so he did, on a mattress next to the couch. When Ryan wanted to talk, they talked. When it was quiet, it was quiet. Monty followed Ingrid's advice: Just listen.

Just listen. That Monty could do. It's what he'd done as a Trail Blazers assistant, after Nate McMillan hired him in 2005. Monty's was the door that was always open at the team hotel. He was the coach who had players over for dinner. The guy sharing his own mistakes. Because that's how a real connection grows.

To ask people around the league about Monty is to have your calls returned immediately, to have people cry on the phone, to hear a string of testimonials. Durant, who worked with Monty for a season in OKC, says, "He'll hate that I say this, but he's the best man that I know. And that's no slight to my dad, my godfather, my uncle or any coaches that I've had." For Durant, lots of men have tried to fill the role of mentor. Most had lots of advice; few wanted to listen. Fewer still shared the hiccups in their own life. "Monty listens, allows you to vent," Durant says, "but then he'll bring you back in and keep it real with you."

Which is why when Durant needed advice last summer, while trying to decide whether to sign with the Warriors, he called Williams. A man most recently employed by the team he was considering leaving. (Williams didn't try to sway him: "The only way I could help was to say, 'Look, don't let anybody else make this decision for you. Your family or your boys or your shoe company. It's your decision.'")

Says Durant, "I was on the phone with him the second I made the decision, right after, right before. A lot of people keep their mind in this basketball bubble and he looked at the whole life. He was there for me as a friend first."

All those people who flew out for the service? Maybe you're starting to understand why. They'd come to support Monty and to honor Ingrid's life. Still, most had no idea what to expect when he spoke.

Watching in the audience, Presti tried to keep it together. He had been the first to receive a call on the night of the accident, awoken at 2 AM by the hospital pastor. Presti had first met Monty in 2004, when they were both with San Antonio. Both men had moved on but, as with so many, remained part of the Spurs family. So Presti had thrown on some clothes and hurried to the hospital. In the hours to come, he'd sit with Monty all night, rubbing his back so hard that, "it was like I was trying to start a fire." Throughout, Presti thought about everyone he now represented and how he felt, "a huge amount of responsibility to make sure I was handling this the way Pop would handle it. This was on my watch, and I had to live up to the standard that Pop expects of us all. I had to fulfill an obligation that's much greater than basketball." In Monty's case, his indoctrination to the Spurs had come in 1996, when San Antonio traded for him, hoping for scoring. ("Turns out he couldn't shoot a lick," says Popovich.) He and Pop didn't get along at first. Monty chafed at Pop's tirades, thought he deserved more playing time, more touches. Pop saw him as a role player. Pop also noticed a darkness to the young man. "He was kind of a Debbie Downer, always expecting the worst to happen," Popovich recalls.

Still, Monty responded to the Spurs' culture. Bible study with David Robinson and Avery Johnson. Post-game parties at Sean Elliott's house. In particular he bonded with Duncan, the player he would come to hold up as the standard as a teammate and a leader. A man who became so close with the Williams family that he coined a nickname for Ingrid on account of how she juggled the kids and everything else, and always put Monty in his place: Legend.

Then, before the 1998 season, the Spurs let Monty go. He ended up sitting on his couch in June, crying as he watched San Antonio celebrate the first of five titles, filled with regret. In the years that followed, Monty and Popovich stayed in touch. Despite what Monty may have thought, Pop always liked the young man, thought he was intelligent and a hard worker. "And we're always looking for those kind of guys," says Popovich, "because you can't teach intelligence and it's pretty tough to get someone to have a work ethic if they don't have already have one." So when Monty called him in 2004, despondent after bad knees had forced him to stop playing, Pop encouraged Monty to come hang out around the team. See if you like it. Soon enough, Pop slapped a label on him: coaching intern. Meanwhile Pop, a sucker for projects, pushed Monty to take chances, try new stuff. He introduced him to different foods, talked to him about politics and reveled in cursing around Monty, who never cusses. ("That's his way of saying I love you," Monty explains.)

Monty learned what so many others already had. Once you joined the Spurs you were in for life, as long as you operated by certain principles. It was never about you. Pay it forward. Basketball is important, but not as important as family and relationships. In June 2005 the Spurs won their third title, the one that had eluded Monty as a player. As the confetti fell, he stood behind the bench, part of the team but still feeling like an outsider, when he felt someone tackle him from the side. He turned to see a grinning Pop. "You got one," Popovich shouted. "You missed out before, but now you got one."

Funny then, that Monty's most important game as a head coach, on the last day of the 2014–15 season, was a win over Pop's Spurs that put the Pelicans in the playoffs. Afterward, as players celebrated and Ingrid brought the kids onto the court, Pop and Monty embraced at midcourt. It felt like a crowning moment.

It'd be easy to see it as karma of sorts: Good things happen to good people, right? But in this case, not long after the Pelicans lost to the title-bound Warriors in the first round, Monty was fired. That same day, a TV reporter knocked on Monty's front door. Monty came out in a T-shirt and spoke for four minutes. He said a lot, thanking the city for its support and the ownership for the opportunity, but one line stood out. "Life's not fair," Monty said. "Don't expect it to be."

And now here was Monty, a guy who always expected the worst, confronted with about the worst situation imaginable. Yet he stood up on stage, projecting calm as he built to what he termed, "the most important thing we need to understand." That's what drew the millions who would later watch video of the speech. What led to all those packages and letters, the ones that continued for half a year, flooding the Thunder offices. What led Popovich to decide that he needed to show the eulogy, in its entirety, to his players.

"Everybody's praying for me and my family, which is right," Monty said, left hand jammed in his pocket like an anchor. "But let us not forget that there were two people in this situation. And that family needs prayer as well." He paused. "That family didn't wake up wanting to hurt my wife.

"Life is hard. It is very hard. And that was tough, but we hold no ill will toward the Donaldson family, and we"—he made a circling motion with his right hand, indicating the whole room—"as a group, brothers united in unity, should be praying for that family because they grieve as well. So let's not lose sight of what's important."

Not long after, he wrapped up with a simple message: "And when we walk away from this place today, let's celebrate because my wife is where we all need to be. And I'm envious of that. But I've got five crumb-snatchers that I need to deal with."

Monty paused as some in the crowd chuckled. "I love you guys for taking time out of your day to celebrate my wife. We didn't lose her. When you lose something, you can't find it. I know exactly where my wife is."

As he left the stage, Monty didn't notice the reaction in the room, or if he did, he doesn't remember it. But those who were there describe a stunned silence. "He was saying to us what we should have been saying to him," says RC Buford, the San Antonio GM. David West turned contemplative. "We always talk about physical strength, but it's nothing compared to mental and emotional strength," West says. "You realize your own deficiencies, because I don't have that type of courage or strength or fortitude to stand as courageously as he did in that moment." Later, on the plane ride home, Popovich told West and Duncan that it would be "years before we understand the totality of that moment." Says Popovich now, "I was in awe. I could not believe that a human being could muster the control and command of his feelings and at the same time be as loving and magnanimous."

The theme at the heart of the speech—forgiveness—was simple, and not unique. Still, the effect was profound. Maybe it was Monty's delivery; it felt sincere. Maybe it's because, right or wrong, we don't always expect such empathy from professional athletes. Maybe it was that, for a message steeped in faith, it never felt preachy. In the weeks that followed, video of the memorial spread, and the reaction was immediate. OKC staffers made pins embossed with w7—that's what people always called the Williams family. Donations poured in to Faithworks, the nonprofit Ingrid believed in so much, from strangers, from a half dozen teams, from players Monty had never met.

Meanwhile, concerned friends offered help. All those people he and Ingrid had poured into over the years? "Now we all wanted to pour back into him," says Durant. His phone beeped constantly, only Monty didn't want any advice or help. On the exterior, he may have appeared strong, and in control. Inside, he was falling apart. He just wanted everyone to leave.

Everyone who loses a loved one processes grief differently. Some focus on coping mechanisms. Disbelief. Denial. Others become disorganized, acting out of character and making rash decisions. Still others try to "intellectualize" the loss, analyzing the situation leading to a loved one's death in intricate detail. To Monty, the world lost its grays; everything was either pitch black or blinding white. One moment he was fine; the next, a tiny thing would set him off. His appetite disappeared and sleep became impossible on many nights. He wanted to lash out, even feared that he'd hurt others. So he did what he'd always done and closed up, turning away from the world to only his family. After all, he and Ingrid had never needed help before. He didn't need it now.

Friends worried.

"I got this," he told Popovich.

"No, you don't have this," Pop answered. "You're going to have days you're pissed off and want to punch a wall, and you have to let it go. And other days when you'll be more together and in both situations you're going to need people, and friends and mentors, and it's O.K., it's O.K., you're not a f——— island."

Still, he tried to go it alone. He woke at 5:30 for Bible study, then he got the kids up and was out of the house by 7:30. He wandered the aisles of the grocery store, in search of the darn bread. Fought with the laundry. At 11 he picked up Micah from nursery school, and then he was with the kids all afternoon, driving around Edmond, Okla.–to basketball, track, school, plays, doctors. He could handle breakfast and lunch, but many nights, dinner was Chick-fil-A. By the end of the day, he was so exhausted he'd fall asleep by 9:30.

Meanwhile, people kept saying he needed to take time for himself. It made him mad sometimes. Time? He didn't have time. And what did that even mean, anyway? What was he going to do, go get a massage?

The nights were the worst, once the kids were in bed but before sleep took hold. That's when the darker thoughts emerged. Popovich remembers talking to him in such moments, and how Monty sounded "like a wounded animal."

Many days Monty fought the urge to check out. And he might have if it weren't for Ingrid's voice in his head. Just take care of the kids. Just take care of the kids.

How in the world is this my life?

The pain and confusion never goes away, this is what Monty's learned. But it does recede. It's now January of 2017, and he ticks off the milestones. The first birthday without Ingrid, the first Thanksgiving, the first graduation. All that's left now is the anniversary of the crash itself.

It's a warm afternoon and he's driving back from practice in San Antonio, where he moved the family in June, to get away from the memories in Oklahoma City and to be closer to Ingrid's parents. He is back with the Spurs for the third time, now as executive VP of operations—"basically a job I made up for Monty," says Pop. He doesn't travel, so he can be home at night. After practices he can often be seen playing one-on-one with Duncan, whose friendship has been instrumental in helping Monty regain some sense of normalcy. Eventually, Pop just gave the two of them their own lockers in the coaches' room, next to each other.

The final month in Oklahoma City wasn't easy. He got through it on his faith and the generosity of others. It was Lawson, coming over to do the stuff that bewildered him, taking the girls shopping for bras. It was Presti and coach Billy Donovan, checking on him, and Pop calling, and Ingrid's parents, and Pastor Bil, reminding him that, "grief is the price of love." It was Tonja Ward, an old friend, pushing him until he hired a cook, to ease his burden.

Teams had reached out about coaching vacancies, and the kids had pushed him to get back into it, thinking it would make their dad happy. But it was too soon.

In August he'd lived a dream, serving as an assistant for the U.S. Olympic team. Upon returning from Rio, he developed something resembling a rhythm. Exercise to work out his anger. Focus on being a dad. Work toward being ready to coach again. Be O.K. delegating: to a cook, a cleaner, his in-laws.

To visit his home now is to enter a whirl of activity. There are the two boys, running outside to shoot hoops in the driveway, Monty stopping Micah—"Put some socks and shoes on, dude!"—and then turning to Elijah. "What do I always tell you?" Monty asks.

"Do. Not. Dominate him," Elijah responds. Monty nods, makes him repeat it again.

In the kitchen Faith makes herself a snack. Ingrid's mom, Veda, stops by—Monty says she has become his best friend over the last year. She brims with life, just like Ingrid, laughing and hugging and ribbing Monty because, after all these years of giving her grief, suddenly he's drinking coffee. (The Spurs' sports science people told him it was good for him.) Monty lets out the family's dog, a border collie named TZ.

To walk the halls is to see memories everywhere. Just off the entrance, a large framed picture of Monty with a grinning Popovich in the back of a limo while wine-tasting in Napa with friends, another of Pop's attempts to force Monty to liven up a bit ("You're not gonna order iced tea, you're gonna sit at dinner and try the damn wine and sit and talk with us"). Photos of the family line the walls. All seven of them, most in white, at a picnic in Oklahoma City. Monty and the kids, in the Turks and Caicos, their first vacation after Ingrid's death. He leads the way to his study. A tiny blue pair of Micah's shoes rests next to other mementos: nerf rims Elijah has broken, all-district plaques from the girls, Ziploc bags containing first lost teeth. A collection of framed photos of Ingrid occupies one corner. Next to it is his wedding ring. For a while he wore it, then put it on a chain around his neck. But that began to feel wrong. He's 44 with five kids. He has half his life ahead of him. He knows he won't stay single forever. She'd be upset if he did.

He puts on a good face, but talking about what happened, as he does over the course of the next three days, often pausing for minutes at a time, remains difficult. "I just couldn't understand it," he says. "And never will. But my faith in God never wavered. Just, sometimes your faith and your feelings don't line up."

He tries to put the grief in its place, as Pop always advises him to do. Compartmentalize. Still, he sometimes texts her, even though he knows she won't respond. Other times, he looks up, thinking she'll walk around a corner. "I can't say that I feel her presence. I just see so much of her in the kids and so many things remind me of her," Monty says. Sometimes he goes outside and talks to her. "And I don't even know what that's about. I just—I'm not grieving for her, you know. She's in heaven, she's with the Lord, she's like, balling right now. You grieve because you don't have what you had."

Moving forward, for Monty, means returning to the bench. He thinks he's ready, that it will center him. Indeed, he'll start getting more calls. In March, after making it through the first anniversary of her death with the help of friends, he'll turn down the top job at Illinois, wishing to focus on the NBA. People around the league will say it's a matter of time—perhaps by the time you read this story—until he's offered a head coaching job.

It will be weird, coaching without her. She was his sounding board, "his battery pack," as West puts it. But that's the reality of loss. You never fill certain voids.

Besides, he's still learning from her, even now. For example, Monty hates candy. Has ever since he suffered toothaches as a kid. So he made a rule: no candy in the house. Still, every once in a while, he'd be cleaning and find a bag of Snickers or M&Ms. "What's this?" he'd ask the kids. They'd hem and haw and finally one of the girls would answer. "Mom lets us have these when you're gone."

When he'd confront Ingrid, she'd stand her ground, as she always did. "Back off," she'd say. "They need to live."

Now if you go into the kitchen and open the cabinet, you'll find the stash. Lollipops and chocolate. It's a small thing, but it's something. They need to live. So he made certain Lael—the one everyone says is so much like Ingrid and who'd been a rock the week of the funeral, making medical decisions, caring for her sisters, and helping plan the service—went off to college at Wheaton, rather than stay home. And he guards against becoming too protective. By no means does he have it figured out, but he's trying.

That's why Monty hates when people call him a role model. He's just a guy who's been tested, again and again. A guy trying to make it through, like all of us.

So maybe it's best to focus on Monty in the real, human moments, like this one. It's early evening and the winter sun is going down. The boys are getting a little crazy—"Dude, calm down," he yells. He still needs to check on homework, and pick up the bombs that the dog left out in the yard, and figure out what to do about the pool, which is on the fritz. He turns to a visitor, watching, and apologizes. "Sorry, man," he says. "I need to go deal with all this."

And so he does.

— POSTSCRIPT —

In reporting this story, I worked closely with Williams, and the Spurs. Popovich has a great affection of Monty, and was protective of him. It took months of discussions before the team signed on.

As for Williams, he hoped the story might help others dealing with grief. Secondarily, he hoped that, by reliving the experience in detail, he'd have something to point to when asked about it in the future. It's a story he only wanted to tell once.

It took two years but, in May of 2019, Williams got another shot as head coach, with the Suns. In 2021, he led them to the NBA Finals. A year later, after leading Phoenix to the best record in the league, Williams was named Coach of the Year.

POWER

APRIL 29, 2013

Pop Art

How Gregg Popovich—a foodie, former spy (maybe), Russian literature lover, French New Wave cinephile, wine enthusiast, curmudgeon, father figure, defensive guru turned offensive mastermind and the longest-tenured coach in American professional sports—created a masterpiece in San Antonio

BY JACK McCALLUM

Picture a parking lot in a small Texas town in the early 1990s, heat curling up from the blacktop like incense from an altar, a few dozen fans watching a crew-cut assistant coach named Gregg Popovich patiently explain the rudiments of basketball. Accompanying Popovich on this annual San Antonio Spurs Caravan are a future star, Sean Elliott; a strangely coiffed center, Dwayne Schintzius; and the Spurs' mascot, called, for obvious reasons, the Coyote.

It is difficult to reconcile that man with the Popovich we know now: impatient, vibrating with energy, eager to get on with it, the Popovich whose Spurs began their 16th straight postseason appearance on Sunday with a 91–79 win over the Lakers. The late, great Schintzius's mullet alone might have prompted Popovich to start kicking cones and get in the faces of potential ticket buyers—to "go Serbian," as Popovich himself describes the cyclone of anger that sometimes engulfs him. *Do you hear what I'm telling you about the rocker step? Do you really want to be a season-ticket holder?*

But that was a different era, before the Spurs were four-time champions, before they put up 14 straight 50-win seasons (which would be 16 if not for the labor strife of 1998–99), before they routinely sold out the 18,581-seat

AT&T Center, before Popovich was a two-time Coach of the Year, before he was elevated to team president as well as coach ("The buck stops with him," says general manager R.C. Buford) and before *Pop* joined *Magic* and *Larry* as one-named NBA entities.

Popovich is the sometimes snarling face of that rare Model Franchise, known for winning, consistency, brand loyalty and a penchant for keeping controversy (hell, keeping almost everything) in-house. Pop has sent forth many of his loyal flock to positions of prominence around the NBA—having been part of the Larry Brown coaching tree, Popovich now has a tree of his own—and most continue to abide at least partly by this code of omertá.

Certainly that is true of Sam Presti, who began as an intern with San Antonio and is now general manager of the Thunder, the team that knocked off the Spurs in last year's conference finals and finished two games ahead of them in the West this season. During an interview about his mentor, Presti jumped off and on the record like a guy adjusting the temperature of the shower, not because he was saying anything remotely controversial but because he didn't want Pop to think he was talking out of turn by dispensing fulsome compliments. Presti mentioned that the coach had bought a book for him recently, but after some deliberation he decided he couldn't divulge the title. "In some way," says Presti, sheepish, "I guess I'm still wearing those Spurs stripes."

While affection for this master of mystery is hardly universal, there is a grudging respect in most quarters—including that quarter at 51st Street and Fifth Avenue in New York City. Popovich and NBA commissioner David Stern have had a couple of well-publicized battles over the coach's decision to rest key players on road trips, the last one (after Pop sent Tim Duncan, Manu Ginóbili and Tony Parker home from a nationally televised TV game in Miami on Nov. 29) resulting in a $250,000 fine to the franchise. "I have always enjoyed my personal interactions with Pop," says Stern. "He brings an extraordinary worldview to the NBA."

Parsing Stern (which, admittedly, can be treacherous), one sees intent in his choice of "worldview." True, a certain Belichickian atmosphere hangs over the Republic of Pop, where the Spurs consider league rules governing media access to be the most casual of suggestions and where the statement "Tim Duncan will not be available today" circulates on an endless loop. But one also discovers a certain charm within the Republic of Pop, stemming largely from the antic disposition of its ruler. "I offer this with hesitation," says Jeff McDonald, who has been on the Spurs beat for the *San Antonio Express-News* for six years, "but when you cover Pop, there's a kind of Stockholm syndrome. You start to feel affection for your captor."

Popovich is described by all who know him well as smart, funny, compassionate and even warm. Indeed, upon revisiting with the man after a yearslong absence, it was disconcerting to be given a sincere bro-hug even as you knew he wished you were climbing on the first plane out of San Antonio International. "If it doesn't fit the mission," says Hall of Fame center David Robinson, who joined the Spurs in 1989, when Popovich was one of Brown's assistants, "Pop just doesn't care about it."

One thing that almost never fits the mission is talking to sideline reporters during games, an NBA-mandated task for head coaches. That difficult assignment has fallen most memorably on TNT's fascinatingly coutured Craig Sager, whose give-and-take with Pop has produced much outstanding theater. "I try to ask questions that he can't answer *yes* or *no*," says Sager, "but that usually doesn't work out. 'What are your impressions of the first quarter?' I might ask, and Pop says, 'None.' Or I'll ask, 'How come you're getting outrebounded?' and he'll say, 'What do want me to do? Get rid of players during the game? Send them to the D-League?'"

On one occasion, Sager saw Pop before the game looking even more out-of-sorts than usual.

"You look like your dog died," Sager said, to which Pop responded: "Actually, that's exactly what happened." The reporter whipped out his notebook to get details, but an alarmed Popovich stopped him. "You mention that on the air," he said, "and I'll wake up tomorrow morning with a thousand dogs on my front step."

Still, Sager, like most people in the press, feels some level of affection for him: "People will ask me, 'Isn't Gregg Popovich a jerk?' and I say, 'Actually, he's one of the greatest in any sport.'" Pop knows just how far to push the jerk thing; even as he's jawing at Sager, he's liable to reach over and wipe sweat onto Sager's pocket handkerchief, which has happened on at least one occasion.

All that makes San Antonio's only major sports franchise a "culture"– Pop Culture, if you will. "Whenever I talk to players on other teams about certain situations," says Spurs guard Ginóbili, "what I end up hearing is, 'Yeah, but you're on the Spurs.' They mean, 'Okay, you'll figure it out and go on winning.'"

For 16 years now, keeping Duncan happy and healthy has been at the top of Pop's mission list. Pop and Tim: tough and steadfast, different sides of the same coin, the Auerbach and Russell of the modern NBA. Pop is one of the few subjects the Big Fundamental will talk about without looking like someone is torturing him with thumbscrews. "Pop has always taken care of me, whether I knew it or not," says Duncan. "Pop has been a mentor for me, a father figure. I know it's incredibly rare. And I know I'm lucky to have it."

Yes, Popovich has come a long way: from the man Elliott thought was "a typical jarhead," when he got a load of Pop's crew cut and his hard-charging ways on those hot afternoons in towns like Eagle Pass and Del Rio, to someone Elliott now describes as "kind of a Renaissance man," his tutor on matters both cinematic and oenophilic. Back in the Caravan days, Pop and Elliott were San Antonio's version of Siskel and Ebert, debating movies on a local TV channel. While Pop recommended titles such as François Truffaut's *400 Blows*—"He liked anything that was obscure, had subtitles and nothing happened," says Elliott—the player tended to go Schwarzeneggerian. "If it had Arnold shooting a gun or somebody crashing a car," says Pop, "Sean was sure to give it an A." But as the years have rolled on, Elliott finds himself gravitating to independent films. "Pop's influence," he says, shrugging his shoulders.

Pop's knowledge of wine is the best-known personal fact about him: his part ownership of the Oregon-based A to Z Wineworks, his 3,000-bottle home wine cellar, the staggering sums he has spent on wines, and the disquisitions on Brunellos and Malvasias that have fallen on deaf ears when he takes his staff out to dinner on the road, an inviolate ritual. "I used to like all these Australians and California Cabs," says Elliott, "and now I'm Old World. That's Pop again."

His sophistication goes well beyond the grape. Popovich talks to Serbian players in their native language; reads the Russian writers Dostoyevsky, Turgenev and Lermontov (in English); has begun collecting rare first editions; counts among his friends one of the top scholars of Swedish history and politics in the U.S.; and makes his restaurant choices by, as he puts it, "triangulating" information in *Travel + Leisure, Condé Nast Traveler, Decanter* and Andrew Harper's *Hideaway Report*. Popovich also owns up to being a political liberal, which gives an interesting edge to conversations with his old buddies on the Air Force Academy endowment committee and with Spurs owner Peter Holt, a GOP contributor.

Oh, yes. Pop was also Larry Brown's best man.

One does not interview Popovich so much as scrounge for scraps, rather like a pigeon at a park bench. "It's an Academy thing," said Pop, a 1970 graduate of Air Force, declaring that he would not talk about himself. After some negotiation, he agreed to a short session of fact-checking, which morphed into a sit-down with the tape recorder running. "I know what you're doing," he said. "I'm a coach, so I know what it means to bull--." He made it clear: He would not be bamboozled into talking.

Popovich grew up in Sunnyside, a mixed-race neighborhood of East Chicago, Ind., not far from Gary: "a white family here, a Puerto Rican family there, a Polish or Czech family over there," he says. He was a tough, raw-boned forward at Merrillville High but drew no major-college interest. "Valdosta State and Wabash College wanted me," says Pop, "and nobody else did."

Convinced that he could play at least mid-major ball, he got his Air Force Academy appointment and earned a spot on the team. He was still on the junior varsity as a sophomore, and it rankled. He was ultracompetitive, hardheaded and, by his own admission, "a wiseass." Nothing has changed in that respect. He got booted out of practice several times by coach Hank Egan, but it never altered his opinion that he should be a varsity starter. "I kicked the varsity's ass every time we played them," says Pop. "But when I complained to Hank that I should be playing up, he always had the same response: 'Shut up and play.'"

By his senior year he was team captain and a scholar-athlete, still the wiseass but also a determined cadet who loaded up with tough courses, such as advanced calculus, analytical geometry, and engineering—astronomical, electrical and mechanical.

He earned a degree in Soviet studies—which made sense for a kid of Eastern European descent—triggering the most intriguing aspect of the Popovich legend: that he was once a spy. He did have intelligence training, he did apply for a top-secret government job in Moscow (the paperwork was delayed, and he didn't get it) and he did briefly serve as an intelligence officer in eastern Turkey, on the borders of Iran and Syria. He has always either laughed off or refused to discuss this mysterious part of his past, but he did come clean (we must assume) in the NBA-sanctioned *History of the San Antonio Spurs*. "People had me carrying guns like I was some kind of spy," Popovich told Texas writer Jan Hubbard. "The more I would deny it, the more they'd roll their eyes and say, 'Yeah, sure. Come on.' I was stationed on the border, but it wasn't like I was James Bond."

From a lifetime perspective, a more valuable Air Force posting for Popovich was at Sunnyvale (officially, Moffett Federal Airfield), once a Naval air station in Northern California. "Napa Valley was just exploding as a center for wine and food," says Pop. "Myself and a buddy could head up there, hit the wineries, pretty cheap, no crowds. That's where I started to learn about wine, and from wine you learn about food."

But Pop has always loved defense more than decanting. He spent part of his active-duty time captaining the U.S. Armed Forces basketball team that won the AAU championship in 1972, and he was an early cut on that year's Olympic team. Pop also tried out for the Nuggets but was axed by Larry Brown, the head coach at the time. As we shall see, Pop didn't take it personally.

After active duty Pop returned to the Academy as Egan's assistant in 1973, picked up a master's degree in physical education and sports sciences from the University of Denver and served as a hoops emissary between good buddies Egan and Brown. In 1979 he took the head job at Pomona-Pitzer, two small California schools known for academics that share an athletic department.

Pop, who was also an associate professor at Pomona, reveled in the college atmosphere. He even moved his family—his wife, Erin, and their two kids—into a dorm for a year. "I was in awe of the brilliance on that campus," says Popovich, who around campus was called Poppo as much as Pop. He taught phys-ed classes but gravitated to the mainstream of college life by serving on committees. "I chaired the committee that investigated fraternities," he says. "I was scared s--less going in, but the dean wanted someone from athletics who wouldn't pussyfoot around. We made a lot of changes with the way frats were operating. I was a member of the women's commission, too. We looked into issues of gender equality, discrimination against gays, abuses in athletics. Those kinds of things are what I really enjoyed."

Popovich is as competitive as any coach in the NBA, but there are grace notes of humility in the man, the kind that stem from, say, going 2–22 in his first season at Pomona and losing to Caltech, the program that would later gain national attention by dropping 310 straight conference games. Indeed, a couple of days after Caltech ended that streak with a 46–45 win over Occidental in February 2011, coach Oliver Eslinger entered his office to find a crate of Pop's Rock & Hammer wine and a note that read, "Congratulations to you and the players for showing the true spirit of sport you display. I am thrilled for you, and as a former loser to Caltech, I wish you more wins."

It might be a leap to say (as do many around Pop) that he would be just as happy coaching in Division III—his approximately $6 million salary buys a lot of high-end vino—but it's obvious that his time at Pomona has stuck with him. It partly explains why in training camp Pop handed his players DVDs of a 2012 presidential debate or why he discusses Argentine politics and political conspiracies with Ginóbili, somewhat the conspiracy theorist. "It is not sufficient to say merely that Gregg is smart," says his friend Steven Koblik, the former president of Reed College in Portland, author of such basketball staples as *Om Vi Teg* (a book about Sweden's response to the Holocaust that translates as *If We Remain Silent*) and Pop's academic adviser at Pomona. "He is also intellectually curious. Now, you combine that with basketball smarts and street smarts and add someone who's a very good judge of people, and that makes for a very unusual person."

Koblik, who is now the president of the Huntington Library in San Marino, Calif., one of the nation's largest research and rare-book libraries, visits Popovich a couple of times per season, and on his last trip he took Pop one of the four volumes of Robert Caro's biography of Lyndon Johnson. "He devoured it," said Koblik. "One of my roles in life is to make sure I read something that Pop will like and give it to him."

In his eighth year at Pomona, 1986–87, Pop took the sabbatical permitted to professors and interned with Brown at Kansas. "It was obvious right away that he was the whole package," says Brown, now at SMU, his 13th head coaching post. "Pop has great character, great passion for the sport and great intelligence. Pretty much all you want." Brown didn't have a permanent spot for Popovich then, so Pop returned to Pomona and scheduled a game against the Jayhawks in Allen Fieldhouse just for the experience of it. His Sagehens lost 94–38 to the team that won the NCAA championship that season.

Popovich left the warm bosom of campus life for good in 1988, following Brown to become an assistant with the Spurs. The team's then owner, Red McCombs, let go Brown and his entire staff in 1992, and two years of franchise unrest ensued before Popovich—who went to Golden State as Don Nelson's assistant—returned as general manager. Pop jettisoned coach Bob Hill, installed himself, heard thousands of boos, built a team based on defensive principles, drafted Duncan, brought order to chaos, won a championship, closed the curtain and settled in for a long run as the pasha of the Republic of Pop.

"Okay, watch what they do here on defense against Oklahoma City," says Kings assistant Jim Eyen. "It's simple, but they do it almost every time." Eyen is in his room at the San Antonio Westin, studying film of the Spurs in preparation for an April 12 game at the AT&T Center. (San Antonio would win 108–101.) "You can see how much Parker is shading [Thunder point guard Russell] Westbrook to the sideline," says Eyen. "That's where their defense starts. They take you where they want you to go so they can load up. And once the ball is on the sideline they don't make it easy [for you] to reverse it. You almost never go one-on-one against them. You're going one-on-five."

Oklahoma City's Kevin Durant sets a pick for Westbrook, but Spurs swingman Kawhi Leonard switches and prevents a drive to the basket. "They're not always aggressive in switches," says Eyen. "You know how the Celtics always jump out and hedge hard? The Spurs play it a little softer, depend on their wits."

Now the 6'9" Durant has the 6'2" Parker guarding him. "But [the Spurs] recognize the mismatch right away," says Eyen. "See, here comes [forward

Danny] Green to help. And look at the other defenders. Their eyes are on that ball."

The Spurs might be vulnerable to Thunder guard Thabo Sefolosha cutting to the hoop from the weak side. "But look at Duncan back there," says Eyen. "He's shaded that way. If Sefolosha cuts, Tim will knock him out of the lane with his chest." The Spurs' de facto zone forces Durant to give it up to forward Nick Collison, who is just above the free throw line. Duncan steps up to guard him. "See Duncan in that position," says Eyen. "He's tracing the ball. They all do that. They all make it tough to make even the easy pass."

Collison swings it to Sefolosha, who has moved out on the perimeter to space the floor. "So the guy who ends up with the ball is the guy you want with the ball on the perimeter," says Eyen. Sure enough, the sequence ends with Sefolosha missing a shot. "They don't have a [Bruce] Bowen now, a real lockdown guy," Eyen says of the Spurs, "and Tim is no longer a shot-blocking force, although he's still damn good. But their team-defense concepts are just as strong as ever."

The Kings assistant switches to offense, cuing up a basic play, which begins with Duncan posting up on the right block. "Okay, Collison decides to front Duncan and keep him from getting the ball," says Eyen. "So what happens? [Spurs big man Tiago] Splitter reads it immediately and comes out to the high post. Parker gets it to him...they already know what they're going to do...Duncan pins Collison, gets the lob from Splitter...and scores easily. So they penalize you for trying to play great defense.

"A lot of teams throw that entry pass directly from the wing. But the Spurs get it to the middle, because that's where it works. And see what else is happening on the weak side? The guys are all active, moving, staying aware of cutting lanes. So it's hard to load up on Duncan, because he will find someone for an even better shot."

It's not that the Spurs do anything magical. It's just that they do whatever they do consistently, from game to game, year to year, decade to decade. "The first thing I think about with them is that they're well drilled," says Eyen. "You know you have college teams, Kansas and Duke, that play a certain way? The NBA version is the Spurs. They are as close to a *program* as you have in the league."

The program, though, is not nearly as immutable as some might think. Things change. Bowen retires, Duncan (who turned 37 on April 25) gets older and Parker gets better, so the Spurs transition into a team that relies almost as much on offense as on defense. San Antonio finished the season seventh in offensive efficiency and tied for third in defensive efficiency. "Most teams are skewed one way or the other, but not the Spurs," says Nets coach P.J.

Carlesimo, the lead assistant under Popovich for five years beginning in 2002. "What that amounts to is you have a team that rarely beats itself, because it can win any game either way."

Changes to the Spurs' system are bottom-lined by Pop, but there is much input. By all accounts the coach revels in an environment of swirling opinions. "The one way you will not make it here," says his top assistant, Mike Budenholzer, a Pomona grad who started in the Spurs' video room in 1994, "is to be a yes man." That goes for players too. Several years ago Parker went to Pop and announced that he didn't want to be the next Avery Johnson, the Pop-molded point guard with whom the Spurs won their first title, in 1999. "I told Pop I didn't want to be a point guard who just runs the team," says Parker. "After that Pop adapted his coaching more to my play and Manu's play. You can talk to Pop. A lot of coaches, you can't."

In that respect Pop's basketball life resembles that of his mentor, Brown. The Republic of Pop is a kind of hoops version of ancient Greece: learned men discussing their science, their philosophy, their lifeblood, Socrates to Plato to Aristotle, Brown to Popovich to Jacque Vaughn (Orlando Magic) or Monty Williams (New Orleans) or Budenholzer, who might someday get the call to coach his own team.

Still, there are crucial differences between Popovich and his tutor. "Larry will listen to a wino if he thinks he has the perfect out-of-bounds play," says Buford, "and that's not Pop." There is also a time when Socratic discourse must cease. "If Pop is really mad, then you drop the discussion," says Ginóbili. "We might talk for 10 minutes about how to defend the pick-and-roll, and he may change his idea. But once he is convinced that is the way, then that is *the way*. And if you don't follow, you end up in the Pop doghouse."

The Pop doghouse has many rooms: one for snooty sommeliers, another for out-of-town TV suits who want to know if Duncan is too old, another for NBA schedule makers. There are also rooms for Spurs superstars and role players alike. Much has been written about Pop's willingness to go after Duncan, who confirms that it's true, but to fully grasp operations in the Republic of Pop, it is just as valuable to note how he handles the non-Duncans.

Steve Kerr, a role player for four seasons under Pop, tells of a time during the 2000–01 season when he was out of the rotation and sulking. He would sit on the floor rather than the bench as a way of protesting. "After a couple games Pop pulled me aside and said, 'Your body language is terrible,'" says Kerr. "'I know you're not playing, but you're a pro who's always handled yourself well, and now you're not. It doesn't look right, and I need you on the bench.' He was absolutely right. So I returned to the bench."

But there is egress from the Pop doghouse and reentry into the Republic, even for those who leave angry, like Monty Williams, an early and unhappy citizen. For 2½ seasons beginning in 1996, Williams chafed under Pop's tongue, left for free agency and, as a member of the Magic, tried to persuade Duncan to leave the Spurs in 2000. Around Alamo City, that was tantamount to dressing up as Santa Anna on Sam Houston Day. But Popovich took Williams back as a coaching intern before the '04–05 season, which ended with a championship and with Williams standing behind the bench in San Antonio after Game 7, soaking it all in.

"I was alone in the middle of all this celebration," remembers Williams, "when all of a sudden somebody tackled me from the side. 'You got one,' Pop said to me. 'You missed out before, but now you got one.' I'm not a real emotional guy, but it almost makes me cry when I think about it: Pop saw something in me that I didn't see in myself."

Handling people—more specifically, people within the Republic of Pop—is his strength, his Pop art. He and Duncan talk as kindred souls, he and Ginóbili as political analysts, he and Parker as old guy to young guy. When Bowen, a master of disingenuousness, was there, their lingua franca was sarcasm. "You're doing it again. You're doing that Eddie Haskell bullcrap," Popovich would say, dropping an appropriately old-school *Leave It to Beaver* reference. "I don't want Eddie Haskell."

Pop's ability to lead comes from...who knows where? Some complex mosaic of East Chicago, the Academy, Pomona, all that fine wine, the cauldron of NBA competition, a dozen other places. He visits the subject of his leadership with reluctance but, once started, with zeal.

"The only reason the word *military* is used to describe what goes on around here is because I went to the Academy," says Pop. "But the correct word is *discipline*. And there are disciplined people in Google, in IBM and the McDonald's down the street.

"Yes, we're disciplined with what we do. But that's not enough. Relationships with people are what it's all about. You have to make players realize you care about them. And they have to care about each other and be interested in each other. Then they start to feel a responsibility toward each other. Then they want to do for each other.

"And I have always thought it helps if you can make it fun, and one of the ways you do that is let them think you're a little crazy, that you're interested in things outside of basketball. 'Are there weapons of mass destruction? Or aren't there? What, don't you read the papers?' You have to give the message that the world is wider than a basketball court."

Pop is getting antsy, worried that he's talking too much. The curtain is closing.

"As far as innovation goes..." one question begins.

"Oh, hell, I don't know anything about innovation," he says, rising. "Here is my innovation: I drafted Tim Duncan. Okay? End of story."

And then he is off, back to the locker room, back where he can dispense blame and blessing in equal measure, back where the Republic of Pop functions best, nuanced and noisy but pretty much unheard in the outside world.

— POSTSCRIPT —

Jack McCallum: "Tell Jack not to come."

"Tell Pop I'm coming anyway."

That was roughly the exchange between Tom James, the San Antonio Spurs director of media relations, and myself in 2013 when I told Tom, gently, that I would be in the Alamo City to report a story on Gregg Popovich, whether or not the coach cooperated. I eventually got Pop to agree to sit down before a game "just to confirm some facts," and out of that conversation he did reveal some portion of himself. "By the way," he said as our session drew to a close, "I know what you're doing." He did, too, but between what he told me and the trove of observations from others, I got what I thought was a good story.

OCTOBER 31, 1983

The Gospel According to Hubie

New York Knicks Coach Hubie Brown preaches X's and O's, teaches defense and screeches about anything that pops to mind

BY BRUCE NEWMAN

Around SI, legend has it that Hubie vowed never to speak to the magazine again after this story.

CHARLEY: *Willy, when're you gonna realize that them things don't mean anything?...The only thing you got in this world is what you can sell. And the funny thing is that you're a salesman, and you don't know that.*

WILLY: *I've always tried to think otherwise, I guess. I always felt that if a man was impressive, and well liked, that nothing—*

CHARLEY: *Why must everybody like you? Who liked J.P. Morgan? Was he impressive? In a Turkish bath he'd look like a butcher. But with his pockets on he was very well liked.*

—DEATH OF A SALESMAN

All day long the colorless sky had brooded over Phoenix like a flat and ugly threat. All that remained as night came was heat lightning and the roll of distant thunder. Soon the storm would begin.

Just as Hubie Brown stood up and moved quietly to the front of the crowded hotel conference room, jagged bolts of lightning split the night

410

air and the rain lapped at the roof in sheets. For several moments the coach of the New York Knicks stood in silence, his eyes closed and his head tilted back. The 75 Litton Industries Credit Corporation executives, who had gathered for their national sales meeting, sat perfectly still. Then Brown slowly drew up his arms and remained that way—in the manner of someone who had been nailed to a cross—until he began to speak.

"The toughest thing...in my life...was to be 48 years old...extremely successful...and to get fired," Brown said, his voice booming through the room. "Remember...every day when you get up...you're just half a step away from the street. My father told me that when I was young. And if that doesn't make you give a hundred percent every day of your life, nothing will."

Many in the audience had come expecting to hear a little uplifting chalk talk sprinkled with a lot of the usual palaver about the power of positive thinking. But Brown has taken Norman Vincent Peale, stood him on his head and dressed him in a brown shirt and a blue collar. It is not the dress-for-success look, but Brown is not selling success, he's selling fear of failure. He preaches the work ethic and the out-of-work ethic in equal measure. "I don't give them all this boola-boola, rah-rah stuff," he says. "When I went to New York," he tells the salesmen, "there were 12 players on the team. Before the first game I got rid of nine. That's how you send a message!"

As Brown speaks, his chin is stuck out and his head is tilted back slightly, so that his nose seems always to be the highest point on his body. His eyes are set deeply and they seem to be measuring something far away. When Brown was 10 years old, his left eye was damaged in a playground accident, and the resulting muscle damage left him slightly walleyed, a condition that allows him to see someone standing almost behind him. For many people who approach Brown, the fact that they're never sure which eye to look him in is often just the start of what can be an unsettling experience. Brown knows he intimidates some people with his long, withering gazes, which even his best friends call The Stare. But Brown was doing little staring and lots of selling, at one point even holding up a book called *The Greatest Salesman In The World* and calling it "the bible." After an hour and a half of preaching his message, Brown slumped into a chair as the salesmen responded with a long standing ovation.

Brown's message is simple: The street made you, and someday it will take you back. It happened to him when he was fired by the Atlanta Hawks in 1981; it can happen to you. Three nights earlier he was selling it to a thousand vacuum-cleaner salesmen in Syracuse, and before that in Schenectady and Gainesville and Daytona. "I'm no different than you," he tells the credit salesmen. But in a way they seem to understand better than he does. Brown is clearly not one of them. By his own estimation, Brown is better than everyone else. In the salesman's line, that is a dangerous thing to be, for you will spend your whole life selling, but never selling out.

Someone once said that Hubie Brown burned his bridges before him. That speaks volumes about the effect Brown's personality has on people. Brown makes little effort to conceal his contempt for many of the other 22 head coaches in the National Basketball Association, and yet he is plainly wounded by their disdain for him. He tells his players he doesn't want them to love and doesn't care if they like him, but then expects them to play harder for him than they have played for any coach in their lives. And he has waged warfare with the front office of virtually every pro team that has employed him.

"Hubie can't stand to have anybody above him," says Cotton Fitzsimmons, coach of the Kansas City Kings, who likes Brown but recognizes his flaws. "He can't believe that anybody else is doing as good a job as he does. Sometimes when you talk to Hubie you get the impression that he invented this game."

Even Brown doesn't believe he invented the whole game, but he did have a great deal to do with reinventing pro basketball in New York last season. In 1981–82, the year before Brown arrived, the Knicks had turned Madison Square Garden into a kennel club of yapping malcontents and strays, woofing to a 33–49 record under Coach Red Holzman. A year ago, no one expected them to do much better than that, but after a dreadful 14–26 start New York won 30 of its last 42 games. In the playoffs, the Knicks wiped out the Nets in two games before falling to the eventual champion 76ers in a series that was far more competitive than the 4–0 margin indicated. Three of the games were decided in the final seconds. In part because of the Knicks' impressive turnaround, Brown's salary was increased to a reported $300,000 a year.

Brown is one of the NBA's best technicians, a wizard of X's and O's. He started calling every play from the bench when only football coaches were doing that, and he was the first coach in the NBA to try to use 10 players in every quarter and to press for 82 games. He is the only coach whose substitution rotation is determined entirely by the clock, completely ignoring the rhythmic flow of the game. "We do a lot of radical things that pro basketball doesn't want to accept," he says. "But if you are an innovator, you will always be attacked. You can't ever allow that to stop you. The easiest thing is to just say you're going to let the players do their dance and let the talent win it or lose it. I want complete control."

While many of the league's other coaches recite a standard litany of Brown's failings, they prefer to do so off the record, a crutch Brown rarely uses. Denver Coach Doug Moe is an exception. "He's overrated," Moe says. "He's everybody's conception of what a good coach should be, but what has he done? His winning percentage [.497 in six NBA seasons] isn't that good. He got a lot of credit for what he did with the Knicks last season, but he had a great cast. When they were losing early in the year, he said it was because they had lousy players; and when they started to win, it was good coaching. Hubie's very insecure and an average coach who happens to be great at promoting himself. Plus, I defy anybody to say his teams aren't boring."

Brown reserves his greatest scorn for critics like Moe, and for most of the other former players who he believes are unworthy of his profession. "Who are these guys to attack me?" he says. "Down at one level you've got some children who were players—guys like Billy Cunningham and Kevin Loughery—who never coached a game and walked into jobs where there was all kinds of talent. Then you've got all the other guys, who I personally have no problem with. And way up here—so far from the rest of them we're practically on an island—you've got Jack Ramsay, Dick Motta and me."

Brown's island became even more deserted when he was censured by the NBA coaches association in September of 1982. The action came during a dramatic and bizarre meeting on Long Island following the playing of a tape on which Brown is heard criticizing Cunningham. On the tape, Brown told a roomful of high school and college coaches that Cunningham had been unable to handle a simple zone trap that the Lakers ran throughout the 1982 championship series, and that had caused the Sixers to lose. What made the remark especially incriminating was that Brown was at least partly right—Philadelphia hadn't responded with a consistent attack against the trap.

When Ramsay, who is president of the coaches association, gave Brown a chance to respond, everyone in the room thought that Brown would be forced to apologize. "At that point it was like backing an animal into a corner," says Atlanta Coach Mike Fratello, who was then Brown's assistant. "He defended himself the way he knew best."

Brown was practically trembling when he stood up to speak. "I told them, 'How dare you come into my classroom and tape two minutes of a three-hour clinic, then play it like this to try to embarrass me? How dare you? I do more clinics in a year than all the rest of you put together, and every time I speak I raise every one of you up to my level of X's and O's, just because you are NBA coaches like me. You think he couldn't handle a simple 1-3-1 trap? You're bleepin'-A right he couldn't! So deal with it and move on.'" He went on like that for several minutes. "There were 44 guys in that room," says Brown, referring to the 22 head coaches and their assistants, "and not one of them had the guts to tell me that I was wrong. I was wild. Jack Ramsay was standing next to me, and when I finished, Jack was as white as a sheet.

I destroyed the guy [Cunningham] in front of the whole group. I destroyed all of them."

And he wasn't finished. Subsequently, Brown got into a fix over his criticism of Phoenix Coach John MacLeod. "I got killed for talking about MacLeod during a clinic, but all I said was that you can't expect to win a [championship] ring when your teams average so much more during the regular season than in the playoffs," Brown says. "When I speak at clinics, I use myself as an example, and if I can accept it, why can't they? What's wrong with these guys? They say they're in the stratosphere of coaching, but they don't want to talk about the possibility they made mistakes."

MacLeod, for one, didn't want to talk about it. "I have to wonder about the self-esteem of someone who has to promote himself at the expense of others," MacLeod says. "He sets himself up as some kind of paragon, but all he's done is load the gun 22 times. You don't think every time we play in New York or when I've got his ass here that I'm not loaded for bear? This is a tough job, and we just can't have that sort of thing."

Brown says he is weary of the controversies, and yet his honesty—which he frequently wields like a bludgeon—doesn't prevent him from diving into new skirmishes. He describes former CBS color analyst Bill Russell as "a moron," and CBS play-by-play announcer Dick Stockton as "a jerk," after having worked with both when he was out of coaching two seasons ago. Of the coach of the New Jersey Nets, he says, "Stan Albeck is a washerwoman who calls six people every day to find out the latest gossip. A nice man." And Brown doesn't stop there. "We've got maybe five general managers in the NBA who know anything about basketball," he says. "The other 18 are stealing their money."

Michael Gearon, president of the Atlanta Hawks and the man who put Brown on the street in 1981, says, "Is it a coincidence that in every [professional] relationship the guy has ever had, the friendships aren't there? In fact, it's almost as if they're all his mortal enemies. I think Hubie really has a contempt for people."

If that is so, then it is truly a paradox because Brown's hard-nosed brand of basketball has made him very popular with fans. "There are NBA coaches who are popular with the players, popular with management, popular with the other coaches," Fratello says, "but what coach in the league is more popular than Hubie with the people in the stands? There are people there every night just to see him." Part of his appeal is his ability to turn a word beginning with F into a noun, adjective and direct object all in the same vile sentence. "I'm more offensive in an empty building than one that's packed," Brown says. "In a packed building I'm known as colorful."

He was colorful in Atlanta, until the Hawks fired him just before the 1980–81 season ended. The Hawks claim they cashiered Brown because his abusiveness toward the players had reached a point of diminished returns. Finally, when Brown's harshness stopped working, there was nothing soft to fall back on.

"People say, 'You're too critical, you attack too much,'" Brown says. "But the real test is to hold your ground when they try to back you down and knock you on your ass. It's easy to be loved, but you have to remember that the only ones who really love you are the people who sit around that dinner table with you at night. Everybody else is trying to cover his own ass."

Hubie Brown was born on Sept. 25, 1933 in the little town of Hazleton, Pa., not far from Bethlehem and Nazareth. In the manner of Catholic families at that time and place, Anna and Charlie Brown named their son for a saint, calling him Hubert Jude, the latter being the patron saint of desperate causes. Hubie was an only child, and Anna and Charlie worshiped him and raised him like their own desperate cause.

When Hubie was three, Charlie moved the family to Elizabeth, N.J., which at that time was an industrial city of 125,000 people, many of them immigrants who worshiped in the city's 15 Catholic churches. "When I was growing up, you never talked about the street you lived on," Brown recalls. "You just said what parish you were from."

The Browns settled in St. Mary's parish, in a four-family apartment house hard by the railroad tracks that came stretching out of Manhattan, 20 miles away. When one of the old steam-driven locomotives rumbled by, not 50 feet from the Browns' front door, you could gauge its speed and the number of boxcars behind it just by pressing your cheek against the window and feeling the vibration in the glass. The Browns never had a telephone or a car, and in the wintertime the furnace warmed only three of the apartment's five rooms. Anna Brown rarely left home, except to go to church almost every day, preferring to stay in the apartment with her rosary and a damp mop. "We could never use the front stairs," Hubie says, "because my mother used to wax them three times a week."

Hubie and Charlie usually called each other "Chief," as friends might. Charlie worked as a foreman at the federal shipyard in nearby Kearny until the end of World War II, helping to ferry completed ships to Navy yards up and down the coast. When the war ended, the shipyards began closing down, and Charlie was laid off. To remind his players how close they are to the street, Hubie frequently tells the story of how his father was thrown out of work after 19 years' service at the shipyard. In fact, Charlie worked at the facility for only 10 years before he lost his job there.

For a while Charlie worked as a maintenance man at the Singer sewing-machine plant in Elizabeth, but when the shipyard reopened he decided to go back. Three months later the docks were closed again, and this time there were no other jobs to be had. "My parents lost everything they had," Hubie says. Charlie was out of work for eight agonizing months, a period of despair for both the father and his son.

"Then one day," Hubie says, as if recalling a miracle, "my father became the janitor at my school."

To this day Brown cannot talk about his father for more than five minutes without choking up. Rather than deny Charlie this most fundamental tribute, Hubie will simply stop speaking while he stares off into space, lost in a private reverie about what, for him, was clearly the best time of his life. "My father was a giant," Brown says.

"Charlie's whole life was his son, and he was always there," recalls Jim Murphy, a standout basketball player at St. Mary's during the 1940s. "When he was watching Hubie it was just like he was watching a little puppy." Charlie never missed a game his son played throughout grammar school and high school. "You wouldn't know Charlie was there," says Al LoBalbo, who was the basketball coach at St. Mary's and now is an assistant at St. John's University. "But he was there. Sometimes I'd see him watching our practices through the window."

To Charlie, failure was a very personal act of denial. That was at the root of Hubie's own obsession with eliminating mistakes. "A lot of Hubie's life has revolved around the fact that his father wanted him to have a better life than he did," says Hubie's wife, Claire, "and that he could make that happen through sports."

Hubie soon learned that you were never far from the street, even with someone who loved you. Once after Hubie had gone 0 for 4 in a baseball game, Charlie wouldn't—or couldn't—bring himself to speak to his son. "It's not like somebody stood there and said, 'I don't love you today because you didn't get a hit,'" Claire says, "but that's what it was. When a person gets all his sense of worth in that one way, in the long run it hurts the person's sense of self-worth. The tendency is to say, 'If I lost today, then I'm not a good person.'"

If there was one thing that Brown practiced even more seriously than sports, it was Catholicism. St. Mary's was run by the Sisters of Charity, and Hubie seemed to consider their stern guidance divine. He began serving as an altar boy while in grammar school, and he hustled weddings for tips. From the fifth grade until he graduated from St. Mary's, Hubie served a daily 6:30 a.m. Mass at St. Elizabeth's Hospital for a dollar a week and breakfast with the staff. After eight years of this, when he was ready to leave for college, one of the nuns at the hospital presented him with a card of thanks and $50. "You have to understand that in 1951, fifty dollars was my father's weekly paycheck," he says. "I was stunned."

It seems odd somehow that this angry man, the most profane coach in pro basketball, should have been most strongly influenced by these vessels of God. "Some of the most important women in my life have been nuns," he says.

After Brown graduated from Niagara University in 1955 (he was a low-scoring, great-passing guard for what was one of the top teams in the country), he spent a year as the phys ed teacher at St. Mary's Academy in Little Falls, N.Y. Like many of his Niagara classmates, Brown had joined the ROTC in college, but when it became evident that the ROTC guys were taking their commissions and going to Korea, Brown quit and was drafted into the Army.

Like many good athletes, he had a way of making the Army work for him. Stationed at the Presidio in San Francisco, Brown spent two years touring the country with various Army basketball, baseball and volleyball teams. "That was a great time for me," he says. "These other guys were all coming back from Korea, where they had been freezing their asses off, and there I was with a tan and no uniform."

When he was mustered out, Brown returned to Niagara in 1958 to get his master's degree in education, playing basketball on weekends for Rochester in the Eastern League. That was also the year he met Claire and, typically, made a vivid first impression. "A friend who was a priest had borrowed a car to take some students to the beach," she says. "Suddenly another car pulled up and a man got out and yelled, 'Father Murray, that's the last time I let you borrow my car. You told me you were going on a sick call!'" Claire remembers looking up and asking, "Who's the maniac?" It was Hubie. Father Murray of the Wayward Car married them two years later. They have four children: Molly, 22, is a recent graduate of Auburn; Ginny, 21, is a senior nursing student at St. Mary's of Notre Dame; Julie, 18, will enter the College of Charleston (S.C.) in January; and Brendan, 13, is in the eighth grade of Atlanta's Marist School.

Starting in 1959, Brown spent five years coaching baseball and jayvee basketball and serving as defensive line coach for the football team at Cranford (N.J.) High School. After that he moved to the varsity basketball coaching job at Fair Lawn (N.J.) High School. The school might as well have hired St. Jude, because the basketball team had won only four of 36 games the preceding two seasons. "When I got to Fair Lawn," Brown says, "basketball was the prelim to the wrestling matches." The first thing he did was cut all the seniors from the squad. That's how you send a message! It was a move that, predictably, caused some acrimony among parents in the community. "I got brought up before the Board of Education for that one," Brown says. The team finished 2–16 his first year. The next season Fair Lawn got hot and won five games. Everyone seemed fairly satisfied that the new coach had fallen flat on his face.

Brown taught business, economics and business law at Fair Lawn, and it was there that he learned to use the classroom as a stage. "You're always selling yourself," he says. "Those kids had a choice between five different winter sports, so when I went in that classroom, I had to give them 55 minutes of dynamite, just blow them away. If I wasn't in the top three for Teacher of the Year every year, I was ticked off. That's how good a teacher I thought I was." For all the notoriety he has achieved in basketball. Brown has spent more time standing at the blackboard in classrooms than he has as a head coach in the NBA. By his third year at Fair Lawn he had turned the program around, and the Cutters posted what was for them an impressive 14–9 record.

Brown says he was happy coaching at the high school level, but in 1967 he decided to take a chance—and an $11,500 pay cut—to become an assistant coach at William & Mary. His salary: $7,000 a year. Eight months later he was offered the freshman coaching job at Duke, also for $7,000, and he took it. For four years he was the chief recruiter at Duke, whose coach at the time was Vic Bubas, and he had the difficult task of "trying to get the best white players with the high college boards." It was a chance to further refine his salesman's pitch, so he talked and talked and talked. "Guys in the business used to say to me, 'You kill the mothers,'" he says. "And I said, 'That's right, because all those moms, they like to talk.'" Talking was something Hubie Brown could always do.

In 1972 Larry Costello, who had been Brown's teammate at Niagara, called to offer him the job as his assistant with the Milwaukee Bucks. It is fair to say that Brown would not be one of the highest paid coaches in basketball today were it not for Costello, a debt that Brown readily acknowledges. "He gave me my start," Brown says. "That was big."

Brown worked with Costello for two seasons in Milwaukee. When Charlie Brown died on Thanksgiving Day in 1973, Hubie drew closer to Costello and threw himself even further into his work. It paid off the next season when he was hired as head coach of the ABA's Kentucky Colonels, a team that included Artis Gilmore, Louie Dampier and Dan Issel. On Oct. 18, 1974, the night of Hubie Brown's first game as head coach of the Kentucky Colonels, one of the empty seats in Louisville's Freedom Hall was between two of Brown's old friends. The seat was for Charlie. "One of the toughest things in my life was that my father never got to see me as a head coach in the pros,"

Hubie says. The Colonels won the ABA championship in 1974–75, Brown's first year, but the next season they were eliminated in the second round of the playoffs. When the ABA and NBA merged after the 1976 season, Kentucky owner John Y. Brown decided to take what cash he could grab in the merger settlement and fold his tent. During this turbulent period, Hubie could not even bring himself to utter the owner's name, referring to Brown as the man who "destroyed the Kentucky Colonels basketball team." To this day, Hubie bears a grudge against Brown, who would later own and all but destroy the Boston Celtics. John Y. Brown is now governor of Kentucky.

With his team and his job gone, Hubie Brown was on the street and, presumably, frantic. As much as anything, that is what would later fuel the speculation—most of it ill-informed—that he stabbed Costello in the back by campaigning for his Milwaukee job. Costello suggested that Brown had done exactly that, and in the years that followed he repeated the charge often to other coaches.

Brown says that when the Colonels disbanded, he was approached by three NBA teams that wanted him to be head coach. He says he never pursued the Milwaukee job and that he had already come to terms with Atlanta.

CHARLEY:... *For a salesman, there is no rock bottom to the life.... He's a man way out there in the blue, riding on a smile and a shoeshine. And when they start not smiling back—that's an earthquake. And then you get yourself a couple of spots on your hat, and you're finished. Nobody dast blame this man. A salesman is got to dream, boy. It comes with the territory.*

The Hawks won only 31 games in Brown's first year, and in midseason Ted Turner bought the team and subsequently instructed Brown to get rid of all the high-priced talent. What followed may have been Brown's greatest triumph. Taking a motley assortment of castoffs and no-name players (Brown had recruited a 27-year-old, 5'8" guard named Charlie Criss from the Eastern League the year before), whose salaries totaled $800,000, Brown pushed and bullied and goaded the Hawks into winning 41 games and making the 1977–78 playoffs, Atlanta's first postseason appearance since 1972–73.

Brown's blue-collar image was forged in those years. He took his so-called "overachievers," taught them the importance of defense, and won 46 and 50 games the next two seasons. "You must make them play to their potential," he would say, "and you must make them cry for mercy." The work ethic that he preached had a special appeal in Atlanta, where most of the fans were white and most of the players were black. Brown had become a sort of working man's hero, an image that was sneered at by other coaches and even the Hawks' management. "That's a sort of demagogic thing," says Gearon, who was uncomfortable with the idea that Brown had become a bigger star than the players. "A lot of people feel the players are overpaid, and they like to see somebody who will kick them in the butt."

Brown was such a dazzling success with the Hawks that at one point Turner tried to persuade him to manage his Atlanta Braves. Brown almost went for it, but eventually decided the scheme was too crazy to work.

Even as the Hawks grew more successful, Brown drew further and further away from his players. "Hubie always dealt in groups," says Tom McMillen, who played with the Hawks during Brown's coaching tenure. "I think that was because it was hard for him to talk to people on an individual basis. When you motivate in a group, you sacrifice the idiosyncrasies of the individual."

One of the most idiosyncratic Hawks was John Drew, the All-Star forward to whom Brown regularly referred—both in front of his teammates and to the press—as "cement head," "moron" and "cinder head," those being among the least harsh and more printable epithets he applied to Drew. In a painfully public way, Drew had become the ultimate whipping boy. Brown never flinched from his role of bully. For his part, Drew refused to say an unkind word about the coach. But by that time, Drew, by his own subsequent admission, was a heavy user of cocaine. The season the Hawks won 50 games, 1979–80, Brown rode Drew mercilessly, a tactic that further alienated him from many of his players. "In terms of depression," says Gearon, "that year was the worst. That was brutal."

In addition to Drew, Brown blamed Guard Eddie Johnson, who would later admit that he had used cocaine, and yet a third player, whom Brown accused of being both a cocaine user and a homosexual, whenever anything went wrong. Gearon disputes the notion that for his last two years in Atlanta Brown was some kind of lone ranger crusading against cocaine, and yet he rather blithely dismisses the impact of Drew's erratic behavior. "John Drew didn't give us any problems after Hubie left," Gearon says. "He may have been a drug user, but it never caused him to be late or to miss practice. John Drew is a very stable person."

Following the Hawks' 4–1 loss to Philadelphia in the Eastern Conference semifinals in 1980, Brown says he spent $1,200 seeing a psychologist who "took my personality and put it into the drug scene." He says the sessions helped him cope with the problem of drug abuse. "So why," he wonders, "did I flip out the next year? I have no answer for that."

The Hawks were beset by injuries during the 1980–81 season, and for the first time Brown could not push his players through the pain. He spent most of his time very close to the edge. "My last year in Atlanta," he says, "I got so paranoid about the drug thing that I became distracted from my job. Every night when the locker room door closed, I was right in their faces, offering to fight them. I should have backed off, but I couldn't. In spite of the problems, I became more obsessed than ever with making the playoffs. I had no peace of mind, ever. You can't believe this creation of yours is being destroyed." The Hawks were 31–48 and in chaos when Brown was finally fired with three games left in the season.

During the months that followed, Brown convinced himself that the people in his suburban Atlanta neighborhood were whispering about him because he had lost his job. "He felt embarrassed, humiliated," says Brown's best friend. Rich Buckelew, "and he went into a shell." He began to accelerate the pace of his speaking engagements, doing 40 coaching clinics and another 40 motivational speeches during the next 18 months. (It is that kind of intensity, said Dr. Norman Scott, the Knicks' physician, that contributed to the mild case of angina and forced Brown to spend four days in New York's Lenox Hill Hospital last week.) He also earned acclaim for his work as an NBA color analyst for both the USA cable network and for CBS, although he found his experience with CBS somewhat disillusioning.

"Everybody thinks football is an incredibly complex game, run by scientific minds," Brown says, "and that's because TV analyzes every play with statistics, breaking it all down. Well, football's not nearly as intricate as basketball, but people don't realize that because CBS doesn't want that kind of analysis. Pro basketball is a beautiful, complex game, played by great athletes. But CBS doesn't want to get too technical because they think that's just for the junkies. They told me, 'Our audience doesn't want to hear that stuff, so keep it on a sixth-grade level.'"

Brown feels particularly strong about Bill Russell, who was one of the game's great centers in the 1950s and '60s when he played with the Celtics and who had done the CBS telecasts for four years before he was replaced prior to this season. "That moron has done more to cause the game's popularity to regress than anyone or anything else," Brown says. "He doesn't know anything about the game and he can't articulate anything. The guy does not prepare.

"Everybody was afraid to say anything to him because—ooh ooh—this is Big Russ. I mean who the hell is Bill Russell? The coaches didn't like him, the fans didn't like him, the guys at CBS didn't like him, but he was allowed to ruin the game. Bill Russell is a terrible human being."

When Brown became coach of the Knicks last year, a columnist wrote in *The New York Times* that after 26 years, of coaching, "Hubie Brown was home."

There was something smug in that, of course, and Brown heard the implied Jersey joke, even if no one else did. "Everybody tells me I'm where I belong now, but that's bull," Brown says. "I belong across the river. I'm a Jersey guy."

All of New York at his feet, king of the hill, top of the heap, and the only thing Brown ever wanted was to be a Jersey guy. "Jersey guys stick together," Brown explains. "There is a unification of guys." When Joe Taub, a Jersey guy who owns the New Jersey Nets, began hinting just before the end of last season that he wanted to lure Brown across the river, the Knicks gave Brown a raise and contract extension. "The truth is, I was ready to go," Brown says, "but the Knicks wouldn't give me permission."

It had been just a few months earlier that Brown had thought he heard the street calling him again. After two weeks, the Knicks were 0–7, and in New York that's not a start, it's an invitation to a funeral. Brown just kept pushing, and taking names along the way. "People say I don't ever forget," he says, "and they're right. Once we got it going [last season], everybody jumped to the front of the parade, and I was a genius. But what had changed?"

Some things never change, just as some people never do. For now, Brown is content to bask in the heat of his own genius. But another winter is coming, another season. And sooner or later a salesman has got to go back out into the street. It comes with the territory.

OCTOBER 30, 2000

The Last Laugh

It's easy to mock Knicks coach Jeff Van Gundy for his
rumpled look and sad-dog demeanor. But don't be fooled
any longer by the disguise. He's shrewd and he's fearless

BY S.L. PRICE

*Price is one of the most observant writers ever to work at SI and here he
provides an indelible portrait of Jeff Van Gundy, a man who chooses to meet
for a national magazine interview at Pizza Hut. Here, we learn about his
origins and what drives him (and his brother, Stan). The last line is perfect.*

This is his game. That's what the world doesn't understand, may never
understand, because the big chance dropped in his lap, and he was handed
a team fat with talent, and there he was, suddenly transformed from
faceless third assistant to millionaire leader of men. Yes, the question
lingers: Has there been any coach luckier than Jeff Van Gundy? A man
with no portfolio, no storied past, no *shoulders* for god's sake, yet now he's
lording it over Madison Square Garden, striding before tycoons and stars,
folding his arms, pursing his lips, leaving Pat Riley in tears, waving Pat
Ewing goodbye, piloting one of the NBA's most prized franchises, the New
York Knickerbockers, for going on five years already. And he fell into the
job—didn't he?—like some yahoo striking oil in his backyard. The guy must
spend each night counting his blessings, thanking the deity in charge of
such things....

No. This is his game, though he never played it very well. His game, because he has never known anything, other than family, that he cared about more. His game, because nothing—not his big brother's bruised ego, not the supposed wisdom of his elders—has ever convinced him otherwise. Sons of coaches, Van Gundy will tell you, are "the biggest assholes to deal with," and coming up, the son of a small-college coach, he was a classic. As an eighth-grader in Martinez, Calif., Van Gundy began playing summer league with his brother, Stan, a high school star. Early in their first game together Stan was running downcourt, hearing his little brother "jump my ass about something he didn't like, for taking a bad shot or not playing defense," Stan recalls. "It just pissed me off: Who the heck is he? He'd never even attended a day of high school. But it was his show: *I'm taking control.* He's always had that attitude."

He doesn't show it much. Van Gundy will say all the right things, and mean them: *I had incredible mentors. I got unbelievable breaks. I'm amazed that I'm coaching the Knicks.* But pat answers don't necessarily make him a predictable man. To get what he wanted, Van Gundy made sacrifices that few others would dare even consider. Imagine you're a 5'9", 150-pound senior coming out of Brockport High in upstate New York in 1980, one of those floor-burned hustlers with no hops and no quickness; you're a B-plus student, and you eked out 1,040 on your SATs, but, thanks to basketball, you get accepted by Yale. So what if the Elis' coaching staff cuts you after watching you play pickup, before fall practice even begins? You're in, and this is *Yale,* you fool: Ivy League prestige, a lifetime of connections. You don't do what no one in the history of higher education has done. You don't transfer after one year from Yale to Menlo Junior College in Menlo Park, Calif., because you're sure you need to play college ball somewhere, *anywhere,* to be a coach.

"I thought he was insane," says Van Gundy's wife of 12 years, Kim, who met Jeff in high school. "I mean, do you know anybody who does that? How do you explain that?"

About as easily as you explain Van Gundy's bizarre summer of 1999, after the Knicks became the first No. 8 seed to reach the NBA Finals. Talk about lucky: In the end it all hinged on guard Allan Houston's last-second runner that bounded twice off the rim before dropping to eliminate Riley's Miami Heat in Game 5 of the first round. Had Houston missed, New York would have been finished, and Van Gundy, for one, is "absolutely" sure he would have been fired.

Time after time that season he had seen his face plastered on the TV screen while pundits said his job was in peril. Garden president Dave Checketts, who'd demoted close friend and general manager Ernie Grunfeld to special consultant over dessert one evening that April, assured Van Gundy, who had one year and $2 million to go on his contract, that he was in good shape. Then, during New York's second-round series against the Atlanta Hawks, the truth emerged: Checketts had interviewed former Chicago Bulls coach Phil Jackson, revealing himself to be someone quite capable of patting Van Gundy on the back, then shoving him into a ravine.

By the time the postseason run was over, though, and New York had fallen to the San Antonio Spurs in five games in the Finals, Van Gundy had become a Big Apple hero, his name chanted by the Garden crowd. His return was assured in everyone's mind but his. "You get to a point where you believe in yourself," Van Gundy says. "And in your mind—you never say it—but in your mind? *F-- it. If you don't want me, somebody else will. And I'll go.*" He sat at home in Chappaqua, N.Y., for two weeks, thinking about quitting. He came close. It sounds absurd. Walk away from the Knicks? The way he'd walked away from Yale? Van Gundy's stubborn belief in himself had a way of propelling him in some odd directions. "I was thinking, What is best? Maybe it's best for me and the team to get a fresh start," he says. "Did I want to continue? Was it worth it?"

Sure it was. That season had hardened him, and Van Gundy had learned the ultimate NBA lesson. "Trust," he says, "all comes back to contract." When they finally met two weeks after the Finals, Checketts offered Van Gundy a long-term extension, which, after negotiations were complete, wound up guaranteeing him $14 million over four years. Van Gundy spent last season becoming richer and more entrenched, guiding the Knicks as far as the Eastern Conference finals. Since the summer New York has taken on a different look: smaller and softer. When Ewing, Van Gundy's staunchest ally when the coach's job was on the line, was traded to the Seattle SuperSonics on Sept. 20, a franchise long dominated by the glowering big man fell fully into the hands of the hangdog little one.

In talking to Checketts that day 15 months ago, the 37-year-old Van Gundy insisted on one thing: He had often heard Checketts use the phrase *great young coach* to describe him, and Van Gundy wanted him to stop. It made him uncomfortable. Drop it, he said to Checketts. Drop the young.

He hears what people say. *Raccoon eyes. A kid in his father's suit.* He reads the stories in the papers, every word. He is not one of those coaches who pretends that the gibes slide off his back; he knows who said what and when and where, and he remembers it all because it hurts. *Yes*, he wants to shout, just once, *Yes, my scalp resembles a scorched field, and my skin looks like skim milk under the arena lights, but can we move on now? Can we get past this?*

But the one-liners aren't about to stop, are they? There was the one Kim saw in the *Chicago Tribune* calling him "a sad-eyed mortician...who appears to have inhaled too much formaldehyde." People aren't quite so harsh when they meet him; no, they simply ask, "Do you have fun? You don't look like you're having fun." But he knows what they really mean. They mean he looks sick; they mean he looks as if he's come down with something you'd want a second opinion on—or worse. By midseason, as Florida coach Billy Donovan puts it, "the guy looks like he was run over by a truck." They mean Van Gundy looks like death out there.

In another time no one would notice that much. But this is the era of perception and image, a time when coaches all seem to be angling for the same trifecta: the Armani wardrobe, the book on leadership, the motivational-speaking gigs. It doesn't help Van Gundy that his boss is the tall and handsome and well-turned-out Checketts, or that his primary mentor was the tall and rugged and well-turned-out Riley, or that the NBA's current genius is the tall and imposing and well-turned-out Jackson. Van Gundy has a 190–129 record, one trip to the Finals and an All-Star Game coaching berth on his résumé despite being, at 38, one of the youngest coaches in the league. Still, he never looks anything but overwhelmed. To see him from afar, from up in the aqua seats at the Garden, is to swear Woody Allen finally got the Knicks job.

Up close, too, Van Gundy hardly makes a formidable impression. When Rick Pitino hired him as a graduate assistant at Providence in 1986, he stood up, shook Van Gundy's hand and said, "Congratulations, Jim." After their second season in New York together, Riley took Van Gundy aside and told him, "You can be a head coach in this league, but you've got to start dressing better." When Don Nelson took over the Knicks in '95, after Van Gundy had already spent five-plus years as an assistant in New York to Stu Jackson, John MacLeod and Riley, the first thing Nelson said was, "I don't think I've ever seen you before."

In March '96, when Checketts fired Nelson and needed an interim coach for the last 23 games of the season, he didn't turn to Van Gundy because he expected greatness. Van Gundy simply lent credence to Woody's famous pronouncement that 90% of success is just showing up. "Jeff was just there," Checketts says.

All of which would be enough to give a guy a complex, except that Van Gundy never seemed to care. There are times, in fact, when he's his own best punch line. No one can detail his Mr. Magoo driving skills more hilariously: Over the years Van Gundy has hit a gas pump, rammed into his garage door, even run a stoplight and crashed into another car, all because he was preoccupied with thinking about basketball. No one has better summed up how he looked when he wrapped himself around Alonzo Mourning's leg ("like a little muskrat") during the Heat-Knicks brawl in Game 4 of the first round of the 1998 playoffs. No one can better describe the sad-sack moment—after Game 5 of last spring's Heat-Knicks series—when his '95 Honda Civic, parked at Westchester County Airport, was destroyed by a blast of exhaust from the team plane's jet engines. ("Where the f-- is my car? It was just here!")

As a Yale freshman Van Gundy and 12 guys in his dorm each tossed $100 into a pool: Whoever landed a date with Oscar-nominated classmate Jodie Foster won it all. "So I'm walking back from the gym one night, and I'm right by this great candy store and these sirens start whipping by, so I stop," Van Gundy says. "They go by, and I'm watching, and now they're gone, and a voice says, 'Boy, that popcorn smells good.' I turn around, and I'm about to say, 'Yeah, it does'...and it's *her*. By herself. And I choked. A box of popcorn, and I could've said it was a date. But I couldn't get anything out. Just, 'Uh-huh.' Then I turned and ran off."

But something doesn't fit here. If he's such a wuss, how did Van Gundy meld the anarchic Knicks of 1998–99, with personalities like Ewing, Larry Johnson, Latrell Sprewell and Charlie Ward, into a unit that made one of the more astonishing runs in recent memory? If he's such a small-timer, why did MacLeod and Riley and Nelson find him indispensable? If he's such a naïf, how did Van Gundy survive in Madison Square Garden—a political snake pit that has consumed one coaching legend after another—for 11 years? "He hasn't survived," Riley corrects. "He's flourished."

Yes, some Knicks object to the way Van Gundy micromanages the offense and plays favorites, but even they respect his work ethic and attention to detail and rigid adherence to defensive principles. Also, says Sprewell, "Jeff understands personnel; he recognizes strengths and weaknesses. It's tough to juggle minutes, but you don't hear as much bitching on this team as you do on others."

If some still can't resist categorizing him as a cola-swilling, junk-food-loving, ankle-nipping schlemiel, they're missing the essence of Van Gundy—that he is, in fact, fearless. In 1996–97, when nobody wanted to provoke Jackson and the mighty Bulls, Van Gundy mockingly called the Chicago coach Big Chief Triangle. A year later, when opponents seemed more interested in kissing Michael Jordan's four NBA championship rings than in beating him, a disgusted Van Gundy called Jordan "a con man." After scoring 51 on the Knicks the next time they met, Jordan walked past him and snapped, "Calm down, you little f--."

Van Gundy didn't care how it played with the public. He never has. When guard John Starks questioned Van Gundy's play calling in a huddle later that season, Van Gundy lit into him for all to hear. "F-- you!" he yelled. "F--you! F-- you! F-- you! F-- you!"

"No matter how big you are, it doesn't matter with him," says Starks, whom the Knicks traded after the 1997–98 season. "He may be small in stature, but he has a big heart and a very strong mind. Players see that, and they respect that."

It is dinnertime on a recent Saturday night, and Van Gundy has chosen to meet at a Pizza Hut near the Knicks' longtime practice facility in Purchase, N.Y., because, he says, "It's the only place around here I know." He is wearing blue sweatpants, a blue sweatshirt, sneakers. He eats a couple slices. His tenure with the Knicks is longer than Pitino's or Riley's; his winning percentage (.596) is better than that of any other New York coach except Riley's (.680). No one in the restaurant appears to notice him.

Asked later to name his favorite book, Van Gundy blurts out *The Prince*, then laughingly tries to retract it, because, he says, it will feed into "the anti–Van Gundy forces." There are critics who believe that since his days as a subservient assistant, Van Gundy has become more Machiavellian, more adept at playing politics. He shrugs this off. "At first you can play into the naiveté that people think you have because you don't dress well," Van Gundy says. "They almost give you the benefit of the doubt. But when success comes, that's no longer a good angle, so now you're 'a political animal.' It's all based on perception. Was that perception of naiveté correct?" He pauses, takes a bite of pizza. "I've always thought you have to know the landscape," he says. "I've always been aware of the landscape."

The silence began with a conversation. It was May 1997, Heat forward P.J. Brown had flung Knicks point guard Charlie Ward over his hip in Game 5 of the conference semifinals to touch off the first of many Miami–New York contretemps, and both teams had flown to New York for Game 6. Stan Van Gundy, Riley's assistant head coach, phoned his brother. After the usual pleasantries Stan said, "I can't believe what Charlie Ward did," and soon the two of them started screaming. "Forget Charlie Ward!" Jeff snapped. "P.J. Brown, that mother--ing coward!" Then came more curses, more accusations, two brothers taking each other apart until Jeff slammed the phone down.

The Knicks and the Heat have played three hotly contested postseason series since—"It's much more electric than the Finals," Jeff says—and each year Stan and Jeff have decided not to speak during those weeks. It is the only way to keep the peace. The worst Mother's Day that Cindy Van Gundy ever spent came during that '97 series, when Stan and Jeff arranged for their parents to come to the Garden from Brockport for Game 3. The couple sat there, paralyzed, as the Knicks won 77–73, and after the game tried to say the right thing to each son. "Too difficult," Cindy says. "One doesn't want to talk, and the other is too busy and too happy to talk." Ever since, the parents have refused to attend a New York–Miami game. They watch at home, Bill in one room with the sound down and Cindy in the other with the volume turned up.

They try to stay neutral, but Stan is sure that his parents root for his brother, because Jeff is a head coach and a loss could hurt Jeff's career more than it could his. Now when the two teams play, Stan avoids talking to Bill and Cindy, too. "I don't really want to be with people who are not in my corner," he says. In the spring of '97, when Jeff was finishing his first full season as Knicks coach, Stan had his last conflicted moment: He wanted to win but couldn't be sure a New York loss in the second round wouldn't cost Jeff his job. Now? "Whether we beat him in the playoffs or not, he's financially secure, and it's established that he can coach in this league," Stan says. "I don't worry any more if we beat him. *Poor guy, what's going to happen to him?* He's set."

Riley knows Stan as well as he once knew Jeff, and what he has seen go on between them for five years leaves him shaking his head in admiration and concern. "It tells you something about their obsession," Riley says. "You hope that everybody understands and that the two of them don't break anybody's back with it."

Bill and Cindy have been bending with the force of this gale for years now, and, as she says, "it all just proves that insanity is contagious." The lunacy can be traced to Bill, although Cindy, as an Indiana schoolgirl, fell in love with basketball while watching Alex Groza and Wah-Wah Jones play for the NBA's old Indianapolis Olympians. A lifetime small college coach who made stops at Cal State–Hayward, SUNY-Brockport and Genessee Community College in Batavia, N.Y., Bill was your classic wildman on the sideline—kicking chairs, throwing his coat. Whenever he could, Bill would take Stan, the elder brother by 2½ years, or Jeff with him when scouting opponents. Instead of houses with curlicue chimney smoke, the boys picked up crayons and drew X's and O's.

When Jeff was 10, Bill started having blackouts. He passed out twice while driving the car and once in his office before doctors diagnosed a brain tumor. The surgery to remove the benign growth lasted 9½ hours, and the memory of that December day in 1971 still leaves Jeff's eyes red and wet. While his dad was recovering at home, laid out on the bed with splitting headaches, Cindy drove the two boys to scout an upcoming opponent. Bill wanted to be back on the bench by the new year. The boys watched the players, tried to pick up patterns and wrote it all down. Cindy charted shots. The kids were never told how close they had come to losing their dad, and no one really knew how scared Jeff had been until later at school, when he cut out a photo of doctors in an operating room and wrote a story about his friend "Billy" who had a tumor.

The two boys had the sardonic sense of humor necessary to survive their father's hired-to-be-fired existence, but Jeff always knew how to push Stan's buttons. "We argue all the time, about everything," Stan says. "I start getting pissed off and raising my voice. He just sticks to his guns and tells you what you think is stupid."

The first time Jeff and Stan were on opposite sides of the court in a game that mattered came during the final of a four-team tournament in 1984. Stan was coaching Castleton (Vt.) State. Jeff, playing point guard for Nazareth College of Rochester, N.Y., had nine points and six assists in Nazareth's victory and was named the tournament's MVP. Once both had become coaches, the brothers were more supportive of each other. When Pitino protege Stu Jackson, who'd been an assistant with Jeff at Providence and later brought him to the Knicks, became Wisconsin coach in 1992, Jeff called Jackson and said of Stan, "He's a better version of me." That was enough for Jackson, who hired Stan as an assistant. (After Jackson left two seasons later, Stan was the Badgers' coach for a year.) When Riley left New York for Miami in 1995, he tried to take Jeff with him, but Checketts wouldn't release Van Gundy from his contract. Jeff drove to Riley's house in Greenwich, Conn., and asked one favor: Talk to Stan; you'll hire him. Riley did. When Jeff became the Knicks' coach, it was Stan who gave him the best advice about the media, the players, the way people change.

Through it all, the brothers would talk hoops—sets, screens, defenses, specials, winning, losing, every game they coached and watched—spending hours on the phone rehashing play after mind-numbing play. Yet when Stan and Jeff talk on the phone in the pressurized days leading up to a Heat-Knicks series, or in the awkward days after, they talk about the weather, vacations, anything trivial. Once in a while during the regular season Jeff might try to land a jab or two. "Running a lot of flares after timeouts, huh?" he'll say, just to show Stan he's watching. All he gets back is silence.

Jeff has this dream: One day he and Stan will coach together. But Stan has no interest in being Jeff's assistant. "I can't see that," Stan says. "I'm used to being on even ground in arguments. I'm as convinced that my side's right as he is, and I always will be."

It is a curious time. Two days after the Knicks severed their 15-year relationship with Ewing by trading him to the Sonics in a four-team, 12-player deal, no one in the New York organization is crowing. They unloaded an aging and unhappy center for six players, including swingman Glen Rice and center Luc Longley, as well as four draft choices, yet no one even bothers to sell the notion that the team came out ahead. Despite the widespread assumption that another shoe will drop—some kind of grab for Dikembe Mutombo or Chris Webber—Van Gundy and general manager Scott Layden insist this undersized crew will be the team they take into the season.

No one doubts that Miami and the Orlando Magic improved their teams with off-season moves (though the Heat later learned that center Alonzo Mourning is suffering from kidney disease and will be lost for the season). The Knicks? "Oh, there's huge doubt," Van Gundy says. "We've got a glut of perimeter players, all our inside players have durability issues, and, other than Larry Johnson, none of the inside players have averaged more than 11 points a game. We took our best rebounder and traded him. Hell, there are a lot of worries. It's my job to make it work."

Don't bet against him. The man whose only previous head coaching experience was an 8–12 season at McQuaid Jesuit High in Rochester has now bested Riley in the playoffs three years running—and earned his mentor's abiding respect. In 1999, after Houston's shot did in the Heat, Riley stayed up all night. At 5:33 a.m. he picked up his pen. When Van Gundy arrived at his hotel room in Atlanta for the start of the second-round series against the Hawks, he found an envelope waiting for him. He got nervous when he recognized the writing. He had given his only child, daughter Mattie, now 5, the middle name Riley. But the two men hadn't spoken since sniping at each other after Van Gundy grabbed Mourning's ankle the year before, and Van Gundy worried that their relationship had been irreparably damaged.

The envelope was addressed to Coach Van Gundy—with Coach underlined. Riley had never called Van Gundy that. But Houston's shot, and the fact that Van Gundy ran the perfect inbounds set with 4.5 seconds left, proved to Riley that his former assistant had come into his own. "That's what he's about: He has them ready, and he has something for them when they need it," Riley says. "That's exactly what I wrote: 'You had it. You had a play for them.'"

He also wrote, "No matter where I go or what I do, the name Van Gundy will have a long-lasting, positive imprint on my life." Van Gundy carries the letter with him in his work bag wherever he goes.

Checketts believes all that sentiment only obscures the obvious. "Jeff's a better coach than Pat is," he says. "I've worked with both of them, and so much of what Pat does is to maintain Pat's image, and it takes away from his ability to focus on coaching. Jeff is consumed with getting his players to play in a way that will help him win. He's the perfect coach for New York."

That Checketts's support of him is now so glowing speaks loudly of Van Gundy's political skill. He has always been smart enough to stay close to the players, and that, in the end, saved his job when Checketts was deciding between Van Gundy and Grunfeld during the 1998–99 season. Yet Van Gundy was also aware enough of the landscape to cultivate reporters on the Knicks' beat and, once he'd heard Grunfeld was gunning for him, savvy enough to give them off-the-record critiques of Grunfeld, his methods and the June 1998 trade—against Van Gundy's wishes—of workhorse Charles Oakley for the oft-injured Marcus Camby. There's no doubt that when Checketts demoted Grunfeld in April 1999, Van Gundy's head was next on the block. He did everything he could to survive.

"It's gotten twisted around since I was the one left standing," says Van Gundy, who now says he was wrong about the Oakley trade. "Dave has told me that Ernie was coming to him 20 games into the year, weekly, trying to fire me. He was unhappy with my performance; I wasn't necessarily unhappy with his. I don't have any power to fire him. He wanted to fire me, but you know what? I got along with him." (Grunfeld declined to comment for this story.)

When, later that summer, Checketts was choosing between Knicks acting G.M. Ed Tapscott and Utah Jazz vice president of basketball operations Layden to replace Grunfeld, Van Gundy didn't hide the fact that his preference was Layden—the former assistant, the son of a coach. Tapscott now works for Grunfeld as a Bucks consultant. "Yeah, I want to control everything that goes into winning or losing," Van Gundy says. "I want to have a say, and I'm going to fight for what I think is right for our team."

Look at him: Hollowed-out eyes, skin the color of parchment—and training camp is still weeks away. Forget all the coaches with their mousse and high-fashion. Look at Van Gundy. On his face is evidence of all the lousy food, sleepless nights, bad news, clashing egos and injuries that every coach endures. On his face is written the job's dirty secret. Winning doesn't help.

"Losing has an unbelievably negative impact on me," Van Gundy says. "I read somewhere that failure is an event, not a person, but I never feel that way. It's who I am."

Pity him. He has never been happier.

DECEMBER 14, 2015

Ponytail Express

Before her pioneering role as an NBA assistant, Becky
Hammon was an overlooked recruit in South Dakota and
an underestimated point guard in the WNBA. Nothing has
come easy for her, and she wouldn't have it any other way

BY ALEXANDER WOLFF

One moment in one game in a risk-taker's city is all it took for Becky
Hammon to transform herself from feminist novelty into an NBA head-
coach-in-waiting.

The city was Las Vegas. The game, against the Knicks last July, was
Hammon's first in charge of the Spurs' entry in the NBA's premier summer
league. And the moment—with possession, down three, 23 seconds to play—
tested San Antonio coach Gregg Popovich's decision 11 months earlier to
make Hammon the first woman to serve as a salaried, full-time assistant for
a major pro sports team.

The Las Vegas Summer League is a cross between cattle call and last-
chance saloon, with all the Wild West untidiness those analogies suggest. A
coach's first challenge is to keep a player from turning every scarce moment
with the ball into an advertisement for himself. "She reminded us to just
bring those Spurs habits to Vegas, to play D and play with one another,"
recalls forward Kyle Anderson, the sole holdover from the franchise's
wintertime A team. "And—one thing that's big in San Antonio—she did a
great job coaching out of timeouts."

So it was that Hammon drew up a play, then watched with alarm as
Anderson and an assortment of rookies and free agents minced through

their first steps. "I could see that they weren't quite sure what to do," she says. "I probably didn't explain it well enough." Eight seconds later, she called another timeout.

Hammon reiterated what she wanted—"a punch play," where the ball goes into the post and out again, followed by a "misdirect flare screen." That's when it finally presented itself, what's known in the trade as a good look....

Where Hammon is involved, the smooth path seldom presents itself. Or, as she once put it in a blog post, "a rose has to push through some fertilizer (or another word for fertilizer, lol) to get to the sunlight to blossom." As a senior at Stevens High in Rapid City, S.D., she found most Division I schools turned off by her 5'6" frame and backwater pedigree. "Average white girl," thought Tom Collen, then an Arkansas assistant. Several years later Collen found himself the coach at Colorado State, where Hammon was already well on her way to scoring 2,740 points, more than any WAC player, male or female. She led a program that had never reached the Top 25 to the Sweet 16, sextupling attendance in the process.

But she had the bad timing to leave Fort Collins right after the demise of the American Basketball League, which flooded the market with experienced talent in 1999. So Hammon took a free-agent flier as one of 20 invitees at the training camp of the New York Liberty, who already had four veteran guards. Two of them, co-captains Teresa Witherspoon and Vickie Johnson, pleaded with management, as one of them put it, to "keep that little white girl who keeps getting up when we knock her down." The Liberty did, and soon Hammon began to trace a steady path: from spot duty off the bench as a rookie, to double-figure points in her second season, to team leader in scoring and shooting percentage in her fifth—before tearing her right ACL. "I've had 17 NBA All-Stars, and nobody drove and finished better than Becky Hammon," says her coach for six summers in New York, Richie Adubato. "Michael or Kobe or [Derrick] Rose could elevate and slither, but Becky is 5'6" and only jumps an inch. When she drove you couldn't see her in the crowd in the lane—just the ball coming out of there and into the basket."

In April 2007, just after turning 30 and suffering a bad left-ankle sprain, the Liberty traded her to San Antonio. There she logged eight more seasons with the Stars and, in 2011, was named one of the top 15 WNBA players of all time. Throughout her career she supplemented meager WNBA wages by playing winters in Italy, Spain, Israel and Russia—a country that crops up in her story again and again.

In 2007, Hammon completed her finest WNBA season to date, finishing second in the MVP voting, the highest among American players. But she wasn't included in the initial U.S. player pool for the 2008 Beijing Games, and though she was eventually invited to try out, her agent confirmed with USA Basketball that she wasn't in serious contention to make the team. So to fulfill a childhood dream of playing in the Olympics, she chose to become a Russian citizen. "She didn't say no to USA Basketball," says Chicago Sky coach Pokey Chatman, who coached her at Spartak Moscow Region. "*They* didn't say yes to *her*. But I don't think she ever came out and put it that way."

The U.S. coach, Anne Donovan, called Hammon's decision "not patriotic." Yet Hammon regards it as an inflection point in her life. "I know I can take a lot of crap when I follow my heart," she says. "To that point I represented the very all-American girl next door, with the ponytail from the Midwest. But that proved I'm not afraid to take a risk. And I risked a lot. My reputation— people said terrible things about me."

But Hammon has a highly developed sense of the silver lining. If the play you call looks shaky, you take another TO to give it a better chance to work. As she says, "My journey had been divinely orchestrated, with one step leading to another."

If she hadn't grown up in South Dakota, where the basketball season then took place in the fall and recruiters gave it a miss, she wouldn't have landed at a Rams program aching for leadership. If she hadn't gone undrafted, she wouldn't have been forced to refine the skills that made her a WNBA legend. If she hadn't hurt her ankle, she wouldn't have been traded to San Antonio and crossed paths with Popovich. If she hadn't been snubbed by Team USA, she wouldn't have become a basketball Russian, which synced up with the academic interest of the Spurs' coach, a Soviet specialist at the Air Force Academy—which would have meant that, when the two found themselves seated next to each other on a flight back from the London Olympics in 2012, they might have been left with nothing to talk about but basketball. Of Hammon and basketball, Popovich already knew plenty; instead they covered just about everything else, which gave the famously worldly Pop his first nuanced sense of her.

Hammon's decision to play for Russia impressed him all on its own. "It was pretty brave, because you knew there'd be people of the ilk of 'That's unpatriotic or shortsighted,'" he says. "It's not about any of that. It's about being a competitor and living a life that lasts not very long, and taking advantage of all life's opportunities without hurting anybody else. She seizes the day."

That the two happened to be in the same row on the same flight—that was just happenstance, right? "I don't think that anything," Hammon says, "is happenstance."

Rapid City was founded one night in 1876 when 11 men around a campfire took honest stock of their lot. Their dreams of finding gold on what is now the western fringe of South Dakota had come to nothing. So they raffled off 11 plots of land among themselves, pledging to "lay out a Denver" for the Black Hills. It was a better bet after a lesser one failed to pay off, but a risky one just the same.

Marty and Bev Hammon arrived from Minnesota a century later in the same prospecting spirit. With Marty assigned new territory as a regional sales rep for a fire sprinkler company, the family moved into a trailer park with daughter Gina, son Matt and infant Rebecca Lynn. Several years later the Hammons built a house with 30,000 acres of the Black Hills National Forest spilling from its door. "Becky would be sitting on the stairs waiting for me to get home from work, and we'd go out and have an adventure," says Marty, who would take neighborhood kids along too. "I promised to never bring 'em back clean."

By the time she turned 12, Becky had learned to hunt pheasant and grouse and handle a shotgun—an heirloom Browning over-under 12-gauge. With Bev brushing the snarls from her hair after a day at what friends called Camp Marty, Becky picked up the nickname Beckaboo, which eventually morphed into Boo-Boo, then Bubba. On snowmobiles, three-wheelers and four-wheelers she crossed creeks and transited ravines, developing the fearlessness, sense of balance and what she calls "overall general alertness" that helped her thrive as a point guard.

During family trips to the Florida Keys, Becky would swim with manatees and dolphins and sometimes sharks, spearing fish for dinner. "If we were all camping, she'd tell us what to do," Popovich says. "She's one of the few women I know who could have survived pioneer days and lived off the land."

In 1993, when Becky was 16, Marty started his own fire sprinkler business. He took out a second mortgage. He paid the penalty for dipping into his IRA. For seven months he didn't see a paycheck. Matt Hammon and his siblings bought out his father three years ago, and Rapid Fire Protection, Inc., is now a $24 million-a-year business with 170 employees. "My dad has a very fearless approach to life," Becky says. "He's smart but not afraid to take risks."

Throughout her childhood Marty had supplied his daughter with reality checks. He first disabused her of dreams of dunking. Then he explained why she'd never play in the NBA.

"I didn't," he says, "say anything about coaching."

Hammon's tear of her left ACL, in July 2013, couldn't have been better timed. It came shortly before the Spurs assembled for training camp and led Popovich to offer her unlimited access to the team's inner sanctum. "Because

I respected her so much, when she got hurt I thought, This young lady can't just sit around all year," he says. "I wanted to see what else was there."

At Colorado State she had been an exercise and sport science major with a concentration in teaching and a coaching minor. Breaking in as a WNBA benchwarmer, Hammon got her first look at pro ball as a coach sees it, learning to assess how a game's rhythm and flow might be altered or exploited. She was already friendly with her Spurs counterpart at point guard, Tony Parker. "She knows when to speak and knows when to shut up," Popovich has said of Hammon, a description that reminds former teammate Rebecca Lobo of the player who had the ability to connect in any corner of the Liberty locker room: "In a coaching situation, just like in a social situation, she knows how to fit in."

Popovich liked another thing about her. "It was just a kick to watch her play, chewing her gum and directing traffic," he says. "She exuded leadership on the court, and players reacted to that. R.C. [Buford, the Spurs' general manager] and I never gave it a second thought. We just did it."

Her hiring became official after that year's apprenticeship and her final WNBA season the following summer. NBA rules mandate that she sit behind the bench because she's not one of Popovich's top three assistants. But there's no duty her boss doesn't trust her with, whether preparing a scouting report or putting a player through an individual workout. She blends seamlessly into the practice-court tableau, except for the occasional splash of color in a headband that pops from the ambient silver and black. "At the beginning I was concerned," Ettore Messina, Popovich's lead assistant, says. "How can we joke? How can we curse? But she's perfectly *there*, and not because she wants to act like a man. She's a woman with a touch of class. In Italian we have the word *femmininilita*, meaning the class of a woman. She has that, even in a men's environment."

Hammon credits the WNBA with professionalizing her through the rigor of weight work and film study. The league also helped her earn respect from NBA players, notwithstanding what she calls "the Joe Schmoes" who might still deride the league. "LeBron James and Chris Paul, they watch it and enjoy it," she says. "Especially the young guys, many of them watched me play. But the biggest was Pop. He and R.C. saw me run a thousand pick-and-rolls. A pick-and-roll is a pick-and-roll no matter who's running it.

"Character is genderless. Leadership is genderless. If you're a great leader, you're a great leader. Patience, service, the ability to listen—either you have it or you don't."

Months after that Las Vegas fortnight, Anderson can still hear Hammon telling him not to "get too cute out there." That sound, he says, "is the voice of authority. I hear it regardless."

Hammon could have any women's coaching job she wants right now, WNBA or major college, but she's in the second year of a two-year deal with San Antonio. "I'm in a great learning space, and this year I'm so much more comfortable," she says. "Then, we'll see."

That shot Hammon engineered at the end of her first game in Las Vegas, a three-pointer from the corner, failed to go in. Afterward she received a consolatory text from her former Stars coach Dan Hughes: *You did what great coaches do. You gave your players a chance to win.* That didn't keep her from revisiting her mistakes through a sleepless night. But over the rest of the competition the Spurs won six straight, including four by five points or fewer, even coming back from 15 down in the second half to beat the Hawks in the semifinals. After they tripped the Suns 93–90 for the title, Hammon's players made the ultimate gesture of acceptance, giving her a Gatorade dousing—although with no cooler handy, the shower came in the form of a dozen players emptying a dozen bottles. It was a Hammonesque moment, making the best of the situation.

Popovich cites the hug that Anderson, the summer league's MVP, fixed her with after the final. "That was heartfelt and genuine and told me a lot," he says. "That's the new generation. Kyle is 21 or 22, and not too cool to do that."

Months later, the day after being named coach of the U.S. men's team for the four-year cycle following next year's Rio Olympics, Popovich sat in his office at San Antonio's AT&T Center and fielded a question: Might there be a place on his U.S. staff for the former point guard of Russia's women's team?

Popovich stiffened as if he had just spotted a Craig Sager sport coat at 10 paces. He began ticking off politic disclaimers. And then he permitted himself a smile. Perhaps he suddenly realized that he might not want to transit the badlands of international basketball without his own Laura Ingalls Wilder. "It is," he said, "a pretty cool thought."

— POSTSCRIPT —

Alexander Wolff: During 36 years on staff I can't think of more than a time or two when I wasn't given the time and resources to do a story properly. Even in the 2010s, with the magazine's budget tightening, editors let me tick the requisite boxes on this story. They sent me to Fort Collins, Colo., to talk to those who remembered Becky from college; to Rapid City, Iowa, to speak with her dad and see the Black Hills that had nurtured her sense of adventure; and of course to San Antonio. The Spurs can be a tough nut to crack, and when I first approached them about doing the piece, they were reluctant to cooperate. (They wanted Becky's private life off-limits, a condition I couldn't come up with a good reason not to accept.) But a year earlier, working on a long feature about the Spurs' Aussie guard Patty Mills and his complicated story, I'd dealt extensively with Gregg Popovich and won his trust. Pop prides himself on recreating the wild diversity of the wider world on his team—he really believes that the Spurs derive strength from their differences—and I have to confess I'm a sucker for that attitude. If writing about pro basketball in the 21st century is rewarding, it's because no other staging ground in sports has more disparate elements colliding and throwing off the sparks that make for a good story.

NOVEMBER 11, 1991

For Whom the Bulls Toil

Bulls coach Phil Jackson used diplomacy—and occasional
strong-arm tactics—to keep a firm hold on his NBA champs

BY JACK McCALLUM

*During his time in the league, Phil Jackson masterfully crafted his own
narrative. He cozied up to reporters. He wrote a series of books, detailing his
relationships with Kobe, Shaq and MJ. Here, Jack McCallum captures Jackson
early in his coaching career, after his time as backup forward for the Knicks
but before his run of titles with the Bulls and Lakers, providing a markedly
different view of the man who would come to be known as the Zen Master.*

On Labor Day weekend of 1962, Philip Douglas Jackson snuck out of the
house and went to the drive-in movies, hardly unusual behavior for a soon-
to-be 17-year-old male with raging hormones. Except that he went with his
older brother, Joe. And the feature was *Seven Brides for Seven Brothers*. And
it was the first movie that Phil ever saw.

Jackson could go to dances, but he wasn't allowed to dance. He could
play sports, but only when they didn't conflict with church functions. He
didn't have a favorite TV program because his parents forbade a boob tube.
He could read the Bible, *Reader's Digest* and *Illustrated Classics*, but, aside
from textbooks, that was about all—no comics, no pulp fiction, no nonsense.
He could sing in church and school choruses (and he was good, first as a
tenor, then, after he began to grow, a baritone), but he couldn't listen to
rock 'n' roll. Most Saturday evenings found him at the dining room table for

"family game night," flicking wooden disks around a rectangular board in a game called Carooms—Jackson calls it Christian pool—or dealing a couple of hands of Rook, a game with faceless playing cards, the kind that didn't send you straight to hell. And on Sundays he stood outside the Assembly of God Church in Williston, N.D., next to his father, Charles, the Pentecostal preacher man, exchanging handshakes and small talk with fellow believers, a gawky greeter in the service of the Lord.

Not many years later, Phil Jackson had long hair, a beard and a restless spirit. He read books on Eastern religion by day, threw elbows around for the New York Knicks by night and dabbled in recreational drugs somewhere in between. He played like a wolf on the prowl, yet ate a careful diet that, for a while, consisted only of vegetables and vitamin supplements. He tested all the rules and all the patience of his coach, Red Holzman, yet he hung on the older man's every word, filing them away for later use. He loved New York City, yet later settled his family in Woodstock, N.Y., among the artisans and bohemians. He longed to coach in the NBA, but showed up in Chicago to interview for an assistant's job with the Bulls wearing a Panama hat with a macaw's feather, and then tried to explain the legend of the feather to his prospective boss, Stan Albeck.

"His eyes glazed over very early in the interview," says Jackson, who did not get the job.

So what does the sum of all that experience make the Phil Jackson of today, the 46-year-old Phil Jackson who last season guided the Bulls to their first NBA title?

"A man with a great perspective, a great base of reference, a lot of dimensions," says Knick coach Pat Riley. "These days coaches have to offer more. You've got to bring more to the table. And Phil Jackson brings more to the table than most coaches I can think of."

"Meekness in itself is nothing else than a TRUE KNOWING and feeling of a man's self as he is. Any man who truly sees and feels himself as he is must surely be meek indeed."

That quotation, from a book called *The Cloud of Unknowing*, written by an anonymous 16th-century Christian mystic, is printed on an index card and tacked to a wall in Jackson's office at the Multiplex, the Bulls' suburban practice center in Deerfield, Ill. Jackson put it there partly as a reminder to himself, partly as an irritant to assistant coach Johnny Bach, whose view of life is anything but beatific. They argue about it from time to time—Bach, the former Navy gunnery officer and father of a California state trooper, holding that might makes right; Phil, the former flower child, clinging to the view that a man can be humble, passionate, fearful and even self-doubting, yet still be a warrior and a winner.

Everything about Jackson's background suggests a man who has learned to weigh the warring impulses inside him and pursue a system of beliefs and behavior that eludes precise characterization. Compared to most coaches, he comes across like a philosophy professor, a little soft, a little trippy, a little abstract. But put him outside the athletic world, and he would probably come across like an ex-jock or a coach—competitive and driven. Jackson is comfortable on his philosophical tightrope, reaching out to touch something over here, then something way over there, straddling two worlds, listening to all sides, getting along with everyone.

"Phil's like lubricating oil," says June Jackson, his wife of 17 years. "He keeps everything moving."

The art of the compromise—that is what Jackson has mastered. And if his accommodations sometimes come out looking like paradox, then so be it. The Bulls have the greatest open-court player in the history of the game, yet Jackson resolutely—many said stubbornly—stuck to a patterned offense last season that was devised a decade before Michael Jordan was born. There were times during the playoffs, though, when Jackson scrapped the patterned "triangle offense" devised by Bulls assistant Tex Winter in favor of the screen-rolls and isolations used by most NBA teams. Jackson is by nature egalitarian, yet he admittedly bends team rules to accommodate Jordan. He wrote a controversial and candid book about his career (*Maverick*), and Lord knows he could be happy only in an open society, yet he's extremely wary of the press and somewhat secretive about team matters.

The Bulls' 1990–91 championship season brought Jackson dozens of invitations to clinics and corporate gatherings, yet the only thing that drew him away from his isolated family retreat along Flathead Lake in Montana over the summer was a low-paying appearance at a holistic summer camp near Woodstock. He is determined not to become a human billboard like Mike Ditka, his counterpart with the Bears (whom, somewhat incredibly, Jackson has never met), yet he did sign on for one local commercial with a Cadillac dealer because—hold on to your love beads all you '60s devotees— he drives one. "I didn't want to turn the championship into a capitalistic conquest," said Jackson. "But, let's face it, I took the commercial, and *any* commercial is basically self-serving." Had Jackson, a liberal Democrat, been invited to the White House by a conservative Republican president 10 years ago, he might not have gone, yet when the call came for the Bulls to visit with George Bush last month, Jackson shrugged his huge shoulders and climbed into his suit because he felt he owed it to the franchise. Predictably, Jackson did not join the storm of protest, both within the Chicago organization and without, when Jordan passed up the ceremony. "It was a personal choice," said Jackson, referring to Jordan's absence.

And while Jackson is now uncomfortable with institutionalized religion, he gathers with the other members of his family (June, daughters Chelsea, 16, and Brooke, 14, and 12-year-old fraternal twins Ben and Charley) once a week in their home in Bannockburn, a Chicago suburb, to talk about spiritual subjects and other matters of the heart. (Another daughter, Elizabeth, 23, lives in Washington.)

Such efforts go largely unappreciated in Bigfork, Mont., where Phil's mother, Elisabeth, an erstwhile soul-saving, street-corner evangelist in her own right, who's alone now that Charles has gone to his just reward, prays often for her son's soul. "My mother still tells me, 'Fifteen hundred people witnessed you being given to God, given to the service of the Lord,'" Jackson says. "She really sees that as the fulfillment of my life, not basketball. I guess in some small way she considers me a success, certainly by financial standards. But spiritually? She has her doubts."

Growing up in Williston, then a hard-scrabble town of about 11,000 near the Montana border, Jackson heard more than his share of Holy Roller jibes, but he was never an outcast. If there was a school activity, chances are he was in it. His parents did not hold him back as long as fundamentalist doctrine was not violated. He took piano lessons, played trombone in the school band and acted in high school productions. He was a split end, a defensive lineman and linebacker (now *there's* a trio) in the fall, a high-scoring center in the winter, a pitcher-first baseman in the spring.

An ambitious young basketball coach named Bill Fitch first visited with Jackson on a bitter spring afternoon in Williston, where, in Fitch's car with the heater running, the coach persuaded Jackson to come to the University of North Dakota. Williston's cold, windy weather—"You can fly a kite there forever," says Fitch—made the people tough and competitive, and the loose-limbed Holy Roller was as tough and competitive as anyone. Jackson's fastball drew the attention of baseball recruiters, but Fitch wanted him only for basketball. "It was the right choice," said Fitch, who went on to coach in the NBA with Cleveland, Boston, Houston and, now, New Jersey. "He couldn't find home plate with a Geiger counter."

One of the turning points in Jackson's life occurred late in his freshman year at North Dakota when he took a long drive with his older brother, Joe, then a graduate student at the University of Texas. Joe had become skeptical about the validity of fundamentalism, and Phil, slowly but surely, was beginning to question his own beliefs, too. The changes within him were wrenching ones—he was, after all, a kid who came to college unable to accept the principles of Darwinism taught in biology class because they conflicted with the biblical story of creation—and he couldn't ignore them. He began to choose courses from all over the North Dakota curriculum, finally ending up with a composite major in psychology, religion and philosophy—three good reasons to read a lot of books and get into a lot of heady, late-night discussions. Having been a prisoner of rigid dogma for so long, Jackson found great joy in simple intellectual freedoms that others took for granted. Certainly he was not the first college student to rebel against his background, but the difference is that once Jackson started to question, he never stopped. His life became—and to a certain extent still is—a constant reexamination, a desire, as he puts it, "to see what doors I could open."

"I think the myopic way I grew up—and that's the best word to describe it—led to my experimentation," says Jackson. "Everything that happened to me in the 1960s was in tune with my background. The whole psychedelic experience or an LSD trip was, as Timothy Leary said, 'a religious experience.'"

The number of professional coaches who quote Timothy Leary is, to be sure, quite small. And as a forward for the Knicks from 1967–68 through '77–78, Jackson opened a few doors that made his coaches a little skittish. But even when he was living a mild version of the psychedelic life, there was something about him that was stable, something eminently sensible. "He's the most comfortable person I've ever known, and that comes through to people," says Charley Rosen, Jackson's co-author of *Maverick* and later his assistant coach in the Continental Basketball Association. "Often he walked to games in New York, and everybody talked to him—bums, kids, cops, businessmen. It didn't make a difference. Everybody just somehow trusted Phil."

Jackson's revelation in *Maverick*, published in 1975, of his occasional drug use caused a stir. "I was quick to realize that you don't get dropped on the stage without a certain price," says Jackson. He doesn't regret his candor in *Maverick*—regret isn't his style—but June despises the book. "People forget that everyone changes," she says. "What Phil was—or any of us were, for that matter—15 years ago is not what he is today."

Jackson feels that he was distrusted by certain segments of the NBA establishment for a while, but these days his counter-culture leanings are generally forgotten or treated with humor. After he lit a smudge stick of sagebrush in his office a couple of seasons ago, for example, a few players stuck their heads in the door and said, "Oh, back to smokin' a little dope, eh, coach?" Actually, in some Indian tribes the lighting of sage is a ritual of purification—one just doesn't see it much in the NBA.

Anyway, whatever Jackson was questioning in the late-1960s and mid-'70s, it was never his love for basketball. He and Rosen coined a saying early in their friendship, and they still repeat it often: "Basketball's not a metaphor for life. Life's a metaphor for basketball."

On the court, Jackson was never confused with a ballet dancer—his movements still suggest one of those loose-jointed skeletons that get nailed to the front door on Halloween—but he played the game intensely, intelligently and unselfishly. Before Holzman had an assistant, he sometimes sent Jackson to scout the opposition (telling him to buy a meal on the team in exchange for his work), because he trusted Jackson's basketball mind. They didn't have anything in common—the traditional, conservative New Yorker in his Brooks Brothers suits, and the bearded, inquisitive, tie-dyed soul from the north—except for a mutual respect.

Jackson appreciated what he calls Holzman's "tender touch," his knack for compromise and conciliation. "He never overloaded you with advice. He doled it out in small packets and in a variety of ways," says Jackson. "He had a featherweight punch that hit you like a knockout blow." Some of Jackson's off-the-court coaching stratagems—giving his players books to read on road trips, taking a bus instead of a plane so they could see the countryside—are really new-age Holzman.

Still, no one figured Jackson for the coaching type—including Jackson himself, who wrote in *Maverick* that coaching wasn't for him because he couldn't deal with the egos and eccentricities of the players. But after he was traded to the New Jersey Nets in 1978 and became a player-assistant coach under Kevin Loughery, he found he liked coaching.

Jackson's playing career ended in 1980. He ran a health club in Montana for a year and then rejoined the Nets as a TV commentator for a season before taking the head coaching job with the Albany Patroons of the CBA in 1983. He moved his family to Woodstock, trading the 110-mile round-trip commute to Albany for the experience of living in a counter-culture environment. When Bulls general manager Jerry Krause called him in 1985 to interview for an assistant's job with Albeck, he felt he was ready for the NBA but not necessarily ready to fit the mold. "I wanted jobs, but I wanted them on my terms," says Jackson, "and I was still young enough to believe that could happen. I wasn't flaunting anything. I wore suits—don't forget I spent my whole boyhood in Sunday clothes—but, yes, I had the beard." And he had the Panama hat, a model that he had picked up in Puerto Rico, where he had been supplementing his income with summer coaching stints, to protect himself from the sun. "It's not just a hat," says Jackson, who still has it, "it's a *great* hat." Albeck took one look at it and wouldn't let Jackson sell ice cream to his team, much less coach it. "And this from a guy who frizzes his hair," says Jackson, smiling.

Jackson stayed with the Patroons for almost five seasons before tiring of the CBA and quitting after the 1986–87 season. He was considering graduate school and filing for unemployment when Krause called again in September '87 to ask him to interview for an assistant's job that had opened up under Doug Collins. "This time, Phil," said Krause, "come in here the right way." Hatless, featherless and clean-shaven, Jackson was hired. And when Collins was fired after the 1988–89 season, Jackson was elevated to the head job as, according to Krause, "the only candidate I ever considered."

Two major reasons Collins was fired were his emotional volatility (initially a strength because he was able to motivate a young team, later a problem because the Bulls started tuning him out) and his refusal to accept Winter's offensive system. Jackson was clearly of more even temperament than Collins and, just as clearly, had more respect for Winter. Collins, who would not comment for this story, has said that he believes that Jackson worked behind the scenes to backstab him, partly by guaranteeing that he would accept Winter's triple-post system if he got the head job. Both Jackson and Krause vehemently deny that there was any politicking to get Collins fired. "It's a move that had to be made," says Krause. "I remember when Phil told me he was going with Tex's system, and it was well after he was hired. Frankly, yes, I was glad to hear it because I happen to think Tex Winter is a genius. But it was not a condition of Phil's hiring."

If there was one question about Jackson as a head coach, though, it was not whether he would paint the locker room black or hire Jerry Garcia as a scout—it was his ability to come up with an offensive game plan. As a player he averaged only 6.7 points per game in a 13-year career, during which he concentrated on defense. "In his ability to guard every position on the floor, he was ahead of his time defensively," says Holzman.

"Tex's system is exactly what I was looking for," said Jackson. "When I got here, there was a feeling of impotence among some players who were eliminated from the process of ball movement. I came from the Knick system that incorporated all five players. Tex's system made a lot of sense."

It was Jackson's job to sell the system to the players, particularly Jordan, who openly derided it. The coach and the superstar played a constant game of give-and-take, Jackson at times turning the game over to Jordan in exchange for Jordan's sometimes sacrificing points for passes. "It was a difficult sell to Michael," says Jackson, "and it will continue to be difficult."

The compromise system worked to perfection in The Finals against the Lakers, as did Bach's stifling defense; the Bulls were simply an overpowering team in June. Whether or not they will be as overpowering this season is anyone's guess, but, obviously, Jackson's continued rapport with Jordan will be a major factor.

"Phil spent the first half of the year trying to build a solid foundation, getting everyone involved, and I understood that," said Jordan recently. "Yes, I was frustrated at times in the system, but, basically, I understood it. And in the second half of the season he was a little more free-wheeling, a little more willing to open it up. It worked. You have to say it worked, and I give him credit for it. Phil was good for our team, and that's what matters."

Off the floor, any coach of Jordan's has an even more difficult time. Before they almost magically peaked in June, the Bulls were not a particularly harmonious band of merry men. There was grumbling about Jordan from his teammates and complaints about the special treatment afforded him, much of it soon to become public in a book entitled *The Jordan Rules*, written by Sam Smith of the *Chicago Tribune*. Both Jackson and Jordan are awaiting its publication in late fall, though not eagerly. Jackson defends whatever he did and still must do to accommodate Jordan.

"My first concern when I got the job was trying to treat Michael as equally as possible on the court," said Jackson. "That's what our offensive system is all about. But there is no possible way to treat him like every other player off the floor. He cannot walk downstairs in a hotel without being mobbed. I've walked past his room and seen eight, sometimes 10 service people—hotel employees!—outside his door, lurking to see if he comes out, flowers and candy all over the place. Unlike other players he has to have people travel with him to filter some of this out. We made our rules strict. His friends couldn't ride on the team bus or the team charter, but they could be with him on the road. There is a difference in the way he's treated, yes, but there's also a difference in the way he produces. A *big* difference. And that must be weighed. There are jealousies that other players must overcome. If they do, we'll be a great team. If they don't, it's going to be a long season."

If some Bulls resented the special treatment given Jordan, almost all of them appreciated the individual treatment they received from Jackson.

"This is not an easy team to coach," says veteran center Bill Cartwright. "There are so many guys who can really play, who really want to take all the big shots, and there were lots of times, of course, when Michael felt he could simply take over. One of the things Phil did was get Michael to accept his role. And the other thing he did was coach his players like individuals. With me, for example, he wanted to make sure I was healthy, make sure I was getting enough rest. And the fact that he cares about his players off the court gets through, too."

In some respects, 26-year-old Scottie Pippen is as difficult for a coach as Jordan is. Pippen's game was rough and undisciplined, and it was a constant struggle for Jackson to harness Pippen's extraordinary natural ability. Pippen is a proud and emotional man, too, and it took of every bit of Jacksonian diplomacy not only to teach him the finer points, but also to convince him they were necessary. Pippen improved so much last season that he landed a spot, with Jordan, on the 1992 U.S. Olympic team.

"The best thing that happened to us was that Scottie took to our coaching and trusted our intuition," says Jackson. "We encouraged him to provide certain skills. He worked, for example, on different backboard angles on his shots, when to take his shot, knowing when he had to score and when he didn't. The maturing of Scottie Pippen as a player was a major factor in our winning."

Indeed, Jackson searches constantly for ways to enlighten his players, to expand the limited frame of reference held by many modern-day athletes. The books, the side trips, the subliminal and overt messages he slips into game films, his prattling on about the lessons of history—all those, he hopes, will have some kind of effect. "I'd like to do more," says Jackson. "When we're in Washington I'd like to take the team to the Senate chamber instead of shoot-around. I'd like us all to go to an art museum. College coaches are able to do that kind of thing once in a while, but as a professional I have to be careful. Having to win the game gets in the way." But Jackson, somewhat the cockeyed idealist, plunges on, seeking to redefine the role of coach, to find a way to make a difference, probing, weighing, compromising. And one wonders when his restless mind will tell him to move on.

"Tell you the truth, I'm surprised he got into coaching," says Fitch. "Not that he couldn't handle it, but because I thought he'd be a Bill Bradley type, maybe a senator from North Dakota." Says Holzman, "I still think he could go back and be governor of North Dakota." June Jackson suggests that her husband's secret dream is to head the Bureau of Indian Affairs in a Democratic administration of Bradley's, who is still a close friend. Jackson has a deep interest in Native American culture and is surely the only NBA coach with a Xeroxed copy of a postcard of Sioux sign language on his desk, right there next to Winter's *Triple-Post Offense* and John Wooden's *Practical Modern Basketball*.

"Well, I do want to do something worthwhile after basketball," said Jackson, "but I'm just not sure what it is. Everything comes with a price. Indian Affairs? Sure, it would interest me. But I've got time. I'll study my options."

Of course he will. A few summers ago, Jackson went to a Pentecostal service back in Bigfork just to please his mother. During the sermon the preacher began hammering upon the point that there were three sinners in the congregation, three influential men who had turned their back on the Lord by staying away from the church.

"Come forward now and save yourselves!" he shouted. "Come forward and receive the blessings of God!"

Jackson recognized the technique—Lord knows he had seen it enough— but he stared straight ahead. Two of the men finally gave in to the altar call and went forward to be saved. The preacher kept hammering away at the one who didn't. But Jackson stayed in his seat, expression unchanged.

"Sometimes you just have to harden your heart," he said later, "and wait it out."

− POSTSCRIPT −

Jack McCallum: For years after I did this story on Jackson and his Pentecostal background, I used to say to him: "Hey, Phil. You played any Carooms or Rooks lately?" He became more elusive in his later years of coaching the Bulls and the Lakers in Los Angeles, but, though we never spoke of it, I think this 1991 story established a bond between us.

FEBRUARY 12, 2007

Lord Jim

For the NBA's most confounding franchise, the spotlight
is on the tempestuous, blues-strumming owner—cable-
television tycoon Jim Dolan—and a much maligned
coach who will either build a winner or lose his job

BY S.L. PRICE

*To be a basketball fan in the first decade of the 2000s was, in large part, to
detest Jim Dolan. Piece by piece, he dismantled a storied franchise. In this
searing feature, S.L. Price uses an avalanche of details to provide a telling
portrait of Dolan. The opening scene—Hawaiian shirt, Springsteen parody,
lack of self-awareness—is unforgettable.*

One night in September 2000, on a makeshift stage in a resort ballroom on
Sanibel Island in Florida, Cablevision Systems CEO Jim Dolan stood before a
captive audience of subordinates—six or seven dozen senior managers from
Madison Square Garden and its sports properties—and began to sing. It was
a lark, one of those gags designed to blow off steam after a day of meetings.
Still, barely a year had passed since Dolan had taken full control of the
Garden and its two main tenants, the New York Knickerbockers and the New
York Rangers, and many in the room had had only glimpses of an owner
who, for his entire adult life, had been overshadowed by his father, cable-TV
pioneer Charles Dolan. The tales of Jim's drug-and-drink-addled past, his
volcanic temper, his shifting moods, were already legendary, fueling the

image of a spoiled boy who had been handed the keys to perhaps the most prized property in all of U.S. sports. No one expected a song.

Yet there Dolan was, fronting a band consisting of Garden employees in Hawaiian shirts and belting out a parody of Bruce Springsteen's "Born to Run." In the audience was Garden president Dave Checketts, who had helmed the most profitable run in Garden history: 10 years of record attendance and revenues that coincided with the exorcism of a 54-year championship curse on the Rangers in 1993–94 and the Knicks' rides to the '94 and '99 NBA Finals. Now there was talk that Checketts, whose relations with Dolan were strained, would bolt to Salt Lake City to rescue the troubled 2002 Winter Olympics. So Dolan was wooing him in a Long Island accent ravaged by years of substance abuse, the boss channeling the Boss.

Dave, this company rips the bones from your back:
It's a death trap, it's a suicide rap.
You should have got out while you were young...
Because I have something to tell you: I'm Chuck Do-lan's son!

Some in the audience cheered. Looking back, most see the moment as a highlight of Dolan's speckled tenure at the Garden. The disastrous trade of future Hall of Famer Patrick Ewing, which would hamstring the franchise financially for years, wouldn't happen for another two weeks. As the music rolled on, Dolan sang that he wanted to be Checketts's friend, offered to rewrite Checketts's contract, even made fun of his own diminutive (5'6") stature. "It was a great moment," says one executive in the crowd that night. "He showed a human side, and everybody was really relieved."

But some also found the moment startling. Dolan was lampooning himself, yes, but he was also bellowing his power with a pride that could be taken as menacing. After all, he ended his musical valentine with a warning:

Someday, Davey, I don't know when,
We're going to get to that place where we really want to go,
And we'll have some fun.
As long as you remember:
I'm Chuck Do-lan's son!

Nine months later Checketts left to start his own sports media and entertainment company. Since May 2001 Dolan has been the undisputed king of the self-styled World's Most Famous Arena, neither franchise has won a playoff series, and the Garden air is thick with bad feeling. Dolan is reviled by New York fans and media for piling up overpriced talent to no avail. The Rangers, aided by the outside discipline of the NHL salary cap and by a stellar year from Jaromír Jágr, showed a bit of playoff life last season before sinking back this winter into bland inconsistency. Meanwhile, for the Knicks, '06 was perhaps the most spectacularly awful year in NBA history.

Consider: Last January team president Isiah Thomas, after amassing the league's highest ($123 million) and most underachieving (14–30) payroll, was accused of sexual harassment by then Knicks vice president Anucha Browne Sanders, who charged that the married father of two twice told her he was in love with her and suggested trysts "off-site." Last spring the team's first-year coach, Larry Brown, engaged in a tabloid-fueled ripfest with his star player, guard Stephon Marbury, over Marbury's role on the team. In June, after letting Brown dangle for 40 days following the season, Dolan dismissed him and came dangerously close to suggesting that the coach had engaged in fraud by never intending to finish out his contract. Then Dolan announced that Thomas would coach the Knicks and, at the ensuing press conference, declared that he had just one season to demonstrate "significant progress" toward winning a championship. "If we can't say that, then Isiah will not be here," Dolan told the team's beat writers on June 26 as a stunned Thomas looked on. "It is his ship to steer, to make go fast, to crash."

Coaching has never been the most secure profession, but it's unheard of for an owner to publicly place the head of his president and coach on the chopping block. "That was a pretty bizarre situation," Miami Heat president and coach Pat Riley says of the Knicks' coaching shuffle. "I've never seen anything like it."

Not content to supply the NBA with the year's worst front-office scandal, ugliest player-coach conflict and most clumsily handled coaching change, the Knicks, on Dec. 16, also engaged in the worst brawl (a 10-player melee with the Denver Nuggets seemingly sparked by Thomas), prompting the league to suspend seven players and levy $1 million in fines and Denver coach George Karl to label Thomas "a jackass." Before the smoke cleared, though, the number 1 question was what impact the fight would have on Thomas's future, highlighting yet again the franchise's uniquely bizarre nature. In the ultimate players' league, these Knicks revolve around two men who never touch the ball. But whether Thomas lasts six months or six years, Dolan seized center stage when he handed Thomas the ultimatum. For the first time, publicly, the Knicks were all about Jim Dolan—and to some who have worked for him, it didn't come as a shock.

Since his first taste of performing in public, on Sanibel Island, the 51-year-old billionaire has made even the band all about him. He built a rehearsal studio on the grounds of his Long Island estate and replaced the Garden's amateur musicians with professionals; today the band is a five-piece blues outfit called J.D. and the Straight Shot. Dolan wears a fedora onstage, plays rhythm guitar and sings lead. For his sporadic performances at New York clubs, attendance by staffers is expected and noted.

"Jim actually doesn't care whether you love him or hate him, as long as you *know* him," says one former Garden executive. "Why else does he sit in the very front row? Why else does he come in late? He wants everyone to know: *I am in charge.*" Indeed, at home games Dolan sits courtside just steps from the Knicks' bench, dressed in funereal black, slumping conspicuously lower the further the Knicks fall behind. Yes, Dolan agrees, he's sending a message to his players.

"There's somebody here who's the owner of the joint," he says. "They're playing for somebody. It's me. I'm actually looking at them and saying, 'I sign your check. When you do great, I feel great, and when you do bad, I feel bad.'"

Dolan has no regrets about the squeeze he's put on Thomas. Sitting in his 26th-floor office across the street from the Garden one evening last month, sipping coffee, Dolan says, "From the day we hired Isiah, we embarked upon a strategy. It was Isiah's strategy, and it relied heavily on the choices he made. Where we ended up last year? It was sort of like, O.K., you've gone to the grocery store, you've gotten all your groceries, and you think we can be successful with what you've brought back? *Go cook.* Let's see if you can cook something good."

Isiah Thomas is ready with a joke. When the subject of the brawl comes up one January afternoon in the lunchroom at the Knicks' training center in Tarrytown, N.Y., he interrupts, "I did not order the Code Red." He laughs long and hard, though what he means isn't exactly clear.

Thomas is referring, of course, to Jack Nicholson's turn as Col. Nathan Jessup in *A Few Good Men*, in which Jessup at first denies ordering the fatal punishment of a man under his command. But Jessup did order the Code Red, so is Thomas coyly admitting that he did warn the Nuggets not to run up the score against New York just seconds before Knicks guard Mardy Collins horse-collared Denver's J.R. Smith on a breakaway and sparked the melee? The laugh isn't much of a clue.

Besides, anyone who has watched the 45-year-old Thomas this season can see he's trying to set a tone. Since becoming coach, he has seemingly taken on all of pro basketball. He took verbal shots at ESPN analyst Greg Anthony for his criticism of the Knicks' first-round draft choice, Renaldo Balkman; got into an altercation with New Jersey Nets coaches in the preseason; jawed at San Antonio Spurs forward Bruce Bowen in November and was heard telling his team to "break his f---foot." Thomas, the leader of the Detroit Pistons' infamous Bad Boys in the late 1980s, wants his team to grow a spine. If a few rules get broken along the way, if he only inspires more Isiah-haters around the league, too bad.

"Every arena we go to, they boo him," says Knicks forward Malik Rose. "Why? Did he shoot the Pope or something?"

Thomas has long had a reputation for being manipulative at best and devious at worst: a sweet-smiling operator who, despite being the smallest man on the court, could always charm, bully and dominate the bigger men surrounding him. He led Detroit to two NBA championships, but along with his Hall of Fame grit came an oily *Who, me?*, the classic instigator's mock innocence. He's always been the guy who started the food fight but went unpunished. His karmic payback would be a second act spent working in an NBA that refused, despite his dazzling accomplishments, to rank him alongside the league-saving trinity of Magic, Michael and Larry—and a Machiavellian image that prompts some serious rationalizing. Thomas says, "I always felt the reason why some of those guys said bad things about me was not because that's how they felt about me personally, but because they hated that they lost to me."

Whether he actually believes that is another thing entirely. Thomas has been blessed with a soft voice and a face that all but glows on camera; the contrast between his angelic façade and his street fighter's edge, between TV-ready Isiah and the hard-eyed operator his pals call Zeke, lends to his two-a-day meetings with the New York media an undercurrent of tension: *Will he crack? Will he lash out?* But he never does. "If I ever had to learn how to play poker, it'd be from Isiah," says Rose. "No one knows how he feels."

After a mediocre stint as vice president of the Toronto Raptors from 1994 through '97 and a disastrous two years as principal owner of the soon-bankrupt Continental Basketball Association, Thomas spent three decent years as the Indiana Pacers' coach until the arrival of his old nemesis Larry Bird as team president in 2003 ensured his firing. That summer Thomas finally seemed to have used up all the shine from his playing days. He bounced around the country visiting NBA training camps and college campuses, but no job offer came up. Then, in December '03, his cell phone rang: Steve Mills, president of the Garden, dangling a job interview. Thomas didn't care what the position was. He all but raced to the plane.

Impressed by the success Thomas had had with the Pacers' young players and needing a quick replacement for the miscast Knicks general manager Scott Layden, Dolan gave Isiah what may well be his last shot. It was, as Thomas likes to say, "a bloody job": Checketts's decision, in October 2000, to trade Ewing in the final year of his contract—instead of letting him play it out and then rebuilding the Knicks with room to maneuver under the salary cap—had saddled the team with a slew of long-term contracts. Dolan and Layden only compounded the problem by signing weak-kneed shooting guard Allan Houston to a preposterous six-year, $99 million contract in '01. But in the three years since Thomas took over as Knicks president, his rebuilding strategy has been as fluid as it has been puzzling. He's gone through three coaches. He stockpiled a listless combination of talented veterans and players with expiring contracts before switching last year to a stress on youth. The higher the payroll got, the worse the team played. Attendance dipped. Thomas made more enemies.

"He has lost all my respect," says Houston Rockets center Dikembe Mutombo, whom Thomas traded at the end of the 2003–04 season. "He insulted me. The first day, he pulled me aside and said, 'I want you to go away on vacation.' When we play the Knicks, I cannot look him in the face." Thomas says he doesn't recall the incident. Mutombo doesn't care. He says, "F–- Isiah."

But the most surreal moment came when Dolan announced that Thomas would coach. The two men had met beforehand and, Dolan says, discussed the one-year ultimatum. But according to sources familiar with the day's events, including film director and Knicks fan Spike Lee, Thomas was blindsided when Dolan made the ultimatum public. "I asked Isiah, 'Did you know he was going to say that?' and he said, 'I didn't,'" Lee says. Told of Lee's account, Thomas all but sputters, "I don't know if I...I think that day in terms of my reaction to kind of it being so public and everything else... you know." He pauses, then finishes with, "Hey, it is what it is," and laughs. Definitely not joking.

When the subject of Sanders's sexual harassment suit comes up, Thomas's eyes narrow and the smile dissolves. "I look forward to my day in court," he says. "[The suit] is baseless and without merit." After an in-house Garden investigation found Sanders's claims "not supported," she was fired. Dolan was later added to her suit on grounds that her dismissal was retaliatory. In September the Equal Employment Opportunity Commission, following its own investigation, found "probable cause" for a violation of Sanders's civil rights and backed her right to sue.

Meanwhile, Thomas fights daily for his professional life. He has won few raves for his front-office work over the last three years, but at 21–28 through Monday, the Knicks are well ahead of Brown's anemic pace last season (14–35). Despite some huge defensive lapses, Thomas's team is more cohesive and competitive. Yet he's walking a wire: just one rolled ankle, one long losing streak from falling into the abyss. "It's a sick kind of thing," Thomas says. "You don't want pressure, but you kind of like it. I grew up [in Chicago] having to walk outside of my house and you had to look at a guy and had to determine quickly if he's robbing you—and you can't make a mistake. It keeps you sharp."

Whether it makes sense to have a coach operate under such conditions isn't Thomas's concern. Dolan is the owner: It is what it is. "This is who we work for," Thomas says. "He calls the shots."

He shouldn't be alive. That's how bad it got for Jim Dolan, in his mind at least: endless liquor, all manner of illicit drugs. "Everything," Dolan says. "I was completely obsessive-compulsive, and I didn't like who I was at all. I kept trying to be somebody else, be what other people wanted me to be. That's impossible to do, so I medicated myself to death trying to convince myself I was somebody I wasn't. It was just horrible."

In August 1993 he bottomed out, and his father personally put him on a Northwest jet bound for the Hazelden clinic in Center City, Minn. Jim came through the fire of recovery, and the 12-step process boiled his worldview down to one brute fact: I've got to be me.

There's a shorthand formulation from antiquity that divides men into two categories, the fox and the hedgehog. "The fox knows many things," wrote the Greek poet Archilochus, "but the hedgehog knows one big thing." With his knack for working boardrooms and pressrooms, his embrace of innovations such as putting ads on pro soccer jerseys or offering free food at NHL games, Checketts, now part owner of Major League Soccer's Real Salt Lake and the NHL's St. Louis Blues, is a fox. Thomas survived Bobby Knight, Dennis Rodman and a host of mistrustful peers en route to the Hall of Fame as a player, and he has survived a host of disgruntled owners and his own reputation to climb into one of the NBA's premier front-office positions—a fox through and through. Dolan? He's thick and gruff and shaggy, but he's a hedgehog more because he was saved, he's sure, by one big thing. "It completely changed my life," he says of recovery. "I had to be honest with myself. And my honesty is completely intertwined with my sobriety. That's how I try and live my life: I try to be honest with myself and with others."

What Dolan means by honest, though, isn't so much about telling the truth. It's about being Jim Dolan—not some second-rate edition of his father, not some slick corporate suit who fills the air with false politesse—no matter whether people hate or love or fear Jim Dolan. Let the cards fall. Sure, the deck is stacked: He's the billionaire, the boss; his employees have no choice but to accept his ways. "If there's nothing else you appreciate about me," he says, "it's at least that you get to see the real me."

The real Jim Dolan, though, can be anything but pleasant. He cut his business teeth in the Darwinian world of 1970s cable television, a zero-sum game in which everyone was an enemy and monopoly was the goal. Saved by the 12-step process, he lards his speech with references to "sticking to the plan" and "following the strategy." When someone doesn't, there's trouble. In March 2001, Dolan was due to show up at Radio City Music Hall, which Cablevision also owns, to help review a dress rehearsal of an upcoming production. Trying to give the workshop a sense of occasion, Seth Abraham, then head of Radio City and soon to be president of the Garden, and Jay Smith, the show's executive producer, put on usher's jackets and waited along with cast members, Radio City staff and a clutch of Garden executives to greet Dolan in the lobby. Dolan, who arrived in a white limo, grew livid at the stunt. "Get in your suits!" he shouted at Abraham and Smith. "I'm controlling this process! I run this f---company!"

Abraham and Smith got back in their suits. Dolan went inside, calmly took a seat and said, "O.K., show me what you got."

In January 2003 the Grammy Awards announced its nominations live on network TV from the Garden. Dolan was due to be onstage with the artists and music industry types. But despite being warned not to direct his limousine up a specific Garden ramp because it would be congested, Dolan insisted on it, walked into the Garden late and was steaming backstage as the show went on. "Find me a room so I can yell louder than I've ever yelled before," he told subordinates. For 45 minutes he raged at the Garden managers. "Absolutely out of control," says one former Garden executive. "And everybody in the room had done his job—and done it well."

"He flies off the handle, and there's no rhyme or reason," says a former sports executive at the Garden. "We'd walk out and say, 'That was a good meeting.' Why? Because no one was torn apart."

"It's basically his way or the highway," says former Garden vice president of security John Fahy, who was fired after Dolan saw a suitcase under a nearby chair during the Knicks' last playoff game in 2004. "Whether or not it's right, it doesn't matter. I'd put some [security] on him, and he'd scream at the guy to get away from him. But when somebody's not on him and there's a problem? He wants to know where somebody is. You can't win with the guy."

Both current and former high-level employees from the Knicks, the Rangers, Madison Square Garden and MSG Network testify to Dolan's need to constantly reassert his place at the top of the food chain. They speak of a "reign of fear" or "culture of paranoia" in which people are more concerned with pleasing Dolan than doing an exemplary job. Most speak only under a guarantee of anonymity. "They hate to be challenged," Bob Gutkowski, a longtime New York sports executive and president of the Garden from 1991 through '94, says of the Dolans. "Cablevision has always been a fighter: 'Never give up, never give in, we're right, and we will do whatever we can do to win the battle.' That's the most important thing: *We can't be wrong.*"

None are shocked by Dolan's dismissive reaction to Sanders's lawsuit against Thomas—"absolutely baseless." A judge and jury will decide whether he's right. But Sanders's dismissal is in keeping with Dolan's knee-jerk combativeness. Since taking over the Garden he has fought the Nets and the Yankees over cable rights; beat the Jets, Mayor Michael Bloomberg and proponents of holding the 2012 Olympic Games in New York City over a proposed West Side stadium that would have competed directly with Madison Square Garden; and enraged Knicks fans by jettisoning longtime broadcaster Marv Albert from MSG Network because of his on-air criticism of the team.

Alcoholics Anonymous members use a phrase, dry drunk, to describe "somebody who is not drinking but hasn't changed who they are," Dolan says, raising two fists into the air. "Part and parcel of a dry drunk is white-knuckling: No, I'm not going to have that drink—even though I really want that drink. They're hanging onto their sobriety. My sobriety is who I am now. I don't think every day about being sober." But at his worst Dolan can exhibit every trait commonly attributed to dry drunks: exaggerated self-importance, rigidly judgmental outlook, impatience, childishness, irresponsible behavior, irrational rationalization, projection and overreaction. "If you have most of these, call your doctor," says one former Garden executive. "He's got every one."

Columnists continually question Dolan's intelligence, and three former high-level employees use the word *dumb* to describe him. But that's simplistic. After all, he envisioned and helped organize the poignant Concert for New York City just five weeks after 9/11, outpointed his father in Cablevision squabbles and outmaneuvered Bloomberg in the stadium fight. (Dolan oversees Cablevision's telecommunications services as well as its sports and entertainment properties; his father has little to do with the hockey and basketball franchises.) "He's not dumb," a New York sports executive with close knowledge of Dolan's Garden says of Jim. "He's reckless. He was reckless with his personal life, and now he's reckless with the teams."

But Dolan is not always oblivious to the damage he does. "I'm still working on not losing my temper," he says. "I'm always trying to be a better person, always trying to be smarter, more compassionate, more successful in my relationships.... I hate it when I bring somebody down.... And I've had to apologize for myself."

The most memorable instance came in an October 2004 meeting at which Dolan took one look at the projected costs for hockey broadcasts on MSG Network in '05, with numbers far higher than those for '04, and started shouting. Mike McCarthy, the president of MSG Network, tried to point out that the '04 NHL lockout had kept costs down. Dolan wouldn't hear it, thinking he was somehow being taken, though the higher '05 budget reflected only the assumption that the lockout would end and games would be played. McCarthy quit soon after, and all he has said since then is that "it was time for a change." Dolan tried to make amends, e-mailing an apology to McCarthy and everyone else who had been in the room. It was too late.

"I tell you: After you do that, it makes it easier to control yourself," Dolan says. "If you go and apologize, I'm not saying it fixes it, but it at least helps me. I hope I'm getting better at it. Quitting smoking didn't help."

So maybe the common wisdom is right: Jim Dolan = Disaster. The New York *Daily News* just made him its Anti-Sportsman of the Year. Knicks and Rangers fan sites all but catch fire with incendiary rips of Dolan's stewardship. "He should stick to his band," Fahy says.

"Jim has tremendous passion," says Abraham, who left the Garden in 2004. "But if you're not careful, passion becomes zealotry. What he does well is bring a tremendous love of the Garden and its occupants. This is not a toy to him." Asked if he thinks the Knicks can ever win with Dolan as their owner, Abraham pauses and then says, very carefully, "The Knicks can't win as they are presently constituted."

Yet Abraham is right about Dolan's love for the teams. If the man has a soft spot, it's for talent. Dolan loves playing guitar because, he says, "I don't play basketball, I don't play hockey, I don't hook up television sets, I don't produce television shows. I'm an executive who manages those things, and I think what I do has a lot to do with how successful they are. But I don't actually *do* anything." Players play, however, and for those with great talent, Dolan will do plenty.

"You couldn't ask for a better owner," says former Edmonton Oilers and Rangers great Mark Messier. "He'll do anything in his power to create an environment that's exactly what a player's looking for: state-of-the-art facilities, willingness to spend money to try to win, the way the team is treated. There's not a better place to play in the league, period. He's taken a bad rap. Jim would do anything for a championship ring with the Knicks or Rangers and has proven he will. Almost to a fault."

Wayne Gretzky, who played for the Rangers from 1996 to '99 and is now the Phoenix Coyotes' part owner and coach, calls his experience with Dolan "tremendous. He would call players in if they had family issues, or their wives were pregnant or somebody was sick, and he would personally get involved. That's someone who genuinely cares."

Mutombo says he's "shocked" by Dolan's continuing support of his $29 million hospital project in Kinshasa, capital of his native Democratic Republic of Congo. Not only did Dolan put Knicks and Garden resources at Mutombo's disposal when he played for New York, but also, in 2006, two years after Mutombo left the Knicks, Dolan was still clearing space on MSG Network and Cablevision systems and on the JumboTron during Knicks and Rangers games to run hospital fund-raising ads. "Incredible," Mutombo says of Dolan. "Every time I need money, I just have to make a phone call and ask him."

In 2005 Dolan took a particular interest in Vin Baker, the four-time All-Star whose career was derailed by alcohol abuse. He met with Baker five times during the one season Baker played for the Knicks, sharing his own struggle, acting less like a boss than "like a person in recovery, like a sponsor," Baker says. In the summer of '04 Dolan stunned Baker by showing up at his golf tournament in Hartford. "I had no idea he was coming," Baker says. "I gave him a great big hug. He was just checking on me."

But then, in those instances Dolan was dealing with people who respected him and his "process": sticking to whatever plan he laid out. In response to the tabloid face-off between Knicks coach Jeff Van Gundy and general manager Ernie Grunfeld during the 1999–2000 season—which, Dolan says, "blew the organization apart"—Dolan instituted media training for all Garden employees who might deal with the press and an ironclad rule against team personnel criticizing others in the organization. The result is the hovering presence of Garden public relations staffers during all interactions between press and personnel, and a Big Brother reputation unsurpassed by any other team in sports. The first time former NFL coach Bill Parcells called one Knicks coach, he asked, "Is this a clean line? Have you had your phone checked to make sure it's not bugged?" The coach giggled uneasily. "I wouldn't be laughing," Parcells said. "They're listening in."

"They're more paranoid about what's written in a 50-cent newspaper than they are about handing out $5 million a year to somebody who can't play," one former high-ranking Garden official says of Dolan's staff. "Winning the media game is more important than winning the game."

Which brings us to Larry Brown. In October the Knicks and Brown agreed to an $18 million settlement on the remaining four years of his contract—effectively handing Brown an absurd $28 million for coaching one season, badly—and agreed to never talk about each other again. In retrospect it's amazing that either side ever thought their relationship could work. The 65-year-old Brown had a well-known history of bashing his players in the press, and Dolan, who soured on Latrell Sprewell and Marcus Camby in 2002 because they walked out on media training, was just as infamous for his intolerance on the matter. Brown's nonstop lineup changes and his public critiques of players Trevor Ariza, Nate Robinson and especially Marbury made Dolan furious. By the time Brown was fired, the air was thick with

Knicks-spawned tales about Brown undermining Thomas by calling teams with proposed deals, refusing to speak to Thomas and, finally, demanding that Dolan buy out half the roster and start over.

But in a sense the details aren't important. What's most telling is the endgame, and what it says to anyone who wants to work in Dolan's world. At his final meeting with Brown, on June 22, Dolan still hoped to salvage things. He walked in with a piece of paper listing Brown's transgressions and ways he could correct them. But, Dolan said last June, Brown "would not acknowledge that there was a problem." Brown, who is now a vice president of the Philadelphia 76ers, declined to comment, but his agent, Joe Glass, said, "You do not admit to anything you haven't done. It's a chapter best forgotten. Thank God we can move on to freer, fresher air."

But for a recovering addict, saved by a process requiring the daily acknowledgment of his problem, what could be worse than Brown's lack of contrition? Brown's pride clashed with Dolan's one big thing, and the relationship died. The fact is, three men were responsible for the Knicks' troubles—Dolan, Thomas and Brown—and for Knicks fans the jury is still out on two of them. The one with the Hall of Fame résumé, the knack for turning around the worst of teams, is gone.

It's hard, these lean days, to feel any magic at Madison Square Garden. Banners and announcements still batter visitors with the idea that it's the world's most famous arena, but the building is 39 years old—and looks and smells like it.

The concrete floors are often filthy, even before the fans roll in, and in certain places there is the faint but unmistakable stench of an unflushed toilet. In recent years the NBA rated a Knicks game experience near the bottom in terms of "satisfaction," though how much that has to do with the team and how much with the joyless environment isn't clear.

Dolan wants to renovate or to move to a new Garden nearby and says he hopes to know which in the next six months. So with the future looking like years of construction dust piled atop years of neglect, the only thing left, it seems, is to dwell on the past. For months MSG Network has been counting down its *50 Greatest Moments* from the Garden's history, and on Jan. 18 it took a few thousand season-ticket holders, sponsors and VIPs back to the glory days at a party announcing the top five moments. There, outside the MSG Theatre, was a tableau designed to take any New York fan's breath away: 1970 Knicks gods Walt Frazier and Willis Reed chatting; boxer Joe Frazier gabbing about his epic '71 win over Muhammad Ali; Messier, Adam Graves and Mike Richter reliving the '94 Stanley Cup run. Then everyone poured inside to watch the countdown, and Walt led the crowd in singing "Happy Birthday" to Mess.

The first discordant note came in the buildup to the number 1 moment: Reed's dramatic Game 7 walk on court during the '70 Finals. Suddenly there was Marv Albert's voice—the exile returns, if only in spirit—calling out in horror when Reed went down in Game 5: "Willis is *hurt!*" The second note came when Mike Bair, president of MSG Network, tried to thank Jim Dolan from the stage just after host Al Trautwig had told the crowd that they gave "this round piece of concrete its soul." The soul spoke, filling the room with boos. Dolan wasn't there. But the noise rang in the ears of all his loyal lieutenants, Mills and Bair and the rest of the managers who hadn't left in the long executive exodus.

Whether goodwill can ever be recovered, whether the Garden will ever again feel like it did in 1970 or '73 or '94, is impossible to say. Dolan's recent bid to take Cablevision private led to rumblings about the possible sale of the Garden and the teams, but it's not a scenario he'll talk about. "I don't think about selling," Dolan says.

There are those who think he never will. "He wants to be known as a sports/show business maestro, and he knows that if Cablevision ever sold the Garden, he would go back to being 'Jim Dolan, the cable guy's son,'" says one former Garden executive. "The Garden gives him a chance, with the teams and Radio City and the Rockettes, to be somebody completely different."

For Knicks fans, though, there is one glint of hope. And Thomas brought it to them. He's the one, after all, who in October 2005 gambled a slew of first-round draft picks—including this year's possible lottery pick—on Eddy Curry, the 6'11" center who has had episodes of irregular heartbeat. Thomas is the one who this season persuaded Marbury to accept second billing, began running the offense through Curry and stayed patient through a rough start to see the 24-year-old underachiever emerge as a strong low-post threat. "It's like the game has really slowed down for me," says Curry, who was averaging 19.5points a game through Monday. "I'm not forcing anything. I used to look up at the scoreboard and think, Man, this the second quarter, I've got two points and two rebounds, I've got to make something happen. But I always knew if I could stay consistent, things would change."

Curry has been a revelation, ranking fourth in the league in shooting percentage and getting better each day at passing out of double-teams. "He's our all-star," Marbury says. "We're basically piggybacking off of him." And compared with the dour and egocentric Marbury, Curry is by all accounts humble and happy, a personality to build around—"the foundation," Thomas says, "of everything we have moving forward."

The team Thomas took over is essentially the same one Brown coached, but Thomas stabilized the lineup and made it clear he'd make no drastic changes, and the players instantly felt less threatened. "Last year the guys weren't really in the mood to do anything—talk, hang out, catch a movie, play a video game, anything," says Malik Rose. "This year we're friends."

One other way that Thomas cemented the squad was with a simple message: The league, the teams, the refs, the media, the other coaches all want to see you fail, so lean on each other. "He's made us aware of all the powers that are against us, top to bottom," Rose says, "and it was an eye-opener." The fallout of the brawl with Denver, of course, was a perfect us-against-the-world teaching moment; since that game the Knicks have played .500 ball, second-year forward David Lee has emerged as a force and the team has shown more heart and resiliency than it ever did last season. If this keeps up, Dolan may well look at the disgraceful black eye as a plus when mulling his decision on Thomas's future. He certainly doesn't mind his coach's pugnacity with the rest of the league. "That's part of what I like about him," Dolan says.

Another thing he likes is next year's big drop in payroll. With four high-priced contracts, including Houston's, coming off the books at season's end, the Knicks will still be far over the salary cap, but Thomas will be able to point to that decline—the first for the Knicks in more than a decade—as evidence of fiscal sanity. "New York has turned the corner," Pat Riley says. "It's not [going to be] a $130 million payroll anymore, it's going to keep getting down. They have a lot of good young players. They've just got to be patient now. So embrace it."

Dolan isn't there yet. He says he'll make no decision on Thomas until season's end. But sitting in his office before a game against New Jersey in late January, he says he likes the team's "build." He likes Thomas. "I think he's grown quite a bit," Dolan says. "He really feels he has control of his destiny. I think he's learning just how good he can be, and I think he's better than even he might have thought he was going to be—as a person, as a coach, as a basketball professional. I've enjoyed watching him, particularly this year, apply himself. I don't enjoy watching him suffer. But I suffer too. We do it together."

Not quite. Dolan knows he will be here next season. He doesn't, as Thomas does, daily face the same half-dozen reporters who've roasted him plenty over the past three years, called into question his every move, his ability—and now monitor each utterance, each pause, for signs of cracks in his composure. In mid-January, right after Philadelphia 76ers forward Chris Webber had become a free agent, Thomas was giving a post practice briefing and was being pressed on possible deals, on whether he'd stand pat or shake things up. He tried to make it clear that he isn't interested, that he's staying with youth. The questions kept coming, though; stories had to be written. "A lot of back pages to fill," said one reporter. Thomas nodded and tried to explain: He doesn't want to rule out some unforeseen move, either, and then be called a liar a month from now. More questions, but he was smiling, patient—Isiah at his best. Finally, the pack surrendered. "Ahh," said one beat writer, "we're just trying to make chicken salad out of chickens––."

Everyone went quiet. The word hung out there. Thomas shrugged, turned to leave, but stopped. He turned back, and for a split second a flash of Zeke crossed his face. Everyone leaned in. Was this the moment he lashed out at last?

"Are you calling me chickens––?" Thomas asked.

But then his eyebrow rose, and he laughed deep and loud, and then the writers laughed, too. The next day's back pages would say nothing about the Knicks. It was a nice little win. EXTRA! EXTRA! *Jim Dolan's team survives another day.*

FEBRUARY 24, 2022

You Really Should Know Connie Kunzmann

Long before the WNBA, there was the WBL. And there was Kunzmann, who scraped and hustled her way to relative fame in a shoestring, sexist league. You might know her name today, if not for a horrific act 40 years ago

BY CHRIS BALLARD

More than 40 years ago, a group of women did their best to get the first pro league off the ground. In this feature, I wanted to use the tragic tale of Connie Kunzmann to tell a larger story about both a league and a generation of players whose legacy has been increasingly lost to time.

Two days before she was murdered, Connie Kunzmann played the game of her life.

It was the evening of Feb. 5, 1981, and Connie, a long-limbed 24-year-old with a halo of curly brown hair, was matched up against the best women's basketball player on the planet, Dallas Diamonds point guard Nancy Lieberman. The face of the nascent Women's Professional Basketball League, Lieberman was as skilled a passer as she was a scorer. Kunzmann? She was a 6'1" reserve forward for the Nebraska Wranglers known for her tenacity, defense and exuberance. If Lieberman was the WBL's Magic Johnson, then Connie, as friend and one-time teammate Molly Bolin puts it, was "our Kurt Rambis."

From the time she picked up a basketball, as a seventh-grader, Connie had devoted herself to the sport. A standout in high school and college, she'd jumped at the opportunity when invited to try out for the WBL, the first women's pro league. The job wouldn't pay much, but she didn't care. She was all in.

Since then, Kunzmann had been a key cog on the Iowa Cornets and then the Wranglers. She set a WBL single-game record with 11 steals, won her team's Hustle Award and played in the league's first two championship series—and she had a blast doing it, traveling coast to coast, goofing off in the back of the bus, seeing cities she'd only read about. But after a slow start to the season, Kunzmann found herself on the bench. Three days before the game against the Diamonds, Steve Kirk, the Wranglers' humorless coach, told her he didn't know whether she could cut it anymore. Play better, he reportedly told her, or you won't travel with the team. Kirk's words cut hard. Usually self-confident and extroverted, Connie began fretting and had fallen into dark moods.

In the second half against Dallas, though, Connie had a chance to redeem herself. Sent in to guard Lieberman, she took a charge and stole a pass. The bench roared. Kunzmann went on to lead the Wranglers with 19 points (she averaged 3.0 per game) and 10 rebounds. Even in defeat, Kirk praised her afterward. Lieberman, too, was impressed. "I remember driving down the middle and she was so strong that it was like hitting a wall," she says. "Connie wasn't flashy, but she was the player you needed on your team if you wanted to win."

With the performance, Connie solidified her spot on the Wranglers. That Saturday night, still buzzing from the game, she headed out to her favorite sports bar in Omaha, Tiger Tom's, to meet friends and celebrate. She was the type of person who could strike up a conversation with anyone over a beer, or three. She greeted strangers like friends and delighted in talking about the WBL. On many evenings like this, her roommate and teammate Genia Beasley came along. On this one, though, Beasley stayed in.

The next morning, Beasley noticed her friend hadn't returned home. She figured Connie had stayed over with someone and would be back soon. It was only when she missed practice that Beasley, and others, began to worry.

Today, a young girl staring up at a poster of Candace Parker or Diana Taurasi on her bedroom wall wouldn't think twice about a career as a pro basketball player. For her the WNBA, which just celebrated its 25th anniversary, has always existed. A talented teenager can play AAU ball, earn a college scholarship and, with the advent of new NIL rules, perhaps earn a little money on the way to a pro league with a $60,000 minimum salary.

Such opportunities would have been hard to fathom in Connie's era. This was before Cheryl Miller scored 105 points in a high school game, before Lisa Leslie dunked her way onto ESPN highlights. UConn was not yet UConn, and Rebecca Lobo was in elementary school. The NBA, meanwhile, was emerging from its own tenuous period, with Finals games relegated to tape delay and rosters beset by substance use problems. College basketball was the more popular men's game, and March Madness for women wouldn't even begin until 1982. Plenty of high schools didn't even have girls basketball programs.

But Connie was fortunate: Of all the places for a basketball-loving girl to grow up in the 1970s, you'd have been hard-pressed to pick a better one than Everly. A town of 700 in Iowa's northwest corner, Everly was known for corn, soybeans and hoops. The Everly High Cattlefeeders' girls team was a local institution, winning a state title in 1966 and qualifying for the tourney almost every year for a decade. In Iowa, where girls teams routinely outdrew the boys and 15,000 fans packed Veterans Auditorium for the state tournament, this was a big deal.

Connie had grown up going to games with her father, Ray, who served in the Army Air Corps in World War II before settling into farming and raising cattle. She took after him: hardworking and competitive. But her world capsized at 13 when Ray died of a heart attack. That year she spent more time helping out on the farm. She also went out for the basketball team.

Back then, girls in Iowa still played six-on-six, with three "guards" on defense, three "forwards" on offense and neither unit allowed to cross half court. Strong and tough, Connie excelled on D and made the Cattlefeeders' varsity as a freshman. Her senior year, switched to offense, she averaged 34 points and was all-state. Around town she was a celebrity; her younger brother, Rick, remembers people "always patting me on the back" just for being related to her. Later, on scholarship at Wayne State, Connie set a slew of school records, once pulling down 25 rebounds. "She kind of pitched her tent in the gymnasium," Chuck Brewer, Wayne State's coach, later told one writer. "Whatever you asked for, she always gave you more."

Meanwhile, women's basketball was slowly gaining in popularity. The sport had been around since 1892, when a Smith College physical education teacher named Sandra Berenson adapted James Naismith's rules, creating the six-on-six format, outlawing steals and limiting players to three dribbles. But for almost another century the women's game would be hindered by a lack of resources, Byzantine rules and antiquated and sexist views about women's sports that limited opportunities. This all began to change in 1972, after the passage of Title IX, the landmark civil rights law that prohibited discrimination based on sex at any school that received federal funds.

Top college teams, like Immaculata, started drawing big crowds, as did the barnstorming All-American Red Heads. After Billie Jean King's televised defeat of Bobby Riggs in the 1973 Battle of the Sexes drew 90 million viewers worldwide, CBS greenlit a series of gender battles that included Red Heads star Karen Logan facing the Lakers' Jerry West in H-O-R-S-E. (Logan won.) And in '76 the Olympics finally added a women's tournament. (The men had been competing since '36.)

Bill Byrne, for one, believed the time was ripe for a women's pro league. Part huckster, part visionary, part b.s. artist, he had run a sporting goods store and then founded an NFL scouting service and a short-lived pro softball circuit. Impressed by ticket sales at women's college games and hoping to get in early on the next big sports wave, Byrne vowed, one night over beers in 1977, to start a league. He recruited Logan (who designed the 28.5-inch women's ball, today's standard) as a player-coach and came up with the league name, which he marketed as the WBL, instead of WPBL, because it sounded more like the NBA and the NFL. Then, to lure investors, he set about making a bunch of promises about scope and reach and return—some of which he even kept.

It worked. Sort of. In the spring of 1978 the WBL held tryouts across the country, followed by a draft. A few of the biggest names taken, including future Hall of Famer Carol Blazejowski, chose to retain their amateur status for the '80 Olympics. Plenty of other draftees had no idea the league even existed: One day they were making their postcollegiate plans, and the next a friend or relative told them they were part of the WBL.

That December the league launched a 34-game season with eight teams, four fewer than hoped. Franchises cost just $50,000 and player salaries could be as low as $3,000. (Kunzmann, after a tryout, signed with the Cornets for $7,500.)

The WBL did garner press, though. FEMALE PROS MAKE HISTORY, announced *The New York Times*. On the night of the league opener Walter Cronkite ran a four-minute report on the *CBS Evening News*. Then, in front of 7,824 fans, the Chicago Hustle beat the Milwaukee Does, one of a handful of teams (the Minnesota Fillies, the Dayton Rockettes...) that bore awkward gendered names.

Much about the league felt makeshift. Teams traveled great distances by bus and occasionally played in high school gyms. Players stayed in cheap hotels, sometimes six to a room. Depending on the club, and the owner's liquidity, a paycheck's arrival could be more a matter of *if* than *when*.

Franchises, which lost an average of $260,000 in that first season, launched and folded in the span of months.

Connie, though, got lucky. Not only were the Cornets close to home, but they also were relatively flush, owned by George Nissen, a collegiate gymnastics champion who went on to invent the trampoline and start a sporting goods business. While other teams made do, Nissen handed out $100 bills at his Christmas party and bought a Greyhound team bus (dubbed the Corn Dog) that he outfitted with TVs, a refrigerator and a stereo system. On long rides, players slept on the carpeted luggage racks. Kunzmann and her teammates played cards, talked about *Saturday Night Live* and rocked out to AC/DC.

Right off the bat, Connie bonded with Bolin, the Cornets' star guard, a fellow small-town Iowan who had gained renown—and the nickname "Machine Gun Molly"—for her deadeye jump shot. While Bolin led the Cornets (and later the WBL) in scoring, setting a league record with 55 points in one game, Kunzmann was a fan favorite. She averaged 11 points and 11 rebounds, and she led Iowa in steals. In photos you could see the bruises on her legs from diving for loose balls. She was the one who cracked up teammates by wearing Groucho Marx glasses or putting smiley faces on everything; the one who served champagne into plastic glasses after the Cornets made the finals their first season. She introduced herself, "Hi, I'm Connie Kunzmann and I play for the Iowa Cornets." She kept a chalkboard in her room, on which she wrote inspirational maxims and she competed at everything, constantly playing a handheld electronic football game, the beeps of which Bolin can still recall to this day.

Connie and the Cornets won both because of and in spite of the men in charge. After hiring and firing three coaches before the first season, ownership settled on Kirk, who, like the majority of his WBL peers, had never before coached women. (Nearly all of the WBL's coaches were male.)

Though players recall Kirk as a mostly effective tactician, he seemed lost when it came to relating to 21- and 22-year-old women. He tried to micromanage everything from the fast break to his players' social lives, laying down a series of rules, with fines for breaking them. He prized discipline and motivated by criticizing. "He felt like he could coach us the same way he coached the men," says Bolin. "He didn't have a high level of tolerance." (Kirk died in 2014 at age 71.)

When the team goofed around in the rear of the bus, Kirk would storm back and holler, "Get your game faces on!" Which, of course, never helped. It was, says Bolin, "like being in church and not being able to laugh."

Banned from smoking or drinking, players would stash single-serving wine bottles from airplane trips and break them out in their hotel rooms.

They held team parties, sang and performed skits, imitating their coach's scowling demeanor. They gawked as they passed the strip clubs in New Orleans, marveled at the beaches in California and tried to sneak into Studio 54 in New York City, wearing their green satin team jackets.

Through all of this the Cornets flourished, racking up wins and leading the WBL in attendance two years in a row. But the league's fortunes seesawed. Some teams, like Chicago, drew thousands of fans; others, hamstrung by poor leadership and a lack of promotion, drew crowds in the low hundreds. Byrne had expanded the WBL to 14 teams before the second season, and that stretched thin the talent and resources. Two franchises collapsed within the first 10 games.

When the league did receive press, the focus often wasn't on the game. A 1981 story in *Sports Illustrated* centered on Bolin, who was pictured wearing a skintight leotard. The lede ended: "Suffice it to say that if beauty were a stat, Molly Bolin would be in the Hall of Fame."

Meanwhile, players chafed at the league culture. According to former WBLers interviewed for this story, plenty of male coaches slept with at least one of their players, which led to favoritism, among other problems. Women say they were expected to look like sex symbols or to show up in pigtails, without makeup. Early on, Logan, one of the few players with leverage—she was the first woman to receive a Nike contract: $3,500 to endorse waffle running shoes—tried to lead a union drive. As a result, she says, she was blackballed, unable to find a team for the WBL's second season. "The message was: Don't come here, because we don't want any trouble," she says. "The power structure was male and certainly didn't want women to unite and have any kind of voice."

By the end of the second season, the WBL was foundering, Iowa included. To publicize his team Nissen had poured $1 million into a movie called *Dribble*, an uncomfortable comedy, never released, that starred Pete Maravich alongside the Cornets. (The movie's tasteless tagline: "A battle of the sexes...who'll end up on top?") Facing losses, Nissen divested most of his stake, and the next owner started bouncing checks. Even though they made the finals for a second time—falling to the New York Stars in the clinching Game 4, despite 20 points and 12 boards from Kunzmann—the Cornets folded that fall.

The players dispersed. Bolin headed to San Francisco, enticed by the chance to play for coach Dean Meminger (an NBA champion as a guard with the Knicks). She tried to recruit Connie and might have succeeded if not for the formation of the Wranglers, a new Omaha franchise, closer to home, where Kirk took the head coaching job.

To this day, Bolin wonders how things might have turned out if only she had persuaded her friend to join her.

Missing one practice was weird. But two? That was unheard of for Connie, especially since each absence came with a $50 fine.

Still, her older brother, Craig, tried to stay optimistic, even after their mother, Eleanor, called him on Feb. 9, 1981, to say that she had heard from a police sergeant in Omaha, and that Connie hadn't been seen in more than a day. A handwritten missing persons report stated: "This person is a pro basketball player for the Wranglers.... She has never missed practice in the past like she has for the past two days."

That night, Craig and Rick drove to Eleanor's house. Craig did his best to comfort her. "Connie has always been able to handle herself," he recalls saying.

Indeed, she had. She had settled into Omaha. The Wranglers were winning, fueled by the dominant post play of top draft pick Rosie Walker and the floor leadership of point guard Holly Warlick, both All-Stars that season.

Omahans had responded, thousands coming out to the Civic Auditorium on winter nights. Even so, the franchise struggled under the ownership of Larry Kozlicki, a Chicago tax attorney who, like many WBL stakeholders, knew little about basketball but enjoyed the publicity and hoped to cash in on the next big thing. Kozlicki had already run one team, the California Dreams, into the ground the previous season; players had walked out over months of unpaid salaries. (Perhaps it had to do with allocation of funds; Kozlicki reportedly enrolled the whole team in John Robert Powers charm school, where they learned how to apply makeup and walk runways.)

That Kozlicki got another chance is evidence of how desperate Byrne and the WBL had become. On the occasions when the Wranglers did get paid, it was often by personal check or cash in an envelope. Management forced players to wear Wrangler boots, cowboy hats, jeans and red-and-white checkered shirts when they traveled. ("Godawful," says Beasley.) Sometimes, on the road, they had to hitchhike from the hotel to the arena because Kozlicki was too cheap, one player says, to pay for buses.

As in Iowa, Connie was the heart and soul of the team. Even though she came off the bench, she was named captain. "You could count on her," says Warlick. "She was just a solid person."

Not long after arriving, Connie had adopted Tiger Tom's as her local hangout, always arriving in her yellow Mustang, with kunz license plates. She even wrangled a personal sponsorship from the pub, and for a while she dated one of the bartenders, Tom Christensen, who was surprised by how open and friendly she was. After meeting only once, she began writing him letters. "Connie was the most upbeat person I have ever known," he later told *Inside Sports*. "She made you feel at ease."

Connie wasn't looking to settle down, though. In January 1981 she had gone to Tiger Tom's to help promote the WBL, handing out free tickets, and she hit it off with Lance Tibke, a security guard at a nuclear power plant. At the time, the 25-year-old Tibke was either engaged or about to be. It seems unlikely, though, that he told this to Connie. That night, after hanging out over beers, the pair left together and spent the night at Kunzmann's place.

They didn't see each other again until late in the evening of Feb. 6, when Tibke dropped off his fiancé at her house and then swung by Tiger Tom's a little after midnight. Spotting Connie leaving the bar in her satin green Wranglers jacket, he pulled over.

She said she was headed out to meet friends at an all-night diner. Tibke offered to give her a ride.

Even 40 years later, the details of what happened next are difficult to relay. Connie got in the car and Tibke drove toward a quiet, private area, turning down a gravel road beside a cemetery and parking where they had a view of Omaha, lit up at night. Tibke later told police that he intended to have sex with Kunzmann, but precisely what occurred remains unclear. He would say that he felt guilty and backed off, angering Connie. Those who know her, though, doubt this. They think it's far more likely she was the one who said no.

One thing is clear: Tibke snapped. He attacked Connie with a pocketknife, then grabbed a tire iron that he kept under his seat, hitting her "five or six times" in the head, according to his police statement.

Connie fought back. Friends and family take a sliver of comfort in the fact that Tibke was left bruised and battered in the end. "She didn't go down easy," says Warlick. "That guy had scratches on his face. She fought to the end."

At some point Tibke realized that Kunzmann was dead. Panicking, he buried her jacket and wallet in the cemetery and drove to Dodge Park, along the Missouri River, where he backed his truck up to the icy water, lugged out Connie's body and then let the current take her away.

At 4:30 a.m. on Feb. 10, three days later, Tibke, at the urging of his father, arrived at the Omaha police department and confessed to the murder.

The weeks that followed remain a blur for those who loved Connie. Eleanor proved inconsolable; when her sons came to tell her of the confession, she "just kept saying, 'No, no, no,'" according to Craig. Friends and teammates were crushed. Since the police hadn't yet found a body, some clung to hope that Connie was still alive.

"Just disbelief," says Warlick. "You kind of think she's going to come through the door any second." Beasley still vividly remembers small details, such as how, when police officers finally arrived at their apartment two days after Connie's disappearance, her game-worn uniform remained damp with sweat in her bag.

Those looking for an explanation found none. Tibke had neither an obvious motive nor a history of violence. He had no criminal record—"hadn't even gotten a parking ticket," says Craig. When Tibke spoke about it, a year later for a story in *Inside Sports*, he provided no reasoning. "I couldn't control it," he said. "I began to pound her and pound her and pound her. She said, 'Stop it, stop it, stop it. Please don't.' But I couldn't stop. I don't know why."

As the community grieved, national media picked up the story. FEMALE BASKETBALL PLAYER MISSING AND BELIEVED SLAIN, ran *The New York Times* headline; A DEATH STUNS THE WBL, wrote *The Washington Post*.

The Wranglers postponed their game that week and, after a team meeting, decided to wear black armbands the rest of the season. They released a statement that began: "Connie was more than our teammate. Connie was a member of our family. In any situation, in any game, in any relationship, she gave more than she had to get.... Never did you hear her complain about her position on the team or in life.... People like Connie do not come along every day.... Her memory will remain with us forever. Her life will become ours. We will live and play as Connie would have, as Connie would want us to do."

Seven weeks after the murder, on March 28, two boys fishing along the banks of the half-frozen Missouri spotted Connie's body in the water. An autopsy determined the cause of death as "blunt force trauma," from the tire iron. Tibke would be convicted of second-degree murder and sentenced to 40 years. Slowly, and then all at once, the finality sank in for relatives and teammates.

Everly is not an easy place to get to, and the Kunzmanns didn't know how many mourners to expect at Connie's funeral. But friends—from childhood, from college, from the WBL—kept arriving. The church balcony filled, then the chapel, then the basement. Craig recalls little about that terrible time, but he can still picture the funeral and the outpouring of people whose lives his sister had touched.

That April, the Wranglers' season came to a bittersweet end. They finished atop the standings and swept the Hustle in the semis to set up a best-of-five showdown against Lieberman and the Diamonds. It should have been reason to celebrate, the reward for all the hard work. Instead, players grieved...and worried about their futures. They reportedly hadn't been paid in months and considered walking out, as the Hustle and the Fillies had a month earlier. But they wondered what that would accomplish. "You can't boycott, because there's no money," says Warlick, who estimates that she received about half her salary that season. "You can't sue them; they'll go bankrupt. So we decided to play it out."

At least the finals provided a thrilling showcase. Walker and Lieberman each averaged more than 30 points. Seven thousand fans showed up for each game at Moody Coliseum in Dallas, and 3,500 in Omaha. During the series, the league awarded the Connie Kunzmann Hustle and Harmony Award, honoring a player, New Orleans Pride captain Sybil Blalock, who personified Connie's attitude and spirit. To watch the surviving footage of that series—a bit shaky, filmed by someone in the stands—is to get a glimpse of what the WBL might have been. The crowd, men and women and kids of all colors, in suits and in bellbottoms, is raucous. The players move with pace, nailing midrange jumpers, pressing on defense and, in Lieberman's case, whipping one-handed passes.

On April 20, 1981, in what would be the WBL finale, the Wranglers beat the Diamonds 99–91 to take Game 5, and the title. Had Connie lived, she would have become not only a champion but also the only player in league history to make all three finals.

When the end came, the WBL went out with a whimper. No confetti fell after the clinching game in Dallas. "We didn't even have a party," says Beasley. Most of the players were too preoccupied with how they would find a way home after the season.

That fall the WBL finally, officially disbanded. And while the ensuing decades were littered with well-meaning attempts to start new leagues—the WABA, NWBA, WBA, ABL and the regrettable LPBA, with its 9'2" basket and skimpy leotards—none lasted more than a few years.

Finally, in June 1997, the inaugural WNBA season tipped off with eight teams. New heroes arose—Leslie and Sheryl Swoopes and Cynthia Cooper. The league had its ups and downs but survived and ultimately thrived, providing a measure of stability in the women's professional game.

The original WBL players went on with their lives. Many became coaches. Others became biochemists, college professors, athletic administrators, doctors, businesswomen, lawyers and real estate agents; wives and mothers. Many lost touch with one another and the world moved on.

While the NBA has gone to great lengths to venerate its foundational stars, the women's game doesn't display the same institutional memory. As a result, the saga of Connie Kunzmann and her fellow trailblazers has been increasingly lost to time, preserved only in faded game programs, grainy VHS tapes and the memories of those who lived through the WBL. The best feature written about Connie at the time, by Ira Berkow for *Inside Sports*—an article that was instrumental in piecing together the story you're currently reading—isn't online. When Nissen died, in 1996, his 800-word *New York Times* obituary didn't even mention the Cornets. The only book about the league, *Mad Seasons* (another valuable resource for this story), was written as a labor of love by Karra Porter, a Salt Lake City lawyer who represented women's players, and published by a university press in 2006.

And so it seemed that, as coaches and players moved on or passed away, all memory of the league threatened to go with them. That is: until 2018, when a group of alums, led by former New Jersey Gems shooting guard Ann Meyers and Hustle coach Doug Bruno, lobbied and pushed and pestered the Women's Basketball Hall of Fame long and hard enough. That June, more than 100 of the original WBL players walked onto a stage in Knoxville, Tenn.

There was Warlick, now an assistant at Tennessee. And then Notre Dame coach Muffet McGraw. And Lieberman, the most famous WBL alum, who'd gone on to become a WNBA coach and the first female NBA assistant, with the Kings. And, in a bright blue dress, there stood Bolin. (She now goes by Molly Kazmer.) The WBL's all-time leading scorer (25.4 points per game) played briefly in the WBA and the LPBA, and she even shot a Spalding commercial with Larry Bird. She joined her peers, signing autographs for fans and laughing about old rivalries. That afternoon, the museum enshrined every WBL player into its Trailblazers of the Game wing, where Connie's uniform is featured prominently. Now, any young girl or boy who comes can read about WBL stars, right alongside presentations on Pat Summitt and Dawn Staley.

Only a fraction of the history is there, of course, and it captures mostly the good stuff. Those who played in the WBL readily acknowledge its flaws. Though the league was intended to be a progressive venture, too many of those in power were men motivated not by progress but by entrepreneurial dreams, or having a franchise of their own to brag about. Plenty who played wonder what their lives would have been like if only they were born a decade or two later. Just imagine the endorsement opportunities for players like Lieberman or Walker or Bolin, who says, "Everybody knew that women's basketball was going to make it. We just didn't know when."

Bolin in particular suffered due to the chauvinistic attitudes of her era. When she and her first husband divorced, after the WBL folded, she lost custody of their young son, based in part on the argument that, as a professional basketball player, her travel and promotional duties had made her an unfit parent. (A year later, the Iowa Supreme Court overturned that decision and gave Bolin full custody.) Teams, meanwhile, profited off her looks, once posing her for a swimsuit poster. But when Bolin decided to take control of her image and sell her own posters, to add to her paltry $6,000 team salary, press and management criticized her. "What I did was super conservative, as far as the cheesecake photos and marketing and promotions—but it was such a big deal," she says. "Now, nobody would even blink at it. Not only that, I might have a million followers on Instagram."

Some, like Logan, look back on that part of their lives as a painful period. They believe that pain makes it all the more important that they preserve the whole history, so others can learn from it. "I'm not trying to be old and bitter; I want to be authentic and honest," Logan says. "Ours is the story of the struggle for women's basketball to get off the ground. The struggle has some not-so-nice parts to it, and some nice parts."

In this way, the story of Connie Kunzmann's death is inextricably tied to the WBL, its darkest moment. It's also a marker of the league's struggles. After years of courting the country's press, the most attention the WBL received after its founding came not when its players thrived, but when one was murdered. (Decades later, it's part of why this story is being told.)

Maybe that can change, though. Elizabeth Galloway-McQuitter, a defensive specialist on the Hustle who went on to coach high school and college for 28 years, was sick of hearing people refer to the WNBA as the first professional women's league. She kept asking: "Whose responsibility is it to tell the history?"

Fed up, she decided it was hers. So, after the Hall of Fame ceremony, she and a group of WBL players founded a nonprofit, Legends of the Ball, geared toward raising awareness of the league. Galloway-McQuitter organized meetups, wrote a mission statement and, to inspire her peers, quoted Maya Angelou: "How important it is for us to recognize and celebrate our heroes and she-roes!"

Now, as Title IX nears its 50th anniversary and the WNBA moves into its next quarter century, there is talk of a documentary, maybe even a scripted TV series, like *GLOW* for basketball. Galloway-McQuitter aims even higher, hoping for a permanent display in the women's Hall of Fame. And induction into the Naismith Basketball Hall of Fame. And then the Smithsonian.

Bolin just wishes her friend was here to be part of it.

Like so many small farm towns in the Midwest, times haven't been easy of late in Everly. In 2019, the middle school and the high school shuttered, taking with them the Cattlefeeder legacy.

That's why it was so exciting for the Kunzmann family when the Everly Heritage Museum opened its doors last fall. Sure, it's just one room in a community center on Main Street, and it's open only two days a week, by appointment. But that doesn't matter to Craig and Rick. What matters is that Connie has her own display, with photos, plaques, news stories, trophies and her yellow WBL travel bag.

For the most part, the Kunzmanns have left Everly. A bunch of relatives headed to the West Coast. Rick is in South Dakota. But Craig is still in town, where he co-owns a construction business. Eleanor died in 1993. "She never quite got over Connie's death," says Craig. "Like part of her was gone." It particularly vexed Eleanor that Tibke served only nine years of his 40-year sentence, getting paroled in '90. "She wanted to go after him and put him away for as long as she could. I said it wasn't worth putting yourself through that."

Those who knew Connie wonder now how her life might have played out. Warlick thinks she may have gone back and worked on her parents' farm, adding, "She would have been a good coach, too. She'd have had a family and a bunch of kids by now; I'm positive about it."

Craig and Rick agree that she'd be coaching. "I think she'd be there, supporting some kids who were saying, 'I don't think I can do this,'" Craig imagines. "She'd say, 'Yes, you can. I know you can. I did, and I know you can do it, too.' She'd be right there, pushing, not getting upset."

On occasion Rick still hears from his sister's teammates. Tanya Crevier, a guard on the Cornets, once came into the auto shop where he worked. Bolin recently sent him some old photos. She hopes that people remember Kunzmann not just for how she died, but for how she lived.

In Everly, people still know Connie's name. As Craig points out: "It's a small town, and people here don't move much. Most of them know me."

Outside of town, largely, it's different. Still, every once in a while, out of the blue, Craig says someone will hear his last name and pause for a second. "They'll say, 'Kunzmann? I think there was a girl who played for the Cornets with the name. Any relation?'"

MAY 26, 2014

Adam Silver Is His Own Man

The first 100 days of the NBA czar's administration has been
like no other in sports history. But a life both privileged
and unconventional prepared him for this moment

BY LEE JENKINS

*In 30 years at the helm of the NBA, David Stern led a floundering league to
unprecedented growth. His retirement was both triumphant and carefully
choreographed. On Feb. 1, 2014, after a nice round anniversary, Stern turned
the job over to his hand-picked successor, Adam Silver. Six months later Stern
was inducted into the Hall of Fame.*

*Following Stern was no easy task. In this, the first in-depth story
published about Silver, Lee Jenkins provides a textured portrait of the quiet,
bespectacled man leading the NBA into the future.*

Masawani Jere, a chief of the Ngoni tribe, presides over a village of 120
in Malawi, a small, landlocked nation in southeastern Africa. The village,
called Emchakachakeni, sits on a hill at the edge of a forest. Most Malawians
live in rural areas and work in agriculture. Many of the 6,000 Ngoni,
descended from the Zulus of South Africa, are timber merchants. Those in
Emchakachakeni own no televisions or computers. But their chief must
maintain some connection with the modern world, so he has a BlackBerry,
on which he created a Facebook account. When Jere logged in on the
last day of April he was struck by a story that all his cyberfriends were
discussing about the bold new NBA commissioner, who had permanently

banished the league's longest-tenured owner for making racist remarks on a leaked audiotape. "Oh, yes," the chief thought as he scrolled through the commissioner's forceful words. "This sounds just like Adam."

In 1977, Jere went to a house party in Rye, N.Y. He was a sophomore at Rye High, having moved to Westchester County three years earlier, when his father became a counselor to Malawi's United Nations ambassador. Jere was desperate to fit in at the new school, even though he couldn't help but stand out. He was one of the few black students in his class. At the party, kids downed beers before heading off to *The Rocky Horror Picture Show* in New Rochelle. As Jere tried to blend in, a long-limbed, clear-eyed freshman introduced himself. "That was Adam Silver," Jere recalls. "All we had in common is we were the two who weren't drinking."

Rye is a posh suburb of New York City, just shy of the Connecticut line, and among its 15,000 residents were wealthy corporate executives and investment bankers. Silver's father, Ed, was one of the most prominent labor lawyers in New York City. His mother, Melba, was a teacher and community activist. Adam grew up in a large Georgian house with a formal garden about a block from Long Island Sound. At Rye High he was an A student, a class president, a member of the cross-country team and editor-in-chief of *The Garnet & Black* newspaper. He played the stock market with the help of a broker on Main Street who indulged his modest trades. Mas, as Jere is known, was a soccer star who struggled with schoolwork. But he and Silver had more in common than their backgrounds indicated.

When Silver was 10 his parents separated and his dad moved to an apartment in Manhattan. By the time he turned 14, his three older siblings were off to college, and his mom was spending winters in Boca Raton, Fla. He was alone in that big colonial, along with Mas, whose parents regularly traveled back to Malawi. "He took me in," Mas says. "He became my brother, and I became his." Adam tutored Mas in history and algebra. He invited him to concerts and sporting events in the city. He took him to fancy restaurants. He even sold Mas his car, a Volkswagen Scirocco, for $2,000 on a layaway plan. "Adam was really Mas's guide through the American experience," says Roy Bostock, a Rye resident and the former Yahoo chairman, who has been a mentor to Silver since he was a teenager.

Mas's other guide was Regan Orillac, a class president one year younger. The trio would drive to the Rye Nature Center after school, grab Tiger's Milk bars and frozen yogurt and head to Adam's. They pored over *New Yorker* cartoons, deconstructed the Abscam scandal and listened to Earth Wind & Fire. They stayed up late picking at pistachios and watching Johnny Carson. "I'm Irish Catholic," Orillac says. "Mas is African. Adam is Jewish. We were an odd group, but we made a little family."

Melba Silver employed a housekeeper, Eudel Baker, during the day and rented a back unit to adults with the understanding that they'd keep an eye on her youngest son. She also opened a charge account for Adam at Playland Market, a mile away, but getting there presented logistical challenges: Adam, at 15, occasionally had to drive there without a license. "I think that whole experience gave Adam skills that other people may attain later," Orillac says. "You don't hem and haw. You don't ask a thousand people for advice. You just get it done, because no one else is around to get it done."

Adam was a cosmopolitan kid, as comfortable at Blind Brook Country Club for Easter brunch as at Carnegie Hall for the Spinners' show. He once mimicked their act, pink tuxedo and all, for a school talent show. At Duke he introduced his freshman-year roommate to Al Green as well as to New York City mayor Ed Koch, who called their dorm looking for Ed Silver the day Adam moved in. "When we were all reading *The Wall Street Journal* for the market, Adam was reading the *Journal* and *The New York Times* for the market and the editorial page," says Jim Zelter, the roommate, now a top executive at the private equity firm Apollo Global Management. Adam also had *The Village Voice* delivered to his campus mailbox.

In December 1983, Silver was a junior political science major visiting his mom in Boca Raton for winter break. Jere was a junior at Concordia College in suburban Bronxville, N.Y., eager to reconnect with old friends home for the holidays. Three nights before Christmas, Jere drove to a bar in New Rochelle with a high school buddy named Chris Pinto, who was pre-med at Johns Hopkins. According to Jere, they drank a few beers before returning to their neighborhood pub in Rye, The Maple Tree. They left after midnight: Jere, Pinto and a young woman Pinto had met inside. Jere and the woman reached the car first. "I was about to open the door," Jere remembers, "and [she] said, 'I'm not getting in the car with a n——.'" Jere demanded an apology and looked around for Pinto, who was talking animatedly with two men on the other side of the street. A fight broke out, and Jere sprinted across the street to help, but the brawl left him bloodied and Pinto unconscious. The hoodlums ran away. An ambulance rushed Pinto to the hospital. He died several days later.

Jere was inconsolable, and, again, Silver was there. He flew up from Boca Raton, coaxed Jere to Pinto's funeral and handed him a black blazer to wear. Jere blamed himself for Pinto's death, and Silver explained that Jere too was an innocent victim. Jere never even learned what Pinto and the two men were fighting about. Detectives investigated the case and interviewed Jere and the alleged assailants, but a grand jury declined to hand down indictments. Jere underwent counseling. He nearly dropped out of college.

In 1986 he moved back to Malawi, and Silver shipped him the Scirocco. Six years after that, Jere and his wife, Annie, had a son, whom they named Christopher. Silver sent the boy a Spalding basketball hoop, and he shot jumpers in the village. Now that boy is 22, and his father's pal is recognized around the globe.

"Christopher," Mas says, "has become a big fan of Adam Silver."

Fifteen floors above Fifth Avenue the commissioner sits in a modest conference room at the NBA's Midtown headquarters, sipping a cup of coffee. His navy suit jacket is draped over a chair. His red-and-blue-striped tie hangs loose around his neck. The window behind him looks out eight blocks north to Central Park, where Silver walks every night with his Labrador retriever, Eydie. He is used to being recognized by NBA junkies, who for more than seven years watched him announce second-round draft picks as the deputy commissioner, but now he is approached by observers who wouldn't know a post-up from a pin-down.

Silver does not seem tired, though he just returned the night before from Los Angeles, where he watched the Clippers play the Thunder at Staples Center in Game 4 of the Western Conference semifinals. It was his first trip to L.A. since April 29, when he announced he was banning Clippers owner Donald Sterling for life and vowed to force a sale of the franchise. Club employees swung by his seat in the lower bowl to thank him for ridding them of a wretched boss, who built a reputation as the worst owner in pro sports by bungling hires, skimping on contracts and heckling his own players. Disney chairman and CEO Bob Iger, who sat with Silver, flashed back to the All-Star Game, which they attended together in New Orleans three months earlier. "The attention he got [in L.A.], the appreciation that was shown, the connection fans wanted to have with him, was completely different," Iger says. Silver struggled to accept the adulation.

"This book is far from written," he says in his first sit-down interview since he expelled Sterling. "I still feel I'm very much in the middle of it. I know what is appropriate here. I have no doubt. But it is one thing to have said what I said and another to execute it—to move the NBA through this chapter to a better place. I feel that obligation. I feel the weight of it on my shoulders." Roughly three hours later Sterling will appear on CNN and issue perhaps the clumsiest public apology in history. The reality show continues.

The NBA is girding for a legal battle with Sterling and his wife, co-owner Rochelle, when they conclude their interview circuit. Proceedings will last months. What matters most to those Clippers staffers, after 33 years under Sterling's thumb, is that someone has finally taken up the fight. Silver also sat with Magic Johnson during Game 4, and to get a sense of the commissioner's standing in L.A., one fan strode past Magic and asked for a picture with Silver.

Johnson holds a prominent place in Silver's biography. In February 1992, Silver was a third-year associate at Cravath, Swaine & Moore in New York City, working 110 hours a week on cases he knew would never go to trial. He had to record the NBA All-Star Game on his VCR, and when he finally returned to his Upper West Side apartment after midnight, he popped in the tape. "Magic made that shot at the end," Silver remembers, "and I was sitting there alone with tears in my eyes." Five months later he quit his career as a litigator and took a job with the NBA as a special assistant to commissioner David Stern.

So began 22 years in the league office, at the lapel of the commissioner, as both adviser and apprentice. Silver is the reason the NBA was the first league to launch its own cable network, in 1999, and the first to incorporate team websites, in '95. He helped negotiate the current eight-year, $7.4 billion TV deal and end the 2011 lockout. He did more than anyone but Stern to make basketball an international sport, and he was such an obvious successor to the commissioner that the owners never bothered conducting a search. Silver "always had a global view," says David Schreff, a former NBA executive who now runs Bedare Sports and Entertainment. "He was David's liaison, but they didn't think identically. They thought collaboratively." On April 18, Silver oversaw his first NBA Board of Governors meeting as commissioner. He started with a written speech.

"It was all about respect and transparency," recalls an owner who was there. "Respect for each other, respect for different personalities, respect for different viewpoints." Sterling was in the room. He heard every word. One week later TMZ released the tape in which Sterling scolds his mistress for bringing African Americans to games, namely Johnson.

As deputy, Silver played a major role in resolving the Pacers-Pistons melee in Detroit and the point-shaving scandal involving referee Tim Donaghy, but nothing could have prepared the freshly minted commissioner for the sound of Sterling. The story, which broke late on April 25, would cross over the next day from sports to entertainment to politics to business—all in the time it took a charter jet to fly from New York City to Memphis, where Silver was headed for a first-round playoff game. Before he departed early in the afternoon of April 26, Silver spoke with Clippers coach Doc Rivers and point guard Chris Paul, assuring them he would investigate the offensive audio. Over the next few hours a Clippers crisis morphed into a national uproar, but Silver was in the air without Internet access. He could not see the storm clouds forming in front of him. He was greeted at the Memphis airport by televisions tuned to ESPN, the ticker teasing a Silver press conference on

Sterling. Silver did have a press conference scheduled at FedEx Forum, but it was supposed to be about the Grizzlies.

He ducked into an airport meeting room for 15 minutes to ponder his reply with his girlfriend, interior designer Maggie Grise, and NBA senior vice president of production Jarad Franzreb. The public craved outrage, but Silver needed evidence. He could not condemn Sterling without verifying his voice. Silver's town car got stuck in traffic outside downtown Memphis, so he power-walked the last four blocks to the arena, arriving 30 minutes late. True to his Cravath roots, he handled questions delicately, promising Sterling due process.

No one will remember that press conference. During the next 30 hours Silver attended playoff games in Memphis, Portland and then Golden State, where he watched the dispirited Clippers lose by 21. Along the way he chatted with players, coaches, team employees and many fans. What initially drew him to Masawani Jere as a boy was a desire to see the world through a different prism. Once again Silver was searching for other perspectives. "You looked at people, and there was a pain in their eyes," he says. "It wasn't even anger as much as hurt."

Players were suggesting boycotts. Fans were planning protests. Sponsors were fleeing the Clippers. "Obviously there were pragmatic factors at play," says one owner. "If people thought the NBA was not sensitive to civil rights even for a moment, it would have been permanently damaging. But there were personal factors also." For decades Silver and his colleagues had defended the NBA from coded racist attacks: complaints about Afros, then cornrows, then tattoos. "This wasn't an outsider taking shots," Silver says. "To have these references come from within an institution that is—while far from perfect—as egalitarian as there is in society made a particular impact."

Silver returned home on April 28 and stayed up until 1 a.m. writing a speech in his apartment. He read sections aloud to Grise. Since the audio was authenticated, he wanted to exile Sterling for good, but he still had not met with NBA lawyers. He tried to focus on the message rather than the punishment. "I got a lot of advice from owners, CEOs and business partners," Silver says, "but they all seemed to come back to this: *Reflect on your life experiences. Then go with your gut.*"

In 1965 famed New York City developer Robert Moses announced plans to build a bridge connecting Long Island and Westchester. The bridge would run from Oyster Bay to Rye. Melba Silver would not have been directly affected. Her house was nowhere near the proposed entrance. But Melba was an environmentalist who hosted fund-raisers for progressive political candidates. She was concerned about the effects of pollution on her children and her hometown. She started a campaign called Ban the Bridge. Her youngest son, Adam, wore BAN THE BRIDGE buttons to elementary school. He saw his mom on TV, and he rejoiced with his family when plans for the bridge were scuttled.

Melba served as president of the Rye library and chairwoman of the town planning commission. She cofounded an alternative high school in White Plains called EduCage, which emphasized the arts and allowed students to smoke in class. Melba taught English and history while puffing on her king-sized nonfiltered Chesterfields. Adam was a regular at EduCage as well as at Proskauer Rose, the Manhattan law firm where his father was chairman. Adam would take the Metro-North Railroad to Grand Central Station and hang out in his dad's office, admiring plaques awarded to him by New York mayors John Lindsay and Abe Beame for helping to settle transit, garbage and other major strikes as the city's special counsel in labor disputes. "He was the kind of lawyer who was discussed with almost as much praise on the other side of the table," says Brad Ruskin, co-chair of the litigation department at Proskauer. The halls bustled with young associates, including hotshots named Gary Bettman and David Stern.

Those city jaunts hooked Silver on law and sports. His father was soft-spoken and reserved, except at Madison Square Garden. There Ed cheered the Knicks and the Rangers—or heckled them—while Adam chuckled. When Ed and Melba split, the games kept father and son together, as did the bouts. The family's favorite athlete was Muhammad Ali, whose poster adorned Adam's bedroom wall and whose fights were broadcast at a theater in New Rochelle. The Silvers appreciated Ali because he embodied the civil rights movement they felt a part of. "I thought Adam could be a great sportswriter," says former SI managing editor Mark Mulvoy, a family friend who lives in Rye. "But he was so intelligent."

Silver yearned to explore the country outside the tristate area, one reason why he went south to Duke, spent a year assisting a U.S. congressman from Oregon in Washington, D.C., and attended law school at Chicago. He and President Barack Obama are both 52, and while Obama worked on the South Side as a community organizer, Silver was the most active law student at Mandel Legal Aid Clinic in the same area. The cases he handled at the clinic, all pro bono, were mainly for victims of housing or employment discrimination who could not afford private counsel. "He tended away from the corporate side of things," says Michael Alter, a law school classmate who now owns the WNBA's Chicago Sky. "He believed in larger ideals of justice and equality, and this was a way he could make an impact."

Silver arrived at Duke the same year as Mike Krzyzewski, and in Chicago a year after Michael Jordan. He could saunter into Cameron Indoor Stadium five minutes before tip-off, and later buy Bulls tickets at the box office on game days. He was no face-painter, and he never considered a career in basketball, but he could not deny that the sport kept finding him.

His first post out of law school was a clerkship under newly appointed federal judge Kimba Wood in the Southern District of New York. Within a month he informed Wood that she did not need to prepare for an upcoming case because he had talked the lawyers into a settlement. "I was astounded," Wood recalls. Silver settled dozens of cases for her, demonstrating an unusual ability to locate middle ground and nudge both parties toward it.

"Could he have become managing partner of a big fancy New York law firm?" asks Jan Uhrbach, his co-clerk under Wood. "Of course he could have." Instead, three years later, Silver wrote a letter to his father's old associate. He was asking for career advice, not a job, but Stern eventually gave him one anyway. (Four years after that, Uhrbach also left her law firm, to become a rabbi.)

Silver did, in some ways, marry the NBA. His mother died in March 2004 of lung cancer, and his father passed away that October from pancreatic cancer, yet Silver still flew to preseason games in China that fall. "This is my other family," he told himself. His oldest brother, Erik, is the tennis pro at Boca Raton Resort & Club; his older sister, Ann, runs an environmental nonprofit in Carson City, Nev.; Owen is an entrepreneur in Boulder, Colo. Late in '04, as the siblings mourned the loss of both parents, they received a gracious letter from a family counselor in Cleveland named Emily Geier. Emily, four years younger than Adam, explained that their father had had a relationship with her mother while they worked in the same office in New York City. She was their sister.

Adam was not surprised. He had fielded a few calls from Geier's mother, starting in high school, but was afraid to confront his dad or tell his mom. "Life is complicated," Silver says. "We embraced her, and we have become good friends. I'm an uncle to her two children. She has become an important part of our family."

New York lawyers sometimes compare Silver with his father, but Adam is far more open, more engaging. His bookish appearance, bald and bespectacled, belies his social dexterity. As the former president of NBA Entertainment, he works the greenroom at All-Star weekend, mingling with Ice Cube, Faith Hill and Ashton Kutcher. He bro-hugs LeBron James. He forwards reviews of Philip Roth books to Rebecca Lobo, the former Connecticut and WNBA star he met in 1996. When Silver received the first shipment of regulation basketballs with his signature, he sent one to Lobo. Attached was a two-word note: Don't Laugh.

Last fall Silver decided to build his relationship with Paul, the Clippers star and players' association president. Silver called Howie Nuchow, whom he befriended 20 years ago when Nuchow worked in the ticket office of the Nets. "Adam is great to people before they have any influence," Nuchow says. Today Nuchow coheads vaunted CAA Sports, which represents Paul. Nuchow arranged a meeting in Philadelphia before a game against the 76ers. Silver and Paul chatted amiably, getting to know each other. Five months later they reconvened at Golden State, under vastly different circumstances. Whether or not the summit in Philly helped prevent a boycott in Oakland, an underpinning of trust had been established. "We have an opportunity," Paul says, "to be partners in everything we do."

Because Silver spent so long at Stern's side, many predicted he would keep the NBA's status quo. But in that initial Board of Governors session he told the owners he wanted to take a fresh look at everything from the lottery system, with its incentive for teams to tank, to the playoff format, with its imbalance between East and West. His first priorities, one owner said, were raising the minimum age for draft eligibility from 19 to 20 and establishing a command center in Secaucus, N.J., for replay reviews. All those enticing ideas were overshadowed by Sterling.

Silver left the law yet still wound up a judge. "There are similarities," he acknowledges, "but these [NBA] cases are unfolding in real time. You can't ask for a delay."

He woke up with a cold on April 29. He took a draft of his speech to the office, and in a 10 a.m. meeting with NBA lawyers learned he could carry out his plan. He kept in contact with a handful of advisers, including Stern, but the final call was his. "I had to take responsibility and own whatever I did," Silver says. "I took in all points of view, but ultimately this was something that had to be mine." His childhood, so often spent unattended in that sprawling house by the water, may have wired him for a solo act. "I've always been very independent because of that," Silver says. A little before 2 p.m. he read over his final draft for the first time at the Hilton Hotel, though he was far more concerned with the substance than with the performance.

His cadence was more deliberate than usual, his tone more forceful, his expression more fierce. Insiders say Silver can be tough in a tactful way—"The kind of guy you appreciate even when he says 'screw you,'" as one puts it—and here was the evidence. "He's like Bjorn Borg," says former tennis pro Justin Gimelstob, an ATP board member who once ran the New York City Marathon with Silver and came in more than nine minutes behind him. "His pulse doesn't have a huge range, but his intensity level does. That speech was the most overtly intense I've ever seen him."

Gimelstob was reminded of a time last fall when Silver called him, incensed at something he had done, which Gimelstob prefers not to share. Silver said, "Realize in this business your friends are very few. Make sure to treat them specially. You have to be willing to be tough with everyone else, and you need to be O.K. with that." Gimelstob remembers the words because he wrote them on a Post-It note and stuck it to the top of his computer monitor.

Of all the passages in the speech, this is the one that will be played and replayed, cited whenever Silver retires: "I am personally distraught that the views expressed by Mr. Sterling came from within an institution that has historically taken such a leadership role in matters of race relations and caused current and former players, coaches, fans and partners of the NBA to question their very association with the league. To them, and pioneers of the game like Earl Lloyd, Chuck Cooper, Sweetwater Clifton, the great Bill Russell, and particularly Magic Johnson, I apologize. Accordingly, effective immediately, I am banning Mr. Sterling for life."

Silver earned raves from players, political leaders and the most casual fans. *Saturday Night Live* parodied him. ("I've gotten more high fives from random black people this week than any week in my life—and I've learned many wonderful new handshakes," said Silver impersonator Taran Killam.) Charitybuzz auctioned a lunch with him, and online bids reached $12,500 in the first six days. At the Conservative Synagogue of the Hamptons in Sag Harbor, N.Y., Rabbi Uhrbach mentioned Silver before blessing the wine at the end of Shabbat services. "I always ask the community if anybody is celebrating anything," Uhrbach says. "I wanted to celebrate Adam because I believe in a sense of calling. I believe there are moments we have an opportunity to rise to the occasion and make a difference. I felt he was blessed with that opportunity and rose to the occasion."

This year's playoffs have showcased the best and worst of the NBA. The first round featured eight overtimes and five Game 7s. In the second round the Clippers came back from 16 points down to the Thunder with nine minutes left to win Game 4, and the Thunder came back from 13 points down with four minutes left to win Game 5. But the specter of the Sterlings hovers over each NBA arena, and whenever they open their mouths, they breathe fire through the league.

The Board of Governors will vote them out, but no one knows exactly how they will leave, quietly or combatively. The NBA hopes for the former but braces for the latter: Sterling has refused to pay his $2.5 million fine and has hired an antitrust lawyer. In the league's 15th-floor conference room, Silver slips on his suit jacket and tightens his tie. He is headed into the New York twilight, across the bridge to Brooklyn, for Game 4 of the Eastern

Conference semifinals between the Nets and the Heat. LeBron James will score 49 points at the same time Sterling badmouths Magic on *Anderson Cooper 360*. Silver will issue another statement, reiterating his intention to remove Sterling as soon as possible, which for many won't be soon enough.

From Malawi to the Hamptons, on BlackBerrys and in synagogues, the world follows basketball's righteous chief.

— POSTSCRIPT —

Lee Jenkins: Mark Mulvoy retired as managing editor of *Sports Illustrated* in 1996, a transformational figure in the history of the magazine. With the encouragement of Chris Stone and Mark Bechtel, my managing editor and NBA editor at SI, I tried calling Mulvoy out of retirement in April 2014 to help guide a profile of NBA commissioner Adam Silver, who had been on the job for two months and was already facing his first crisis, banning Clippers owner Donald Sterling from the league for racist comments made on a leaked audiotape. Mulvoy lived in Rye, N.Y., Silver's hometown, and his daughter happened to be Silver's former babysitter. Feature reporting is filled with happy coincidences. Mulvoy connected me with several of Silver's childhood friends, who connected me with another, Masawani Jere. Before Jere was chief of the Ngoni tribe in southeastern Africa, he attended Silver's high school, and for a while lived in Silver's home. Connecting with Jere, by phone from Malawi, was only slightly more challenging than arranging an interview with Silver, who eventually agreed to a sit-down at the NBA office in New York, presumably to stop me from harassing any more of his old friends. He was engaging and insightful, especially about "Mas," whose experiences in Westchester helped inform a future commissioner's views on race, and eventually, his landmark speech banning Sterling.